I0126222

Hawkins County, Tennessee

WILL BOOK

1786–1864

Eugenia L. Messick

Heritage Books
2024

HERITAGE BOOKS
AN IMPRINT OF HERITAGE BOOKS, INC.

Books, CDs, and more—Worldwide

For our listing of thousands of titles see our website
at
www.HeritageBooks.com

A Facsimile Reprint
Published 2024 by
HERITAGE BOOKS, INC.
Publishing Division
5810 Ruatan Street
Berwyn Heights, MD 20740

Originally published
Mountain Press
Signal Mountain, Tennessee
1992

— Publisher's Notice —
In reprints such as this, it is often not possible to remove
blemishes from the original. We feel the contents of this
book warrant its reissue despite these blemishes and

International Standard Book Number
Paperbound: 978-0-7884-9075-0

CONTENTS

The original will books of Hawkins County, Tennessee were destroyed in 1863. Some time after the end of the Civil War, The County Court
Clerk copied all the original wills from surviving originals that he
was able to decipher. The originals of most of the older wills are pre-
served.

The Tennessee State Library and Archives microfilmed the re-copied
will books, and it is from the microfilm that all the wills appearing
in this volume were transcribed. Due to the great number of wills contained in the microfilm, it was felt that two volumes would be necessary;
therefore, Volume I covers the period beginning with the earliest will,
1786, and ends with wills dated in 1864.

The transcriptions in this volume are essentially verbatim copies
of the re-recorded wills. Some of the standard religious preambles in
use during the time span of this book were omitted or condensed for
the sake of space.

It appears that the County Court Clerk, when he undertook the
enormous job of re-copying into books the original wills, attempted to
preserve the many inconsistencies and errors in spelling and punctuation.
If a surname was spelled variously in a will, he copied it as he read
it, but usually underlined the spelling in question. Vernacular words
and expressions mirror the former region of many of the testators, only
adding to the value and interest of the document.

When extracting the microfilm, I was careful that my transcription
would be a verbatim copy of the clerk's work, except in those instances
in which the microfilm was illegible, forcing me to guess at the faded
or missing word. In those places I underscored the questionable word
or blank space.

Many of the last wills and testaments contained in this volume
reveal rich genealogical and historical content. From the surnames we
recognize men who went into politics and became prominent in forming
one of the earliest examples of democratic government. The names include traders who built stations and became wealthy; veterans of the
American Revolution who took up new land; land speculators, land
surveyors and their followers who swarmed into the new area to grab the
cheap land. The first to arrive claimed the best land; later arrivals
took up poorer acreage. Then, there were the people who came into the
frontier to escape hardships in their former homes.

The people who settled Hawkins County were predominently Scotch-
Irish, Welch, English, Irish and German. The Scotch-Irish and Germans
had come down the Valley of Virginia from Pennsylvania, many having
sojourned in Virginia or North Carolina before moving onto the frontier.
Each group bore its ethnic mark. The thrifty Germans became successful
farmers, mechanics and professionals who, at the end of their lives,
bequeathed their wealth to their descendants. Also successful as farmers,
land speculators, minors and professionals were the Scotch-Irish, Welch,
Irish and English.

From the last wills and testaments we are able to glimpse into the
lives of the people: their dress, speech, religion, politics, their
homes and farms, churches, burying customs, their homespun industries
and their educational institutions. We learn that they built grist and
saw mills, leather tanneries, made shoes, saddles, harnesses, wagons.
Most farms had a still. There were cabinet makers who turned out plain
as well as quality furniture. The women carded the wool, flax and cotton
and spun the thread, made the cloth, then fashioned the clothing. They
plucked the feathers from the geese and made the featherbeds and pillows.

Clothing was valued—not to be discarded as soon as new styles were
introduced. Rather, we see the inhabitants of Hawkins County passing on
their used clothing to their legatees. Mary Burns, widow of Revolutionary
War veteran Robert Burns, bequeathed to her daughter all her clothing.
Ruben Craycraft directed that all his just debts, together with his
sickness and funeral expenses be paid out of his worldly goods, consisting
of one brown mare, one blue broadcloth coat and jacket, one corduroy
breeches, one brown cloth coat and a white cloth jacket, one fine shirt,
one pair thread stockings, one pair new shoes, one pair of silver knee-
buckles, one cotton coat and three yards of homemade fustian, two pairs
of garters and one old saddle bag. T. A. Fletcher bequeathed his son
John P. "one lindsey suit of clothes now wore by me, consisting of coat,
jacket and pantaloons".

Many people owned slaves, but many abhorred slavery. Instructions
were spelled out in many wills for the special care or the emanciation
of their slaves at their death. John Grigsby stipulated: "My negro
man Will is to be no longer a slave after the death of me and my wife
Winney Grigsby." Nancy Hord wished her slave Hanna to be freed at her
death. Joshua Phipps "enjoined it upon the Guardian of my son Mac to
take good care of my old servant Andy, that he be not overworked or exposed, but be employed in the oversight and feeding of stock, attending
to the fields &c, lighter duties suited to his age and faithful character".
Hezekiah Hamblen freed his mulatto man Harry, but gave his various
other slaves to his children. Malinda Kenner emancipated her "old negro
woman Rachael and gave her one cow and calf and one year's provision..."

Eugenia Lauderdale Messick
6437 Heather Drive
Memphis, Tennessee, 38119

EARLY MAP OF EAST TENNESSEE

On the reverse of this page is a copy of an early map of east Tennessee. When established, the boundaries of Hawkins County extended from the North Fork of Holston River west and southwest to the Suck in the Tennessee River near Chattanooga. In 1792 Knox County was formed from Hawkins County; in 1796 Grainger County was formed from Hawkins and Knox. In 1801 Claiborne was erected from Hawkins and Grainger. In 1844 Hancock County was erected from Hawkins and Claiborne, and in 1870 the old 13th District of Hawkins became part of the new county of Hamblen. From 1787 to 1790 Hawkins County was in North Carolina; from 1790 to 1796 in the Territory of the United States South of the River Ohio, and since 1796 in Tennessee.

The county seat is Rogersville, established by the North Carolina Legislature in 1789 and built at Joseph Rogers' on Crockett's Creek. Other principal villages are Mooresburg founded by Hugh G. Moore; Bull's Gap, named for John Bull, the first settler in the vicinity; New Canton, Rotherwood, Surgoinsville, established in 1815 upon land owned by James Surgoin and Arthur G. Armstrong; Austin's Mill; War Gap; Stony Point and Persia.*

*For the above facts regarding the history of Hawkins County, we are indebted to Goodspeed's History of East Tennessee and to Prentiss Price in his Tennessee Marriage Records, Vol. 2.

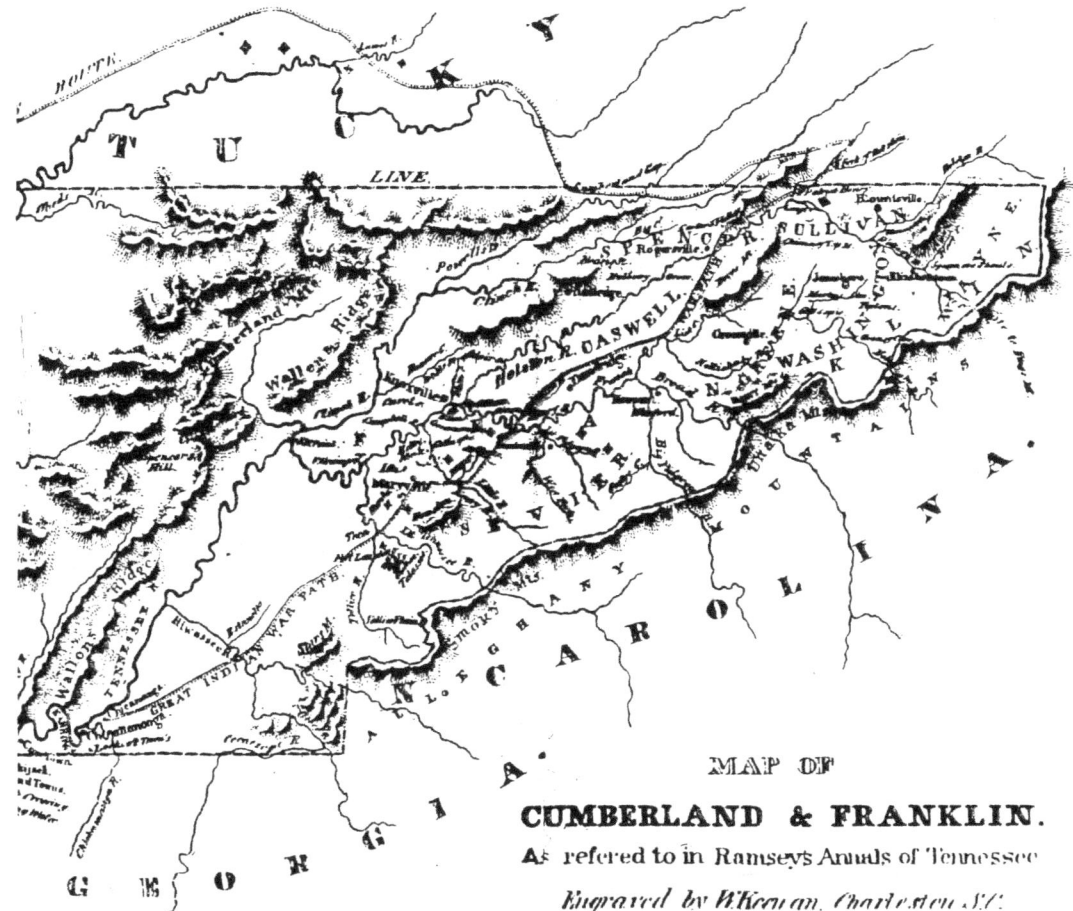

MAP OF
CUMBERLAND & FRANKLIN.
As refered to in Ramseys Annals of Tennessee
Engraved by W.Keenan. Charleston S.C.
For Ramseys Annals of Tennessee

****

Wills represented by the following index generally fall into the period, 1871-1886, and may be found in the re-copied Will Book, Pages 512-581, or on the microfilm from which the wills appearing in this book were transcribed.

*Michael Dougherty was murdered on April 8, 1806 by his 14-year-old daughter Mary. See Knoxville Gazette for April 23, 1806, and Tennessee Reports Overton II 80.

WILLS OF HAWKINS COUNTY, TENNESSEE

WILL OF THOMAS AMIS

Page 1   November 16, 1797

In the Name of God, Amen. I, **Thomas Amis** of the State of Tenn. and
County of Hawkins, knowing that it is ordained for all men once to die, &
being sick and weak but of sound mind & memory do make and ordain this my
last Will and Testament in manner and form following, (Viz):

First. I bequeath my self to Almighty God fully believing in his
Almighty wise providence & mercy to all his creation, after this life to
rest in peace. And as to my worldly goods and chattels that he has been
pleased to put in my care in this life, I dispose of in manner and form
following:

Item. I give and bequeath unto my wife **Lucy** all my cash in hand at
my decease with all my stock of every kind & species. Also, all my plantation tools & utensils including waggons &c and all my household and kitchen
furniture of every kind & all the present crop of all sorts whatever to her
and her heirs forever. I also lend to my said wife all my lands on Bigg
Creek containing 350 acres in three tracts including the place I now live.
Also the tract of land whereon **Polly Brooks** now lives containing 200 acres,
adjoining the land my son **Willis** lives on—with my mills, stills and the
utensils thereunto belonging and my smith tools all of which said loan I
lend her during the time she remains my widow, and at her death or marriage,
I give the same to my son **Baynes Amis** & his heirs forever.

Item. I give to my son **John Amis** what may be received from the cargo
seized from me by the Spanish Commandant at Fort Natchez in June 1786. I
also give him the tract of land he now lives on adjoining the town of
Rogersville and lying the east side of the main road. Also, the lower part
of my 640 acre tract of land to be laid off by a line to run square with
the upper end of the tract he now lives on, to him and his heirs forever.

Item. I give to my son **Lincoln Amis** the five lots in the town of
Rogersville which I purchased of **Daniel Hamblen.** I also give him all my
lands lying the west side of the main road and adjoining the town of
Rogersville.

Item. I give to my son **Thomas Gale Amis** all the Certificates by
me funded in the Continental Loan Office in North Carolina the 22nd of
August, 1791—Number 106, amounting to $2,262.40. To him and his heirs
forever.

Item. My will is that the rest of my Estate consisting of slaves,
bonds, notes, Judgement Book accounts &c shall be equally divided between
my wife **Lucy Amis** and my children except **Thomas Gale Amis** and **Baynes Amis**
as I consider their legacies to be made equal otherways with the rest of
my children. Also the following deductions to be made (Viz) out of my
daughters **Tabitha's** and **Mary's** shares, six hundred and sixty-six and two
thirds dollars each & out of my daughter **Fanny's** and my son **John's** shares,
three hundred & thirty-three & 1/3 dollars each. I make these deductions
for negroes already given them. It is my will and desire that my friends,
**John Ray, Esq'r, Col. James Armstrong, William Armstrong, Esqr, James
McMinn, Esq'r,** and **William Howard,** Surveyor, or a majority of them do make
the division of the above mentioned slaves, Bonds, notes, Judgement Book
accounts &c, such division when made to be made of record in Court which
shall stand good in law, and if any of my children die without leaving a
lawful heir, then I will their legacy to be equally divided amongst tose

of my children who have a share in the last mentioned legacy of slaves,
bonds, notes, book accounts, or their lawful representatives. It is
also my will and desire that my Library of all my books be kept together
for the use of my school.

And lastly, I do appoint my wife **Lucy** my Executrix to this my last
Will and Testament, revoking all other will or wills by me made.

In witness whereof I have hereunto set my hand & seal this Sixteenth
day of November, One Thousand Seven Hundred and Ninety-Seven.

                                        Thomas Amis (P L)

Signed and sealed in presence of:
Milton Ford, Jurat
Isaac Lambert,
James Herbart Irvin
Spencer Ball, Jurat

WILL OF WILLIAM AMIS

Page 3   Dated December 30, 1809

Meditating on the uncertainties of life, I make this my last Will
and Testament. I bequeath my soul to the mercy of my maker Almighty God,
and bequeath my worldly Estate in the manner following:

I bequeath to my beloved brother **Baynes Amis** my negro **Tom.** I bequeath to my beloved brother **James Amis** my negro boy **Frank**, also what is
now coming to me in the State of Kentucky. I bequeath to my dear beloved
sister **Nancy** my negro girl **Milly**, and I wish my brother **Baynes Amis,** Exec.,
to settle my affairs and do bequeath **Daph** and **Joe** to him for his trouble
__ ? my brother **Haynes Amis** and should the debts due me not discharge
what I justly owe, I wish the negroes to be hired out until there is
money collected to discharge the same. Given under my hand and seal this
Thirtieth day of December, 1809.

                                        Wm. Amis (seal)

In presence of:
Peter Burum (?) Jurat
Jas Cox
Jno. T. Rogers, Jurat

WILL OF WILLIAM ARMSTRONG

Page 3   Dated: February 17, 1810

In the Name of God, Amen. I, **William Armstrong,** of Hawkins County
and State of Tennessee, considering the uncertainties of this mortal life
and being of sound mind and memory, do make and publish this my last Will
and Testament in manner and form following, that is to say:

First. I give and bequeath unto my beloved wife **Abinah Armstrong**
all of my estate to be possessed and enjoyed by her forever, deducting the
following legacies (that is): To each of my sons and daughters, I bequeath
the sum on One Dollar, each which said several legacies or sums of money
I will and order shall be paid to the said respective Legatees within
twelve months after my decease, likewise all my just debts to be paid, and...

Lastly. As to the rest, residue and remainder of my estate of what kind or nature soever, I will and bequeath unto my said beloved wife, **Abinah Armstrong,** and I hereby appoint her Executrix and **Thomas Jackson** Executor of this my last Will and Testament, hereby revoking all former wills by me made.

In witness whereof I have hereunto set my hand and seal. This seventeenth day of February, in the year of our Lord, One Thousand Eight Hundred and Ten.

Wm. Armstrong (seal)

Signed, sealed, published and declared by the above William Armstrong to be his last Will and Testament in the presence of us who have hereunto subscribed our names as witnesses in the presence of the Testator.

Henry Marshall

Jesse x Brown

(his mark)

Cans. (Cornelius?) Regan

WILL OF JOHN ARMSTRONG

Page 4   Dated: April 17, 1813

In the Name of God, Amen. I, **John Armstrong,** of Hawkins County and State of Tennessee, considering the uncertainty of this mortal life and being of sound and perfect mind and memory, blessed be Almighty God for the same, do make and publish this my last Will and Testament in manner and form following. (That is to say):

First. I give and bequeath unto my beloved wife **Jane Armstrong** my plantation in Carter's Valley, together with all my stock of every kind-- farming utensils & household furniture, deducting and reserving what is hereafter specified, likewise both my negro women **Catt & Sall,** and my negro fellow **Spencer** to be enjoyed by her during her natural life. I will and bequeath unto my daughter **Jane Armstrong** my negro woman named **Sall,** the eldest, to be freely possessed and enjoyed by her and her heirs forever. To my son **Thomas Armstrong,** I will and bequeath my negro man **Minor** to be freely possessed by him and his heirs forever. To my son **Baker Armstrong,** I will and devise that plantation now occupied by him (in) Stanley Valley and also my negro boy **Ambrose,** to be freely possessed and enjoyed by him and his heirs and assigns forever. To my son **John Armstrong,** I will and bequeath my negro girl named **Aggy,** to be freely possessed and enjoyed by him and his heirs forever. To my daughter **Annes Baker,** I will and bequeath my negro girl named **Milly,** to be freely possessed and enjoyed by her and her heirs forever. To my daughter **Mary Armstrong,** a single woman, I will and bequeath my negro woman **Nancy** and her increase, to be freely possessed and enjoyed by her and the heirs of her body forever, and also a good horse and saddle, a bed and bedding, household furniture, two cows and calves, a sow and pigs, to be freely possessed by her and her heirs forever. And my will and desire is that my wife **Jane** may, if she chooses, sell my plantation and all my personal estate in her possession, reserving for herself such part of said personal property as she may think convenient for her use and necessity, and live with any of her children that she may think proper, and at her decease, it is my will and meaning that

Spencer shall belong to my son **Baker** and also that **Jesse** and **Sal** shall belong to my son **John Armstrong** forever. And likewise, my will and meaning is that at my wife's death the residue or remainder of the amount of the sale of said plantation, personal estate, money and debts shall be equally divided between all my children, and I hereby appoint my son **Thomas Armstrong** and **John Young** Executors of this my last Will and Testament, hereby revoking all former wills by me made.

In witness whereof I have hereunto set my hand and seal this (blank space) day of (blank space), in the Year of our Lord, (blank space).

(blank space) (seal)

Signed, sealed, published and declared by the above named John Armstrong to be his last Will and Testament, in the presence of us who at his request and in his presence have hereunto subscribed our names as witnesses to the same.

STATE OF TENNESSEE)

HAWKINS COUNTY   )   An Article of Agreement made and concluded on between the wife and Legatees of **John Armstrong,** dec'd, though not witnessed nor signed by him, the said **John Armstrong,** dec'd, but the wife and Legatees from different reasons believing it to be his will and desire that his estate should be divided in the manner and form prescribed by said will, and we the parties doth mutually agree to abide and stand by the said will, and that we and each of us will appear at our next County Court of Pleas and Quarter Sessions on the fourth Monday of May next and give our consent to have the said will recorded, and that we the under-named subscribers do ever hereafter the benefit of any other will as the laws of our country respecting the said estate of the said **John Armstrong,** Dec'd., and for the true performance we and each of us do bind ourselves, our heirs &C in the penal sum of One Thousand Dollars, as witness our hands and seals. This 17th day of April, 1813.

Test.

John Young   **Jean x Armstrong** (seal)

Jas. Armstrong   (her mark)

Thomas Armstrong (seal)

Wm. Armstrong (seal)

B. Armstrong (seal)

John Armstrong (seal)

Sam'l Armstrong (seal)

James Armstrong (seal)

WILL OF WILLIAM ARMSTRONG

Page 6   Dated: May 10, 1817

Being confined to my bed in sickness, though perfectly in my natural sense, I am about to make my last Will and Testament.

First. I bequeath to my beloved wife **Elizabeth** the plantation with all the farming implements and stock, during her natural life, and at her decease, all to fall to my son **John,** with the exception of a certain horse beast and a cow to my daughter **Jane**. Also, a horse beast and a cow to my daughter **Anna**. I will and bequeath to my son **Thomas** the tract of land whereon he now lives. I will and bequeath to my daughter **Jane** a certain negro girl named **Lettie**; and also to my daughter **Ann_**, a negro girl named **Lyd--Lyd's** oldest child, if any, to belong to **Jane** at her mother's decease. In case either of my three children now living with me should die without issue,their portion of the property (is) to be equally divided between the other two, and to my daughter **Nancy Forgey**, I bequeath Fifty Dollars at my wife's decease.

In testimony whereof I have set my hand and seal.

William Armstrong (seal)

Test.
W. T. Armstrong
John Armstrong

N. B. At my wife's decease, all the household furniture to be equally divided among the children of **John, James & Ann_**.

WILL OF LUCY AMIS

Page 6   December 17, 1818

I, **Lucy Amis**, widow of the late **Thomas Amis**, Dec'd., of Hawkins County and State of Tennessee, being weak in body but in sound mind and memory, meditating on the uncertainty of human events, ordain and request this my last Will and Testament.

First. I bequeath my soul to Almighty God, the giver of it, and request my worldly affairs...in the following manner. It is my desire that my son **Baynes Amis** have all my Estate of every description, and (for) him to pay my son **James Amis** and **Nancy Howel** the value of **Milly** and **Joe**, the two oldest children of **Polly**, which I consider to be worth six hundred dollars, which will be three hundred dollars to each--to be paid in two years after my death. Also, pay to **Tabitha Cox**, **Francis Grantham**, **Polly Rogers**, the heirs of **John Amis**, **Rachael Hogan**, **Willis Amis**, **Alla Gordon**, **Lincoln Amis** and the heirs of **Thomas G. Amis**, one dollar each. And to **Lucy N. Amis** youngest daughter of **Lincoln Amis**, I wish to have my negro boy **Charles** which I purchased of the said **Lincoln Amis**. And it is my desire my step grandson **John A. Rogers** act as my Executor in this my last Will and Testament, and I hereby revoke all other wills.

In witness whereof I have hereunto set my hand and seal. This 17th day of December, 1818.

Lucy Amis (seal)

Signed, sealed & acknowledged in presence
of: Witnesses:
    William E. Cocke
    Rachael Armstrong

WILL OF DAVID ANDERSON

Page 7   August 6, 1822

This Indenture made this sixth of August, in the year of our Lord 1822. **David Anderson** of the County of Hawkins and State of Tennessee,

being weak of body but of sound mind and memory, knowing that all men is born to die and after death to go to Judgement, do make this my last Will and Testament. In the Name of God, Amen.

I wish and devise to my son, **David M. Anderson,** one muly cow, a shovel plow and falling **ax**, and my daughter, **Elizabeth Christian**, I devise and leave her my Bible, and I devise and leave to all my lawful sons and daughters one dollar each, in twelve months after my decease, if applied for, and I will a(nd) bequeath to my beloved wife **Elizabeth** all my real and perishable property of every kind and all my household and kitchen furniture of every kind, and I hereby constitute and appoint my wife **Elizabeth Anderson** my Executor to this my last will. In Testimony whereof I, **David Anderson**, have hereunto set my hand and seal the day and date above written. In the Name of God, Amen.

David Anderson (seal)

Attest:
James Johnson
John F. Johnson
George Winegar

WILL OF DEBORAH ALEXANDER

Page 8   Dated: December 23, 1827

In the Name of God, Amen.

I, **Deborah Alexander** of the County of Hawkins in the State of Tennessee, being weak of body but of sound mind and memory, do make and ordain this my last Will and Testament.

I recommend my soul to Almighty God, and as to my worldly estate, I make my youngest and beloved son **Dicks Alexander** my sole heir and bequeath unto him all that I possess, consisting principally of a Note of Hand on my son **William Alexander** for $1,248.77, on which several payments have been made, and all that my son **Dicks** has received on said note--which note is dated Seventh of June, 1808, and secured by a mortgage on real estate dated One July, 1808 by **William Alexander**. Also, a Bond executed by **Amos Farquhar** and **Jonathan Jessop** of the Borough of York in the County of York, State of Pennsylvania, for $554.00, to secure the payment of $277.375, dated September 13, 1815.

Also, a Note or Bill single executed by **Jonathan Jessop** of York, Pennsylvania for the sum of Fifty Pounds and dated 13 June, 1809.

And lastly, I appoint my beloved son **Dicks Alexander** my sole Executor. In testimony whereof I have hereto set my hand and seal this Twenty Third day of December, Year of our Lord, One Thousand Eight Hundred, Twenty Seven.

Deborah Alexander (seal)

Witness:
Hu A. Walker
W. A. Walker

WILL OF WILLIAM ARMSTRONG, SEN'R

Page 8   Dated: January 13, 1835

I, **William Armstrong, Sen'r.** of the County of Hawkins and State of Tennessee, being of sound mind and memory, do make this my last Will and Testament.

First. I will and bequeath unto my daughter-in-law **Rachael** and her five children, **Elizabeth, Mary, Joseph Rogers, Alice Louisiana** and **William Pitt Armstrong,** the tract of land on the south side of Holston River in the county aforesaid known as the Caldwell Place and on which she has heretofore resided—containing by estimation 350 acres—which tract I heretofore conveyed to them to be equally divided according to the provisions of said conveyance. I further give unto the said **Rachael** and her children above named, a negro woman slave named **Rinda** and her increase in lieu of certain improvements made by my son **Arthur** on town lots in the town of Surgoinsville. Said negro and her increase to be equally divided among **Rachael** and her children before named.

2nd. I give and bequeath unto my son **William Armstrong, Jr.** the plantation in Carter's Valley originally owned by my father and lately sold by my son **William Armstrong** to **J. B. Galbraith,** containing by estimation 240 acres. Also one other tract adjoining the same containing by estimation 46 acres which he has also sold. Said lands being conveyed by me to my son **William** several years since. I also give and bequeath unto my son **William** a negro or mulatto man slave named **Stephen,** which slave he has also had in possession for some years. I also give him all stock and donations of whatever kind received by him heretofore from me.

3rd. I give and bequeath unto my son **Clinton Armstrong** a part of the tract adjoining the place whereon I now live and which tract my son **Clinton** has sold unto my son **William** and which I have heretofore conveyed unto my son **Clinton,** containing by estimation 300 acres. I also give and bequeath unto my son **Clinton** all the stock and other donations of whatever kind which he has heretofore received from me, and I further give and bequeath unto my son **Clinton** my negro man slave named **Ben.**

4th. I give and bequeath unto my daughter **Polly Amis** the tract of land whereon she now lives in **Carter's** Valley containing 500 acres which tract has been conveyed by me some years since. I also give and bequeath unto her a negro woman slave named **Fanny** and her increase. Also, I give unto her all stock and other donations of whatever kind heretofore received by her.

5th. I give and bequeath unto **Elizabeth Bradford,** my daughter, a negro woman named **Clarissa** and her child **Pocahontas** which slaves she has received some years since with their increase younger than **Pocahontas.** I also give unto her all stock and other donations of whatever kind which (she) received from me as such heretofore. My daughter **Elizabeth** has in her possession a negro boy named **Isaac,** son of **Clarissa.** I will that she pay to me or my Executor &C the sum of twenty-five dollars yearly for the hire of said boy **Isaac** from the time he becomes sixteen years of age until my death, then said boy to be offered to her at a fair valuation and should she decline receiving at such price as he shall be valued, said **Isaac** is to be sold with the rest of my negroes, &C.

6th. I give and bequeath unto my son **Carry A. Armstrong** a certain tract or parcel of land lying on the main stage road adjoining the land of **William Lyons** in the county aforesaid, containing by estimation 15 acres— which tract of land was conveyed by me to him some years since. I also give unto him all the stock and other donations made to him by me heretofore. And, I further will and devise that should my son **Carry** return and get married within three years after my decease that he have the river plantation, including the mill, still house, Old Tavern &C as hereinafter

7

described, but should he not return aforesaid of three years after my death and marry and settle himself, it is my will that said tract of land be sold and divided among all my other children, giving unto the heirs of my son **Arthur** one equal share of the proceeds of the sale of said lands and the rents that may accrue thereon.

7th. I give and bequeath unto my daughter **Sally B. Bord** two negroes named **Nancy** (and her increase), and **Wiley.** Also all stock and other donations of whatever kind heretofore received by her from me.

8th. I give and bequeath unto my daughter **Louisiana DeWolfe** two negroes named **George** and **Linda** with her increase, also all the stock and other donations of whatever kind heretofore received of her by me.

9th. I give and bequeath unto my daughter **Margaret E. Cook** two negroes named **Eliza** and **Rufus,** also all stock and other donations of property heretofore received by her from me. I also will that she be paid the sum of Two Hundred Dollars extra of her division.

10th. I give and bequeath unto my daughter **Julia Armstrong** two negroes, namely **Bill** and **Harriet** with her increase. And I further will and devise that the sum of Three Hundred Dollars be paid over to my daughter **Julia** extra over and above her equal share as herein provided for with her other sisters, **Elizabeth, Sally, Margaret and Louisiana.**

11th. I will that the tract of land on which I live be divided as follows, to wit: Beginning at the Brick Spring House, running down the spring branch, thence down the mill branch to the lower end of the little meadow on the west side of the branch. Thence a straight (line) with the lower end of the meadow fence to the back line adjoining **Mrs. Surgoine's** land. Thence with my line to the river. Thence up the river to my son **William's** line. Thence with his line to where it strikes the mill branch. Thence up the same to where the road crosses opposite the Brick Spring House. Thence to the beginning which aforesaid described tract I allot to the Old Tavern which is to include the mill, still house, &C.

To the Brick House lot to the division, I assign from the branch at the lower end of the little meadow aforesaid out to the back line adjoining **Mrs. Surgoine's** land aforesaid. Thence, along the same to the line of the long tract. Thence with the same to the northwest corner thereof near the Wolfe Spring on the Barrett Tract lately sold to **Mr. Grigsby.** Thence with my lines to the Meeting House lot with the lines of the same and the lines of my son **William's** to the branch. Then down the branch until nearly opposite the Brick Spring House. Thence a straight line to the spring house. Thence down the spring branch and mill branch to the beginning at the lower end of the little meadow aforesaid.

11th. I will and devise that my land adjoining the above described tracts be laid off into three lots as near as may be of equal value, and that said lots of land also the tract attached to the Brick House as above described. Also my lots in the town of Surgoinesville (excepting one given to **William Amis**). Also a tract of land in Stanley Valley on Marshall's Creek, also all my negroes not herein otherwise disposed of, also my stock and other personal property be sold and the proceeds thereof be divided equally among my five daughters, **Elizabeth Bradford, Sally Bord, Louisiana DeWolfe, Margaret Cook,** and **Julia Armstrong,** after having first paid all my just debts.

8

12th. I further will and devise that the titles for 5000 acres of land on the waters of Bear Creek from **Zachariah Cox** &c be divided among all my children equally providing that should any one of the heirs take on them the trouble and expense to secure the title of said lands from the Government of the U. States, I will devise to that heir two shares of said land in said division.

13th. I will that the river tract herein conditionally given to my son **Cary** remain in the possession of my Executors until the expiration of the three years, unless my son **Cary** should sooner return and comply with the conditions of this my will.

14th. I will and devise that all other property that I may die possessed of and not herein named whether real estate or personal, be sold and divided among all my children.

16th. I will and bequeath that my grandson **Wm. A. Amis** have a lot in the town of Surgonsville, lying opposite where **Mrs. Carter** lately lived, said lot lying and being on the south side of the main street. I will that the Sulphur Spring lot remain unsold for the benefit of all my children.

Lastly. I will that **William Armstrong, Jr.** and **James Amis** be made the Executors of this my last Will & Testament.

W. Armstrong (seal)

Signed, sealed and acknowledged
in presence of:
William Lyons,
Aaron Grigsby
G. M. Lyons

I, **William Armstrong, Sen'r.** being still of sound mind and memory but weak in body do add this Supplement to the foregoing--my last Will and Testament, viz: I will that the donations in money &C heretofore given to my daughters **Margaret & Julia** by my wife in her lifetime be considered a part of my will, and that my daughters **Margaret & Julia** retain the same and I further will that my daughter **Julia** have a good horse in addition to what I have herein bequeathed unto her.

I further will that the dividing line between the river tract and the tract attached to the Brick House be altered and that from the lower end of the little meadow down, that the creek be the line.

Given under my hand and seal this 13th day of January, 1835.

W. Armstrong (seal)

In presence of: ...

WILL OF HAYNES AMIS

Page 13   Dated: July 27, 1847

In the Name of God, Amen.

I, **Haynes Amis** of the County of Hawkins and State of Tennessee, being weak in body, but of perfect mind and memory and considering the uncertainty of human life have concluded and determined to dispose of the worldly _____ with which the Lord has intrusted me in the manner

hereinafter mentioned, and I do by this my last Will and Testament revoke and annul all other wills and devises of my said Estate.

To my sons, **Thomas J. Amis** and **James H. Amis**, I give and bequeath the land on which I reside included in several adjoining tracts containing 800 acres or upwards to be divided between them by the following lines, Viz: Beginning at a point in **Mr. William's** line on the east side of Big Creek, so that a direct line from thence through the site of the burnt smith's shop shall pass to the center of the spring, thence up a branch to a sugar tree, thence a southwest course to the western line including my dwelling house, mills and other improvements. I hereby give to my said son **Thomas** with the personal property owned by him and in his possession.

All of my land lying southward of said line, including the tan yard, the stock therein and other improvements on said southern portion of the land I hereby give to my said son **James**, together with the personal property owned by him and in his possession.

To my daughter, **Lucy H. Amis**, intermarried with **John Hagan**, I give and bequeath a tract of land of about 170 acres on which they have lately resided, a negro man named **Joe** about 30 years of age, and a negro woman now and for several years in their possession named **Mary**, about 20 years of age, and $200.00 in money.

To my daughter **Martha**, intermarried with **John Kershner**, I have heretofore given a tract of land of 150 acres which they having relinquished to my sons, it is now a part of the bequest to my son **Thomas.** I have also given my said daughter a negro girl for many years in her possession and I now give her $300.00 in money.

To my daughter **Mary**, intermarried with **Lazarus Spears**, I have heretofore given a negro woman named **Nancy** and her three (now four) children. I also give her a negro man named **Jack** about 25 years of age and $200.00 in money.

To the children of my deceased daughter **Sarah Amis** (late wife of **James M. Armstrong**): To **Louisiana Armstrong** I give a horse, saddle & bridle worth one hundred dollars. To **Lucy Ann Armstrong** I give two negro girls named **Francis** and **Harriet** and $200.00 in money.

Any and all other property belonging to me at the time of my death to be equally divided between my four daughters above named and their heirs.

I hereby constitute and appoint my son **Thomas J. Amis** Executor of this my last Will and Testament, hereby ratifying and confirming all such lawful acts as he my said Executor shall do and perform in relation to the aforesaid Estate.

In witness of all which I have hereunto set my hand and seal this 27th day of July, 1847.

Haynes Amis (seal)

Test:
Richard Grantham
George Hale
John Larkin

WILL OF JONATHAN ANDERSON

Page 14   Dated: March 3, 1849

I, **Jonathan Anderson** do make and publish this my last Will and Testament hereby revoking and making void all other wills by me at any time made.

First. I do direct my funeral expenses and all my debts be paid as soon after my death as possible out of any money that I may die possessed of or may first come into the hands of my Executor.

Secondly. I give and bequeath unto my two grandsons, to wit: Rien Anderson and Carter Anderson one dollar each.

Thirdly. I do give and bequeath unto my daughter Rhody Anderson as once was, but now Rhody Sizemore, one dollar.

Fourthly. I do give and bequeath unto my daughter Catherine Anderson as once was, but now Catherine Herd, one dollar.

Fifthly. I do give and bequeath unto my daughter Mary Anderson, as once was, but now Mary Smith, one dollar.

Sixthly and Lastly. I do hereby nominate and appoint Beverly C. Ford my Executor. In witness whereof I do to this my will set my hand and seal. This 3rd day of March, One Thousand Eight Hundred and Forty-nine.

Jonathan x Anderson (seal)
(his mark)

Signed, sealed & published in our presence, and we have subscribed out names hereto in the presence of the Testator. This 3rd day of March, 1849.

James C. x Ford
(his mark)

Jarel Ford

John x Herd
(his mark)

Page 15

WILL OF ISAAC AMYX

Dated: October 13, 1849
Proven: February, 1850

State of Tennessee, Hawkins County:

I, Isaac Amyx, do make and publish this my last Will and Testament, hereby revoking and making void all other wills by me at any time made.

First. I direct that my funeral expenses and my debts be paid as soon after my death as possible out of any money that I may die possessed of or may first come into the hands of my Executor.

Secondly. I give and bequeath to my son Samuel Amyx and his heirs the following boundary of land, Viz: Beginning on a white oak corner, running westwardly to the high bluff of the ridge. On then with the west side of the ridge to the cross fence and with said fence to the apple orchard, and then to a sugar tree so as not to include any of said orchard. Then southwest to the top of a spur, then with the top of the spur to the top of Clinch Mountain, and with the top of the mountain eastwardly to Samuel Amyx's line and with said line to Riley Winstead's line and thence to the beginning.

Thirdly. I give and bequeath to my daughter Elizabeth, now Elizabeth Snider, and her heirs the following boundary of land, Viz: Beginning on a dogwood, my beginning corner--running thence northeast to (a) hollow that comes down from Jones and Goodman's field opposite to the spring branch and with the same to said Samuel Amyx's boundary. Thence westwardly with said Amyx's boundary to near the orchard. Thence westwardly to the War Gap road. Thence with Charles Snider's line to the beginning.

Fourthly. I give and bequeath unto my daughter Polly Amyx 20 acres of

land on the upper end of my farm joining Polly Pearson's land.

Fifthly. I give and bequeath to my daughter Prissilla, now Prissilla Davis and her heirs a boundary of land as follows: Beginning at the above named Amyx & Snider boundary near the orchard; thence southeast with Samuel Amyx's boundary to the top of the Clinch Mountain. Thence westwardly with the top of the mountain to Samuel Amyx's line. Thence northwardly with said line to Wm. Drinnen's line. Thence with said line to Charles Snider's line. Thence with said line to War Gap Road and thence with said Snider's line to the beginning.

Sixthly. I direct that my wife Mary Amyx shall have a decent maintenance from the said Samuel, Elizabeth & Prissilla Amyx during her life, and I further direct that in one year after the death of my wife Mary Amyx that the aforesaid Samuel Amyx, Elizabeth Snider & Prissilla Davis shall pay to the following named heirs $500.00 in good, current bank notes according to the value of each of their boundaries of land aforenamed, Viz:

To Elenor, now Nancy Drinnon, $100.00.
To Nancy, now Nancy Lawson, $100.00.
To Lucinda, now Lucinda Drinnon, $100.00.
To Susannah, now Susannah Jones, $100.00.
To Sarah, now Sarah Davis, $100.00.

(It is to be understood that the improvements on the aforenamed boundaries of land are not to be valued).

Seventhly. I give and bequeath to my wife Mary Amyx all of my household and kitchen furniture to dispose of as she may think proper.

Eightly. I direct that all my personal property be sold on twelve months' credit and the proceeds equally divided between all of my above named children.

Lastly. I do hereby nominate and appoint my son Samuel Amyx my Executor. In witness whereof I do to this my will set my hand and seal. This 13th day of October, 1849.

Isaac Amyx (seal)

Signed, sealed and published in our presence, and we have subscribed out names hereto in the presence of the Testator. This 14th day of October, 1849.

Witnesses: Rial Johns, James Johnson, W. C. Wilder

Page 16

WILL OF AARON ANDERSON

Dated: August 13, 1855
Proven: December Term, 1855

We the undersigned John Begley & John Templeton, both of Hawkins County--the first named of the age of forty-nine years; the last named of the age of twenty-three years, state that on the first Wednesday in August, 1855, being the first day of said month, we being present at the house of Aaron Anderson who was then lying sick and who being made aware of the probable approach of death, in contemplation of his decease which took place on the Sunday following, said Anderson called upon us to remain with him while the company retired, and when left alone with us, John Begley mentioned to him the subject of death on which he stated he was not afraid

to die but was ready to go at any moment. He then said all the property
that he had—land, negroes, and other property—everything he possessed
in the world, he wanted **Bitha**, his wife, to have during her life, to dispose of as she pleased. At the death of his wife he wanted **William Stapleton's**
eldest child **Solomon Stapleton** to have the two fields in the possession of
William Stapleton, where said **Wm. Stapleton** has been tending the last five
or six years, and to include with said fields the land from the field to
the back line of the tract running with the fence westwardly to the lane
that runs by said **Anderson's** house and with said lane from the corner of
said field southeastwardly as far as the lane goes. Then the same direction to the back line of the said tract of land on the mountain. He said
he thought the said land would make the little boy a right good home if he
lived.

He then said that **Henry Hart** had lived with him tho' he said **Anderson**
had raised him pretty much; that he was poor and had for him, said **Anderson**,
(done) many days hard work and that he thought it right to do something
for him. He said he wanted **Henry** and his two negroes **Alfred** and **Betty** to
have his land after his wife's death, provided the law would allow the
negroes to be free and stay on it, but if it would not, they were to belong
to his wife, to dispose of as she pleased. In case the said negroes could
not be freed, he said he wanted **Henry Hart** to have half the land after his
wife's death to be so divided as (to) give water to each part and his wife
to dispose of the balance.

He further said he did not want his people to have a dollar that he
had worked for...that they had always been against him from the time he was
a boy, and that his wife had helped him work for it and he wanted her to
have it, and he wanted it fixed so that his people could not trouble her
after his death.

He then said this is my will—the way I want my property disposed of
after my death. If I have two or three days I will have it put in writing.

At the time of the above, the said **Aaron Anderson** was in his senses
and of sound and disposing mind and memory, in full possession of all his
faculties.

In testimony whereof we have hereto set our hands this 13th day of
August, 1855.

> John Begley
> John Templeton

WILL OF WILLIAM ALTOM

Page 18   Dated: May 29, 1857
                                           Proven Sept., 1857

In the Name of God, Amen.

I, **William Altom** of the County of Hawkins and State of Tennessee,
being of sound mind and memory and considering the uncertainty of this
frail and transitory life, do therefore make, ordain, publish and declare
this to be my last Will and Testament. That is to say:

First. After all my lawful debts are paid and discharged, the
residue of my estate I give and bequeath as follows, to wit:

To my beloved wife, the land and appurtenances on which I now live
during her natural life, and to have the rents and proffits on the land

on the east end of s'd lands to a cross fence running from the back of
Cloud's Creek north toward Stone Mountain, on the east side of my son
John's house in which he now lives, together with fifty dollars cash and
all my household and kitchen furniture which I may die in possession of—
one red cow with a white face and her calf and one brindle heifer, one
white spotted sow and four chaised hogs, also all the corn, bacon and
wheat that I now have on hand.

Secondly. I give to my son **John** the west end of my farm after the
death of my beloved wife, running north and south crossing Cloud's Creek,
a straight line with a cross fence east of son **John's** house in which he
now lives, about fifty or sixty yards of said house, to have possession
of said lot of land now free from rents but the not to be invested in him
until after the death of my wife, then to have title to said lot of land.

Thirdly. My will is that after the death of my wife the remainder of
my land to be sold and the proceeds arising from sale of said lands to be
equally divided between my two daughters (to wit): **Mary Elkins** and **Sarah
Carpenter** share and share alike.

Fourth. I give and bequeath to my grandson **John Carpenter** my brown
colt in which I am now in possession.

Fifth. My will is that if it should be the will of the Almighty God
to call me from the walks of society before the crop to which I now have on
hand, my will is that the balance of my personal property be sold at public
sale but not to be sold until the present crop is made and the proceeds
arising from said sale be equally divided between my wife and three children, share and share alike. Likewise, I make, constitute and appoint my
son **John Altom** and S. D. Brooks to be my Executors of this my last Will
and Testament, hereby revoking all former wills by me made.

In witness whereof I have hereunto subscribed my name and affixed my
seal. This 29th day of May in the year of our Lord, One Thousand Eight
Hundred and Fifty-seven.

                              (his)
                    William x Altom (seal)
                              (mark)

The above written instrument was subscribed by the said **Wm. Altom** in our
presence, and acknowledged by him to each of us, and he at the same time
published and declared the above instrument so subscribed to be his last
Will and Testament, and we at the Testator's request and in his presence
have signed our names as witnesses hereto.
R. M. Bishop
Thomas Everhart

WILL OF SETH ARMSTRONG

Page 19   Dated: July 11, 1859
                                 Recorded: Jan. Term,1878, p.3
                                 Proven: Jan. 7, 1878

I, **Seth Armstrong** of the County of Hawkins in the State of Tennessee,
do make and publish this my last Will & Testament in manner and form following, hereby revoking and making void all former wills by me at any time
made. And as to such other worldly goods as it has pleased God to entrust
me with, I dispose of as follows:

First. I direct that all my just debts and funeral charges be paid as soon as possible after my decease out of any money that may come to the hands of my Administrator from any portion of my Estate, real or personal. I further will and bequeath to my daughter **Milly M. Hicks** and to her heirs one half of my tract of land in Hawkins County in the State of Tennessee, on the waters of the Holston River, adjoining the land of **George Arnold** and **Thomas Marshall**, also one half of a tract known as the Mountain Tract, containing by estimation, 104 acres, and the first mentioned tract contains by estimation 146 acres, together with all the issues, rents and profits arising therefrom to have and to hold said lands during her natural life, and then to her heirs, to her own separate use, benefit and behoof—free from the control of her husband, **Thomas Hicks**, and free from all the debts, liabilities and judgements which now exist or may hereafter exist against her said husband. I further will and bequeath to my daughter **Milly M. Hicks** one-half (interest ?) in three negroes—one negro man called **Ben** about 60 years and one negro woman **Pagey** aged about 60 years, and one negro **Leta** about 19 years, to be divided equally between my two daughters, share and share alike as may be agreed upon by themselves, together with their increase during her natural life, and free from all his debts, judgements, liabilities of any whatsoever, but at the death of my said daughter, should she have no children living, I will that all the Estate herein created shall fall back to my other daughter.

I further will and bequeath to my said daughter **Ann** half of all money that I may be possessed of at my decease, or that may come into the hands of the Administrators, arising out of the sales & otherwise from any portion of my Estate to her own separate use and benefit, free from the control of her husband and free from his debts, judgements and liabilities of every kind—to be paid to my said daughter upon her separate receipt upon ? examination.

I further direct that my beloved wife **Elizabeth Armstrong** (if I should die first), shall have a child's part of my estate during her natural life or widowhood, but in case she shall marry a second time, then my will is that she shall have and be governed by the Law of Dower then existing in this State, and she shall be governed by the same.

I further will to my grand daughter **Dorothy An. Hicks** one sorrel horse called Jim, to be from the date of the delivery thereof her own, for her own use and the entire right of said horse is hereby vested in her. I also give to my daughter, **Sary Christian**, a horse of equal value to the horse above mentioned.

I further will and bequeath to my daughter **Sary Catharine** the other half of my estate, share and share alike with the before-mentioned daughter **Milly M. Hicks** in every particular and to her heirs. But in default of heirs of my said daughter **Sary Catharine**, then I will and direct that the estate herein created shall fall back and go to my other heirs then living by the rules of descent of this state then existing.

In testimony whereof I have hereunto set my hand and seal this 11th day of July, 1859, by making his mark, being unable to write his name.

Seth x Armstrong (seal)
(his mark)

Attest:
William Mullins: Stephen x Hicks
(his mark)

Page 21

WILL OF JOHN K. ARNOLD

Dated: Oct. 10, 1859
Proven Dec. 3, 1860
(Recorded P. 418)

In the Name of God, Amen.

I, **John K. Arnold**, do make this my last Will and Testament.

First. I will and bequeath to Almighty God my soul, who gave it.

Secondly. It is my will that my wife **Martha Arnold** have my plantation whereon I now live during her natural lifetime to do with as she pleases while she lives. I also will that my wife have all the household and kitchen furniture and all the stocks on hand, say horses, cattle, hogs and sheep, and all the crop or grain that may be on hand at the time of my death.

Thirdly. I will that my two sons **William** and **Andrew J. Arnold** have at the time of the death of my wife the entire plantation that I have willed to my wife, and that my two sons, **William** and **Jackson Arnold** pay to each of my children Five Dollars apiece, that is to say: **John Granville, Thomas Greenberry, Eliza, George, Alfred, Sarah, Juliann** and **Harvey Arnold.**

Fourthly. It is my will that my wife **Martha** pay all my debts and funeral expenses as soon as she can after my death out of any property or money that I may die possessed of. This the 10th day of October, 1859.

John K. x Arnold
(his mark)

Signed, sealed and delivered in our presence:

Robb Cooper
George P. x Arnold
(his mark)

Page 21

WILL OF WILLIAM M. ARNOLT

Dated July 29, 1860
Proven: Aug. 6, 1860
[Recorded P. 389]

I, **William M. Arnolt**, being of sound and well disposing mind but in feeble health do make and publish this as my last Will and Testament, hereby revoking and making void all other wills by me made at any time.

First. I will that my funeral expenses and all my just debts be paid as soon as possible after my death out of any money that I may die possessed of or may first come into the hands of my Executor.

2nd. I will to **William A. Charles** my nephew have 100 acres of land to be run off of the lower end of my farm where it joins the lands of **Wiley A. Grigsby** and **Thomas Moore.**

3rd. I will to my father **William Arnolt** all the rest of my land embraced in the deed made to me by my father, by him given up the bond given by myself to him on the 13th day of June, 1854, for Two Thousand dollars, conditioned for the maintenance of himself and mother, together with the note that I executed to him on the same date of the bond for ____ dollars.

4th. I further will and bequeath to my beloved wife the 22½ acre tract of land known as the Wax Tract, during her lifetime or widowhood, and at her death or marriage, said land to go to my brothers and sisters and their heirs, and that she further have all the property and household furniture that she had when she and I were married, and one cow, (she to choose), and the sorrel blazed faced filly and three hundred dollars in cash, all the increase of the stock on hand of the stock she had when she came to live with me, and to have two-thirds of the corn crop that is on hand, one-third of the oats that is on hand, half of the hay that is now made, and is to have my Bureau during her lifetime or widowhood, and at her death or marriage, the Bureau to be sold and the proceeds be equally divided between my brothers and sisters or their heirs &c.

5th. I further will that my father William Arnolt have all the grass on hand that is now uncut, and half the hay that is now made, all the wheat on hand, one-third of the corn crop, two-thirds of the oats on hand.

6th. I will that all the rest of my personal property be sold and that the proceeds be equally divided between my brothers and sisters or their heirs, my wife Sally being made an heir with them, except fifty dollars that I will my niece Isabella Rader is to have.

7th and lastly. I appoint James Hearick as my Executor to this my will. Whereunto I do set my hand and seal to this my will. This the 29th July, 1860.

William M. x Arnolt
(his mark)

Signed, sealed and published in
our presence, and we have subscribed
our names in the presence of the Testator
on this 29th day of July, 1860.
James H. Walker
Thomas Moore

WILL OF WILLIAM ARMSTRONG

Page 23

Dated: Feb. 16, 1860
Proven: Sept. 3, 1860
[Rec'd Page 392]

Hawkins County, State of Tennessee

I, **William Armstrong**, considering the uncertainty of this life, and being of sound mind and memory do make and publish this my last Will and Testament in manner and form following (that is to say):

1st. I give and bequeath to my son **Henry C. Armstrong** a negro slave named **Moses**, which I consider worth Four Hundred Dollars.

2nd. I will and bequeath to my daughter **Mary E. Powel**, wife of Sam'l Powel two negro slaves named **Rhoda** and **Riceton** which I consider worth Four Hundred Dollars, also one town lot in Rogersville—said lot conveyed to me by **William Dick Alexander** as a trustee of **James Bradley**; also the Military Land Warrants containing 120 acres, (The town lot and Land Warrants I consider worth Three Hundred Dollars). The above bequest amounting to Eleven Hundred Dollars.

In addition to those bequests I have paid to my daughter **Mary E. Powel** and her husband **Samuel Powel** $1,550.00, all of said payments amounting to $2,600.00 they have received from me. I further will that the further sum of $1,850.00 be paid to **Mary E. Powel** before or after my death.

4th. I will and bequeath to my son **William L. Armstrong**, one negro slave, **David**, my land lying and being in the County of Hawkins and State of Tennessee, on the north side of Holston River, in 8th Civil District. I divide in the following manner (to wit): Beginning on a small willow box elder and sycamore on the Holston River at low water mark, running thence south eighty-two and one-half degrees, west seventy poles to a small double sweet gum at the foot of the rise of the bottom; thence north 10 west twenty poles to a maple at the foot of a stony bottom; thence north seventy-two (a) half. West sixty-eight poles to a mulberry, the upper side of the old orchard field. Then south fifty, west sixteen to a sycamore at the creek back of the old stable. Thence north to west up the creek as it meanders one hundred and twenty poles to a large, flat rock in said creek about three poles below where the sawmill dam now is. Thence north forty-two degrees and east twenty-seven poles to a white oak oak corner of the N. Providence Church lot. Thence along the south west end of said church lot to a black oak corner of same, it also being the corner of the teacher's lot. Then along the line of the teacher's residence lot to a small ironwood sapling near the creek corner of said lot; thence north seventy-eight, west forty-six poles to a stake. Thence north 73, west 92 poles to a poplar near the spring known as Wolf Spring. Thence north 48, west 73 poles to a stake in the branch (**Larkin's** Branch) west of where an old cabin now stands. Thence 65 west up **Larkin's** Branch, 74 poles to a poplar and beach corner - corner of a tract of land formerly owned by my father, a part of which was sold to **Baker Armstrong**. The above described line I make to divide my land, making two tracts of the same. My tract of land I dispose of in the following manner:

1st. I consider my land worth $12,000.00, and I give and bequeath to my son **Harry C. Armstrong** $4,000.00 which sum he has already received of me when he started...and moved to Missouri. This amount I consider due him for his interest in my land.

2nd. I give and bequeath to my son **Alfred Armstrong**, his heirs and assigns, all that part of my land north and east of the dividing line adjoining and bounded by the lands of the heirs of **Baker Armstrong**, dec'd., **Dr. Robert Johnson** and the heirs of **William Bradley**, dec'd., along the lines of same to a black walnut on the river bank and two sycamores corner of **William Bradley's** heirs and my corner at low water mark. Thence down the Holston River to the willow box elder and sycamores (beginning of the dividing line), him to have and to hold with all appurtenances thereto belonging &c, with this incumbrance. The said **Alfred Armstrong** is to pay me or my Executor $1,500.00 toward my son **Henry's** interest in my land, $1,278.00 of which he has paid to me as will appear from my receipt to him.

The other part of my land I give and bequeath to my wife **Mary Armstrong**, with all its appurtenances thereto belonging, or in anywise appertaining, during her natural life. At her death, I will and bequeath the same to my son, **William L. Armstrong**, the lands being bounded as follows, to wit: By the dividing line before mentioned, thence along my lines to the corner between the heirs of **Baker Armstrong** and **Dock Larkins**. Thence with said **Larkins** to **John Young's**. Thence along said **Young's** to **Wm Lyon's**. Along

WILL OF CHARLES D. ALVIS

Dated March 22, 1861
Proven Feb. 3, 1862
[Recorded p. 526]

his to Conrad Fudge's lines. Thence to Surgoin's and others to David Lyon's; along his to Wesley A. Phipps' line to his ash and Lyon's corner on the Holston River; thence to low water mark. Thence up the river to the willow box elder and sycamore near low water mark, the beginning corner of the dividing line. To my son William L. Armstrong, I bequeath the same to him to have and to hold with all the appurtenances thereunto belonging, to him and his heirs and assigns subject to the encumbrance—that he pay me or my Executors the sum of $2,500.00, that being the amount I paid for him to my son Henry for his interest in my land.

I give and bequeath to my wife Mary Armstrong my negro slaves not other-wise herein disposed of, namely (to wit): Stephen, Betty, Jefferson, Arthur and Sidney and her three children, Harriet, Lousanna and Jane—her Jefferson, my son William L. Armstrong (to have) Stephen, Betty & Arthur. I allow my wife Mary Armstrong to divide Sidney and her children in the way and manner she may think best. It is my will that my two old servants Stephen & Betty be well provided for and made comfortable while they live.

I give unto my wife Mary Armstrong what money I have—notes & other evidence of debt, all my stock consisting of horses, cattle, hogs, and sheep; also all my farming utensils, household and kitchen furniture, her to have and hold the same and to be at her disposal in any manner she may see proper, she being responsible for the payment of all my just debts, funeral expenses and all other necessary and contingent expenses.

It is my will that my son William L. Armstrong live with his mother and take charge of the farm and hands and him to have half they make after paying all expenses, until he pays the amount of the encumbrance. I allow him to pay for his land. If my wife should die before Mary B. Powel is paid, then the balance of Mary's Dower which she has not heretofore received from me, must be paid out of the proceeds of my personal Estate, stock & otherwise.

The division is as follows: I consider all my land worth $12,000.00. I divide my land between my two sons Alfred and William L. Armstrong—they to pay me $4,000.00 which sum I paid to my son H. C. Armstrong when he moved to Missouri which will appear from his receipt to me for the same. To my son, H. C. Armstrong, in money and negro, $4,400.00. To my son Alfred Armstrong in land and negro, $4,400.00. To my daughter Mary B. Powel two negroes and sundry other made and to be paid $4,400.00. To my son William L. Armstrong, land and negro, $4,400.00.

The rest of my property, if any, I wish divided equally among my legatees.

I hereby appoint my wife Mary Armstrong my Executrix and my son Alfred Armstrong my Executor of this my last Will and Testament. In witness whereof I have hereunto set my hand and seal this sixteenth day of February, One Thousand Eight Hundred and Sixty.

Wm. Armstrong

Witnesses thereunto:
Jesse M. Lyons
Jos. B. Galbraith

I, Charles D. Alvis, senior, of Hawkins County, State of Tennessee, being in good health and in my right mind do make and publish this my last Will and Testament hereby revoking and making void all other wills by me at any time made.

1st. I bequeath my soul to God who gave it.

2nd. I direct that my funeral expenses and all my debts be paid as soon as possible after my death out of any money that I may die possessed of, or may first come into the hands of my Executor.

Third. I do will and desire that my well beloved wife Susannah Alvis have the use of my mansion house and a comfortable support of ten pro-ceeds of my farm. Also William Henry a yellow boy slave twenty-two years of age; also Sharlot a black girl slave twenty-one years of age during her natural life or widowhood—if she remain in the state. I will and desire that my slaves that I have willed to my well beloved wife be set free at her death or leaving the state or marriage.

Fourth. I do will and bequeath to my son Charles D. Alvis, Jr., my mansion house and ten acres of land running with James Brooks' line to James T. Brice's line, thence round so as to square ten acres.

Fifth. It is my will and desire that the balance of my land and property be equally divided between my three children, Charles D. Alvis, Jr., Mary Ann Susan Klepper and Joseph H. Alvis and their children after their deaths.

Sixth. I do will and bequeath to my son Elias H. Alvis Fifty Cents. To my son William A. Alvis, Fifty Cents. To my son George W. Alvis, Fifty Cents. To my son Thaddeus J. Alvis, Fifty Cents. To my son Thomas J. Alvis, Fifty Cents. To my daughter Virginia Rebecca Johnson Fifty Cents. To my son John M. Alvis' heirs, Fifty Cents.

Seventh. I do will and bequeath to my well beloved wife, in addition to the third item of this will, all of my household and kitchen furniture and necessary property for farming consisting of one horse and set of farming tools, one yoke of oxen, two cows and calves, pork sufficient to meat her one year, or hogs to make it. Two sows and pigs or shoats, thirty barrels of corn and twenty bushels of wheat and twenty bushels of oats, an also my wife Susannah Alvis is to have my three slaves above named during her natural life and the increase of Sharlot is to be set free during life. After her death, the aforesaid slaves and the increase of Sharlot is to be set free in the state.

Eighth. I reserve a square at the graveyard for a burying ground.

Lastly. I do hereby nominate and appoint Charles D. Alvis, Jr., my Executor. In witness whereof I do to this my last Will set my hand and seal This 22nd day of March, 1861.

Charles D. x Alvis, Sr.(seal)
(his mark)

Signed and published in our presence and we have subscribed our names hereto in the presence of the Testator. This 22nd day of March, 1861.

Barney M. Klepper

N B: I appoint Charles D. Alvis, Jr. to attend to my beloved wife and to manage for my slaves as laid down in this will.

WILL OF HUGH BROWN

Page 28   Dated: July 4, 1789

In the Name of God, Amen.

I, **Hugh Brown** of the State of North Carolina and County of Hawkins, farmer, being very weak and frail in body, but blessed be God of perfect mind and memory, and calling to mind the mortality of my body and knowing that it is appointed unto all men once to die, therefore, I do make, constitute and ordain my last Will and Testament. And being thus composed in mind, first and principally, I do give and recommend my soul to God who gave it me, and my body I recommend to the earth to be buried in a decent Christian-like manner at the discretion of my Executors, nothing doubting but at the general judgement I shall receive the same again by the mighty power of God. And as to such worldly Estate wherewith it hath pleased the Lord to bless me in this life, I do give, bequeath and dispose of in the following manner:

Imprimis. After all my just and lawful debts are paid, I do give and bequeath to my dearly and well beloved wife **Rebecka Brown** my negro wench named **Jean**.

Item. I do give and bequeath to my dearly beloved daughter, **Sarah Brown**, my negro girl named **Atne**.

Item. I do give and bequeath to my dearly beloved daughter **Margaret Brown** my negro boy named **Sam**.

Item. I do give and bequeath to my two dearly and well beloved sons, **John Brown** and **William Brown** all my houses, lands, tenements and whole estate until they come to the age of 21 years or until some one of my daughters should be married and then their part Viz: The girls shall be given them and when my sons come to the age of 21, they shall equally divide the remainder between themselves.

And furthermore, I do appoint, constitute and ordain my true and trusty friend, **Rob't. Black** and my dearly and well beloved wife, **Rebecca Brown**, to be the whole and sole Executors of this my last Will and Testament, and I do hereby utterly break, disannul and make void all and every former will or wills or testaments at any time, or in any way by me made, and I do acknowledge this and none other to be my last Will and Testament.

In witness whereof I have hereunto set my hand and seal This fourth day of July in the year of our Lord One Thousand Seven Hundred and Eighty-nine.

                          Hugh x Brown (seal)
                              (his mark)

Signed, sealed, published and pronounced by the said **Hugh Brown** as his last Will and Testament in the presence of us who in the presence of the said **Brown** and in the presence of each other have hereunto witnessed our names.

Jas. Cunningham
Ananias McCoy
James White

WILL OF EBENEZER BROOKS

Page 29   Dated: April 23, 1799

In the Name of God, Amen. I, **Ebenezer Brooks**, late of the County of Washington in the State of Virginia, now of the County of Hawkins in the State of Tennessee, being in a lingering state of health, but of sound mind and memory, to provide against that mortality to which we are all liable and by which I am now particularly threatened, do ordain this to be my last Will and Testament, confiding in the unbounded goodness of God and the certain foundation of Christian hope, I commend my soul to the keeping of my Heavenly Father, hoping to obtain a Resurrection among the just. Should my present disease put a period to my earthly abode, I commit my body to the care of my trusty friends **David Caldwell** and **James Caldwell**, to be by them decently buried at New Providence Meeting House. To defray the expenses of which I leave to them ten dollars in cash at **John Campbells** in Washington County, Va. and notes payable on demand now in my possession, but should that not be sufficient, I leave my mare and colt now at **John Campbell's**, and my riding horse for that purpose, and also such other property as I have in Washington County, Virginia, or in Hawkins County, Tennessee. But should what cash I have and my debts be sufficient to defray my funeral expenses and charges, then I will and bequeath my riding horse to **David Cunningham**, eldest son of said **John**, my mare to his daughter **Polly**, and the colt to his daughter **Betsy**.

I will and bequeath to my friend and cousin, **William Montgomery** of Sumner County, Tennessee, and to his heirs forever all my landed property and claims following, to wit: A tract of land containing 900 acres between Silver and Paint Lick Creeks, one other tract containing 1,000 acres on the waters of Station Camp Creek above Boonsborough, one other tract containing 4,812 acres on Cabbin Creek, all lying in the State of Kentucky. Also one other tract of land containing 640 acres on Stone's River, one other tract containing 640 acres on Little Harpath, both on the waters of the Cumerland River in Tennessee; also, a military claim of 500 acres on Little Miami, part of the claim of **Col. Joseph Crockets** in the State of Kentucky, to the sole use and behoof of the said **William Montgomery** and his heirs forever, yet with this reservation and on the condition that should **William Montgomery** recover my lands in the State of Kentucky and my two tracts in the State of Tennessee, that then he should pay unto my half sister **Jean Davis** of Washington County in the State of **Delaware** $1,575.00, if she shall require it, but should he only obtain possession of the two tracts in the State of Tennessee, he is only to pay her $1,000.00. But if my said sister **Jean** is dead, or should die before this will is carried into execution after my death, or should not require of **William Montgomery** the above specified legacy, then, and in that case, the said **William Montgomery** is to have the fee simple estate in the above mentioned lands without any reservation to my sister (**Jean**), or condition whatever. I will and direct that the money arising from my two Manuscripts, the one--**A Reply to Paines Age of Reason**, the other, **A Treatise on Stenography**, be applied to the use of my sister if living. If not, I will them (the proceeds) to **William Montgomery**. Should the provision I have made for my funeral expenses be insufficient, I will that **William Montgomery** settle and pay the balance and the value of the legacies to the person to whom they are bequeathed. Also, that he erect over my grave at New Providence a decent tombstone.

I empower and authorize John Campbell of Washington County, Virginia to settle my estate in that county and David Caldwell of Hawkins County, Tennessee to settle my affairs in the counties of Sullivan and Hawkins, and do hereby nominate and appoint my friend and cousin William Montgomery Executor of this my last Will and Testament, hereby revoking all other wills by me made and declaring this to be my last Will and Testament.

In testimony whereof I have hereunto set my hand and seal This twenty third day of April, in the year of our Lord, one thousand seven hundred and ninety-nine.

    Ebenezer Brooks (seal)

Signed, sealed and acknowledged in the presence of us who in the presence of the Testator and at his request signed our names as witnesses thereto.

    John Campbell
    Baker Armstrong (Jurat)
    David Caldwell (Jurat)
    David Campbell, Jun'r.

WILL OF RICHARD BYRD

Dated: March 5, 1803   Page 31

In the Name of God, Amen. I, Richard Byrd of the County of Hawkins and State of Tennessee South of the River Ohio, planter, being in and of imperfect health of body, but in and of perfect mind and memory, thanks be given unto God. Calling to mind the mortality of my ( ) blank space), and knowing that it is once appointed for all men to die, do make and ordain this my last Will and Testament. That is to say, principally and first of all, I give and recommend my soul into the hands of Almighty God that gave it and my body I recommend to the earth to be buried in decent Christian burial at the discretion of my Executor, nothing doubting but at the general resurrection I shall recieve the same again by the mighty power of God.

And, as touching such worldly estate wherewith it has pleased God to bless me in this life, I give, devise and dispose of the same in the following manner and form:

1st. My three eldest sons, naming first, William Byrd, second, John Byrd, third, David Byrd. I also give to my son David Byrd 175105 in the form of his land, and two daughters, Jean McDaniel and Ann ____ day and my two younger sons, Michael Byrd & Richard Byrd, I, Richard Byrd, do consider that they have equally received of my estate one hundred dollars each. And I give and bequeath to my four younger children—two sons and two daughters: first, Elizabeth Byrd, second, Mary Byrd, likewise, James Byrd and Charles Byrd, one hundred dollars a-piece as they come of age.

Also, I bequeath to Elizabeth, my dearly beloved wife all the remaining horses, cattle, sheep, hogs and slaves and household goods and movable effects, together with the land and plantation on which I now live containing 200 acres, to be by her freely possessed during the term of her widowhood, at the expiration of which time, or at her death, I will the said land to my two youngest sons, James and Charles Byrd—the plantation

to be divided. The hollow the wagon road runs up shall be the line betwixt them. The end of the land which I now live on I do will to my son Charles and the other end to my son James. If the title of the land stands good, or is made good by the substances of the place when they receive the said hundred dollars before mentioned and said land they are to have no part of the balance of the property; if the land is lost they are to have an equal part in the balance of the estate.

The slaves that I will to my wife during her life or widowhood, my will is that she shall give them at her decease to her children that she thinks will use them well, and they are to be valued and they receive them is to pay up the value of them in good trade at cash price with reducing their own part out. I say my will is that my five eldest sons and four daughters: William, John, David, Michael and Richard, Jane, Ann, Elizabeth and Mary shall have an equal part in my estate at the death of my wife, Elizabeth, that is left in her hands.

I also constitute, make and ordain my dearly beloved wife Elizabeth, and my son William Byrd the sole Executors of this my last Will and Testament, and I do hereby utterly disallow, revoke and dis-annul all and every other former testament, wills, legacies, bequeaths and Executors by me before named, willed and bequeathed—ratifying and confirming this and no other to be my last Will and Testament.

In witness whereof I have hereunto set my hand and seal This 5th day of March in the year of our Lord, one Thousand eight hundred and three.

    Richard Byrd (seal)

Signed, sealed and published, pronounced, declared by the said Richard Byrd as his last Will and Testament, in the presence of us who in his presence and in the presence of each other have hereunto subscribed our names.

Test.
    John Walker

WILL OF MICHAEL BACON

Dated: August 6, 1804   Page 33

In the Name of God, Amen.

I, Michael Bacon of Hawkins County and State of Tennessee, farmer, being very sick and weak in body, but of perfect mind and memory, calling to mind the mortality of my body, do make this my Will and Testament. That is to say: as touching my worldly estate which it hath pleased God to bless me in this life, I give, devise and dispose of in the following manner and form:

First. I give and bequeath unto my daughter Catherine all that is now called hers (viz), two milk cows and two heifers, her bed and furniture and saddle.

Secondly. I will that my beloved wife Isabella keep full and inter-rupted possession (of) all my estate until the marriage or death of my daughter Catherine, and then the whole to be valued and equally divided between my wife and three daughters (viz): Mary, Sarah and Catherine. And

Catherine to have my negro man James at his valuation in her part of the Estate, except one hundred dollars that I bequeath for the education of Samuel Lee, son of Thomas Lee and Mary Lee his wife.

I appoint Thomas Lee and Dubart Murphy Executors of this my last Will and Testament. In witness whereof I have hereunto set my hand and seal. This sixth day of August, One Thousand, Eight hundred and four.

Michael Bacon (seal)

Signed, sealed and published in presence of Isaac Barton, Michael Byrd and Job x Hale
    (his mark)

WILL OF HENRY BRAY

Page 33   Dated: May 11, 1827
In the Name of God, Amen. I, Henry Bray, of Hawkins County and State of Tennessee, being very sick and weak of body, but perfect mind and memory, Thanks be to God, calling unto mind the mortality of my body and knowing that it is appointed unto all men once to die, do make and ordain this my last Will and Testament, that is to say, principally and first of all: I give and recommend my soul unto the hand of Almighty God that gave it and my body I recommend to the Earth to be buried in decent Christian burial at the discretion of my Executor, nothing doubting but at the general resurrec-tion I shall receive the same by the mighty power of God. And as touching such worldly Estate wherewith it hath pleased God to bless me in this life, I give and devise and dispose of the same in the following manner and form:

First. I give and bequeath to Margaret my dearly beloved wife all that I possess--lands and stock of every kind--to pay my just debts, and whats left, to raise my children on. And I do hereby utterly disallow, revoke and dis-annul all and every other former testament, wills, legacies, bequests and Executors by me in anywise before named, willed and bequeathed, ratifying and confirming this and no other to be my last Will and Testament in writing. Whereof I have hereunto set my hand and seal This 11th day of May, One Thousand eight hundred and twenty-seven.

Signed, sealed, published, pronounced and ordained by the said Henry Bray to be his last Will and Testament. Signed, sealed and acknowledged in the presence of:
Attest:
Benjamin Bray, Jr.
Benjamin Bray, Sr.   Henry x Bray (seal)
                                                (his mark)

WILL OF JAMES BREEDEN

Page 34   Dated: Sept. 6, 1815
In the Name of God, Amen. I, James Breeden of the County of Hawkins in the State of Tennessee, being in a low state of health, but of sound mind, do make this my last Will and Testament in manner following, to wit:

It is my will and desire that my two tracts of land that lie joining on the south side of Holston River known by the name of Brown Town be divided into three equal parts. I give and bequeath to Winney, Mack, Ruthy, Polly, Nancy, William and Betsy Rutherford, children of John Rutherford and his wife Betsy, the third part of said land to them and their heirs forever.

I give and bequeath unto James Smith, Pulcherry Smith, Polly Smith, Winney Smith and Wade Smith, children of Samuel B. Smith and Judy his wife, one other third part of said tracts of land, to them and their heirs forever.

I give and bequeath one other third part of said tract unto Louisiana Smith and McKinney Smith, children of James Smith and Polly his wife, to them and their heirs forever. It is my will and desire should the said John Rutherford and his wife Betsy have any more children here-after that they shall have an equal interest in the lands left to those named, and it is also my will that if Samuel B. Smith and his wife Judy Smith should have any more children than those named, that they shall have an equal interest in the part left the other children of the said Samuel and Judy Smith. It is my will and desire that in case James Smith and Polly Smith should have any more children than those named, that they shall have an equal interest in the land left those named.

It is my will that John Rutherford's children's part shall be laid off to include the house and plantation rented to Old Mr. Hinton. And it is my will and desire that Thomas Jackson, Samuel Smith and Richard Mitchell divide and allot the said land or any two of them.

It is my will and desire that John Rutherford and wife, Samuel B. Smith and wife, and James Smith and wife may reside and live on the parts left their children during their respective lives, but if either doth refuse to do so, their land and share may be occupied by those that may choose to live upon their respective parts, but it may not be rented out.

It is my will and desire that my negro woman Charlott be, and I do hereby set free and liberate my negro woman Charlott after my decease. I give and bequeath unto the before-named children of John Rutherford and Betsy Rutherford his wife, and to those they may hereafter have, all the children my said negro woman Charlott now has or may have before my death, together with my negro girl Easter now in possession of Joseph Huffmaster; also my negro man named Simon, to them and their heirs forever. It is my will and desire that the said negro children, negro girl Easter and negro man Simon, remain in possession of Betsy Rutherford during her natural life, and at her death the before named children to have the sole right and title to them and their increase forever. I give and bequeath to Betsy Rutherford my negro girl named Nancy, to her and her heirs forever.

It is my will and desire that all the rest of my Estate, both real and personal be sold to pay my just debts, and if there should not be a sufficiency to pay all debts, dues and demands, it is my will that my negro man Simon above named be sold to make up the deficiency. And if there should be any left after paying my just debts, I give all the residue of my estate to Judy Smith the wife of Samuel B. Smith, to be given to her in such manner as my Executors hereafter named may think proper for the purpose of raising and supporting her children so as the said Samuel shall have no control over the same. I will to my negro woman Charlott (that I

WILL OF HENRY BUREM

Dated February 4, 1816

In the Name of God. Amen. I, Henry Burem of Hawkins County and State of Tennessee, knowing the frailty of man and the uncertainty of this life, and being of sound mind and memory, do make and ordain this my last Will and Testament in manner and form as follows: After recommending my soul to God and my body to the dust from whence it came, to be buried in a plain decent Christian-like manner (after my decease), and covering such worldly goods as it has been pleasing to the Almighty to bestow on me, I do bestow and dispose of in the following manner:

First. I desire my funeral charges to be paid out of my goods and chattels at the discretion of my Executors whom I shall hereafter name, and my debts to be paid in like manner. My goods and chattels of every description to be sold on a credit of twelve months, my lands to be divided in the following manner, that is to say:

The road tract to make one part and my home tract to be divided in the following manner: With straight lines from the river to the back line, to make four parts. Each tract will have the same appearance so that the lower and upper tracts will contain eighty acres, and the two middle tracts will have equal number of acres, and each of the three parts which do not contain the spring, to have liberty of a pathway to it. I do allot for my sons Pitser, Paskill H., Henry, John and Absalom to have the said tracts, pieces or lots of land and they—my said sons—to draw lots for the tracts of land. And I give to my daughter Polly one hundred and fifty dollars. And my children will not be of age at my decease to be raised and schooled out of any money which will be in my Executors' hands, and as for my son Peter Burem and my daughters Betsy Carter, Darcus Kenner and Sally Charles, I have heretofore given them what I consider an equal share. And as for the residue which may remain in the hands of my Executors to be divided in the following manner (Viz): My sons, Henry, John and Absalom to have fifty dollars each, and the balance to be equally divided

have freed) one cow and calf for her support, also one sow and pigs to her own use.

I appoint Samuel Powel Executor to this my last Will and Testament, hereby revoking all former wills made by me, publishing this to be my last Will and Testament.

In witness whereof I have hereunto set my hand and seal this sixth day of September, in the year of our Lord, one thousand eight hundred and fifteen.

James Breeden (seal)

Sealed, published and declared in presence of us:

Test.
Sam Smith
Richard Mitchell
James x Sanders
(his mark)

WILL OF HENRY BUREM

Dated: April 28, 1822

In the Name of God, Amen. I, Henry Burem of the County of Hawkins and State of Tennessee, being of sound mind and memory, do make and ordain this my last will and testament in writing, in manner and form as followeth:

First. I recommend my soul to God and my body to the Earth to be buried in a Christian-like manner, and such worldly goods as has come to my possession I bestow in the following manner. First, I desire that all my just debts shall be paid out of my Estate, my goods and chattels of every kind, together with the negroes to be sold at a twelve-month credit and the land to be divided in five equal parts so that each lot will have an equal distance on the river.

Item 1st. I give unto my son Paskill H. Baren the lot lying up the river on the upper end of the tract.

Item 2nd. I give unto my son Henry Burem the second lot up the river adjoining Paskill's lot.

Item 3rd. I give unto my son Charles Pitser Burem the middle lot which will adjoin Henry.

Item 4th. I give unto my two sons John Burem and Absalom Burem the two lower lots and for them to cast lots for the choice at any time after my son Absalom arrives at the age of sixteen.

Item 5th. My son Peter Burem I allow to get no more of my estate as I have heretofore given him a full share...

Item 6th. My daughter Darcus Kenner I have also heretofore given what I consider a full share. I therefore give her no more of my estate.

Item 7th. My daughter Sally Charles I have also given heretofore what I consider a full share. I therefore give her no more of my estate.

Item 8th. I give and bequeath unto my daughter Polly Haus one hundred and fifty dollars to be paid her 18 months after my decease.

Item 9th. My daughter Betsy Carter I have heretofore given an equal share. I therefore give her no more of my Estate.

between Pitser, Paskill, John, Henry and Absalom.

I do appoint and request my beloved son C. Pitser Burem and Jacob Miller to be my Executors of this my last Will and Testament in writing, and do by these presence revoke, disannul and make void every other will or wills by me made.

In testimony whereof I have hereunto set my hand and affixed my seal this 4th day of February in the year of our Lord, 1816.

Signed, sealed, published and declared by Henry Burem to be his last Will and Testament in writing, in presence of us who was subscribing witnesses thereto.

Henry Burem (seal)

John Laughmiller
Wm. Hagood

Item 10th. The lands which I have given to my sons **Charles P.,**
Paskill H., Henry, John and **Absalom L.,** I give with the following conditions: That is, that neither of them shall convey their right to a
stranger, but may to one another and should they presume to do that, the
conveyance shall be void and of no effect.

Item 11th. As for what may remain in the hands of my Executors which
I will hereafter name, I wish to be equally divided between all my children.
That is, **Polly Haus, Betsy Carter, Darcus Kenner, Peter Burem, Sally**
Charles, C. Pitser Burem, Paskill H. Burem, Henry Burem, John Burem and
Absalom L. Burem.

And to carry this my last Will and Testament in writing into execution and effect, I constitute, nominate and appoint my beloved son **Paskill**
H. Burem and **Jacob Miller** my Executors, annulling, revoking and making
void all other wills by me made.

In witness whereof I the said **Henry Burem**, have hereunto set my hand
and affixed my seal. This 28th April One thousand eight hundred and
twenty two.

Signed, sealed published and declared in presence of us who at the
request of him the said **Henry Burem** became subscribing witnesses thereto.

                                        H'ry Burem (seal)
                    WILL OF WILLIAM BERRY
Page 39   Dated Sept. 13, 1823

In the Name of God, Amen. I, **William Berry** of the County of Hawkins
and State of Tennessee, being of sound mind and perfect memory, considering the uncertainty of this mortal life and being of sound mind, blessed
be God for the same do make and publish this my last Will and Testament
in manner and form following, that is to say: First my debts to be paid.
Then one dollar unto my daughter **Elizabeth Walker**; one dollar to my
daughter **Rachael**; one dollar to **Sarah (Mulhel?)**; one dollar to my son
John; one dollar to my son **Thomas**; one dollar to my son **William**; one
dollar to my daughter **Mary**; one dollar to my son **Francis**; one dollar to
my daughter **Hannah**. My will is that my wife **Suanne** shall have all the
household and kitchen furniture for to do with as she thinks proper at
her death, and my will is that **Benoni Morlan** shall have my land for taking
care of me and my wife as long as we live, and my will is that my wife
shall have the use of the farming tools and all the stock after my death
as long as she lives. I do make and ordain **Benoni Morlan** to be my whole
and sole Executor of this my last Will and Testament. I do hereby disannul all wills former and testaments, wills, bequests—ratifying and
confirming this and no other to be my last Will and Testament. In witness
I have hereunto set my hand and seal This 13th day of September, 1823.
                                        William Berry (seal)

Benjamin Morlan
Even C. Morlan

                    WILL OF THOMAS BRAMHALL
Page 40   Dated: January 5, 1827

In the Name of God Amen. Be it remembered that I **Thomas Bramhall** of
the County of Hawkins and State of Tennessee, being weak in body but of
sound mind and memory, but considering the uncertainty of this mortal life
and being of sound and perfect mind and memory, blessed be Almighty God
for the same, do make and publish this my last will and testament in manner
and form following. That is to say:

First. I give and bequeath to my beloved wife **Judith Bramhall** all
my Estate—lands, stock of all kind, together with all my household furniture or freehold estate, I give unto her to dispose of as she sees cause
to do during her life.

Item. It is my desire that at her decease my grandson **Jacob Bramhall**
should have a horse colt, two years old next summer, also one feather bed
and furniture.

Item. It is further my desire that my dear and well beloved wife
should dispose of all my goods and chattels as she sees fit at her decease,
whom I hereby appoint sole Executrix of this my last will and testament,
hereby revoking all former wills by me made. In witness whereof I have
hereunto set my hand and seal this fifth day of January in the year of our
Lord, one thousand eight hundred and twenty-seven.

Signed, sealed, published and declared by the above named **Thomas**
Bramhall to be his last Will and Testament in the presence of us who at
his request and at his presence have hereunto subscribed our names as
witnesses to the same.

Witnesses:
William x Skelton   **Thomas x Bramhall** (seal)
   (his mark)   (his mark)
James x Skelton
   (his mark)
William Feagins

                    WILL OF PETER BARR
Page 40   Dated: April 4, 1829

In the Name of God, Amen. I **Peter Barr, Sen'r** of the County of
Hawkins and State of Tennessee, being of sound and disposing mind and
memory, bringing to mind the mortality of this life, knowing it is appointed for all persons once to die and having a desire to dispose of
such worldly estate wherewith it hath pleased God to bless me do make
and publish this my last Will and Testament in manner following, to wit:

Item First. I give and bequeath unto my beloved wife **Edy** during
her natural life all and every part and parcel of the land and tenements whereon I now live, together with all the entries that I have
heretofore made joining said land at at her death, the aforesaid lands
to be equally divided between my two sons, namely **Jacob** and **James Barr.**

Item Second. I give and bequeath to my wife **Edy** during her natural
life all my personal property of every description composed of the
following articles, to wit: All my stock of cattle, hogs and sheep,

household and kitchen furniture, working tools, &c, together with my sorrel mare, but it is understood that each of my children hereinafter named is to have the privilege of raising a colt from said mare. My son Jacob is to have the first colt that the said mare may bring after the one that she is now in foal with which belongs to my daughter Nancy. My daughters Barbary, Deborough and Susan, each to have a colt from said mare, and if in case my said wife Bdy should marry, all the above property both real and personal, shall descend to my said two sons, namely Jacob and James, with the exception of the colts heretofore named. And in case my said wife should not marry, at her death all the personal property of every description (is) to be divided between my said sons, Jacob and James.

Item Third. And it is further my will and desire that my four daughters, namely Nancy, Barbary, Deborough and Susan should remain with their mother until they arrive to the age of maturity and to have their support out of the proceeds of the property and to have and receive a reasonable portion of schooling, and it is further my will and desire that my said sons Jacob and James should take charge of my said farm and have the use of all my property by supporting myself, their mother and their four sisters heretofore named, but not to have any of the property at their disposal, except for the use of my said property. And it is further my will and desire that after the death of my wife Bdy that my two sons, Jacob and James shall sell so much of my property as will make twenty-five dollars and dispose of it in the following manner: To my son Michael, five dollars; to my son Henry, five dollars; to my son Peter, five dollars, to my son George, five dollars; to my son Mathews, five dollars, and it is my will and desire that they receive no other part of my said Estate.

Lastly. I do hereby constitute and appoint my friend John G (or S.) Wells of County of Hawkins, Executor of this my last Will and Testament.

In testimony whereof I have hereunto set my hand and Seal this 4th day of April, A.D., 1829.

Peter x Barr (seal)
(his mark)

Signed in presence of:
G. McCraw
William x Golding
(his mark)

WILL OF WILLIAM BAILEY

Page 42

Dated: May 30, 1828

I, William Bailey, Sr., of the County of Hawkins and State of Tenn., knowing the uncertainty of life and the certainty of death, and being of sound mind and memory but weak in body, I ordain and declare this my last will and Testament.

First. I bequeath my body to the grave and my soul to Almighty God, the giver of it. My worldly goods, after defraying my burial, I give and bequeath in the following manner, to wit:

I bequeath to my son James Bailey the land on which I lately lived, on the south side of Beech Creek, after deducting or taking from it what has been conveyed to my son William Bailey, Jr. Also, the benefit of an

entry of 100 acres made by him, James, in my name on the 26th of this month on condition he pay to Sally Harmon, wife of David Harmon, fifteen dollars in good trade.

I give to my daughter Frankey Luster, wife of S. D. Luster, that part of (a) tract of land which lies on both sides of Beech Creek. Beginning on a hickory, a corner of the old survey which was originally a sour wood, to run to a stake from thence a corner of said tract at the end of the line of a hundred poles crossing the creek. Then with old line to Luster line. Then to the beginning on condition said Luster relinquish all claims against me. In case he does not relinquish any claims he may have, the land is to go to James Bailey who is to pay the claim of said Luster.

I give to my grand daughter Jude Harmon my bed and furniture. I bequeath to Aggy Stacy, Betsy Christian, Polly Fields, three heirs of Carr Bailey, Samuel Bailey and daughter, Susan Williams, I have given John Bailey and the heirs of Thomas Bailey one dollar each. To my sons their portion heretofore.

It is my wish that James Bailey my son act as my Executor for which and to pay the legacies herewith bequeathed, I give all my remaining personal estate. In testimony whereof I have hereunto set my hand and seal this 30th of May, 1828.

William x Bailey (seal)
(his mark)

Signed, sealed and acknowledged before us the date above.

John A. Rogers
Aln Long
Robb Millar

WILL OF HENRY BRUTINTON

Page 43

Dated: June 10, 1829

In the Name of God, Amen. Be it remembered that I, Henry Brutinton of the County of Hawkins and State of Tennessee, considering the uncertainty of this mortal life and being sick of body, but of sound and perfect mind and memory, blessed be Almighty God for the same, do make and publish this my last Will and Testament in manner and form following. That is to say:

First. I give and bequeath unto my eldest son Jacob all my land where I now live, lying and being in the County and State aforesaid, containing 55 acres more or less, to hold forever with all the appurtenances thereunto. Likewise. I give unto my said son Jacob all my farming utensils with all my stock such as one horse, one cow and calf, nine sheep, eleven hogs, four bee stands and all the household furniture. The latter is to fall to my beloved wife Betsy Brutinton when he comes of age. The above mentioned property my beloved wife Betsy (is) to make use of as she wants it for and the childrens' maintenance. She is to live on the place as long as she chooses and as to the rest of my children (that is to say), my three girls Jinny, Catharine and Polly--when Jacob my son comes of age... is to give unto the girls one cow and a calf a-piece.

And I hereby appoint my beloved wife **Betsy** sole Executrix of this my last Will and Testament, hereby revoking all former wills by me made. In witness whereof I have set my hand and seal The tenth day of June, One thousand eight hundred and twenty-nine.

                                 Henry x Bruthinton (seal)
                                         (his mark)
Signed, sealed published and declared by the above named **Henry Bruthinton** to be his last Will and Testament in the presence of us:
William C. Reynolds
Isaac Laudeback

WILL OF MOSES BALL

Page 44
                                    Dated: December 15, 1831

In the Name of God, Amen. I, **Moses Ball** of the County of Hawkins and State of Tennessee, being weak in body but being in perfect mind and memory, thanks be given unto God. Calling to mind the mortality of my body and knowing that it is appointed for all men once to die, do make and ordain this instrument of writing to be my last Will and Testament. That is to say: First of all, I give and recommend my soul in the hand of Almighty God that gave it and my body I recommend to the Earth to be buried at the discretion of my Executors hereinafter appointed, nothing doubting but at the general resurrection, I shall receive the same again by the mighty power of God, and as touching such worldly Estate wherewith it has pleased God to bless me in this life:

First. I give and bequeath to my son **Spencer Ball** one dollar out of my estate and no more.

Secondly. I give and bequeath to my son **Robb Ball** one dollar out of my estate.

Thirdly. I give and devise to my son **Bennett Ball** a certain parcel of land lying and being between my sons **William** and **Thomas Ball**, and from the southern boundary of my land and running northward to where the Beech Creek road runs through my land and no further. And it (is) my further will and desire that if my wife **Molly** shall have the rent of the said land that I have devised to my son **Bennett** during her natural life for her support. (?)

Fourthly. I give and devise to my grandson **Jonathan Ball** a certain described parcel of land lying on the north side of the Beech Creek road and lying between the said **William** and **Thomas Ball** land and including my apple orchard and running to the northern boundary of my land. And it is my further will and desire that my Executor after my decease shall rent said parcel of land and orchard and the money or property arising from said rent to pay for the Education of my grandson **Jonathan Ball**. And it is my further will and desire that my said grandson **Jonathan Ball** shall have a horse, saddle and bridle out of my Estate.

Fifthly. I give and bequeath to my well beloved wife **Molly** all the residue of my personal estate and money that is owing to me during her natural life.

Sixthly. It is my further will and desire after my wife's decease, the property--if any--is to be sold, except my wearing clothes, and the plank that is in my loft and my books. The planks to remain where they are, my wearing clothes and books to be divided equally between my children as the can (sic), and the money arising from said sale to be equally divided between my daughters, _____ **McDaniel**, **Nancy Warren**, **Polly Ball**, **Sibby Long** and **Sarah Long's** children and my grandson **Jonathan Ball** or their heirs. There was $32.00 that I paid for **William McDaniel** in part pay(ment) for said **McDaniel's** wagon, $16.00 of that, said **William McDaniel** was to pay **John K. Long** who married with my daughter **Sibby**. If **John K. Long** has received that amount, they are to settle with my Executor.

I constitute and appoint my sons **Wesley Ball** and **Thomas Ball** my Executors of this my last Will and Testament, to manage my estate, real and personal, as they think best. I hereby utterly revoke and disannul all and every other former testament, wills, legacies before mentioned, willed...bequeathed, ratifying and confirming this and no other to be my last Will and Testament. In witness whereof I hereunto set my hand and seal This fifteenth day of December in the year of our Lord, One thousand eight hundred and thirty-one.

                                         Moses Ball (seal)
Attest:
Reuben Bernard
John Ball,
Jesse Ball
James Tunnell

A NUNCUPATIVE WILL OF JOEL BOYLES

Page 45

That my negro boy named **Sam** be free and all my other property be sold at public sale and be applied to public school, and I want to be buried on my own land near the poplar on the hill that I had cut down (near the Meeting House), as I do not want to be buried as a beggar. **Mrs. David Laughmiller** adds after his debts were paid the balance to be given to the public school (or this district).

Given under our hands This 13th day of April A.D. 1833
John J. Brown
David Laughmiller

WILL OF NATHANIEL BASSETT

Page 46
                                    Dated: December 4, 1834
                                    See Original 1832
In the Name of God, Amen. I, **Nathaniel Basset** of the County of Hawkins and State of Tennessee, being weak in body but of sound and disposing mind and memory, bringing to mind the mortality of this life, knowing it is appointed for all persons once to die, and having a desire to dispose of such worldly estate wherewith it hath pleased Almighty God to bless me with, I do make and publish this my last Will and Testament in manner following, to wit:

First. I will that all my just debts be paid.

Secondly. I give and bequeath unto the heirs of my son **Burwell**

Bassett namely, **Elvira**, **Ketturah**, **Adaline**, **Alexander** and **Richard** and **Nathaniel Bassett** and any other lawful heirs that the said **Burrell Bassett** may hereafter have, all that part of my land whereon I now reside including the dwelling house and other buildings in the following boundary, to wit: Beginning at a stake four poles west of my stables, running due south to the top of the knob, then eastwardly with the top of said knob to **Sterling Cooke's** line, then with said **Cooke's** line to the stage road, then with **Thomas Poindexter's** line north to a red oak near **George Matlock's** house, then with said line to the south side of said road, then west to a stake on my old line, then with said line north to the back line of my said old tract, then west with the line of said tract so far that a due south line will strike the first station near said stables. To have and to hold the before described tract of land, appurtenances to them and their heirs forever.

Thirdly. I give and bequeath unto the heirs of my son **Spencer Bassett**, namely, **William**, **Louisa**, **John**, **George**, **Isaac** and **Joseph Bassett**, and any other lawful heirs that **Spencer** may hereafter have, all that tract of land whereon I now reside, lying west of a line designated to the heirs of **Burwell Bassett**. That is to say: Beginning at a stake four poles west of my stables, running thence due south to the top of the knob, then westwardly with the top of the knob to **Willie B. Kyle's** line. Then with the line of said tract east so far that a line run due south will strike the beginning at the stake near said stables, to have and enjoy the before described tract of land with the appurtenances, to them and their heirs forever. And it is further my will that the heirs of the said **Spencer Bassett** is to have free and un-interrupted privileges of the spring that I now make use of for water, and to have equal privilege of said spring with the heirs of said **Burrell Bassett**, and to have a passway to said spring. And it is my further will that the said **Burrell** and **Spencer Bassett** (shall) have and enjoy the before-described tract of land with appurtenances during that lives subject to the following conditions: Now, if from extravagance, intemperance or imprudence, the said land or the life estate of the said **Burrell** and the said **Spencer Bassett** should be likely to be sold for their debts, then and in that case my said Executors hereinafter nominated shall have full power and authority to sell either or both lots of said land for the best price that can be had and the money arising therefrom to go to the use of said heirs heretofore named, agreeable to the value of their...lots.

Fourthly. I give and bequeath unto my daughter **Polly** who has intermarried with **Valentine Matlock**, the following described negro, namely **Minne** and her three children, estimating the said four negroes together with the hire of said negro **Minne**, say fourteen years, at one thousand dollars which is equal to one lot of my land heretofore disposed of between the heirs heretofore mentioned, to her and her heirs forever.

Fifthly. I give and bequeath unto my son **Hugh Bassett** my negro woman **Jenny**, which negro I estimate her value at four hundred and fifty dollars, to him and his heirs forever. And I further give and bequeath to my said son **Hugh**...my gray horse at the price of one hundred and fifty dollars and two feather beds and furniture at forty dollars each, which makes his part six hundred and eighty dollars.

Sixthly. I give and bequeath unto **Hugh Armstrong**, who intermarried with my daughter **Ketturah Bassett**, my negro boy **Aaron** which negro I estimate his value together with his hire for sixteen years at one thousand dollars which (is) equal to the above named three first shares, to him and his heirs forever.

Seventhly. I give and bequeath unto my daughter **Peggy** who has intermarried with **George Matlock**, my negro woman **Winney** and my negro woman **Sidea** and her child, a girl about two years old, which three negroes, together with the hire of **Sidea** eight years, I estimate their value at nine hundred dollars, to her and her heirs forever. And I further give to my said daughter **Peggy** two beds and furniture at forty dollars each which makes her share worth nine hundred and eighty dollars.

Eightly. And it is further my will and desire that my negro man **Dick**, at my death, shall be free and that he be allowed reasonable portion of said farm during his life to make a support. And I also give to said **Dick** my old sorrel horse to dispose of as he may think fit. And it is further my will and desire that my said son **Burwell** shall see to **Dick's** welfare so long as both shall live and it said **Dick** should become so infirm that he cannot support himself, then and in that case the said **Burwell** shall provide for him.

Ninthly. It is my further will and desire that all my said property that is not otherwise disposed of shall be sold by my said Executors hereinafter named for the best price that can be had for it and the money arising from said sale in the first place to go towards carrying (out) this my last will into effect, and the balance to go to my son **Hugh Bassett** and my daughter **Peggy**, to make their shares equal to the rest of the shares, or to make their shares worth one thousand dollars, and if there should be any balance remaining, my said Executors shall divide it equally with my said heirs.

Tenthly. And it is further my will and desire that if any of my said heirs shall be dissatisfied with this my last will and shall go to law for the purpose of preventing my will from being carried into effect, then and in that case the one so offending or trying to break my said will shall forfeit all claims to any part of my estate, and the part allotted to him or them shall be equally divided amongst the rest of my heirs.

Lastly. I do hereby constitute, ordain and appoint my friends **James L. Etter** and **Gabriel McCraw** my Executors to this my last will and Testament, revoking and making void all former wills heretofore made by me, and ratifying and confirming this my last will and Testament. In testimony whereof I the said **Nathaniel Bassett** have hereunto set my hand and affixed my seal. This fourth day of December in the year of our Lord, One thousand eight hundred and thirty-two.

Nathaniel Bassett (seal)

Test: **Thomas Poindexter**, Sanford Johnson

Note: The word "live" in the 26th line and the word "dollars" in the 109th line were interlined before signed. Balance illegible.

WILL OF DANIEL BLOOMER

Page 49   Dated: May 23, 1838

In the Name of God, Amen. I, **Daniel Bloomer** of the State of Tennessee, Hawkins, County, being very low in body, but in perfect mind and memory, thanks be given unto God. Calling into mind and mortality of my body and knowing that it is appointed for all men once to die, do make and ordain this my last Will and Testament, that is to say: Principally and first of all, I give and recommend my soul into the hands of Almighty God that gave it, and my body I recommend to the earth to be buried in a decent Christian burial at the discretion of my Executor, and as touching such worldly estate wherewith it has pleased God to bless me in this life, I give, devise and dispose of the same in the following manner and form:

First of all, I give and bequeath to **Lucy** my dearly beloved wife, half of this plantation or the benefit thereof, my dwelling house and kitchen and all the furniture belonging to them and all the property that I now claim during her life, and for her to pay all my just debts and further for her to pay my daughter **Lucy** one hundred and sixty dollars at her marrying or coming of age.

Also for the land I have in Scott County, Virginia, I will and bequeath to four of my sons which is **William Bloomer** who is to have from the lower end of the survey up to a beech and hickory. Thence a southeast course with a conditional line between him and **Nehemiah Bloomer's** field. **Joseph Bloomer** is to have from the last conditional line up to a cucumber (tree) and back near the upper end of **Joseph Bloomer's** field. Thence southeast course to the creek. Thence running with the creek to a double lyme. **James Bloomer** is to have from this conditional line to the upper end of the survey; these lines are also to extend across **Iham Young's** entry that I have made.

The house where **Jesse Bloomer** now lives, I bequeath to him; also the other half of this home plantation and at the death of my wife, the whole of this plantation is to be his.

I bequeath at the death of my wife all the personal property, household and kitchen furniture, money and negroes to my six girls: **Mary, Elizabeth, Milly, Phebe, Marthy, Lucy**, and I further request my wife to have full power to sell or convey these negroes at any time for her decent support. I further bequeath **Lucy** have one falling leaf table and corner cupboard extra of her one hundred and sixty...

And I do hereby utterly disallow, revoke and disannul all and every other former testament, wills, legacies, bequeaths and Executors by me in anywise before named, willed and bequeathed--ratifying and confirming this and no other to be my last Will and Testament.

In witness whereof I have hereunto set my hand and seal, and I appoint for my Executors, **William Walling, Jr.** and **James Bloomer.**

                                    Daniel x Bloomer (seal)
Test: (his mark)
Ezkiel x Sullivan
(his mark)
Claiborne Roberson

WILL OF THOMAS BARRETT

Page 50   Dated: June 26, 1838
                                 Proven: Feb. and April
                                 Term, 1855

In the Name of God, Amen. I, **Thomas Barrett** of the County of Hawkins, State of Tennessee, being in a low state of health, but of sound and disposing mind, memory and understanding--considering the uncertainty of death and the uncertainty of the time thereof, do ordain and constitute this my last Will and Testament in manner and form following, Viz:

First. I commend my soul into the hand of Almighty God and my body to the earth to be decently buried at the discretion of my Executors hereinafter named.

Item. To my beloved wife **Winefred Barrett**, I leave one horse, two milk cows, one feather bed and furniture, and all the lands on this side of the creek between the lines of **William Reynolds** where he now lives and where he formerly lived, including the dwelling house and other houses, also the lands on the other side of the creek between the lands of **John Barrett** and **William Reynolds**, to her so long as she remains my widow. At her death the lands (are) to belong to our youngest son **Alfred Barrett.**

Item. The land on which our two sons, **Pleasant** and **Hugh** now live to be divided between our sons, **Hugh** and **Pleasant's** children. The children (are) to have the lower end of the land including the house they live in and as far as they have enclosed in a fence and then up the hollow to **Anderson's** line.

Item. To our son **John Barrett**, I leave all the lands in the following bounds: Beginning on a stake, corner of the bank of the branch opposite the great hollow that leads down to the creek on the left of my Sugar Camp. Thence up the fence by the side of the branch to a cross fence, then down cross fence to the creek. Then up the creek to the road. Then with the road to my line. Then with my line to the head of aforesaid hollow, then down the hollow to the beginning.

To my other two sons, **Nelson** and **Thomas Barrett**, I leave a tract of land I purchased of **James Donelson**, to be divided between them. The line to run with the creek where it will strike the creek after leaving the little meadow near the barn on **Thomas'** side. **Nelson** to have the upper end including the dwelling house. The land in Big Poor Valley adjoining the **Donalson** Tract also to be divided between **Nelson** and **Thomas.** My wife to have the care of **Thomas** until he is of sufficient age to go to himself.

Item. My other land in Big Poor Valley to be divided between our sons **John** and **Alfred.**

Item. I leave to **Thomas** and **Alfred** the colts already given them. I leave unto my daughters **Polly**, **Nancy** and **Malinda** each one bed and furniture and to each one a milch cow.

Item. After my just debts are paid, what money may be left and... the balance of my property sells for, I wish to be divided between our daughters **Holly Ford**, **Betsy Reynolds**, **Louisa Grose**, **Polly**, **Nancy** and **Malinda Barrett.** **Betsy Reynolds** to pay $20.00 to the other girls except **Holly Ford** out of her portion.

Item. To **William Reynolds** I leave all the lands he has under fence where he formerly lived, except a small timothy lot which will belong to **Alfred** at his mother's death.

Item. The land whereon **William Reynolds** now lives he purchased of our son **Clinton Barrett.** I leave to said **Reynolds**—the lines to run as specified in the articles between us now held by **Jim Barrett.** Our sons **John** and **Nelson** are to pay $10.00 each to be divided between our daughters **Polly, Nancy** and **Malinda.**

As I have previously given to our son **Clinton** his portion, I now give him the sum of $2.00 to let him know he still lives in my affec-tion.

And for the purpose of carrying into effect this my last Will and Testament, I appoint my sons **John** and **Nelson** Executors, to see that it is done. In testimony whereof I have hereunto set my hand and seal this twenty sixth day of June, in the year of our Lord one thousand eight hundred and thirty eight, in the presence of:
(interlined before signing)

Thomas x Barrett (seal)
(his mark)

B. W. Vaughan
David x Anderson
(his mark)
Elijah D. x Gillenwaters
(his mark)
Anthony Smith

WILL OF DAVID BLACKWELL.

Page 52
Date: No date given

I, **David Blackwell,** in the Name of God, Amen, ordain this my last will and testament, that is to say:

In the first place I give and bequeath to my dearly beloved wife **Anny** my whole estate, real and personal, to do with and make use of in what like manner she may see fit during her lifetime, then to my children to be equally divided amongst them. Whereunto I have set my hand in the presence of:

David Blackwell

Benj. Hawkins
John Bunch (Jurat)
Henry Lewis

WILL OF ALEXANDER BALLARD, SR.

Page 52
Dated: May 6, 1839

To all whom these may concern, I, **Alexander Ballard, Sen'r.,** in the Name of God, Amen, being sound in mind and memory, but frail in body do make and ordain this my last Will and Testament.

First. I give and bequeath unto my grand daughter **Sarah Ann Ballard,** the daughter of my son **Alexander Ballard, Jr.,** my dwelling house and all my household furniture, to wit: One bed and furniture.

one corner cupboard, one chest and one table and two chairs, one pot, one frying pan. To the said **Sarah Ann Ballard,** for her service to me in my old age, to be the said grandchild's forever after my death. In witness whereof I have set my hand this day and year above written.

Alexander x Ballard, Sr.
(his mark)

Test:
Andrew Coffman
Thomas x White
(his mark)

WILL OF ALEXANDER BALLARD, SR.

May the 6th, One thousand Eight hundred and thirty-nine. To all whom these presents may concern. I **Alexander Ballard, Sr.,** in the name of God, Amen, being sound in mind and memory, but frail in body do make and ordain this my last Will and Testament.

My will is that my grandson, **James Mauley Ballard,** son of **Alexander Ballard, Jr.,** first, my saddle and bridle and big coat, the same to be **James M. Ballard's** after my death, and also he—the said **James Mauley Ballard,** is to have one hundred dollars in silver when he is twenty one years of age, which I will to him after my death. And last of all, my will is that my son, **William Ballard** or his heirs, one dollar; **John Ballard,** one dollar; **David Ballard** one dollar; **Joshua Ballard, Alexander Ballard, Jr., George** and **Jesse Ballard** one dollar each, and to my daughter **Jane,** one dollar. All my burial expenses (to be) paid out of my estate.

In witness whereof I set my hand this date and year as above written.

Alexander Ballard, Sen't

Test:
Andrew Coffman
Thomas x White
(his mark)

WILL OF NICHOLAS BALDWIN

Page 53
Dated: July 26, 1840

In the Name of God, Amen.

I, **Nicholas Baldwin** of the County of Hawkins in the State of Tennessee, being in great bodily affliction and believing my corporeal existance near an end, yet being in my mind perfect and mental faculties pure, do hereby make this my last Will and Testament in words and figures as follows:

To my dear wife, **Alicy Baldwin,** I do bequeath all my land and stock and household furniture to raise her children on that she has now and to have full power to sell and apply any personal property to the use and maintenance of the children during her natural life or widowhood, to give to each and every one as they come of age what she may think a reasonable portion, and when they all come of age for her if she yet lives, to have the land for her maintenance. But should she marry again, the property to be sold on a twelve months' credit by my Executors that I shall hereafter name—all but one bed and furniture which she shall have and all the land I want in that case to be rented by my Executors for cash or other property, and if property, to be sold for cash and the money kept at usury, and at the youngest coming of age, the money and land to be equally divided among the children, taking into consideration what the older ones have got as they grew up. And should the children want any money for schooling in the case my wife **Ailcy Baldwin** marries, the Executors shall advance what they think reasonable for their school-ing and should she marry a sober, pious man that the children would be willing to live with, in that case, if she choose to live on the land, she shall have half the cleared land to stay on till the youngest child comes of age, then a division as before stated take place and the other half of the land be rented, and but so long as she remains single, she is to have the sole control of the tendings of the land, and the right of the personal property till the youngest child comes of age, then to have a third of the land during her life or widowhood.

And, I do hereby appoint my friends **Richard Mitchell** and **Henry Byrd** my true and lawful executors to this my last Will and Testament, and I do hereby make this my last will, revoking all former wills by me. And in full testimony of the above...will, I have set my name and af-fixed my seal on the 26th day of July in the year of our Lord, one thousand eight hundred and forty. In presence of **Joseph Brooks** and **John Byrd** who are subscribing witnesses hereto.

Nicholas x Baldwin (seal)
(his mark)

Witnesses:
Joseph Brooks, John Byrd

WILL OF JOHN BOLIN

Page 54

Dated: July 29, 1839
Proven: Nov. 1839

In the Name of God, Amen. I, **John Bolin** of Hawkins County, State of East Tennessee, being sick of body but of sound disposing memory, do resign my soul to Almighty God who gave it and after a decent burial my will is that all my just debts be paid and the balance of my worldly goods I give and bequeath as follows:

Item. I give and bequeath to my beloved Father and Mother all my land together with all my crop and all other property I possess during their lives, and after their death...

Item. My will and desire is that **James Bolin** should live with his father and mother and take care of them as long as they live and at their death for **James Bolin** to have all of the said property that is left.

I acknowledge this to be my last will and testament. July 29, 1839. I appoint **James Bolin** my Executor.

John x Bolin
(his mark)

WILL OF JOHN BEEIL

Page 55

Dated: July 24, 1840
Proven: Aug. Term, 1840

In the Name of God, Amen.

I, **John Beeil** of Hawkins County and State of Tennessee, being very sick and weak in body, but good perfect mind and memory, thanks be given to God, do make and ordain this my last Will and Testament. I recom-mend my soul into the hands of Almighty God that gave it any my body I

recommend to the earth to be buried in a decent and Christian burial, and as touching such worldly estate I leave it at the discretion of my Executors in form and manner following:

First. I give and bequeath to my beloved wife **Eve** the plantation whereon I now live...and all the property belonging to said land to have and to hold until her death, and after her death my daughter **Catherine** shall have the land and $150.00 worth of said property to be valued to her, to have and to hold during her single life and good behavior, and also there is a certain tract or parcel of land lying between **Martin Beeil's** lines and **Jacob Maxe's** that my son **David** has bought of me, and there is $145.00 that is coming to me for the land, and I also give that to my beloved wife **Eve** and whenever my son **David** shall pay this money she shall make him a lawful deed for said land. And I also leave **Joseph Wright** and **William Keeler** to be Executors on my whole Estate. As witnesses my hand and seal this 24th day of July, 1840. Signed, sealed and delivered in the presence of **John Beeil**. This is his last Will and Testament.

John Beeil (seal)

Test.
Joseph Wright
William Keller

WILL OF BURWELL BASSETT

Page 56

Dated: June 14, 1842

I, **Burwell Bassett**, of the County of Hawkins and State of Tenn., being weak in body but of sound and disposing mind and memory, bring-ing to mind the mortality of this life, knowing it is appointed for man once to die and having a desire to dispose of such worldly estate which it has pleased Almighty God to bless me with do make and publish this my last will and testament in manner following, to wit:

First. I will that all my just debts be paid, that my Executor hereinafter named shall sell so much of my personal property as will be sufficient to pay all my just debts, and the balance of my personal estate I give and bequeath unto my beloved wife **Martha Bassett** during her naturl life or widowhood. And I further give and bequeath unto my said wife all the tract of land with its appurtenances whereon I now live, and in case she should marry, then and in that case my Executors hereinafter named shall have full power and authority to sell all my personal property, together with my negroes and the proceeds of such property to be equally divided between my said wife **Martha** and my chil-dren hereinafter named, to wit: **Elvira Bassett** who intermarried with **Joseph Vaughan, Ketturah Bassett, Adaline Bassett, Alexander Bassett, Richard Nathaniel Bassett, James N. Bassett, Martha** and **Helen Bassett**, share and share alike, but it is further my will and desire that in case my said wife **Martha** should marry, that my said Executors shall divide the tract of land whereon I now live equally between my said wife **Martha** and my children before named, reserving to themselves the right to lay off and set apart to my wife a lot to include the mansion house where I now reside with the privilege of water from the spring that I now make use of, which lot of land and building my wife shall have and enjoy during her natural life, and at her death the said lot of land to be equally divided amongst my said children. And in case my wife should remain single and keep my said property together, that she raise and school my said children out of the proceeds of the property and farm free from cost. And it is further my will and desire that as my said children heretofore named shall marry that my wife, with the advice and consent of my said Executors shall set apart so much of my personal estate as they may think my said wife can conveniently spare so as to make the balance of my said children equal to what my daughter Elvira has received.

And it is further my will and desire that my wife Martha remain in possession of all my real and personal property during her natural life or widowhood, and that she have and enjoy all and singular my real estate subject nevertheless to the foregoing conditions stipulated above.

And lastly, I do constitute and appoint my friends James L. Etter and Joseph Vaughan of the County of Hawkins and State of Tennessee my Executors of this my last Will and Testament, revoking all former wills heretofore made by me.

In testimony whereof I have hereunto set my hand and seal this 14th day of June, in the year of our Lord, A.D., 1842.

Burwell W. Bassett (seal)

Signed, sealed and declared in presence of: William McCraw,
Spencer Bassett
G. McCraw

WILL OF WILLIAM BRADLEY
(Abstracted)

Page 57

Dated: October 1, 1842
Proven: May 6, 1845

In the Name of God, Amen. I, William Bradley, of the County of Hawkins and the State of Tennessee, being advanced in years, but in good health, and of sound mind and memory and understanding do make and ordain and publish this my last will and testament in manner following, that is to say:

First: I desire that any just debts which I may owe shall any remain at my decease, be paid by my Executors hereinafter named, out of the money on hand or debts due to my Estate.

Second. To my grand daughter Nancy B. Phipps, the only issue at present born of the marriage between my daughter Louisa and Joshua Phipps, I give and devise the lands I bought of Jacob Felkner and William Armstrong, situated in said County of Hawkins, and also the land lying behind them from the stage road, to have and to hold the same, to the said Nancy B. Phipps, during the term of her natural life, with remainder to her issue in fee simple, if any she should have. But in the event the said Nancy B. Phipps at any time hereafter shall have any brother or brothers, sister or sisters born, the issue of said marriage of my daughter Louisa and Joshua Phipps, my will and intention is that such after-born issue, if any such there should be, shall take hold and enjoy said lands equally, in all respects with Nancy B. Phipps,

to them and the survivor of them and their heirs in fee simple. And should the said Nancy B. die without issue, and without brother or sister or brothers, sister or sisters...then my will and intention is that said lands shall go to and rest in my son Orville Bradley in fee simple, if living, or to his lawful heirs should he be dead. And in case my said son should be dead without leaving lawful issue, my will and intention is that said lands shall go to my own lawful and proper heirs, according to the statutes of descent of Tennessee. My will, desire and intention being in relation to the said lands, and also in relation to all the other lands and property hereinafter mentioned, that the same and every part thereof remain vested and descend to my own proper heirs and lineal descendants and their issue, as far as practicable, from generation to generation. I furthermore desire that the said Nancy B. Phipps shall be let into the full possession and enjoyment of the foregoing devise upon her attaining the age of 21.

Third. To my only daughter Louisa Phipps, the wife of Joshua Phipps, I give and devise the lands on which I now live adjoining G. Leeper on the river above and the Felkner place below, including the houses and improvements where I reside; also all my homeplace not included in the foregoing devise of the Felkner Place to the said Nancy B. Phipps, west of the creek on which G. Lyon's grist mill stands. To have and to hold the same to my said daughter during the term of her natural life, and at the death of my said daughter, Louisa, my will and intention is that the estate in remainder of said lands shall rest in my grand daughter, the said Nancy B. Phipps, during her natural life, and then in her issue, if any she should have, in fee simple. To have and to hold the same in like manner, and upon the same terms and conditions in all respects as are set forth and specified in the foregoing devise to Nancy B. Phipps; that is to say, in the event there shall be any other issue hereafter born of...Louisa and Joshua Phipps...such after-born issue shall take hold and enjoy said Estate in remainder equally in all respects with Nancy B. Phipps, to them and their heirs forever, and to the survivor of them, and should the said Nancy B. die without issue, and without brothers or sisters, or the lawful issue of such, my will and intention is that...estate in remainder shall go to and rest in my son Orville Bradley and his heirs in fee simple, if living and in case he should be dead...leaving no lawful issue, my will and intention is that the estate in remainder in said lands shall go to and rest in my own lawful and proper heirs according to the statutes of descent in Tennessee, in like manner in all respects as provided in the second devise of this my last will and testament.

Fourth. To my son Orville Bradley, I will and devise all the rest and residue of my lands and real estate wheresoever situated, to have and hold...to him and his heirs in fee simple. I also give and bequeath unto my son Orville all the money on hand; also all the notes, bonds, debts and evidences of debt belonging to me on hand at my death, also all my negroes not previously or otherwise disposed (of) or conveyed... by me.

Fifth. All my stock of grain, stock of every kind, household and kitchen furniture, farming utensils and all my other personal property not previously disposed of...except my Pianoforte, shall be divided between my son **Orville** and my daughter **Louisa Phipps** in manner following: Two thirds of same I will and bequeath to my son **Orville**, and the remaining one third to my daughter **Louisa Phipps** to her sole and separate use with full power and authority to dispose of the same in such manner as she shall deem proper, by gift, deed, will or otherwise.

Sixth. It is my will and desire that should my son **Orville** die leaving no lawful issue, the negroes above given and bequeathed to him and their increase...shall go to and rest in the said **Nancy B. Phipps**, if living, or if dead, to her lawful heirs. And should there be any brothers or sisters hereafter born, the issue of **Louisa Phipps**, such after-born issue shall share said negroes equally with **Nancy B. Phipps**...

Seventh. I give and bequeath my Pianoforte to **Nancy B. Phipps**.

Eighth. I do hereby nominate and appoint my son **Orville Bradley**, and my friend **Jesse Lyons** Executors of this my last will and testament.

And Lastly. I do revoke and make utterly void all former wills by me at any time heretofore made, declaring this to be my last Will and Testament.

In witness whereof I have hereunto affixed my hand and seal This 1st day of October, 1842.

William Bradley (seal)

Signed, sealed and declared by the said **William Bradley** as his last will and testament in the presence of us who have hereunto affixed our names as witnesses at his request, and in his presence, the date above written.
J. P. McCarty
Jas. M. Hord
John T. Brice

WILL OF WILLIAM BALDWIN

Page 60
Dated: May 4, 1844
Proven May 5, 1845

I, **William Baldwin**, do make and publish this my last will and testament, hereby revoking and making void all other wills by me made (at) any time.

First. I direct that my funeral expenses and all my debts be paid as soon after my death as possible out of any money that I may die possessed of or may first come into the hands of my Executors.

Second. I give and bequeath unto my son **William** the west end of my plantation where I now live, also the tract I purchased of **McCraw** by him paying my present debts, and also my son **Nicholas** fifty dollars (on?) a horse when he becomes of age.

Thirdly. I will and bequeath unto my son **John** the east end of my home plantation, by him paying to my son **Nicholas** fifty dollars in a horse when he becomes of age.

Fourthly. I give and bequeath to my beloved wife **Mary** the use of my plantation during her widowhood.

Fifthly. I will and bequeath that my daughters, Viz: **Mary Ann**, **Esther** and **Elizabeth Jane** have each a good feather bed and clothing and one good cow each.

Lastly. I do hereby nominate and appoint my son **William K. Baldwin** my Executor. In witness whereof I do to this my will set my hand and seal This the 4th day of May, 1844.

William x Baldwin (seal)
(his mark)

Signed, sealed and published in our presence...of the Testator this the 4th day of May, 1844.
Witnesses:
Anderson Campbell
Joseph Garland
John x Byrd
 (his mark)
John Davis

WILL OF ORVILLE BRADLEY

Page 61   Dated: September 27, 1845
In the Name of God, Amen.

I, **Orville Bradley**, being of sound and disposing mind and memory, but feeble in body, do publish and declare this to be my last will and testament.

1st. It is my will and desire that out of whatever money I may have on hand at my death, or debts coming to me, that all my just debts be paid. And should there not be sufficient to pay them, then and in that case, out of my personal estate, and the expenses attending my funeral.

2nd. It is my will and desire that all my estate both real and personal which I may be possessed of at my death shall be vested in **Hugh Walker** and **George R. Powel** for the benefit of my niece **Nancy Bradley Phipps**, the daughter of **Joshua** and **Louisa Phipps**. And should the said **Nancy Bradley Phipps** die without leaving heirs of her body, then it is my will and desire that all my property both real and personal, at her death be sold by my Trustees hereby appointed, and a permanent fund raised for purposes of General Education in the County of Hawkins and the interest of said fund applied to the use of common schools.

3rd. It is my will and desire that should my Trustees hereby appointed believe it to be for the interest of my said niece, **Nancy**, that all my lands lying in the Western District, Tennessee should be sold, they may at their discretion within five years from this date, sell the same either at public or private sale as they may think most desirable, for the use and benefit of my niece...and the proceeds of said sale to be loaned out as an accumulating fund by my Trustees, as aforesaid until my said niece shall have attained the age of 21 years.

4th. It is my will and desire that all my negroes and my stock should remain on my farm as they are now, and the proceeds of my said farm applied to the payment of my debts or encumbrances which may lawfully arise against my estate otherwise to be an accumulation fund as aforesaid.

5th. It is my will and desire that if in the judgement of my Trustees hereby appointed, any of my slaves should become refractory or unmanageable or useless to my estate, that they may dispose of them at private or public sale as they in their discretion may think advisable. It is my will and desire that my Trustees for their trouble in carrying out the provisions of this my last will and testament, shall be allowed a reasonable allowance to be paid them out of my estate.

September 27, 1845.

Orville Bradley (seal)

Signed, sealed published and declared in the presence of us the undersigned:
D. Alexander
S. D. Mitchell
Chas. J. McKinney
Samuel Neill, Sr.
Robert H. Hale

WILL OF JACOB BOWMAN

Page 62

Dated: July 19, 1847　　Proven: Sept. 6th, 1847

I, Jacob Bowman of the County of Hawkins and State of Tennessee, do hereby make and constitute this my last will and testament hereby revoking all former wills by me at any time made.

1st. My will and desire is that all my just debts be paid out of any money I may die seized or possessed of, or that may first come into the hands of my Executors.

2nd. My will and desire is that my beloved wife Mary may have and hold possession of my house and farm...during her life or widowhood.

3rd. My will and desire...my son David have the farm whereupon he now lives, and pay $100.00 to the other children at the end of five years.

4th. My will and desire...my son Jacob...have all my farm at his mother's death and live with and take care of her during her life or widowhood. Except what I shall hereinafter mention and bequeath to others, and that he pay $1,000.00 for the benefit of my four youngest children, and that my son Jacob...

5th. My will and desire is that my son William have the saw and grist mill, and 100 acres of land on both sides of Big Creek, including all on the east side and in direction with the creek and the west side... and that he pay $1,000.00 for the benefit of my four youngest children, in equal proportions to them as they become of age, and also to have all my carpenter tools.

6th. My will and desire is that my son David have 20 acres of land lying at the upper end of my farm on both sides of the creek and running so as to include the house where David Thacker now lives parallel.

with the upper line, and 100 acres of land in the knob back of John Harlan's farm, also to have my blacksmith tools.

7th. My will and desire is that my daughters Anna and Rebecca, my sons John and Samuel have $500.00 each when they become of age of the proceeds of the sale of my personal property, and a piece of land lying on the south side of Bunker Hill which I wish to be sold.

8th. My will and desire is that what there is of the proceeds of my Estate over the bequests to my four youngest children after my debts is paid, I want my beloved wife Mary to have. In testimony I have hereunto set my hand and seal this 19th day of July A.D., 1847. I also wish my sons Jacob and William and Christian Sensabaugh appointed Executors to this my last will and testament, the date above written.

Jacob x Bowman (seal)
　　　　　　　　　　(his mark)

Witnesses:
Jacob Isenberg
Jacob Simmons
Thos. J. Amis

WILL OF MORDECAI BEAN

Page 63

Dated: March 11, 1853　　Proven: July Term, 1853

I, Mordecai Bean do make and publish this my last will and testament hereby revoking and making void all other wills by me at any time made.

First. I desire that my funeral expenses and all my just debts be paid as soon after my death as possible, out of any money that I may die possessed of or may first come into the hands of my Executor.

Secondly. I give and bequeath to my wife Katharine Bean all my household and kitchen furniture, stock of all kinds, my plantation and all its appurtenances, all the grain and forage, together with everything that I possess, during her life with full privilege to sell and use the same to pay any debts that may be owing, or for her support and all other legal purposes. I have heretofore given to all my children what I allowed them, unless there should be something remain (sic) after my wife's death, which (is to) be equally divided among my children.

Lastly. I do hereby nominate and appoint my wife Katharine Bean my executrix and that without giving any security. In witness whereof I do to this my last will set my hand and seal. This 11th day of March, 1853.

Mordecai Bean (seal)

Signed, sealed and published in our presence and we have subscribed our names hereto in the presence of the Testator. This 11th March, 1853.

Robert Wright, Eld(ridge) Hord; John Winn.

Note to foregoing: **Eld. Bord** witnessed this will on 19th of April, 1853, in presence of **Mordecai Bean** and **John Winn.**

WILL OF WILLIAM D. BROOKS

Page 64

Dated: May 3, 1854

Proven: June Term, 1854

I, **William D. Brooks** do make and publish this as my last Will and Testament hereby revoking and making void all other wills by me at any time made.

First. I desire that all my funeral expenses and debts be paid as soon after my death as possible out of any money I die possessed of, or may come first into the hands of my Executor or Administrator.

Secondly. I give and bequeath to my wife **Susannah**...all the interest that I have in 160-acre land warrant which will be located in Missouri, Newton County. Also to have one gray mare and colt, one four-horse wagon, one yoke of oxen and two milch cows, household and kitchen furniture.

Thirdly. I direct that my lands, all where I now live, be sold and all the balance of my personal property, after giving to my wife **Susannah** the above-named property, that my wife have a child's part of the money arising from the sale of my property.

Fourthly. I give and bequeath to each of my children (to wit): **Margaret Mooney, George Brooks, James Brooks, Cillina Pachal, Mary Webb, Susannah Bassett, Lafayette Brooks, Thomas Brooks, John Brooks, Rachael Paschal, Albert Brooks, Leah Brooks, Nancy Brooks,** I now give to each of the above named children an equal portion of the money arising from the sale of my land and personal property, each of them to have their part as soon as my Executor or Administrator may have time to sell and collect as the law directs, except those who are now minor children. Their portion I direct remain in the hands of my Executor or Administrator until they become of age or (are) competent to manage for themselves.

Fifthly. I also direct my two sons **John** and **Albert** have one horse each to be bought by my Executor...out (of) any money that I may die possessed (of) when they become 21 years of age. The above horses to be worth $65.00.

Sixthly. I...nominate my son **James Brooks** my Executor. In witness whereof I do to this my last will set my hand and seal. This 3rd day of May, 1854.

Wm. D. Brooks (seal)

Witnewsses: **John Altom, S. Brooks**

WILL OF JOHN BARNETT

Page 66

Dated: october 18, 1855

Proven: Dec. Term, 1855

I, **John Barnett** of the County of Hawkins and State of Tennessee, do make and publish this my last will and testament, hereby revoking all other wills by me heretofore made. I direct that my body be interred on my own farm in a manner suited to my condition in life, and for the worldly estate that it has pleased God to intrust me with, I dispose of as follows:

1st. I direct that all my just debts and funeral expenses be paid as soon after my decease as possible.

2nd. I will and bequeath to my beloved wife **Tempy** all my real estate and personal property during her natural life. At her death I direct that my daughter **Adaline Barnett** have one third of my real estate, also one cow and calf and one side saddle. The balance of my real estate and personal property to be sold and equally divided among my three daughters, **Adaline Barnett, Lucy Barnett** wife of **John Barnett, Jr.** and **Emily Miller** wife of **John Miller.** I hereby constitute and appoint my beloved wife **Tempy** and **William W. Johnson** my sole Executrix and Executor.

It is also my desire that **John Barnett, Jr.** live on and attend a part of my lands and pay my wife a reasonable rent for the lands he may attend. In testimony...I have...set my hand and seal, Oct. the 18th, 1855.

Test.

Daniel Harrell

N. H. Coldwell

John x Barnett (seal0

(his mark)

WILL OF THOMAS K. BALDWIN

Page 66

Dated: May 16, 1856

Proven: July Term, 1856

I, **Thomas K. Baldwin** being in feeble health but of disposing mind and memory, do make and publish this my last Will and Testament, hereby revoking and making void all other wills by me at any time made.

1st. I direct that my funeral expenses and all my just debts be paid as soon after my death as possible out of any money that I may die possessed of or may first come into the hands of my...Executors.

I give and bequeath to my beloved wife **Cassander** during her natural life all my stock of horses, hogs, cattle, sheep, household and kitchen furniture, one new wagon, farming utensils &c, together with the entire growing crop of corn, wheat and oats for the comfort of my beloved wife and family. I wish them settled on a farm on which they may be able to make a support and in order to effect that object, I wish my wife with the advice and consent of my Executors to have the privilege of purchasing a farm on which to live ranging in cost somewhere from twelve to eighteen hundred dollars, and in order that the means may be had to make said purchase of land, I wish that my property of any kind or description that in the judgement of my wife and my Executors can be spared that such property be sold upon such terms and conditions as may be agreed upon my and between my wife and Executors, and that the proceeds thereof be applied to the purchase of said farm, and that the balance of the amount necessary to pay for said farm be taken out of the first payments which will hereafter fall due to me for lands I have sold to **John N. Williams**, and after said farm shall have been purchased and my family settled thereon as above contemplated, I wish my said wife to have the privilege of purchasing for her own use a negro girl to be paid out of the proceeds of my said land sold to John N. Williams, but in the event that my said wife shall not choose to make the purchase of said negro girl, then the said fund arising from the land sold to John N. Williams... shall be loaned out by my Executors until my youngest child shall arrive at the age of 21, then said amount with interest thereon to be equally divided between my four children, and at the death of my beloved wife, the remaining portion of any property and effects of every kind...to be equally distributed between my legitimate heirs so as to make each one share and share alike.

I do hereby constitute and appoint William Davis of the County of Hancock and Thomas J. Lee of the County of Hawkins, Executors of this my last will and testament. I wish that my Executor William Davis be al-lowed to give security in his respective County of Hancock.

In testimony I have hereunto set my hand and affixed my seal. This 16th day of May, 1856.

Thomas K. Baldwin (seal)

Signed, sealed and published and we have subscribed our names in the presence of the Testator.

R. H. Drake
Henry D. Chesnutt

WILL OF JOHN BURCHELL

Dated: June 29, 1856
Proven: Sept. Term, 1856

I, John Burchell do make and publish this my last Will and Testament, hereby revoking and making void all wills by me at any other time made.

First. I direct my funeral expenses to be paid as soon as possible after my death out of any moneys that I may die possessed of or may first come into the hands of my Executor.

Secondly. I give and bequeath unto my daughter Sally Hicks one dollar.

Third. I bequeath to my son John Burchell one dollar.

Fourth. I bequeath to my daughter Elizabeth Barr one dollar.

Fifth. I bequeath to my daughter Nancy Davis one dollar.

Sixth. I bequeath to my daughter Jane Collins one dollar.

Seventh. I bequeath to my daughter Catherine Burchell one dollar.

Eighth. I bequeath to my wife Rebecca Burchell all the remainder of my estate consisting of horses, cattle, hogs, sheep, household and kitchen furniture, farming utensils and all the present growing crop... consisting of corn, wheat and other vegetables.

Lastly. I do nominate and appoint George Phillips my Executor.

In witness whereof I do to this my will set my hand and seal this 29th day of June, 1856.

John x Burchell (seal)
(his mark)

Signed, sealed and published in our presence and we have subscribed our names hereto in the presence of the Testator. This 29th day of June, 1856.

Test:
B. A. Creech
John Whitaker

WILL OF HUGH BARRETT

Dated: August 25, 1857
Proven: May Term, 1860

I, Hugh Barrett of the County of Hawkins and State of Tennessee, being of sound and disposing mind and memory do make, ordain and publish this my last will and testament hereby revoking and making void all other wills by me at any time made.

First. It is my wish and desire that my funeral expenses be paid as soon after my death as practicable out of the first money that may come into the hands of my Executor.

Second. It is my wish and desire that all my just debts be paid and my property whatever may be left, disposed of as follows:

To my son, John Nelson Barrett, I will and bequeath one half of my landed estate, being half of the farm whereon I now live including the house and other buildings, the farm to be divided agreeable to quantity and quality, and further that my wife Maria shall have a maintenance or life estate in said half of farm so willed to my son John Nelson Barrett, in case she lives a widow, but in case she marries, her maintenance or life estate in said parcel of land to be at an end and descend to my son John immediately. And further, my son John Nelson Barrett shall pay to his sister Elizabeth Laurie Barrett $150.00 in good property or money to be paid to her when she arrives at the age of 21 years. John, Elizabeth and their mother to live on said piece of land. My wife Maria, mother of John and Elizabeth, to have management and control of said piece of land in case she lives a widow until John becomes 21 years old at which time he is to have control of the place. The balance of farm, being the other half, I will and bequeath to my two sons William and Thomas, to be equally divided between them.

Thirdly. It is my wish and desire that my movable property, what-ever I may die possessed of, shall be sold and the proceeds divided as follows: To my two daughters Sally and Orlena, I will $25.00 each, and the balance, whatever it may be, equally divided between my five daugh-ters, Matilda, Mary, Louisa, Sally and Orlena.

Fourthly. I appoint my brother, Thomas T. Barrett, my Executor of this my last Will and Testament.

In testimony whereof I hereto set my hand and seal. This 25th day of August, 1851, in presence of the subscribing witnesses.

Hugh Barrett (seal)

Attest:
Wm. x Hutchisson
(his mark)
T. T. Barrett
A. P. K. Barrett

WILL OF WILLIAM N. BARRETT

Page 70

Dated: September 11, 1858
Proven: May Term, 1860

I, **William N. Barrett**, of the County of Hawkins and State of Tennessee, being of sound and disposing mind and memory, do make and ordain this to be my last will and testament, hereby revoking all other wills by me at any time made.

First. It is my wish and desire that my funeral expenses be paid out of any money that may first come into the hands of my Executors.

Second. It is my wish and desire that my beloved wife **Nancy** shall have one third of all my lands, including my dwelling house, and all my out buildings during her life in case she lives single, together with all my notes, books and papers of every kind and all my movable property of whatever kind it may be.

Third. It is my wish and desire that out of my money and notes and other movable property, my debts shall be paid by my wife **Nancy** and nothing sold except at her discretion.

Fourth. It is my wish that the remaining two thirds of my land shall be divided between my eight children, to wit: **Wm. C. Barrett, Sarah Adaline, Ezekiel Haynes, James Arthur, Mary Elizabeth, Peggy Jane, Thomas Orville** and **Martha Cornelia**, that they shall each receive their part as they reach 21 years of age.

Fifth. It is my wish and desire that at the death of my wife, the above-named property bequeathed to her shall be equally divided between the...eight children, and in case she marries the same to be divided between the children at her marriage as at her death.

Sixth. It is my wish and desire that my wife **Nancy** and **Thomas T. Barrett** be, and they are hereby constituted and appointed my Executors of this my last Will and Testament.

In testimony whereof I have hereunto set my hand and affixed my seal This 11th day of September, 1858 in the presence of the subscribing witnesses.

Attest:
Wm. Hutchisson
A. P. K. Barrett

William N. x Barrett (seal)
(his)
(mark)

NUNCUPATIVE WILL OF JOSEPH D. BECKNER

Page 71

Dated: November 1, 1858
Proven: Nov. Term. 1858

We, **Malcom D. Moore & Abraham Beckner** do state that the nuncupative will of **Joseph D. Beckner** was made by him on the 20th day of September, 1858, in our presence to which we were specially required to bear witness by the Testator himself in the presence of each other; that it was made in his last sickness in his own habitation or dwelling house, as follows:

It was his will and desire that his effects should be disposed of after his decease in the following manner:

1st. That all his debts and funeral expenses be paid.

2nd. That his son **Abraham B. Beckner** is to have the privilege of building himself a house on a site somewhere near spring and that he is to have it for himself and family a home.

3rd. That beloved wife, **Sarah Beckner** to have use of all the rest of estate during her lifetime or widowhood, except the provisions hereinafter mentioned. That **John F. Beckner** is to live with his family until age of 21, is to have a good horse, bridle and saddle and a good suit of clothes, and that his son **Abraham B. Beckner** should see to him getting the same.

4th. That his two daughters, **Nancy** and **Rhoda** be permitted to live on the place with their mother, and after his wife is done with the estate, all be equally distributed between his heirs, and his grand daughter **Mary Beckner** is to be an heir with his children, receiving an equal share of the estate with them. Made out by us and signed this 1st day of November, 1858.

A. Beckner
M. D. Moore

WILL OF BENJAMIN L. BUSSELL

Page 72

Dated: July 29, 1859 (or 23)
Proven: Sept. Term, 1859

I, **Benjamin L. Bussell**, do make and publish this as my last will and testament, hereby revoking and making void all other wills by me at any time made.

First. I direct that my funeral expenses and all my debts be paid as soon after my death as possible, out of any money that I may die possessed of or may first come into the hands of my Executor.

Secondly. I give and bequeath unto my well beloved wife **Polly Bassell** during her lifetime or widowhood the plantation on which I now live, together with all houses, barn and other outbuildings, and all the household and kitchen furniture that I may die seized and possessed of, farming tools, &c on the plantation and all the slaves and stock of every kind that is upon or may be upon the plantation at the time of my death.

Third. At the death of my wife **Polly Bussell**, or in case of her marriage, I give and bequeath plantation and improvements to my five sons, namely: **James M. Bussell, George W., John R., Calvin P.** and **Absalom T. Bussell** to be equally divided, share and share alike. The division to be made in any manner they choose to adopt.

Fourthly. I give and bequeath the tract of land known as the Mill Place, consisting of several tracts (to wit) a fifty-acre entry purchased from **John Jones**, a forty acre entry and an eleven acre entry and the land I purchased from **Joshua and Louisa Phipps**, that portion of it on which there is no encumbrances, together with the grist and saw mills and all other machinery, emprovements erected thereon, to my sons, namely: **Benjamin Sanford Bussell** and **Burwell W. Bussell**, to be equally divided between them, share and share alike. And in the event of the death of either of them without bodily heirs, then and in that case the other to heir the whole premises to his own proper use and benefit.

Fifthly. I have heretofore given to my daughter **Virenda Charles** a negro girl which I estimate to be worth $450.00 at the time of the gift; and I also gave to my daughter **Sarah Ann Rutherford** a negro girl which I estimate to be worth $550.00 at the time of the gift. And I also gave to my daughter **Mary Ann Prater** a negro girl which I estimate to be worth $500.00 at the time of the gift.

Sixthly. It is my will and desire that at the time of the death or marriage of my wife **Polly Bussell**, my Executor hereinafter appointed shall proceed to sell all the property on hand at the time, consisting of slaves, stock of all kind, wagons, gearing and farming tools, and household and kitchen furniture of every kind and description. And when the proceeds of sale of said property shall have been collected, he shall make the following distribution thereof, that is to say: (I have heretofore paid to my sons **James M., George W.** and **John R. Bussell** $275.00 each). He shall pay to my sons **Calvin P., Benjamin Sanford, Burwell W. &** **Absalom T.** each the sum of $275.00, and to my daughter **Virenda Charles** $425.00...daughter **Sarah Ann Rutherford** $325.00 and daughter **Mary Ann Prater** $375.00 to make them all equal with my sons to whom I have heretofore made advances.

Seventhly. After payments heretofore provided shall have been made, if there is a surplus of money remaining in the hands of my Executor, he shall make equal distribution between both sons and daughters, share and share alike, till the whole is exhausted.

Lastly. I do hereby nominate and appoint my sons **Calvin P.** and **Absalom T. Bussell** my executors. In witness whereof I do to this my will set my hand and seal. This 23rd day of July, 1859.

B. L. Bussell (seal)

Signed, sealed and acknowledged in our presence. **John Ball, J. M. Charles, Burum Harrison**

WILL OF REBECCA BURTON

Page 74

Dated: July 17, 1859
Proven: Aug. 1862

July the seventh day, 1859. In the name of God, Amen. I, Rebecca Burton, do make and publish this my last will and testament.

First. I direct that my funeral expenses and all my debts be paid as soon as possible after my death out of any money that I may die possessed of or may first come into the hands of my Executor.

Secondly. I will and bequeath to my daughter **Elizabeth** all my interest in one tract of land containing 25 acres.

Thirdly. I will all my personal property to my daughter **Elizabeth.** I hereby set my hand and seal to this my last will.

July 17, 1859.   Rebecca x Burton (her mark)

Signed, sealed and published in our presence and we have subscribed our names in the presence of the Testator. This the 17th day of July, 1859.

Witness: **Nehemiah B. Hurley; Jasper N. Murrell**

COPY OF WILL OF WESLEY BALL

Page 74

Dated April 23, 1860

I, **Wesley Ball**, do make this as my last will and testament, revoking and making void all former wills at any time by me made.

First. I direct that my funeral expenses and all my debts be paid as soon after my death as possible out of any money that I may die possessed of, or that may first come into the hands of my Executor herein to be appointed.

Secondly. I give and bequeath to my beloved wife **Jane Ball** two good beds and clothes &c that should belong to them, table, knives & forks, cooking utensils and all other furniture of my house that would be necessary for housekeeping. I will and bequeath that my Executor pay to her, my said wife, $100.00 cash. I will that my wife shall have one horse, saddle and bridle, her choice, and that she shall enjoy and keep possession of my house that I now live in as her own during her life or widowhood, but at her death or marriage, the house is to belong to my son **S. H. Ball**, of whom I will hereafter speak. My will and desire is that my wife shall have one choice cow, and if she chooses, five sheep, three or four hogs.

I will and bequeath unto my son **John Ball** all the land he lives on, it being the land I bought of **John Ball, Sr.**, also all the place at the forks of the road called The Old Voting Ground where he--John--now has his store and I purchased of **D. Bailey.**

I will and bequeath unto my son **Spencer H. Ball** all of my home place extending to the top of the mountain each side, even with the lower and upper end, to have full possession of my house after the death or marriage of my wife, but to have full control of all the lands and out buildings when this will takes effect.

I will and bequeath unto my daughter **N. Lucas**, formerly **Nancy Ball** all of the place she lives on and to the mountain top each way as described in the place I gave **Spencer.** My will and desire is that my daughter **Patsy** who married **Jacob Morelock** and now resides in the state of Missouri shall have paid to her for the use of her and her own children by my Executors, $600.00 cash.

I will and bequeath unto my daughter **Polly** and her husband **Jonathan Bernard** all the tract of land that **John Smith** now lives on which land I bought of **John Bernard** and all of the land adjoining the same on the side of **Bay's Mountain** to the top of the same; and in addition to this land I desire my daughter **Polly Bernard** to have paid to her by my Executors $500.00 which I think will make her equal with her sister **Nancy Lucas.** I will and desire that my son **John Ball**, owing to his place in my opinion being an over share, shall pay to me or my Estate $200.00, and that my son **Spencer H. Ball** in like manner pay $500.00. I further enjoin upon my two sons **John & Spencer** to support my wife with a decent support during her life or widowhood, the expense to be born in equal proportions with both. This I do because their lands are valuable and hence they should support my wife.

And finally, all other property personal and real, debts, money and every species, shall be sold and collected by my Executors, and equally divided among my five children or their heirs. I do hereby nominate and appoint my two sons **Spencer H. Ball & John Ball** my Executors of this my last will and testament. In witness whereof I do to this my will set my hand and seal. This 23rd Day of April, 1860.

(his)
Wesley x Ball
(mark)

Signed, sealed and published in our presence, and we have subscribed our names hereto in the presence of the Testator. This 23rd Day of April, 1860.
Jacob Miller, David Bailey,

State of Tennessee) .I **James R. Pace,** Clerk of the County
Hawkins County ·)   Court of said county do hereby certify
)   that the foregoing is a true and perfect copy of the last will and testament of **Wesley Ball** Dec'd. now on file in my office, this the 2nd day of February,1863.
Jas. R. Pace, clerk

WILL OF SAMUEL BRYANT
Page 76

                 Dated: June 15, 1860
                 Proven: Sept. Term, 1860

I, **Samuel Bryant,** considering the uncertainty of this mortal life, and being of sound mind and memory, do make and publish this my last will and testament in manner and form following, that is to say:

First. I give and bequeath unto my beloved wife **Sarah Bryant** the lands I now live on and possess during her natural life, provided in the event she and my executor together believe they can better her condition by selling the land and purchasing others--or the proceeds kept unless she should come to actual want. If so relieve her wants by using the means in her possession. I also further give to my wife **Sarah** all the rest, residue and remainder of my personal estate, goods and chattels of whatever kind and nature for her use and benefit during her life, and after her death, if anything remains, it shall be sold and the proceeds equally divided among my three daughters (to wit) **Mary Elizabeth, Martha Ann, Lucinda Cornelia,** and as **Mary E.,** now **Mary E. McAnnally** and **Martha A.,** now **Martha A. Wolfe** have had some property (namely) a bed, saddle and cow - for which I wish **Lucinda Cornelia** to be made equal by my Executors.

I hereby appoint my beloved wife **Sarah** and **Leeroy Wolfe** my Executors of this my last will and testament by revoking all former wills by me made.

In witness whereof I have set my hand and seal this 15th day of June, one thousand eight hundred and sixty.

Samuel x Bryant (seal)
(his mark)

Attest: **B. Blackburn & B. Golden**

WILL OF MARY M. BURNS
Page 77

                 Dated: March 4, 1851
                 Proven: Dec. Term 1851

In the Name of God, Amen.

I, **Mary Burns,** being of sound and disposing mind and memory but feeble in health, do make, publish and declare the following to be my last will and testament, hereby revoking and making entirely void all other wills which I have at any time heretofore made.

First. It is my will and desire, and I so direct that after my decease, I shall be buried according to the mode of Christian burial, and that my Executors hereinafter named shall pay all the expenses attending my funeral.

Secondly. I will and bequeath unto my sons **William** and **John** all my interest in a land warrant which has not as yet come to hand, for 160 acres of land, on account of service rendered by my deceased husband **Robert Burns** in the Army of the United States in the War of 1812, and whereas I have heretofore executed a Power of Attorney to **Samuel Powel,** my son-in-law authorizing him to do all the business necessary to procure said land warrant and to obtain a pension. It is my will and desire that the business be taken out of the hands of **Samuel Powel** and that my Executors hereinafter named and appointed shall have the sole and exclusive control of the whole business and that the said **Powel** shall have nothing further to do with said business.

Thirdly. It is my will and desire and I so direct that out of the money which may arise from the sale of said land warrant that my Executors pay unto my daughters **Jane E. Davis** and **Sarah Ann Powel** each the sum of five dollars.

Fourthly. It is my will and desire that if I should obtain a pension from the Government of the United States, that the same be equally divided between all my children, share and share alike.

Fifthly. I will and bequeath to my son **John Burns** my bed and furniture.

Sixthly. I will and bequeath unto my daughters **Jane E. Davis** all of my clothing of whatsoever kind or character that I may possess at my death.

And Lastly. I do hereby nominate and appoint my two sons **John & William** my Executors of this my last will and testament.

In witness whereof I do to this my last will and testament set my hand and seal this 4th day of March, 1851.

Mary x Burns (seal)
(her mark)

Signed, sealed and published in our presence and we have subscribed our names hereto in the presence of the Testator. This 4th day of March, 1851.

George R. Powel
J. R. Armstrong

WILL OF BENJAMIN COX

Page 79   Dated: June 13, 1791

In the Name of God, Amen. I, **Benjamin Cox**, of Hawkins County in the Western Territory, South of the Ohio, being weak in body but perfect in sense, praised be God, I do make this my last will and testament.

Item. Promise. I do hereby give unto my brother **William Cox** all my lands unto him and his heirs forever.

Item. I do hereby give unto my father **William Cox** all my movable effects and living stock, unto him and his heirs forever, after all my just debts are paid. I do appoint m loving and trusting father my sole Executor of this my last will and testament, hereby revoking all former wills and testaments.

In witness whereof I do to all and every part of the above said will and testament I have hereunto set my hand and seal this thirteenth day of June in the year of our Lord, 1791. Sealed, published and delivered by the written name of **Benjamin Cox** for his last will and testament in the presence of us:

Jesse Cox
Solomon Cox (Jurat)
Marjery Cox

Benj. Cox (seal)

WILL OF RUBEN CRAYCRAFT

Page 79   Dated: April 6, 1791

In the Name of God, Amen. I, **Ruben Craycraft**, being through the a-bundant mercy & goodness of God though weak in body yet of sound and perfect understanding & memory do constitute this my last will and testa-ment, and desire it may be received by all as such.

Imprimis. I most humbly bequeath my soul, to God my Maker, beseech-ing His most gracious acceptance of it through the all-sufficient merits and mediation of my most Compassionate Redeemer, Jesus Christ who gave Himself to be an Atonement for my sins and is able to save to the utter-most all that come unto God by Him, seeing He ever liveth to make inter-cession for them and who I trust will not reject me, a returning penitent sinner when I come to him for mercy in this hope and confidence. I ren-der up my soul with comfort hereby beseeching the most blessed and glo-rious to prepare me for the time of my dissolution and there to take me to Himself, into that peace and rest and incomparable felicity which He has prepared for all that love and fear His holy name, Amen.

Next, I give my body to the earth from whence it was taken in full as-surance of its resurrection from thence at the last day. As for my burial, I desire it may be decent, without pomp or state at the discre-tion of my dear friend and my Executors hereafter named who I doubt not will manage it with all requisite prudence.

As to my worldly estate, I will and positively order that all my just debts be paid, together with all my sickness and funeral expense out of the same, that is to say, one brown mare about seven years old, one blue broadcloth coat and jacket, one corduroy breeches, one brown cloth coat and a white cloth jacket, one fine shirt, one pair thread stockings, one pair new shoes, one pair of silver knee-buckles, one cotton and three pairs of homemade fustain; two pairs garters and one old saddle and saddle bags and bridle. All of which the above-mentioned articles I will and positively order the balance after the above mentioned debts or ex-penses is paid, to give the remainder to my father, **William Craycraft** when he makes application for the same. And I do constitute **Thomas McLaughlin** and **Thomas Murrell** Executors of this my last will and testament and Trustees of the same. In witness whereof I have hereunto set my hand and seal this 6th day of April in the year of our Lord, One Thousand, Seven Hundred and Ninety-one.

Ruben x Craycraft (seal)
(his mark)

Witnesses: **Matthew Sims, Jacob x Graff, Elisha Walling**
(his mark)

Note: The word "my" before burial interlined before signing &c.

WILL OF COLLIN CRILLY

Page 80   Dated: July 4, 1793

In the name of God, Amen. I, **Collin Crilly**, of Hawkins County and ceded territory, South of Ohio River, being weak in body but in natural sense doth make this my last will and testament, and do make void all former wills. At my death I give and bequeath unto **Elizabeth Musgrove**, wife to **Saul Musgrove**, all my estate both in bonds and property accepting two dollars in tred (trade), one to **William Crilly** and one to **Jane Thompson Crilly**. And I do appoint **John Young** my Executor. As witness my hand and seal this 4th day of July, 1793, in presence of:

Collin Crilly (seal)

Test:
John Young, Henry Larkin

WILL OF EDWARD CROSS

Page 81   Dated: July 21, 1794

In the Name of God, Amen. I, **Edward Cross**, being sick in body though perfect in memory, knowing it is appointed for all men once to die, do make and ordain this my last will and testament in manner...as follows:

In the first place, I recommend my soul to Almighty God who
gave it, and my body to the earth to be decently buried at the
discretion of my Executors, hereafter mentioned, and as for what
worldly goods it hath pleased God to bestow on me, I give and bequeath in manner and form as follows:
In the first place, I give and bequeath unto my beloved wife
Rebecker, all my estate both personal and real, to her during
her natural life or widowhood, and at her death or marriage, I
desire my whole estate to be equally divided amongst all my
children, i.e. **rebecker Parmely**, **Robert Cross**, **Elizabeth Cross**,
to have ten pounds less than the rest of my children on account
of former presents made to them. That is to say, to be divided
betwixt **Rebecker Parmely**, **Robert Cross**, **Elizabeth Cross**, **Deaner
Cross**, **Mary Cross**, **Nancy Cross**, **William Cross** and **Gibbins Cross**,
Patty Cross and **James Cross.**
I appoint my beloved wife my executrix and **W. Thomas
Gibbins, Sr.** and my son **Robberd Cross** my Executors. In witness
whereof I have hereunto set my hand and seal This 21st day of
July, 1794.
Signed and sealed in the presence
of: **William Molsby**   **Edward Cross** (seal)
    John Bean
    W. Elzey

WILL OF JOHN COX

Page 82   Dated August 25, 1798
   In the name of God, Amen. I **John Cox** of the County of
Hawkins and State of Tennessee, being sick and weak, but of
sound, disposing mind and memory, do make and ordain this to
be my last will and testament, in the manner and form as followeth, viz:
Item. I give unto my lawful wife **Tibitha Cox** all my land and
mill & all my negroes excepting one named **Mille**, likewise all
my stock excepting one horse colt. Likewise, all my household
furniture and working tools during her widowhood. I will and
bequeath unto my son **Thomas** one young horse colt, and I likewise
bequeath unto my daughter **Ellice Cox** one negro girl named **Mille**,
to her and her body heirs forever, and all her increase. Likewise, the said **Thomas Cox** and **Ellice Cox** is to have an equal
share with the rest hereafter. It is my will and request that
my brother **Edward Cox** should take the remainder of the goods
and to settle my accounts below as far as the(y) will pay, and
if there should not be as much as would satisfy the debts, the
said **Edward Cox** should have power to settle the books as far as
to pay the amount. And finally, I do acknowledge this to be my
last will and revoking all others.
   Witnesseth my hand and seal This 25th day of August, 1798.
Witness present: **John Cox** (seal)
Samuel Vernon, James Dougherty, Abraham Vernon

WILL OF WILLIAM CRAWFORD

Page 82   Dated July 8, 1804
In the name of God, Amen. I, **William Crawford**, being of sound
and perfect memory, blessed be God, do this eighth day of July
in the year of our Lord one thousand eight hundred and four make
and publish this my last will and testament in manner following,
that is to say:
I do give and bequeath unto my loving wife all and singular my
goods and chattels, together with all my debts and movable effects, by her freely to be possessed and enjoyed during her life.
And I do hereby make and ordain my worthy friend **Christopher
Wilflee** Executor of this my last will and testament. In witness
whereof I, the said **William Crawford**, have set my hand and seal,
the day and year above written.

                                     William Crawford

Signed, sealed, published and
declared in presence of: **Robert McMinn, Samuel Morrison**

COPY OF SALLY COLEY'S WILL

Page 83   Dated March 9, 1807
   In the name of God, Amen. I **Sally Coley**, of Goochland
County and State of Virginia, being in a weak state of body, but
of perfect mind and memory and knowing it is appointed for us
all one time to die, have ordained this my last will and testament in the words and form as followeth:
Item. It is my will and desire that all my negroes to be emancipated after my death, to wit: **Lucy, Burton, James, Lewis,
Frankey, Harrison, Martha and Mary**, all being the children of
the first-named **Lucy** - and it is further my will and desire that
after my dec'd that these my above mentioned negroes shall be
all sot free that they may have the use of my plantation one
year after my death - together I give my stock of all kinds to
my above mentioned negroes to be equally divided among them all.
I further give unto my above mentioned negroes my plantation
tools, to them my negroes, whome my will is they shall be sot
free.
Item. I give unto my sister **Nancy Coley** one large puter dish and
one large bason.
Item. I give unto **James Coley**, son of **Peggy Coley**, my bead
and furniture together (with) the bead stead, card &c, provided
he, said **James Coley**, comes in thise county in the corse of two
years after my dec'd, and should he not apply in that time for
sd bead and furniture, it is my desire for **Wm Coley** to have it,
who is son of **Molly Colley**. It is further my will and desire
that my above mentioned negroes shall after my death have the
balance of my household and kitchen furniture, to be equally
divided among them, and likewise for them, my said negroes to
have the growing crop and the crop that may be already made, if
any on hand.
Item. It is my further will and desire that my land whereon I

WILL OF JACOB COX

Page 85

Dated: July 1, 1808
Prov. Nov. 28, 1807

In the Name of God, Amen. I, Jacob Cox, of the County of Hawkins and State of Tennessee, being weak of body but of perfect mind, do make, constitute and ordain this my last will and testament in the following manner, to wit (Viz):

Item. It is my will and desire that all my just debts be paid. It is my will and desire that my loving wife **Mary Cox** shall have my black mare called Cate without any Legence. It is my wish, my will and desire that the tract of land whereon I now live shall be divided in the following manner (Viz): That my loving wife **Mary Cox** shall have the one third part her lifetime and the remaining two thirds to be equally divided between my loving children hereafter named.

It is my will and desire that all my other lands shall be equally divided between my three sons, to wit: **John, Witner** and **Pharoah,** by three dis-interested men. It is my will and desire that all my personal estate and household furniture shall be equally divided between my loving wife and loving children hereafter named as they becomes of age if they stand in need of it, to be valued by three dis-interested men and delivered to my loving wife **Mary** and loving children: **Lucy, Betsy, John, Polly, Witner, Pharoah, Nancy** and **Emmaline.**

It is my will and desire that if there is more stock than will be considered for use of the place it shall be sold as they think proper. It is my will and desire that my loving children shall be educated out of the estate as my Executor may think proper.

I do make, constitute and ordain **Thomas Hopkins,** my wife, **Mary Cox,** & **Martin Rowler** my three lawful Executors of this my last will and Testament. Given from under my hand and seal this twenty-first day of July in the year of our Lord, one thousand eight hundred and eight.

Jacob Cox (seal)

Test. Continued.
Martin Roller

Also, I do will being my desire and having the same mind and since fore-going was wrote, I have a son that we have named **Samuel** share equally with my other sons as within mentioned. My wish is that at the time of a regular division of my personal estate that our daughter **Lucy** may admit of a credit from a sorrel mare supposed to be worth $100.00. It is my will and desire that my son **John Cox** should have a certain horse named Polleat, together with a new saddle, bridle and a rifle gun charged one hundred dollars which will be deducted out of his legacy.

It is also my will and desire that the negroes shall be hired out or kept on the premises as shall be thought best by my Executors and family for the term of ten years, and at the end of said term of ten years for them and their increase to be equally divided amongst my children: never-theless, it is my will and desire that my dearly beloved wife **Mary Cox** have her choice of the negroes during her lifetime and then to fall to my children again.

Given from under my hand and seal this 27th June 1809.
Jacob Cox (seal)

---

know live to be sold to the highest bidder, one-third of the money to be paid in hand, the other two-thirds to be paid in two annual payments. It is further my will and desire that my Executor hereafter mentioned shall fix my within mentioned negroes of with a lite horse carte and one horse worth aboute fifteen pounds and should the horse I have now on hand be dead or not able to help my within mentioned negroes move oute of the State as the laws of the land calls for them so to do, it is my will and desire their should be another horse provided for them by my Executors and two mens' saddles and bridles; the second horse, it wanting, should be at fifteen pounds - or there abouts. It is further my will and desire that my negro woman **Lucy's** receipt give to my Executors for what I have left she s'd and her children so as to clear my Executors from her-self & her children as they are at this time under age. So that **Lucy's** receipt shall be good and a clear discharge for my Executor, and further it is my will that if my negro woman **Lucy** will not goe oute of the state with her biggest children, that **Burton, James & Lewis** shall have the two horses and saddles above mentioned and goe oute of the state. It is further my will and desire that my just debts be all paid oute of the last two-thirds of my land money and that my Executors shall be suf-ficiently satisfied oute of the same two-thirds of s'd land money, and further, the above-mentioned saddles and bridles are to be new ones got for my negroes above mentioned, and it is further my will and desire that the balance of my land money, if any left after payment of my debts and fixing of my negroes for their journey and satisfy (satisfying) my Executors for their trouble with my worldly affairs to be equally divided between **Molly Coley, Nancy Coley, Frank Coley, Betsy Coley, Peggy Coley, Wm. Coley & James Coley,** and I do further appoint **Charles Massie** and **William Turner** Executors of thise my last will and testament, revoking all other wills made heretofore. In witness whereof I have hereunto set my hand and seal this 9th day of March, 1807. (Interlined before signed in severall places.)

Sally x Coley (seal)
(her mark)

Witnesses:
Pleasant Turner
Rob't x Singleton
(his mark)
Hazard x Singleton
(his mark)

(Page 85) At a monthly Session Court held for Goochland County at the Court House on Monday the 19th day of Sept. 1808, the within was presented in Court and proved by the oaths of Pleasant Turner, Robert Singleton and Hazard Singleton to be the last will and testament of Sally Coley, dec'd, and ordered to be recorded. Then Charles Massie and William Turner, the Executors herein named appeared in Court and formally and solemnly re-nounced all rights as Executors under this will and refused to be quali-fied as such.

Test. Wm. Miller C.G.C.

A Copy

Test.
Henry A. Hall, Matthew Cleck, Dennis Condray, John Miller, Martin Roller, (J),
Jacob Wills (J), Presley Buckner

WILL OF JAMES CALDWELL

Page 87
Dated: March 30, 1812
Proven: August 1812

In the Name of God, Amen. I, **James Caldwell** of the County of Hawkins
and State of Tennessee, being weak in body and in a low state of health,
but sound in mind and memory, and calling to mind the mortality of our
nature that it is appointed unto all men once to die and after that the
Judgement, I commend my soul to God and my body to the earth to be buried
in a decent Christian manner, hoping they again will be united at the
general resurrection of the Just, and I do make and ordain my last Will
and Testament in the form following, to wit:

In the first place, I allow my just debts to be paid.

Item. I leave and bequeath to my beloved wife **Jane** my dwelling house
and kitchen with all the furniture in them as long as she needs them, and
then to be distributed amongst my children at her discretion. Also the
third part of the plantation I live on, both clear ground and woodland
during her natural life. I also leave her the negro fellow **Bob** to her
during her life, to work her land under the direction of my son **St. Clair.**
I also leave her the negro girl **Ciz** during her life. Also I leave her a
horse, she to have her choice when she pleases to make it. I allow to my
wife one third part of my stock of cattle, sheep and hogs.

Item. I also give and bequeath to my son **St. Clair** the other two
thirds of my plantation I live on both clear ground and woodland and at
his mother's death the whole plantation forever, also all the farming
tools of every kind, also I leave my negro **Bob** and the negro girl **Ciz** at
the death of his mother to my son **St. Clair.**

Item. I give and bequeath to my son **John** the price of a place
lately sold in Tennessee Valley, Rhea County, amounting to seven hundred
and thirty-five dollars, also a negro boy named **App**, also a horse named
Rock.

Item. I give and bequeath to my daughter **Ann**, a bay filly now in
the possession of her husband, in addition to what she has already got.

Item. The leaving (sic) I have given to my son **Silas** must in a
measure stand for his fortune, but as his education is not finished, I
give and bequeath to him a negro boy **Park**, also $300.00 to complete his
education.

Item. I give and bequeath to my daughter **Jane** a negro girl named
Vicey, also a good horse and saddle, also two cows and calves. The
residue of stock, horses, cattle, hogs and sheep to remain as a fund to
pay debts, finish **Silas'** education, and the balance I leave to **St. Clair.**

Item. My negro woman **Hannah** and her child **Prise** I allow to be
either continued on the place, hired out or sold at the (discretion)
of my Executors, hereafter to be named. Should the above fund of
stock not answer the end contemplated, I allow the proffits of **Hannah**
the negro woman and her child **Price** to make it up whatever disposition
may be made of her and so as to leave **St. Clair** a sufficient stock to
carry on his farm. The balance, if any, to be equally divided among the
legatees.

I appoint my beloved wife **Jane** and my sons **John** and **St. Clair** to
execute this my last will and testament.

Given under my hand this 30th of March A.D., 1812, in the presence
of
(witnesses)
George Maxwell   James Caldwell
John Young

WILL OF JOHN C. CHURCH

Page 88
Dated: May 30, 1813

In the Name of God, Amen. I, **John Christian Church** of Hawkins
County and State of Tennessee, being very sick and weak or imperfect
health of body, but perfect mind and memory, thanks be to God for the
same, and calling to mind the mortality of my body and knowing that it
is appointed once for all men to die, do make this my last Will and
Testament (Viz):

Principally and first of all, I do give and recommend my soul into
the hands of God that gave it and my body I recommend to the earth to
be buried in a decent Christian burial at the discretion of my Executors,
nothing doubting but at the general resurrection I shall receive the same
again by the Almighty power of God. And as touching such worldly estate
wherewith it hath pleased God to bless me in this life, I give, devise
and dispose of the same in the following manner and form, Viz:

First of all, I give and bequeath to my three sons, **Henry, Thomas**
and **George** an equal share of all I possess (i.e.) my land, messuages,
tenements, including all my household furniture, still and utensils of
every kind.

Secondly, I leave my wife **Eleanor Church** a child's part during her
widowhood, and after her decease, her part to be equally divided among
the three above-mentioned boys.

Thirdly, I give and bequeath to my daughter **Mary Anne** Staples one
dollar.

Fourthly, I give and bequeath to my daughter **Mary Anne's** daughter
Nancy twenty dollars.

Fifthly and lastly. I give and bequeath to my three sons, **Henry,
Thomas** and **George** all that is coming from **William Warren's** note after
William Armstrong is satisfied. I do hereby utterly disallow, revoke and
disannul all and every former testaments, wills, legacies, bequests by
me in anywise made, confirming this and no other to be my last Will and
Testament. In witness whereof I have hereunto set my hand and affixed
my seal This 30th day of May, A.D., 1813.

John C. x Church (seal)
(his mark)

Signed, sealed, published, pronounced and declared by the said John C. Church as his last will and testament in the presence of us who in his presence and of each other have hereunto set our hands.

Test. Names of witnesses illegible.

WILL OF JOHN CROSON

Dated Feb'y 6, 1814

In the name of God, Amen. This, the last will and testament of **John Croson** of Hawkins County and State of Tennessee is as followeth, viz: He the said **John Croson** finding himself sick and weak of body, but in perfect mind and memory, blessed be God therefore, and calling to mind the frailty of this life and the certainty of death, I do ordain and make this my last will and testament in form and manner as followeth:

Imprimis: I do recommend my soul unto the hand of God who gave it and my body to the earth to be interred therein with decent and Christian burial at the discretion of my executor hereafter named. And as for what worldly goods it hath pleased God to bless me with, all I do will and bequeath in manner and form foloweth, viz:

Item. I give and bequeath to my beloved wife **Drusiller Croson** all my horse creatures, cattle and hogs, with all my household and kitchen furniture and working tools, to be her during her natural life, and at her decease if anything remains, then to be equally divided amongst all my children. This I do make to be my last will and testament. And I do hereby have my beloved wife **Drewsiller Croson** and **John Croson** my son to act for me as my Executors. This the 6th day of February, 1814.

Test. **Francis Winstead**   **John x Croson** (his mark)
Test. **Samuel x Burton** (his mark)

WILL OF MICHAEL CLICK

Dated July 28, 1814

In the name of God, Amen. I **Michael Click** of Hawkins County and State of Tennessee, being weak of body, but of perfect mind and memory. Thanks be given to God, & calling unto mind the mortality of my body and knowing that it is appointed unto all men once to die, do make and ordain this my last Will and Testament: That is to say, principally and first of all, I give and recommend my soul unto the hand of Almighty God that gave it and my body I recommend to the earth to be buried in decent Christian burial at the discretion of my Executors, nothing doubting but at the general resurrection I shall receive the same again by the mighty power of God, and as touching such worldly estate wherewith it has pleased God to bless me in this life, I give, devise and dispose of in the following manner; and:

First. I give and bequeath to my three daughters, viz: **Margaret**, **Elizabeth** and **Katharine** all my cattle, sheep hogs, beds, clothing and all household furniture. Also, one bay mare known by the name of Cate, to be equally divided among them (My sons **John**, **George**, **Michael** and **Matthias** have all received their shares). Also, I give to my son **Jacob** all my land including the plantation whereon I now live and two small tracts adjoining it; also all my farming utensils out of which he will pay all my lawful debts and provide for and furnish his mother with everything necessary to her comfort and support during her live, leaving her to possess my new dwelling house, garden, &c.

Lastly. I constitute and ordain my wife **Margaret Click**, my son **Jacob Click**, and grandson **Jesse Huggard** my sole Executors of this my last will and testament. And I do hereby utterly disallow, revoke and disannul all and every other former testament or will obligation, &c by me in any way before named, willed or bequeathed, verifying and confirming this and no other to be my last will and testament. In witness whereof I have hereunto set my hand and seal. This twenty eighth of July in the year of our Lord, one thousand eight hundred and fourteen.

Signed, sealed published, pronounced and declared by the said **Michael Click** as his last will and testament in the presence of us who in his presence and in the presence of each other have hereunto subscribed our names.

Thomas Larkin (jurat)   **Michael x Click** (seal)
John Larkin (his mark)

WILL OF JOHN COX

Dated: May 16, 1816   Proven: Nov., 1820

In the Name of God, Amen. I, **John Cox** of the State of Tennessee and County of Hawkins, being of sound sense and memory, though in a declining state of health, do this sixteenth day of May, eighteen hundred and sixteen, make and publish this my last Will and Testament in writing.

First. I desire after decease to be buried in a plain and decent manner.

Item. I do give the following children one dollar each, (viz): **Patty Matlock**, **Nancy Sims**, **Elizabeth Sims**, **Sally Cocke**, **Katy Looney**, **Josiah Cox** and **Absalom Cox**.

Item. I do give the balance of my property both real and personal to my son **George Cox** on condition that he takes good care of his mother and my wife **Frances Cox** during her life, except my sorrel horse colt.

Item. I do give my grandson **Russel Cox** my sorrel horse colt.

Item. I appoint and request my son **George Cox** to be my Executor of this my last Will and Testament, and do hereby revoke and void every other will or wills by me made. In witness whereof I, the said **John Cox**, Testator, have hereunto set my hand and affixed my seal, the day and date above written.

John x Cox (seal)
(his mark)

Test.
John Howell
John Laughmiller

WILL OF REBECCA CRAFT

Page 92
                                    Dated: February 5, 1818
                                    Proven: Feb. Session 1818

In the Name of God, Amen. I, **Rebecca Craft** of the County of Hawkins
and State of Tennessee, calling to mind the shortness of this mortal
life and knowing that it is appointed for all persons once to die, do
make and ordain this my last Will and Testament, that is to say:

Principally and first of all, I give and recommend my soul into the
hand of Almighty God that gave it. And as touching such worldly estate
wherewith it has pleased God to bless me in this life, I give, demise
and dispose of the same in the following manner and form:

First. I give and bequeath to my brothers and sisters the sum of
ten dollars to be equally divided between my brothers and sisters or
their heirs, excepting my sister **Sarah Light**. It is also my will that
my negro girl named **Anna** should be freed, agreeable to the law of the
state, at twenty-one years of age. And it is also my will she should
have one puter dish and coffe pot, one pewter bason and six pewter plates,
a set of knives and forks, six spoons and one tin cup; one feather bed
and furniture and one velvet riding dress and one bed stead and one chest.
And I give to my sister **Sarah Light** two pewter dishes, six pewter plates,
seven spoons, three small pewter basons, three tin plans, and five tea
cups, one peper box and a worm of cotton cards and one coffee pot, one
stone jug, one pickling pot(?), and one bed and furniture and bedstead,
and two pots, one oven, and one dresser, one iron shovel and one cow,
and it is also my will that **Vachel Light** and his three sons should have
fourteen head of hogs to be equally divided between them. I likewise
constitute, make and ordain **Vachel Light** my sole Executor of this my last
will and testament. And I do hereby utterly revoke and disannul all and
every other former will. I do ratify and confirm this to be my last will
and testament. In witness whereof I have hereunto set my hand and seal.
This fifth day of February in the year of our Lord, One thousand eight
hundred and eighteen.

Signed, sealed and published and declared by the said **Rebecca Craft**
in presence of:
(Attest)   Rebecca x Craft (seal)
Reuben Barnard (Jurat)   (her mark)
James Morrison (Jurat)
George_____ (name illegible)

WILL OF CORNELIUS CARMACK

Page 93   Dated: December 29, 1818

In the Name of God, Amen. I, **Cornelius Carmack** of the County of
Hawkins and State of Tennessee, being sick in body but of a sound and
disposing mind, memory and understanding, considering the certainty of
death and the uncertainty of the time thereof and being desirous to
settle my worldly affairs and thereby be the better prepared to leave
this world when it shall please God to call me hence, do therefore
make this my last will and testament in manner and form following, Viz:

First and principally. I commit my soul unto the hands of Almighty
God and my body to the earth to be decently buried. I then demise and
bequeath to son **Isaac** the tract of land on which he now lives according
as it was laid off to him and his heirs, and fifty acres to be taken off
across the lower end, which fifty acres I demise and bequeath unto my
son **John**, together with the tract which was laid off for him and (he)
now lives on, to him and his heirs and assigns. I also give, demise and
bequeath unto my son **William** the tract of land on which he now lives, together with twelve rods wide across to be taken off the lower end of the
plantation on which I now live. I also give and bequeath unto my son
Cornelius the plantation on which I now live according to the pattine
(patent?) to him the said **Cornelius**, his heirs and assigns. I also cause
my above named sons for the named land above demised and bequeathed to
them - pay unto my Executors hereinafter mentioned the sum of two
dollars per acre which is to be paid within three years after my death
to the Executors with all debts.

I also give and bequeath unto my grand children, children of my
daughter **Rachael**, the sum of two hundred dollars to be equally divided
among them by my Executors. I also give and bequeath unto my daughter
Elizabeth the sum of five dollars, to her and her heirs. I also give and
bequeath unto my other daughters, Viz: **Susannah, Sally, Polly, Nelly,
Nancy**, and **Catharine** the money then remaining in the Executors' hands to be
equally divided among them—share and share alike. And,

Lastly, I give and bequeath unto my son **Cornelius** and my two daughters
Nancy and **Catharine** all the rest and remainder of my estate then remaining
on the plantation, to be equally divided, share and share alike. And
lastly, I do constitute and appoint my sons **William** and **Cornelius** to be sole
Executors of this my testament, revoking and annuling all former wills by
me heretofore made, ratifying and confirming this my last Will and Testament.

In testimony whereof I hereunto set my hand and affixed my seal This
twenty ninth day of December, one thousand eight hundred and eighteen.

                                    Cornelius Carmack (seal)
Signed, sealed, published and declared by **Cornelius Carmack**, the above
Testator, as and for his last will and testament in presence of us at his
request and in his presence and in presence of each other have subscribed
our names in writing hereto.
Jacob Grove (seal)
William Carmack (seal)
Cornelius Carmack, Jr. (seal)

Page 94

WILL OF SAMUEL CURRY

Dated: February 22, 1812

Considering the uncertainty of this mortal life and being of sound and perfect memory, blessed be Almighty God for the same, do make and publish this my last will and testament in manner and form following. (viz)

After all my legal debts are paid:

First. I give and bequeath unto my beloved wife Mary Curry the third of my estate both real and personal. I do also give and bequeath unto my youngest two sons George and Samuel the plantation whereon I now live. I also give and bequeath unto my three daughters, (viz) Rebecca, Ann and Margaret Curry three cows and calves and four sheep, a feather bed and bed clothes to each, likewise a horse and saddle, the horse not exceeding eight years old, nor under fourteen hands high. I do also give and be-queath unto John McPheeters, Arch'd Simpson, John and James Curry and Reuben Skelton the sum of one dollar each. And lastly, as to all the rest, residue and remainder of my personal estate, goods and chattels of what kind soever, I give and bequeath the same to my said beloved wife Mary Curry whom together with Samuel McPheeters, Executor and Executrix of this my last will and testament, hereby revoking all former wills by me made. In witness whereof I have hereunto set my hand and seal This twenty second day of February in the year of our Lord, one thousand, eight hundred and twelve.

Samuel Curry (seal)

Signed, sealed published and declared by the above named Samuel Curry to be his last will and testament, in the presence of us who at his request and in his presence have hereunto subscribed our names as witnesses to the same.

Thomas Connilly
John Marshall

Page 95

WILL OF DANIEL CAREY

Dated: December 27, 1820

In the Name of God, Amen. I, Daniel Carey being weak of body, but of sound mind and memory and recollecting that all men have once to die, do make and ordain, publish and declare this to be my last will and testament in the words and figures following.

First. I give my soul to God from whom it came and my body to the clay, to be decently and plainly buried, and the funeral expenses paid to-gether with all my just debts.

Item 2nd. To my daughter Sally Carey in Nelson County, Virginia, I give that tract of land known by the name of Lee's Place, containing 44 acres in said County of Nelson (County) Virginia.

Item 3rd. To my daughter Rebecca Carey of said County of Nelson, Virginia, that part of land in said county...known by name of Cooper's Old Place, on the headwaters of Rockfish River, adjoining land with Soloman Carey and Samain Shropshire, containing one hundred and seven acres,be the same more or less.

Item 4th. To my daughter Mary An Carey, I give that tract of land known by the name of Foxes Place, containing eighty acres, lying in said County of Nelson, adjoining land with Richard and Samuel Fox & Robert Henderson.

And should there be another child by my wife Susannah which I mout have been the father of, it shall share equally with Mary An in the above de-scribed 80 acres of land. The before described lands and children are all in the State of Virginia.

Item 5th. To Polly Hollin I gave possession of all the property both real and personal, that is, that I hold in Hawkins County during her natural life or widowhood, and at her death or marriage, as the case may be, my son Daniel Carey is to be and fall heir to all of said estate in said County of Hawkins, both real and personal. And should the said Polly Hollin accept of said estate, it shall be on these conditions: That she gives my son Daniel Carey good schooling until he be fourteen or fifteen years old, at which time I wish him put to some trade or business that he may earn a living by. As to this my last will and Testament in force at my decease, I constitute, nominate and appoint my worthy friends Thomas Ingram and Jacob Miller...Executors to this my last will in force, revok-ing and disannulling all others heretofore made.

Item 6th. At my decease, I wish a sale of all my property at a twelve months' credit, except two milk cows, all the household and kitchen furniture, farming tools and one mare, bed and bedding, together with the grain and meat on hand and half of my stock of hogs, which named articles I wish left on the farm unsold.

In testimony whereof I the said Daniel Carey have set my hand and af-fixed my seal This 27th day of December, 1820, in presence of

Luke Pannel,
James x Henry
    (his mark)
Thomas Ingram and Ja'c Miller

Daniel Carey (seal)

Page 96

WILL OF LEWIS CHRISTIAN

Dated: May 1, 1822

In the Name of the Father, Son & Holy Ghost, three persons but God.

I, Lewis Christian, Sr. of the County of Hawkins and State of Tennessee, calling to mind the certainty and yet the uncertainty of the time when—do make and ordain this my last will & Testament in the words and form following, to wit: After commending my soul to God and my body to the dust, to be buried in a decent Christian manner, hoping they will again be united at the resurrection and enjoy a glorious immortality, I dispose of my worldly goods as follows:

I allow all my just debts to be paid in the first place.

I bequeath to my sons, John, Thomas, Lewis, Jr., Allen and James, to each one dollar.

I bequeath to my daughter Lucinda the lower end of my place, begin-ning at a mulberry at the mouth of a hollow, at the upper end of the old peach orchard on south side of the creek and including the field and all the land to the lower end of the survey.

I give and bequeath to my daughter Peggy the upper end of my place beginning on Maxwell's line, running forty poles down the river and then a straight line across the upper end to the mountain. I give and bequeath to my daughters Betsy, Polly and Nancy each one dollar. Also, I give and bequeath to my daughter Nancy and her children 49 acres of land whereon she lately lived, joining **Francis Godard**.

I give and bequeath to my son **Lewis** 50 acres of land joining his old survey, **Alex'r Smith** and **Alex'r Patterson** whate in lines more or less. I give to my grandson **Thomas** the place whereon my son **Thomas** now lives, containing 52 acres reserving to my son **Thomas** the use of the place during his life. I bequeath to my grandson **William**, the son of my daughter **Sally**, dec'd, 50 acres of land lying between my son **Thomas** and **Samuel Bailey** with the improvements. I give and bequeath to my son **William** the place I now live on joining **Cindy** below and **Peggy** above, with the buildings and improvements. If my wife **Peggy** should outlive me, I allow **William**, **Cindy** and **Peggy** to give her 30 bushels of corn per year during her natural life. I also nominate her Executrix of this will. I also allow **Peggy** my wife to divide the household and kitchen furniture between her three youngest children at her discretion. I allow her also to have use of the mansion house and one third of the farm during her life. I also nominate my son **William** my other Executor. Whereas I have been informed that my son **Lewis Christian, Jr.** has a bond in possession with my mark or signature to it, purporting to be a title bond with a penalty of $1,500.00 in default of making him a title to certain lands, I have no recollection of any such transaction, and if he has any such bond, he obtained it in an unfair manner when I was not in my right mind. In testimony whereof I have hereunto set my mark this 1st day of May, 1822.

Lewis x Christian, Sr.
(his mark)

Acknowledged in presence of us:
Geo. Maxwell, Reuben Skelton, Geor. Curry

A Codicil of my Will &c, Supplement or Addition

I, **Lewis Christian, Sr.** of the County of Hawkins and State of Tenn., do this 15th day of December make and publish this Codicil to my last Will & Testament in manner following, that is to say: I give to my grand daughter **Sally**, the daughter of **Cindy Christian** one bed and furniture, one puter dish, one tin pan, one dozen tea cups, three bowls, one pitcher, two glass tumblers and six plates, one table cloth and one set of curtains: also one cow and calf, one sow and pigs, one horse colt. And whereas, in my last Will & Testament I have given to my daughter **Cindy** the lower end of my place, beginning at a mulberry at the mouth of a hollow, also, I do bequeath to her a part of the two last locations I make below the same hollow. And lastly, my present codicil be annexed to and made a part of my last Will and Testament, to all intents and purposes. In witness whereof I hereunto set my hand and seal this 15th day of December, 1828.

Lewis x Christian, Sr. (seal)
(his mark)

Signed, sealed and declared by the above named **Lewis Christian, Sr.** as a codicil to be annexed to his last will and testament in the presence of:
William Feagins, James Lyons
N.B. It is my desire that the above mentioned property be equally divided between heirs of my daughter **Sindy's** body at her decease.

Lewis x Christian, Sr. (seal)
(his mark)

William Feagins, James Lyons

A codicil or supplement to my will &c, &c:

Whereas I in my former will gave or bequeathed to my grand son **Thomas Christian** 52 acres of land, I now in this my last will bequeath and give the aforesaid 52 acres of land to my son **Thomas Christian**, being the same land whereon he then lived, to be his just right. In witness whereof I have hereunto set my hand and seal this 26th day of March, 1830.

Lewis x Christian, Sr. (seal)
(his mark)

Signed, sealed, published & declared by the above named **Lewis Christian, Sr.** as a codicil to be annexed to his last will and testament. In the presence of:
William Feagins, James Feagins

November 20, 1830:

To the gentlemen of the Court of Rogersville. It is the wish of **Margaret Christian** that **James Bailey** do administer to the estate of **Lewis Christian**, dec'd for I am not able to attend to it myself owing to sickness and old age. Also, it is the wish of **William Christian** son of the dec'd; also we both stand as security.

Margaret x Christian	**William Christian**, Witness
(her mark)	**James Christian**
	(his mark)

WILL OF JOSEPH W. CARDEN

Page 99   Dated: Sept. 29, 1824

I, **Joseph Carden**, being in his sound mind desires this to be his last will and testament & it is my desire that my property may be distributed as I may hereafter mention in this my will. First, that all my debts be paid out of any money that is due me and the remainder to be put to interest in the education of my children. I desire that all my landed estate be given to my son **Christopher Columbus Carden, Charlotte & Frank**. Also to **C. Columbus Carden** with a sufficient part of the proceeds of said estate to give him the said **C. C. Carden** a classical education and complete his studies. It is also my desire that **C. C. Carden** study law profession. My wife **Judith** is now pregnant and should she have a son, it is my desire that he may have the same benefits of an education and share one half of the above property given to my son **C. C. Carden**. I desire that my daughter **L. Josephphene** have **Maria** a negro girl and her four children and their increase, and the property arising from the firm of **Carden & Rubel** in Rogersville and that she have the third of the negroes from **Mrs. Kenner** my part as one of the legatees. It is also my desire that she be sent to school until she has a competent English education. Should my wife have a daughter, she (to) be educated as well as her sister **L. Josephphene** and have one half of the before described property given to my daughter **L. Josephphene**. My wife **Judith** (is) to have peacable possession of the plantation whereon I now live, also to have the negroes before named during her life or marriage, provided she should marry a prudent man, and the proffits of said Estate to be given to my s'd children before mentioned, otherwise the said property to be distributed between my s'd children at the age of twenty-one years. I desire that Miss Elizabeth Parteplilo to live with my wife or children while she is single and to have a decent support from said estate. It is my desire that Cealy a negro girl be set free at the age of 23. Whatever I shall get of my father's estate at the death of my mother I wish equally di-vided among my children. Should all my children die without heirs, at the death of the last one all the before (named) negroes and their increase be free and my landed property and money if any should be on hand be put in a fund & to interest (?), and the interest thereof to be laid out for the education of poor honest children.

It is also my desire that my wife have all the stock, household and kitchen furniture of every kind that may be on s'd plantation whereon I now live without sale at my death, to do as she pleases with.

I also desire that my friend, Judge S. Powel (or G. Powel) ad-vise with my wife and give and instructions concerning the education of my children, and dividing the property and keeping same to-gether.

J. W. Carden

Attest:
C. Backney
second name torn off

Page 100

WILL OF JOHN COLE

Dated Sept. 11, 1826

In the Name of God, Amen. I John Cole of Hawkins County, Tennessee being very sick and weak but thanks to God of sound disposing mind, and knowing that we all must die, do make and or-der this my last will and testament in manner following. It is my will and desire that all my just debts be paid and all the balance of my property of every kind and description both personal and real I give and bequeath unto my beloved wife Margaret. And whereas I heretofore sold to Joseph Cole (my grandfather) a tract of land lying in the State of Virginia, Washington County for $700.00 which he was to have paid down but I have only received $435.00, the balance to bear interest from the 23rd November, 1825. I also sold a small tract to my brother James Cole for $55.00, containing five acres which when the above sums are paid, my wife Margaret (will) make deeds for said lands sold. And I do appoint my beloved wife sole Executrix of this my last will and do not require her to give security. In witness I have hereto set my hand and seal This 11th of September 1826.

John x Cole (seal)
(his mark)

Witness: Richard Mitchell
Thomas W. Bell

Page 101

WILL OF ELIZABETH COOPER

Dated: February 8, 1828

I, Elizabeth Cooper being of sound mind, but weak in bodily strength, do declare this to be my last Will in writing. This eighth day of February in the year of our Lord One thousand eight hundred and twenty eight.

I do bequeath and give unto my son James Cooper my lot of land whereon I now live, containing 70 or 80 acres, be the same more or less & my two head of horses, and my son James is to pay all my just and honest debts.

And all of the balance of my property to be equally divided between my children.

And that my son James Cooper is to be my Executor of my last Will & Testament. Given under my hand and seal, Feb'y 8, 1828.

Elizabeth x Cooper (seal)
(her mark)

Witness:
Jas. Francisco
Henry Larkin

Page 102

WILL OF SAMUEL CURREY

Dated: August 14, 1830

In the name of God, Amen. I, Samuel Currey of the County of Hawkins and State of Tennessee, being in a low state of health, but of sound mind & memory, do make this my last will and testament in writing. First, recommending my soul to God who gave it and my body from whence it came.

Item 1. I give unto my wife Jane Currey, after all my just debts are paid, all my personal Estate, together with the profits of the third of my land during her natural life.

Item 2. I will that the residue of my land be rented and for the support of my children until the youngest becomes 21 years of age, and then to be sold and the proceeds to be equally divided amongst all my children.

Thirdly. It is my will that my sons should learn useful and profitable trades. Wherefore, I will that they be bound out to pious men to learn trades. It is my desire that James Lynn and Frederick A. Ross should have any of my children bound to them should they wish to do so.

To put this my last Will & Testament in force & executed, I nominate and appoint my worthy friends Frederick A. Ross and James Lynn my Executors...In witness whereof I, the said Samuel Currey have hereunto set my hand and seal This 14th day of August, One Thousand eight hundred and thirty.

Signed, sealed & published the above date in presence of us who are subscribing witnesses thereto.

Ja' Miller
Charles P. Miller   Samuel Currey (seal)
Sarah Miller

In the Name of God, Amen.

I hereunto make an alteration to my last Will and Testament so far as it respects my youngest child whom **Anna Campbell** desires to have, and daughter to whom I will that she remain during her single state subject to the said **Anna Campbell**. In testimony whereof I set my hand and seal this 16th day of August 1830.

Sam'l Curry/Currey

I also will my four sons, **James C.**, **William G.**, **George** and **John** remain with their grandfather **Robert Campbell** during his life or soundness of mind, then this section to be done in void.

In testimony whereof I have set my hand and seal this day and date above written.

Samuel Curry

Signed, sealed and acknowledged in the presence of us:
Anderson Campbell, James V Campbell

WILL OF TABITHA COX

Page 103   Dated: September 13, 1831
In the Name of God, Amen.

I, **Tabitha Cox** of Hawkins County and State of Tennessee, being in good health but knowing the uncertainty of death, of sound mind and memory and knowing that all must die do make this my last Will and Testament in the manner following to wit: I will my soul to God who gave it and my body to the earth from whence it came, to be buried in a decent Christianlike manner. And as to worldly goods it has pleased the Almighty to bless me with, I give and bequeath in the following manner to wit: It is my will that all my just debts be paid out of my estate. It is my will that my grandson **James Roling Henderson**,   have my tract of land of 100 acres on the west side of Robinson's Creek; it is my will that the balance of my lands be equally divided between my two grandsons, **Thomas G. A. Cox** and **Thomas H. Cox**. It is my will that my executors pay to the Trustees of the **Methois** Church twenty dollars out of my estate. It is my will that my negro fellow **Joe** be emancipated at my death.

It is my will that my Executors pay to **Edward Cox**, **James Cox**, **John Cox**, **Alice Hale**, formerly **Alice Cox** and **Francis Taylor**, formerly **Francis Cox** one dollar each out of my estate. It is my will that my daughter **Elizabeth Cox** have all my household and kitchen furniture of every kind and all my stock of every kind.

It is my will that my grand daughter **Elizabeth V. Cox** have the balance of my Estate consisting of cash and lands.

I do hereby appoint my friends **James Grantham** and **James Bradley** of Grainger and Hawkins County, Tennessee my Executors to this will, revoking all others by me made. And I, the said **Tabitha Cox** do hereby acknowledge this and no other to be my last Will and Testament.

In witness whereof I have hereunto set my hand and seal. This 13th day of September, 1831.

Tabitha Cox (seal)

Test: **Joseph Lackey**
       Jas Carden

WILL OF JOHN COOPER

Page 104   Dated: December 7, 1831

In the Name of God, Amen. I, **John Cooper** of the County of Hawkins and State of Tennessee, being weak in body, but of sound mind and memory, considering the uncertainty of life and being of sound and perfect mind &c. blessed be Almighty God for the same do make and publish this my last Will and Testament in manner and form following, that is to say: First, I give and bequeath unto my eldest daughter, **Jane Cooper** a negro girl called **Mary**. I also give and bequeath unto my daughter **Elizabeth Cooper** a negro girl named **Agnus**. I give and bequeath unto my daughter **Mary Cooper** a negro girl named **Mariah**. I also give and bequeath unto my son **William Cooper** a negro boy named **Spencer**. I also give and bequeath unto my son **James Cooper** four negroes to be divided after our deaths, equally between **William**, **John**, **Robert**, **Wiley**, **Absalom** and **Henry Cooper**, by the boys above named getting **Jane**, **Elizabeth** and **Mary Cooper** a horse, saddle and bridle a-piece.

I also give and bequeath to my seven sons, **James**, **William**, **John**, **Robert**, **Wiley**, **Absalom** and **Henry** all my lands and tenements lying and being in the County of Hawkins and State of Tennessee. For them to have and to hold and dispose of agreeable to their will. At my death, my seven sons above named is to go equal shares in paying a bank debt that is against me. And as for my stock and household and kitchen furniture (it) is to be divided among all my children, with the exception of my eldest son **James Cooper**. This is my last will by me made.

In witness whereof I have hereunto set my hand and seal. This Twenty seventh day of December in the Year of our Lord, one thousand eight hundred and thirty one.

John x Cooper (seal)
(his mark)

Signed, sealed, published and declared by the above named **John Cooper** to be his last Will and Testament in the presence of us who have hereunto subscribed our names (as) witnesses in the presence of the Testator.
George Morrison
Robert Cooper

Hawkins County, State of Tennessee

We, the under assigned legatees of **John Cooper** dec'd, after seeing his last Will and Testament, believing that it has been forgotten or neglected by him to make such provisions for our mother as he intended, we the undersigned do agree that she shall have as follows: The dwelling house and kitchen, including the orchard and garden, then along the lane past the old barn, thence a straight course with the fence until it strike the great road, that she is to have her lifetime all the land east of said line until it strikes **King Caid's** line. Likewise, she is to have the disposal of her household and kitchen furniture and stock of every kind. Likewise, a neglect naming the negro boy that was left to **James Cooper**, in the will whose name is **Ben**. We, and each of us, do bind ourselves in the sum of $500.00 to stand to the above agreement. As witness our hands and seals, This 24th of August, 1832. Signed,sealed and acknowledged in the presence of us: **George Morrison, Robert Cooper**.

James Cooper(seal)
William Cooper(seal)
John Cooper (seal)
Robert Cooper (seal)
Wiley Cooper(seal)
Jane x Cooper (seal)
(her mark)
Elizabeth x Cooper (seal)
(her mark)

Note: The above will of John Cooper was proven August Session, 1832.

WILL OF JOHN CHESTER

Page 106   Dated: June 7, 1832
In the Name of God, Amen.

I, John Chester of the County of Hawkins and State of Tennessee, being weak in body but of sound mind and memory and calling to mind that it is appointed for all men once to die, so make and ordain this my last will and testament.

In the first place, it is my will that my beloved wife Mary have and enjoy all my estate both real and personal as long as she continues to be my widow, to dispose of as she may think best, and to sell off any part to pay my debts. Only it is my desire that my old mare be kept by her as long as she may live. If my wife Mary should marry, it is my will that she should have my negro girl Sarah, one cow, my old mare and one bed and bedding, some household and kitchen furniture, and at her death my negro girl named Sarah and all the property to return to my children to be divided as hereafter expressed.

Item. It is my will that at the death or marriage of my beloved wife, that all my real or personal Estate be equally divided between my children after deducting from each one's share the amount they have severally rec'd from me, according to my account against each.

Item. It is my will that my negroes that may remain at the death or marriage of my wife, after the payment of my debts, remain in the family and be not sold, and if my children cannot agree among themselves as to the division of them, let them be valued by three dis-interested men of their own or my Executors' choosing, and whoever of my children they may fall to, let him or them pay to the other their part of the valuation.

Item. It is my will that my shop tools be valued with my negro man Dick, and let them go to my children with him.

Item. It is my will that the part of my Estate that may fall to my daughter Elizabeth Roberts, at the marriage or decease of her mother, should be kept by my Executors for the use and benefit of my daughter and her children to be given to them as they may need it, at the discretion of my Executors.

Item. It is my will that my daughter Catharine and my son Archibald be raised, clothed and schooled out of my Estate without charge as long as they stay with their mother, and at her death or marriage, go receive (an equal share) of my estate as their other brothers and sisters.

I do hereby constitute and appoint my two sons Sam'l G. Chester and John K. Chester Executors of this my last Will and Testament not requiring them to give any security for the Execution of the same.

In witness whereof I have hereunto set my hand & seal this 7th day of June, 1832.

John Chester (seal)

Signed, sealed & ack'd in
presence of us:
Sam'l Grer (Chester?)
Benjamin Boyd
Test. Wm. Bradley

WILL OF JACOB CHARLTON

Page 107   Dated: July 4, 1834
In the Name of God, Amen.

I, Jacob Charlton of Hawkins County, State of Tennessee, being weak in body but of sound mind & memory & convinced of the uncertainty of life & the certainty of death, do make, ordain & publish this my last Will and Testament in manner following, that is to say. It is my desire and wish after my death that Polly Gilliam, wife of John Gilliam shall have & receive whatever sum of money shall at that time be due and owing to me as pension of the United States for my services during the Revolutionary War, in consideration for her services and attention to me at various times during my sickness, and in order to carry into effect the bequest in this will, I appoint John Gilliam Executor of this will, and he is not required to give security.

Jacob x Charlton (seal)
(his mark)

Witness: W. O.Winston
Anthony Smith

WILL OF BENONI COLDWELL

Page 108   Dated March 1, 1837
In the Name of God, Amen.

I, Benoni Coldwell, of Hawkins County & State of Tennessee, being weak in body but of sound and perfect mind and memory, calling to mind the uncertainty of this present life, do make this my last Will & Testament in the words following (To wit)

Imprimis. I give my precious immortal soul to God who gave it and as to my personal Estate my will & desire is that it be divided in the following manner, after all my just debts and funeral expenses are paid.

Item. I give & bequeath unto my beloved wife Elizabeth Coldwell all that part of the plantation whereon I now reside, lying south of the Stanley Valley Road, including the dwelling and out houses, during her life or widowhood, also a negro man named Nelson, one other negro man named Henry, also a negro girl named Milly, also four head of horses, her choice out of my stock, also my stock of cattle & hogs, ten ewes and lambs, also ten head of other sheep... Also my stock of geese and ducks for the purpose of my wife and daughters making themselves beds. Also my youngest sons to have benefit of beds if their sisters think proper to make for them. Also a new wagon part made contracted to be made by **David Kestren** for her to have finished and keep as her other property, the balance to be paid for finishing the wagon out of my estate. Also, all my household and kitchen furniture, farming utensils and all other property...also my wife to have the present crop of wheat that is now growing in the field on the north side of the Stanley Valley Road, adjoining **George Walters'** land.

Item. I give & bequeath unto my daughter **Sally Greenway** and her heirs a negro girl **Isabel**.

Item. I give and bequeath unto my son **Thomas K. Coldwell** the tract of land whereon he now resides containing 200 acres more or less, also $100.00 to be made out of my Estate.

Item. I give and bequeath unto my daughter **Lettice Young** what she has already received of my estate as her part at the present.

Item. I give and bequeath unto my daughter **Mary Galbraith** she she has already received of my estate as her part at the present.

Item. I give and bequeath unto my daughter **Betsy Bryan** what she has already received of my estate as her part at the present.

Item. I give and bequeath unto my son **Benoni F.Coldwell** what he has already received of my estate as his part at the present.

Item. I give and bequeath unto my two sons **John & Nathaniel** the two tracts of land, one called Stubblefield's Place, and the other called Baker's Place, also the entries around them, to be equally divided between them agreeable to quantity and quality. **John's** part to be laid off at the lower or west end, including where he now lives.

Item. I give and bequeath unto my two sons **Percy C. & Volney Coldwell** all that part of the tract of land whereon I now reside, lying north of the Stanley Valley Road until the death of their mother, then the whole tract to be equally divided between them. Also, I leave a 50 acre entry in the Caney Valley Knobs to support the tract I live on with timber.

Item. I give and bequeath unto my four daughters **Delphi Ann, Rachael, Eliza & Julia Ann Coldwell**, each, five hundred dollars, to be paid out of my estate in addition to the beds they have or may hereafter make. My will and desire is that after the death of my wife all the property she may (have) be sold and proceeds equally divided among all my children enumerated above. My will and desire is that the following property be sold to carry my last will & testament into effect, to wit: Two tracts of land lying in Big Poor Valley, one containing 50 acres and the other 100 acres; one negro man **Edward**, one named **Leroy**, one negro boy named **Jesse**, one negro girl named **Lucy**, also my old wagon, the balance of my stock of hogs and sheep, two stills, still tubs & other vessels, one set of blacksmith tools and coopers tools.

I do hereby constitute, ordain and appoint my brother **Thomas Coldwell** & my wife **Elizabeth Coldwell** my sole Executor and Executrix to carry this my last Will & Testament into effect & that

they be not required to give security for the faithful execution of the same.

In testimony whereof I have hereunto set my hand and seal this twenty first day of March in the year of our Lord, 1837.
                                        B. Coldwell(seal)
Test.
Philip S. Hale
John Shough
Rob't Johnson

WILL OF GEORGE CROBARGER
Page 110   No Date

I, **George Crobarger**, of the County of Hawkins and State of Tennessee, being of sound mind and memory, Blessed be God, do make and ordain this my last Will and Testament as follows,that is to say:

My wish and desire is that my daughter **Hetty Crobarger**, now **Hetty Seaver** shall have one dollar of my estate and no more.

My wish and desire is that my loving wife **Mary Crobarger** shall after my just debts are paid, have the whole of my personal Estate at her disposal during her life and to dispose...in any manner she may choose. If my Executors think it best to make a sale and dispose of any part of the stock and other articles which may be to spare, I leave it with them to do as they think best.

I do also constitute and appoint my wife **Mary** and **John Critz** my lawful Executors of this my last Will &c.
                                        George x Crobarger (seal)
Signed, sealed and acknowledged   (his mark)
before us:

        John Gibbons
        John Boyd
        Robert McMinn

WILL OF SIMEON COLLINS
Page 110   No Date

Simeon Collins being of sound and perfect mind & memory did make and publish this his last Will & Testament in manner and form following. He desires and requests that his wife **Frankey** should have and keep all his property, both real and personal for the purpose of keeping her children together and to raise them on what he left as his wife **Frankey** had labored with him for all they possessed which said Will and Testament was made while on his death bed and no opportunity of committing his last will to writing as he was soon after taken dangerously ill and died somewhat unexpected and appeared not to have had his mind engaged on the subject no more, which last Will and Testament was declared in presence of the undersigned subscribing witnesses.

N.B. He the said **Simeon** further requested that all his just debts be paid and satisfied & the balance retained for the purpose

above stated.
Sardy x Collins, Morgan x Collins, Charlotty x Collins, Millenton
  (his mark)   (his mark)   (her mark)
Collins, Allen Collins

WILL OF JOHN COCKREHAM

Page 111   Dated: January 5, 1839
                            Proven: 7th April, 1845 Term

In the Name of God, Amen, I **John Cockreham** of the County of Hawkins and State of Tennessee being in a bad state of health, but of sound mind & memory, blessed be God, calling to mind the mortality of this life & knowing that it is appointed for all men once to die, do make and publish this my last Will and Testament in manner following, viz:

First. I give & bequeath to my beloved wife **Sally** the use of all my land & negro slaves during her life or widowhood...also to my wife **Sally** as much of my stock of horses, cattle, sheep, and hogs as she shall choose to set apart for herself and I also give to my wife...all my household furniture and kitchen and farming utensils, all my corn, bacon, wheat and other provisions on hand, also one wagon and two yolk of oxen.

Secondly. I give & bequeath after the death or marriage of my wife...to my sons, **Thomas G. Cockreham, John H. Cockreham, Daniel H. Cockreham, William H. & Abner W. Cockreham,** and to my daughters **Maria McCollough, Elizabeth Tharp, Louisa McBride, Emily H. Cockreham & Amanda Cockreham** all my estate both real and personal to be equally divided among them, share and share alike, after deducting the following sums from the respective shares for property that I have heretofore advanced to some of my said sons & daughters, to wit: I have heretofore advanced to my son **Thomas G. Cockreham** property to the value of Five hundred and twenty seven dollars. I have heretofore advanced to my son **John H. Cockreham** property to the value of four hundred & fifty seven dollars. I have heretofore advanced to my said son **Daniel H. Cockreham** property valued at Four Hundred and Fifty seven dollars. I have heretofore advanced to my said son, **William H. Cockreham** property valued at One Hundred, Eighty Two dollars. I have heretofore advance to my said son **Abner W. Cockreham** property valued at One Hundred Fifteen dollars. I have heretofore advanced to my daughter **Maria McCollough** property valued at Two Hundred, Forty eight dollars. I have heretofore advanced to my daughter **Elizabeth Tharp** property valued at One Hundred and Eighty two dollars. I have heretofore advanced to my said daughter **Louisa McBride** One Hundred Eighty Two dollars, all advances to be taken into consideration in their respective shares of my Estate, so that all (finally) receive an equal share of my Estate to them and their heirs forever. It is my desire that whenever my Executors shall have a considerable sum of money in their hands arising out of my estate either from the sale of property or from collecting debts due to me, that they shall divide the same among all my said sons and daughters equally taking into consideration the advances aforesaid.

Fourthly. I do hereby nominate and appoint my two sons **Thomas G. Cockreham** and **John H. Cockreham** Executors of this my last Will and Testament. In witness whereof I have hereunto set my hand & fixed my seal This fifth day of January in the year of our Lord, 1839.
                          John x Cockreham (seal)
                                (his mark)

Signed, sealed published & declared by **John Cockreham** the Testator as his last Will & Testament in the presence of us who have hereunto subscribed our names as witnesses in the presence of each other.
John Williams, Ephraim Parvin

WILL OF SARAH CHARLES

Page 113   Dated: March 22, 1839
                            Proven: April, 1839

In the Name of God, Amen. I, Sarah Charles of the County of Hawkins and State of Tennessee, being in low state of health but of sound mind, do make this my last will and testament in manner following, to wit: I will and bequeath to **Mary Charles** my daughter one bay mare, one cow and calf, one bed and clothes, one cupport and one big cattle. I will and bequeath to my son **James Charles** one rifle gun, one man's saddle and all the crop after it tis made after all my just debts is paid out of it. **Darcus Jane** my daughter I will and bequeath one red heifer, one coverled and notted counterpin. I will and bequeath to **Malinda** one bed and clothes, one chest, one pot or oven and lid &c, and one fall leaf table. To **Lucinda** one bed and clothes, one old chest. I will and bequeath to **Jasper** my son one gray colt and one heifer. I will and bequeath **Eldridge Charles** one dollar. I will and bequeath unto **Manecy** one bed and clothes. The hogs ise to gon to the youse of the family that is now living with me. I will and bequeath to **James Charles** one cow I got (from) **Wiley Hord.**

Publishing this to be my last Will and Testament. In witness whereof I have hereunto set my hand seal this twenty second day of March in the year of our Lord one thousand eight hundred and thirty nine.
                        Sarah x Charles (seal)
Witness: (her mark)
Wade H. Smith

WILL OF HENRY CHURCH

Page 114   Dated: November 5, 1844
                            Proven: December Term, 1844

I, **Henry Church**, do make and publish this my last Will and Testament hereby revoking and making void all other wills by me at any time made.
First. I direct that my funeral expenses and all my debts be paid as soon after my death as possible out of any moneys that I may die possessed of or may first come into the hands of my Executor.

Secondly. I do give and bequeath to my beloved wife **Allice Church** all the residue of my property consisting of all my household and kitchen furniture with all the stock to wit: Horses, cattle, hogs, sheep, geese and poltry of all kinds. Also all my farming tools & machanicle tools, also one still cup and worm and a quantity of tubs and all the grain that is upon the farm during her life or widowhood.

Thirdly. That I do will and bequeath unto my two daughters **Matilda** and **Sarah** out of the above named property one good bed and furniture, one cow and calf and equally otherwise as much as the other daughters that is married off.

Fourthly. I do will and bequeath unto my four three sons, **George, Enoch** and **Henry** when they become 21, for them to have a horse, bridle and saddle.

Fifthly. I desire after the death of my wife **Allice Church** that the remainder of the above named Estate to be sold and equally divided between all my daughters.

Lastly. I do hereby nominate and appoint **William Church & Beverly C. Ford** my Executors. In witness whereof I do to this my last will set my hand and seal this, the fifth day of November, 1844.

Henry x Church (seal)
(his mark)

Signed sealed & published in our presence and we have subscribed our names hereto in the presence of the Testator Nov. the 5th, 1844.
B. C. Ford, David x Hickman, Henry Reed
(his mark)

WILL OF JOHN CHRISTIAN

Page 115   Dated: March 4, 1845
                            Proven: Sept. 1, 1845

I, **John Christian** have on this the 4th day of March in the year of our Lord, 1845 in my proper mind, made & published this my last Will & Testament hereby revoking all former wills by me at any time heretofore made. **First.** I desire that my body be intered decently according to the custom of the country, that my burial & funeral expenses together with all my just debts be paid out of any money that I may die sezed of or the first that may come into the hands of my Executor from any of my real or personal Estate.

Secondly. I give & bequeath to my beloved wife **Nancy** my entire landed Estate not hereinafter bequeathed, during her natural life provided she never marries, together with all my household and kitchen furniture, one horse, three cows and twelve sheep & twelve hogs.

Thirdly. I give to my son **William L. Christian** five dollars, having previously provided for him.

Fourth, Fifth, Sixth, Seventh and Eighth. I give to **Margaret Arnald, Ruthy Felken/Felkner, Lewis Christian's widow** and lawful heirs, **Thomas Christian, Nancy Long** (all) $5.00 each having previously provided for (each of them).

Ninth. I give to **John Christian** one-half of a certain Island known by the name of **Felkner's Island** and $5.00.

Tenth. After paying all my debts & the above cash bequests at the above named death or marriage of my wife **Nancy** I give and bequeath to my four youngest sons, **Allen, Seth, Jas & George Christian,** all my landed Estate together with any stock, farming utensils &c, leaving my wife **Nancy** to dispose of the personal property left her to who she pleases at her death.

Eleventh. I do hereby nominate & appoint my two beloved sons **William L.** and **Thomas J.** my Executors to this my last Will & Testament. In testimony whereof I have this day set my hand & affixed my seal the day & date above written.

John x Christian(seal)
(his mark)

Signed, sealed & delivered in
presence of the Testator & each
other, the day & date above written:
Test: P. x Henderson
(his mark)
David x Lyons, Jr.
(his mark)
Adam Patterson

I **John Christian** have this day in my proper mind made and published this codicil and attached it to my last Will & Testament and declared it a portion of the same...my son **Allen** in the division of my real estate shall have his interest at the upper or east end of the plantation so as to include my present dwelling and out houses. This shall not be so construed as to revoke or make void any portion of my will to which it is attached. In testimony whereof I have set my hand and affixed my seal this 28th of May, 1845, in presence of:

John X Christian (seal)
(his mark)

P. x Henderson Pro Sept. 1, 1845
(his mark)
Emanuel x Rutledge Jan. 5, 1846
(his mark)

WILL OF JOHN CROZIER

Page 116   Dated: July 25, 1845

I, **John Crozier** make and publish this my last Will and Testament hereby revoking and making void all other wills by me at any time made, being of sound mind and memory.

First. I direct that my funeral expenses and my debts be paid as soon as possible after my death out of money that I may have or that may first come into the hands of my Administrator.

Secondly. I give and bequeath to my beloved wife **Elizabeth** all my land and personal property consisting of the following, to wit: All my household and kitchen furniture and all my stock of every description consisting of horses, cattle, hogs, sheep and many other articles too tedious to mention, as long as she lives, at her death all land and personal property remaining after paying all her expenses and the land be equally divided between my four daughters (viz) **Susannah, Agnes, Casander** and **Nancy Isabella,** and if any of them be dead...heirs to have their mother's part and also all the personal property whatever there may be of every description shall be equally divided between the above named daughters or

WILL OF CASANDER CROSIER

their children as aforesaid.

Thirdly. The heirs to choose some three disinterested persons that is suitable to make said division if they can agree about it, and if there be any orphans, their guardian to superintend on their part, otherwise the County Court to appoint someone to act for them, but if they cannot agree about persons to make said division, then and in that case the Administrator if any may be proceed and ask the County Court to appoint men as aforesaid to make said division, and in case there should be a disagreement among the heirs about that, the Administrator shall forthwith proceed to give lawful notice by advertisment and sell all the property both real and personal to the highest bidder on a twelve months credit. And if there be no Administrator then and in that case any one of the heirs shall or may complain to the County Court which shall appoint an Administrator and take bond and security according to law and sell the same as above mentioned, and shall divide out equally among the several heirs accordingly but should they make a division of the property the husbands of the daughters shall have power to sell the lands and make titles for the same, but should the wife be made the guardian of the orphans, shall have power to sell the property or rent it out as may be deemed best and shall be governed according to law in other cases. In witness whereof I do to this my will set my hand and seal 25th day of July, 1845.

John Crozier(seal)

Signed, sealed and published in our presence and we have subscribed our names hereto in the presence of the Testator This 25th day of July, 1845.

Test: Nicholas x Beckner, William x Grigsby, Joseph Jenkins
(his mark)   (his mark)

Page 117

WILL OF CASANDER CROSIER
Dated August 3, 1847
Proven in open Court Sept. 6
1847

A written Will and Testament.

I, Casander Crosier, do make and publish this my last Will and Testament hereby revoking and making void all other wills by me at any time made.

First. I direct that my funeral expenses and all my debts be paid as soon after my death as possible out of any money that I may die possessed of or may first come into the hands of my Executor.

Second. It is my will that my mother Elizabeth Crosier shall have all my personal property and real Estate during her natural life, and at the death of my mother, it is my will that my sister Nancy Isabella Crosier shall have the remainder of my real and personal property.

Lastly. I do hereby nominate and appoint William Grigsby sen. my Executor. In witness whereof I do to this I will set my hand and seal this August 3rd, 1847.

Casander x Crosier(seal.)
(His mark)

Page 118
WILL OF DANIEL CARMICHAEL
Dated: May 28, 1848

In the Name of God, Amen.

I, Daniel Carmichael, being of sound and disposing mind, though feeble in body do make and ordain this my last Will and Testament, revoking all others that I may heretofore have made.

First. To my beloved wife, I will and bequeath my landed Estate, with the exception of one small tract containing about 30 acres of cleared land and 10 acres of timbered land adjoining John A. McKinney's, being a part of the tract on which Mrs. Kenner lived, on the right hand side of the Dodson Ford Road, which said tract of 40 acres I give to my trusty old servant Dick during his natural life on condition he keep an orderly house at all times.

Sec'd. To my beloved wife, I will all my slaves during her widowhood with the exception of Dick whom I wish liberated at my death, and with the exception also of a boy named Joe whom I have given to my nephew James Ayres and also a boy named Hilyon 12 or 13 years old whom I wish to be sold to assist in paying my debts.

Third. At my wife's death, or whenever she marries again, it is my will that all my slaves that I have willed to her be emancipated immediately.

Fourth. At my wife's death, it is my will that Hamilton Carmichael, son of Fanny Moore, whom I believe to be my son, although not born in lawful (?) should have all my real estate, but provided Hamilton Carmichael dies before my wife, then it is my will that my landed estate be divided into two equal parts—one half of which is to be at the disposal of my wife, the other half to be equally divided between my two nephews, James Ayers and Pleasant Carmichael, son of James Carmichael. It is expressly my will that my two nephews should not have possession of the said land until after my wife's death.

I have agreed with my wife, and I hereby bind myself to fulfill said agreement that if she should die before I do, and if I should re-marry, the three slaves that I have willed to my wife are to be liberated.

All my money and drafts in the hands of John Blevins amounting to over $4,000.00 are to be appropriated to payment of my just debts, and if there should be a deficit, then enough of my personal property be sold to pay all my debts.

All my personal property, after paying my debts, I will to my wife without reserve.

In witness whereof I have hereunto set my hand and seal This 28th day of May, 1848.

Daniel Carmichael

Signed, sealed and published in our presence and will (?) names hereto in presence of the Testator this date above written.

Witnesses: William Moore, Thos. M. Arnott

(witnesses)
Sarah A. Savage
Matilda L. Shields
George Savage
Wm. W. Shields

It is my will that **Absalom Kyle sen'r** and **James K. Neal** be appointed by the Court Executors without requiring them to give security.

WILL OF YELBERTON CARPENTER

Page 119   Dated June 15, 1848
In the Name of God, Amen.   Proven April term 1848

I **Yelberton Carpenter** of the County of Hawkins and State of Tennessee, do make and publish this as my last Will and Testament.

First. I direct that my funeral expenses and all my debts be paid as soon after my death as possible out of any money that I may die possessed of or may first come into the hands of my Exec.

Secondly. I **give** to my beloved wife **Hannah Carpenter** the use of my tract of land in the County of Claiborne, State of Tennessee for her comfortable support and maintenance, and it is my will that my grand daughter **Nancy Orlena Carpenter,** daughter of **Anderson Carpenter** remain with my wife **Hannah** and have life support from said land during my wife's life, and I further give to my wife **Hannah** all my household and kitchen furniture one choice cow, one brood sow, three choice stock hogs, thirteen pigs, four sheep, one choice heifer, &c. It is further my will that at any time my wife may think best she is to give to my grand daughter **Nancy Orlena** one bed, one cow, some kitchen utensils, a small start in hogs and sheep.

Thirdly. It is my will that after the death of my wife, that the above named tract of land in **Claiborne County** be divided between my sons **Jackson** and **Wilson** in the following manner, to wit: Beginning at the mouth of the spring branch. Thence with the meandering of said branch to a cross fence at the upper end of the rocky field. Thence a straight line to a gum corner to said land and corner to **Michael Person's** land. **Jackson** to have north side of dividing line, with improvements, to descend after his death, to the lawful children that he now has or may hereafter have to be divided equal between them. And the said **Wilson Carpenter** to have the south side of said dividing line, with improvements thereon during his natural life, and after his death to descend to his lawful children that he now has or may hereafter have, to be divided equal between them.

Fourthly. I give and bequeath to my son **Allen Carpenter** the tract of land whereon I now live, together with a tract of land on Clowd's Creek in Hawkins County, purchased by me from **William Altom.**

Fifthly. I give and bequeath unto my son **Jesse Carpenter** fifty dollars in trade, it being one-half of a debt due me from my son **Anderson Carpenter.**

Sixthly. I give and bequeath to my son **Anderson Carpenter** fifty dollars due from him to me after paying the above bequest of fifty dollars to **Jesse Carpenter.**

Seventhly. I give and bequeath unto my sons **William, John, James** and my daughter **Mary Spradler** all my stock consisting of horses, cattle, hogs, and sheep not disposed of in the foregoing bequests, to be equally divided between them. It is my request they divide the stock themselves, and

Lastly. I do constitute and appoint my friend **James Conner** and my son **John Carpenter** of the County of Hawkins...my Executors of this my last Will & Testament. In witness whereof I have hereunto set my hand, affixed my seal this 15th day of June in the Year of our Lord, A.D. 1845.

                  Yelberton x Carpenter(seal)
Signed, sealed & delivered in   (his mark)
presence of **James L. Etter, Edmund Lovin**

WILL OF THOMAS COCKE

Page 121   Dated: August 9, 1849
                  Proven: March Term, 1862
                  (J. H. Vance, Clk.)

In the name of God, Amen.

I, **Thomas Cocke** of Hawkins County in the State of Tennessee, being in the full possession of my ordinary powers of mind, but contemplating the uncertainty of life and being desirous of making such disposition of my worldly property and effects as after mature deliberation my own judgement and sense of duty appeares and as I anxiously desire for sufficient reasons to be carried into effect after my death do make ordain and publish this my last Will & Testament in manner and form following that is to say:

First. I desire that all my just debts if any should remain unpaid at my death, shall be paid out of my estate and I direct that any money which may be on hand and debts which may be due to me at my death and my personal estate as far as necessary shall be first applied to this purpose.

Second. For considerations satisfactory to my own mind, I give and bequeath unto my wife **Lucinda** absolutely for her own separate use and benefit 200 acres of land situate in County of Hawkins including the house wherein I now reside to be laid off as she may direct to have and to hold the same and every part and portion thereof in absolute fee simple, together with all my household and kitchen furniture, waggon, yoke of oxen and farming utensils of every description, the one fifth part of my live stock of every kind and description and also my two negro women slaves, **Nancy** and **Catharine.**

Third. All the residue of my estate property and effects of every kind and description real, personal or mixed in possession or in action wheresoever situate, including the tract of land wherein I now reside situate in said County of Hawkins, joining the lands of John B. Proffitt, William Mays and the heirs of Thomas Stubblefield, dec'd and known by the name of Mulberry Grove es-timated to contain 1200 acres more or less, I give, bequeath and devise unto William S. Creed, Mary A. Read, wife of Thomas R. Read, formerly Mary A. Creed, and Maryaner Moore wife of George W. Moore, formerly Maryaner Creed, to them and their heirs jointly and equally in fee simple subject to charges that my just debts which remain unpaid at my death be payed at my death.

Fourth. I direct that as soon after my death as practicable my Executors hereinafter named shall sell and dispose of all my per-sonal effects and property, the proceeds thereof after paying my just debts and funeral expenses shall be paid equally to the said William S. Creed, Mary A. Read and Maryaner Moore. I do hereby nominate constitute and appoint William S. Creed, Thomas R. Read and George W. Moore Executors of this my last Will and Testament, here-by revoking and making void all former or other wills by me hereto-fore made and declaring this to be my last Will and Testament, and I deem it proper here solemnly to declare to my relations and friends and to all other persons that the foregoing disposition of my property is made upon reflection and deliberation and is such as satisfies my own feelings and sense of justice. Let no one question or attempt to disturb it after my death.

In testimony whereof I have hereunto affixed my hand and seal. This ninth day of August in the year of our Lord A.D. One thousand eight hundred and forty-nine.

Signed sealed and acknowledged   Thomas Cocke (seal)
by the said Thomas Cocke in our
presence to be his last Will and
Testament who have witnessed the
same at his request in the presence
of each other and in his presence the
date above written. Test:
Elisha Dodson, Hugh Cain, Jr.

Page 123

WILL OF ETHELDRIDGE CHARLES

Dated: March 29, 1842
Proven: May 2, 1842

In the Name of God, Amen. I Etheldridge W. Charles of Hawkins County & State of Tennessee, being in low state of health but of sound mind do make this my last Will & Testament in the manner following, to wit:

I will & bequeath to my wife Susannah Charles one bay mare and side saddle and bridle, one red spotted cow, one white sow and five shoats, two beds and clothing, one cupboard and furniture, and beauro and clock and four chairs and one common dining table, one large pot, one small pot and one bake oven, one small oven, one skillet, one loom and one pair of horse gears and plow & the balance of my property to be sold to pay my just debts, and if anything over, it is to go to my three children, William A., Susannah E. and Carsha J. Charles, & I will and bequeath to my brother Hughy J. Charles my saddle & I will that my s'd wife

---

have the sole benefit of the plantation and buildings where I now live until the youngest child, Barsheba J. Charles, comes of age and then the lands to be sold and equally divided amongst my three named children.

In witness witness hereof, publishing this to be my last Will and Testament, I have hereunto set my hand and seal this the 29th (twenty-ninth) day of March, One Thousand eight hundred and forty-two.

B. W. x Charles (seal)
       (his mark)

Witness:
Martin Phillips

Page 124

WILL OF THOMAS COLDWELL

Dated: November 15, 1852
Proven: March Term, 1853

Know all men by these presents that I, Thomas Coldwell, being of sound mind and body, but calling to mind the uncertainty of human life, and desiring to settle my worldly affairs, do ordain and publish this my last Will and Testament, revoking and annulling all others.

First. I direct that all my just debts and funeral expenses shall be paid.

Secondly. I will and bequeath to my beloved wife Sally...during her natural life or widowhood one third of the plantation on which I live, including the dwelling house and out houses thereto attached. Also, all my household and kitchen furniture, farming utensils, including wagon or wagons, blacksmith tools and one half of the stock on my farm at my death; also all my slaves.

Thirdly. To my son James, I bequeath all my lands including--after her death--the part willed to my wife, also after the death of my wife, I bequeath unto my son James all the personal property, including wagon or wagons on my farm and blacksmith tools, except the slaves which has been devised to her and also one half the stock of all kinds, and grain on hands at my death.

Fourthly. To my son Benoni I will and bequeath in lieu of his Benoni's interest in my land and personal property, that James pay him-- the amount proposed in the agreement made and entered into between them, James and Benoni, heretofore. In addition to which, after the death of my wife, I direct that my slave Pompey be left to Benoni.

Fifthly. To the children of my son Anderson F. Coldwell, dec'd., and after the death of my wife, I will that my slave Ellen be sold and the proceeds of her sale be equally divided to said children of Anderson F. Coldwell.

Sixthly. To my son Abram Coldwell, I bequeath after the death of my wife, my slaves Frank and Susan.

Seventhly. To my daughter, Indiana Chesnutt, during her life and after the death of my wife, I will my slave Mary, and after the death of said Mary and her increase be equally divided among the children of Indiana.

Eighthly. After the death of my wife, it is my will that my son James shall have my slave Bob and that he shall maintain Old Cynth.

Ninthly. It is my will that if my slaves should increase hereafter during my life or the life of my wife, that the two oldest of the increase living at the death of my wife shall belong to my son **James**, and the balance of such increase, if any such, shall be equally divided between (the children of) my son **Anderson F. Coldwell**, dec'd, for one part, and my son **Abriam** and my daughter **Indiana**, but to go to my daughter **Indiana** and her children in the same manner as the slave **Mary** is willed.

Tenthly. It is my will that all my property not otherwise devised shall belong to my wife during her natural life or widowhood and to pay my son **James** after her death, and my wife and son **James** are charged with the payment of all my just debts, and are hereby appointed Executor and Executrix of this my last Will and Testament.

In testimony whereof I have hereunto set my hand and affixed my seal. This 15th day of November, 1852.

       Thomas Coldwell (seal)

Signed, sealed and acknowledged in presence of us:
H. Wallerson, Jesse M. Lyons, John Young

WILL OF DANIEL CHAMBERS

Page 125   Dated: December 4, 1852
           Proven: July Term, 1852

I, **Daniel Chambers**, do make and publish this as my last Will and Testament, hereby revoking and making void all other wills by me at any time made.

First. I direct that my funeral expenses and all my debts be paid as soon after my death as possible out of any moneys that I may die possessed of or may first come into the hands of my Executor.

Secondly. I give and bequeath unto my beloved wife **Sarah** all the land which I now own on north side of Holston River whereon I now live, together with part of my plantation on south side of said river. Say, from the barn up the river. I also give and bequeath to her my wife **Sarah Chambers** my negro man named **Charles** and also his wife **Fan**. I also give and bequeath to my wife two horse beasts and three cows, her choice; my yoke of oxen and waggon, one large plow, one shovel plow, two pair of gears and so much of my household and kitchen furniture sufficient for her use, also my hogs, sheep and stock. All of which named property I leave to her during her natural life, or so long as she remains my widow, then the above named negro woman **Fan** is to have the liberty of choosing with whom of my children or grandchildren she will live. But the above named **Charles** to be valued and have choice to live with either of my children who will pay valuation—which valuation to be divided equally into three parts; one part going to children of each of my three daughters, namely, **Amanda Francisco's**, **Lois Miller's** and **Rachael Miller's**. I do further give and bequeath to my wife **Sarah** two feather beds and furniture, as much as she thinks proper, also her Bible and Saddle, which last named articles I leave at her own disposal.

Thirdly. I do give to my son **William S. Chambers** all the land I own on the south side of Holston River, containing 310 acres, also all the land which I own on the north side of said river from the spring branch down to **Stephen Bagood's** line, to have possession of at my wife's death or intermarriage. But he, **William S. Chambers**, is at

all times to have the use of timber on said lands. I further bequeath to **William S. Chambers** my negro man, **Isaac**.

Fourthly. I give and bequeath to my daughter **Amanda Francisco's** children...**Mary Simmons**, $200.00, and to **Amanda's** other children, namely **Thomas**, **Daniel** and **Sarah Francisco**, I give and bequeath the land whereon I now live, from the spring branch up the river adjoining the lands of **T. Coldwell** and **James Bagood**. The land to be at my wife's death (sold?), and the proceeds divided equally between the three last named children of my daughter **Amanda Francisco**.

Fifthly. I give and bequeath to my daughter **Lois Miller's** three children, namely **Daniel C. Miller**, **Rachael D. Miller** and **John P. Miller** my two negro boys, **Lewis** and **Charles**. I further give and bequeath to my grandson **John P. Miller**, one horse and saddle worth $100.00.

Sixthly. I give and bequeath to my daughter **Rachael Miller** my negro woman named **Susan** and her two little daughters, namely **Sarah** and **Julia**, during her natural life and then to said **Rachael Miller's** children.

Seventhly. The residue of my personal property undisposed of in the foregoing bequests, I direct to be sold and the proceeds of said sale to be equally divided between my three daughters, namely **Amanda Francisco's**, **Lois Miller's** and **Rachael Miller's** children.

Lastly. I do hereby nominate and appoint my son, **William S. Chambers** my Executor. In witness whereof I do to this my last Will and Testament set my hand and seal. This fourth day of December, 1852.

       Daniel Chambers (seal)

Signed, sealed and published in our presence and we have subscribed our names hereto in presence of the Testator.
H. Watterson
C. C. Miller

WILL OF LEWIS CLICK

Page 127   Dated: Feb'y 21, 1853
           Proven: Sept. Term, 1853

The last Will and Testament of **Lewis Click** of Hawkins County, Tenn. I, **Lewis Click**, considering the uncertainty of this mortal life and being of sound mind and memory do make and publish this my last Will and Testament in manner and form following:

First. I direct that my funeral expenses and all my debts be paid as soon after my death as possible out of any money that I may die possessed of or may first come into the hands of my Executor.

Second. I give and bequeath unto my beloved wife **Rosannah** all the household and kitchen furniture or as much as she may need.

I further give and bequeath to my wife **Rosannah** the farm and mansion house where I now reside, to have and to hold with all its appurtenances, for the term of ten years, and at the expiration of the said ten years, I hereby give and bequeath to my wife **Rosannah** the fifth part of the above named farm, together with all its buildings. I give and bequeath to my son **William** the fifth part of the above named farm. I further give and bequeath to my son **Robert** the fifth part of the above named farm. Also, I give and bequeath to my son **Peter** the fifth part of the fore-mentioned farm. Also, I give and devise to my youngest son **George** one yoke of black steers and one Rifle gun. Also at the death or marriage of my wife, **Rosanah,** I give and bequeath to my youngest daughter **Rosah** the fifth part of the aforementioned farm, or the part I laid off for my wife. I will and desire that all stock, grain, farming utensils and slaves not excepted shall be sold subject to my debts after my death, or at such time as my Executor may deem proper. I further give and devise to my son **Arthur** one sorrel mare that he took from me last fall for his full share, debarring him from getting holt of whatever may come into the hands of my representatives from my Estate. I further give and devise to my son **John** $500.00 that I paid to **Rogan** and **Edwards** for him, that being his full share of my estate. Also, I want **John** to attend to my suits and my Executor will pay him for his services. I further give and devise to my son **James** $500.00, the full amount of his share of my Estate, being a part of $1,000.00 I paid for him at the Rogersville Bank. I want my Executor to collect the remaining part as soon after my death as he can and pay it to my creditors. I give and bequeath to my daughter **Mary** $300.00, is the sale of the land I sold to her husband. I further give and devise to my daughter **Eliza** $200.00 which shall be paid to her at the expiration of ten years by **William, Robert, Peter** and **George,** each one to pay her $50.00.

I hereby appoint my beloved wife **Rosanah** the sole Executrix of this my last Will and Testament, hereby revoking all former wills by me made. In witness whereof I have hereunto set my hand and seal. This 21st day of February, 1853.

Lewis x Click (seal)
(his mark)

Signed, sealed and published in our presence and we have subscribed our names hereunto in the presence of the Testator. This 21st day of Feb., 1853.

James W. Davison

James W. Clarke

WILL OF HAMILTON J. CARTER

Page 129
Dated: March 9, 1855
Proven: May Term, 1855

In the Name of God, Amen.

I, **Hamilton J. Carter,** being weak in body, but of sound mind and memory do publish this my last Will and Testament, revoking all other wills by me at any time made.

First. I require my Executor to pay my funeral expenses with all my just debts out of any moneys that I may die possessed of or may first come into his hands.

Second. I will and bequeath unto my wife, **Highley Carter,** all my household and kitchen furniture.

Third. I also will and bequeath unto her my plantation so long as she sees proper to live upon it, but if she chooses to leave it, then it is to belong to my two brothers, **Charles** and **Allen Carter.**

Fourth. I give unto my daughter **Lucinda Carter** one spotted heifer, and no more of my Estate.

Fifth. I nominate and appoint **George Kenney** my Executor and allow him to administer without security.

Given under my hand and seal this the ninth day of March, 1855.

Hameltn Cater (seal)

Witnesses:
Bird Smith, John x Bord
(his mark)

Witnesses depose that they saw Testator sign the will and believed him to be of sound mind and memory.

Hila Carter, widow, appears in open court & dissents to the will.

WILL OF JAMES M. COX

Page 130
Dated: March 6, 1857
Proven: April Term, 1857
[Recorded p. 44]

I, **James Cox** of the County of Hawkins and State of Tennessee, being of sound mind and memory and feeling certain that my natural life is drawing to a close, do therefore make publish and declare this to be my last Will & Testament, that is to say:

First. That my body be buried in a decent and respectable manner, and that my burial expenses be paid out of my Estate.

Second. I will that my lawful debts be discharged out of any money that may come into the hands of my Executor, which I will hereafter name in the will, and the residue of my Estate, both real and personal, I will bequeath and dispose of as follows:

Third. I will and bequeath to my two nephews **John James Cox** and **George Van Cox,** sons of **John T. Cox,** the tract of land on which I now live containing 50 acres more or less, to be divided equally between them when they arrive at a lawful age, and that **John T. Cox** or some other suitable person have full control of my land until they become of age, and that my mother have her home and support off the said land during her natural life.

Fourth. I give, will and bequeath to my brother **John T. Cox,** the following notes and interest thereon: One note on **John R. Charles** for $122.31, dated January 5, 1857; one note on **E. D. Faris** for $11.66, dated 12th Jan.., 1857; one note on **Jesse M. Lyons** for 25, dated 29th August, 1856; one note on **Nelson Campbell** for $181.09, dated Aug. 6, 1856; one note on **Jas. Miller** for $33.42, dated April 9, 1856; one note on **T. T. Barrett** for $241.62, dated Jan. 25, 185.; one note on **C. C. Miller** dated March 18, 1850 for $15.00, due 15 October, 1856; one note on **John T. White** and **James White** for $42.63, dated March 5, 1857; one note on **Jim Lyons** for $25.00, dated Jan. 28, 1853; one note on **Dan Green** for $65.28, with a credit of $35.00, June 27, 1855. One Receipt on **Elias Beal** for $200.00, dated October 23, 1856, and that the said **John T. Cox** pay out of said notes the sum of $17.00 to **George Cox.**

Fifth. I give and bequeath to **Sarah S. Cox,** wife of **John T. Cox,** one note on **Wm. White & Bro.** for $98.31.

Sixth. I give, will and bequeath to **John T.Cox & Sarah S. Cox** his wife all my household and other articles too tedious to mention.

Seventh. I will that my Executor pay to **George Cox** the sum of $22.50 out of the money I now have on hand.

Eighth. I appoint, make and put on **John T. Cox** for my Executor to this my last Will and Testament.

Ninth. I will and desire that my said Executor pay to **Thomas T.Cox** my brother and **Polly Bray** my sister the sum of one dollar each, out of my Estate. Interlined before signed.

In testimony whereof I **James Cox** hereunto set my hand and affix my seal The 6th day of March A.D. 1857.

James M. Cox (seal)

Witness: **Wm A. x Owen & R. M. Sensabaugh**
(his mark)

WILL OF WILEY COBB

Page 131   Dated: June 12, 1857
         Proven July 6, 1857
         [Recorded P. 71]

I, **Wiley Cobb** of the County of Hawkins and State of Tennessee be afflicted and not knowing whether I shall live long or not, I do this day make and ordain this my last Will and Testament in manner and form following.

First. I will and bequeath my land to my three sons and one daughter, **Joseph, Jackson, Thomas** and **Elizabeth** to be divided equally among them when they become free. I want my son-in-law **Dyer D. Lawson** to have the land till the heirs all comes free to maintain the children upon, also I want **Dyer** and the children that is here with him to have all the grain that is growing on the place, and all the corn, wheat, oats, bacon, &c that is here now if he stays here with me and takes care of me as long as I live. I also will and bequeath to my three sons and one daughter namely **Joseph, Jackson, Thomas** and **Mary** all my beds and bed clothing, to be equally divided among them and the three boys to have the cupboard. I also will and bequeath to my three sons my horses to keep here on the place for the purpose of using them here among them all that is here on the place. I want **Joseph** to have his oxens that he now claims, I also want my cow kept here among them to milk, and I also want them to keep the hogs to make them meat for next year, and I want **Dyer** and the boys to finish paying for the land in corn if **Joel Cobb** will wait with them till they can and if he wont why, they must sell one of the horses to pay it. I want **Dyer** to keep all the farming utensils here on the farm to use, and I want **Dyer** and **Elizabeth** to keep the house and kitchen furniture. I also will my side saddle to my daughter **Elizabeth**, and the other saddle I will to my son **Joseph**. I will my sheep to them all that is here to keep them here among them till they become free and then divided them among equally and I want the geese to stay here among them all that is here.

I lastly will to my two daughters **Catharine** and **Mandy** five dollars to each of them to have when they become free, and also my

daughter **Mary** $5.00 to have when she becomes free.

And, Lastly. I hereby constitute and appoint **Dyer D. Lawson** to pay all of the heirs the money as they become free. This my last Will and Testament. In witness whereof I have set my hand and seal This June the 12th, 1857.

Wiley x Cobb (seal)
(his mark)

Attest:
A. O. Lawson
H. E. Lawson

WILL OF SUSANNAH CRITZ

Page 132   Dated: December 19, 1857
         Proven: Feb. Term, 1861

I, **Susannah Critz** do make and publish this my last Will and Testament, hereby revoking and making void all other wills by me at any time made.

First. I direct that all expenses and all debts be paid as soon after my death as possible out of any money that I may die possessed of, or may first come into the hands of my Executor.

Second. I give and bequeath my riding mare to **Mary Kinkead.**

Thirdly. I give and bequeath a one year old horse colt to **Samuel A. Kinkead** and all the cash, notes and accounts and all my rent, grain of every description.

Fifthly and lastly. I give and bequeath to **Mary Kinkead** one cow and calf and all my household and kitchen furniture and my bed and all my bed clothing.

Lastly. I denominate and appoint **David Kinkead** my Executor. In witness whereof I do to this my will set my hand and seal. This the 19th day of December, 1857.

Susannah x Critz (seal)
(her mark)

Signed, sealed and published in our presence and (we) have subscribed (our) names hereunto in the presence of the Testator. This 19th day of December, 1857.
James M. Bellomy, W. A. Pearson, Hiram x Wills
(his mark)

WILL OF ELIAKENN COX

Page 133   Dated: December 13, 1860
         Proven: Sept. Term., 1862

I, **Eliakenn Cox**, do make and publish this my last Will and Testament, hereby revoking and making void all othr wills by me at any time made.

First. I direct that my funeral expenses and all my just debts be paid as soon after my death as possible, out of any money that I may die possessed of or may first come into the hands of my hereinafter named Executor.

WILL OF A. CARMICHAEL
[Dr. Archibald Carmichael]

Dated: December 19, 1860

Proven: February Term 1861

In view of the uncertainty of life & the certainty of death,

I, Archibald Carmichael, of the County of Hawkins, Tennessee, being sick in body but of sound and disposing mind & memory, do make publish and declare the following to be my last Will & Testament, hereby revoking & making void any other wills heretofore made by me.

First. It is my will & desire that all my funeral expenses should be paid.

Secondly. It is my will & desire that all my just debts should be paid and discharged.

Thirdly. In as much as it is my opinion that my personal effects will not be sufficient to pay off and discharge my debts, it is my will and desire that Executor & Executrix hereafter named shall sell my real estate at public or private sale as in their discretion they may think advisable & for the interest of my dearly beloved wife & children & shall sell the same on a credit of six or twelve months, the purchaser/s giving bond with security & with interest from day of sale for the purchase money, a lien retained until the purchase money is fully paid.

Fourthly. It is my will & desire that after all my just debts shall have been paid, the residue of my Estate shall be handed over to my dearly beloved wife to be laid out in the purchase of a comfortable house for herself & family and the residue if any, to go to the use of the family in their education & training &c.

Fifthly. It is my will and desire that my dearly beloved wife shall use occupy & enjoy said property or house so purchased for & during her natural life & at her death the same to be equally divided amongst my four children, to wit: **Mattie Ellen, William Andrew, Whitfield and Ann,** share and share alike, and in the event my beloved wife shall in her good judgement think it best to marry a second time, then & in that case whatever property she may have purchased or may have saved of my Estate shall be divided equally between her and my four children, share & share alike.

Lastly. I do hereby nominate, constitute & appoint my dearly beloved wife my Executrix & appoint my esteemed friend **George R. Powel** Executor of this my last Will & Testament. In witness whereof I have hereunto set my hand & affixed my seal this 19th day of December A.D., 1860.

A. Carmichael (seal)

Witness: Bu Walker, Audley Anderson

Secondly. I give and bequeath to my wife **Elizabeth Cox** my farm for her own use. After the death or marriage of my wife Elizabeth, I give and bequeath the said farm to my youngest son **Hugh Cox,** provided he will come and live upon it, and if he will not come and live upon the farm, then I give said farm to my grandson, **Eliacium Bardin.**

Third – Twelve. I give and bequeath to my following children one dollar each: **Ann Hardin, Mathew Cox, Margaret Johnson, Rachael Foster, Martin Cox, Mariah Foster, Eliacium Cox, Lucinda Johnson & William Cox.** Said money to be paid by my Executor as soon as may be convenient.

Lastly. I do hereby nominate and appoint **Daniel M Sheffey** Executor. In witness whereof I do to this my last Will and Testament set my hand and seal this 13 day of December 1860.

E. Cox (seal)

Signed, sealed and published in our presence and we have subscribed our names hereto in the presence of the Testator. This 13 day of December, 1860.

Thos J. x Lee (his mark)

Gale x Walker (his mark)

WILL OF JOEL COBB

Dated: Feb. 18, 1861

Proven: April 1861

I, **Joel Cobb** of the County of Hawkins and State of Tennessee, do make and publish this my last Will and Testament, hereby revoking and making void all other wills by me at any time made.

First. I direct that my funeral expense and all my debts be paid as soon after my death as possible out of any money that I may die possessed of or may first come into the hands of my Executor.

Secondly. I give and bequeath to my son **Winsted D. Cobb** and his heirs all my Estate, real and personal, to wit: The tract of land whereon I now live of 50 acres more or less, joining the lands of **Wiley Cobb's** heirs and **P. G. Murrel** and others, one yellow mare, one muley red, brindle cow, one cupboard, one bureau, all my beds and bed clothing, one kettle and one clock, all my bacon and lard, together with everything I may die seized and possessed of.

Thirdly. My son **Winsted D. Cobb,** one year after my death is to pay **Pleasant G. Murrel** $40.00, and to my daughter **Sally Trent** $5.00, and to my grand daughter **Polly Frazier** $1.00, and to the heirs of **Wiley Cobb,** $1.00, and to my daughter **Polly Murrel,** $1.00, and to my daughter **Fanny Murrel,** $1.00, and to the heirs of **Jacob Bow** $1.00, and to my son **Edward Cobb,** $1.00.

Lastly. I appoint my son **Winsted D. Cobb** my Executor. In witness whereof I do to this my will set my hand and seal. This 18th day of February, 1861.

Joel x Cobb (seal) (his mark)

Signed, sealed and acknowledged in the presence of:

Wm. J. Pearson, Banks x Lawson, Thomas x Lawson (his mark) (his mark)

WILL OF WILLIAM CARMACK

Page 136

Dated: March 23, 1861
Proven: May term 1861

I, **William Carmack** of the County of Hawkins and State of Tenn. being advanced in years but of sound mind and memory, do hereby make and declare this to be my last Will & Testament, to wit:

First. I give and bequeath to the heirs of my son **Cornelius**, dec'd the proceeds of a note on my son **William E. Carmack** for $1,000.00 dated February 21, 1861 and due five years after date to be divided amongst the children of said **Cornelius Carmack**, share and share alike.

Second. I give and bequeath to my daughter **Polly Ann** who married **Lewis Long** one dollar.

Third. I give and bequeath to my three sons James, Wiley & Epps Carmack the proceeds of a note on my son **William E. Carmack** for $63.97 due one day after date and dated 23rd March, 1861, to be divided equally.

Fourth. I give and bequeath to my said three sons above named to wit: **James, Wiley & Epps Carmack** a Land Warrant issued by the United States to me for 80 acres as the proceeds of said Land Warrant, if sold by me during my lifetime or by my Executor or Administrator after my death to be divided amongst them, share and share alike.

Fifth. I give and bequeath to my son **William E. Carmack** all the remainder of my estate whatever there may be.

Lastly. I hereby appoint **Cornelius C. Miller** Executor of this my last Will & Testament, hereby revoking all other wills by me at any time made.

In testimony whereof I have hereunto set my hand and affixed my seal. This 23rd day of March 1861.

William Carmack (seal)

Signed, sealed & acknowledged in our presence the 23rd day of March 1861.

J. H. Vance, C. E. x Carmack, A. J. x Camp
           (his mark)   (his mark)

WILL OF GEORGE S. CHILDRESS

Page 137

Dated: June 20, 1861
Proven: Aug. Term, 1861

I, **George S. Childress** of the County of Hawkins in the State of Tennessee, being in feeble health, but of sound and perfect mind and memory do make, publish and declare this to be my last Will and Testament. As regards my estate, real and personal, I desire to dispose of the same as follows:

First. I will and desire that all my indebtedness and my funeral expenses be paid as soon as practicable after my decease.

Secondly. I will and devise to my dearly beloved wife **Sarah T. Childress** my entire interest in the negroes, land and other personal property which belong to the heirs of **James M. Childress**, dec'd, late of Sullivan County, State of Tennessee, said lands are situated in Sullivan County upon the waters of Reedy Creek. Said negroes and lands are undivided between the heirs of **James M. Childress**, dec'd.

And Lastly. I do hereby appoint (and nominate) **Andrew Leslie, Esq.** of Sullivan County, Tennessee my Executor of this my last Will and Testament. In testimony whereof I have hereunto subscribed my name and affixed my seal on this 20th day of June, 1861.

G. S. Childress (seal)

Signed, sealed and acknowledged in our presence and in the presence of the Testator on 20th day of June, 1861. Signed after interlining.
Witness: **R. G. Netherland, S. Richardson**

WILL OF WILLIAM L. CHRISTIAN

Page 138

Dated: August 11, 1861
Proven: October, 1861

I, **William L. Christian**, do this day make and publish this as my last Will and Testament, hereby revoking all former wills that may have been made by me at any time heretofore.

First. I will and bequeath that my funeral expenses, together with my debts shall be paid out of any money that I may die seized and possessed of at my death, or the first money (that) may come into the hands of my Executor.

Second. I will and bequeath unto my wife **Elizabeth Christian** the home place.

Third. I will and bequeath to my son **William L. Christian** the east end of my place. Beginning at the bridge on the branch running from **Mary Skelton's**. Thence with the branch at a mouth of a ditch, thence due north to **John Skelton's** line.

Fourth. I will and bequeath to my daughter **Mahaly St. John** and the heirs of her body the north part of my land. Beginning at the line fence on **Wullran** line, formerly the line fence of **John Skelton**, dec'd. Thence with said fence as it has formerly run to a mulberry. Thence a straight line to the corner aup (and up ?) next Alex Mountain of a twelv_ a_ ahalf acre entry bought from **John Skelton, Sr.** Thence with the several courses and distance to the beginning.

Fifthly. I will and bequeath to my son **James Christian** the part of my land joining **Mahaly St. John**. Beginning at the mulberry, **St. John** Corner, thence a straight line to the creek to a beech tree on the bank of the creek with the meanders of said creek aup to a blackhaw bush. Thence northwest to a sycamore. Thence a west course straight to the beginning. Also, one half of the 25-acre entry on the side of Alex Mountain adjoining my land.

Sixthly. I will and bequeath to my son **David Christian** the part adjoining **James**, including my buildings of every description on said part. Beginning at the gum, **James'** Corner, thence with the old line crossing the creek to a walnut tree at the foot of the hill. Thence with the fence to the lane. Thence a straight line to an elm, then with the drain to the line between me and **Mary Skelton**. Then with the line to the road, to a black oak and sweet gum. Thence with the road to the head of the ditch, thence with the ditch to the creek.

Seventhly. I will and bequeath to my daughter **Mary B. Christian** and to the heirs of her body all the land lying adjoining Mary Skelton & **William L. Christian, Mahaly St. John &** James Christian, also one half of the entry on Alex Mountain -- that half to **James** and the other to her -- her half to be laid off at the east end of said tract.

Eighthly. I will and bequeath to my daughter **Rachael M.** Christian and the heirs of her body all the part of my land lying south of **David** and joining his part, also to have one half of the forty acre entry under the Big Mountain, and **David** to have the other half of said entry.

Ninthly. I will and bequeath to my four children to be equally divided among them to wit: **Stephen Christian** to have where he lives to include his house: **Eldridge** to have where he now lives: **Jesse** to have where he now lives: **Joseph F.** his part adjoining **Jesse Christian** and **Stephen Christian** and **Polly Bailey** next the Big Mountain, on the north side of said mountain.

Tenthly. I will and bequeath that my children, namely: **Eldridge, Stephen, William L., Jesse, Isaac** shall each pay $5.00 for seven years and **Mahaly St. John** to pay $5.00 for five years.

Eleventh. I hereby nominate and appoint my wife **Elizabeth** Christian my Executor. In testimony whereof I have hereunto set my hand and seal. _This the 16th of August, 1861._

William L. x Christian (seal)
(his mark)

Signed, sealed and delivered in our presence. This the 16th day of August, 1861.

Attest:
T. A. x Long
(his mark)

Acknowledged in our presence This 13 Day of September, 1861.
John Ball, James Feagins, George D. Wagner

WILL OF SAMUEL CHESNUTT

Page 139

Dated: May 7, 1862
Proven: July Term 1862

I **Samuel Chesnutt** do make and publish this my last will and Testament, hereby revoking and making void all other wills by me at any time made. **First.** I direct that my funeral expenses and debts to be paid in the manner I shall hereinafter direct.

Secondly. I give and bequeath to my beloved wife **Susan** all the household and kitchen furniture that she brought with her, also one negro woman named **Amanda** during her life. Also, if she chooses to remain with the family she is to have one room of the house and to have her support from the proceeds of the land which I shall give and bequeath to my daughter **Caroline** and son **Samuel**. **Thirdly.** I give and bequeath to my daughter **Polly Kirkpatrick** and her children the land on which she lives as laid off to her, also a negro woman named **Ester** and her youngest child.

Fourthly. I give and bequeath to my daughter **Catherine Cobb** and her children the land on which she now lives as laid off to **P. A. Cobb**. Also one negro man, **Lilbourne** when my son **Samuel** attains the age of 22 years.

Fifthly. I give and bequeath to my daughter **Sally Morell** and her children one negro woman **Sydney** and her twin children.

Sixthly. I give and bequeath to my son **Thomas** one black boy named **Charles** and one-third of the tract of land where I now live also a small lot lying down west of the mill adjoining Simpson's lands.

Seventhly. I give and bequeath to my daughter **Margaret Phillips** and her children one negro girl **Ann** and a negro woman **Amanda** at the death of my wife.

Eighthly. I give and bequeath to my daughter **Caroline** and her children one negro girl **Mary** and one third of the tract of the land on which I live.

Ninthly. I give and bequeath to my son **Samuel** one negro boy **Bob** and one third of the tract of land on which I live. I wish the land divided without respect to quality but equal in number of acres. **Thomas** to have his third off the upper end of the farm **Caroline** next & **Samuel** the lower end including the dwelling house. I wish **Lilbourn** to remain with and work on the farm for the support of the family until my son **Samuel** attains the age of 22 years.

Tenthly. I give and bequeath to my grand daughter **Muscadore Smith** one negro boy named **Elbert**. If she should die without issue then said boy **Elbert** revert to my estate and be equally divided. I wish my negro man **Jo** to be sold and the proceeds applied to payment of my debts, together with the moneys that are due me. After my debts are paid, if there remains any surplus, I wish it equally divided amongst my children. If the debt due me known as the mule debt be collected, I give $300.00 of that to daughter **Margaret**, in addition to what I have heretofore given her. My farming tools, waggon, horses and all my stock I wish to remain on the farm for the use of the family. Also the balance of my household and kitchen furniture I give to my daughter **Caroline** and son **Samuel**.

Lastly. I nominate and appoint my brother **Rodham Chesnutt** Executor of this my last will and Testament. I wish my old negro woman **Lydia** to live with any of the family that she may choose. I desire that my Executor shall not be required to enter into bond with security.

In testimony whereof I have hereunto set my hand and affixed my seal this 7 day of May, 1862.

Sam'l Chesnutt (seal)

Signed, sealed and acknowledged in our presence:
Thos J. Lee, C. F. Hobbs

I hereby acknowledge myself satisfied and consent to the above disposition of property as made by the Will and Testament of my husband.

Susan Chesnutt (seal)

Thos. J. Lee
C. F. Hobbs

WILL OF ALLEN CARTER

Page 141   Dated: July 29, 1863

I, **Allen Carter** of the County of Hawkins and State of Tenn. hereby revoking and making void all former wills by me made and first: I direct that my body be decently buried in a manner suitable to my condition in life, and as to such worldly Estate as it has pleased God to intrust me with, I dispose of as follows:

First. I direct that all my debts and funeral expenses be paid as soon after my death as possible out of any money that I may die possessed of.

Second. I will and bequeath to my wife **Tempyrance (Tempey)** and my children all my lands and stock, household and kitchen furniture of all kinds. My wife is to have the above bequeath her lifetime or as long as she remains my widow. Whenever my wife ceases to be my widow, the entire Estate is to be equally divided amongst my children.

In witness whereof I **Allen Carter** have hereunto set my hand and seal this 29th day of July, 1863.

Attest: A. D. Johnson   **Allen x Carter**(seal)
       Stephen Darter   (his mark)
       David Hickman

WILL OF PHAROAH COBB

Page 142   Dated: March 18, 1823
In the Name of God, Amen.

I **Pharoah Cobb** of the County of Hawkins in the State of Tenn., being in perfect health and of sound, disposing mind and memory and knowing that all must die, do make this my last Will and Testament in manner and form following, to wit: It is my will and desire that all my just debts be paid.

I give and bequeath unto my beloved wife **Barsha** four negroes, **Stephen, Lucy** his wife and her two children **Cairy** and **Eliza** with all my household and kitchen furniture, to her and her heirs forever. It is my will and desire that my wife **Barsha** should enjoy and have the use of the house and kitchen that we now occupy with as much of the cleared and woodland as may be deemed sufficient for her support her life, with two of my horse beasts, her choice, and four cows and calves of her choice with as many sheep and hogs as she may need for her use and support, and at her death the same to be sold by my Executor hereafter named. I also leave to my said wife a negro boy named **Peter** during her lifetime, and at her death he is to be sold as above.

Whereas I have heretofore given to my son-in-law **Julias Conner** property to the amount of $3,000.00 which is all that I ever intend to give him. I have also given to my grandson (   ) **Conner** one young negro woman worth $500.00 for the express purpose of supporting and taking care of his mother. I have heretofore given to my son **Richard Caswell Cobb** $3,000.00 worth of property. To my son **William** $2,000.00 worth of property. To my son **Arthur Cobb** $2,000.00 worth of property. To my son-in-law

Absalom Kyle $2,000.00 worth of property. And to my son **Jesse Cobb** $2,000.00 worth of property. A part of the property that I heretofore have given to my son **Jesse** is a negro woman named **Charity** then having two children, but has now five. And since that gift was made a certain **Julias Conner** has filed his Bill in Equity for the recovery of said negroes and to guard against the event of the suit, I do hereby set apart six negroes, to wit: A negro **Esther** and her two children, and **Hamilton, Wyly** and **Frankey** which is for my son **Jesse Cobb** provided he should lose **Charity** and her five children, but should my son **Jesse** gain the suit and keep negro **Charity** it is then my will that negro woman **Esther** and her two children and **Hamilton, Wyly** and **Franky** should be divided as hereafter mentioned. My Executors shall pay to my daughter **Barshaba Kyle** and to my grand daughter **Barshaba Cobb**, daughter of my son **Arthur Cobb** dec'd one thousand dollars each in negroes and money out of my estate. And it is further my will and desire that my Executors...shall lay off all my negroes not otherwise disposed of into three parcels of equal value or as nearly so as convenient, putting as many of one family into the same parcel as can be done with convenience, and draw by lot...one lot or third part to my daughter **Barshaba Kyle**, one third part to my three grand daughters, **Eliza, Barshaba** and **Sally**, children of my son **Richard Caswell Cobb** dec'd and one third part to my grand daughter **Barshaba Cobb**, daughter of my son **Arthur Cobb**, dec'd. And it is my will and desire that all the rest of my personal Estate not by this will devised, my blacksmith tools excepted, be sold by my Executors and the money arising therefrom be equally divided in the following manner, to wit: One third part to my daughter **Barshaba Kyle**, one third part to my three grand daughters, **Eliza, Barshaba** and **Sally** children of my son **Richard C. Cobb**, dec'd. And one third part to **Barshaba Cobb**, daughter of my son **Arthur**, dec'd. to them and their heirs forever.

It is my will that if in allotting of my negroes as above mentioned that one lot or lots should be of more value than the others, that those drawing the highest price lot shall pay to those drawing the lower price lot so as to make them all equal as my Executors may think proper. It is further my will that the property left my wife her lifetime and directed to be sold, that the money be divided into three parcels and given in the above manner. I give and bequeath to my sons **William** and **Jesse** the tracts of land I live on to be divided in the following manner: The Island to be equally divided by running a line across the same, giving to my son **William** the lower part and **Jesse** the upper part. Then to begin at the upper elm tree standing on the bank of the river a little distance above a Spanish oak and several elms, a small distance above the point of the island and above a cliff of rock. Then to run an east or nearly an east course to a stake or stone that I may hereafter set up. Then north or nearly north to a Spanish oak and cherry tree standing close together on the point of a hill near the creek, then up the middle of the creek to the lower end of a new meadow made since I purchased from **William Lee**, then along the line of the meadow fence and to continue that course as near as may be up to **Galbraith's** line, leaving all the flat meadow ground to the north of the line up to Galbraith's line, which if I do shall be the dividing line, unless I may hereafter make a line from the meadow and I give to my son William the lower part of said land, and to Jesse the upper part, reserving to my wife as before mentioned. I give and bequeath to my sons William and Jesse the mill I give to them and their heirs forever. I give to my son Jesse all my blacksmith tools.

And, I appoint my friends George Hale, Andrew Galbraith and Richard Mitchell my Executors to this my last Will, revoking all others by me made.

In witness whereof I Pharoah Cobb hath hereto set my hand and seal. This 18th day of March 1823.

Note: Interlined between the 19th and 20th lines before signing.

Pharoah Cobb (seal)

Signed, sealed and acknowledged on the 5th day of May, 1823 in the presence of

G D. Mitchell
R. H. Mitchell

WILL OF RALEIGH DODSON (SR.)

Page 145
Dated: July 20, 1793

In the Name of God, Amen. I, Rayleigh Dodson Sr. being in an infirm state of health but of sound mind and considering that I may shortly leave this life, I have thought it necessary to make this my last Will & Testament, revoking all former wills by me made, and in the first place I resign myself to the disposal of my Creator hoping for mercy & forgiveness. In respect of my Earthly affairs, To my wife I leave and bequeath my whole Estate real & personal to her use during her natural life, after which I leave to my son Rayleigh Dodson the plantation on which I now live with all the appurtenances, also one other piece of land joining, butted and bounded as appears by the patent in my name, also all my working tools, horses, except a motherless colt, three cows with their calves, one feather bed with the furniture, half the pewter, and one half pot metal, also what hay I may have remaining.

To my grandchildren Mary and Nancy Shelton, the remainder of my cattle equally divided, also the remainder of the pewter and pot metal to be equally divided between them, and to Mary Shelton one bed and furniture, also the motherless colt, one linen wheel and half the cards, the other wheel & cards to Nancy.

There is a bond due to me of fifteen pounds from Henry Rowan to be collected and my debts paid out of it. Peggey Manafee my eldest daughter having by her husband obtained credit for sixty pounds for which I have his note, I hereby direct my Executor to give up said note. My sons Lazarus and Tolliver I have done a Fatherly part by and hereby acquit them of all demands that I may have against them. My daughter Nelly the wife of John Saunders I consider I have done enough for, having given her husband the land he now lives on.

My son James to whom I have (already) given several things, I now bequeath my claim on Thos. Jackson for share of some land to be obtained by a warrant up by me given to said Jackson to be laid on the halves provided said warrant obtains a title for land. Warrant was for 300 acres.

I also appoint my son Lazarus and my neighbor Rodham Kenner my Executors and do authorize and direct them to put this my said Will & Testament into effect.

In witness whereof I have hereunto set my hand and seal This 20th day of July A.D. 1793.

Test.   Rayleigh x Dodson (seal)
                                    (his mark)
Thos. Jackson
Rodham Kenner
Mary x Shelton
                    (her mark)

WILL OF EDWARD DOWDALL

Page 146
Dated: December 28, 1818

This is to certify that I Edward Dowdall late of the County of Frederick and State of Virginia being in perfect health and of sound mind and disposing memory do mind the uncertainty of human life and being about to proceed upon an eventful journey and not knowing that I shall live to return to Hawkins County in Tennessee from whence I now depart and hope to return but in case of my decease before I should return to said place of departure, it is my sincere wish that Michael McCann of Hawkins County, Tenn. should have all the estate both real and personal of which I am entitled to as being the lawful heir of Joseph Raverhill, dec'd late of Knox County, Tennessee, which estate is now in the hands of Hugh L. White of Knoxville, Tennessee. And in case of my death before I should return to Hawkins County, State of Tennessee, it is my wish that the said Estate of said Joseph Raverhill, dec'd go to said M. McCann or his lawful heirs. Given under my hand and seal this 28th day of December, 1818, and in the presence of: J. Wilson
                    Larkin Willis

WILL OF FRANCIS DALZELL

Page 147
Dated: December 4, 1823

In the Name of God, Amen.

I Francis Dalzell of the County of Hawkins in the State of Tennessee being weak of body but of sound mind and memory do make and ordain this my last Will and Testament. I recommend my soul to Almighty God. And as to my worldly Estate, I dispose of it as follows, that is to say. I will that my just debts be paid by my Executor and for that purpose that the debts owing to me be collected. The money which I have now on hand I bequeath to my beloved wife Nancy. I also give and bequeath to her the use of my negroes during her live, and at her death they all shall be set free. I also devise to my wife Nancy the house and lots on which I now live with the appurtenances, and the use of my plantation adjoining George Hale and John A. McKinney to her during her life and after her death the plantation to go to

the children of my brother **William** and I make the same disposition of my
river plantation if it be gained in law as a suit is now depending respecting it. All my stock and household furniture and farming utensils I also
give and bequeath to my beloved wife. And I appoint my friends **Dicks
Alexander** and **John A. McKinney** the Executors of this my last Will and Testament.

In witness whereof I have hereunto set my hand and seal This the first
day of December A.D. 1823.

Fran's Dalzell (seal)

Test. **A. McKinney, Samuel Neill**

WILL OF WILLIAM DYKES

Page 148   Dated: October 14, 1825
In the Name of God, Amen.

I **William Dykes** senr. of the County of Hawkins and State of Tennessee,
being very weak but in perfect mind and memory, Thanks be given unto God.
Calling unto mind the mortality of my body and knowing that it is appointed
for all men once to die, do make and ordain this my last Will and Testament.
That is to say, principally and first of all, I give and recommend my soul
unto the hand of Almighty God that gave it, and my body I recommend to the
Earth to be buried in a decent Christian burial at the discretion of my
Executor, nothing doubting but at the general resurrection I shall receive
the _____ same again by the mighty power of God. And as touching such world-
Estate wherewith it has pleased God to bless me in this life, First of all,
I give and bequeath to **Susannah Dykes** my beloved wife my dwelling house and
all the land on the south side of the road on Beech Creek, Hawkins County,
and bounded on the west by the land of **Jacob Light** and on the east by
Flower Mullins, during her life, and at her death my son **William Dykes** is to
have that part of my land that I have devised to my wife. and also I give
to **Susannah Dykes** all my personal estate, or as much as she sees cause to
retain, and after her decease all my personal estate to be sold by my Exec.
hereinafter appointed, and money arising therefrom to be equally divided
between my four daughters, **Mary Hase, (Hale?), Prissilla Cooper, Sarah
Mullins** and **Ann Raseberry.** I give and bequeath that part of my land on the
north side of Beech Creek Road between **Thos. Mullins** and **Flower Mullins** to
my son **Isum Dykes** to dispose of as he thinks proper.

I give and bequeath to my son **John Dykes** 250 acres of land, be the
same more or less joining the land of **Flower Mullins** on the head of Beech
Creek on the waters of Walkers fork to dispose of as he thinks proper. I
give to **David McCatley** a colt that my bay mare is now with foal, provided
s'd **David** pays the season. I add nothing now to my son **James Dykes** (as) I
have made ample provision heretofore.

I consitiute make and ordain my son **John Dykes** the sole Executor of
this my last Will and Testament and I do hereby utterly disallow, revoke and
disannul all & every other former Testament, Wills, Legacies, bequests and
Executors by me in anywise before mentioned, willed & bequeathed, ratifying
and confirming this and no other to be my last Will and Testament.

In witness whereof I have hereunto set my hand and seal, This 14th
day of October in the year of our Lord, one thousand Eight hundred and
twenty five. Signed, sealed published, pronounced and declared in presence of:

Reuben Bernard
Wright x Mullins
  (his mark)
Joseph x Dykes
  (his mark)

William x Dykes (seal)
  (his mark)

WILL OF THOMAS DODSON

Page 149   Date: None
In the Name of God, Amen.

I **Thomas Dodson** of the County of Hawkins & State of Tennessee, being
weak & sick in body but of sound mind and disposing memory, calling to mind
the mortality of my body do make and ordain this my last Will and Testament
in form and manner following. That is to say. First. I give my soul into
the hands of God, and my body I resign to the earth to be buried in a Christian like manner at the discretion of my Executors hereinafter named, and as
to touching my worldly Estate wherewith it hath pleased God to bless me, I
give and dispose of in the following manner.

First. I will that my loving wife **Jamima Dodson** possess & enjoy my
whole Estate both real and personal, in this wise. She, my s'd loving wife
Jamima is to raise and bring up my children hereinafter named in the best
manner that her ability will admit, she my s'd wife **Jamima** being hereby empowered to lay out so much of my Estate in schooling & educating all my
children as shall be sufficient to answer s'd purpose, and also my..wife
with my Executors is hereby empowered to collect and receive all money due
me on bonds, notes of hand or otherwise; also to sell any such personal
property as she and my Executors shall think proper &c. And further, I will
that my s'd wife have hold, possess & enjoy my whole Estate both real &
personal until my youngest child arrives at the age of twenty one years,
except my s'd wife **Jamima** should marry before that time, and if that be the
case, and should my Estate appear to be wasting and destroying, my Executors
to take charge until my youngest child **Rolly** arrives at the age of twenty
one years at which time legal division be made of my whole Estate, both real
and personal between my wife and four children, viz: **James, Sarah, Elisha**
and **Rolly Dodson** and further, if **Thomas Robinson** and **John Robinson** live and
abide with my wife and behave orderly and well until they are twenty one
years of age, then each of them is to have a horse and saddle worth $100.00
out of my Estate.

And further, I appoint my loving wife **Jamima** my lawful Executrix and
James Johnson & **Samuel Riggs** my Executors of this my last Will and Testament.

Signed, sealed, published & declared by the said **Thomas Dodson** as his
last Will & Testament, in presence of,
James Dodson,
Richard Hellson
Richard Roberson, Jurat

Thomas x Dodson (seal)
  (his mark)

WILL OF ROBERT DODSON
Dated: December 20, 1830

Page 151

In the Name of God, Amen. This 20th day of December, 1830, I **Robert Dodson** of the County of Hawkins and State of Tennessee, being sick and weak of body but of sound mind and memory, and calling to mind that it is appointed for all men once to die, do make and ordain this to be my last Will and Testament in manner and form following, to wit:

First and Principally: I give my soul unto the care of Almighty God who created and gave it.

Second. My body to the earth to be buried in a decent Christian like manner at the discretion of my hereinafter named.

Third and Lastly. My Earthly Estate wherewith I may die seized and possessed. To my beloved wife **Jane** I give and bequeath in manner following. I give and bequeath a bed and furniture, a milk cow and flax wheel, and one sheep, one small oven and a skillet, six geese, a bible and my Hymn book. I give and bequeath to my son **John A.** the tract of land where I now live, to-gether with the following articles: one plough and a log chain, one ax, one iron wedge and weeding hoes, a set of mowing machines, turning lathe irons, a slate, one steel faced hammer and one half of my magazine books. I give and bequeath to my daughter **Mary Ann** a bed and furniture, a pair of fire irons, two books, **The Christian Arter** (Writer?) and **Zion's Pilgrim.** I give and bequeath to my daughter **Nancy Jane** a cup-board and iron kettle and the one half of the magazines. It is my wish that **Jane** my wife is to have equal benefit of the tract of land aforesaid as long as she lives a single life after my decease.

Item. The foregoing I declare to be my last Will and Testament, in all its parts, publishing and declaring it as such. Disannuling and revoking all others. In testimony whereof I have hereunto set my hand and affixed my seal this day and year first before written.

Robert Dodson (seal)

Signed, sealed, published and declared in presence of we:

John Long & Jacob Bechner

WILL OF JOHN DODSON
Dated: Jan. 2, 1838

Page 151

Knowing all men by these presents that I, **John Dodson, senr.** of the State of Tennessee and Hawkins County, do hereby make my last Will and Testament in the words and figures following, to wit: I do will and bequeath to my be-loved grandson **George Dodson** a certain tract of land containing 50 acres more or less bounded as follows: Being in the County of Hawkins and State aforesaid, on the south side of Holston River, on the head waters of Dodson's Creek. Beginning on a white oak near the ___ of the path agoing from my house to **Thomas Berry's.** Thence, a north east course to a cedar tree. Thence south east to **Anna Coward's** line near where **John Walker** cut a locust tree at or near the mouth of ___ branch. Thence with **Mitchell's** line round to the beginning. I also will and bequeath to the said **George Dodson** one dollar in **Manis** one dollar out of my Estate. I also will and bequeath to my son **John Manis** one dollar out of my estate. I also will and bequeath to my daughter **Mary/Mary** money out of my estate. I also will and bequeath to my son **John** the remainder of my land including my old possessions containing 224 acres be it the same more or less. I also will to my son **John** all the balance of my property that I possess consisting of a variety of articles too tedious to mention.

I hereby set my hand and seal this second day of January in ___ of our Lord One Thousand Eight hundred and thirty eight, in presence of:

Attest: Nicholas Bechner

John x Dodson (his) (mark) (seal)

Wm. Smith
John Walker
John Berry

WILL OF LARKIN DAVIS
Page 152

Dated June 28, 1847
Proven Aug. 2, 1847

This I leave as my last Will and Testament being in my right mind, sober senses, first will and bequeath that my wife **Louisa** shall have full posses-sion, control and management of the tract of land she now lives on and all the proceeds arising therefrom, to maintain my children as long as she re-mains in widowhood, and if **Louisa** should marry, I will that the Court should appoint some suitable persons to manage the affairs for my children and that the land and all personal property be equally divided between **Leanier Jane** my eldest daughter, **Mary** my second, and **William Henry,** third, **James Madison** fourth, **Larkin** my youngest son, with the exception of a two year old colt. I will and bequeath that **Solomon Overton** or **Seals** have a two year old colt provided he stays and works for my family until he is 21. I further will that if it is accertained that my wife **Louisa** should have the appearance of squandering said property, the Court to appoint some suitable person to manage said affairs. This I leave as my last Will and Testament. this given under my hand and seal this twenty eighth of June in the Year of our Lord 1847.

Larkin x Davis (his) (mark)

Attest:
Wm. Wilder, Batice x Cantwell (his mark), Madison Davis, James Davis, Jr.

Proven in open Court by the oaths of Madison Davis & James Davis, Jr. on the 2nd day of August, 1847.

John H. Ellis, Clk.
By J. H. Vance, D. Clk.

WILL OF JOHN DODSON
Page 153

Dated: November 30, 1852
Proven: March Term., 1853

In the Year of Our Lord one Eight Hundred and fifty two, November the 30th day 1852, I, **John Dodson** have this day made & do make this my last Will and Testament and publish this as the same, hereby revoking and making void all other wills by me at any time made &c.

2nd. My will and desire is that as soon after my decease as is prac-ticable, I wish my just debts and funeral Expenses be paid by my representa-tive or representatives out of any money that may first come to my said re-presentatives

3rd. I give to my wife **Rebecca Dodson** all my land and all the buildings thereunto belonging during her life or widowhood with this exception, viz:

4th. I will to my little son **William Dodson** a certain piece of land which I now describe as follows: Beginning at a stake in the branch below my house, **E. Walker's** corner. Then eastwardly to a white oak corner on **Couche's** line. Then with **Couche's** line to the foot of the mountain. Then with **Anna Coward's** line to the beginning. This piece of land I desire that my wife have full control of the same during her life or widowhood, or until my son is twenty one years of age, then to him or his representative. I also give to my son **William** my Rifle gun, shot pouch and horn, and an equal portion of the proceeds of the sale of my perishable property should there be any.

5th. My will is that my six other children have all of my tract of land not otherwise disposed of, Viz: My daughter **Lany (Delaney) Dodson**, son **Arthur Dodson**, my daughters **Ann Dodson**, **Elizabeth Dodson**, **Mary Dodson**, **Winny Dodson** &c, to be equally enjoyed and divided among them all at the time above mentioned, &c.

Lastly. I do nominate and appoint my friend **Edward Walker** my Executor of my last Will and Testament.

In witness whereof I do __ this my last will set my hand and seal. This 30th day of November, 1852.

John x Dodson (seal)
(his mark)

Signed, sealed and published in our presence the day and date above mentioned.
Attest: **Wm. Smith**, **Edward Walker**

WILL OF WILLIAM S. DICKSON

Page 154

Dated: Nov. 1, 1852
Proven: Feb. & Mar. 1853

I, **William S. Dickson** of Hawkins County and State of Tennessee, do make and publish this my last Will and Testament, hereby revoking and annulling all former wills by me made.

1st. My Executor to be hereinafter appointed shall so soon as it can be done after my death, proceed to collect the debts and claims due me, and out of the proceeds thereof first pay and discharge all my debts and liabilities that may be outstanding...at my death, as well as all the expenses incident to my last illness, burial &c, and secondly, to pay (after retaining his compensation for his services) the balance of the fund so to be collected by him over to the Guardian of my children, to be hereinafter appointed.

2nd. It is my will and desire that my wife, **Jane S. Dickson**, shall be comfortably provided for, and so situated as that she may be able without burthen to raise, support and clothe my children. I therefore give to my wife **Jane S.** the entire personal property of which I may die possessed of every description whatever, including my horses, hogs, cattle, household and kitchen furniture, farming utensils, carriages, &c, and all other personalty (except my negroes, cash, chose in action, notes and accounts due me), to be her absolute property to dispose of as she may see proper. I give and bequeath to my wife my two negro women, **Polly & Nicey**, to have and to hold as her absolute property, to dispose of as she may deem proper. I also give to my wife for and during her lifetime the farm on which I now live at Mooresburg, Hawkins County, together with the store house and lot, and all other real estate of which I may die possessed, in and around Mooresburg, Hawkins County, Tennessee. And at her death, it is my will that

said Real Estate be disposed of as hereinafter directed. I furthermore give and bequeath unto my wife during her life or widowhood the possession and services of my two negro boys **Houston** and **Nelson** to enable her to carry on the farming business for the support of herself and children. But should my wife **Jane S.** marry, then it is my will and desire that the Guardian of my children to be hereinafter appointed shall take possession and control of said negro boys **Houston** and **Nelson** and hire them out as hereinafter directed for the benefit of my children.

3rd. I have now at the date of the preparation of this my will, two children, a son named **William S.** and a daughter named **Eliza D.** and my wife is now <u>Enscient</u> and looking forward to birth of a third child which, if in the Providence of God it shall be born alive (whether before or after my death) shall in all respects be equal with my other two children, and in all expressions throughout this my last Will & Testament where the word "children" is used, it is intended to embrace as well such third child (should one be born & live) as my two children now living.

4th. As one of the negro women hereinbefore willed to my wife is at this time afflicted with rheumatism and it is uncertain whether she will recover or not, so as to be servicable to my wife, and as it is my purpose so to provide for my wife as to render it right and proper for me to charge her said bequest & devises with the support and maintenance of my children free of charge. It is my will and desire, and I hereby direct the Guardian of my children to be hereinafter appointed to set apart of the funds to be paid into his hands for the use of my children, the sum of Eight hundred dollars which he shall loan at interest and the interest yearly arising therefrom he shall pay over to my wife as an additional provision for her to...better support herself and children, which yearly payment Guardian shall continue to make until said negro **Nicey** shall die or become incapacitated by disease from labor, in which event to wit: the death or inability of s'd **Nicey** it is my will and desire and I hereby direct, empower and require the Guardian ...to purchase a negro woman with the Eight hundred dollars so set apart of the funds of my children which negro girl so purchased...be permitted to serve my wife free of hire during her natural life, and at her death, s'd negro woman with all her increase shall belong to my children and shall be disposed of by said Guardian as hereinafter directed. And it is expressly directed that if the contingency arises on which said girl is to be purchased ...then the yearly payment of the sum accruing as interest on Eight hundred dollars shall cease, but should said contingency not happen, then said Guardian shall keep said sum funded until my children all come of age, at which period Guardian may call in said sum and distribute the same among my children provided they secure to their mother the annual payment of interest on Eight hundred dollars, and should my children refuse to secure the payment of said sum, then the Guardian shall continue said fund at interest as before directed and pay the interest to my wife as it is my purpose will and desire that my wife shall during her natural life have paid to her yearly the interest arising on Eight hundred dollars, unless it becomes necessary to purchase another slave, in which event she shall have the service of said slave free from hire during her natural life.

5th. In consideration of the ample provision made for the comfort and support of my wife (having a due regard to my circumstances & condition), it is my will and desire that she shall keep my children together, support, clothe and maintain them free of charge, and I hereby declare the support and maintenance of my children to be and constitute a charge and lien on the devises and bequest herein made to my wife. By the word "clothe" as used in the above clause, is intended to be comfortable, everyday clothing and not extra clothing.

6th. I give and devise unto my children the fee simple Estate and remainder interest in the farm, store house and other real estate in and adjoining Mooresburg that I have in the second clause of this will devised to my wife for life, hereby declaring it to be my will and desire that my children shall have said real estate as Tenants in Common, subject to be partitioned or sold at the death of my wife, and after my eldest child shall become of age as in the opinion of the Guardian...aided by the direction of the Chancery Court upon an application ...made for that purpose..shall be deemed best, should my wife die and my oldest child require severance of possession of said real estate before my youngest child shall become of age.

7th. I give and bequeath unto my children (subject to rights of my wife in the second clause of this will) my two negro boys **Houston** and **Nelson**, and as it is now impossible for me to foresee the exegencies that may arise, whether all my children shall be alive at the death or marriage of my wife, or when my youngest child shall become of age, I must therefore give to the Guardian of my children (to be herein after appointed) full power and discretion to act as his judgement may direct, keeping in view the interest of my children. It is my desire...that one of my children shall each own each of said boys provided they shall remain as honest and faithful as slaves as they now are. But should either of them become dishonest, get to drinking ardent spirits to excess, or otherwise become unruly and valueless as slaves, the Guardian is empowered to sell them either at public or private sale,... to the best interest of my children. If said slaves prove faithful and no necessity arises compelling (their) sale, ...on the death or marriage of my wife and coming of age of my youngest child, the Guardian, ...if there be more of my children alive than there are slaves, (to) put said slaves up to be bid for by my children alone, and the highest bidder...shall have the slaves conveyed to...them, her or him, and the aggregate amount thus bid for the slaves or slave shall be divided into as many equal parts as there are children alive, and the purchaser or purchasers shall pay to the child or children that does not get a slave his, her or their equal portion of the value of slave/slaves.

8th. I am the owner of ten shares of the Capitol stock of the E. Tennessee and Virginia Rail Road Company, several calls upon which I have paid. I give and bequeath to my children as Tenants in Common, or joint owners said ten shares in the Capitol stock in said Company. And I will and direct that the Guardian of my children out of the funds willed and given to them pay all the calls regularly as they may be made upon said Capitol stock.

9th. I am the owner of two half-acre lots in the town of Greenville, one on each side and both adjoining the lot conveyed by me to my sister **Margaret Irvin**, wife of **David Irvin**, and on which **David Irvin** now lives. I devise said lots to the Guardian of my children in trust for the following uses...I have agreed with **Margaret Irvin**...and her husband that if **David Irvin** will pay the Guardian ten dollars annually for eight years, then the lots will be conveyed to **Margaret Irvin** and her children in fee. I therefore direct and empower said Guardian (to be appointed) to convey said lots in pursuance of said agreement, provided said payments of ten dollars per year are regularly made. Said payments to be made on the first day of Jan. each and every year, and if not punctually paid to bear interest from and after the day of payment.

10th. I am also the owner of a house and lot in the town of Greenville on the southeast side of town and adjoining the lands of **John Dickson**, being the house in which my sister **Isabella Enart** now lives, and in which my father formerly lived, which house and lot it is my will and desire that my sister **Isabella Enart**, shall be permitted to occupy for three years should she desire to do so, free of rent, and at the end of said term of three years or whenever my sister shall surrender the possession thereof, should she desire to do so before the expiration of three years, it is my will and desire that said house and lot shall by the Guardian of my children be sold at public sale to the highest bidder on a credit of one and two years, taking bond and security for the purchase money.

11th. I am at this time engaged in merchandising, in partnership with **William McFarland** at Spring Vale, Jefferson County, Tenn., which partnership does not expire until about the _____ day of June 1855. As said, business is believed to be prosperous and as I have the utmost confidence in my partner, it is my will that business shall continue if partner is willing, until expiration of the partnership for benefit of my children to whom I bequeth my entire interest in said partnership business.

12th. I hereby nominate and appoint **Robert M. Barton, Esq.** the Guardian of my children, and vest in him all the rights and powers necessary for him to carry out fully every bequest herein before or hereinafter made, or to be made. He is hereby authorized to make such disposition of their slaves hereinbefore willed to them as in his judgment he may decree necessary, and should said **Robert M. Barton, Esq.** from any cause find it necessary to renounce his guardianship, he is hereby authorized to resign said trust to the Chancery Court, who shall be empowered under the direction of said Court to discharge all the trusts and perform all the duties by this my last will required to be performed and discharged by my friend **Robert M. Barton, Esq.** whom I have chosen as the Guardian of my children, and to the end that the provisions of the Eleventh clause of this will may be fully carried out, said Guardian is fully empowered to make settlements with my partner and to require of him Exhibits of the business. He may at his discretion, by the consent of the partner, draw out before the expiration of the business whatever profits may be made.

13th. As I do not wish to involve my friend whom I have chosen as Guardian of my children, it is my will that if any misfortune should befall the partnership business after my death, **Robert M. Barton, Esq.** shall not be liable on account thereof, nor be required to give security for or on account of partnership business, or any of the other trusts imposed upon him, nor shall he be accountable for any loss sustained by reason of any of said trusts, other than such as may arise from gross negligence or fraud on part of the Guardian.

14th. I furthermore declare it to be my will...that said **Robert M. Barton, Esq.** as Guardian of my children shall(share in) the management and control of their education in connection with their mother. That he shall out of their funds provide for said additional clothing (other than the clothing required by this will to be furnished by my wife), as in his judgement is suitable to their state and condition in society.

15. By the first clause of this will I direct my Executor to collect all debts &c due me. I hereby declare and direct that all claims of whatever character due the firm of **McFarland & Dickson**, in the Eleventh clause of this will mentioned shall be excepted out of the operation of said first clause, as it is my will and desire that said partnership business shall be exclusively under the management and control of the children's Guardian.

16th. If in the opinion of the Guardian it will be to the interest of my children to continue said mercantile business, said Guardian is hereby fully authorized to continue said business for such length of time as he may think best, under the same terms as are specified in the present Article of Partnership.

17th. I hereby constitute and appoint my friend **James Etter**, Executor of this my last Will and Testament.

18th. If under this Will it becomes necessary for the Guardian of my children to purchase a negro woman, then at the death of my wife, it is my will and desire that said negro and her increase shall be disposed of for the benefit of my children, or divided among them, as I have in the Seventh Clause of this Will directed the slaves **Houston** and **Nelson** to be disposed of or divided. Note the words "bequeath" on the first page, "on" on the fourth page were interlined, and the words "she paying the losses thereon" were erased before the signing of this my Will.

In witness whereof I have hereunto set my hand and seal. This 1st day of November, 1852.

Wm. S. Dickson (seal)

Signed, sealed and acknowledged in the presence of us, the subscribing witnesses who were called upon and requested by said **William S. Dickson**, the Testator, to witness the attestation of this his last Will and Testament which is written on the **nine** foregoing pages. Witness This the 1st day of November, 1852.

John B. Logan, Felix G. Moore

WILL OF DANIEL DELP

Page 161

Dated: April 1, 1853
Proven: Sept. Term. 1860
J. H. Vance, Clk.

State of Tennessee, Hawkins County. A written Will and Testament.

I, **Daniel Delp**, do make and publish this as my last Will and Testament, hereby revoking & making void all other wills by me at any time made.

First. I direct that my funeral expenses & all my debts be paid as soon after my death as possible out of any money that I may die possessed of or may first come into the hands of my Executor.

Secondly. I give and bequeath to **Margaret Delp** my wife all my personal property & debts, dues and demands that is owing to me in any wise. Also, the tract or parcel of land where I now live containing by estimation 100 acres, be the same more or less, adjoining the lands of **John Manis** and **Christian Pearson** and others during her life, or as long as she remains (my) widow.

Thirdly. I give and bequeath that after her death or marriage, I give unto all the heirs $1.00 each, except **Andrew J. Delp**, my youngest son.

Fourthly. I give and bequeath to **Andrew J. Delp**, my youngest son, the above named parcel of land after **Margaret Delp's** death, his mother, or at any time that she marries and conditions that he manage and takes care and helps provide for his mother during her lifetime or during her widowhood. If he does not take care of her she shall have the liberty to sell the above named tract of land or dispose of it to suit her own convenience at any time that he fails or refuses to heop provide for his mother, except hindered by Providence.

Lastly. I do hereby nominate and appoint **Stephen Delp** my Executor. In witness whereof I do to my will set my hand and seal This the first day of April in the Year of our Lord, One thousand eight hundred and fifty three. Interlined before signing.

(his)
Daniel x Delp (seal)
(mark)

Signed and sealed in our presence and have subscribed our names hereunto in the presence of the Testator. This the 1st day of April, 1853.
Witness: **C. A. Manis, William Anderson, John x Roberson, Pleasant Begley & C. Edison**
(his mark)

WILL OF MARTHA DODSON

Page 163

Dated: August 4. 1853
Proven Nov. Term, 1855

In the Name of God, Amen. I **Martha Dodson** commonly called **Patsey Dodson** of Hawkins County and State of Tennessee being weak of body but of sound mind and memory, calling to mind the mortality of this life, and knowing it is appointed unto all persons once to die, having a desire to dispose of such worldly estate wherewith it hath pleased God to bless me, do hereby make and publish this my last Will & Testament in manner and form following, to wit:

I give and bequeath to my dearly beloved children, **Penelope Mays**, wife of **Beverly Mays, Eliza Dodson, Thomas L. Dodson, William E. Dodson, James H. Dodson, Sanford Dodson & George Dodson** jointly the following named negro slaves, to wit: One woman slave named **Nice**, one negro boy slave named **Jack**. one negro girl slave named **Sis**, likewise one other boy slave named **Dick**, which several named slaves were willed to me by the last Will and Testament of my deceased father **Thomas Johnson**, and are all children of the said negro slave **Nice**.

Item 2nd. It is my wish and desire that all my above named children have jointly an equal interest and share in the above named slaves, arrangement to be made by my Executor hereafter named as shall insure each and every one of my said children their just part and share therein so that they each have share and share alike.

Lastly. I hereby nominate and appoint ___(blank)___ sole Executor of this my last Will and Testament aforesaid.

In testimony whereof I have hereunto set my hand and seal this fourth day of August A.D. 1853.

(her mark)
Martha x Dodson (seal)

___ng and acknowledged in the presence of us:
Test. **Wm. F. Lee**
Test. **Thos. Johnson**

WILL OF JOHN DYKES

Page 164

Dated: February 19, 1855
Proven: June Term, 1855

I, **John Dykes** do make and publish this as my last Will and Testament hereby revoking and making void all other wills by me at any time made.

First. I direct that my funeral expenses and all my just debts be paid as soon after my death as possible out of any money that I may die possessed of or may first come into the hands of my Executor.

WILL OF ASA DAVIS

Dated Dec. 13, 1857
Proven: Jan. Term, 1858

In the Name of God, Amen.

I, Asa Davis of the County of Hawkins and State of Tennessee, being in sound and perfect mind and memory, blessed be God. Calling to mind the uncertainty of this life, do this 13th day of December in the year of our Lord, 1857, make this my last Will and Testament in manner following, viz: I here-by lend to my wife Polly all my property both real and personal during the time that she lives single or during her natural life, and at her death or marriage, I do hereby give and bequeath all my property both real and personal to my sons and daughters, share and share alike to them and their heirs forever.

I do hereby appoint Lilborn Davis Executor of this my last Will and Testament. In witness whereof I the said Asa Davis have to this my last Will and Testament set my hand & seal the day and year above written.

Asa x Davis (seal)
(his mark)

Signed and acknowledged in the
presence of: John Hamblen, C. A. Charles,
Hezekiah Davis

Secondly - I give and bequeath unto my well beloved son Joseph's heirs one dollar.

Thirdly - I give to my son William one dollar.

Fourthly - I give to my son Henry's heirs the sum of one dollar.

Fifthly - I give to my son James one dollar.

Sixthly - I give to my son John one dollar.

Seventhly - I give to my son Thomas one dollar.

Eighthly - I give to my daughter Mary who intermarried with James Mullenix one dollar.

Ninthly - I give to my daughter Susannah who intermarried with James Simpson one dollar.

Tenthly - I give to my son Isham Dykes the sum of one dollar.

11th (sic) I give to my grand daughter Mary and daughter of Susannah Simpson one cow and calf, one bed and furniture, which sums as above mentioned I will and desire that my Executor pay over out of any money that may come to his hands and further my will and desire is that my well beloved wife Susannah have all the remainder of my personal property, money &c that I may die possessed of, also the tract of land whereon my son John now lives, it being a part of a 100 acre entry I bought of G. McCrain and joining the piece I sold to James Simpson, William Dykes & others, supposed to contain about 50 acres, be the same more or less containing the houses, buildings and all improvements pertaining thereto.

And Lastly. I nominate and appoint my son Isham Dykes my Executor to transact all business pertaining to this will.

This 19th day of February, 1855.

John x Dykes (seal)
(his)
(mark)

Signed and acknowledged in our presence:
Branch Tucker & George M. Long

WILL OF EDWARD ERWIN

Dated: Jan. 31, 1794

In the Name of God, Amen.

I Edward Erwin of the County of Hawkins in the Territory South of the River Ohio, being of perfect mind and memory do make ordain, publish and de-clare my last Will and Testament in manner and form following, viz:

I allow my body to be buried in a decent manner, also my worldly goods that divine Providence has in this life blessed me with, I dispose of in manner following:

I allow all my just debts to be paid.

I give and bequeath to my beloved wife after my decease all right and title to the plantation I now live on during her natural life. Also one negro woman named Mariah, one negro boy named Dan, also all the stock of horses, cows, &c, together with all the implements belonging to the farming business.

I give and bequeath to my daughter Frances Erwin one dollar.

I give and bequeath to my son John Erwin one dollar.

I give and bequeath to my son William Erwin one dollar.

I give and bequeath to my son Edward Erwin one dollar.

I give and bequeath to my son Andrew Erwin one dollar.

I give and bequeath to each of the following one dollar: Elizabeth Erwin, my daughter, my sons Robert and Samuel, daughter Mary, son Benjamin.

I give and bequeath to my daughter Sarah Erwin after the death of myself and my wife one half of all my movable Estate except such parts as shall here-after be specified.

WILL OF REBECCA DODSON

Dated: March 2, 1861
Proven: Apr. Term, 1861

I Rebecca Dodson do make this day my last Will and Testament, being of sound mind and usual knowledge, do this day will and bequeath my bay property as follows, Viz: I give unto my youngest son William Dodson my bay horse, second choice of beds and one year's provisions of what I have. I secondly give unto my youngest daughter Winnie Dodson first choice of beds and Bureau and one year's provisions, and all of my table ware and cooking vessels. I thirdly give unto my grandson John Hamilton the bed that I once gave his mother Anna Hamilton, dec'd, which bed was left with me and son in my care, and one year's provisions.

And the rest of all my personal property to be sold at out cry to the highest bidder, and the residue with my present claims be used in paying my just debts and that the remainder of the residue be equally divided between my children, Viz: Delana Stanberry, Arthur Dodson, Elizabeth Yates, Winny Dodson, William Dodson, John Hamilton, and that Arthur Dodson take John Hamilton to raise if it seems to my Executor that William Dodson cannot manage him to an advantage. I give to Wm. M. Arnott possession of the land willed to me for my lifetime and then to my children by my husband John Dodson which has been sold to said Wm. M. Arnott by them. I further appoint Wm. M. Arnott as my Administrator of this my last Will & Testament. This the 2nd day of March, 1861.

Rebecca x Dodson (seal)
(her)

Witness: Wm. M. Arnott
Anderson x Stanberry
(mark)
(his mark)

I give, devise and bequeath unto my daughter **Margaret** my plantation on which I now live, containing 200 acres or more, to her and heirs forever, subject however to the reservation aforesaid in favor of my wife, also one negro girl **Sarah** with all her issue, at my decease. Also one half of my movable Estate at the decease of myself and wife.

I do hereby constitute and appoint my trusty friends **Samuel McPheeters** and **Joseph McMinn** Executors of this my last Will and Testament. And I do hereby revoke, make null and void all and every other past Will and Testament heretofore by me made, ordaining, publishing, making and declaring this and no other to be my last Will and Testament. In witness whereof I have hereunto set my hand and seal. This thirty first day of January A.D. 1794.   **Edward Erwin**

Signed, sealed, published, declared and acknowledged by the said **Edward Erwin** to be his last Will and Testament, in the presence of us who were present at the same time.

Joshua Phipps
Ar. G. McCra
Joseph McMinn

WILL OF JOSEPH EPPERSON

Page 167   Dated: Sept. 26, 1814

In the Name of God, Amen.

I **Joseph Epperson** of the County of Hawkins and State of Tennessee, planter, being in and of imperfect health of body but in and of perfect mind and memory, thanks be given unto God. Calling to mind the mortality of my body and knowing that it is appointed once for all men to die, do make and ordain this my last Will and Testament. That is to say, principally and first of all, I give and recommend my soul to the hands of Almighty God that gave it, and my body I give to the Earth, to be buried in a decent Christian burial at the discretion of my Executors, nothing doubting but at the General Resurrection I shall raise the same again by the mighty power of God. As touching such as my worldly Estate whereas it has pleased God to bless me in this life, I give, devise and dispose of in the following manner and form.

First. I give and bequeath unto my dearly beloved wife **Jane Epperson** and my children all my stock of horses, cattle, hogs & cows, house furniture, and movable effects, together with my plantation on which I now live containing 100 acres, to be by her freely possessed during her widowhood. At the expiration of her time, or at her death I will that the same property except the land should be sold and equally divided between the eight children: **Betsy, Allen, Nancy Epperson, John Epperson, Polly Epperson, Peggy Epperson, Thomas Epperson, Hester Epperson, Patsey Epperson,** Then I will said land to **John & Thos. Epperson** my two sons as their right and property. I also constitute and ordain my dearly beloved wife **Jane Epperson** and **Jesse Epperson** the sole Executors of this last Will and Testament. And I do hereby utterly revoke and disannul all and every other former will, testament, _____, Executors by me before named, willed, bequeathed, ratifying & confirming this and no other to be my Will & Testament. In witness whereof I have hereunto set my hand and seal, This 26th Sept. 1814.

Signed, sealed, published and pronounced and declared by the said **Joseph Epperson** as his last Will and Testament in the presence of us who have hereunto set our names in the presence of each other.

Attest: **Henry Crawley,   Francis Aubraken,   Joseph Epperson** (seal) **Joseph Davis**

WILL OF WILLIAM EPPERSON

Page 169   Dated: _____ Dec., 1823
                                          [See Original 1828]

I, **William Epperson** of the County of Hawkins, State of Tennessee, being weak of body but thanks be to God, of sound mind & memory, do make constitute and ordain this my last Will & Testament in the manner and form hereafter described, that is to say: My will and wish is that after my decease my Executors pay all my just debts, and further, my wish is that he pay to my daughter **Huldy** now **Huldy Boyd** the sum of fifty cents, also pay my daughter **Phanny**, now **Phanny Beard** fifty cents, also my son **Hopson Epperson** fifty cents & also pay my daughter **Sina**, now **Sina Bradshaw** fifty cents and also pay to my daughter **Kassia**, now **Kassia McCleane** fifty cents & also pay to my son **Stephen Epperson** fifty cents, also pay to my daughter **Susannah**, now **Susannah Dickard** fifty cents, & for the many good services my daughter **Nancey** have rendered us, my will and wish is that she have her cow, her wheel, bed and furniture. The remainder of my property of every description I do give and bequeath unto my loving wife **Nancy Epperson** during her life, and after her decease, all such property on hand after her just debts is paid be given to my dutiful son **Harrison Epperson**, together with the like sum of fifty cents. And I do further constitute, make and appoint my son **Harrison Epperson** my lawful Executor of this my last Will and Testament.

In witness thereof I have made my mark This ____ day of December, 1823.

In presence of: **William x Epperson**
John Gibbons, Rob't McMinn, Stephen Epperson   (his mark)

WILL OF CHRISLEY EVERHART

Page 169   Dated May 28, 1842

In the Name of God, Amen.

I, **Chrisley Everhart** have this day published this my last Will and Testament in manner and form as follows, to wit:

First. My will and desire is as soon after my decease as practicable, I desire that all my household and kitchen furniture of every kind, all my farming tools that belong to the farm of every kind, all of my stock of each and every kind except that which I will hereafter mention be sold, and out of the proceeds thereof all my just debts and funeral expenses be paid.

Second. I give and bequeath to my wife **Lizzy Everhart** my cupboard and furniture that belongs to the cupboard. I give to her one cow, and my flax wheel.

Secondly. I give to my three sons all my tract of land (Viz) **John Everhart, William Everhart** and **Samuel Everhart**, to be equally divided between them. I also give to my son **William** my wagon and the gearing that belong to it and no more.

Third. I give to my son **Jacob** one dollar of my Estate and no more.

Fourth. I give to my son **James** one dollar of my Estate and no more.

Fifth. I desire that after all my property is sold and all my just debts are collected and expenses paid, then the balance of the proceeds be equally divided between my three daughters, **Elizabeth Spears** and her heirs, **Sarah Stewart** and daughter **Polly Everhart** and my grand daughter **Anny Smith**.

Sixth. My will is that my wife **Lizzy** have free privilege to live in my house where she now lives during her life if she chooses, and then to be supported by my three sons that I gave my land to, Viz: **John, William** and **Samuel**, and after my wife's death, the property I willed her be equally divided between her said daughters that are living at the time of my wife's decease.

In witness whereof I have hereunto set my hand and affixed my seal, on the 28th day of May, Eighteen hundred and fifty two.

Attest: Christley x Everhart (seal)

Jim Arnott
(his mark)

David Reynolds

WILL OF JOHN ELLIS

Dated: June 6, 1840

Know all men by these presents that I, John Ellis, Sr., of Hawkins Co., Tennessee, being of sound mind & memory but taking into consideration the uncertainty of human life & being desirous to settle my worldly affairs, do ordain & establish this my last Will & Testament.

Imprimis: I give and bequeath to my oldest daughter Joanna Ellis the following lot of land, being a part of the tract on which I now reside. Beginning at the old beginning corner on King's Old Line, a white oak and some gums. Then running with King's Old Line to the stage road, then along the stage road to within 52 poles of the middle of the passage between the two pins of the houses in which I reside to a stake in the middle of the stage road. Then square off at right angles to the road 30 poles to a stake, then 52 poles parallel with the stage road to a stake in the apple orchard, opposite the middle of the passage of my dwelling house, so as to include the row of apple trees, south of said line. Thence southwardly to include the kitchen, passing through the passage of the house to a stake in the middle of the stage road. Then along the stage road to the race or branch, then along the race to the lower end of the meadow, then to include four die of the stage road. Then a straight line to the beginning, including a right of way and water to the spring I use & including a right to use the timber for firewood and repairs off any of the lands I now own.

To have and to hold during her natural life and at her death to be equally divided among the heirs of her body if any she have then living & in default of heirs of her own body, then to descend to my own right heirs, share and share alike. I also give to her one horse beast to be worth one hundred dollars, also two cows & calves & three beds & furniture which her mother gave & which she has since made (feather beds?), and also what she may make hereafter, also the cupboard & dairy and half the furniture in them. Also her chest & my own, also two pots & two ovens, one desk. I also bequeath to Joanna my negro boy George and my negro girl Francis.

In the second place, I will & bequeath to my daughter Betsey one horse beast & saddle to be worth one hundred and twenty dollars, two beds & furniture which her mother gave & what she has since made or may hereafter make for herself. Also one cow & calf & one heifer. Also my Mulatto girl Harriet, a slave for life. Also two pots and two ovens & one half of my cupboard furniture, also her chest. Also a Bureau, one book case. Also while she remains single she is to have the use of the west end of my dwelling house & small room adjoining & the stable between the house & spring.

In the third place, I give and bequeath to my sons William and John as trustees in trust for the use and benefit of my daughter Nancy Fisher one tract of land where John Richardson lives amounting to one (100) hundred acres, or thereabouts, on the west end of the tract including the land in possession of Richardson, and one thousand dollars in money. The trustees

Page 171

aforesaid are to loan out said money at interest on the best security & to vest it in some safe stock yielding an annual or semi-annual interest & to collect and pay over annually the interest to her separate use and benefit during her life unless her husband James Fisher should die or be divorced from her before her death. In that event, the principal may be paid over to her if said trustees should deem it advisable; but if she dies before James Fisher and (is) not divorced from him, then said one thousand dollars and interest shall pass to her heirs, if any. If none, then it is to be equally divided among my own right heirs. The tract of land on which Richardson lives is to vest in my sons William and John, their heirs and assigns forever, in trust for the separate use and benefit of said daughter during her natural life, and at her death to the use of her heirs if any, and in default of her heirs then of my own right heirs. During the intermarriage of my daughter Nancy & James Fisher the exclusive control of the land shall be vested in said trustees and they shall have full authority either to put it into the possession of my said daughter herself or to rent it out to some body else & pay over to her the annual rents as they may deem most for her advantage.

In the fourth place, I give & bequeath to my son John Ellis one cow & calf & one bed & furniture.

In the fifth place, it is my will and desire that all the rest of my real estate not otherwise disposed of be equally divided between my sons William, Guy & John Ellis & my daughters Jane Butts & Betsey Ellis, share and share alike, to them & their heirs forever, and that Orville Bradley, William Hord and Philip S. Hale be commissioners and divide the land between them.

In the sixth place, it is my will that all my negroes and other personal Estate not otherwise disposed (of) be sold and after the payment of all just claims against me, the legacy to Nancy Fisher's use, be equally divided between my sons William, Guy & John and daughters Jane Butts & Betsey Ellis, share and share alike to each.

It is my wish that my son, William Ellis, and my friend Philip S. Hale be Executors of this my last Will & Testament.

In witness whereof I have hereunto set my hand and affixed my seal.
This 6th day of June, 1840.   John Ellis (seal)

Witnesses present:
Orville Bradley & Wm. M. Alexander

Codicil to my will heretofore made, to wit, on the sixth of June, 1840 & witnessed by Wm. M. Alexander & Orville Bradley, said will is hereby confirmed in all particulars except as it is altered by this codicil. It is my will that the following alterations and additions be made...My daughter Joanna shall have the girl Mary instead of the boy George. Instead of the land and pounds given her by said will on the north side of the stage road, she shall now have the whole of my house & yard & garden & three rows of the apple orchard joining thereto and instead of four acres at the lower end of my meadow, she is to have four acres at the upper end of said meadow. I also will & bequeath her a piece of the land I bought of Wm. Ellis adjoining the land willed to her on the south side of the stage road, beginning on the stage road at or near a white oak near the new barn. Thence southwardly to include my turnip patch & Thence on the same course to C. McKinney's line & thence along said line to the lines of the land heretofore willed to her.

The land now willed is to be held in the same manner as that devised in my will of 1840. **Joanna** shall also have the other bureau and my clock in the east room, and **Betsey** (is to have) the clock in the west room. I hereby reduce my legacy by one thousand dollars given by my former will for the use of **Nancy Fisher** to Seven Hundred and fifty dollars. I give to my son **John Ellis** in fee simple 45 acres of the land I bought of **William Ellis**, to be laid off adjoining the land given to **Joanna**, running from the stage road to **McKinney's** line to be bounded by parallel lines. The balance of the land I bought of **Wm Ellis** lying between the tract devised to **John Ellis** & the lands of **Orville Bradley**, I will to my son **Guy Ellis** in fee simple. Given under my hand & seal this 24th day of July, 1843.

Witnesses Present: **John Ellis** (seal)
Orville Bradley & Wm. M. Alexander

The following codicil I make to my will of 1840 & the aforesaid codicil, confirming them in all respects except as altered by this codicil: It is my will that the following alterations be made in the devise of the **Richardson** Place to my daughter ___ **Fisher**, viz: The line shall begin at the orchard to include the orchard and clover field fence. Then a straight line with the clover field fence to the new fence, then with the new fence a straight course to my back line & this to be the line between & whoever of my children may get the adjoining land, to be held in the same way & same uses as provided in my first will above named, and her legacy of seven hundred and fifty dollars to be reduced to five hundred dollars to be held as vested, as provided for in my will aforesaid. It is my will that my son **John Ellis** shall after the death of my daughter **Joanna** have the house I live in & the lots around it, on the north side of the road devised to said **Joanna** on the north side of the road, provided **Joanna** should die without heirs of her body. If **Joanna** leaves children the said house & lots to vest in them.

It is my will that my daughter **Fisher** shall have the separate use of & benefit of my black girl **Sarah** in the same way that I have given the land to her. The said **Sarah** is therefore willed to my sons **John & William** as trustees to do with said slave and her increase in the same way as already provided in my will they are to do with the land. Given under my hand & seal this 27th Feb'y, 1844.

Witnesses present: **John x Ellis**(seal)
O Bradley   (his mark)
Josephine A. Crauder

WILL OF THOMAS ELLISON

Page 175   Dated: Mar. 29, 1852
                                      Proven: 1855

I **Thomas Ellison** do make and publish this as my last Will and Testament, hereby revoking and making void all other wills by me at any time made.

First. I direct that my funeral expenses and all my debts be paid as soon after my death as possible out of any money that I may die possessed of or I will that my wife **Elizabeth Ellison** sell property off the farm to pay off the same.

Secondly. I will and bequeath to my wife **Elizabeth Ellison** all my land during her natural life time and all my property of every description so long as she may live. Then after her death, I will and bequeath that my

wife **Elizabeth Ellison's** two grand children, **Thomas Ellison** and **Frances Ellison**, shall have all my land and possessions equally divided between them so as to divide the house that each one can have a room and all the property of every description, except what is otherwise disposed of.

Thirdly. I will and bequeath that my son **Edmond Ellison** shall have ten dollars at the death of my wife **Elizabeth Ellison**.

In witness whereof I do to this my will set my hand and seal. This 29th day of March, 1852.

                              Thomas x Ellison (seal)
                                      (his mark)

Signed, sealed and published in our presence, and we have subscribed our names hereto in the presence of the Testator. This 29th day of March,1852.
Attest: **Urial Boms (Bones), Rob't Cooper, John H. x Arnold**
                                      (his mark)

WILL OF POLLY EVERHART

Page 176   Dated: May 19, 1852
                                      Proven: July Term, 1852

I, **Polly Everhart**, do make and publish this my last Will and Testament, hereby revoking and making void all other wills by me at any time made.

First. I direct that my debts be paid and my other expenses out of any money that may be coming to me.

Second. I give and bequeath to my sister, **Sally Stewart**, my bed and bed clothing, also my flax wheel and reel, all my clothing, also my clock.

Lastly. I do hereby nominate and appoint **David Stewart** my Executor. In witness whereof I do to this my will set my hand and seal This 18th day of May, 1852.

                              Polly x Everhart (seal)
                                      (her mark)

Signed, sealed and published in our presence and we have subscribed our names hereto in the presence of the Testator. This 18th of May, 1852.
Jac Arnott, William x Everhart
            (his mark)

WILL OF WILLIAM EIDSON, SR.

Page 176   Dated: Jan. 24, 1859
                                      Proven: March Term, 1859

I, **William Eidson**, Sr. do make and publish this my last Will & Testament, hereby revoking & making void all other wills by me at any time made.

1st. I direct that my funeral expenses and all my debts be paid as soon after my death as possible out of any money I may die possessed of or may first come into the hands of my Executor.

2nd. I will, give and bequeath to my youngest son **Larkin W. Eidson**, all my land containing 375 acres, lying in Hawkins County, Tenn., Dist. #3, adjoining the lands of **Swinefield Eidson, Isaac Bloomer** & others, to have said land after my death and my wife's after which he must pay to **Creton Eidson**, my oldest son, $265.00 and each of my children now living the like sum, to wit: **Willson Eidson, Wm. Eidson, Samuel Eidson, Elizabeth Frost, Martha Hunter;** likewise my will is...he pay to my grand children, to wit:

Swinefield Bidson, John Bidson & William Klepper, $50.00 each. The above
money to be paid to the above named heirs at the expiration of three years
after my death and my wife Martha Bidson's. My will is that Larkin W.
Bidson has the hole control of all my lands after my death and that he take
care of and provide for his mother during her lifetime.

3rd. It is my will and desire that all my personal property be sold
after my death except one choice cow, one sow and pigs and all the household and kitchen furniture which I will to my wife Martha Bidson.

4th. I will and bequeath to my son Creton Bidson, $100.00 after my
death out of the proceeds of my personal estate.

5th. I will and it is my (desire) that after my debts is all paid out
of my property that the balance of the proceeds of my personal Estate go to
my son Larkin W. B. son if anything left.

Lastly. I nominate & appoint my son Larkin W. Bidson my Executor to
this my last Will & Testament.

In witness whereof I do to this my will set my hand and seal This the
twenty fourth day of January, Eighteen Hundred & fifty nine.

William x Bidson (seal)
(his mark)

Signed, sealed & published in our presence, and we have subscribed our names
hereto in presence of the Testator this January 24th, 1859.

C. A. Manis, John Starnes

WILL OF ANDREW FORGEY

Page 178

Dated: February 8, 1809

In the Name of God, Amen.

I, Andrew Forgey of the State of Tennessee and County of Hawkins, being
for sometime past in a declining state of health, but of sound mind and memory, and calling to mind the mortality of all men that it is appointed to all
once to die, do by these presents publish and declare this to be my last will
& Testament in writing in the following manner, Viz: After commending my
soul to God and my body from whence it came, to be buried in decent and Christian manner, hoping they will be again united to the general
resurrection (sic) and received into the favor of God. And concerning such
worldly goods as it has been pleasing to the Almighty to bestow on me, I do
dispose of in the following manner, that is to say. I desire all my just
debts to be paid out of my movable property at the discretion of my Executors
whom I shall hereafter name.

Item. I do give and bequeath to my son Andrew Forgey, Junior a part of
the tract of land I now live on butted and bounded as followeth: Beginning
on the main road opposite a cross fence about half way between where I now
live and where my son Andrew lives, then along said fence and to continue
the course thereof to the back line of said tract. Then with said line to
a chestnut corner of said tract. Then along the line dividing my land from
a tract whereon Benoni Coldwell now lives to the old road that is nearest
to my son Andrew's fence. Then with said road to the beginning, including
the house and plantation whereon my son Andrew now lives.

Item. Whereas I had given to my son John Forgey another part of said
tract and have made him a right to the same which he has since sold to my son
James Forgey and has received payment, and I being anxious to secure the said
part to James for the considerations above, I do therefore bequeath to James
Forgey the said part which is bounded as followeth: Beginning on the road

at the place where Andrew Forgey's began, opposite the before mentioned
cross fence, running the course of the same so as to make a straight line
across the valley from one line of the grant to the other, and all the
land contained in my grant between said line and the line of the tract
whereon Benoni Coldwell now lives, and on the opposite side of the above
mentioned road from where my son Andrew now lives, including the improvements made by John Forgey whereon Hugh Forgey now lives.

Item. I do lend to my beloved wife Margaret Forgey my negro boy
Bacchus during her life, and after her decease to be equally divided
between my sons Andrew and John.

Item. I do lend to my said wife the other part of my plantation (from
the before mentioned cross fence) with the appurtenances during her life
and after her death the title thereof to be vested in my son James Forgey.

Item. I do lend to my said wife all my goods and chattels not otherwise disposed of during her natural life and after her decease to be equally
divided between all my daughters.

Item. I do give to my son Hugh Forgey $100.00 to be paid to him by my
son James out of his part of the plantation.

Item. I appoint and request my beloved son James Forgey and my trusty
friend Benoni Coldwell to be my Executors of this my last Will and Testament
in writing. And do by these presents disannul and make void every other
will or wills by me made.

In witness whereof I have hereunto set my hand and affixed my seal This
Eighth day of February, One thousand eight hundred and nine.

In presence of us: Andrew Forgey (seal)
James M. Bellomy
Isam Looney

WILL OF HENRY FELCKNOR

Page 179

Dated: Feb'y 15, 1810

In the Name of God, Amen.

I Henry Felcknor of the County of Hawkins in the State of Tennessee,
being sick and weak in body but of sound mind &c, considering the certainty
of death and the uncertainty of the time thereof, and being desirous to
settle my worldly affairs and thereby be the better prepared to leave this
world when it shall please God to call me hence, do therefore make and
publish this my last Will and Testament in manner and form following, that
is to say. I give and bequeath unto my wife Rosanna Felcknor all my household
goods of every kind, and all my stock of cattle consisting of cattle
and sheep and hogs (as for horses, I have not any), during her life and then
to be sold by my Executors and equally divided amongst my daughters and my
grand daughters, Polly Lewis Felcknor, daughter to Louis Felcknor, deceased,
(Catherine, wife to Anthony Baker, Charlotte, wife to George Baker, Elizabeth
wife to Stophel Shotts, Tweday wife to Phillip P. Baker, Susan wife to Jacob
Sensabaugh and my grand daughter Polly Lewis Felcknor). I allow my Executors
to take an inventory of my stock at my death. I give and bequeath unto my
sons Phillip and George Felcknor the tract of land they now live on, to be
equally divided between them, to their use forever. I give and bequeath unto
my son Jacob Felcknor the tract of land I now live on and all my lands adjoining said tract, and further I injoin it on my son Jacob to furnish his
mother with every necessary she stands in need of during her life. I give

and bequeath to my daughter **Elizabeth Shotts** the one half of the tract of land I own in Sullivan County or the value thereof when sold. I give unto my sons **Phillip, Martin, George & Jacob** each an equal part of 100 acres of land I purchased lying near the Muscle Shoals and if sid land should not be obtained, I leave my son **Jacob** to pay my son **Martin** one hundred dollars, and lastly, I do hereby constitute and appoint my son **Jacob Felcknow** and **Arthur Galbraith Armstrong** to be my sole Executors of this my last Will and Testament.

In testimony whereof I have hereunto set my hand and affixed my seal. This fifteenth day of February in the year of our Lord, One Thousand Eight hundred and Ten, in the presence of the subscribing witnesses.
Test: **Henry Felcknor** (seal)
W. Armstrong, George Argenbright, Jacob Livingston

WILL OF JAMES FINLEY

Page 181   Dated: Feb'y 23, 1814
In the Name of God, Amen.

I, **James Finley**, of the County of Hawkins and State of Tennessee, being weak in body, but of sound mind and memory, do make this my last Will and Testament, revoking all others.

Item. To my two sons **Samuel** and **William**, I bequeath the plantation I now live on, to them and their heirs forever, with all my lands adjoining said tract, to be equally divided between them, they are to maintain my wife decently during her life.

To my daughter **Nancy McCollough** I give and bequeath my negro girl **Eliza**, to her and her heirs forever. To my daughter **Sally Argenbright** I give and bequeath my negro child named **Sid**. Should my negro woman **Jin** have any children hereafter, I give and bequeath the first born to my daughter **Prudence Finley**. Should she not have any more children, I give and bequeath her to my daughter **Prudence Finley** at the decease of my wife. I give and bequeath my negro woman **Jin** to my wife **Prudence** to dispose of as she thinks proper, her and her issue except such as is heretofore disposed of. To my wife **Prudence** I give and bequeath the buildings where I now live with all the movable property to dispose of as she thinks proper. And lastly, I appoint my wife **Prudence** and my son **Samuel Finley** to be my sold Executors of this my last Will and Testament. Given under my hand and seal This twenty third day of February in the year of our Lord one thousand Eight hundred and fourteen.
Witness: **James Finley** (seal)
A. G. Armstrong (Jurat)
Samuel Finley

WILL OF ROBERT FROST

Page 181   Dated: Mar. 21, 1819
                                             Proven Aug. Term, 1819

This is my last Will and Testament made in the year of our Lord 1819. I want the land on (the) South side Clinch River equally divided betwixt my three eldest sons, **Thomas Frost, William Frost & Simeon Frost**, and I want **Wm. Farmer** and his wife **Elizabeth Farmer** to have the upper end of survey down to the steep gut which lies on the north side of said river.

The remainder part of the land and what other property is left for **Sarah Frost** to raise the children in during her widowhood, & as the children grows up I want **Sarah Frost** the widow of **Robert Frost** to divide the land and property to be as near equal with the other children as possible. Interlined before assigned. (sic) This being my last will and Testament, whereunto I set my hand and seal, March the 21st, 1819.
Witness: **Robert x Frost** (seal)
R. W. Lovin   (his mark)
William Farmer

WILL OF ANDREW FORGEY

Page 182   Dated: August 13, 1830
In the Name of God, Amen.   [See original will]

I, **Andrew Forgey** being weak in body but sound in mind and memory do make this my last Will & Testament in manner and form as follows, to wit:

I do will and bequeath unto my beloved wife **Isabella** my house and one third part of the plantation, with all my farming tools, wagon excepted, which is to be given to my son **John** at my decease, and all my household and kitchen furniture and my negro man **Bachus** to my wife during her life. I do also bequeath unto her all my stock of horses, cattle, hogs & sheep so long as she may live except one horse to the value of fifty dollars and a saddle and bridle to be worth seventeen dollars which is to be given to my bound boy **Harvey Taylor** when he shall arrive at the age of 21 years old. At my death I do bequeath unto my son **John** the two remaining thirds of my land, and at the death of my wife, I do will unto said **John** my negro man **Bachus**, together with the dower that is set apart for my wife which includes all my landed possessions and all the property, stock, household, and kitchen furniture remaining at the death of my wife is to be equally distributed between my two daughters **Margaret Crawford** and **Rebecah Crawford**. And I do hereby nominate and appoint **Smith Hale** and my son **John Forgey** Executors to carry this my last Will & Testament fully into effect. In witness whereof I have set my hand and seal, This 13th day of August, 1830.
                                             Andrew Forgey (seal)
Attest: **B. Coldwell**
         Thomas Coldwell

WILL OF GEORGE FELKNER

Page 183   Dated Oct. 13, 1830
I, **George Felkner** of the County of Hawkins and State of Tennessee, being afflicted in body but yet sound in mind and feeling sensibly the uncertainty of this mortal life & the certainty of death, do make this my last Will and Testament.

First. My desire & will is that after my death my mortal remains be decently interred & that my funeral expenses be defrayed.

2nd. That my just debts be paid, then my property real and personal be disposed of in the following manner:

1st. I bequeath unto my wife **Susan Felkner** all my lands during her widowhood, but should she marry again my will is that she have her Dower as allowed by law & then my children to have their share in the lands laid off to them respectively.

2nd. I also give and bequeath unto my son **John Felkner** one sorrel horse three years old next spring. The remaining part of my personal property I give and bequeath unto my wife **Susan Felkner** including my stock of horses, cattle and hogs, sheep, farming utensils and household and kitchen furniture and other property in common not herein named which I am possessed of to her use for the purpose of raising and supporting my children, but at the expiration of her widowhood, the personal estate to be sold and equally divided among my children. I also will that my wife **Susan** be my sole Executrix.

In testimony whereof I have hereunto set my hand & affixed my seal, This 13th of October, 1830. In presence of:

Philip Felkner, Jacob Felkner, Wm. Armstrong, George x Felkner (seal)

(his mark)

WILL OF JAMES FORGEY

Page 183   Dated: May 13, 1831

In the Name of the Father, Son and Holy Ghost, three persons but one God, I **James Forgey** of the County of Hawkins and State of Tennessee, calling to mind the certainty of death and yet the uncertainty of the time when, do make and ordain this my last Will and Testament in the words following, Viz: After commending my soul to God and my body to the dust to be buried in a decent Christian manner, hoping they will again be united at the general resurrection, and enjoy a glorious immortality, I proceed to dispose of my worldly goods and chattels that God has blessed me with in the following manner, Viz: I allow all my just debts to be paid out of my movable property.

Item. I leave the use of the plantation I live on and my household furniture of every description to my beloved wife **Margaret** during her life. And the household furniture to be disposed of at her discretion, and at her decease I leave my said plantation to my son **James Reynolds,** together with the appurtenances, stock of all kind and farming utensils, except the lower end of the farm where I settled my daughter **Polly** on and her husband **Dickerson Thurmon.** Beginning on a hickory on or near **Jacob Miller's** line which had a block chopped out of it some time past and which stands in a hollow opposite the middle of the field we call the Forty Acre field, then running straight across the Forty Acre field so as to include half of said field. Thence in the same direction to **Jacob Miller's** line on to the top of the ridge, all the land on the west side of above described line I bequeath to my daughter **Polly** and her heirs.

Item 3. I give to my daughter **Rachael** a lot of land joining to the one I gave to **Polly.** Beginning on **Miller's** line on the south side of the Forty Acre field on the same hickory that **Polly's** began on and running east with **Miller's** line to an ash and sassafrass, each of them has three chops of a tomahawk and stand on the east side of a wet weather branch and on the south side of a little field we call the Wet Patch and running from thence thru said wet patch and across the road to the cross fence on east side of the old clover field, then with the course of said fence to the top of the ridge, all of the land west of said line and east of **Polly's** line I give and bequeath unto my daughter **Rachael.** I also give and bequeath to my daughter **Rachael** all the land that I own on the east side of the creek where I live joining **Lijah Kincheloe, Thos Coldwell** and **David Laughmiller** with the appurtenances. I also give and bequeath to my daughter **Rachael** a little yellow boy named **Tom** going on one year old. I also allow my daughter **Rachael** a good horse.

Item 4. I give and bequeath to the heirs of my daughter **Ellen** to be enjoyed by her during her life time and then to her heirs in fee simple forever, the lot of land lying on the south side of Holston River, containing

73 acres or thereabouts, being the land that I bought of **John Coldwell** some years ago for $800.00, also 100 acres I entered joining it and **Square William Armstrong's** land on the lower side of the creek, and likewise, the 50 acres I bought of **William Elzy** on the lower side of the creek.

Item 5. I give and bequeath to my daughter **Matilda** one other lot of land joining above the one before described conveyed to me by **Lijah Kincheloe,** containing 63 or 64 acres, also one lot conveyed to me by **Joseph Woods** containing three or four acres, likewise one lot of one acre, a mill seat. I also bequeath to my daughter **Matilda** one little yellow girl named **Sarah** about three years old. I also allow **Matilda** to have a good horse.

Item 6. I give and bequeath to my daughter **Betsy** and her husband **John Harlan** one other lot of land joining still above which I bought of **Soloman Walters** and joining to **John Lyon's** land, containing 64 or 65 acres with an equal share of what upland I own on the upper or east side of Terrels Creek.

Item 7. I give and bequeath to my two grand daughters **Eliza** and **Malvinia Rogers** the 160 acres of land I bought of **Alexander M. Broom** lying in Illinois, also the 160 acres of land I bought of **Thomas Bray** lying in Missouri or Ark., and each of them to have an equal interest in both.

Item 8. I request my son **James** to give to my grandson **John Rogers** a tolerable good horse, saddle and bridle, say worth sixty or seventy dollars.

Item 9. All the up land that has not been named in the above items that I own on the south side of Holston River I wish to be divided between **Matilda** and **Betsy.**

Item 10. I leave my yellow boy **Joseph** and his wife **Peggy** to my beloved wife during her life, and at her decease for them and their issue to be equally divided amongst my daughters, and it is my request that **James** would keep them at a moderate price and for them not (to be) separated themselves, but their children may be divided between the girls.

Item 11. All the land that I own on this side of Holston River that has not been disposed of in any of the above items I leave to my son **James** at the decease of my beloved wife.

And I do hereby appoint my said beloved wife **Margaret** and my said son **James Reynolds** Executors...of this my last Will and Testament.

In testimony whereof I have hereunto set my hand and seal This thirteenth day of May, in the year of our Lord one thousand eitht hundred and thirty one.

N.B. The word "plantation" and the words "I leave my said plantation" on first page were interlined before signing.

James Forgey (Seal)

Signed, sealed, published and declared by the said **James Forgey** to be his last Will and Testament in the presence of us:

S. Powel, William Lyons, Thomas Coldwell

Codicil to the last Will and Testament of **James Forgey.** Whereas I **James Forgey** of the County of Hawkins and State of Tennessee did make and execute my last Will & Testament bearing date of 13 May 1831, and still remaining of sound disposing mind for which I do thank Almighty God for his kind favor bestowed on me, and wishing to alter and amend said will in the following particulars:

1st. It is my will that instead of my debts being paid out of my movable property that they be paid by my son **James Reynolds Forgey** except as hereafter excepted. I consider the land I willed to him of more value than any other lot.

2nd. It is my will that the lots devised by my will to my daughter **Polly's** heirs, my daughter **Rachael,** and my son **James R.** run no further north nor out of the land I purchased of **James Hagan** except as hereinafter described. That is, all the land that I own lying north and west of said tract purchased of **Hagan** to be equally divided between the three according to quality and quality.

3rd. It is my will that the land I purchased of **John Coldwell, Soloman Walters and Elijah Kincheloe,** lying on the south side of Holston River and not included in what is known as low ground or river lots that is all the land that I own back of the river lots to be divided equally between my three daughters, **Ellen Rogers, Matilda Miller** and **Betsy Horton** agreeable to quality and quantity, to be laid off that their back lands will join their river lots.

4th. It is my will that at the decease of my beloved wife, my boy **Jo** have the choice of a master amongst my children for himself and wife. Said negroes to be valued at a moderate price to whomsoever of my children **Jo** may choose to live with, and their value to be equally divided between my daughters **Ellen, Matilda, Betsy** and **Rachael** and the children of my daughter **Polly** dec'd. **Polly's** children together to have an equal share with my daughters, but if I should hereafter contract debts the proceeds of said negroes is to be applied to debts with balance being divided among my children and grand children.

5th. It is my will that my two small negroes **Alsy & Robert** be disposed of as follows: **Alsy** to son-in-law **John Harlon** and **Cornelius C. Miller** in trust for my daughter **Ellen** during her life; my daughter to have the use of and control over her during her life and at her death said negro to go to her heirs. I will and bequeth the said boy **Robert** to my daughter **Betsy.**

6th. In addition to what I have already bequeathed to my son **James,** I bequeath to him at the decease of my beloved wife all the personal property that may be then on hand and not disposed of by my (earlier) will and this codicil. In testimony whereof I have herewith set my hand and seal This 29th day of August, 1834.

James Forgey (seal)

Signed, sealed, published & declared by the said **James Forgey** to be a codicil to his last Will and Testament.

S. Powel, Geo. R. Powel, Thomas Coldwell

WILL OF RACHAEL FORGEY

Page 187   Dated: Mar. 27, 1837
State of Tennessee, Hawkins County

Whereas human life is at all times uncertain and whereas I, **Rachael Forgey** am weak in body but of sound disposing memory, and whereas it is my wish to dispose of my property myself and arrange my own affairs, therefore, I do ordain and publish this my last Will & Testament, revoking and annulling all others. In the first place, it is my will that all just claims against me for my funeral expenses and of all other descriptions shall be first paid. In the second place, it is my will that after such payment of debts & charges all the rest of my property both real & personal shall go to my mother, **Margaret Forgey** for her in fee simple to be at her absolute disposal by deed, will or otherwise except that I will to each of my sisters: **Rogers, Harlon & Miller** each one feather bed and furniture, & it is also my request that my mother shall divide what household articles I may leave at my death among my sisters. & I do hereby constitute & appoint my brother **James R. Forgey** Exec. of this my last Will and Testament. In testimony whereof I the said **Rachael Forgey** have hereunto set my hand & affixed my seal This 29th day of March, 1837.

Rachael Forgey (seal)

Signed, sealed and acknowledged before
us: **Orville Bradley**
    Thomas Coldwell

WILL OF DANIEL FLORA

Page 188   Dated: June 19, 1838
State of Tennessee)
Hawkins County   )   Know all men by these presents that I, **Daniel Flora** of the County of Hawkins and State aforesaid do make, ordain and foreordain this to be my last Will and Testament. First and foremost, I want my body to be buried in good Christian burial. Next, I want all my just dues, debts and demands satisfied. I bequeath unto my wife **Charlotte Flora** one year's substance. I bequeath unto my son **Joseph** one fourth part of my land including the building where I now live by him maintaining my wife **Charlotte** during her life. The rest to be divided among my three sons: **Jacob, Daniel** and **Abraham** by giving **Daniel** $30.00, **Jacob, Joseph** and **Abraham** to pay the $30.00 out of the value of their part in the land. I bequeath unto my five daughters each $100.00 apiece, Viz: **Nancy, Charlotte, Polly, Lucinda** and **Evline.**

I leave my son **Joseph** Executor of my will and also Guardian of the minor heirs by his giving bond and approved security.

Daniel x Flora
(his mark)

Signed and delivered and acknowledged in the presence of us in the year of our Lord the 19th of June, 1838.
Thomas Chesnutt
Jacob Beal

WILL OF DANIEL FLORA

Page 189   Dated: April 28, 1840
Be it remembered that I, **Daniel Flora**, of the County of Hawkins and State of Tenn., being weak in body but of sound mind and memory, do make this my last Will and Testament.

First. My will and desire is that all my just debts and funeral expenses be first paid and satisfied out of my Estate.

Secondly. I will and bequeath to my beloved wife **Nancy** all my estate of every description whatever, consisting principally of horse beasts, cattle, hogs, some farming utensils and household furniture, and do hereby nominate and appoint my said beloved wife **Nancy** Executrix of this my last Will and Testament, and my will and desire is that my Executrix be not required to give and security for the due execution of this my said last Will and testament.

In testimony whereof I have hereunto set my hand and seal This 25th day of April, in the year of our Lord one thousand eight hundred and forty.

Daniel x Flora (seal)
(his mark)

Signed, sealed and acknowledged in the presence of us:
S. Powel
Jas. M. Armstrong

WILL OF THOMAS A. FLETCHER

Page 189   Dated: November 30, 1841
In the Name of God, Amen.

I, **Thomas A. Fletcher** of the County of Hawkins in the State of Tenn., being of perfect sound mind & memory, but at the same time knowing the certainty of death and the uncertainty of life and being far advanced in

First. To my son John P. Fletcher I give and bequeath one Lindsey suit of clothes now wore by me, consisting of coat, jacket & pantaloons.

2nd. To my son William I give a receipt in full for all he owed me.

3rd. To my son Thomas I give a clean discharge of all debts due me and the same to my son James.

4th. To my daughters Janey Hettin, Polly O Daniel, Peggy Fletcher & Frankey Etter I also give receipts in full for all claims I hold on them and their husbands.

5th. And in consideration of the kind treatment and attention I have & am now receiving from my son-in-law Anthony Smith & his wife Elizabeth, my daughter, at whose house I am now living under their care and attention, I give and bequeath all the remainder of my Estate both real and personal for the reason that I have given my other children their full share of my Estate, and they have no cause to complain. Inasmuch as my dearly beloved daughter Elizabeth and her husband Anthony Smith have been supporting and taking care of me, and still intend to do so therefore, I more cheerfully make them my sole heirs and devisees of what ever estate I may possess at my death.

6th. I desire that I may be decently intered at the place where I am now living, at Anthony Smith's in Hawkins County.

7th. I hereby nominate and ordain said Anthony Smith to be my sole Executor and request that the Court shall not require any bond and security of him as Executor of my Estate.

In testimony whereof I hereunto set my hand & seal This thirteenth day of November in the year of our Lord, 1841.

Test.   T. A. Fletcher (seal).
Stephen Johnson Decease
Matilda Johnson
Beverley O. Ford
William D. x Johnson
          (his mark)

(Note: The following clause was written below the names above)

"Sole heirs an devisees of whatever Estate I may leave at my death."

Page 190

WILL OF MARGARET FORGEY

Dated: Dec. 20, 1843
Proven 6th April 1846

In the Name of God, Amen, I Margaret Forgey of the County of Hawkins and State of Tennessee, being sensible that according to the law of nature that I must shortly leave this world and trusting and hoping to receive the reward of the righteous made perfect in the world to come: and being of sound mind and disposing memory do make and publish this my last Will and Testament in the words and figures following, to wit:

First. I give and bequeath unto my son James R. Forgey two tracts of land and one negro boy named Tom, being the same tracts of land and negro which were bequeathed to me by my beloved daughter Rachael, but my son James is to pay all the just debts against the estate of my daughter Rachael, and all my debts and funeral expenses out of the bequest. And he is further to pay out of the bequest above written, Four hundred dollars to Eliza M. Cocke and Malvina M. Conner, they being my grand daughters, which said sum of Four

hundred dollars is to be equally divided between my grand daughters, and the same to be paid to them in a short time after my death, and after which pay-ment above directed, an absolute title in fee simple to the lands and negroes aforesaid is to vest in my son James Forgey and his heirs forever.

Secondly. I give and bequeath to my grand daughters Eliza M. Cocke and Malvina M. Conner, all the right title, claim and interest I have in and to the slaves Joe and Peggy and the issue of Peggy, which was bequeathed to me by my beloved daughter Rachael, to be divided equally between my grand daughters aforesaid, to have and to hold to them and their children forever.

And further, having full confidence in the fidelity of my son James R. Forgey, I do hereby nominate, appoint and constitute him Executor of this my last Will and Testament, hereby revoking all former wills and codicils, which I may have made and published.

In witness whereof I have hereunto subscribed my name This 20th day of December, 1843, in presence of:

R. B. Reynolds   Margaret Forgey (seal).
James Coldwell
David Laughmiller

Page 192

WILL OF JOHN FLETCHER

Dated: October 3rd, 1844
Proven: March 3, 1845

October the 3rd, 1844

Decently buried and all the just debts to be satisfied, his wife Christine its his will that what properties and lands &c is to be given up to her as her own title and properties to dispose of at her wish and the heirs is to have one dollar each, and at her death is to be equally divided among the heirs. it is his request also that an unjust note from Ann Strong and Fulkerson that he swore off before Pleasant Begley an acting Justice of the Peace which is not to be paid and by these presents he has set his hand and fixt his seal in the presence of

Robert Frost, Russel F. Belcher   John Fletcher (seal)
William A. Hix, Henry Fletcher
Polly x Smith
          (her mark)

Page 192

WILL OF JAMES L. FULKERSON

Dated: Jan. 31, 1849
Proven: April Term, 1849

I James L. Fulkerson do make and publish this my last Will and Testament hereby revoking and making void all other wills by me at any time made.

First. I give & bequeath to my wife Alice G. Fulkerson all my personal property, household and kitchen furniture, beds & bedding, all the cash and all the debts due to me, and out of which I direct her to pay all the debts owed by me.

Secondly. I give and bequeath to my wife Alice G. the lot of ground bought by me from Wm. R. Armstrong on the street opposite Doctor H. Walker, the plantation owned by me in Grainger County, Tennessee, formerly owned by my father Abram Fulkerson and where now resides (sic) to be sold and out of sale $1,400. shall first be paid over to my wife Alice G., and whatever over

that amount the land may sell for to be placed in the hands of my brothers
Sam'l V. Fulkerson and Francis M. Fulkerson as Trustees who will loan out on
safe security the amount received by them at the close of each year thereafter to pay all the interest accruing on said amount to my mother Margaret
Fulkerson during her lifetime for her sole benefit and use, and at her death
I bequeath the principal to my two sisters Harriet and Catharine Fulkerson,
to be equally divided between them.

   Lastly. I do hereby nominate & appoint my wife Alice G. Fulkerson
Executrix and brother Sam'l V. Fulkerson Executor. In witness whereof I do
to this my last Will set my hand and seal. This 31st day of January 1849.
Test.   James L. Fulkerson (seal)
A. Carmichael, Hiram Fain

WILL OF NICHOLAS FAIN

Page 193   Dated: June 24, 1849

I Nicholas Fain of the County of Hawkins and State of Tennessee do hereby
make and publish this as my last Will and Testament, hereby revoking and
making void all other wills by me heretofore made.

   First. I direct that my funeral expenses and all my debts be paid as
soon after my death as possible, out of any money I may die possessed of, or
that may first come into the hands of my Executors.

   Secondly. I will and bequeath to my wife Elizabeth my negro woman Polly,
also one half of my household and kitchen furniture, excepting my secretary
and book case, also a good riding horse, saddle and bridle.

   Thirdly. It is my will and desire that the portraits of myself and my
wife Elizabeth, painted by Samuel Shaver be the property of Elizabeth until
her death, after which they shall belong to my son Richard G. Fain and his
wife Elizabeth R. Fain.

   Fourthly. It is my will and desire that my Executors hereinafter named
shall pay to my wife Elizabeth nine hundred dollars in cash provided she will
receive the same in lieu of her dower.

   Fifthly. I will and bequeath to my son Hiram Fain my silver patent lever
watch.

   Sixthly. It is my will and desire that my Executors pay to my son
Richard G. Fain three hundred dollars in cash to indemnify him for putting
up a more costly dwelling house than was at first contemplated, on that part
of my tract of land leased by me to him, and also to indemnify him for his
part of a supposed loss sustained by the firm of R. G. FAIN & CO. on account
of the debts sold and transferred by me to the firm.

   Seventhly. I will and bequeath to my son John H. Fain my negro man
Alexander, usually called "Ellick", a blacksmith by trade, to be hired out
by my Executors for the benefit of my said son John and the hire to be paid
to him semi-annually, and my said Executors are hereby authorized to sell said
negro man Ellick with the consent of my son John if they shall consider it
advisable to do so, and the proceeds of said sale shall remain in the hands
of my Executors and be subject to their control as a trust fund for the benefit of my son John, to be kept regularly loaned out at interest in safe hands,
and the interest paid semi-annually to my son John H. Fain.

   Eightly. It is my will and desire that my Executors pay the sum of one
hundred and fifty dollars to my son George G. Fain to indemnify him for his
part of a supposed loss sustained by the firm of R. G. FAIN & COMPANY on

account of the debts sold and transferred to said firm, also to son George
all of my law books.

   Ninthly. It is my will and desire that all the residue of my property
of every description, both real and personal, not hereinbefore specifically
bequeathed or disposed of, shall be equally divided share and share alike
between my wife Elizabeth and my six children (to wit): Hiram Fain, Nancy
McCarty, Richard G. Fain, John H. Fain, Eliza Ruth Powel and George G. Fain,
and in making this last mentioned distribution of my property among my wife
and children, each one of my said children shall account for all advances
heretofore made by me to them respectively, without interest thereon, which
advances were specifically set forth in my hand writing, in a red Morocco
memorandum book with my name printed in gilt letters on the side thereof,
and with said distribution my sons Richard G. and George G. Fain who constituted the firm of R. G. Fain & Company shall account for the balance that
may be due at my death on a note which I hold on the firm of R. G. Fain &
Company, also the balance that may be due me at my death on a note held by
me on George R. Powell, shall be accounted for in adjusting or settling
the distributive share as above set forth to my daughter Eliza Ruth Powel,
also the balance that may be due at my death on a judgement in the Circuit
Court of Hawkins County in favor of R. G. Fain & Company against James R.
McCarty and transferred to me by R. G. Fain & Company, shall in like manner
be accounted for in adjusting or selling the distributive share as set forth
above to my daughter Nancy McCarty, and it is also my will and desire that
the interest on the two above last mentioned notes and also the interest on
the above mentioned judgement shall cease at my death.

   I hereby constitute and appoint my two sons Hiram Fain and Richard G.
Fain Executors of this my last Will and Testament.

   And I do hereby fully authorize and empower my said Executors to sell
or dispose of at public or private sale, either the whole or any part of
the property not herein before specifically bequeathed or disposed of, and
to make all needful transfers or conveyances therefor, provided they shall
in their discretion consider that such sale will be for the interest of
the distributees and will facilitate a fair distribution and speedy settlement of my estate.

   Lastly. It is my will and desire that in the general distribution of
my property herein before set forth in the Ninth item, whatever distributive
share shall fall to my daughter Nancy McCarty or to my son John H. Fain,
shall be deemed and held in the hands of my Executors as a trust fund for
the benefit of said distributees during their natural lives, the interest or
profits of which shall be paid to them respectively semi-annually, and at
their death their respective distributive shares shall be equally divided
among their legal heirs. And if my son John H. Fain should die without
legal heirs, it is my will and desire that in that event his distributive
share as herein before set forth shall be equally divided among his brothers
and sisters or their heirs. And in case of the death or removal of my said
Executors, or their refusal to take upon themselves the execution of the
trusts above set forth, or the trusts set forth in the Seventh item hereof,
then and in that case, it is my will and desire that the Chancellor of the
Chancery Court of the District including the County of Hawkins shall appoint
a Trustee who shall enter into bond with security to be approved by the
Chancellor for the faithful execution of said trust. The word "dollars"
in the twentieth line and the word "three" in the twenty-fifth line, both
on the first page, interlined before signing.

In testimony whereof I have hereunto subscribed my name and affixed my seal. This 24th day of June, 1849.

N. Pain (seal)

Signed by Nicholas Pain the Testator in the presence of us, who in his presence have subscribed our names as witnesses.

S. D. Mitchell
Sam Powel

WILL OF JAMES R. FORGEY

Page 196
Dated: May 12, 1853
Proven: Jan'y Term, 1854

Calling to mind the uncertainty of human life, I make this my last will and Testament in the following manner:

I appoint my wife Executrix to have full power to manage my property without security, and in the first place that she pay all my just debts. And I further give all my property, notes, cash and all claims to my beloved wife, except hereafter mentioned in this my will.

I give the East end of my farm, the line to run with fence on through straight between the large field joining C. C. Miller and the flat field on the road, to my son Gabriel at the death of my wife. I give my daughters each a horse, saddle and bridle, or one hundred dollars in cash, as my wife may choose, and also that each of my daughters have two servant girls to be selected by my wife. Given under my hand and seal the date above written.

J. R. Forgey (seal)

Witness: John Young, David Laughmiller

WILL OF JOHN H. PAIN

Page 196
Dated: August 26, 1853
Proven: Sept. Term, 1853

I John H. Pain do hereby make and publish this my last will and Testament, hereby revoking and making void all wills by me at any time heretofore made. First. I will and bequeath that all my just debts and funeral expenses be paid out of the first money that may come into the hands of my Executor. Secondly. I will and bequeath to my brother George G. Pain Two hundred dollars. Thirdly. I will and bequeath to my brother Hiram Pain, one hundred dollars. Fourth. I will and bequeath to my sister Nancy McCarty formerly Nancy Pain Fifty dollars. Fifth. I will and bequeath to my sister Eliza R. Powel formerly Eliza R. Pain, Fifty dollars. Sixth. And whatever may remain after satisfying the above bequests, I will and bequeath that the same shall be equally divided between my brothers Hiram Pain, Richard G. Pain and George G. Pain. Lastly, I appoint George G. Pain my Executor. In testimony whereof I have hereunto set my hand and seal this 26th day of August, 1853.

John H. Pain

Signed, sealed and published in our presence and we have subscribed our names in the presence of the Testator. This the 26th day of August, 1853.

Sam Powel
Hiram Pain Junior

WILL OF JAMES FRANCISCO

Page 197
Dated: 27 Dec., 1855
Proven: Aug. 1, 1865 [Min. P.41]

I James Francisco of Hawkins County, State of Tennessee, viewing the uncertainty of life and the certainty of death, wishing to dispose of my Estate both real and personal in the manner that seems right and just, do make this my last will and Testament in writing, revoking all wills by me made before this date. First, my wish and desire that all my just debts be speedily paid with my burying expenses.

Secondly. I give to my daughter Phebe Adaline Vaughan, formerly P. A. Francisco, a tract of land including the house and other buildings on said land. Lot #1 which will show by the platt herein enclosed. The division lines between Phebe A. & my son Jackson W. Francisco - Beginning on the side of Stage Road, on the southwest corner Elizabeth Vaughan's lot of six acres. Then with the dividing line of the two lots Phebe A. Willloy & Elizabeth Vaughan, N23 W18 poles to a stake in the middle of the great road. Corner of two lots. Then running with the middle of the pass way to the head of the spring. N23 W 18 poles to a stake in the middle of said pass way. Then west two poles to stake. Then N24 W14 poles to a stake opposite to nearly so- to the spring. Then N35 W170 poles passing through the field to a black oak & hickory on the ridge about two poles west of the northwest corner of the field. Then west six poles to three white oaks on the top of a ridge. Then N36 W26 poles to a white oak on a rockey point. Then N37 E18 poles to a large Spanish oak on the side of a small ridge. Then N2¾W50 poles to two white oaks on Barnes' line, which line passes through a pond on the top of the ridge. which lines of the division between Phebe A. & Jackson W. I give all my land on the north side of the Stage Road & on the east to said divis- ion lines to P. A. Vaughan and her heirs, containing 180 acres, be the same more or less. I also give Phebe A. my daughter all my household & kitchen furniture with my weaving loom, except my cooking stove, my beds and steads, clock, cupboard & Bureau with all that is in my house and kitchen furniture and charge her seventy five dollars for the same. Also she is to have a horse or fifty dollars that as she never had advanced to her when married. She shall be charged advanced say property (sic) to the value of fifty dollars in the settlement of my Estate that she 2 when married.

Thirdly. I give my son Jackson W. Francisco all my land west of the division line which more fully show by the platt herein enclosed (sic), in- cluding the house where Jessy Cloud now lives on the south side of the road. The house where Les King lives and the old comfort houses containing 270 acres more or less, and charge him with money and property advanced to him, say $500.00.

Fourthly. I give to my son William B. Francisco his heirs, three slaves Carson 45 years old a man, Lucy a woman 33 and her daughter Mary 16 years and charge for property advanced to him $100.00. All the above land and negroes shall be valued by the following men: Robert Cooper, Nathan Wells, Eldridge Hord, Joshua Phipps, Robert Netherland & Phillip Critz, and if any of the (above) named men should die or leave the country, any three to be sufficient and their valuations shall be final. The lands to be valued and negroes at cash valuation the land & improvement. (sic) Each lot shall be valued and a deduction made on each lot of of $400.00 on account of the land of their mother is attached to said lots as they have divided their mother's land to take effect at my death which I have included their deeds in this will. I got two negroes by Jack and Adaline's mother worth, say $400.00 each after paying them each four dollars. My wish is for my

Executors to divide my Estate equally among my three children, agreeable to the valuation of the property and negroes, debts, and what money, if I have any on hand, the balance of my property and land shall be sold by my Executors and the money divided equally among my three children, share and share alike. I hereby empower my Executors herein named to sell three shares I have in a tract of land in Virginia, Scott County (of) 400 acres, which is a fourth of said tract including the Calebriate Spring, which is undivided, if I do not sell the same before I die and make a special warrantee deed of conveyance to the same—either at private or public sale—the same to be equally divided as heretofore. My will is that if I have a crop commenced that my family and stock should be permitted to remain with the premises until the crop is all gathered, that my son **Jackson** shall see that nothing shall be destroyed—no more than can be helped. The family shall remain as if I was living until said crops shall be gathered, and may be divided equally among my children without a sale of the same. And any property I have not specially willed may be divided by my children if they so wish and can agree to the same without a sale. My daughter **P. A. Vaughan** and her children, she being an unfortunate person, I hereby agree that she and her children shall not be charged anything by my Executors or by **Jackson** or **Wm. B. Francisco** for my raising, Educating and keeping them or what money I have laid out for their benefit as she agrees for us to be even & no charge to be made by either of us. As my son **Wm. F.** has received the estate that came by the **Burris** family, I think it right and just that **P. A.** (and) **Jackson** shall in value what their mother had at the time of our marriage.

I hereby appoint **Robert Cooper** & my son **Jackson** my Executors of this my last Will and Testament in writing. My wish is that after defraying necessary expenses and paying for their services that they may divide my estate equally among my three children, agreeable to my directions herein set forth—that they keep a valuation of the land & negroes & return the same to Court so that there may be a record of the same, a account of value of my other property & take a receipt from each child what they have rec'd.

I will enjoin it on some of my Executors at my death to take an inventory of my property that is not specially willed and the same returned to Court. In furnishing this my last will, I have been influenced outly by what I consider is right & just. I wish my children to act like Brothers and Sisters and be friendly.

In Testimony whereof I set my hand & affix my seal, Dec. 27th, 1855.

James Francisco (seal)

Signed and acknowledged before us:
**Asa Hopkins, Joseph W. Clark,
Charles x Murdock, Jeremiah x Cloud.**
(his mark)   (his mark)
Mathew Marcus Lynch, John P. Hamilton

We, **Robert Cooper, Phillip Critz & (E.) Hord** appointed commissioners by the Will and Testament of **Jas. Francisco**, dec'd met this day at the house of s'd **Jas. Francisco**, dec'd, and have proceeded under the will to value the land, lot No. 2 as described in the will at $2,833.33 1/3 to **J. W. Francisco**, and lot No. 1 to **Phebe Adaline Vaughan** at $2,032.33 1/3, and five negroes: **Carson** at $350.00, **Lucy** at $333.33 1/3, and **Mary** and her children at $1,111.33 1/3 to **W. B. Francisco**.

El^d **Hord, P. Critz, Rob't Cooper**

Note: The Plat mentioned in foregoing will of James Francisco is reproduced and shown on page 250 in the Addendum.

ELM

State of Tennessee)
Hawkins County   )   Personally appeared before me, **James Lackey,** Clerk of the County Court of said County **Jeremiah Cloud** and **Charles Murdock** subscribing witnesses to the foregoing agreement, who being duly sworn according to law depose and say that they are personally acquainted with **Phebe A. Vaughan** and **Jackson W. Francisco** the makers thereof and heard them severally acknowledge the same to be their act and deed for the purposes therein contained. Witness my hand at office the 7th day of August, 1865.

James Lackey, Clk
By J. H. Vance, D. Clk.

WILL OF RACHAEL FORGEY

Page 202
Dated: November 24, 1856
Proven: Dec. Term, 1856

I, **Rachael Forgey** knowing the uncertainty of life and the certainty of death and being weak of body but sound of mind and memory, do hereby make and constitute the following my last Will and Testament, to wit:

Item First. My will and desire is that my body be decently buried in a plain manner, and that all my funeral expenses and just debts be paid in the first place.

Item Second. My will and desire is that my two step daughters, **Manerva** and **Matilda Forgey** and my own daughter **Susan Forgey**, have each one negro girl, in addition to those left them by their father, all to be set apart to them by my Executors hereafter appointed, each of them two good beds and furniture, to be set apart in like manner.

Item Third. My will and desire is that my son **James R. Forgey** have in fee simple all the lands that I may die seized and possessed of, it being the land I inherited by the last Will and Testament of my husband **James R. Forgey,** and in addition to the land, my Executors to pay to him, the said **James R. Forgey** the sum of six thousand dollars in cash or negroes belonging to my Estate, to be decided by them and paid accordingly. The reason for this bequest is that his father provided for my son **Gabriel** in his will and did not for **James**, and this, I think, will make **James** nearly equal with **Gabriel**.

Item Fourth. My will and desire is that my Executors sell all the residue of my property of every kind whatever and such credit as is usually given in such cases, and out of the proceeds of the same, and out of the residue of my Estate of all kinds, I desire them, first, to pay my daughter **Susan Forgey** Three thousand dollars ($3,000.), if so much there be, and all the residue if any to be equally divided between my three children, **Susan, Gabriel** and **James R. Forgey.** I further request that my two step daughters, **Manerva** and **Matilda** and my daughter **Susan** have a home with my son **Gabriel** at the old place, so long as they remain single.

I do hereby nominate and appoint **C. L. Miller** and **John Young** Executors of this my last Will and Testament. In testimony whereof I have hereunto set my hand and seal This 24th day of November, 1856.

Signed, sealed and acknowledged   **Rachael Forgey** (seal)
in presence of us,
**Jacob Miller
David Laughmiller, John Young**

WILL OF ALEXANDER GRANT

Dated: June 12, 1789

In the Name of God, Amen.

I, Alexander Grant of Hawkins County in the State of North Carolina, being weak in body but of sound mind and memory and understanding, do make and publish this my last Will and Testament in manner & form following, to wit:

First. It is my will and desire that my just debts be honestly paid and as for the Estate real and personal that it hath pleased the Almighty God to bestow on me; I give & bequeath to my son & daughter, Thomas & Mary Grant, their heirs, &c forever. But in case one of the said children should die under age, the surviving child is to have the whole of the Estate, real and personal, after my loving wife Ellinor Grant's decease, and she is to have her living out of said Estate as long as it may please God to let her live. My landed estate doth contain 200 acres more or less, including the plantation I now live on which is to be equally divided between my children, Thomas & Mary Grant. In witness whereof I have hereunto set my hand & seal, This 12th day of June in the year of our Lord, one thousand seven hundred and eighty nine. By the above named Alex'r Grant for his last Will and Testament. In presence of us who have hereunto affixed our names as witnesses:

Thos. King
Nathan Watson
Jno King

(his)
Alexander x Grant (seal)
(mark)

WILL OF ELIZABETH GROVE

Dated: March 13, 1805

In name of God, Amen.

I Elizabeth Grove of the County of Hawkins, in the State of Tennessee, being of sound mind but in an infirm state of health have thought fit to make this my last Will & Testament; and by these presents do will and bequeath all the effects I am now possessed of to my son-in-law David Sensabaugh and his wife, except my wearing apparel which I bequeath to my daughter Elizabeth How. In witness whereof I have set my hand and seal this 13th day of March 1805.

(her)
Elizabeth x Grove (seal)
(mark)

Test:
Thomas Jackson, Joseph Clipper

WILL OF THOMAS GIBBONS

Dated: June 13, 1809

In the Name of God, Amen.

I, Thomas Gibbons of the County of Hawkins & State of Tennessee, being weak in body but of sound and perfect memory, blessed be Almighty God, do make and publish this my last Will & Testament in manner & form following (that is to say) —

It is my will that all my personal estate which I now claim be equally divided between my children, Thomas Gibbons, Nancy Howard, Betsy Chisolm, Edmond Gibbons, William Gibbons, Sally Gillenwaters and Epps Gibbons and a child's share to be equally divided between my grand children, Nancy Isham,

Garrett Fitzgerald & Elizabeth Babb, children of my daughter Molly Fitzgerald.

I further bequeath to my son Edmond Gibbons two hundred pounds in lieu of land over and above his share. I also give and bequeath to my daughter Rebecca Bell one dollar. I also give & bequeath to my son John Gibbons one dollar, also my son James Gibbons one dollar, they having already received their share of my Estate. I hereby appoint my son-in-law Wm. Hord & my son Edmond Gibbons Executors of this my last Will & Testament, hereby revoking all former wills by me made. In witness whereof I have hereunto set my hand and seal, This 13th day of June, A.D. 1809.

(his mark)
Thos x Gibbons (seal)

Signed, sealed Published & declared by the above named Thos. Gibbons to be his last Will & Testament, in the presence of us who at his request and in his presence have hereunto subscribed our names as witnesses to the same.

Jon [Jonathan] Spyker
John Starnes (Jurat)
Joel Gillenwaters (Jurat)

WILL OF CHRISLEY GROSE [Chrisley]

Dated: October 16, 1809

In the Name of God, Amen.

I, Chrisley Grose of Hawkins County within the State of Tennessee, being of full age and sound memory do make and publish this my last Will and Testament in the words and figures following (to wit):

Item. I give and bequeath to James McVay of said County a certain tract or parcel of land lying in said County of Hawkins containing 150 acres, lying near the lands of Thomas Ingram and John Young between Carters and Stanleys Valley. Also, I give unto said McVay one still containing sixty-five gallons, and that this my last will may be more understood, I do ordain that said James McVay be sole and entire heir of all the property that I now have both real and personal. In testimony whereof I have hereunto set my hand this this sixteenth day of October, 1809.

Test: Nath'l Henderson
Patrick McVay

(his mark)
Chrisley x Grose (seal)

WILL OF PHILADELPHIA GRILLS

Dated August 13, 1789 [see Original]

In the Name of God, Amen.

I Philadelphia Grills being in sound judgement and memory, calling to mind my latter end, being willing to have what little fortune that it hath pleased God of his goodness to bless me with divided in the manner following. The six negroes that I claim as my right and property, that is Mall and her five children, Launar, George, Walker, Robing, and Silve, my desire is that they be sold and the money divided in the manner as follows, that is: To my loving husband John Grills my desire would be that he would have the sum of fifteen pounds paid to him yearly by the hands of the Legatees, each paying an equal portion to him out of their part, and the whole amount of the negroes that was the property of the late **Philadelphia Grills** deceased is to be equally divided between **Richard Grills, Ellinar Ingles, Mildred Johnson, Martha McAdow** and **Elbert [Ellet] Grills**. Said Legatees is each of them to receive their part as soon as sale can be made and the money collected. Only **Mildred Johnson**, and her part to be kept in the hands of a trustee to be divided among the heirs of her body at her death. Only the interest, she-**Mildred Johnson**- is to receive yearly. And further, I desire that **Richard Grills** should have the sorrel horse that I the deceased **Philadelphia Grills** claimed as my property. And I leave my bay mare to **Mildred Johnson** and said mare's colt I leave to **Ellinar Ingles**. And to **Martha McAdow** I leave the black mare. And said mare's colt I leave to **Elbert Grills**.

And I do here appoint and constitute **Thomas Ingles, John McAdow** and **Elbert Grills** to be my Executors to put this my last will and Testament into execution, and I do disannul and revoke all wills that hath been heretofore made and I do acknowledge this to be my last will and Testament as witness my hand and seal This 13th day of August, 1789.

Philadelphia Grills (seal)

Signed in presence of:
Jeremiah Chamberlain
James Carmichael

And it is my desire that my husband **John Grills** have any of the horses that he should make choice of that is mentiont to the aforesaid Legatees in the other part of the will and said horses is to be returned to said Legatees at his death and whos ever lot it is that the said **John Grills** chooses their horses that is mentiont to them in the aforesaid will each of them is to have the sum of ___ five pounds paid out of the estate. And further, I leave to my son **John Grills** the sum of twenty five pounds to be paid out of said Estate. And to my daughter **Elizabeth Cox** the sum of fifteen pounds, and to my son **Elbert Grills** I leave the new Bed that I am making up. And the Bed that I ly on, after the death of his grandfather **John Grills**, I leave to **Washington Johnson**. In witness whereof I the said **Philadelphia Grills** have to this my last will and Testament set my hand and seal this 12th day of October, 1789.

Philadelphia Grills (seal)

Signed, sealed and delivered by the said **Philadelphia Grills** as and for her last will and Testament in the presence of us who were present at the signing and sealing thereof.
Jeremiah Chamberlain
Thos Flippere

WILL OF JOSEPH GALBRAITH

Page 207   Dated: Sept. 26, 1811
In the Name of God, Amen.

I, **Joseph Galbraith** of the County of Hawkins and State of Tennessee, being weak of body, but of perfect mind and memory and calling to mind the mortality of my body that it is appointed for all men once to die, do make and ordain this to be my last Will and Testament in manner and form following, to wit:

First and principally of all. I give my soul into care of Almighty God who created and gave it.

Second. My body to the Earth to be buried in a decent and Christian like manner at the discretion of my hereinafter named Executors.

And third and lastly. My earthly estate wherewith I may die seized or possessed, I give and bequeath in manner following:

To my beloved wife **Mottlenia** all my household and kitchen furniture without reservation to her use and benefit forever, also two cows and calves and $300.00 out of the money and personal property I may be possessed of at the time of my decease. My negro woman **Ibb** I give and bequeath to the Infant (or Infants) of which my wife is now pregnant should it survive, to its use and benefit forever. And during its minority it is my wish that the said negro may remain under the direction of one of my herein named Executors and her labor to go towards the support of my said wife and child during the minority of my child and widowhood of my said wife, and in case of her marriage, then ever after to the benefit of my said child. But in all cases it is my wish that should said negro have children, they should be for the use and benefit of my child, and in case of my said child's death and death or marriage of my wife then said **Ibb** I give to my nephew **Joseph Carrington** to his use and benefit forever.

Item. I give to my said child should it survive, all the estate personal (sic) that I may be possessed of at the time of my decease, after paying all debts and the hereinbefore named legatees, and in case of its death, then and in that case, I give $300.00 more to my said nephew **Joseph Carrington** out of said money that may be on hand.

Item. I will that my tract of land containing 500 acres in Roan County (Poplar Creek) shall be sold when recovered, and it is my wish that my brother **Andrew Galbraith** shall have the sole direction of all matters touching said land while in dispute and full power to sell and dispose of the same when recovered, and be hereby authorized to dispose of any part of said land in prosecuting said suit until recovered for the purpose of obtaining the land-- that he may think proper.

And it is my will that if said land is recovered, when sold and all costs and charges defrayed that my wife **Mottlenia** have one third part of what may remain of the price of said land, and the remaining two thirds to my aforesaid Infant to be disposed of for its use during its minority as my said Executors think proper. And in case of its death the said two thirds of said land to be equally divided between the following persons, (Viz): To my sister **Margaret Young**, my brother **Andrew Galbraith**, **Harvey Young** (son of my sister **Sally Young**), my sister **Julia Davis**, my nephew **Pleasant Henderson** (son of my sister **Tabitha Henderson**) and **Eneas S. Galbraith**, to each of the above named persons, share and share alike. It is further my will that any money that may be belonging to my estate not already herein disposed of shall be divided equally between the above six persons last named.

Item. It is my will that in case my said Infant lives and my wife decease, remove, or marry that my Executors shall have direction of my child's education in every manner whatever.

Item. The foregoing I declare to be my last Will and Testament in all its parts, publishing and declaring it as such, disannulling and revoking all others. In testimony whereof I have hereunto set my hand and affixed my seal this 26th day of September in the year of our Lord, 1811.

Item. I hereby constitute and appoint my two brothers **Andrew Galbraith** and **Aeneas S. Galbraith** Executors to this my last Will and Testament. This I further publish and declare to be part of my last Will & Testament:

Item. I will in case my said negro should have children and my said child decease during its minority and my wife decease or marry, then and in that case, it is my will that my said nephew **Joseph Carrington** shall have negro child or children as well as negro **Ibb**.

This I also declare to be the part of this my last Will and Testament. In testimony of all and every part herein contained, I hereunto set my hand and seal the day and year first before herein written.

Joseph Galbraith (seal)

Signed, published &
declared in presence of us:
Robert x Young
(his mark)
Arthur x Young
(his mark)

Page 210
WILL OF ARTHUR GALBRAITH
Dated: Feb'y 23, 1818

I Arthur Galbraith of the County of Hawkins and State of Tennessee, being weak in body but of perfect mind and memory and calling to mind the mortality of my body and that it is appointed for all men once to die, do make, ordain, publish and declare this to be my last Will and Testament in manner and form following:

First and principally of all. I give my soul into care of Almighty God who created and gave it. Second. My body to the Earth to be buried in a decent and Christian like manner at the discretion of my Executors. And Third and lastly. My Earthly Estate wherewith I may die seized or possessed I give and bequeath in manner following: First. I allow all my just debts to be paid.

Second. I will to my son John Galbraith my negro boy Albert and my negro girl Araminto and $200.00 in money, also my old servant negro man Aaron, the said negro having been a faithful servant and it is his wish to reside with my said son John.

Third. I will to my daughter Elizabeth Armstrong my negro boy Mitchell.

Fourthly. I will to my son Andrew Galbraith the sum of ten dollars which I consider his part having heretofore provided for him.

Fifthly. I will to my son Aeneas S. Galbraith my negro woman Minna and her youngest child Nancy to my grand daughter Elizabeth Galbraith, daughter of my son Aeneas.

Sixthly. I will that all my stock of every kind, household furniture, farming utensils and money on hand and every kind of property not heretofore disposed of to be sold and the money arising therefrom to be equally divided among my herein named children, share and share alike (To wit): My daughter Margaret Young, Elizabeth Armstrong, Polly Looney, Sally Young, Julia Davis, Tabetha Henderson and Lucinda Carrington.

Fourthly and Lastly. I constitute and appoint my two sons John Galbraith and Aeneas S. Galbraith Executors of this my last Will and Testament. The foregoing I publish and declare to be my last Will and Testament, revoking all others.

In testimony whereof I have hereunto set my hand and affixed my seal This 23rd day of February, 1818.

Arthur x Galbraith (seal)
(his mark)

Signed, sealed, published and declared in presence of:
James Amis, Jurat
Henry Brown, Sen'r, Jurat
Henry Brown

Page 211
WILL OF JAMES T. GAINES
Dated: Dec. 29, 1820

I, James Taylor Gaines of the County of Hawkins and State of Tennessee being weak in body but in sound mind & memory meditating on the uncertainty of human events ordain & desire this to be my last Will & Testament – first giving up to Almighty God my soul & body the giver & maker of it.

1st. It is my wish & desire that the tract of land whereon I now live with all the lands adjoining the same, purchased of Joseph McMinn and my part of an undivided tract granted to David Kinkead be sold on condition (that) $8,000.00 can be had for them and do hereby authorize my Executrix and Executors hereinafter named to convey the same to any person or persons that may pay that amt. for the same or secure the payment for that amt. for the same & subject to the following conditions, to wit: I wish my Father and Mother to reside in the house where they now live or in the house at the head of the Spring where James Childress lately resided at their option & to hold during their natural lives with the following premises the upper field or field above the branch with the boat yard field as low down as the first drain that empties into the river from the long ditch with the orchard field but not the exclusive privilege of the fruit but an equal share of it. Also have free privilege of the large wood land pasture for the use and bene-fit of their stock. It is further my wish and desire that they have my sorrel horse Kiswil by the name of the Big Sorrel, also Old Ball a sorrel horse, one-half of cows and calves from head of young cattle to an average quality, one-half of my stock of hogs on hand, and as much corn and wheat as will be sufficient for their support and family until they can raise or make a crop, & further I desire that my negro Ben be retained by my Mother and Father during their lives to assist in making a support. After their death(s), I wish Ben sold with any of the property that may be remaining on hand herein directed to be put into the possession of my Father & Mother & the money arising from sale to be loaned or vested in some kind of stock that will be most profit-able to my wife and children. I also desire that my Father and Mother have the privilege of half the garden with the before described premises during their natural lives or so long as they think proper to reside on the same.

I bequeath to my beloved sister Sarah Gaines my negro girl Malinda and her heirs, together with my horse known by the name of Pony. I will to Joseph Everett and his heirs the plantation where my sister Childress and her family now reside, but subject the following uses & trusts, to wit: That during the natural life of my said sister Childress, that he shall per-mit her to remain in the use and occupation of the farm or pay over to her for her sole use and benefit the rents and profits of same as shall be most to her benefit & advantage, and after the death of my said sister Childress it is my will that the said Joseph Everett or his heirs shall expose the said tract of land to sale for the highest price that can be procured for the same and then divide the money arising from said sister Childress, share and share alike, to wit: James, Phebe, Edmond, Henry, Elizabeth & Bethelland.

It is also my will that the ten shares I hold of the town of Demopolis in the State of Alabama be sold by my Executrix and Executors, and I do here-by authorize them to transfer or convey the same. The moneys arising from sale be paid over for the use of wife & children equally. It is also my will that all my personal property with 100 acres of land adjoining the lands of Rosses large survey & Alexander's lands be sold except the property above devised or bequeathed & the following negroes to wit: Jack, Dick, Diner, Minerva, Gilbert, John & Rufus, which negroes I wish retained with their increase for the use and benefit of my wife and children Elizabeth Mary and **Frances Gaines**. The money arising from the sale of my property after paying all my debts, I wish equally divided between my wife and my two daughters before mentioned.

It is my will in case my landed Estate whereon I now reside with the adjoining lands cannot be sold for the sum herein directed - That it be rented or occupied by my wife & children as she may think most proper.

It is my will & desire that my beloved wife, **Frances G. Gaines** be & act as my Executrix with my friends **John G. Gaines** & **Clinton Armstrong** as Executors of this my last will & Testament, hereby revoking & making void all former wills by me made whatever.

In testimony whereof I have hereunto set my hand & affixed my seal This 29th day of December, 1820.

James T. Gaines (seal)

Signed, sealed & acknowledged
in presence of us the date above
written.
Jno A. Rogers
P. Parsons
John Shough

WILL OF JAMES GIDEONS

Page 213   Dated: August 20, 1823
In the Name of God, Amen.

I, **James Gideons**, Senior of the County of Hawkins and State of Tenn., being weak in body but of sound and perfect mind and memory, calling to mind the mortality of my body, knowing that it is appointed for all men once to die. First of all, I give my body to the earth to be buried in a Christian burial at the discretion of my Executor and my soul I give to Almighty God who gave it, nothing doubting but at the resurrection I shall receive both at the mighty hand of God. And as it has pleased God to bless me with such worldly Estate wherewith I am blessed with do make constitute ordain and appoint this my last Will and Testament in the following manner and form.

Item First. I give and bequeath unto my son **Edward Giddions** $50.00 to be levied out of my Estate in trade at trade rates. The next place, I give and bequeath unto my son **William Giddeons** one dollar in like manner. Next, I give to my son **James Giddeons** $50.00 to be paid twelve months after my decease in trade at trade rates. Next, I give and bequeath unto my son **Isham Giddions** a certain boundary of my land whereon I now live, beginning on a forked sugar tree, running North to two dogwoods Thence East with a conditional line between **Isham** & **John Gideons** to a horn beam on the old line. Thence a South East course with the old line to a stake near **William Gideon's** house. Thence West with a conditional line made between myself and my son **William Gideons** to a sugar tree. Thence a Southeast Course with a conditional line to the old line to a stake near the top of Clinch Mountain. Thence with the old line to the beginning. Next, I give and bequeath unto my two daughters **Elizabeth Davis** and **Sary Reed** all my household furniture with the exception of one bed and furniture to be equally divided between them at my decease and my wife's. Likewise, I give unto the above named daughters all my stock of every kind, likewise to be divided equally between them. And in the next place I give and bequeath unto my son **John Gideons** one feather bed and furniture. It is further my will that my son **Isham Gideons** be my Executor and I do hereby appoint, constitute and ordain my son **Ishum** my Executor to

attend to the business as my Executor, and it is further my will that my son **Ishum** sees to take care and support my beloved wife **Martha Gideons** of the substances of my Estate during her natural lifetime, and it is further my will that if any of my said heirs are dissatisfied with this my last Will & shall go to law about my property that they forfeit all claim to any part of my Estate, and the part that was allotted to them to be divided amongst the balance of my s'd heirs. Now, I the said **James Gideons**, senior do ratify this to be my last Will and Testament, revoking and disannulling and disallowing all other wills and Tenements.

Signed, sealed and delivered This twentieth day of August in the Year of our Lord One thousand Eight hundred and thirty three in the presence of us who in the presence of each other have hereunto set our names as witnesses.

James x Gideons (seal)
(his mark

Test: **Ab Hawk**
Nicholas Antrikin
James H. Gideons

WILL OF JOHN GRIGSBY

Page 214   Dated: Sept. 28, 1826

Know all men by these presents that I **John Grigsby** of the County of Hawkins and State of Tennessee, being sick and weak of body but of sound mind and memory do this day make my last Will and Testament.

First of all, I give and commend my life into the hands of Almighty God who gave it and my body to the Earth from whence it sprang. I give and bequeath to my wife **Winney Grigsby** my negro man **Will** and his family, Viz: **Susan**, **Frank** and **Gibson**, as long as she lives. I give and bequeath to my son **Nathaniel Grigsby** and **Ashby Grigsby** all my lands and tenements lying on the south side of Holston River adjoining on the west to **James Sanders'** land and to **James Bredens'** line on the east to be equally divided between them. **Nathaniel Grigsby** is to have the part of the land I now live on, together with the buildings. The said **Nathaniel Grigsby** and **Ashby Grigsby** are to have no part of the remainder of my lands. My negro man **Will** is to be no longer a slave after the death of me and my wife **Winney Grigsby**; he shall be allowed to live with any of the children as he pleases or with anybody else.

I give and bequeath to my daughter **Judy Smith** ten dollars out of my Estate and all I have gave her and no more.

I give to my daughter **Elizabeth Rutherford** and **John Rutherford** her husband ten dollars out of the Estate I now have and all I have gave them and no more. I give to my daughter **Fanny Wood**, dec'd and **John Wood** her husband ten dollars out of my estate and all I have gave them and no more. I give to my daughter **Polly Smith** and **James Smith** her husband ten dollars out of my estate and all I have gave them and no more. I give to my daughter **Winney Rutherford** and **John Rutherford** her husband ten dollars out of my estate and all I have gave them and no more.

William Grigsby my son is to have $235.00 out of my estate over and above an equal share of the remainder of my estate lands excepted being indebted for the value and all I have gave him and no more.

James Grigsby is to have an equal share of my Estate, lands excepted. Also **Samuel Grigsby** is to have an equal share of my Estate lands excepted. **John Grigsby** is to have the price of a plantation out of my estate to be worth Five Hundred Dollars and equal part of the estate.

Nancy West and her husband **James West** is to have an equal share of my

and running to Catherine Murphy's line. I further will and bequeath that the balance of my land be equally divided between my three sons, James, William and Cornelius Gross.

I further will that my three sons, James, William and Cornelius, pay my daughter Sally Gilliam $130.00 in current money - half to be paid three years after my death and the balance three years after the death of my wife Nancy, admitting she outlives me. And also, I further will that my three sons, James, William and Cornelius, pay Lewis Gross, son of John Gross, dec'd the sum of $80.00 in current money and Margaret Rorack $15.00, and Mary and Nancy Gross, children of my dec'd son, John Gross $30.00 each - to be paid in like manner. And I will and bequeath unto my daughter Elizabeth Ford the sum of $5.00.

I do appoint my sons James and Cornelius Gross my Executors of this my last Will & Testament in writing, and wish them to enter on the business without giving security. Revoking all other wills by me made. In testimony whereof I have hereunto set my hand and affixed my seal, This 22nd day of December, One thousand, eight hundred and twenty seven, in the presence of us:

James V. Campbell
Stephen Wilson

William Gross (seal)

WILL OF FRANCIS GODDARD

Page 218

Dated: Sept. 27, 1828

In the Name of God, Amen.

Be it remembered that I, Francis Goddard of the County of Hawkins and State of Tennessee, being weak in body but of sound mind and memory, and considering that it is appointed for men once to die, do make this my last Will and Testament in words and form following, viz:

First of all. I commend my body to the dust and my Spirit to God that gave it, that is to say, my body to be buried in a decent Christian order, hoping in the G Resurrection I shall receive it again. Secondly. It is my will that my dear and well beloved wife Sarah Goddard should have and hold all my estate, my lands and all my perishable property, stocks of all kinds, household and kitchen furniture of everykind, together with all my farming utensils and every part and parcel thereof to have and to hold dur-ing her natural life. And at her decease my son Soloman Goddard should have all the land which is 160 acres. Also at my wife's decease, I want all the perishable property to be equally divided between my three single daughters, Polly, Rebecca G. and Suteary G. and those three to have the privilege to abide with their mother as long as they live single.

Item- It is my will and desire that my oldest daughters Caty and Elenor and Sally should have $5.00 each out of my property - that the Legatees previously named should pay them that sum out of the property. Also, I hereby appoint my daughter Nancy to have $10.00 out of the estate. And I do hereby appoint my dear and well beloved wife Sarah as my sole Executrix or Executor.

N.B. The sums mentioned to be trade at that price. Together with William Peagins as assistant and do hereby disannul all former wills by me made, and do hereby acknowledge this to be my last Will and Testament. In witness whereof I have hereunto set my hand and affixed my seal This 27th day of September, 1828.

Signed, sealed and ack'd in presence
of William Peagins, James Pryer,
Isaac D. Cox

Francis x Goddard (seal)
(his mark)

Estate, lands excepted. Lucy Murrel [Hertial—see original] is to have an equal share of my estate, lands excepted, and negro Ede and negro Alcy also. I give to my two grand daughters Louisiana Smith and Minerva Smith a negro girl named Rose and all I have give them shall be theirs and no more.

So this my last Will and Testament whereunto I have set my hand and af-fixed my seal, This twenty eighth day of September, 1826. N.B. I will that my son James Grigsby be appointed Guardian for Louisiana and Minerva Smith, my grand daughters over the negroes I have gave them above mentioned.

Witness: Jesse Creech

John x Grigsby (Seal)
(his mark)

WILL OF WILLIAM GOING

Page 216

Dated: August 21, 1827

In the Name of God, Amen.

I, William Going of the County of Hawkins and State of Tennessee, being of sound mind and memory at present, blessed be God, do this 21st day of Aug. in the year of our Lord one thousand, Eight hundred and twenty seven make and publish this my Will and Testament in manner following, that is to say:

First of all. After paying my just debts, I wish my personal property and the tract of land coming to me from the United States be sold to pay my debts and the over plush money, if there be any, to be divided equally between my heirs, except Sheard and Andrew Going, my two sons, to have 50 acres of land I now live on equally between them if the debts can be settled with-out selling the land. And I do ordain and appoint Nicholas Long my Executor of this my last Will and Testament without his giving bond and security, in the presence of us who are present at the time of his signing and sealing thereof.

Witness:
John x King and William Willeford
(his mark)

William x Going (seal)
(his mark)

WILL OF WILLIAM GROSS

Page 216

Dated: Dec. 22, 1827
Proven: Nov. 25, 1828

In the Name of God. I, William Gross of the County of Hawkins and State of Tennessee, being old and infirm and knowing that all men are born to die, But being of sound mind and memory do make and ordain this my last will and Testament in writing. I wish all my just debts to be paid out of my Estate. Secondly, I give unto my beloved wife Nancy Gross the plantation wheron I now live, including all the land that lies on the south side of Big Creek within the first grant.

I wish my household and kitchen furniture, stock and farming utensils to be sold and my just debts to be paid and if any money should be left after all my just debts is paid, I wish it to be-appropriated to the use of my be-loved wife Nancy during her life. I further will and bequeath unto my daugh-ter Catherine Murphy 60 acres of land, to her and her children during their life. Beginning on Absalom Looney's line and running through the hundred acre tract including the farm where she now lives. I further will and be-queath unto my daughter Polly Grose 40 acres of land. Beginning at Big Creek

WILL OF JOHN GALBRAITH

Page 219   Dated: August 22, 1832

In the Name of God, Amen.

I **John Galbraith** of the County of Hawkins & State of Tennessee, being of perfect mind and memory and calling to mind the imortality of my body, that it is appointed for all men once to die, do make, ordain, publish and declare this to be my last Will and Testament in manner and form following. First and principally of all, I give my soul into care of Almighty God who created and gave it.

Second. My body to the Earth to be buried in a Christian like manner at the discretion of my hereinafter named Executors, and Third and lastly, I give my Earthly estate wherewith I may die seized or possessed of in manner following:

First. I allow all my just debts to be paid.

Second. I give to my son **Andrew L. Galbraith** $1,000.00 in money.

Third. I give to my daughter **Priscilla Wright** a negro girl named Araminta which I consider worth $200.00, also three notes of hand given by her husband **Robert Wright** for $308.00, making in all the sum of $508.00, which sum is to be counted in her dower as part of my estate without interest hereinafter named. I also give her one cow and calf of my stock and one bed and furniture.

Fourth. To my daughter **Sally Watterson** I give one bed & furniture over and above what she has heretofore received.

Fifth. To my son **John Sharp Galbraith** two horse beasts, to wit: One brown horse called his horse & one sorrel mare, a new three horse waggon and $700.00 in money, also two beds and one bed stead and furniture.

Sixth. To my daughter **Juliann** I give one hundred dollars in money, one horse, two beds & furniture.

Seventh. To my son **Arthur Wright Galbraith** I give my large Family Bible, $1,100.00 in money, a negro boy named **Spencer,** a mare and young horse, two beds and furniture, provided he goes to the State of Missouri and settles and remains there, but in case he does not go to said State of Missouri, or if said state should not agree with him and he may return and prefer living elsewhere, in that case I will that he have the tract of land I now live on in Stanley Valley containing 178 acres, also an entry of 50 acres, making in all 228 acres, more or less. The negro boy above named, Book, horses & Beds. The rest of my books I wish equally divided with all my children except **Arthur W. Galbraith,** and my hereinafter named Executors to make s'd division. I will that all my negroes, together with all my stock of every kind, household furniture & farming tools and every kind of property not herein already disposed of be sold and the proceeds of the sale & money on hand be equally divided among my hereinafter named children, share and share alike (to wit) **Priscilla Wright, Matilda Baygood, Sally Watterson, Melinda Sprowl & Juliann Galbraith.**

Lastly. I constitute and appoint my son **Andrew Galbraith** & brother **Aeneas S. Galbreath** Executors of this my last Will & Testament. The foregoing I declare to be my last Will and Testament, disannulling & revoking all others. In testimony I hereunto set my hand and affix my seal, This 22nd day of August, 1832.

Signed in presence of: **John Galbraith** (seal)

H. Watterson, Elijah C. Gillenwaters
Absalom D. Looney

NUNCUPATIVE WILL OF JACOB B. GROVES

Page 220   Dated: January 13, 1837

Be it remembered that on the sixth day of January in the year 1837, we, **Thomas Eidson, William Rogers** and **Jack Sensabaugh,** citizens of Hawkins County, State of Tennessee, being near neighbors of the late **Jacob B. Groves,** and in being in the house of the said **Jacob B.** on the night after said 6th of January and a short time before the said **Jacob B.** died, and whilst the undersigned **Thomas Eidson** was behind the said **Jacob B.** on the bed supporting the said **Jacob B.,** and the undersigned **William Rogers** and **Jacob Sensabaugh** were standing by the bedside of the same **Jacob B,** ...he said, "Tommy, Tommy, I was to make a right to **Howe's** children for the land of **Jacob Howe** but have never made the right. I aimed to make a deed yesterday when I went to town, but I did not go" He continued,"**John** and **Winstead's** wife have no share in it for I have paid them for their shares - and I want the land divided among the balance of the children..." And then he observed, "Men take notice..." Just at that time Mrs. **Fanny Groves,** the mother of said **Jacob B.** approached the Bed, and the said **Jacob B.** continued, "Mother, don't grieve after me, for you have a plenty here to last you your days, and what is mine is all yours." The old lady seemed much affected. Shortly after, his sister **Mrs. Charles** came, and she observed, "You are very sick, Brother",to which he replied, "I am, my days are nearly numbered". And in about one hour after, expired, without saying any thing more as to nis property.

The undersigned **Jacob Sensabaugh** states that he did not pay particular attention to what **Mr. Jacob B. Groves** said in relation to **Howe's** land, but distinctly recollects hearing him state that he did not want the balance of **Howe's** children wronged out of their land. He also distinctly recollects and paid particular attention to what **Mr. Groves** said to his mother, that "What was his was all hers". The undersigned further state that the said **Jacob B.** was of sound disposing mind and memory at the said time. In witness thereof we have hereunto set our hands this 13th day of January, 1837.

                              Jacob Sensabaugh
                              Thomas x Eidson
                                 (his mark)
                              William x Rogers
                                 (his mark)

Witnesses: D. Alexander, W. T. Senter

WILL OF LAZARUS GULLY/GULLEY

Page 221   Dated: March 1, 1837

In the Name of God, Amen.

I, **Lazarus Gully** of the County of Hawkins and State of Tenn., being of sound and disposing mind and memory, blessed be God, do this first day of March in the year of our Lord One thousand Eight hundred and thirty seven, do publish this to be my last Will and Testament in manner and form following, that is to say:

First of all. After paying my just debts, I give and bequeath unto my loving wife **Nancy Gully** all my land and all my other personal property, except one rifle gun. The colt which the mare is with foal now when foaled is to be the property of my son **Nathan.** The rest of the property is to ... remain with my wife **Nancy** during her life or widowhood, for the support of my younger children, namely, Praint, Thomas, Nelson, Isaac, and my daughter Sally Gully. And if my said wife should marry, said property to be sold and applied to the support of my four children as before mentioned, and (I) do appoint my loving wife Nancy Gully sole Executrix of this my last Will and Testament.

In testimony whereof I have hereunto set my hand and affixed my seal the year and date first written in presence of:

Nicholas Long
George Gully   Lazarus x Gully (seal.)
                       (his mark)

WILL OF WILLIAM GRIGSBY, COL'D

Page 222
Dated: July 21, 1839

I William Grigsby, a free man of color, being weak of bodily strength but of sound disposing mind and memory, do make this my last Will and Testament—

First. it is my desire that at my death, I shall be decently buried. It is also my wish and desire that Wade B. Smith be my sole Executor, to attend to my business, and that after my death, he—the said Wade B. Smith—shall attend to the selling of all my property that I have any claim to — to be sold at public sale on a credit of 12 months, and it is my wish and desire that, first of all, all my just debts be paid, and secondly, my wife Susan be decently supported out of the balance of the proceeds of my property as long as she shall live, and if there shall be anything left at her death, (it) to be equally divided between my three children, Sarah, Frank and Gipson.

In witness whereof I have hereunto set my hand and seal. This 21st day of July, 1839.

William x Grigsby (seal.)
         (his mark)

Witness: John Reynolds and Edmond Fitzpatrick

WILL OF THOMAS GILLENWATERS (Sr.)

Page 223
Dated: March 30, 1841

In the name of God, Amen.

I, Thomas Gillenwaters, Sr., of the County of Hawkins and State of Tenn., being afflicted in body but of sound mind & memory, calling to mind the certainty of death, do make and ordain this my last Will and Testament. In the first place, I recommend my soul to that God who gave it, trusting that He will receive it into glory. Next, I recommend my body to the grave in a plain, Christian maner.

As touching my temporal matters, I desire that all my just debts be paid in the first place. I give and bequeath unto my beloved wife Mary my young bay mare, two cows and calves, six head of sheep, one sow, six pigs & Rusia boar, two beds, bed steads and bed furniture, one Bureau, one cupboard, one folding cherry table, one chest, four chairs, one set of plates, set of cups and saucers, set of knives and forks, such of the casting as she wants for her own use, at her own disposal. I further give unto my beloved wife all the proceeds of the remaining perishable property which I may die in

possession of, which property not otherwise disposed of in this instrument shall be sold on a 12-month credit and kept to her use during life, and at her death if there be a remainder, it to be divided among the children. My land whereon I now live I give to my daughter Rachael Kyle and Robert Kyle, her husband, containing 210 acres down to the road called Cove Road, on the condition Robert Kyle will pay $550.00 within five years next after being possessed of s'd farm, to be paid in the following manner: To Betsy Klepper on order $100.00. To Patsy McCann $100.00; to Nancy Klepper $100.00. To Polly Gillenwaters $200.00, and the remaining $50.00 to be paid to my four sons, William, Robert, Joel and Thomas Gillenwaters, each an equal part. I also give to Rachael one bed, bedstead and furniture, one pot, one kettle, three ewes and lambs. I give and bequeath unto my youngest daughter Sally Simmons a tract of land containing 30 acres, adjoining the tract I live on, on Molsbee's Branch: Beginning on a white oak, William Gillenwater's corner near the mouth of Molsbee's Branch, then with Cove Road to my old line and Molsbee's line, then crossing the branch various courses to the beginning. I also give Betsy one bed, bedstead and furniture, one large kettle. And I give to my daughter Polly a kettle. I give Calvin M. Gillenwaters, my grandson, three ewes and lambs and one bed, bedstead and furniture and the crop now commenced for this year by Robert Kyle and Calvin Gillenwaters. Robert is to have 2/3 of all that may be raised and Calvin 1/3, by their continuing to work together until the crop is finished and to have what bacon and corn it will require to do them this year which we have on hand. My great coat I give to Calvin; all my other clothing to be give to my loving wife. In witness whereof I hereunto set my hand and affix my seal. This 30th day of March, in the year of our Lord one thousand eight hundred and forty-one.

(Seal)

A codicil. I further desire that James G. Simmons be appointed My Executor and Administrator and that he make no sale of any goods' or chattels until in August next. Also that said Simmons not be required to give security in this matter. Also I give to my youngest son, Thomas, my Family Bible. I desire that this shall be considered a part of my last will and to be good and valid in fee simple.

In witness whereof I have hereunto set my hand the day and year above written.

Thomas Gillenwaters (Seal)

Attest:
William Gillenwaters
David Patterson
Geo. Gillenwaters

WILL OF SHEPARD GIBSON

Page: 224
Dated: December 7, 1842

I, Shepard Gibson do make & publish this as my last Will & Testament, hereby revoking & making void all other wills by me at any other time made. First, I direct that all my funeral expenses and all my debts be paid as soon after my death as possible, out of any money that I may die possessed of or may first come into the hands of my Executor. Secondly, I gave and bequeath to my beloved wife Matilda all the land whereon we now live and all the lands elsewhere which is in my name, and all my livestock of personally property, horses, cattle, hogs, sheep and all the household and kitchen furniture.

Thirdly. I gave & bequeath to each of my brothers & sisters the sum of one dollar each, paid as soon as it shall come into the hand of my Exec.

Fourthly and lastly. I do hereby nominate & appoint **Vardy Collins** my Executor. In witness whereof I do to this my will set my hand and seal. This 7th day of December, 1842.

Shepard x Gibson (seal)

(his mark)

Signed, sealed & published in our presence & we have subscribed our names hereunto in the presence of the Testator. This the 7th day of December, 1842.
Witness:

Timothy x Williams, **Vardy x Collins**, **B. G. Sullivan**   (Proven: 2nd
  (his mark)   (his mark)   January, 1843)

WILL OF JOHN GIBBONS

Page 225   Dated: May 31, 1852
                                     Proven: Dec. Term, 1858
                                         [by J. H. Vance, Clk.]

In the Name of God, Amen.

I, **John Gibbons** of the County of Hawkins and State of Tennessee, being of sound mind and memory, but weak of body and knowing the uncertainty of life and the certainty of death, do make and publish this as my last Will and Testament, hereby revoking and annulling all others made by me.

First. I direct that all my funeral expenses be paid and all my just debts be paid as soon after my decease as practicable out of moneys in the hands of my Executors hereafter named.

Second. I give and bequeath to my son **William Gibbons** one negro slave named **William**, one bed and bed clothes.

Third. I give and bequeath to my son **James Gibbons** the sum of one thousand dollars in money on the express condition that **James** shall apply in proper person to my Executors within the period of two years from the time Executors shall qualify in Court. Should he not apply for said money, my Executors shall divide among my three children.

Fourth. I give and bequeath to my son **Robert Gibbons** one negro slave named **Bob**.

Fifth. I give and bequeath to my daughter **Elizabeth Larkin** one negro slave named **Julia Ann** and one other named **Mary Ann** which is all I intend my said daughter to have of my Estate.

Sixth. I give and bequeath to my daughter **Mary Godsey** one slave named **Moriah** and one other named **Preston** and one other named **Sealah**, which slaves and their increase are to remain in the possession of my daughter and be subject to her control during her life, and at her death said slaves and their increase are to be divided equally among her children.

Seventh. After my decease, I desire that all the money that I have on hand at my death and all that is due me be divided by my Executors equally among my children, as follows, to wit: My grand children **Mary Ann Gillenwaters**, **Elizabeth Gillenwaters**, **Nancy L. Miller**, and **Susannah A. Gillenwaters**; the children of my daughter **Nancy Kinkead**, dec'd. to draw the portion of their mother and to be equally divided among them, and the balance to be equally divided among **William Gibbons**, **James Gibbons** & **Robert Gibbons**, my sons, and my daughter **Mary Godsey**.

Eighth. It is my will that after my death my slave **Reuben** and **Mary** be set free.

Ninth. The property remaining at my death shall be sold by my Executors and the proceeds thereof divided among the following children, namely my grand children: **Mary Ann Gillenwaters**, **Nancy L. Miller**, **Susannah A. Gillenwaters** the children of my daughter is to draw their mother's part, and **William**, **James** and **Robert Gibbons** and **Mary Godsey**.

Tenth. I do hereby nominate and appoint my friend **Rob't Cooper**, **Esq.** and my son **Robert Gibbons** Executors of this my last Will and Testament and desire that the County Court shall not require bond & security of them.

In testimony whereof I have hereunto set my hand and seal this 31st day of May, 1852.

John Gibbons (seal)

Signed, & published in our presence:
William R. Pearson, **James Carmack**, **Robert Cooper**

WILL OF JAMES G. GUTHRIE

Page 227   Dated: February 12, 1853
                                         Proven: Mar, 1853

In the name of Almighty God, Amen.

I **James G. Guthrie** of the County of Hawkins in thre State of Tennessee being of sound mind and memory do make and publish this as my last Will and Testament hereby revoking and annulling all other wills by me made at any time heretofore.

First. I direct that my funeral expenses and all my just debts be paid as speedily as possible.

Second. I will and direct that my personal representatives hereinafter to be named dispose of such of my property, including my stock in the East Tennessee & Virginia Railroad and my interest in a grant of land on Bay Mountain, whereupon they may deem it advisable to do so either at public or private sale.

Third. It is my wish and desire that each of my children be as well educated as the means I leave in the hands of my beloved wife **Mary Ann** will justify and she may deem proper and advisable.

Fourth. I desire that my beloved wife retain possession of all my effects in the raising and education of our children, except so much as my personal representatives with the assent of my beloved wife may determine to invest in Western Lands - and also if deemed expedient by them to do so, to purchase a farm or homestead for the use of my family, having the fullest confidence in my wife doing justice to each and all of our children, and I hereby expressly leave it with her to apportion to them such property and means as her ability to do so will allow, giving to each child an equal share. At such time during the time she may remain unmarried as she may think proper to do so, and also if deemed most for the interest of my family, my personal Representative may invest such sums or part of the means in their hands belonging to my estate in the mercantile business or any other branch of business, as to them may seem best calculated to promote the interest of my family. And I do hereby invest my said personal Representatives hereinafter to be named with full power and authority to use and control & manage said Estate with the assent of my said wife, as though I were still alive. And to this end I do hereby authorize and empower them to dispose of any of my negroes when deemed advisable & to purchase others with any funds or means belonging to my estate. And if deemed best by them to loan said funds, then to take bond and good security from time to time so as to secure the principal and interest.

Fifth. I desire that my son **William S. Guthrie** remain with his mother and assist her in raising and educating our children and assist in managing her business, and should he prove obedient, kind and attentive to his mother, and I am well assured that he will, then I desire that she and her co-executors hereafter to be named assist my son in going into business, allowing him an equal share with my other children of my Estate besides what she may think he is entitled to on account of the care and attention bestowed by him as above stated toward his mother & the business of the Estate, leaving it discretionary with her to say at what time these shares shall be paid over during her widowhood.

Sixth. In the event that my beloved wife should hereafter conclude to marry again, then and in that case, I desire & direct that my Executors forthwith make a settlement with her and allot to her a child's share of my Estate, and for them to retain in their hands the remainder of the assets &c belonging to my estate, or if it not in their hands then to proceed immediately to recover possession in order to have them distributed among my children or those of them entitled to said assets, as they may respectively attain the age of 21 years. Or should any of my daughters marry, then in their sound discretion my said Executors may pay over to the husbands of my said daughters such shares or balances coming to them respectively; or if deemed most expedient by my Executors, retain in their hands such shares or funds of said Estate until my said daughters shall respectively attain the full age of 21 years, giving to each one an equal share after deducting whatever may have been expended on account of their raising and education & according to equity & justice.

Seventh. I desire that the claims due by me to the late firm of **Neill & Simpson** and to the Estate of **William Simpson**, dec'd, be recognized and allowed in the division of the Estate of said **William Simpson**, dec'd.

Eighth. And I do hereby appoint my beloved wife **Mary Ann** Executrix and my friends **James K. Simpson & Robert Simpson** Executors of this my last Will & Testament, giving them full and plenary powers to manage my said Estate in such way and manner as in their judgement & sound discretion will promote the best interest of my family and estate - and having the fullest confidence in their integrity and ability to manage the same, it is my request that the County Court do not require bond & security of them, but simply that they qualify as my Executors, &c.

Ninth. In case of the death of any of my Executors, if it should be deemed proper by survivors to fill their places thus made vacant by death or wish to resign, then and in that case, I desire that the Chancellor of the district where my property may be, may appoint other suitable persons to fill such vacancies, possessing the confidence of my family or heirs & possessing the discretion & ability to discharge the duties devolving on them.

And lastly, I bequeath my soul to Almighty God who created it, desiring my body to be decently interred in the graveyard of the First Presbyterian church where my children repose.

In witness whereof I have hereunto set my hand and seal This twelfth day of February, 1853.

James G. Guthrie (seal)

Signed sealed & published in the presence of:

D. Alexander, J. B. Vance, John Blevins

WILL OF MARY GILLENWATERS
Page 229

No Date

Proven in part Nov. Term, 1855

In the Name of God, Amen.

I **Mary Gillenwaters** widow & relic of **Thomas Gillenwaters**, dec'd of the County of Hawkins in the State of Tennessee, being weak of body but of sound memory, considering the uncertainty of life and the certainty of death do make and ordain this to be my last Will and Testament, hereby revoking and annulling all others by me made. I commit my soul into the hands of Almighty God and hope to enjoy eternal happiness when He shall please to call me from this mortal life, and it is my wish and desire that my body shall be buried in a plain, Christian manner, and as to what worldly property it hath pleased the Almighty to place in my hands, I dispose of the same in the following manner, that is to say. I do hereby give and bequeath unto my beloved son-in-law **Thomas Gillenwaters** for his use and that of my beloved daughter **Polly** who intermarried with him, all my personal property which I may possess at my death, consisting of all my stock on the farm, household and kitchen furniture, bedding and clothing - in short, all that I possess for their benefit.

And I do hereby nominate and appoint my said son-in-law **Thomas Gillenwater** Executor of this my last Will and Testament and request the County Court of Hawkins County not to require him to give bond and security as is usual, having confidence in the said **Thomas** that he will act faithfully in the matter.

In testimony whereof I have hereunto set my hand & seal and acknowledged this to be my last Will and Testament in the presence of the following witnesses:

Mary x Gillenwaters (seal)
(her mark)

Test: Elijah C. Gillenwaters
Joel C. Gillenwaters
David Molsbee

WILL OF WILLIAM GILLENWATERS
Page 230

Dated: October 25, 1856

Proven Jan. Term, 1857

[Proven 5-Jan 1857, Rec'd P.5]

In the Name of God, Amen - I give my body to the mother dust and my immortal soul to God who gave it.

The first. I wish to be buried in a Christian manner.

Second. I wish my burial expense paid out of my Estate.

Third. I will to my beloved wife **Sally** her lifetime all my property and one half of my plantation I bought in the State of Kentucky in Monroe Co. of **James B. Thomas**, and the half belongs to my beloved son **George** in the partnership purchase, and at my death and my beloved wife **Sally**, I give him the whole of my plantation to my son **George**, and I bind him in this my will to pay my beloved daughter **Lucritia Wax** the sum of $400.00 in cash. Also, to pay my daughter **Malvinia King** $100.00 in cash, to be paid in two years after my death & my wife **Sally**. Also I give all the money I have on hand to my son **George** to lift my bond from **James B. Thomas** for the above tract of land, and my personal property to be sole at my death and my beloved wife, and to be equally divided between my children. I also bind my son **George** to pay all my just debts.

In testimony given under my hand and seal This 25th day of October, 1856. In presence of us,

Test: **Elijah C. Gillenwaters**   **Wm x Gillenwaters** (seal)
       A. Carmichael   (his mark)

WILL OF ANDREW GALBRAITH (Sr.)

Page 231   Dated: November 17, 1857
                                  Proven: Dec. Term. 1860

In the Name of God, Amen, November 17, 1857.

I **Andrew Galbraith, Sr.** of the County of Hawkins and State of Tennessee, being of sound mind and memory but calling to mind that it is appointed for all men once to die do make and ordain this my last Will and Testament in manner and form following: I give my soul to God who created and gave it, my body to the earth to be decently buried at the discretion of my Executors, and lastly, my earthly estate in the manner following. I will that all my just debts be paid. I give to my daughter **Louisa McCanse** the sum of $5.00, in addition to what she has heretofore received at the time of her marriage. I give to my son **Alexander M. Galbraith** the sum of $200.00, in addition to what he has heretofore received. To my son **John M. Galbraith** the sum of $5.00 in addition to what he has heretofore received. To my daughter **Anna Maria Galbraith** one feather bed and furniture and one half of the proceeds of a plantation sold to **Nelson Getser** in July or August, 1853, it being the farm on which said **Getser** now lives, containing 300 acres more or less which was sold for $5.00 per acre, that the proceeds and interest arising thereon be managed and controled by my Executors for her benefit and support as I deem her incompetent to manage her own property. The proceeds and interest of the other half I will and bequeath to the heirs of my daughter **Elizabeth Lee**, dec'd. I give to my daughter **Sarah Elmore** my negro boy **Page** and girl **Laura**, also one equal divide of any other children my girl **Harriet** may have previous to my death not otherwise disposed of by this will. I also give her my young gray horse Bob, which horse is given in trust for the benefit of her son **William Porter Elmore**. I give to my daughter **Amanda McCarty** my girl **Harriet** and her sons **Orange** and **Wesley** and an equal divide with **Sarah Elmore** of any other children **Harriet** may have as above provided. If I do not in my lifetme make any arrangements for my daughter **Amanda** a home, my Executors are hereby authorized to invest $800.00 out of any monies belonging to my estate in the lands where she lives for the benefit of her and her children. To my sons **Joseph** and **Andrew** I give the farm on which I live (except the marble quarry) containing 700 acres more or less by them paying to my son **Anderson** $1,000.00, and to the son and daughter of **Audley Galbraith**, dec'd $2,000.00, and to my son **William** $500.00 with interest on these sums from one year after my death till paid. They may have indulgence if they desire it on the money to be paid the son & daughter of **Audley Galbraith**, dec'd, until they are of age, by paying the interest.

It is my will in further relation to the part of the farm given to my son **Andrew**, that should he have no children at his death that it revert back to my other children or their heirs. I give to my son **Andrew** my waggons and gears, also the farming tools, one feather bed and furniture, my negro girl **Sarah**, my desk and book case and rifle gun. My son **Andrew** is to have the part of the farm where I now live, and **Joseph** the other part where he lives, dividing by the lane that now leads to the bottom.

The lands up the river to be divided between them giving each necessary ways to ~~ofrom~~ his lots, this relates to the lands above the Big Spring branch. The money to be paid **Frederick A. Galbraith** and **Mary T. Galbraith**, children of **Audley Galbraith**, dec'd., to be equally divided, share and share alike. The marble quarry on the home place to contain fifty acres more or less, embracing all the marble land on the potato hill, I give in equal interest to all my children and their heirs including both families. The proceeds and profits arising therefrom after my decease to be equally divided amongst all my children or their heirs. **Joseph** and **Andrew** to have the benefit of the rents of any houses on the quarry lands during the present lease, and the proceeds of wood sold during said leases to be equally divided between **Joseph**, **Anderson** and **Andrew..** It is further provided that none of the quarry property shall be sold off in lots or shares, but if ever sold, to be sold altogether and proceeds equally divided between beneficiaries——not to be sold for a less sum than $50,000.00. It is my will that my son **Andrew** have my negro boy **Kader.** I give to **Sarah Elmore** my Clarks Commentary on the New Testament. To **Anderson Galbraith** my History of The Methodist Church. To **Wm.Galbraith** Watson's Institutes. To **Joseph Galbraith**, Fletcher's Checks. To **Andrew Galbraith** my Family Bible. To **William** and **Harvey Galbraith** Benson's Commentary. To **Amanda McCarty** my life of Bascom, Bascom's Sermons, Life of Lady Maxwell and Benson's Sermons. The balance of my books to be divided amongst my heirs by my Executors.

My household furniture or other property not disposed of to be sold and anything remaining after paying the bequests herein provided for, the balance to be divided amongst all my children. I appoint my three sons, **Joseph**, **William** and **Andrew** Executors to this my last Will and Testament. In testimony of all and every part herein contained, revoking all others, I have hereunto signed my proper name and affixed my seal the day and date first above written.

Signed, sealed & acknowledged   **A. Galbraith** (seal)
in presence of: **W. H. Moffett**   Say **A. Galbraith, Sr.**
                A. Blackburn
                J. T. Moffett

August 12, 1860, the foregoing will reviewed and approved in all its parts.

Witness: **James L. Etter, C. C. Etter, William W. Etter, Junior**

WILL OF LEVIN GLADSON

Page 234   Dated: March 19, 1858
                              Proven: Apr. 1858

In the Name of God, Amen.

I, **Levin Gladson** of the County of Hawkins and State of Tennessee, being in sound and perfect mind and memory, blessed be God, calling to mind the uncertainty of this life, I do this 19th day of March, 1858 make this my last Will and Testament in manner following, Viz: I have here before given **Joshua** and **Wilton Gladson** their portions, I make no further provision for them. I do hereby give and bequeath all my property to my sons and daughters, Viz: **Nathan, Elizabeth, Mark S. Gladson, Parmaler Hamben (Hamblen), Polly Brooks**, to them and their heirs forever, share and share alike.

I wish all my property to remain on the place until October next, in the care of **Nathan Gladson.** I do hereby appoint **Nathan Gladson** Executor of this my last Will and Testament provided he qualifies and gives security.

Page 234

WILL OF NATHANIEL GRIGSBY

Dated: Feb. 23, 1859
Proven: March Term, 1859

I, **Nathaniel Grigsby,** do make and publish this my last Will and Testament, hereby revoking and making void all other wills by me at anytime made.

First. I direct that all my debts and funeral expenses be paid as soon after my death as possible out of any money that I may die possessed of or may first come into the hands of my Executor; and should there not be sufficient means in his hands to pay all my debts, then I desire that my Executor sell any personal property that my wife **Elizabeth** may designate sufficient to pay any balance.

Secondly. I give and bequeath to my wife **Elizabeth** all my household and kitchen furniture, together with all the stock (except a small filly) I may die seized and possessed of at the time of my death, and all the farming tools of every description that I may have on hand at the time of my death. Also, my negro man named **Jim** to have and to hold during her natural life, and at her death said property is to be sold and equally divided between the following named sons and daughters, to wit: **Winny** (now **Winny Long**), **Henry, Jesse, Samuel, Sarena, Betsy Jane** and **James.**

Thirdly. I give and bequeath to my son **John** $10.00 out of any funds that may remain in the hands of my Executor after my just debts are paid.

And should there be any money left in the hands of my Executor after paying the $10.00 mentioned in this bequest & all my just debts and funeral expenses, I direct that it shall be paid over to my wife for the benefit of my three youngest children, to wit: **Sarena, Betsy Jane,** and **James.**

Fifthly. I give and bequeath the use and control of the land I may die seized and possessed of at the time of my death, for the benefit of herself and the three youngest children, **Sarena, Betsy Jane** and **James,** during her lifetime, and as my son **Jesse** is now living on my farm with me, my will and desire is that he should he remain on the farm and pay my wife for the use of so much of the same as she may not want for cultivation, 10 bushels of corn and 10 bushels of wheat per annum, during her life, that he should have one third part of the land, but should he from any cause fail or refuse to pay said rent to my wife, then and in that case that part of the land devised to him shall go to my son **James.**

Sixthly. I give and bequeath unto my son **James** the remaining two thirds of all the land I may die seized and possessed of; also the one third part devised to **Jesse** should he fail or refuse to comply with the conditions mentioned in the fifth bequest. I also give my son **James** the sorrel filly I now own.

Seventhly. I give and bequeath to my grand daughters **Mary Ann Couch & Martha Couch,** one dollar and no more.

Lastly. I do hereby nominate and appoint **Jas. M. Hord** my Executor. In witness whereof I do to this my will set my hand and seal. This 23rd day of February, 1859.

Nathaniel x Grigsby (seal)
(his mark)

Joseph F. Hord, William x Jones
(his mark)

In witness whereof I the said **Levin Gladson** have to this my last Will and Testament set my hand and fixed my seal the day and year above written.

Levin x Gladson (seal)
(his mark)

Signed and acknowledged in the presence of:
John Hamblen, George Davis, J. M. Baines, John Shanks

Page: 236

WILL OF ROBERT HAMILTON, SR.

Dated: February 21, 1800

In the Name of God, Amen.

I, **Robert Hamilton,** Sen't of the County of Hawkins and State of Tenn., being in a low state of health & weak in body, but of sound mind & memory, calling to mind the mortality of our nature that it is appointed unto all men once to die, I do ordain this my last Will and Testament in form following to wit: After commending my soul to God and my body to the dust, to be buried in a decent Christian manner by Christian friends, hoping the will be again united at the general resurrection of the just, I dispose of my worldly goods as follows, viz:

I allow the first place, all my lawful debts to be paid out of my movable property. I give and bequeath my plantation I live on, on the south bank of Holston containing 225 acres, to my son **Robert,** he paying his brother **John** who is my son one hundred pounds Virginia money.

Item. I give and bequeath to my son **James** one dollar.
Item. I bequeath to my daughter **Catharine** one dollar.
Item. I bequeath to my daughter **Elenor** one dollar.
Item. I give & bequeath to my daughter **Elizabeth** fifty pounds value in trade to be paid as soon as my two hundred acre survey on the heads of Grassy Creek is sold, to be paid in such trade as rec'd for the land.
Item. I allow my 400 acre entry on the north bank of Holston, between **Thomas Morrison & David Kinkead, Esq.** to be sold and the moneys arising therefrom to be divided as follows, viz: To my grand children **Robert** and **Nathan Page,** each the sum of $50.00, to be paid in the same kind of pay that is got for the land. To **Robert McWilliams** and **Robert Brushire** each the sum of ten pounds as above. To my son **John Hamilton's** two sons, **Robert & William,** each ten pounds. I leave the house I now live in & the part of the crop I now receive from my son **Robert,** to wit: One third & all the household & movable property to my wife **Margaret** during her life, cattle and horses inclusive. I leave a judgement I obtained in Sullivan Court against **John Snodgrass** to **James McWilliams.** I leave my horses, cattle & household furniture after paying all my debts at the death of my wife to be sold & the sums not otherwise appropriated to be divided between my son **Robert,** son **John's** son **William & John Bershire.**

I nominate and appoint **Samuel McPheeters,** my son **Robert Hamilton, George Maxwell,** my Executors. They or a majority of them to execute this my last will & testament, announcing & declaring all former wills by me made null & void, and declaring and ratifying this my last Will & Testament. In testimony whereof I have hereunto set my hand & affixed my seal this 21st day of Feb. A. D. 1800. (The words "in & three" in the will interlined before signed).

Robert Hamilton (seal)

Test: **Wm. Young, John Young,** Jurat; **Robert Young, Jr.**

I, **Robert Hamilton,** Sr., the Testator of the foregoing Will and Testament, having through the mercy of God survived to the present date and being in sound mind and memory, tho weak in body, I think proper to annex the following alterations to the foregoing will, to wit:

I leave the plantation I live on to my son **Robert** on his paying $100.00 to my son **John** and $10.00 to his eldest son.
I allow my negro wench **Silla** after my death to live with either my son **Robert** or **Jesse McWilliams,** my son-in-law, and the one she lives with shall

pay annually to the other $20.00. I give & bequeath to my daughter **Elizabeth** in lieu of the fifty pounds, one dollar. My 400-acre entry on the north bank of Holston between **Tho's Morrison** and **David Kinkead**, I allow my son **Robert** to sell and (proceeds) as follows: To my son **Robert** $110.00. The residue to be equally divided between my grandsons. The Executors named in the foregoing will I approve of. Signed & sealed this 24th day of June, A.D., 1801.

Robert Hamilton (seal)

Signed sealed & acknowledged in presence of us:
Test: **William Brandon** & **George Curry**

WILL OF DANIEL HAMLEN

Page 238   Dated: May 25, 1801
In the Name of God Amen.

I, **Daniel Hamlen** of Hawkins County, being very weak in body but of perfect mind & memory do make this my last Will & Testament.

First, I leave my beloved wife **Rosamond** in possession of all the land and plantation, for the support of my wife and family of children until my son **Pascal** shall rise to the age of 20 years, then for him to take his land in possession which shall be hereafter mentioned and so in rotation with the rest of my sons as they shall rise to the age of 20 years, as their land shall be mentioned hereafter. I also leave her in possession of the land and houses whereon I now live with a reasonable support out of the profits of the land for her support alone during her life or widowhood, and at her death or marriage for the said land to return to the use of my sons.

I also give to my wife one negro man named **Abram**, also my chesnutt mare and black mare, four cows and calves of her choosing, all my hogs, sheep, one big plow & the rest of my farming utensils, all my household & kitchen furniture (except one good feather bed and furniture to each of my daughters not yet married) to her and her heirs forever. I give to my daughter **Polly** one negro girl named **Charity** to her and her heirs forever. I give to my daughter **Susannah** one negro man named **Jacob**, one good feather bed & furniture, to her and her heirs forever. I give to my son **Pascal** 100 acres of land I bought of **Wm. Cox** joining **Henry Burem** & **John Rice**, lying on the south side of Holston River to him and his heirs forever. I give to my son **Edwin** the 100 acres of land I bought of **John G. Fletcher**, to him and his heirs forever. I give to my sons **Henry** & **Frank** the land I bought of **Richard Fletcher** containing 150 acres, to be equally divided between them by running a direct line from the river (Holston) out towards Beech Creek, observing **Henry** shall take the Loeft part and **Frank** the upper part, to them and their heirs forever. Also if one of my three sons—**Edwin**, **Henry** or **Frank**—should decease before coming to the age of twenty years, the deceast's part of land shall be divided between the other two.

I give to my daughter **Sally** $333.33 to be levied of my stock & utensils not yet mentioned, one good feather bed and furniture, to her and her heirs forever.

I also constitute & ordain my wife my sole Executrix of this my last Will & Testament. In witness whereof I have set my hand & seal. This 25th day of May, 1801.

Witnesses Present: **Daniel Hamlen** (seal)
Mary x Buram, **Henry Buram**, **Sam'l x Spears**, **Lincoln Amis**, **James Gordon**
   (her mark)   (his mark)

WILL OF THOMAS HARLIN

Page 239   Dated: August 15, 1811
In the Name of God, Amen.

I **Thomas Harlin** of Hawkins County and State of Tennessee, being very sick and weak, or imperfect health of body but of perfect mind and memory, thanks be to God for the same, and calling to mind the mortality of my body and knowing that it is appointed for all men once to die, do make and ordain this my last Will & Testament, (Viz): Principally and first of all, I give and recommend my soul into the hands of Almighty God that gave it, and my body I recommend to the Earth to be buried in a decent Christian burial at the discretion of my Executors, nothing doubting but at the general resurrection I shall receive the same again by the Almighty power of God. And, as touching such worldly estate with which it has pleased God to bless me with in this life, I give, devise and dispose of the same in the following manner (Viz). I give and bequeath to my loving wife **Elizabeth** all my property (after all just debts are paid) and the use of the land until my son **John** shall arrive at lawful age.

2nd. It is my desire for her to have her third her life time.

3rd. Then it is my desire when **John** comes to age for an equal division of the two thirds to take place, and at her—my wife **Elizabeth's**—death, an equal division of her one third to take place.

In witness whereof I have hereunto set my hand and affixed my seal, This 15th August, A.D., 1811.

Thomas x Harlin (seal)
   (his mark)

Test: **P. Reynolds**, **Thomas Gillenwaters**, **John Carmack**, **Cornelius Carmack**

I likewise constitute and appoint **John Carmack** my Executor to act in the same manner as if I myself were present. As witness my hand and seal the day & date above written.

Thomas x Harlin (seal)
   (his mark)

WILL OF JOHN HERREL

Page 240   Dated: Sept. 9, 1815
In the Name of God, Amen.

I, **John Herrel** of the County of Hawkins and State of Tennessee, being of sound mind and memory but being old and knowing the frailty of man and the uncertainty of this life, do make and ordain this my last Will & Testament in writing in manner and form as followeth: That after recommending my soul to God and my body to the dust from whence it came, to be buried in a plain manner after my decease. And concerning such worldly goods as it has pleased God to bestow on me, I dispose of them in the following manner:

First. I desire my funeral charges to be paid out of my estate, and my debts to be paid in like manner.

Item 1. I give unto my daughter **Polly** ten dollars and all my housel goods at my wife's death.

Item 2. I do allow all the rest of my property including negroes to be sold at the discretion of my Executors which will hereafter nominate, and the moneys when collected divided between my daughters **Sally Norman**, **Tish North**, **Lidy Comes** and **Polly Herrel**. (**Frank** and **Samuel Woods** my grandsons) between

the two to have an equal part with my daughters which I have named and my
sons Brock Harrel and John Harrel, & my daughters Betsy Shark and Winney
Parrott I have heretofore given their shares - the boys in the way of land,
and the girls in a negro apiece which I hope they will be content with, and
I do appoint John Harrel and Jacob Miller Executors of this my last Will and
Testament in writing, and do by these presents revoke, disannul and make void
every other will or wills by me made.

In testimony whereof I have hereunto set my hand and affixed my seal,
this ninth day of September, one thousand Eight hundred and fifteen.

John x Harrel (RLS)
(his mark)

Signed, sealed published & declared
by John Harrel to be his last Will
and Testament in presence of us
who was subscribing witnesses thereto.

David Henshan (?)
Jesse McWilliams
John Grove and L. Wilson

WILL OF JOHN HENSON

Page 241

Dated: October 8, 1816
Admitted to Record Feb. 7, 1817

I John Henson of Hawkins County, State of East Tennessee (sic), do hereby make my last Will and Testament in manner and form following, that is to
say:

First. I desire that all my just debts be paid and satisfied.
Secondly. After the payment of all my just debts, I give to my wife
Elizabeth Henson one half of my Estate, both real and personal. The other
half to my child she is now pregnant with, provided said child should live
to the year of maturity, but if it should please God that the child should
die an infant, I will the whole of my Estate as before mentioned to my wife
Elizabeth, her and her heirs forever.

And lastly. I do hereby constitute and appoint my loving wife Elizabeth
Executrix and my friend Gabriel McGraw Executor of this my last Will and
Testament, hereby revoking all other former wills or testaments by me hereto-
fore made. In witness whereof I have hereto set my hand and affixed my seal.
This 8th day of October, in the year of our Lord, one Thousand Eight Hundred
and sixteen.

John Henson (seal)

Signed, published and declared as and for the last Will and Testament
of the above named John Henson in presence of us.

William P. Richardson, Geo. W. Blincoe, John Ratcliffe

At a Court held for Fairfax County [Virginia] the 21st day of October
1816, this last Will and Testament of John Henson, dec'd was presented in
Court and the same being proven by oath of Geo. W. Blincoe and affirmation
of William P. Robertson is admitted to record.
Test. Wm. Moss, Clk.

The Commonwealth of Virginia, Fairfax County, to wit: I William Moss,
Clerk of the County Court aforesaid do hereby verify that the foregoing is
a true copy of the last Will & Testament of John Henson dec'd from the records
of my office seal. In testimony whereof I have hereunto set my hand and affixed the seal of the said County the 23rd of Nov., 1816, in the 41st year
of the Commonwealth.

Wm. Moss, Clk.

Fairfax County and Commonwealth of Virginia, to wit: I, Richard
Ratcliffe a presiding Justice of the Peace in and for the County aforesaid
do hereby certify that William Moss whose signature and seal of office is
above affixed is duly commissioned and appointed Clerk of the Court of the
said County, and that due faith and credit is to be given all his attestations
as such. Witness my hand and seal this 23rd of November, 1816.

R. Ratcliffe (Clerk)

WILL OF JOHN HOWEL

Page 242

Dated: August 10, 1820
Proven: August, 1820

In the Name of God, Amen.

I John Howel of the County of Hawkins and State of Tennessee, do make,
ordain and declare this instrument which is written by my order thereto
subscribing with my name to be my last Will and Testament, revoking all
others. All my debts of which I owe are to be punctually and speedily paid.
and the legacies hereafter bequeathed are to be discharged as soon as circumstances will permit and in the manner directed.

To my dearly beloved wife Mary Howel, I give and bequeath the use, profit
and benefit of all the slaves that I am now in possession of which is: Luce,
Lilla and Ruth, two horse creatures, black horse and mare, one called Dick
and Trim, and two cows and calves her choice, three beds and furniture and
all the kitchen furniture, and to have possession of the house that we now
live in, and 100 acres of land during life, and at her decease, the land to
fall to my youngest son Willy B. Howel, and my wife to have four sheep, the
pick of the flock, and two of the best sows and shoats and nine killing hogs,
and to keep all her geese and poultry with her cupboard and furniture and one
big bar share plow and shovel, and let Mattison, Elizabeth and Willy have one
heifer apiece and Sara one cow the name of Spot. Clark one cow the name of
Little Brin and 100 acres of land where William Caley now occupies and one
wagon that David Casner filled the wheels lately, one bedstead, bed and furniture, one big bar share plow, one table. To James 100 acres of land lying
in Mitchell's hollow joining John Pack's land, one bedstead, bed and furniture, one cow, two shovel plows and one collar. And Clark and James shall
pay their sisters $50.00 apiece that is, Nancy, Sally and Betsy. And
Mattison to have one hundred acres of land - a place called Tate's Place, and
Willy to have 100 acres of land where I now live house (sic) and to pay
Mattison $150.00 when Willy Arrives at the age of 25 years of age.
And Sally to have a bedstead, bed & furniture and one cow, bedstead,
bed and furniture. And all the rest of my property that is not mentioned here
is to be sold and the money divided between William, Nancy, Sally and Betsy.

Lastly, I constitute and appoint my worthy neighbors David Chambers,
Haynes Amis Executors of this my last Will & Testament. In witness of all
and each of (the) herein mentioned, I have set my hand and seal the 10th day
of August in the year of our Lord one Thousand Eight hundred and twenty.

John Howel (seal)
Test:
Thos. T. Tate
William x McCoy
(his mark)

WILL OF JAMES HAGAN

Page 244

Dated: August 17, 1820
Proven: May Term 1829

I **James Hagan** of Hawkins County and State of Tennessee, being of sound mind and memory but of weak body, knowing the uncertainty of human events, ordain and desire this to be my last Will and Testament. After giving my soul to Almighty God, the giver of it, I devise my worldly affairs in the manner following, to wit: 1st. I devise to my daughter **Frances Hagan** my negro or mulatto girl **Almira**, the daughter of **Cate**. 2nd. I bequeath to my sons **John, Thomas & Alexander Hagan** each a horse, saddle and bridle to be worth $100.00. 3rd. I bequeath to my daughter **Margaret Hagan**, when she arrives at the age of 21 years, a horse, saddle and bridle to be valued at $100.00. 4th. I bequeath to my daughter **Elizabeth R. Hagan** my negro boy **Barney**, son of **Nancy** who is at this time in State of Kentucky in the care of my brother **Alexander Hagan**. The whole of which devises I wish kept under the direction with all my other real and personal estate of my beloved wife **Rachael Hagan** during her life or widowhood. After her death, or in case she should intermarry, my estate both personal and real to be equally divided by five persons chosen by the Court of Pleas and Quarters for the said County of Hawkins, among all my children, Viz: **Margaret, John, Thomas, Alexander, Alice, Mary, Frances & Elizabeth**. It is my desire that my wife **Rachael Hagan** act as my Executrix with my son **John Hagan** when he arrives at the age of 21 years as Executor. Hereby revoking and making void all other wills. Given under my hand & seal, this 17th day of August, Eighteen Hundred and twenty.

James Hagan (seal)

Signed, sealed and acknowledged in our presence the date above written.
Jno. A. Rogers, John H. Smith

WILL OF JOHN S. HILL

Page 245

Dated: May 20, 1823
[Died 1830-34[

Although at present in tolerable health, thanks be to God, yet certain circumstances render it my duty to provide for the disposal of the little property I now possess or may hereafter possess, and while the blessing of health and sound mind offer, I **John S. Hill** of Hawkins County, State of Tenn., make this my last Will and Testament in the following manner:

1st. I request that all the debts I owe may be paid by my Executrix and Executor hereafter named as soon as may be convenient after my decease.

2nd. I give to my sons **Charles Miller Hill** and **James Hill** the sum of five dollars each only - as I consider they have already a full and equal share with what I have hereby to give my other children.

3rd. To my ever dear and respected wife **Martha** I give the whole and every part of the balance of my property - lands, negroes, stock of every kind, household and kitchen furniture, farming utensils &c during her life.

4th. At her decease, my will is that the whole of my property be divided among my children in the following manner: That all those of them who may be under sixteen years of age at the time of their mother's death shall (?) to the amount of $200.00 worth of property each, over and above an equal share with those that may be at that time twenty one years of age or over, and likewise to all those at that time who may be between twenty one

and sixteen years old, $100.00 worth of property each, more than those who may be then twenty one years of age or more.

5th. I give my children **Betsy Hill, Levin Hill, Sally Hill, Martha Hill, Ketty Hill, Ann Augusta Hill & Thomas Robinson Hill** at the death of their mother the whole of my land, also negroes **Fred, Cherry, Dick, Eliza, Martha** and all the children that **Cherry, Eliza** and **Martha** may hereafter have. Also all the stock of every kind, the whole of the household and kitchen furniture, the farming utensils of every kind and the whole of the provisions that maybe on hand at that time, each to have an equal share to them and to each of their heirs.

6th. To **Polly Moore, Benjamin Hill, John Stephen Hill, Peggy Hill, Jenny Boltzell** and **Joshua Hill** I give all and every part of the balance of my property, to be equally divided amongst them (the following few articles next mentioned only excepted) to each of them and to their heirs, to wit: To **Polly Moore** three silver table spoons marked "JBM" and to **Peggy Hill** the three other silver tablespoons marked in like manner with initials of the names of their great grandfather and great grandmother **Joseph** and **Bathsheba Miller**. To **Jenny Boltzell** five silver teaspoons marked "J.M.D.", the initials of the names of her grandfather and granmother, **James** and **Mary Deane**, and likewise all the finger and ear rings, necklaces, locket, &c that formerly belonged to her deceased Mother. To **Joshua Hill**, six silver teaspoons marked "J.M.D." and to **Thomas Robinson Hill**, he being the youngest and there not being a sufficiency worth dividing, I give six silver teaspoons, a large silver soup spoon and a pair of silver sugar tongs, all marked with the initials of his mother and my name, "J.M.H.". And to my son **Levin Hill** my watch, it being an uncommon one, therefore I request him to keep it for my sake.

7th. To provide as much as possible for my childrens' welfare after my decease, and guard against the destructive power of a step-father, my will is that if my wife should take a second husband that she then directly be entitled to no more of my property than the law will allow her, and in that case, hereby revoke all and every bequeath hereby made to her, and that a division of it may take place as soon thereafter as may be convenient.

8th. And lastly, I appoint my dear wife **Martha Hill** and my old friend **Andrew Galbraith** to be the Executrix & Executor of this my last Will and Testament.

In witness of the above, I the said **John S. Hill**, have to this act set my hand and seal this twentieth day of May in the year of our Lord, One Thousand, Eight Hundred & Twenty-three.

John S. Hill (seal)

Signed, sealed and acknowledged by the said **John S. Hill** for his last Will and Testament in the presence of **John Buckhart, Aquilla Jones, Alexander M. Galbraith.**

WILL OF BENONY HARRIS

Page 246

Dated: February 10, 1829

Be it remembered that I **Benony Harris** of the County of Hawkins, State of Tennessee, being low in body but of sound and perfect mind and memory doth make this my last Will & Testament in the manner and form following:

First. I do order that all my lawful and just debts be paid out of my personal property. Then I give and bequeath unto my beloved wife **Rachael** all my personal property during her widowhood, and also I bequeath unto my beloved wife **Rachael** full possession of all my lands during her widowhood. And then I do order that when my two youngest sons, **William** and **Isam** shall become of age, that she shall let them have one horse, saddle and bridle worth $100.00, to make them equal with my two oldest sons, **Absalom** and **James Harris.** And then I do order that as my daughters shall become of age, namely: **Sally, Polly , Janny, Lutey & Elizabeth**, that my wife **Rachael** let each of them have one cow and calf with each of them a bed, and I do order that at the end of my wife's widowhood, the residue of my personal property with all my lands be sold and an equal divide made between all my ears of the money arising from such sale, and I do appoint my wife **Rachael** as Executrix of this my last will testament (sic), revoking all former wills made by me. In witness whereof I have set my hand and seal. February 10th, 1829.

Test:
Benony x Harris (seal)
(his mark)

George White
John Harris

WILL OF GOODLEFF/GOODLAF HUFFMASTER

Page 247
Dated: April 18, 1829
Proven: May Term, 1844

In the Name of God, Amen.

Be it remembered that I **Goodlaf Huffmaster** of the County of Hawkins, State of Tennessee, considering the uncertainty of this mortal life, and being of sound and perfect mind and memory, blessed be Almighty God for the same, do make and publish this my last Will & Testament in manner and form following, that is to say:

First. I give and bequeath unto my son **John** my plantation where I now live, being in the County and State as aforesaid for which he is to maintain me and my wife our lifetime. Likewise, I give my son **John** all my farming utensils for which he is to pay $40.00 at my death in the following manner, that is to say. Unto my son **Joseph** $25.00, son **Jonathan** $10.00, son **Daniel's** heirs by the **Anny** (sic) $5.00, and after my wife's death, all the household furniture, that is to say, two beds, clothes cloth (sic) and in a word all the loose property about the house is to be equally divided among my four daughters, that is to say, **Barbary, Mary, Sally & Betsy**, and for this I appoint my son **Joseph Huffmaster** and **Issac Lauderback** Executors to see to the dividing of property equally of this my last Will & Testament, hereby revoking all former wills by me made.

In witness whereof I have hereunto set my hand and seal the Eighteenth day of April in the year of our Lord, one thousand, eight hundred and twenty nine.

Goodlaf x Huffmaster (seal)
(his mark)

Signed, sealed published and declared by the above named **Goodlaf Huffmaster** to be his last Will and Testament in the presence of us who at his request and in his presence have hereunto subscribed our names as witnesses to the same.

John Walker
(Other witness name illegible)

WILL OF CHRISTOPHER HAYNES

Page 248
Dated: Dec. 9, 1830

In the Name of God, Amen.

I do hereby constitute this my last Will & Testament, revoking all others heretofore made. I now proceed to make the following disposition of my property both real and personal which division shall take place after my death. I give unto my wife **Frances** a negro woman **Peggy**, a negro man **Miles** and a negro boy **Manson** during her widowhood; also one cow and calf, one feather bed and furniture for the same forever. I do give unto the heirs of my son **Thomas Haynes** $15.00 forever. Unto the heirs of my son **Turner Haynes**, $10.00 forever. Unto my son **Drury Haynes**, $25.00 forever; unto **Lazarus Spears** $25.00 forever; unto **James Bradley** $25.00 forever; unto my daughter **Feruby Spears** a negro girl **Lydia** forever. Unto my daughter **Sarah Charles** a negro girl **Edy** forever. Unto my daughter **Jane Hagan** a negro boy **Joe** forever; unto my daughter **Mary Haynes** a negro boy **John**, a negro girl **Margaret** forever. The residue of my property both real and personal I wish to be sold and proceeds thereof to be equally divided between my sons, **John, Christopher, Jesse** and **Francis.** The above loaned negroes to my wife at the expiration of her widowhood to be sold and equally divided between my sons above mentioned-- **John, Christopher, Jesse & Francis.**

I do hereby constitute my son-in-law **James Bradley** and my nephew **Haynes Amis** my sole Executors. In testimony whereof I do hereunto affix my hand and seal, this ninth day of December, A.D. Eighteen hundred and thirty.

Christopher x Haynes(seal)
(his mark)

Witnesses: **John H. Kershner, Hugh Woods, Thomas J. Amis**

WILL OF JAMES HAGOOD

Page 249
Dated: August 9, 1833

Whereas I **James Hagood** of Hawkins County in the State of Tenn., being frail in body but of sound mind, taking into view that all men must die and being desirous so to settle and adjust my affairs that my family may be provided for in the best manner possible consistent with the amount of property I hold, and that all difficulties or grounds for dispute or litigation about this may be removed, do ordain, publish and declare this to be my last Will and Testament, hereby revoking and annulling all former wills.

Imprimis. I give and bequeath so much of my personal property as may be necessary to discharge all my debts and expenses of every kind to my Executors to be sold on twelve months' credit & then collected and paid over till all said debts and expenses are paid.

Item. I give and bequeath unto my beloved wife **Nancy Hagood** my land whereon I live containing 90 acres more or less to have and to hold during her widowhood or life if she shall not marry again, and after the marriage or death of my wife, I will the land to my daughter **Becky Ingram**, wife of **Miller Ingram**, and **Anne Raley** wife of **Phillip Raley** and their heirs respectively in fee simple, share and share alike.

Item. I give & bequeath to my s'd wife **Nancy** the following negroes Viz: **Franky, Jack, Jesse, Betsy & Julia** to have during her widowhood or life if she never marry again, and after her marriage or death to my sons **Benjamin F., James M., & Stephen D.** in full property to be divided among them equally & if there should be any increase of said negroes during the time they are to be helf by my wife, s'd increase to be divided between my sons in same manner.

Item. I bequeath unto my son **Benjamin F.** my blazed face mare called Jen and her sucking colt and a feather bed and furniture and bedstead and the saddle and bridle he now uses and claims.

Item. I give and bequeath unto my son **James M.** my bay mare called Fan, a bedstead, feather bed and furniture and the saddle and bridle he generally uses and claims.

Item. I give and bequeath unto my son **Stephen D.** that my Executors shall upon his coming of age give him out of my Estate as good a mare as Fan, that is left to **James M.**, a saddle and bridle worth $15.00, a bedstead, feather bed, furniture and a good fur hat.

Item. I give and bequeath that after my debts and expenses and all other legacies are paid, all my other stock, household and kitchen furniture and farming utensils shall go to my wife **Nancy** to hold during her widowhood or life if she never marry again, and after her death or marriage to go to my sons **Benjamin F., James M. & Stephen D.**, share and share alike...

Item. I give and bequeath unto my son **William** one dollar, he having already been sufficiently provided for.

I do hereby appoint my wife **Nancy** and my sons **Benjamin F.** and **James M.** Executrix and Executors of this my last Will and Testament, and they are not to be required to give security, and it is also my will that in the event of the marriage of my wife, then my said sons shall be my sole Executors and her power shall cease. And in the event of any dispute or difficulty among my legatees or Executors in reference to my estate or this will, I do hereby appoint **Jacob Miller, Lazarus Spears, Thomas Coldwell, Daniel Chambers & Orville Bradley** as arbitrators to whom said difficulty or dispute shall be referred and any (of) these are sufficient to act and their award to be conclusive and final.

Item. It is my will that my Executors be authorized in any manner they may deem proper by agreement, compromise, or otherwise, to settle and ascertain the boundary line between my lands and the lands of **George**

Francisco, if (this) is not done during my lifetime.

Item. It is my will that the crop on hand shall go to the support of the family. Given under my hand & seal This 9th of August, 1833.

J. Hagood (seal)

Witnesses present who witnessed this will in the presence of & at the request of the Testator:
Orville Bradley, Geo. R. Powel, G. Francisco

I, **James Hagood**, do this 11th day of August, 1833, offer the following codicil or supplement to the above will & do declare it in all respects to be a part thereof. That is to say, that if my wife should either die or marry before the first day of January, 1842, Executors to hold the land until that time to maintain and school my youngest son **Stephen D. Hagood**.

Item. If either of my three sons, **Benjamin F., James M.** or **Stephen D.** should die intestate or unmarried, then in that case the survivor or survivors is to heir what is willed to the three. The five barrels of corn that **Robert Gray** owes me this fall is to be collected and considered as part of the crop. Given under my hand and seal day & date above written.

J. Hagood (seal)

Witnesses present & who witnessed this will in presence of & at the request of the Testator:
G. Francisco, T. Coldwell, Jr.

Whereas I **James Hagood** did make my will in August last & thereby did lend five negroes to my wife during her widowhood & at her marriage or death to be divided between my three sons...since which I have sold one of them to **George M. Lyons.** Now I do offer this schedule to explain my intention concerning the disposal of the proceeds of the sale of said negro. What money, bank notes & bonds may remain on hand at my death, after paying my debts & all expenses, to be equally divided between my wife & three sons, **Benjamin F., James M. & Stephen D. Hagood,** and **Stephen's** share to be put out on interest to some safe hand until he becomes of age, which will be in the year 1841. The will & Codicil annexed thereto is hereby confirmed. Done this 20 July, 1834.

J. Hagood (seal)

In presence of who was desired to witnesseth:
Test: **George Francisco**
      Clinton A. Charles

WILL OF NANCY HORD

Page 252   Dated: October 5, 1837

I, **Nancy Hord** of the County of Hawkins and State of Tennessee do make and publish this my last Will and Testament, hereby revoking and making void all former wills by me at any time heretofore made.

First. I direct that all my funeral expenses and just debts be paid out of any moneys that I may die possessed of or that may first come into the hands of my Executors.

Second. I do give and bequeath unto my children, **Eldridge, Thomas, William** and **Lucretia Rowan,** formerly **Hord,** all the property real and personal that I die possessed of except what (I herein dispose of). That is, that **William's** share be $100.00 less than the others on account of a still that he has received. Also that the children of my son **Stanwix,** dec'd. jointly receive a share equal to one of my own children which shall be divided among them as follows: **Nancy** and **Malvina** **Hord's** share to be equal, **William Stanwix Hord's** share five hundred dollars more than **Nancy** or **Malvina.**

I do further will and direct that my negro slave **Hannah** be freed at my death. I do hereby make, ordain and appoint my son **Eldridge Hord** and **Robert W. Kinkead,** Executors of this my last Will and Testament. In witness whereof I have unto this my will written on one sheet of paper, set my hand and seal, This 5th day of October, 1837. The words "be paid" interlined before signed.

Signed and sealed in the presence   **Nancy x Hord** (seal)
of us who subscribed in the   (her mark)
presence of each other.
N. Fain
Jos. Huffmaster

WILL OF ABRAHAM HAUN

Page 253   Dated: October 23, 1841
                                     Proven: Aug. 2nd, 1847

In the Name of God, Amen,
I **Abraham Haun** being weak in body but of sound mind and memory, do make

Page 253

WILL OF OGDON HALE

Dated: Dec. 13, 1841.

Proven: Sept. Term, 1849

Be it remembered that I, Ogdon Hale of the County of Hawkins and State of Tennessee, being weak in body, but of sound and perfect mind and memory, blessed be Almighty God for the same, do make and publish this my last will and Testament in manner and form following, that is to say:

First. I give and bequeath to my daughter Mary Haynes the sum of one dollar. I also give and bequeath to my daughter Anne Kelly the sum of one dollar. I give and bequeath to my son Harvey Hale the sum of one dollar. I also give and bequeath to my son Thomas Hale the sum of one dollar. I also give and bequeath to my sons Arthur, Jesse and Turner Hale the sum of one dollar. Which several legacies or sums of money I will and order shall be paid to the said respective legatees within two years after my decease.

I also give and bequeath to my daughter Kiziah Hale and my son Samuel Hale all my land in said county, lying on south side of Holston River, on the waters of Beech Creek, together with all my personal estate, goods and chattels; but if either Kiziah or Samuel die, the other is then to have the land and personal property above named, only reserving to my beloved wife Lorina Hale a home and support during her lifetime out of the above named land and personal property, hereby revoking all former wills by me made.

In witness whereof I have hereunto set my hand and seal, Dec. 18, 1841.

Ogdon x Hale
(his mark)

Signed sealed published and declared by the above named Ogdon Hale to be his last Will and Testament in the presence of us who at his request and at his presence have hereunto subscribed our names as witnesses to the same.

Jacob M. Charles, Sally Charles

Page 254

WILL OF SAMUEL HENDERSON

Dated: Mar 30, 1843

Proven: May Term, 1843

In the Name of God Amen.

I Samuel Henderson of the County of Hawkins and State of Tennessee, being weak in body but of sound and perfect mind and memory do make and publish this my last Will & Testament in manner and form following that is to say.

First, I give and bequeath unto my wife the tract of land I reside on during her natural life; after her death it is to go to my sons Pleasant and Samuel Henderson; one bay mare, one black and one brown mare. I bequeath to my wife also my entire stock of hogs. It is my will that my tract of land in the Western District be sold on a twelve-month credit and all the proceeds of sale except $300.00 be divided between my three daughters Betsy, Lucinda and Amanda, and the $300.00 named above to go to my three grand children, i.e. Thomas, George and William. My land on the south side of the river, about 40 acres to be sold on twelve-month credit and my other four grand children, Milly, Bally, Samuel & John to have $100.00 each, and the remainder to go to my three daughters named, equally divided my wife to have two of the plows, two axes, four hoes, three milk cows & yoke of oxen. The rest of my farming tools and waggon and cattle is to be sold, also my bay colt and sorrel horse and proceeds divided equally between my sons Pleasant and Samuel L. Henderson.

My daughter Lucinda is to have a sorrel horse named Jim.

My entire stock of sheep to go to my wife during her lifetime, then to be equally divided between all my children. My four negroes, Sally, Minne, Gibb, and Pack to go to my wife that she may dispose of as she chooses, so they are left among my children, but according to her own notion. I wish my son Samuel L. to collect a debt (from each of the following): David Lyons, Jr., Thomas Taylor, John McWilliams, Orville Bradley, and Jacob Burris, and to account for same on final settlement with Pleasant Henderson. My just debt to be paid out of any money on hand, and if there is a surplus it is to go to my wife. I bequeath to my daughter Amanda one boy per name of Bill.

ALL the grain of every kind to be left for use of the family.

I do hereby appoint Pleasant and Samuel L. Henderson Executors of this my Will & Testament, hereby revoking all former wills by me made. In witness whereof I have hereunto set my hand and seal this 30th of March, 1843.

Samuel x Henderson (seal)
(his mark)

Signed sealed published and declared by the above named Samuel Henderson to be his last will in the presence of us who have subscribed our names as witnesses in the presence of the Testator.

Robert Johnson, Joshua Phipps; William F. McCullah

Page 255

WILL OF ARTHUR HALE

Dated: May 19, 1845

Be it understood that I, Arthur Hale of the County of Hawkins and State of Tennessee, being of sound and perfect mind and memory do make and publish this my last will and Testament in manner and form following, that is to say:

First. I give and bequeath unto my beloved wife Jane Hale the tract of land on which I live during her lifetime or widowhood, then to be divided between my two youngest daughters, Alis and Marthy. Also I give and bequeath to my two eldest daughters a old tract or part of an old tract and entry land joining Barnabas Kelly and David Tate, divided equally between them—

Hiley J. Hale and Betsy Viney Hale. Also, I bequeath to Kindred Hale my son, a tract of land that I bought of Jesse and R. Jackson called the Barber Jay Place, all the above named land lying in said County and on the waters of Beech Creek. Also, I give and bequeath to each heirs and my wife a bed and furniture and stead to be made equal. Also to my wife and children all my property remain in the hands or under control of my wife as long as the children remain with her. When they leave or have a need of it, they to have their proportional part of property. My son Kindred Hale is to have a horse, saddle and bridle. Also that a brown filly be sold and the moneys divided between Hiley J. Hale and Betsy Viney Hale. Also that my wife and my son Kindred sell such surplus property as they do not need and youse the proceeds for support of the family. In witness whereunto I set my hand and fix my seal This 19th May, 1845.

Arthur Hale(seal)

Riley Jones, James Charles, Alexander Hale

WILL OF JOHN HEADRICK

Page 256   Dated: Sept. 23, 1847

In the Name of God, Amen.

    I, John Headrick, being of sound and disposing mind and memory do make publish and ordain this to be my last Will and Testament in manner as follows (Viz): My body I give to be buried in a Christian like manner at the discretion of my friends, and my soul to return to God who gave it. After all my just debts are paid, I wish to dispose of my property, both real and personal in the following manner:

    First. I give and bequeath to my wife Rachael a certain sorrel mare for her own use and benefit, to dispose of as she pleases. The balance of the personal property to be sold, except what she may want to keep for her benefit, except the blacksmith tools is to belong to my son John B. Headrick. I will to my son James W. Headrick one dollar. I will to my son Barnard C. one dollar. I will that the personal property which may be sold...that the proceeds, together with my outstanding debts be collected and the proceeds equally divided between my son Elijah W., daughter Peggy Phillips and my daughter Ann Walker.

    I will that my wife Rachael have the use and benefit of the plantation that I now live on during her life, and at her decease, I will that the plantation be sold and the proceeds divided between Elijah W., Peggy Phillips, & Ann Walker.

    I do hereby nominate & appoint James W. Headrick to be the Executor of this my last Will & Testament, This 23rd day of September 1847.

John x Headrick (seal)
(his mark)

Witness:

Samuel Chesnutt

(name of other witness illegible)

WILL OF BENJAMIN HUTCHISSON

Page 257   Dated: October 13, 1849

In the Name of God, Amen.

    I Benjamin Hutchisson of the County of Hawkins, State of Tennessee, being of sound mind and disposing memory, but somewhat feeble in body, do make and publish this my last Will and Testament.

    First. It is my wish and desire that the expenses attending my death and burial shall be paid out of any money or property that I may have at the time of my death, as soon after my death as practicable.

    Second. It is my wish and desire that my son Rudolph shall have a young bay horse that he now uses called Rover, together with all the money that he has in his hands of mine—the money for which he sold my property.

    Third. It is my will and desire that my grand daughter Margaret, daughter of Rudolph, shall be furnished by my daughter Rebecca with a good bed, bedstead and furniture when she arrives at the age of eighteen.

    Fourthly. It is my wish and desire that my daughter Rebecca shall have all my land consisting of 150 acres, together with all my personal property, books, papers, &c, but in case Rebecca should die before my grand daughter Margaret arrives at the age of eighteen, Wm. Huchisson and Henry Watterson should dispose of my property as they may see proper, and furnish to Margaret the property to wit: the bed and furniture.

    Fifth. It is my wish and desire that William Hutchisson shall be my Executor without security.

    In testimony whereof I hereunto set my hand and seal This 13th day of October, one thousand, eight hundred and forty nine, in presence of:

H. Watterson, Thomas T. Barrett

Benjn Hutchisson

WILL OF JORDAN HUNDLEY

Page 258   Dated: May 14, 1853
                            Proven: Nov. Term, 1853

I, Jordan Hundley of the County of Hawkins, State of Tennessee, make and constitute the following to be my last Will and Testament.

    Item First. My will and desire is that after my death, my body may be buried in a decent manner.

    Item Second. My will and desire is that out of my money or property all my just debts be paid by my Executor hereafter appointed.

    Item Third. My will and desire is that my beloved wife Elizabeth shall have all my lands whereon I now live containing about 60 acres, and at her death, my said land to descend to my beloved son Jordan Hundley who now lives with me, and that he have full title to land at the death of his mother.

    Item Fourth. My desire is that my wife hold all the household and kitchen furniture belonging to me and one cow and yearling if she may choose to keep same.

    Item Fifth. My will and desire is that my Executor pay my son William Hundley one dollar, he having heretofore been provided for.

    Item Sixth. It is my will and desire that my Executor pay my son Joseph Hundley one dollar, he having heretofore been provided for.

    Item Seventh. I desire that the heirs of my daughter Nancy Tucker, wife of A. Tucker, receive from my Executor one dollar, she having been provided for.

    Item Eighth. My desire is that my daughter Lucy Cavin, wife of John Cavin receive one dollar, she having been provided for.

    Item Ninth. My will and desire is that my daughter Phebe Richards, wife of Aaron Richards receive one dollar, she having provided for.

    Item Eleven (No Item Ten). My will is that Elizabeth Cavin (no relationship stated, but assumed a daughter) receive from my Executor one dollar, she having been provided for.

WILL OF HEZEKIAH HAMBLEN

...I further make, constitute and appoint my son Jordan Hundley my Exec'., and that he have all of my personal estate not otherwise herein disposed of out of which to pay my debts and the several bequests herein made, and any remainder to him after the death of my wife, she retaining and using the same during her life, she having the right to dispose (of) to whom she may please of the household and kitchen furniture devised to her.

In testimony whereof I have hereunto set my hand and seal. This 14th day of May, 1853.

Jordan x Hundley (seal)
(his mark)

Witness: Jacob Miller, Abraham Britton

Page 259

WILL OF HEZEKIAH HAMBLEN

Dated: January 22, 1854
Proven: Feb. Term, 1855

In the Name of God, Amen.

I, Hezekiah Hamblen of the County of Hawkins, State of Tennesee, being in good health and in sound and perfect mind and memory, blessed be God, being in the seventy-ninth year of my age and calling to mind the mortality of this life do this 22nd day of January in the year of our Lord, 1854 make this my last Will & Testament in manner following, Viz:

Whereas I have heretofore given to most of my children portions of my property as circumstances suggested, I gave to my son William a whole portion, I gave to my son Henry Hamblen part of his portion, and now I give to Henry all that tract of land I purchased of Thomas Hamblen lying on the waters of Stock Creek which Henry now lives on, which makes up his whole portion. I gave to my daughter Elizabeth Smith her whole portion. I gave to my daughter Mary Smith negro Sam & other things, and I give to her daughter and son Caroline and Moses a negro girl Beckey which makes up the full portion. I gave to my daughter Jane Lauderback her full portion. I gave to my son Abner part of his portion and now I give him Molly and Frank and their increase, to him and his heirs forever. I gave to my son John part of his portion and now I give John negro Jesse. I have given daughter Nancy part of her portion and now I give to Nancy negro Harriet and her increase, to the said Nancy and her heirs as the balance of her portion. I have given no portion to my daughter Priscilla Green, and now I give her negro Eliza and her two children Stokley and Ned. I also give and bequeath to my grandson William Greene a negro boy named Bob. Also to my grand daughter Susannah Greene a negro boy named Peter, which goes for Priscilla's portion. I have given to my daughter Susannah Ely her full portion. I hereby lend to my wife Nancy half of my tract of land upon Caney Creek and the following named negroes - Willis, Marie, Marcia, Ellen, Mary, Florida and Sandy, two of my horses - her choice, five cattle - her choice, during the time she lives single or during her natural life. It is my will that my mulatto man Harry be free and emancipated at my death. Now, my son William and my daughter Mary are dead. I do hereby bequeath the balance of my estate, real and personal--together with the part lent to my wife, after her marriage or death to my sons and daughters, Henry, Elizabeth Smith, Jane Lauderback, Nancy Hamblen, Priscilla Greene, John, Abner Hamblen and Susannah Ely to be divided equally, share and share alike to them and their heirs forever.

I do hereby appoint my three sons, Henry, John & Abner Executors of this my last Will and Testament, or so many of them as shall give security and qualify. In witness whereof I the said Hezekiah Hamblen have to this

my last Will and Testament set my hand and seal, the day & year above written. I leave this among my valuable papers.

Hezekiah Hamblen (seal)

Endorsed: Handwriting to this will was proven by the oath of D. Alexander, Jno D. McFarland, Orville Rice, Alex' Long & John Stipe.

Page 261

WILL OF FRANCES HAYNES

Dated: January 19, 1855
Proven: Feb. Term, 1855

In the Name of Almighty God, Amen.

I Frances Haynes, widow of Christopher Haynes, dec'd, do make and publish this my last Will & Testament, revoking all others by me heretofore made.

First. I want out of what personal property, money or other effects that I may have at my decease, to be buried in a Christian like manner and the expenses of my funeral paid, and after this is done, out of the residue of what I may be possessed of or that may come into the hands of my Exec. in my right in any way whatever, and in particular my pension from the United States due me. If the same shall not be obtained by my Attorney in my lifetime, it is my desire that the be paid according to our understanding for his trouble and the residue after paying off my just debts and liabilities in every way whatever, I give and bequeath to my beloved daughter Fereba Spears wife of Jesse Spears, for the love and affection I bear to her and her said husband, and for the further consideration of the trouble and expense they have had in their kindness and attention to me in my last days.

I do further appoint and constitute my beloved son-in-law Jesse Spears my sole Executor to carry out the provisions of this my last Will. Signed, sealed & published in our presence, and we have signed out names as witnesses in the presence of the Testator, This 19th day of January, 1855.

Samuel Spears
Henry Smith

Frances x Haynes (seal)
(her mark)

Page 261

WILL OF JOHN HARLAN

Dated: Feb. 24, 1860
Proven: Apr. 2nd, 1860

I John Harlan do hereby make and publish this my last Will and Testament, hereby revoking all former wills by me made.

First. I will and bequeath that my just debts be paid in the manner hereafter to be specified.

Secondly. I will and bequeath that a tract of land that I own purchased at a sale of John Groves, dec'd, owned by Groves in his lifetime and sold to pay his debts, containing about 81 acres, adjoining the old Groves farms be sold and the proceeds of said sale be equally divided amongst all my children.

3rd. I will and bequeath to my son Thomas Harlan my Bunker Hill farm containing about 300 acres, said Thomas to pay my daughter Rachael $300.00.

4th. I will and bequeath to my daughter Rachael the above sum of $300.00 to be paid to her by Thomas, I also will and bequeath to the said Rachael my negro boy Jake. I further will to Rachael, if she should marry, an equal amount of property to go to housekeeping with that I have already given my other daughters, **Elizabeth** and **Matilda.** And my wife **Tabitha** is to determine the articles they received, and in the event my daughter **Rachael** should never marry, she shall have a house free of charge upon the old home farm and at my family residence.

I will and bequeath unto my daughter **Matilda** who intermarried with **Joshua Smith**, in addition to what she has received, $300.00, to be raised in the manner hereafter specified. I will and bequeath to my wife **Tabitha** a comfortable support during her natural life, to be raised in the manner hereafter specified. My wife **Tabitha** is also to have control of my dwelling house as long as my son **Cornelius** should remain single. And if my son **Cornelius** should marry then my wife is to have during her natural life, choice of rooms in my house, together with a room to cook in and out houses necessary to make her comfortable.

I will and bequeath to my son **Cornelius** all the balance of my land, together with my two slaves **Henry** and **Malvina**, all my farming utensils, household and kitching furniture, all my stock, my notes and accounts, but my son **Cornelius** is charged with the following payments: He is to pay all my just debts of every description; he is to pay my daughter **Matilda Smith** $300.00. He is also to pay my daughter **Mary Eliza** $800.00 when she marries or becomes 21 years of age. My said son **Cornelius** is to raise and educate my daughter **Mary Eliza** and furnish her a comfortable home as long as she remains single. The said **Cornelius** is also to provide my daughter **Rachael** with a home at the old homestead as long as she remains single, free from charge, furnish her and her sister with a horse to go to church, and **Cornelius** is also to furnish **Rachael** with the same amount of articles to go to housekeeping with that I gave my other daughters, **Matilda** and **Elizabeth** in the event she should marry. My son **Cornelius** is also to furnish my wife **Tabitha** with a comfortable support as long as she lives. She is to have control of the dwelling house as long as **Cornelius** remains single. Should he marry, then my wife is to select what room or rooms she may desire in the homestead with any out buildings she may desire. The above named real estate so bequeathed to my son **Cornelius** is charged with the payment of the above bequests, and my son **Cornelius** is also to have my blacksmith tools, together with all my personal property not herein disposed of.

I will and bequeath to my daughter **Mary Eliza** in addition to the expenses she may incur upon my son **Cornelius** in raising, the following slaves and their increase to wit: **John, Julia** and her child **Sudy** and **Ben**, and the sum of $800.00 when she marries or becomes 21 years of age, which my son **Cornelius** is to pay her. She is also to have a home at the old homestead as long as she remains single. My son **Cornelius** is to support said slaves and their increase and have the use of them until **Mary Eliza** marries or becomes 21. **Cornelius** is also to provide my wife with a good, gentle saddle horse as long as she lives.

I hereby appoint my son **Cornelius** Executor of this my last Will and Testament with full power to sell the tract of land bequeathed by me to be sold, dividing the proceeds equally among all my children... In testimony whereof I have hereunto set my hand and seal This the 24th day of February, 1860.

John Harlan (seal)

Signed and sealed in our presence,
and we have subscribed our names as
witnesses in the presence of the Testator.
A. Carmichael, C. C. Sensabaugh

WILL OF JOHN B. HEADRICK

Page 264   Dated: October 4, 1862

I **John B. Headrick** do make and publish this my last Will and Testament, hereby revoking and making void all other wills by me at any time made.

First. I direct that all my funeral expenses and all my debts be paid as soon after my death as possible out of any money that I may die possessed of or may first come into the hands of my Executor.

Second. I will and bequeath to my son **John Headrick** 50 acres of my land as willed him by my father, **John Headrick**, according to the will of the said **John Headrick.**

Thirdly. I will that the remainder of my land (69 acres more or less) be sold by my Executor to the best advantage at public or private sale, together with any personal property and the proceeds thereof to be equally divided between my four younger children, to wit: **Elizabeth Headrick, Zedic B. Headrick, Daniel W. Headrick** and **Ishinder Headrick.** Lastly, I do hereby nominate and appoint **Daniel M. Sheffey** Executor. In witness whereof I do to this my will set my hand and seal This 4th day of October, 1862.

John B. Headrick

Signed sealed and published in our presence and we have subscribed our names hereto in the presence of the Testator This 4th day of October, 1862.
J. J. Carroll, H. C. Seavers

WILL OF JACOB ISENBERG

Page 264   Dated: April 21, 1859
                                             Proven: Feb'y Term, 1861

State of Tennessee)   I **Jacob Isenberg** being of a sound mind and perfect
Hawkins County   )   memory, do make and publish this my last Will and
                             Testament as follows:

First. I will and bequeath unto my beloved wife **Elizabeth** the mansion house, out house, and her maintenance of her land during her natural life, also all my personal property died poses of (sic) after all my just debts or paid not otherwise bequeathed by me.

Second. I will and bequeath unto my daughter **Marh Isen (Martha Isenberg)** as much of the property as will make her equal to the rest of the children, or as much as they got from home when they was married. And the remainder of my property to be quail divied between all my children.

Third. I will and bequeath unto my three grand children in payment for their lot of land and the child that pay them gits the lot of land pars as follows: To **Jacob J. Malory** $100.00. To **Mary M. Mallory** $75.00. To **Moriah A. Mallory** $75.00, all amounting to $250.00 to be paid as above nam as the become of age.

4th. I will and bequeath all my land to be equal between all of my children. **Simeon Isenberg** is to have **Joseph B. Isenberg's** lot of land & **Elizabeth Mallory** three children is to have the above nam som for their lot of land.

5th. I will and bequeath unto my son **Simeon Isenberg** his mansion house out house and orchard including his lot of land where he now lives. I will and bequeath unto my son **Benjamin Isenberg** his mansion house out house and orchard where he now lives including his lot of land.

6th. I will and bequeath unto the child that waits on or takes care of me and their mother while we live is to have my house where _____ lives, including their lot of land.

Lastly. I nominate my son **Simeon Isenberg** my sole Executor of this my last Will and Testament. Given under my hand and seal this the twenty first day of April one thousand eight hundred and fifty nine.

Jacob Isenberg (seal)

Publish and sealed and delivered in the presence of us wh hereunto subscribed out names in the presence of the above Testator as witnesses.

D—— D. Anderson
Samuel Molsbee

Page 266
WILL OF AQUILLA JONES   Dated: Dec. 15, 1809

In the Name of God, Amen.

I **Aquilla Jones** of the County of Hawkins, State of Tennessee, being in a languishing state of health but sound in mind, expecting ere long for to depart this life, committing my soul to God who gave it and my body to be buried in Christian decency at the discretion of my Executors. And as for my portion of worldly things which God in his providence has bestowed on me, I wish to dispose of in the following manner.

After paying my just debts, I bequeath to my well beloved wife **Mary** my dwelling house and the third of the cleared land, one bed and bedding, stead and furniture during her widowhood. And my land for to be equally divided between my two sons **Martin** and **Enec** according to quantity and quality, also my farming utensils and the balance of my household furniture, also after my daughter **Ruth Williams** one milk cow. The balance of my live stock for to be divided, two thirds to **Martin**, one third to **Enech**. Signed with my hand and dated This 15th day of December, 1809.

Aquilla Jones (seal)

Test:
David Kinkead (Jurat)
Burrough Kincade

Page 266
WILL OF THOMAS JACKSON   Dated: Jan'y 27, 1817

In the Name of God, Amen.

I **Thomas Jackson** of Hawkins County in the State of Tennessee, being of sound mind, do make this my will & desire that my Estate be divided in the following manner. That my sons **Robert** and **James** have their maintenance off the plantation where I now live until they come of age and that my eldest son **Joseph S. Jackson** have all my land in Hawkins County, the farming utensils and household furniture, with a negro boy named **Betty** and the horses to be equally divided among all my children. My land in Overton and on Big Lick creek in West Tennessee to be equally divided between my children **James, Robert** and **Bethunia.** My daughter is to have the negro woman named **Minta.** **James M. Jackson** is to have a negro boy named **Sam**, and **Robert** is to have the boy named **Sandy,** and as there is notes in my desk to the amount of $2,700.00, I desire that my debts may first be paid then the the balance to be equally divided among all my children, and as my son **Joseph** is absent from home, it is my desire that my sons **James** and **Robert** continue to live on my plantation in Hawkins County, and should **Joseph** die before he comes home, then my Estate

in Hawkins County is to be equally divided between **James** and **Robert,** and in that case, **Joe** and **Eve** is to be the property of **Bethunia H. Jackson.** But should **Joe** die before he comes home - he being yet under age. I appoint M. **Neil** and **George Hale** my attornies to see this my will Executed and to them I join my son **James M. Jackson.** As witness my hand & seal This 27th day of January, 1817.

Thomas Jackson (seal)

Test:
Samuel x Spears & James Breeden
(his mark)

Page 267
WILL OF JAMES JOHNSON   Dated: June 26, 1832

In the Name of God, Amen.

I, **James Johnson,** of Hawkins County, State of Tennessee, being weak in body but of sound and perfect mind and memory but calling to mind that it is appointed for all men once to die, do execute and publish this my last Will and Testament.

1st. I leave to my beloved wife **Susannah** the plantation on which I am now living, together with two horses, four cows and calves, 15 hogs, six sheep, all my farming utensils and household and kitchen furniture. Also, **Frank** and his wife, **Old George** and his wife, which she is to have during her natural life. If she should wish to discontinue housekeeping, the Executors may sell the land together with all the property except the negroes, and after making the heirs equal by counting in what I have previously given my children — giving my grandson **James T. Johnson** half as much as one of my children — then the balance of cash kept for the use of my wife **Susannah** until her death to be divided in the manner above named, also the negroes left to her to be sold and the cash divided in the same way as above named. Having due regard to the property heretofore given my children, it is to be understood by this my last will that I have given to my son **Thomas** $100.00. To my daughter **Charity** the sum of $550.00. To my daughter **Lucy** the sum of $146.00. To my daughter **Polly** the sum of $20.00, which several sums are to be taken into consideration and settled out of their several shares at my death, or out of my property that is sold at that time, which is to be all the property not herein mentioned.

I leave to my daughter **Charity—Betsy, Sally** and **Betsy's** youngest child. if she has more than one more child, i.e. the youngest child at my death. I leave to my daughter **Lucy—Bob & Sis** & if **Rachael** has more than one child before my death, **Lucy** is to have the next to the youngest child. I loan to my daughter **Mary—Rachael, Mandy** and **Rachael's** youngest child at my death if she has any more children. I will to my son **Jeremiah—Young George, Henry & Levis.** I will to my son **James—Jacob** and **Katharine** and **William.** I loan to my grandson **James Thomas Johnson—Jacob** and the next child that **Betsy** may have which I want valued at my death and with them take into consideration the $100.00 that his father has had, then at my wife's death, I want him to have enough cash to make what he and his father has had equal to one half as much as one of my own children gets, to have the use of during his life, then unless he should have a lawful heir - a legitimate child - it is my will that what I have loaned him should be equally divided amongst my children at his death. And all the above named property I want valued by three good men that may be chosen by my Executors and each one to have possession of the above named property at that time, but should one of my children's part or negroes, together with what I have given them be estimated at more than another, they are all to be made equal out of what property is sold at that time or with cash.

The above property that I have given to my daughters, or rather loaned, it is my will that they should have the actual possession of it until their death, then to be divided amongst their children equally, but should there be an attempt made in any way to sell the above named negroes, it is my will that my Executors should take them in possession and hire them out and apply the proceeds in what way the Executors may think best to their use. It is also my will that my Executors should out of what I have given my grandson **James T. Johnson** give him good schooling and his part not to be given him until he is twenty one years old. The land over the river together with what property not herein mentioned to be sold at my death and disposed of as above mentioned. And if the negro women should have any more children than what is otherwise disposed of, they are to be sold at my death with the other property. Ratifying and confirming this my last will and Testament. In testimony whereof I have hereunto set my hand & seal This 26th day of June A.D. 1832.

N B Let it hereby be understood that I want my wife to have one year's provision after my death. It is also my will that the old negroes should be sold to the highest bidder; but not to be sold unless the heirs bought them, and so as not to part man and wife.

James Johnson (seal)

Attest: **Bardy Johnson & Elisha Dodson**

N B It is my wish that **James & Jeremiah** execute this my last Will, or some other good man if they both refuse so to do. Given under my hand This 26th day of June, 1832.

James Johnson (seal)

Attest: **Bardy Johnson, Elisha Dodson**

WILL OF NANCY JOHNSON

Page 269   Dated: April, 1842

In the Name of God, Amen, I, **Nancy Johnson** of Hawkins County, State of Tenn., being weak in body but of sound mind, knowing the uncertainty of life, do make and ordain this my last Will and Testament, that is to say. I commit my soul unto the hands of my Maker, and as to my property, I bequeath all to my son-in-law **Jacob Giford** who married my daughter **Judith Giford**. And also I bequeath to Jacob Giford whatever amount may be due or coming to me on account of a pension from the United States which Mr. **Alexander** of Rogersville expects to procure for me on account of services rendered by my deceased husband. I make this disposition of what I have because my said daughter, **Mrs. Giford** did not get from her father near as much as my other children did get from him. And because she and her husband have been maintaining me and intend to do so.

I also appoint the said **Jacob Giford** my sole Executor of this my last Will and Testament and do not wish that Bond & security shall be required of him by the Court.

In testimony whereof I have hereunto set my hand & seal this _____ day of April, 1842.

Nancy x Johnson
(her mark)

Lincoln Amis
Jesse D. Bloomer

WILL OF JAMES JOHNSON

Page 270   Dated: Feb. 11, 1849
                                   Proven: Sept. 1860
                                   (By J. H. VANCE, CLK)

I, **James Johnson** of the County of Hawkins, State of Tennessee, do make and publish this my last Will and Testament hereby revoking and making void all former wills by me at any time made. I direct that my body be interred at my grave yard in said county and suitable to my condition in life, and as to such worldly estate as it has pleased God to bestow upon me, I dispose of the same as follows:

First. I direct that my debts and funeral Expenses be paid as soon after my decease as possible out of any money that I may die possessed of or may first come into the hands of my Executor from any portion of my Estate.

Second. I will and bequeath to my beloved wife **Ann**, my five slaves, to wit: **Charity**, a mulatto woman aged about 53 years, **Martha** a mulatto girl about 19 years and her increase, **Henston** a mulatto boy about 21 and two little girls, **Catherine & Caroline**. My wife **Ann** to dispose of said slaves as she may think proper at her death. I also bequeath to my wife **Ann** two horses, the choice of my stock, one of said horses to do with as she may think fit at her death. Also two milk cows and calves, her choice of my stock, 20 head of hogs and 15 head of sheep, her choice. Also one wagon and two pair of gear, one patent plow, one shovel plow, one bull tongue plow, one log chain, one copper kettle, also all of my household furniture, all kitchen furniture, all my beds, bedsteads and bed clothing. My wife **Ann** to dispose of the beds and furniture at her death as she thinks proper, also all my geese and other fowl.

Third. I will and bequeath to my son **Walter Johnson** $250.00 out of my Estate.

Fourth. I will and bequeath to my son **A. D. Johnson** the balance of the **Isam Looney** tract of land by the said **A. D. Johnson** paying to **Walter Johnson** $200.00, it being a portion of the above bequeath to **Walter Johnson**. It is also my wish that the crop of corn, wheat and oats on hand be left to my wife **Ann** to dispose of as she may think proper. I also will and bequeath if there should be anything left after paying all my debts and filling the above bequests that it be equally divided between all my daughters by my first wife.

I do hereby make ordain and appoint my wife **Ann** and my son **A. D. Johnson** Executors of this my last Will and Testament.

In witness whereof I **James Johnson** the said Testator have to this my last will set my hand and seal This Eleventh day of February in the year of our Lord, one thousand eight hundred and fifty nine.

James Johnson (seal)

Attest:
Samuel A. Kirkead
Absalom Looney

WILL OF THOMAS JOHNSON

Page 271   Dated: August 23, 1854
                                   Proven: Nov. Term, 1861

I **Thomas Johnson** of the County of Hawkins and State of Tennessee, being of sound disposing mind and memory, do make and ordain this my last Will and Testament in manner and form following.

First. I will that my body be decently buried in a manner to suit my condition in life, and that my funeral expenses be paid out of any money that I may die possessed of or may first come into the hands of my Executor.

And that all my just debts be paid.

Second. I will that my wife Elizabeth live on the farm whereon we now live and that she have her maintenance off the same during her life time or widowhood.

Thirdly. I will and bequeath to my said wife half the beds and furniture, tools and the balance of my stock be sold at twelve months credit and the proceeds of said sale equally divided between my five daughters, Elizabeth, Anna, Sally, Patsy and Hanet and my three grandsons, namely: Thomas, Anderson and Abner, sons of Stephen Johnson, dec'd, to have one share equal to one of my daughters.

And lastly, I hereby constitute and appoint my friend Aderson Lawson my Executor to this my last Will and Testament. In witness whereof I have set my hand and seal Aug. 23rd, 1854.   Thomas Johnson (seal)

Attest:
Joseph D. Mitchell, John Mitchell, Alford C. Lawson
Edward P. x Johnson & Harmon E. Lawson
(his mark)

Page 272
WILL OF ROBERT JOHNSON
Dated: May 8, 1861
Proven: July Term, 1861

In the Name of God, Amen. I Robert Johnson of Hawkins County, State of Tenn., being weak in body but of sound and perfect mind and memory do make and publish this my last Will & Testament in manner and form following, that is to say:

First. I give and bequeath unto my wife Eliza M. Johnson $1,000.00. I also give unto my daughter Delph C. Johnson $1,000.00. Also, I give to my son Robert Emet Johnson $1,000.00. Also I give to my son Benoni P. C. Johnson $1,000.00. Also. Also I give to my son Nathaniel Wiley McBride Johnson $1,000.00. And also I give to my grandson Robert J. Looney $1,000.00, the above amount to be made out of a note I hold on John Riley. And also I desire that the above be kept at interest and applied to support of the family, and as they severally come of age to draw their respective shares. And further, it is my desire that my wife Eliza M. Johnson have my farm during her natural life to use in support of the family at her death to be divided between my three sons, Robert Emet, Benoni T. C., and Nathaniel Wiley McBride Johnson.

I also give to my wife all the household and kitchen furniture, also all the stocks of cattle, horses, hogs and sheep. I desire that my wife give each one an out-fit for housekeeping when they commence that business.

Now, out of the balance of my effects — bonds, notes and accounts of every kind, after my just debts are paid, I desire my daughter Delpha C. have $500.00 to be placed at interest to go to the support of the family until they come of age, and what should remain of my effects to be put to interest and the interest to go to the support of the above named children and grand children come of age to draw their equal part.

It is also my will and desire that my son William W. Johnson have $25.00 in addition to what I have given him. Also I desire that my grandson Robert Emet Johnson have $50.00, also my grandson John Wesley Johnson have $25.00, all to be paid over within 18 months after my decease, I desire that my wife have all the farming utensils and all the grain on hand.

I do hereby appoint my wife Eliza M. Johnson my Executor, hereby revoking all other wills made by   . And further I do not require her to give security. In testimony whereof I have set my name and affixed my seal this 8th day of May, 1861.

                                        Robert Johnson (seal)
Attest:
Wm. X Larkin
James Hoffman

This Codicil to the foregoing will, whereas I willed to my grandson Rob't J. Looney in the body of the will one thousand dollars, if he should not live to the age of 21, it is my will and desire that it should be equally divided between my daughter Delpha C., Robert Emet, Benoni P. C. and Nathaniel Wiley McBride Johnson and William W. I hereby subscribe my name and fix my seal, May 18, 1861.

                                        Robert Johnson (seal)
Attest:
Wm. X Larkins
James Hoffman

Page 274
WILL OF JACOB KLINE, JR. *
Dated: June 3, 1807

*Notation made by someone later says Sen'r. - See Original.

In the Name of God, Amen.

I Jacob Kline, Jr., being for some time in a declining state of health, but of sound mind and memory, calling to mind the mortality of all men that it is appointed unto all men once to die do by these presents declare, ratify and announce my last Will and Testament in the manner following, to wit:

After commending my soul to God and my body to the dust from whence it came, to be buried in a decent and Christian manner, believing they will again be united in the General Resurrection and received into the favor of God. I do bequeath and dispose of my worldly goods and chattels in the following manner (Viz):

I allow all my just debts to be paid out of my movable and perishable property. I give and bequeath to my wife Mottena part of my plantation to be laid off in the following manner: Beginning on Doctor Finley's line on the main road, then along the road to the creek - down the creek by the still house to Henderson's line. Then round my lines to the beginning to include two cabbins and stable, two fields with the meadow below the cabbins and also to have the use of a spring that comes out of the opposite bank of the creek below the still house, she is to have the use of said spring and land during her life then to be sold and be divided among my children. I also give her one horse creature, Three cows, Three sheep, six head of hogs - she shall her choice of all my stock, also three beds, bedsteads and furniture. my wagon, one pair gears, a saddle and bridle, one bar share and shovel plow and harrow, one chest and trunk, one table, six chairs and cotton wheels and one flax do four still tubs two barrels and one half of my kitchen furniture and to be provided for one year out of my estate by my Executors. her part of the personal estate to be at her own disposal. There is some of my

children has rec'd part of their portion – them that has shall give an
account of what they have rec'd and my other children shall have as much
given them, then my estate equally divided among all with two exceptions.
I give to my daughter **Mottena** the sum of one dollar and what she would
have by an equal part, to be given her children. And it is my will that if
my son **Jacob** does marry **Polly Brown**, I will give him one dollar and no more,
and if not he shall have his equal part with the rest of my children. I allow all my estate, real and personal, to be sold by my Executors at their
discretion so they can make the best sale that they can. They may sell my
land in one tract or divide the same or as they may think best.

It is my will that my three youngest sons be schooled to <u>rite</u>, read and
ciper, and bound to trades at the age of 18, at their own choice. Also my
four young daughters be <u>larned</u> to read in the Bible. To be paid out of my
Estate: I give my wife $300.00 that is in the hand of **Mical McGurney/
McGunery**, if it can be received. I do nominate and appoint my worthy friends
Benoni Coldwell & Jas Forgey to Execute this my last will and Testament —
revoking all former wills and Testaments by me made heretofore to be null
and void and declaring this to be my last Will and Testament. Signed, sealed
and published. This 3rd of June in the year of our Lord 1807, and in presence
of witnesses:

Benoni Coldwell   Jacob Kline (seal)
Jacob Sensabaugh

CERTIFICATE OF PROBATE OF WILLIAM KING'S WILL

Page 275   Dated: December 20, 1808
Virginia, to wit:

At a Court held for Washington County the 20th day of Dec., 1808.
The last will and Testament of **William King**, dec'd was exhibited into
Court and proven by the oath of **William D. Neilson** one of the subscribing
witnesses thereto who further made oath that he saw **John Daugherty** the other
subscribing witness sign his name thereto as a witness at the request of
the said **William King** – that he the said **Daugherty** if living, resides in the
Mississippi Territory about one thousand miles from this place, and that the
said will except the signatures of the said witnesses is entirely in the hand
writing of the said **William King** the Testator, further that the codicil
thereto appointing **James King** and **William Trigg** Executors and dated the third
day of March, one thousand eight hundred and six is also in the handwriting
of **William King** the Testator – That he believes the codicil was written and
lying under the will when he attested it as a witness and he never saw or
knew of any other codicil – Col^o **James King, Samuel Glen & Jacob Baker** made
oath that the said will and the codicil dated the 3rd day of March, 1806 are
in the handwriting of the said **William King** the Testator except the attestation of the witnesses to the will.

The Court are of the opinion that the said evidence is sufficient, and
it is ordered that the said will and codicil be recorded, and on motion of
William Trigg and **James King**, the Executors named in said codicil who took
the oath of Executor prescribed by law and entered into and acknowledged
themselves bound in the sum of one million five hundred thousand dollars with
**Robert Craig, Jr., Thomas Tate, Robert Delp, John Aperson, Josiah Cole,
Robert White, Basell Talbutt, John Cole, Thomas Moffett, Joshua Burke,
William Duff, William Jones, Benjamin Estill, Samuel Vance, James Bryant,
Michael Shavner/Shauner, Gerrard T. Conn, James Thompson, Enoch Schoolfield,**

**George Spangler, James Key, John McCullock, John Williamson, William
Gray, James Lyon, Alexander Hamilton, Benjamin Langley, Jacob Mungle,
Robert Houston, Reuben Bradley, Valentine Baugh, John Mitchell, Jacob Baker,
John McCormick, Robert Craig, John Athey, John Goodson, Peter Clark, John
Buchanan, James King, Sen'r., Samuel Meek, Samuel Glen, Rufus Morgan, James
Langley, William McHenry, Michael Dechert, Lilburn L. Henderson, John J.
Trigg, David Smith, Robert Dukes, William D. Neilson, Earl B. Clap, Jacob
Long, Welcome Martin, Robert McCullock, Thomas Thornburgh, Mathew Willoughby,
Benjamin Clark, Connally Findley, William King, Joseph Miller, Charles Tate,
Pettus C. Clayton, William Paston, Peter Scott,** Securities conditioned as
the law directs. A Certificate is therefore granted them for the probate of
said will in due form.

In testimony that the foregoing is a true copy, I **John Campbell**, Clerk
of Washington County in the state aforesaid have hereunto Subscribed my name
and affixed the seal of the said County this 24th day of December in the
year of our Lord, one thousand, eight hundred and eight, and the Commonwealth
the thirty-third.

                                  John Campbell

Washington County, to wit:

I **Robert Campbell** presiding Justice of the Court of Washington County
in the State aforesaid do certify that the above attestation of **John Campbell,**
Clerk of the Court of the said County is in due form. Given under my hand
this 29th day of December, 1808

                                Robert Campbell

WILL OF GEORGE KARNES (SR.)

Page 277   Dated: October 14, 1816
In the Name of God Amen.

I **George Karnes, Senior** of the County of Hawkins and State of Tennessee
being of sound and perfect mind and memory (blessed be God) do this 14th day
of October, 1816, make and publish this my last Will & Testament in manner
following, that is to say –

First. I give and bequeath unto my son **Jacob Karnes** a certain tract
and parcel of land lying in the upper end of the tract of land whereon I now
live, bounded as follows: Beginning at Crocketts Creek & running with the
middle fence between where **Jacob Moore** now lives and the above mentioned
Jacob Karnes. Thence to the foot of the hill that the meeting house stands
on. Thence along the foot of said hill to the Meeting House spring. Thence
to the S.E. corner of a field opposite thereto on the north side of the road.
Thence a straight line to run with the eastern fence of said field and to continue beyond it to said **George Karnes'** line at the foot of Cany Creek Knobs.
Thence with his land northeastwardly to **Daniel Lipes'** line. Thence with his
line to ? **Howrey's** line. Thence along said boundary westwardly as far
as it is from the beginning at the creek to **Karnes'** Cedar corner & from
thence a straight line to the beginning, to him and his heirs forever.

Secondly. I give and bequeath to my son **George Karnes** a certain
tract of land lying in the lower end of the tract of land whereon I now live.
Beginning on the southeast boundary of my land at a point that will include
the improvement where **Isaac Barger** tended on the south side of the creek.
Thence a straight line crossing said creek to **Moore's** fence, from thence to
the middle fence between myself & the said **Moore** to a cherry tree, then

follow the middle fence about half way up the hill, then corner and run straight across the field to the fence that runs by the Grave Yard. Then follow that fence to a flat place near the spring branch. Thence a straight line to run so as to take two acres of the lower end of my lower field on the north side of the road to my back line. Thence along my line to George Karnes' line. Thence along his line to the river. Thence up the river to where my southern boundary strikes the same. Thence with my boundary to the beginning, to him and his heirs forever.

Thirdly. I give and bequeath to my loving wife **Elizabeth** the use of half the balance of my land during her life or widowhood.

Fourthly. I give and bequeath to my son **Andrew Karnes** all the balance of my land subject to the use above mentioned, bounded as follows: Beginning at the before mentioned **George Karnes'** beginning corner in my southern boundary & running thence along along the different lines of this land, bequeathed to my son **George** to my line at the foot of Cany Creek Knobs, thence with my line along the foot of said knobs to the line of the land hereinbefore bequeathed to my son **Jacob Karnes**. Thence along the lines of the land bequeathed to my son **Jacob** to my southern boundary. Thence along the same westwardly to the beginning, to him and his heirs forever.

Fifthly. I give and bequeath one third part of all my movable property to my wife **Elizabeth**, to her and her heirs forever.

Sixthly. I give and bequeath to my daughter **Elizabeth Wetty** the sum of $350.00 in specie, to her and her heirs forever.

Seventhly. I give & bequeath all the residue of my personal Estate to my three sons, **Jacob, George & Andrew**, divided equally, share and share alike.

Eightly. I give and bequeath to my son **William Karnes** the sum of one dollar to be levied out of my personal estate.

Ninthly. I have heretofore advanced to my son **John** his full equitable share, therefore I make no further provision for him.

Tenthly. I do hereby make and ordain my son **Jacob Karnes** Executor of this my last Will and Testament. In witness whereof I the said **George Karnes, Senior** have to this my last Will & Testament set my hand & seal the day and year above written.

George Karnes (seal)

Signed sealed published & declared by the said **George Karnes, Senior** the Testator as his last Will & Testament in the presence of us who were present at the time of signing & sealing thereof.
George H. Etter
Daniel Howry

WILL OF JUDITH KENNER

Page 279   Dated: Nov. 16, 1819
In the Name of God, Amen.

I **Judith Kenner** of the County of Hawkins & State of Tennessee, being of sound and perfect mind and memory (blessed be God) do this sixteenth day of November in the year of our Lord one thousand eight hundred & nineteen, make and publish this my last Will and Testament in manner following, that is to say.

First. I give to my mother **Margaret Duguard** the use or profits of all my Estate real & personal during her life, provided nevertheless that the same shall be under the care and management of my Executor from the time of my death and during the lifetime of my mother.

Secondly. I give and bequeath to my daughter **Lucy Beverly Winston** the use of my negro girl **Mary** during her life, and after the death of my daughter Lucy, I give my said negro **Mary** and **Mary's** increase to my grand daughter **Margaret Winston**, to her and her heirs forever.

Thirdly. I give and bequeath to my son **Lawrence Sterns Kenner** one horse, one bed and furniture, and one Beaufat.

Fourthly. I give and bequeath to my daughter **Judith Cardin** one bed and furniture.

Fifthly. I give and bequeath to my daughters **Lucy Beverly Winston** and **Judith Cardin** all my wearing apparel to be equally divided.

Sixthly. I give to my grandson **William Winston Kenner** the tract of land whereon I now live containing 110 acres by estimation, be the same more or less, to him and his heirs forever.

Seventhly. I give and bequeath to my grandson **Roaham Beverly Kenner** my negro girl **Eliza** and her increase, to him and his heirs forever.

Eighthly. I give and bequeath the residue of my estate real and personal to my grand children, equally divided, share and share alike.

Lastly. I hereby make and ordain my worthey friend **William Simpson** of Rogersville Executor of this my last Will & Testament. In witness whereof I the said **Judith Kenner** have to this my last Will & Testament set my hand & seal the day and year above written.

Judith Kenner (seal)

Hezekiah Hamblen
George McCollough

WILL OF ROBERT KYLE

Page 280   Dated: Sept. 21, 1820
State of Tennessee)   In the Name of God, Amen.
Hawkins County   )   I **Robert Kyle** of the County of Hawkins and State of Tennessee, being indisposed, but of sound mind and memory & calling to mind the mortality of life & that it is appointed once for all men to die, do make, ordain and declare this my last Will & Testament, revoking all others by me heretofore made, that is to say:

First. I recommend my soul unto the hands of God who gave it and my body to a decent Christian burial, and after the expense of the same are defrayed, I give and bequeath the residue of my Estate, goods & chattels of which it hath pleased God to bless me as follows:

I will & bequeath to my loving wife **Leah Kyle**, formerly **Leah Brooks** the following property to her use during her life, to wit: My negro fellow named **Mingo** and his wife **Sarah** with **Bass** and a negro girl called **Betty**, daughter of **Comfort** with their increase if any there be, also my wagon and three horses to wit: The gray horse, a horse called Doctor and a sorrel horse called Rock, Five cows and calves, two of the best of my steers, together with two or three of my young steers & heifers with as many of my hogs as she may think proper to take. Three beds & furniture, one Table with as much kitchen furniture as may be necessary for her use, together with as much corn, wheat, rye, oats &c as may be necessary for her support for one year. All of which my wife is to have the benefit of during her natural life & at her death, **Mingo** and his wife to be valued together by my Exec's hereafter to be named and if **Mingo** and **Sarah** choose any of my four Legatees as a master, to wit: **William Kyle**, the heirs of **John Maples**, the heirs of **William Simms** and heirs of **William McCarty**. But the mother of **Maples** heirs and the mother of the **Simms** heirs to have the use of said parts during their natural lives and they are willing to take them at valuation, then and in that case the Legatees that **Mingo** and wife choose as master, if he thinks proper to take at their said valuation as above, then said Legatee to pay the rest of the Legatees their several proportions of said valuation. But if **Mingo** and wife choose any other person for master and that person is willing to take them at their valuation and pays the Legatees their respective shares, then and in that case the Legatees are bound to receive the same, but if neither the Legatees nor any other person chosen by **Mingo** and wife for master, then will not take them, then and in that case **Mingo** & wife are to be ballotted for by the four Legatees above named and which ever draws them to pay the other three their respective shares of valuation, and the negro girl called **Betty** willed to my wife during her life--her and her increase if any there be—to go to my two grandsons **Gale** and **William Kyle**, sons of **Thomas Kyle**, dec'd & the other negro **Bass** willed to my wife during her natural life, I wish at her death to be valued by my Executors and to be drawn for by the following Legatees or by the Executors for them: **McCarty** heirs, **Polly Maples**, **Patty Maples** and **William Kyle**. Whichever one draws him to pay the rest their respective shares of said valuation, share and share alike. But if drawn by **Polly Maples** or **Patty Maples**, at their death to descend to their children which they now have or may have by their husbands. The remainder of said property willed to my wife, at her death to be sold & proceeds equally divided among the above named heirs, including my son **Absalom Kyle** also.

Item. 2. I do further will to my grandson **William Kyle** who now lives with me one negro girl called **Sallie**, child of **Kate**, to him and his heirs forever.

Item 3. I give & bequeath to my grand daughter **Nancy Wilson**, formerly **Nancy Kyle**, daughter of **Robert Kyle**, dec'd, my negro boy **Abraham** with **Mary** daughter of **Comfort**, to her and her heirs forever, provided **Sam'l Wilson**, husband of **Nancy** receipt my heirs in full for all the demands they may have on me as Administrator of **Robert Kyle**, dec'd.

Item 4. For and in consideration of the dutiful and faithful services to me rendered for a number of years by my three slaves, **Baptit**, **Pell** and **Bettie**, **Pell's** wife, it is my will and desire that at my death they be set at perfect liberty and no longer be held in servitude by my heirs or any other person whatsoever.

Item 5. It is my further will and desire that my two grandsons, **Gale** and **William Kyle**, sons of **Thomas Kyle**, dec'd, have the tract of land whereon my son **Absalom** now lives after the death of my wife **Leah**, but my wife to have a life estate in and to the same. Also, I wish said two grandsons to have the following negroes, to wit: My negro fellow **Jack**, my negro girl **Comfort**, her young child named **Jenny**. To them and their heirs forever, and to the above named **Gale Kyle**, I will my rifle gun, to him and his heirs...

Item 6. It is further my desire that the residue of my negroes, to wit: **Kate** with her four children—**Violet**, **Tom**, **Betty** and **Nancy**—together with **Harry** be divided into four equal lots as near as may be by my Executors, to be valued by the same and drawn by them in four lots: One lot for **Polly Maples**, and one lot each for **Patty Maples**, **McCarty** heirs and **William Kyle**, and if lots not be equally divided, the lot or lots of greater value to pay the lot or lots of lesser value the difference in money.

Item 7. It is my desire that my son **Absalom Kyle** have my set of blacksmith tools with my writing desk, to him and his heirs forever.

Item 8. I further will & desire that all the residue of my Estate of every denomination not hereby disposed of be sold by my Executors and proceeds equally divided among the following heirs, to wit: **McCarty** heirs, one share and one share each to **Polly Maples**, **William Kyle**, **Absalom Kyle**.

Item 9. I wish it to be expressly understood to be my will that all the estate devised by this will to **Polly Maples** and her heirs and **Patty Maples** and her heirs is to go to the said **Polly** & **Patty** during their natural lives, then to descend to all their children equally.

Item 10. It is further my desire and wish & I do hereby constitute & appoint my beloved son **Absalom Kyle** and my true & trusty friends **John Young** and **William Hord** my Executors to this my last Will & Testament & do hereby revoke all others heretofore by me made.

In witness whereof I **Robert Kyle** have hereunto set my hand and affixed my seal This 21st day of September in the Year of our Lord, 1820.

Robert x Kyle (seal)

Signed, sealed & acknowledged in the presence of us:
Cleon Moore, **John Brooks** & **Thomas Cox**

WILL OF JUDITH KENNER

Page 282   Dated: February 13, 1829

In the Name of God, Amen.

I **Judith Kenner** of Hawkins County, State of Tennessee, being in perfect health of body, of sound and disposing mind and memory and understanding, considering the certainty of death and the uncertainty of the time thereof, and being desirous to settle my worldly affairs and thereby be the better prepared to leave this world when it shall please God to call me hence, do therefore make and publish this my last Will & Testament in manner and form following, that is to say:

I give and devise to my two grandsons **Rodham Kenner** and **William W. Kenner** all my land containing about 300 acres, their heirs and assigns in fee simple, to be equally divided when **William W. Kenner** comes of age.

I give and bequeath unto my said grandsons **William W. Kenner** and **Rodham Kenner** one negro woman called **Eliza** together with her offspring, equally divided, when **William W. Kenner** comes of age.

I give and bequeath unto my said grandson **Rodham Kenner** my walking cane, marked on the head with **Rodham Kenner**, also my silver table spoons.

I give and bequeath unto my said grandson **William W. Kenner** my silver watch, also I give and bequeath unto the said **William W. Kenner** my silver Teaspoons.

It is my desire that my negro man called **Martin** shall be sold and one half of the money to be put in the hands of my grandson **William O. Winston** for the special benefit of his mother, my daughter **Lucy**, and the other half to be equally divided between my two grandsons **Columbus Carden** and **Joseph Carden**, children of my daughter **Judith Carden**, to be put out on interest till **Joseph** comes of age. In case one of them should die, the whole of said half to go to the survivor.

I give and bequeath unto all my grand children all my claims and interests in the State of Virginia, to be equally divided between them, share and share alike whenever settled.

I give and bequeath unto my grand daughter **Beverly J.** Carden the bed and bed furniture on which I lay.

It is my desire that my negroes called John, **Nann** & **Caroline** shall remain on the place whereon I now live, that all my stock and household furniture and farming utensils shall be kept together and nothing sold till the herein after mentioned, and it is my desire that **Lucy Winston** my daughter shall take possession & live on the place & the house whereon & wherein I now reside till **William W.** Kenner comes of age or so long as my said daughter **Lucy** sees fit to reside on said place till the coming of age of said **William W.** Kenner, it is also my desire that my negro woman Eliza with her children shall remain on the said place, together with John, **Nann** & **Caroline** and assist in making provisions for my two grandsons Rodham Kenner and **William W.** Kenner and my daughter **Lucy Winston** till **William W.** Kenner comes of age, and it is my desire that all things be kept together on said place by my daughter **Lucy** just in the situation as I leave them till **William W.** Kenner comes of age, and then my old negroes John, **Nann** & **Caroline** are to always find a home on the place whereon I now live or live with whomsoever of my daughters or grand children they see fit, that when said **William** W. Kenner comes of age it is my desire that all my stock and household furniture be sold and out of the proceeds of said sale, I give and bequeath unto my grand daughter **Margaret Findley** $60.00, unto my grandson John G. **Winston** $60.00 & unto my grandson Columbus Carden $60.00, and after paying over the said sums, I give and bequeath unto my daughters **Lucy Winston** & **Judith** Carden the residue of said proceeds. And lastly, I do hereby constitute and appoint **William Simpson** to be the Executor of this my last Will & Testament, revoking and annulling all former wills by me heretofore made, ratifying & confirming this and none other to be my last Will & Testament. In testimony whereof I have hereunto set my hand & affixed my seal. This 13th day of February in the year of our Lord, one thousand eight hundred & twenty nine.

Judith Kenner (seal)

Signed, sealed, published & declared by **Judith** Kenner the above named Testator as & for her last Will & Testament in the presence of us who at her request in her presence & in the presence of each other have subscribed our names as witnesses thereto.

O. Rice
G. W. Huntsman

WILL OF ANDREW KING

Page 284

Dated: April 11, 1831

State of Tennessee, Hawkins County:

To all whom these presents may come, Greeting:

I **Andrew King**, in the name of God, Amen. Being sound in memory but frail in body, do hereby make and ardane this my last Will & Testament.

First of all, my desire is to be decently buried and my estate pay the expenses of the same, and next, my will is that all my just debts be paid.

First. I give to my beloved wife **Barbara** the third of all the land I cleared on the plantation where I now live, including meadows and orchards, and I give to my beloved wife a horse and saddle to be valued to one hundred dollars. And it is my will that she is to have my dwelling house with all my buildings, to her only proper use and also too beds and furniture, the loom and all pertaining to it and wheel, kitchen cupboard with all her pewter and one pot, too pair of pot hooks, one oven and lid, one frying pan, one

kettle and one pot rack, tongs and shovel and dog irons, smoothing iron, table and clevis and swingletree (singletree), one pair of chain gears and too cows, fore sheep, six head of hogs – one of them a breeding sow, also one year's provision for herself and her stock, and my will is that all her property that is not perishable to be taken care of & sold and equally divided between my children that I gave no land, to her only proper use during her natural life.

Secondly. I give and bequeath to my son **Jacob King's** heirs a certain tract of land in Hawkins County on the waters of Hunnicut's Creek, lying on the dry fork bounded as follows: Beginning on an elm and ash then due south 50 poles to a stake then west 190 poles to a white oak corner, then due north 20 poles to a stake on **Walker's** line, then due east to the beginning, containing 60 acres, be the same more or less. And my will is that his heirs, when they become of age to sell the land and equally divide the amount, to their only proper use forever. And I hereby give and bequeath to my son **Adam King's** wife five dollars to be paid out of my estate, and that is all I will to her. Likewise to **Adam King's** son **Andy**, I give a horse to be valued at $25.00 and saddle at $10.00, and to his daughter when she becomes to be of age, one bolster and card, one under bed and one feather bed, two sheets, one bedstead and case, one blanket, one quilt, one white counterpin and one good calico dress for her own proper use forever, and I hereby give and bequeath to my son **James King** a certain tract of land lying in the County of Hawkins on the dry fork of Hunnicutt's Creek. Beginning on a stone, then west 190 poles to a white oak corner. Then due south 170 poles to a dogwood and poplar corner. Then due east to a double mulberry, then south 80 poles to a white oak, then east 148 poles to a stake, then north 222 poles to the beginning, containing 247 acres more or less for his use after his mother and father decease. And I give and bequeath to my daughter **Fanny King** a certain tract of land lying in the County of Hawkins on the waters of Hunnicutt's Creek, beginning on a post oak and white oak corner, then due south 170 poles to a dogwood and poplar corner, then due south 170 poles to a dogwood and poplar corner. Then due west 88 poles to a stake. Thence due north 170 poles to a pine corner. Then due east 88 (poles?) to the beginning, containing 90 acres more or less, for her and her children after her death. And she shall have her two beds and her furniture that I have given her for her only proper use forever. And I hereby will to my son **Charles King** a (tract) and parcel of land lying in the County of Hawkins on the north side of Holston River. Beginning on an elm and sugartree on the bank of the Holston River. Then running down said river 52 poles to a black gum and locust on the bank. Then north 42 degrees, east 32 poles to a white oak corner. Then the same course on the water of the hollow, then with the meanders of the branch to **Pain's** Grant to a white oak corner on **Dazeal's** entry. Then with s'd entry line north 54 degrees east 70 poles to a white oak corner. Then with s'd line north 30 degrees, east 100 poles to a white oak and dogwood corner on said line. Then south 80 degrees, east 46 poles to two dogwoods. Then a direct line to the ridge to where I sold to **McCanna**, then along the conditional line with **McCanna** to the old line which comes up from the river, then back to a stake in the field. Then south 150 poles to the beginning down the river to the hollow again and the said **Charles King**, if he sells the land is to pay $75.00 out of the price to me, his father, and the rest to his only proper use forever.

And I give to my daughter **Elizabeth** out of my property so much as will make her equal with the rest of my daughters, for her only proper use forever.

And I give and bequeath to my daughter **Sary** and her heirs after her death so much of my loos property as will make her equal with the rest of my daughter, and if she can give good security after my death, she shall have the money without paying the lawful interest to her only proper use forever. And my will is that 50 acres out of my last grant to be _____ at the highest bidders and the money to make all the daughters equal. In witness whereof I the said **Andrew King** have hereunto set my hand and seal. This eleventh day of April in the Year of our Lord One thousand eight hundred and thirty one. Signed in the presence of the witnesses:

Test: **John Reynolds**   **Andrew x King** (seal)
      William White   (his mark)
      C. H. King

WILL OF ELIJAH KINCHELOE

Page 287   Dated: Feb. 10, 1832
[Old Book A, P. 117]
In the name of God, Amen.

I **Elijah Kincheloe** of the County of Hawkins and State of Tennessee, being for some time past in a declining state of health though of sound mind and memory, Blessed be the Almighty God for his mercies have this 10th day of February, 1832, do make and publish this my last Will & Testament in writing. First, I desire all my just debts to be punctually paid and my body to have a plain and decent burial after my decease.

And concerning such worldly goods as it hath pleased the Almighty to bestow on me, I dispose of in the following manner, to wit:

Item 1st. I give to my wife **Polly Kincheloe** two feather beds and their furniture weighing 25 pounds each, two cows and calves, and the bureau she had at our intermarriage.

Item 2nd. I do lend to my wife during the time she remains my widow her first choice of two of my horse beasts, one side saddle, and bridle claimed by her, my wagon and four pair of gears, all the sheep I own, two sows and pigs, six of the largest hogs, one folding leaf table, two small tables, one dozen chairs, one cupboard and the furniture belonging to the cupboard, one yoke of oxen, all the geese, two spinning wheels, four pair of bedsteads, one clock, one sugar chest, one brass kettle, one candle stand, one large kettle, two ovens and lids, two pots, one shovel and tongs, one loom, one fan to clean grain, two plows, two axes, three hoes, one scythe and cradle one mowing scythe, two sickles, one iron tooth harrow, two cows, two iron wedges, one negro man named **Jack**, one negro woman named **Rose**. At my wife's death or marriage, the above named property lent to my wife is to fall to my three youngest children, and the two negroes **Jack & Rose** is to fall to the same, **Margaret, Sarah** and **James B. Kincheloe**, equally divided. And if either of them should die without a lawful heir of their body, then their property to fall to the above named living children and their lawful heirs.

Item 3rd. I also lend to my wife during the time she remains my widow the tract of land I now live on 157 acres 80 poles, which I purchased of **James Surgoine** and a small lot joining said land and joining the town lots of Surgoinesville. At my wife's death or marriage I give the land lent to my wife to my youngest son **James B.**, and he is to have the half of the land lent to my wife **Polly** when he arrives at the age of 20, and I also give him the tract of land I bought of **Benjamin Thurman** and my silver watch and gun,

and should he die without a lawful child, then my two daughters **Margaret** and **Sarah Kincheloe** to be his heir, and should **Margaret** or **Sarah** die without a lawful child, then the survivor of the three children to inherit all the property above named.

Item 4th. I give my daughter **Margaret** one negro girl named **Malinda** and a bed - the weight 30 pounds - the furniture for said bed also to go with it.

Item 5th. I give to my daughter **Sarah** a negro girl named **Liza** and a bed to weigh 30 pounds and furniture to said bed, and also $100.00 to her and her lawful heirs of her body, and in case of the death of either daughter without a lawful child, the other daughter to have the property given to both, and in case of the death of both without a lawful child, the property to go to my son **James B.** I also give to my two daughters **Margaret** and **Sarah** a bureau to be worth $15.00 apiece, and side saddle and bridle to be worth $18.00 apiece.

Item 6th. It is my desire that my wife have the care of her own children and their property until they come of age, and the expense of **Sarah** and **James**' education to come from the proceeds of their land left to them, and their mother to board them gratis and **James** to have a good English Education.

Item 7th. My three sons, **Thomas O., John** and **George W. Kincheloe** have been provided for heretofore. I therefore give them one dollar each.

Item 8th. My daughter **Polly** has been provided for heretofore, I therefore now give her one dollar.

Item 9th. My daughter **Elizabeth** has been provided for heretofore, I therefore give her one dollar and a bureau which she claims at my house.

Item 10th. My daughter **Nancy** having been provided for heretofore, I therefore give her a bureau worth $15.00 and a side saddle and bridle worth $18.00.

Item 11th. My daughters **Louisa** and **Rachael** have been provided for heretofore as my son **John Kincheloe** holds an obligation on me for their portion. I give each of them beside a bureau worth $15.00 a side saddle worth $18.00 each with the bridles.

Item 12th. It is my desire that the negro I own named **Gideon** go to satisfy the obligation which my son **John** holds on me for the benefit of **Louisa** and **Rachael**, and that the balance of the obligation be filled by the debts now due me by **Mrs. Surgoine, John A. Rogers** and others.

Item. 13th. It is my desire that if there can be money raised to satisfy the last named obligation which my son **John** holds on me...and to satisfy other debts from me, that my wife have **Iceham** during her widowhood, and then he fall to my son **James**. But if there cannot be money enough collected from them that owes me for the above purpose, I desire that **Iceham** be sold to satisfy the obligation and any other debts that may be due from me.

Item 14th. It is my desire that if either of my daughters, **Elizabeth, Nancy Louisa** or **Rachael** should die without a lawful issue, that the property given them fall to the survivors of them.

Item 15th. I desire all my books to be equally divided among my wife and children and each of them to have a Bible bought for them.

Item 16th. It is my desire that my wife take charge of **Old Phillis** and take care of her.

Item 17th. All the property not herein otherwise disposed of to be sold and the proceeds together with what debts may be owing me at the payment of all my just debts and necessary expenses, if any is left, to be equally divided between my six single daughters.

18th. I do appoint my beloved wife **Polly Kincheloe** my Executrix of this my last will and testament in writing and wish her to enter on the duties of her appointment without giving security. In testimony whereof I the said **Lijah Kincheloe** Testator have hereunto set my hand and affixed my seal this day and date above written.

Lijah Kincheloe (seal)

Signed, sealed and published in presence of us who are subscribing witnesses thereto the date above written. "Silver watch and gun" interlined before signed in 48th line.

Jacob Barb
Johnson Lacy
William Lyons
Robert D. Gray

[Old Book A, p. 120]

Be it remembered that on this 4th day of February, 1833, I, **Lijah Kincheloe** of the County of Hawkins, State of Tennessee, remaining still of sound mind and memory do make the following additions to my last Will & Testament in writing bearing date of 10 Feb., 1832. That is, I give to my daughters **Louisa** and **Rachael** my negro boy **Gideon** and my negro girl **Malinda** heretofore given to my daughter **Margaret**, which two negroes to go in full discharge of the obligation that my son **John** holds on me for the benefit of my two daughters, and instead of giving **Malinda** to my daughter **Margaret**, I desire a negro shall be purchased for her with the same funds that was to make the purchase for **Louisa & Rachael**...if there be a deficiency as satisfied in my will, that **Jack** be sold instead of **Isham**. If negro **Rose** shall outlive my wife **Polly** that she be liberated and set free, and should said **Rose** have a child or children, they are to go to my daughters **Margaret** and **Sarah**. And further to conclude: It is my desire that **Nathan Gray** of Granger County, together with my wife be Executors of this my last Will & Testament in writing. In witness whereof I have hereunto set my hand & seal the day & date above written. It is my wish that my Executors do proceed to the execution of this my last will without giving security.

Lijah Kincheloe (seal)

In presence of us:
J. G. Miller, C. C. Miller, A. Sanders

WILL OF MALINDA KENNER (Abstracted)

Page 291   Dated: Sept. 8, 1835

I, **Malinda Kenner** of Hawkins County, State of Tennessee, being of sound mind and memory, do make this my last Will & Testament...I direct that my body be decently buried by my Executors...that all my just debts should be paid by them out of my Estate. I give to my son **James** two negro girls **Sidney** and **Laura** and their increase during his life for his support and maintenance. And whereas my son **James** was born of weak mind so much so that he is not capable of taking care of himself or the property I leave to him for life for his support. It is my desire that my son **Rodham** shall take **James** and the property I leave to him for life and take care of him and treat him with tender kindness as long as **James** may live, and at his death if **Rodham** should do so, I then give and bequeath unto my son **Rodham** the two negro girls **Sidney** & **Laura** and their increase with what other property I may leave to **James** for life. Should **Rodham** die before **James**, I then revoke the bequeath made to **Rodham** and request that my son-in-law **George Savage** take **James** and the property

left to him during his life, and treat him with tender kindness suitable to his unhappy situation, then and in that case I give the property...unto my son-in-law **George Savage** to him & his heirs for their trouble of taking care of **James**. But should my son-in-law **George Savage** die before **James**, then and in that case, I revoke and disannul the bequeath to my son-in-law. But if **James** and myself should die before **Rodham**, it is then my will that **Rodham** shall keep the two negroes, **Sidney** and **Laura** and their increase at their value put on by my Executors, and the money be equally divided between all my children... It is my will and desire that my old negro woman **Rachael** should be set free, and as far as I have the power, I do hereby emancipate and set free my negro woman **Rachael** and give to her one cow and calf and one year's provision to be laid off by my Executors. And all the rest of my Estate I leave to **James** for life for his support, and at his death my will is that it shall go as my will directs my two negro girls to go.

I hereby appoint my two friends **Edwin Hamblen** and **Richard Mitchell** Executors... In witness whereof I have hereunto set my hand and affixed my seal this 8th day of September, 1835.

(her mark)
Malinda x Kenner (seal)

Signed, sealed published and declared by **Malinda Kenner** as her last Will and Testament in presence of us: **Jas. Bradley & W. B. Mitchell**

WILL OF BARBARY KING (Abstracted)

Page 292   Dated: March 18, 1842
                      Rec'd for Record June 5, 1848

State of Tennessee, Hawkins County. In the Name of God, Amen.

I, **Barbary King**, being of sound mind and disposing memory...wish now to dispose of my property, such as it has pleased God to bless me with.

I, **Barbary King**, do make and publish this as my last will and testament, hereby revoking and making void all other wills by me at any time made.

1st. I direct that all my funeral expenses and all my just debts be paid as soon after my death as possible out of any money I may die possessed of or may first come into the hands of my Executor.

2nd. I will that my cupboard and all the cupboard ware, my clock and my wind mill, my two pots and a baker, and one skillet, one bed and bed covers, one pair of steelyards and wire sifter, my gray mare, my red and white pided cow. I have in my possession three notes of hand, one on **Charles Coffin** for $30.00 and interest, one on **Rodham Chesnutt** for $19.00 and interest, one on **John Barnett** for $12.00 and interest.

3rd. After my decease I want my Executor to sell all of the above named property for cash, and also all of my property (that I die owning) and cause to be collected the three notes above mentioned, and out of the money arising, pay it to my children as I shall direct:

First. I will to my son **Adam King** or heirs one dollar.

2nd, 3rd and 4th: To my son **Charles King**; to my son **Jacob King** or his heirs; to my son **James King**, to each one dollar and no more.

5th. I will to my daughter **Fanny Arnott** one dollar and no more.

6th. I will to my two daughters **Sarah Beel** and **Elizabeth Garrison** all the balance of money arising from the sale of my property and notes as soon after my decease as possible.

7th and last. I will that my neighbor **David Reynolds** be my Executor and manage my affairs.

In witness whereof I do to this my last will set my hand and seal This 18th day of March, 1842.

Barbary x King (seal)
(her mark)

Signed sealed and published in our presence and we have subscribed our names hereto in the presence of the Testator, 18th March, 1842.
Attest: Wm. Smith, Sr., David Reynolds

WILL OF WILLIAM KEELE

Page 293

Dated: Jan. 13, 1845
Proven: Mar. 6, 1848

A written Will and Testament.

I William Keele do make and publish this my last Will and Testament hereby revoking and making void all other wills by me made at any time.

First. I direct that my funeral expenses and all my debts be paid as soon after my death as possible out of any money that I may die possessed of or may first come into the hands of my Executors.

Secondly. I sell my son Anthony B. Keele all the lands and possessions that I am seized and possessed of at this time for the sum of $1,200.00. Six hundred dollars to me in hand paid and the said A. B. Keele to have one half of the lands in possession from this date, and six hundred dollars at my death and the death of my wife Livy Ann, and the said A. B. Keele to have all my lands and possession.

Thirdly. I bequeath to my two sons for their interest in my estate, to A. B. Keele 50 acres of land and Jesse Keele, 80 acres.

Fourthly. All the personal property and moneys that is left at my death and the death of my wife Livy Ann is to be equally divided amongst my daughters Elizabeth Coffman, Mary Eavin, Rachael Deriaux, Heneretta Bailey, Matilda Weams, Sibbriney Carter.

Fifthly. My negro man named Archabel shall be emancipated and set at perfect liberty at our deaths.

Lastly. I do hereby nominate and appoint my two sons Jesse Keele and A. B. Keele my Executors. In witness whereof I do to this my will set my hand and seal this 13 January, 1845.

William x Keele (seal)
(his mark)

Signed sealed and published in our presence and we have subscribed our names hereto in the presence of the Testator. This date above written.
John Pogue & Jacob Smith

WILL OF JOHN KIRKPATRICK

Page 294

Dated: June 15, 1846

State of Tennessee, Hawkins County, June 15, 1846. In the Name of God, Amen.

I John Kirkpatrick of the County & State above mentioned do make and publish this my last Will and Testament in the following manner Viz: Being called to mind the uncertainty of life and the true certainty of death, and through the kindness of Providence having enabled me and family to accumulate some property both real and personal to which I feel to thank God for His Kindness toward me &c. Being somewhat afflicted in body but sound in mind and memory to dispose of such of my worldly substance as it has pleased God to bless me with.

First. My will is that as soon after my decease as possible, my administrators or the survivors of them to pay all my just debts and funeral expenses out of the proceeds of the sale of my perishable property.

Second. I give to my son David Kirkpatrick a certain portion of my land, including my mills and all the buildings thereon. Beginning at or near Nathan Vernon's spring on my line in the creek, thence down the creek as it meanders to a bend in the creek, thence across a strip of rising ground by where Thomas Case's grave is to the creek and across the line of said tract of ground, thence running with the said line to where it comes to the creek at the beginning, to include all the land in that boundary, to have full privilege to keep up his mill dam at or near the same place it stands at this time, and...David shall at all times give full privilege for the water to be conveyed from the spring through the dam in logs for the use of those who may occupy the house where I now live, to all intents and purposes that it now is used.

Third. To my sons, Hugh and James Kirkpatrick the balance of my land to be divided between them equally, and that the said Hugh and James are to support and maintain their mother Judith Kirkpatrick during her widowhood, and my wife to have privilege to live in the dwelling where she now lives during the same period above mentioned. Should my wife Judith ever marry after my decease, I desire and my will is for her to have $50.00 out of the proceeds of the sale of the perishable property of my Estate.

Fourth. My son David is to pay to Hugh and James Kirkpatrick $150.00 twelve months after my decease, to be paid in payments of $50.00 per year.

Fifth. Should there be any negroes or money on hand after my decease, I desire that it all be equally divided between my four children, Viz: Eliza Chesnutt, Hugh, James and David Kirkpatrick, also the perishable property or the proceeds thereof be also equally divided between my children or my heirs as above mentioned.

In witness whereof I do to this my last Will & Testament set my hand and seal This 22nd day of June, 1846.

John Kirkpatrick (seal)

Signed sealed and published in our presence and we have subscribed our names hereto in the presence of the Testator. This 22nd day of June in the year of our Lord one thousand eight hundred and forty six.
Attest: Wm. Smith, William Tharp

Now, I John Kirkpatrick having heretofore made my last Will and Testament, do make and declare this as a codicil thereto, to wit: First. I desire that a change be made in my former will and that is that Richard Chesnutt and his wife Eliza have $250.00 out of my Estate and no more, also my wife Judith to have one good feather bed and good furniture for the same &c. It is my desire that this codicil be attached to and constitute a part of my will to all intents and purposes whatsoever.

In testimony whereof I have hereunto set my name and affixed my seal hereunto This 5th day of January, 1848.

John Kirkpatrick (seal)

Attest: Wm. Smith & William Tharp

Page 296
WILL OF JOHN KITE (Senior)
Dated: October 2, 1850
Proven: May Term, 1851

The last Will and Testament of John Kite, Senior, made in the year of our Lord one Thousand Eight Hundred and Fifty, on second day of October. In the name of God, Amen.

I John Kite of Hawkins County, State of Tennessee being of sound mind and memory and wishing to dispose of such of my property as I will herein-after mention in manner and form as follows, viz:

First. My Will and desire is that as soon after my decease as is practicable, I desire that all my just debts and funeral expenses be paid out of any money that may come into the hands of my Executor or Administrator out of the sales of any of my perishable or personal property, or both as the case may be required.

Secondly. My will is that there be any money remaining in the hands of my representative after defraying the above-mentioned expenses, or any other expenses that may become necessary or right to be paid, the balance be equally divided between my lawful heirs viz: with the exception of my son Martin Kite, and to him I will all my tract of land whereon I now live containing 150 acres, lying on Dodson's Creek in District #15, adjoining the lands of Henry Laudeback and others.

NB The reason that I have not given the names of all the persons that will is that no one, or more of my lawful heirs attempt to break this my last Will and Testament.

In witness whereof I have hereunto set my hand and affixed my seal this day and date above written.

John x Kite (seal)
(his mark)

Attest: Wm. Smith, James P. Bradley

Page 297
WILL OF BARNABAS KELLEY (abstracted)
Dated: July 7, 1852
Proven in part at Aug. & Sept.
Term, 1856

I Barnabas Kelley of State of Tennessee, County of Hawkins, being feeble in body, but sound of mind, make and constitute the following to be my last Will and Testament, to wit:

Item. First, I will and bequeath unto my beloved wife Mary all my lands during her life, all my stock, household and kitchen furniture that may be left after my funeral expenses and just debts are paid by her.

Item 2nd. I will and bequeath that at the death of my wife Mary my be-loved son Joseph D. Kelley inherit all my lands and other property that I left my wife that may not be consumed by her. I do also hereby appoint my wife Mary my Executrix, and she not to be required to give security. In testimony whereof I have hereunto set my hand and seal this 7th day of July, 1852.

Barnabas x Kelley (seal)
(his mark)

Witness: Jacob Miller, Bales (Bails) Jeffers

Page 297
WILL OF HUGH L. KIRKPATRICK
Dated: August 8, 1853
Proven. Nov. 1853

In the Name of God. Amen.

I, Hugh L. Kirkpatrick being in feeble health but of sound mind and memory do make and publish this my last Will and Testament in the name of God. following. My body I give to be buried in a Christian like manner and form at the discretion of my family and friends and my soul to return to God who gave it.

2nd. After all my just debts are paid, I bequeath to my beloved wife, Mary, all my land and farming utensils, all my horses, hogs, sheep and cattle, together with my household and kitchen furniture of every kind during her life, or so long as she shall remain my widow, but in the event that my beloved wife should marry again, then my personal property (to be) sold and the proceeds divided according to law between my legal heirs; and my land rented out to the best advantage of my family during the natural life of my beloved wife. And at her death, I wish my land sold and proceeds divided between my several children (un-named). I do hereby nominate and appoint my wife Mary Executrix of this my last Will & Testament.

Witness my hand and seal. This 8th day of August, 1853.

Hugh L. Kirkpatrick (seal)

In presence of: Thos. J. Gill, John A. Mooney

Page 298
WILL OF JOHN W. KNEELAND
Dated: Feb. 5, 1855
Proven: Oct. Term, 1855

State of Tennessee, Hawkins County

I John W. Kneeland of the county and state aforesaid, considering the uncertainty of human life and being in perfect health and in the full pos-session of my mental faculties do make and devise this my last Will and Testament as follows:

First. I give and bequeath unto my beloved wife Mary B. Kneeland all of the property that I possess at my death including my entire estate, real and personal, except the bequests hereafter to be named, and furthermore, I bequeath to the heirs of my sister Polly Clark, dec'd, the sum of $6.00, to be divided equally between the children (there being six), also, I be-queath unto my sister Lucy Huggins the sum of one dollar. Also, I bequeath unto my sister Syntha Messick one dollar. Also I bequeath unto my sister Electa Titus one dollar. To my sister Abial H. Parr, one dollar. To my sister Eliza H. McCorde, one dollar.

And I hereby appoint the said Mary B. Kneeland my Executrix for the fulfillment of this my last Will and Testament.

In testimony whereof I hereunto affix my signature. This fifth day of February, 1855.

John W. Kneeland

Attested by Wm. Faris

Page 299
WILL OF BARSHABA KYLE
Dated: August 29, 1855

Barshaba Kyle's will, August 29, 1855, gives Leonidas Kyle, her son, Jessy, Cook Eliza, Vincent & Cook Eliza's Lucy and their increase. Also, four best beds, bedsteads and furniture and all of her.

stock, farming utensils, horses & buggy, except cow **Barsha** now has and also two other good cows and calves.

Old Lucy, mulatto, to live with any of her children chooses, or if she does not like to live with either, with any other person she may select, and **Leonidas** to furnish her with a decent support...her life & bury her decently.

If the compromise with her children is made for the money she claims from the estate which is about $6,000.00, and they give her the negroes in lieu if said claim, to wit: **George, Bush, Houston & Lucy,** (then) **Leonidas** is also to have **Houston, Clint & George** and all the money that may be on hand at her death, also all my household & kitchen furniture except three beds, bedsteads & furniture, also all my interest whatever it may be in the copper mines in Va.

Barshaba McClure to have all the remaining property during her life, and if she should die before him, the property is to revert to **Leonidas**, to wit: **Bush** and **Lucy** and her increase, also three bedsteads and furniture. No sale of any of her property to be made after her death, and if **Leonidas** should not be of age the property willed to him to be put in the hands of some safe person until he becomes of age.

If compromise be not made, I want the suit carried on for its recovery and if gained, **Barsha McClure** to have the value of **Bush** and **Lucy**, and **Leonidas** the balance. That is to say, my will is that whatever amount be gained of claim of $6,000.00 against the Estate of **A. Kyle**, dec'd, the part above willed to **Barsheba McClure,** my will is that said fund be put out at interest free from the control of my son-in-law **Mitchell McClure**, and my daughter only to have the interest on fund and the principal. If my daughter **Barsheba** dies before my son **Leonidas**, then principal to go to him.

Witness my hand and seal this 29th day of August, 1855.

Barshaba Kyle (seal)

Attest: **Sam Powel, J. H. Vance**

WILL OF JAMES KING
Page 300

Dated: oct. 11, 1855
Proven: Nov. Term., 1855

I, **James King** of County of Hawkins, State of Tenn., being frail in body but of sound mind memory and understanding, do make, ordain and establish this my last Will & Testament...

First. I give my body to be buried decently and all expenses arising therefrom to be paid & all just debts to be paid by my Executor (to be) named.

Second. I give...to my beloved wife **Elizabeth** all my property, real and personal, after paying all just debts during her life provided she remains my widow, then to be equally divided between her two sons, **William J. Tirout** and **James M. Tirout**, but if she should marry...she to have a cow and calf, a bed, bedstead and furniture, and if that should occur, ...my Executor take charge of my property and manage to best advantage for above named heirs **William J.** and **J. M. Tirout**, and then equally divided when **J. M. Tirout** becomes 21.

Third. I nominate and appoint my friend **Rodham Chesnutt** my Executor to this my last Will & Testament, revoking and making void all former wills by me made. This 11th day of October, 1855.

Signed and acknowledged in the
presence of Us: **James Everhart,**
William Everhart, George White

James x King (seal)
(his mark)

WILL OF ROBERT P. KYLE
Page 301

Dated: Nov. 11, 1856
Proven: Aug. Term, 1861
J. H. Vance, Clk.

I, **Robert P. Kyle** of the County of Hawkins and State of Tenn., do make and publish this my last Will and Testament, hereby revoking all other wills heretofore made by me.

First. My will is that all my just debts and funeral expenses be paid by my Executors out of any money I may hve on hand at my death if there is sufficient for that purpose, otherwise to pay said debts and expenses out of sales of my personal property, a sufficient quantity of which I direct to be sold for that purpose.

2nd. I give my plantation known as "Brooks Place" to my three brothers, **Wm. C. Kyle, Absalom A. Kyle,** and **Leonidas Kyle,** divided equally.

Third. The plantation whereon I now reside, I give to my wife **Mary** during her life or widowhood, and at her death or marriage, the said plantation (it being the same one that I bought of **James P. McCarty**), is hereby given to my three brothers on the same terms in all respects as the Brooks Place.

Fourth. I give to my wife all my slaves with the exception of **Lewis, John** and **Nelly.** My wife to have slaves herein given during her life or widowhood, and at her marriage or death, the slaves to belong to my three brothers. At my death the slaves **Lewis, John** and **Nelly** are to belong equally to my three brothers.

Fifth. I also give to my wife my stock of cattle, horses, &c, household and kitchen furniture and whatever grain is on hand, and the farming tools that I may have, but the property given in this clause is subject to the payment of my debts. And it is my will, and all the property given to my wife is given on the condition that she survives me. If she dies first, then my three brothers to have all the property hereinbefore given to her immediately upon my death.

Sixth. I hereby give to my said brothers all my copper interests in the State of Virginia and North Carolina, including what I owned in my own right and what I got from the estate of my father.

Seventh. I hereby nominate **John Netherland** and **Joseph B. Heiskill** Executors of this my last Will and Testament.

In testimony whereof I have hereunto set my hand and seal. This the 11th day of November, 1856. (Interlined before signing).

Robert P. Kyle (seal)

Signed & sealed by the Testator and witnessed by us at his request & in his presences.
Wit: **John Dunlap**

WILL OF WILEY B. KENNER
Page 302

Dated: March 13, 1858
Proven: Dec. Term, 1862
James R. Pace, Clk.

I, **Wiley B. Kenner**, do make and publish this as my last Will and Testament, hereby revoking and making void all other wills by me at any time made.

First. I direct that my funeral expenses and all my debts be paid as soon after my death as possible out of any money that I (may have at my death),

Secondly. I give and bequeath to my wife **Elizabeth** as long as she remains my widow or during her life all the tract of land whereon I now reside or own at my death and all the personal property, household and kitchen furniture.

Third. I desire that at her death all the personal property be sold and my two daughters Polly Ann Webb and Lucinda Snyder shall have each $150.00 in cash.

Fourth. I give and bequeath all my land to my sons, to wit: **James, William, Mark, Houson, Wiley B.,** Doctor Jasper Kenner & Newton Kenner, to be equally divided.

Lastly. I do hereby nominate and appoint my sons **James** and **William** my Executors. In witness whereof I do to this my Will set my hand and seal this 31st day of March, 1858.

Willie B. Kenner (seal)

Signed, sealed and published in our presence and we have subscribed our names hereto in the presence of the Testator. This 31st day of March, 1858.

Rial Jones and **Frederick Brewer**

WILL OF WILLIAMS KINKEAD
Page 303
Dated: Dec. 9, 1859
Proven: Aug. 6, 1860

J. B. Vance, Clk.

I, **William Kinkead, Senior,** of Hawkins County, State of Tennessee, do make and publish this my last Will & Testament, hereby revoking and making void all other wills by me at any time made.

First. I bequeath my soul to God who gave it.

Second. I direct that my funeral expenses and all my debts be paid as soon after my death as possible out of any moneys that I may die possessed of or may first come into the hands of my Executor.

Third. I give and bequeath to my four daughters, to wit: **Mary Ann Gillenwaters,** formerly Mary Ann Kinkead, **Elizabeth Gillenwaters,** formerly Kinkead, **Maney S. Miller,** formerly Kinkead and **Susan Adaline Gillenwaters,** my negro man **Jeff** to be divided equally among them, and it is my request that he be kept in the family.

Fourth. I will and bequeath to my four daughters above named the notes of my sale to be equally divided among them.

Fifth. The balance of my personal property to my four daughters above named to be equally divided.

Sixth. My library of books to be divided between my four daughters and whatever is left of my personate after paying my debt to be divided with my daughters equal. (The interlining was made before signing and annexed).

Lastly. I do hereby nominate and appoint as my Executors **Anderson** Kinkead and Michael **Miller.** In witness whereof I do to this my will set my hand and seal. This the 9th day of Dec., 1859.

Test:
Wms Kinkead (seal)

A. Carmichael, N. Campbell

NUNCUPATIVE WILL OF JESSE KEELE
Page 303
Dated: Dec. 1, 1861
Proven: Apr. Term, 1862

We, **Anthony B. Keele** and **William Shepherd,** do state that the nuncupative will of **Jesse Keele** was made by him on the 26th day of November, 1861 in our presence to which we were specially required to bear witness by the Testator

himself in the presence of each other; that is, it was made in his last sickness in his own dwelling house, and the same is as follows, to wit:

It was his will and desire that his effects should be disposed of after his death in the following manner:

First. It was his will that all his personal property should remain on the farm he lived on, and that his son **William Keele** should come and live on and take charge of said farm and property and see to the raising of the children and settle up all unsettled business and when the children should become of age or marry, they should be portioned off equal to those which has already married, and at any time he is authorized to sell at private or public sale any personal property that may be on hand in order to pay debts or for the benefit of the children, and that his children should remain on the farm or live in the house there until of age or marry, and that his farm in Greene County be rented out by his Executor and the rent thereof used for the benefit of his children and if any surplus left, to be retained until the youngest child becomes of age, and at any time that his Executor should think it more to the interest of his children for said farm in Greene County to be sold he is hereby authorized to sell same farm, make title for same, &c, and when the youngest child is of full age then all his estate real and personal to be equally divided between all my children, and that his son **William Keele** should have yearly out of any surplus property made on the farm a sufficiency to compensate him for his troubles in managing said business, and lastly, he nominated and appointed his son **William Keele** his Executor to this his last will made out by us this 1st day of December, 1861.

A. B. Keele
William Shepherd

WILL OF THOMAS LOYD
Page 305
Dated: April 14, 1789

I **Thomas Loyd,** being in a poor state of health but in my senses do cause this my last Will & Testament to be made and to be in the manner and form following, viz: My beloved wife to retain all my property until her death, unless in case any of the children marry, then it is to be as follows: Upon **John** marriage, or death of his mother, he is to have a cow called Goodluck with her calf, and in case of his mother's death one half of the land I own equal in quality and improvements and under the same situation. **Polly** in like case to have the other half the land (sic) and a cow and calf. **Tom** to have the muly-headed cow and calf and an equal share of my personal effects. **Benjamin** I mention last because he has had his share from me when he married, but notwithstand, I bequeath him one cow and calf upon his demand. All this being my full desire, I request it may be fulfilled. As witness my hand and seal this 14th day of April 1789.

Thos. x Loyd (seal)   (his mark)

Wit: Dennis Cannon, George Brooks

WILL OF GEORGE LAUGHMILLER
Page 305
Dated: Jan. 17, 1789

In the Name of God, Amen.
Hawkins County & State of Tennessee, Jan. 17, 1789.

This day I find myself in a poor state of health and if should not (sic) recover from this, I give up my soul to God and is my will and testament that my body be decently buried and is also my will that my loving wife should have the third of my personal astate, accepting to too mares and she is to have the use of the plantation and the too mares until John my son, gits of age, if not married before for raising my children, as soon as either of these comenses then nomore than the third of the rent and further I wil¹ to my son John my rifle gun and colt and my copers (coopers ?) tools and the plantation when of age at its value which he is to have an equal share in with the rest of my children & my daughter Elizabeth a spinning wheel, and my daughter Rebecca a spinning wheel. This property heir given is as a present to my son and daughter, so that the wife and the rest of the children is to receive no benefit for it. The above mentioned two thirds to be sold and all my children to receive an equal divide as they come of age, and is my will that all debts to be paid out of my astate before divided. And for to execut this my will I choose my trusty friends, Joseph Rogers and Jonas Lockmiller.

So this is my last will and Testament which I publish with my one hand this before mentioned date.

George Loughmiller (seal)
[In German Script]

Signed & published in presence of:
Jacob Miller, Peter Miller

WILL OF JOHN LEE (SR.)

Page 306   Dated: August 22, 1809
In the name of God, Amen.

I John Lee Senior of the County of Hawkins and State of Tennessee, being of the decline of life, though weak in body but of perfect mind and memory, Thanks be to God, calling to mind the mortality of my body and knowing that it is appointed for all men once to die, do make and ordain this my last Will & Testament, that is to day, principally and first of all, I give and recommend my soul to the hands of Almighty God that gave it and my body I recommend to the earth to be buried in a decent Christian burial at the discretion of my Executors nothing doubting but at the general Resurrection I shall receive the same again by the Mighty power of God. And touching such worldly estate wherewith it hath pleased God to bless me with in this life, I give, devise and dispose of the same in the following manner and form:

First. I bequeath to my three sons, Cador, Burrell and John Lee one negro man named Mark, to be divided equally between them, also to my son John one bed and furniture to contain forty weight of feathers to the bed and five to the bolsters. I now bequeath to my daughter Mary Lee, First, a parcel of land being the lower part of my plantation. Beginning on Thomas Lee's line on the north hillside and running along his line to the corner, from thence to the dividing line between my land and Enoch Marrisett. Thence along the dividing line across Dry Creek. Thence along the bank of the creek to the peach orchard fence. Thence along the said fence to a cross fence. Thence along that cross fence to my shop, thence along the other fence to the hog pen by the spring. From thence to an ash at the spring, from thence through the middle of the spring to an ash. From thence across to two persimmons in the Sugar Camp branch. Thence up the said branch to the back lines, from thence to the beginning containing 100 acres more or less, with one horse colt called Snip to her after my wife's death.

The rest of my land to be divided between my daughters Martha Lee and Sarah Patrick. Beginning at the mouth of said Martha Lee's spring branch and running up said branch to a chopt dogwood, thence a direct course to the back line containing 75 acres more or less. Martha Lee to have one colt called Bird after my wife's decease. Also, I give and bequeath to my grandson William Lee one bed and furniture - the bed that me any my wife lies on. The rest of my stock and household furniture to be equally divided between Mary Lee, Martha Lee, Sarah Patrick and William Lee, son of Martha Lee, to be theirs after my wife's decease. Also, I give and bequeath to my grandson William Lee, all my working tools of all kinds.

Also, I give and bequeath to my wife Elizabeth Lee one negro woman named lind, to be hers her lifetime and after her decease to belong to Mary Lee and Sarah Patrick. Also, I give and bequeath to my wife Elizabeth Lee one negro man named Tona to be hers her lifetime and after her decease to be equally divided between my son Robert and my daughters Mary Lee and Sarah Patrick.

I do hereby utterly disallow, revoke and dis-annul all and every other former Testament, Will, legacy, bequeath and executors by me any way before named, willed and bequeathed, ratifying and confirming this and no other to be my last Will & Testament.

In witness whereof I have hereunto set my hand and seal. In the year of our Lord, one Thousand Eight Hundred and Nine, This 22nd day of August.

John Lee (seal)

Signed, sealed, published, pronounced and delivered by the said John Lee as his last Will & Testament in the presence of us who in his presence and the presence of each other have hereto subscribed our names.
John Lee, Edward Lee, James Griffin

WILL OF WILLIAM LEMAR

Page 308   Dated: August 29, 1812
In the Name of God, Amen.

Be it known and remembered that I, William B. Lemar of the County of Fredrick and State of Maryland, now within Hawkins County and State of Tenn., and on my way from the State of Kentucky to my residence in Frederick County aforesaid, and being sick and in a low state of health, but of perfect mind and memory and calling to mind the certainty of death and uncertainty of life do make this my last will and testament, revoking all former wills, deeds of gift, bequests, etc., and in the first place doth will and desire that (after resigning my soul to Almighty God who gave it me), my body to be decently buried at the expense of my Estate. And, Secondly, I give to my son Marine T. Lemar a tract of land which I purchased from John Lewis, the same containing 160 acres situated in Breckenridge County, State of Kentucky, adjoining lands of Joseph Killenbarger, reference to said John Lewis deed to me will be more fully explain. (sic) And, I also give to my son Marine aforesaid one negro boy called Tom, one horse, one cow, and also a note of hand on Perry Rice $128.125.

Thirdly, I give to my two sons Benjamin S. Lemar and Richard S. Lemar the tract of land on which I live including all the land which has not been conveyed to my sons Thos and William Lemar, to be equally divided between Benjamin and Richard, and to Benjamin I also give a negro boy named Andrew, one horse, one cow, and to Richard I give a negro boy named Jack, one horse and one cow. Fourthly, I give all my stock of negroes not heretofore disposed of by this will and excluding such as I have previously bequeathed to my children, to be equally divided between my four daughters, and all my movable estate of every description including bond, notes, &c, excepting the one herein named to wit: The one given to my son **Marine**, to be equally divided between my daughters aforesaid, say, **Henney**, **Sally**, **Susanah** and **Rachael**.

Fifthly, I also give to each of my sons **Benjamin** and **Richard** in addition to what I have heretofore given them by this will.

Lastly, I appoint my sons **William** and **Thomas Lemar** Executors of this my last Will & Testament. Signed, sealed and acknowledged in the presence of those whose names are hereunto set. 29th August, 1812.

William Bishop x Lemar (seal) (his mark)

Daniel Deck, George Morrison, Joseph McMinn

Page 309

WILL OF JOHN LAUGHMILLER

Dated August 11, 1814

In the Name of God, Amen.

I, John Laughmiller of Hawkins County, State of Tenn., being weak in body but in sound memory and perfect mind, thanks be to Almighty God, and calling to mind the mortality of the body and knowing it is appointed for all men once to die, do make and ordain this my last Will – Testament:

1st. I recommend my soul to God that gave it and my body to the earth to be buried in a Christian like manner by my Executors, and my worldly estate

Item. After paying all my just debts, I give and bequeath to my beloved wife **Savana Laughmiller** two cows and a roan mare with one bed & furniture. Also the pewter she had when I was married to her. It is also my desire my wife **Savana** should have one third of all the grain & hay raised on the clear- ed land which I have cleared, and pasture for the two cows and mare above mentioned & in case my wife **Savana** should get married again the above to cease and she is to live on my present place of residence during her life unmolested in case she does not marry. There is also a pot rack, one iron pot and a coffee mill my wife had when I was married to her, which I wish her to retain, also one walnut chest.

It is my desire that all my personal estate be sold at public vendue – such as horses, cattle, sheep, farming utensils & shop tools of every kind, &c., grain and hay excepted, which is to be retained for the use of the family & stock. The monies arising therefrom to be applied to the payment of a debt which I owe my brother **Jonas Laughmiller**.

It is my desire that my daughter **Elizabeth Lutholtz** have $67.00 cash, to be paid by my Executors in the following manner: One half in 12 months after my death. The other half in two years after my death. I also desire that my sons **Jacob** and **George** have paid them the same sums paid in cash that is paid my daughter **Elizabeth Lutholtz**, and in the same manner.

My son **Jacob** is to have a horse beast to worth (sic) $30.00 exclusive of the above-named legacy in cash.

My landed estate I wish divided equally between my sons, to wit: My son **John** to hold the place where he now lives. **Jonas** to hold the place where he now lives, which place is to be equally divided with the 50 acres adjoin- ing the same between my sons **Jonas** and **Frederick** and **Henry**. The place where I now reside is to be equally divided between my sons **David**, **Abram** and **Phillip**, and when divide **David** is to have the place where the buildings now stand, all of which land are to be valued by persons chosen by all my sons above mention- ed, and should any one tract be more valuable than the rest, the ones holding such tracts of land shall pay to my Executors a sum in money to make all lot equal which I wish paid to the ones least valuable. It is my desire that my

seven sons above mentioned who holds my landed estate should pay to my daugh- ter **Sarah Laughmiller** the amount that will be equal to what the average lot – land will be valued at. It is also my desire that **Jonas** and **Frederick** be my Executors to this my last Will & Testament.

John x Laughmiller (seal) (his mark)

Signed, sealed, acknowledged in the presence of the following witnesses. This 11th day of August, 1814.   John A. Rodgers, Thomas Betty, William Lyons

It is my will, in addition to the above, that the buildings and im- provements on the lands here above given to my sons **John** & **Jonas Laughmiller** be not taken into the account in ascertaining the value thereof, except such improvements as were on the same when they first got possession.

John Laughmiller (seal)

William Lyons, George Hale, Thomas Betty (his mark)

Page 311

NONCUPATIVE WILL OF THOMAS LEE

Dated: 29 June, 1816

On the 29th of June 1816, **Thomas Lee**, Senior of Hawkins County, State of Tennessee, being then sick in body but of sound mind and memory told us by word of mouth what he wanted to be done with his negroes after his death as follows, to wit: That he wished his wife **Mary Lee** to have three negroes, to wit: **Rachael**, **Jane** and **George**, and his son **James Lee** he wished to have the negro boy named **Sam**, and the rest and residue to be sold. And on the 2nd day of July following he departed this life and on the 4th of July we reduced his conversation to writing as above. Witness our hands and seals.

Needham Lee (seal)

William Lee (seal)

[see original will]

Page 311

WILL OF WILLIAM LIGHT

Dated: Sept. 25, 1817.

In the Name of God. Amen.

I, **William Light** of Hawkins County and State of Tennessee, considering the uncertainty of this mortal life and being of sound and perfect mind and memory, Blessed be Almighty God for the same do make and publish this my last Will and Testament in manner and form following, that is to say:

First. I leave unto my beloved wife **Patience** all and singular my goods and chattels during her life. Furthermore, I do give and bequeath unto my youngest son **Jacob Light** all my lands and tenements, that is to say, the tract of land where I now live. It is also my will that the rest of my children, that is to say, unto **Vachel Light**, **John**, **William**, **George**, **Wright**, **Joshua** and **Michael** and my daughters **Patience Mullins**, **Susanah Rice**, **Elenor Light** and **Prudence Mortlock** all and singular my goods and chattels (after the decease of my beloved wife), to be equally divided between them. And I do hereby appoint **John** my sole Executors of this my last Will and Testament, hereby revoking all former wills by me made.

In witness whereof I have hereunto set my hand and seal. This twenty fifth day of September, in the year of our Lord, one thousand Eight hundred and seventeen. Signed, sealed and acknowledged in presence of:

attest: Reuben Barnard,
Samuel Mortlock, Wright x Light (his mark)

William x Light (seal) (his mark)

WILL OF MARY LEE

Page 312

Dated: August 19, 1818
Proven: May Session, 1821

In the Name of God, Amen.

Be it remembered that I, **Mary Lee**, widow of **Thomas Lee**, dec'd of Hawkins County and State of Tennessee, being in sound health, memory, and considering the uncertainty of this mortal life and the certainty of death, blessed be God Almighty for the same do make and publish this my last Will & Testament in manner and form following, that is to say:

First. I give and bequeath unto my three daughters **Winnfred Bailey**, **Zilpha Bailey**, **Mary Griffin** all my wearing clothes, them to be equal- divided between the three daughters before named. The rest and residue of my whole estate I wish to be sold and equally divided between all the lawful heirs of my body. And I do hereby appoint **William Lee** and **Edward Lee** sole Executors of this my last Will and Testament. In witness whereof I have hereunto set my hand and seal this 19th day of August, 1818.

Mary x Lee (seal)
(her mark)

Signed, sealed published and declared by the above named **Mary Lee** to be her last will and testament in the presence of us who at her request and in her presence have hereunto subscribed our names as witnesses to the same.
Attest: **Jones Griffin, James Lee, David B. Cumming**

WILL OF MARY LEE

Page 312

Dated: January 17, 1819

In the Name of God, Amen.

I, **Mary Lee**, of the County of Hawkins and State of Tennessee, being in a low state of health but of sound mind and memory, thanks be to God, calling unto mind the mortality of my body and knowing that it is appointed for all mortals once to die, I do make and ordain this my last Will & Testament in writing, to wit: I give and bequeath to my only son **Clinton Lee** all and singular my property real and personal, to wit: A certain tract or parcel of land in the County of Hawkins on the south side of Holston River in Carter's Valley, the same tract of land formerly willed to **Mary Lee** by her father **John Lee**, Senior, dec'd, the same being bounded as follows: Beginning on **Thomas Lee's** line on the north hillside and running along his line to the corner, from thence to the dividing line between my land and the heirs of **Enoch Morrisett**. Thence along the dividing line across the Dry Creek. Thence along the branch of the creek to the peach orchard fence. Thence along said fence to my father's shop, thence along the other fence to where my father had a hog pen by the spring. From thence through the middle of the spring to an ash. From thence across to two persimmons in the Sugar Camp branch. Thence up the said branch to the line, from thence to the beginning, containing 100 acres more or less. This being all of my real property. I now give and bequeath to my only son **Clinton Lee** all and singular my personal property, to wit: all my bedding and furniture, also, all my livestock of horses, hogs and cattle, together with every species of property that I may die seized and possessed of both real and personal.

But if my son **Clinton Lee** should not live to the years of maturity, to wit: to live to the age of 21, then I wish my brother **Robert Lee** have all the property real and personal that I herein willed to my son **Clinton**. I do hereby make and appoint my brother **Robert Lee** Executor of this my last will and testament. I do hereby utterly disallow, revoke and disannul all and

every other former will or testament by me made, confirming this and no other to be my last Will & Testament. In witness whereof I have hereunto set my hand and seal, This 17th January, the year of our Lord, one Thousand eight hundred and nineteen.

Mary x Lee (seal)
(her mark)

Signed, sealed published and declared by the said **Mary Lee** as her last Will and Testament in presence of us. **Jones Griffin, Edward Lee, Mary x Lee**, Sen'r
(her mark)

WILL OF JOHN LANE

Page 313

Dated: Dec. 4, 1823

In the Name of God, Amen.

Know all men by these presents that I **John Lane** of Hawkins County, State of Tennessee, being of advanced age in life and if infirmity of body, do make and put in writing this piece of written papers to be my last Will & Testament.

First. I bequeath to my well beloved wife **Sarah** one horse or mare, saddle and bridle and two cows, 20 head of hogs on the plantation and one feather bed and furniture in the house during her lifetime, and at her death such of them that may be in being (sic) to be equally divided between my said wife's two youngest sons, to wit: **Zadoc** and **John Barnard**.

Second. I give **Zadoc** and **John Barnard** all residue of my property that is on the plantation whereon I live now, both indoors and out that may be on hand at the time of my death, and after my wife get out what I have bequeathed to her in this my last will. And in consideration of and for the reason that the said **Zadoc** and **John** shall have maintained me and my wife in our old days and that they have us buried in a decent manner, also to pay unto my daughter **Sarah Wood**, wife of **John Wood** the sum of $50.00 in current bank notes, or in specie as the mode of payments may be after my death.

And as to all the rest of my children, I having heretofore given them what of my estate I was able, therefore, I say nothing more about them in this my last Will & Testament.

My will is that after death of my wife, all property on hand that she got from her father's estate since the intermarriage of me and her, that is: first to remain hers during her lifetime and at her death, as above, be equally divided between all the children of my wife, share and share alike with all increase arising therefrom at the time of her decease.

In witness whereof the said **John Lane** doth hereby set his hand and seal, and also acknowledging this piece of paper to be his last Will and Testament. This fourth day of December, 1823.

John Lane (seal)

Attest: **Reuben Barnard, Lewis Dalton, Lewis Barnard**

WILL OF JAMES LEEPER

Page 315

Dated: April 13, 1826

I, **James Leeper** of the County of Hawkins and State of Tennessee mediating on the uncertainty of life, being weak of body but of sound mind and memory think it advisable that all men should make joice of disposing of their worldly effects previous to their departure from this life into that of eternity, have thought proper to dispose and bequeath of mine in the following manner.

In the first place, I bequeath my soul to Almighty God, Him who gave it.

My request, then, is that my property be disposed of and is bequeathed.

First, to my beloved wife **Ruthe Leeper** the furniture belonging property, to wit: Two beds and furniture, my cupboard with the furniture belonging to, with the tables and bureau of my house. Also my large chest; likewise, my kitchen table and furniture belonging to kitchin furniture consisting of ovens, pots, kettles and their appendiges, together with every other des- cription of household furniture. Also two work horses to be chosen by her out of my stock, two milk cows and calves, six head of sheep, her choice; likewise, six head of hogs fit for fattening out of the best lot I have for killing, with her stock of geese and pigs. Likewise, her stock of geese and poultry. She is also to keep possession of the dwelling house and farm until my youngest daughter **Sally** becomes 18 years of age, provided she should not live to arrive to that age, to keep possession until the year 1840---to keep also all my negroes until that period of time. They are then to be agree- able to this my will to be sold, all but one which I allow my wife to keep and to wait on her, her lifetime, which ever one she may think proper to keep, and at her death to be sold and the proceeds of them to be equally divided amongst all my children except my sons **John** and **Guion Leeper**. The negroes that are to be sold at the period of 1840, their proceeds are to be divided so soon as the price of them can be lawfully collected. If my wife should die before the period above named, the property given to her for the benefit and purpose of raising and schooling my five youngest children, the property then is to remain on the premises for the support of s'd five children until that period of time arrives, then all that remains which I have bequeathed unto the hands of my wife is to be sold and divided as above named, except one dollar to my son **John** having received heretofore more than any of the rest of my children which I consider his full share of my Estate. Also, my son **Guion** having by this my last Will & Testament my land, I bequeath to **Guion** the possession which he is not to have until the period of 1840, which land was bequeathed to me by my father **Guion Leeper**, but only so much of it as can be spared from the support of my wife and the family which I have named to stay with her until they are raised, sufficient to transact business for themselves, then he is to have title in fee simple by this bequeath, and all the benefits inuring from the same after the period of 1840 is to go to him the s'd **Guion**, my youngest son. I likewise bequeath to him one heifer.

Also, to my son **James**, one heifer; my daughter **Ruthe A.** one heifer; my daugh- ter **Sally** one heifer, also the residue of my cattle except a cow and yearling my daughter **Jane** claims and a cow and yearling my daughter **Nancy J. Leeper's** grandmother gave her are to be sold together with all the rest of my prop- erty not named in my will except my farming utensils which my wife is to keep for the use of herself and children and one horse which I bequeathed to my son **Francis**, my young bay horse. My wife is also to keep as much bacon and grain as will be considered sufficient for one season, together with as much land as she may think proper, also her soap. All the property that is not specially bequeathed is to be sold as soon as practicable after my death, on a 12-month credit and to be equally divided between all my children except such as are excepted above, with my daughters **Margaret** and **Taphena** also from any part of the first sale of my property, but after that **Margaret** and **Taphena** are to come in and share equal in the residuum. My son **Hugh** is to have $45.00 from my Estate before a general division is commenced.

(Codicil) Should my wife die before 1840, none of the property is to be retained as aforementioned but the negroes, but is to be sold as soon as practicable thereafter. My wish is that my friends **William Armstrong** and

---

Guion Leeper be my Executors of this my last Will and Testament, and in this My request, I revoke all others. In witness whereof I have set my hand and seal. This 13th day of April, 1826.

James Leeper (seal)

Attest: James Amis
        Hugh Leeper, Snr.

WILL OF THOMAS LEE

Page 317   Dated: July 13, 1828

In the Name of God, Amen.

This 13th day of July in the year of our Lord, 1828., I, **Thomas Lee** of the County of Hawkins and State of Tennessee being weak in body but of per- fect mind and memory, and calling to mind the mortality of my body and that it is appointed for all men once to die, do make and ordain this my last Will and Testament in the manner following, Viz: My body I give to the earth to be buried in a Christian manner at the discretion of my hereinafter named Executors, my soul to God who created and gave it, and my earthly Estate I give and bequeath in the manner following:

First, All my just debts are to be paid. Then I give and bequeath to my beloved wife **Polly** a mare and colt — this mare known by the name of Peg, to her use and benefit forever, also to my wife the use and benefit of both my plantation and farming utensils during the term of seven years, together with the use and benefit of all my negroes for the same time. At the end of said seven years, it is my will that a division take place of the personal Estate and Killenworth Plantation and the proceeds to be equally divided be- tween my son **James Lee** and son-in-law **Samuel Chesnutt**, daughter **Sally Lee** so far as will make them shares equal with my other hereinafter named children- to whom I will my negroes – making to each share and share alike. I give and bequeath to my daughter **Elizabeth** one negro woman named **Tilda** (her increase excepted). I give and bequeath unto my son **Thomas Lee** one negro boy named **Henderson**. I give and bequeath to my son **Pleasant N. Lee** one negro boy named **Hardy**. I give and bequeath to my son **William D.** one negro boy named **Elbert**. I give and bequeath to my daughter **Polly Ann** one negro girl named **Melvina**. Should either of the negro women have a girl child in four years, it is to go to **Polly Ann**, and **Melvina** to my daughter **Sally**. If there should be no increase of a girl child in four years, **Melvina** to be **Polly Ann's**. Should any of the above-named negroes die previous to the division, then in that case their part is to be made equal to the other heirs.

I give and bequeath to my beloved wife one negro woman named **Nance** during her natural life. Then her and increase to go back to the Estate. I wish the plantation on which I live to remain unmolested and free from division until the youngest child comes of age when a final division can take place. I will that at the time of making the final division, all be made equal and that the heirs of my son **Samuel J. Lee**, dec'd receive his part, and (heirs) of my son **Michael B. Lee**, dec'd, receive his part.

I do hereby nominate, constitute and appoint my son **James Lee** and my son- in-law **Samuel Chesnutt** Executors of this my last Will and Testament in all its parts, disannulling and revoking all others.

In testimony whereof I have hereunto set my hand and affixed my seal. This 13th day of February, 1828.

(The words "and woman" "Deceased" were interlined before signing).

Signed, sealed published and   **Thomas Lee** (seal)
declared in presence of Andrew Galbraith, Edward Lee and Nicholas Lee

WILL OF THOMAS LARKIN

Page 318

Dated: August 18, 1829
Proven: Nov. 16, 1830

In the Name of God, Amen.

The 18th of August, 1829, I **Thomas Larkin** of Hawkins County, State of Tennessee, being weak in body but of perfect mind and memory, Thanks be to God. Therefore calling of mind the mortality of my body knowing it was appointed for all men once to die, I do make and ordain this to be my last Will and Testament. Principally and first of all, I give my soul to the care of Almighty God that gave it and my body I recommend to the earth to be buried in a decent and Christian manner at the discretion of my Executors, and as to this estate wherewith it pleased God to bless me with in this life, I give and devise, dispose of the same in the following manner.

First. I allow my lawful debts to be paid and I give and bequeath to my beloved wife **Ann** the house and land whereon I now live and all privilege of negro **Mill** and **Fill** as long as she lives. And **William** and **Robert R. Larkin** to maintain their mother with the negroes **Mill** and **Fill** as long as she lives, and at her death **William** to have **Mill** and **Robert R.** to have **Fill**. All the stock to be kept on the plantation as long as your mother lives, and I allow **James C. Larkin** the land he now lives on, and **John Larkin** a colt, either from Whitefoot or Snip, for his share of the land. And for **Henry Larkin** I allow him that big colt or the price of him for his share of the land. John, James, Henry, Margaret, Thomas, Mary, David, William Robert R. Larkin. And I allow **Thomas** and **David Larkin** to find out the corner beeches between Gibbons' land and this tract I now live on at this time according to the old original grant, and if you get it—beech corner established—then you are to get 35 acres across the valley apiece, you and **David**, with part of the entry to the crossing of hotus spring branch as the road goes now through the gap of the knobs. And if any of you takes a notion to sell their part, let **William** or **Robert** have it at a reasonable price and sell to no other person, and I allow **William** to have next the hotous branch and **Robert R.** the house I now live in at their mother's death, and **William** I allow the Bureau and **Robert** the cupboard and chest, and I allow the wagon between **William** and **Robert R. Larkin**, and I allow a Bible to be bought for every one of my children, paid for from money in the house at this time, and the rest of it be kept to pay the taxes, and if there is any at your mother's death, I allow it to **Robert R. Larkin**.

NB **William** and **Robert R.**, you both must help (get) **Henry C. Larkin** a horse and saddle when he comes of age. Have no disputing about none of your affairs. I allow this to be my last Will and Testament. Signed and delivered in presence of Test.　　　　　　　　**Thomas Larkin** (seal)

We the underneath subscribers having examined the foregoing will of **Thomas Larkin**, dec'd do jointly and severally agree that the said last Will and Testament as aforesaid shall be good and valid in law and equity and do hereby ratify and confirm the same to be the last Will & Testament of **Thomas Larkin**, dec'd. Given under our hands and seals this 16th November, 1830. Test.

Henry Larkin
Robert McMinn

Widow Ann Larkin(seal)
John Larkin　(seal)
James C. Larkin　(seal)
Henry Larkin　(seal)
James Cooper and Peggy his wife (seal)
continued...

William Davis and Mary Davis,
the late Mary Larkin (seal)
David Larkin (seal)
William Larkin(seal)
Robert Larkin (seal)

WILL OF MARY LOONEY

Page 320

Dated: November 20, 1830

In the name of God, Amen.

I, **Mary Looney** of the County of Hawkins, State of Tennessee, being weak of body but of sound mind and memory and calling to mind the oncertainty of life and certainty of death do make and ordain and constitute this to be my last will and testament, revoking all former wills by me made.

First. Recommending my soul into the hands of Almighty God who gave it.

Secondly. My body be decently buried by my Executor in a Christian like manner.

Thirdly. That my just debts be paid by my Executors out of my Estate, and as to the goods of this world which it has been pleased God to bless me with, I wish to be disposed of in the following manner. First. My wish is that my black woman **Charlotte** be set free after my death by her complying with the law in such cases made and provided and that my Executor use all lawful means in his power to procure her emancipation and freedom.

I give and bequeath to my grand children, children of my son **Benjamin Looney**, dec'd one dollar equally among them. I give and bequeath to my son **John Looney** $5.00. To my son **Isam Looney** $10.00, including $5.00 which I am in due him. To my grand children, children of my son **Robert Looney**, dec'd one dollar equally among them. I give and bequeath to **Alzina Mullins** and **Metildy Looney** daughters of my son **Absalom Looney** all my household and kitchen furniture of every kind and all my stock of every kind, farming utensils, grain and everything else I may die possessed of by him paying the above bequeath sums and my funeral expenses. The bequeath sums to be paid in 18 months after my decease. Having full confidence in the integrity of my son **Absalom**, I nominate and appoint him my Executor to this my last Will and Testament. It is also my wish and desire that he not be bound in security for the execution of said executorship, believing that he will in all things act faithful. In testimony whereof I the s'd **Mary Looney** have hereunto set my hand and seal. This 20th of November, 1830.

Attest: Signed sealed and
acknowledged in presence of
James Johnson, J. S. Johnson

Mary Looney (seal)

WILL OF EDWARD LAWSON

Page 321

Dated: October 28, 1832
Recorded Nov. Ses. 1832

In the Name of God, Amen.

I **Edward Lawson** of Hawkins County, State of Tennessee and citizen thereof, being very weak and low in body yet of sound mind and memory, do constitute this instrument of writing to be my last Will and Testament, desiring it may be received by all and every person and particular_ my relatives and friends. First of all I give and recommend my soul to the Almighty God that gave it me, nothing doubting but that I shall receive it again by the mighty power of God, and as touching my worldly estate wherewith it has pleased God to bless me with, my will and desire is that my wife **Patsy** may have the whole and full power of transacting my estate and first to sell a sufficient part of my property to pay all my just debts on the most advisable terms, and the residue of my Estate after paying my just debts to remain in power of my wife **Patsy** for her own benefit and **Clement Lawson, Jr.** my only son and principal heir to this my will and testament, and at the decease of my wife **Patsy** the remainder whatever it be of my Estate to be the right and property of **Clement Lawson, Jr.** my only heir.

In testimony whereof I the s'd **Edward Lawson** hath hereunto set my hand and seal. This 28th day of October, in the year of our Lord, 1832.

Edward x Lawson (seal)
(his mark)

Witnesses:
E. S. Goodman
Joseph Roberts
Isaac Mendenall

WILL OF ROBERT LEE

Page 322
Dated: April 30, 1834
Proven: Aug. Session 1834

In the Name of God, Amen.

The 30th day of April in the year of our Lord, 1834, I, **Robert Lee** of the County of Hawkins and State of Tennessee, being weak of body, but of sound mind and memory and calling to mind the mortality of my body and that it is appointed for all men once to die, do make and ordain this my last Will and Testament in manner following (to wit:) My body I give and bequeath to the earth to be buried in a Christian like manner at the discretion of my hereinafter name Executors. My soul into care of Almighty God who created and gave it. And my earthly estate I give and dispose of in manner and form following:

First. I allow as much of my property, personal or real, to be sold as will be sufficient to pay and satisfy all my just debts, and also the sum of one dollar to each of my brothers and sisters (to wit:) **James Lee, Hopkins Lee, Kader Lee, Burrell Lee, Sarah Patrick** and **John Lee,** to each I give and bequeath the sum of one dollar.

Second. I give to my sister **Mary Lee** my negro girl **Linda** during her natural life, and it is my will that said negro girl with her increase (if any) shall at my s'd sister's death descend to my sister's son **Clinton** or his heirs and assigns forever. I give and bequeath to **Clinton Lee,** son of my sister **Mary Lee** all of my Estate that may remain, both personal and real, consisting of land, my negro woman **Milla,** her daughter **Mary,** son **March,** son **Peter** and **Noah** with their increase, to him and his heirs & assigns forever. Also all stock, farming utensils and household furniture that may remain after paying my just debts and before named legacies to my brothers and sisters. I give and bequeath also to the aforenamed **Clinton Lee,** son of my sister **Mary Lee,** to his use and behoof forever, and in case of his death without heirs (children of his own), and at the death of my sister **Mary Lee,** then, the laws of the land permitting, it is my will that each of the afore-named negroes with their increase at a proper age may be free. I do con-stitute and appoint my sister **Mary Lee** and **Andrew Galbraith** both of the Co. of Hawkins, Executors of this my last Will and Testament.

And lastly. I do hereby declare the foregoing in all its parts to be my last Will and Testament and do hereby utterly make void all others.

In testimony whereof I have hereunto set my hand and affixed my seal, published and declared it for the purposes herein expressed on the day and year first above written.

Robert Lee (seal)

Signed, sealed and published and declared by the said **Robert Lee** as his last will and Testament in presence of us:
James Lee, Gregory Lee, Benjamin Lavin, Penay x Lavin
(her mark)

WILL OF JONATHAN LONG

Page 323
Dated: April 20, 1839

In the Name of God, Amen.

I **Jonathan Long** of the County of Hawkins and State of Tenn., being old and weak in body but of sound mind & memory, Thanks be to God, calling to mind that it is appointed for all men once to die, do make this my last Will and Testament. First. I give & recommend my soul to God that gave it, my body to the earth from whence it came, to be buried at the dis-cretion of my executors. And as touching such worldly estate as it hath pleased God to bless me with in this life, I give, devise and dispose of it in the following manner and form, Viz:

First. I will that my plantation or land be equally divided between my three sons, **John, David** and **James.**

Secondly. I will to my three daughters, **Sarah, Nancy** and **Polly** $100.00 in money. My personal property to be sold and the residue if any equally divided between my sons **John, David** and **James.**

I likewise constitute and appoint **John Long** & **Rodham Chesnutt** my sole Executors of this my last Will & Testament. In witness whereof I have set my hand and seal. This twentieth day of April, 1839.

Jonathan Long (seal)

James M. Hord, D. Alexander, James L. Falkerson

WILL OF HENRY LARKIN

Page 323
Dated: September 9, 1842
Proven: Feb. 6th, 1843

I, **Henry Larkin** being desirous to dispose of my effects between my children do make and publish this my last Will and Testament, hereby revok-ing and making void all other wills by me at any time made. First. I desire that all my debts be paid by my Executors as soon as practicable. Secondly. I give and bequeath to my son **John Larkin** my negro boy **Edward** and my negro girl **Mary.** Thirdly. I give and bequeath to my daughter **Mary Larkin** my negro girl **Malinda** and my two negro children **Houston** and **Rachael.** Fourthly. I give to my son **Anderson Larkin** my negro boy **Alfred.** I likewise give him the tract of land whereon I reside containing 200 acres, together with all my other property not herein before named, consisting of household and kitchen furniture, farming tools, wagon, horses, cattle, hogs and sheep and my old negro woman **Charity** for which I require him, the said **Anderson,** the payment of the sum of $150.00, to be paid two years after my death to my three children or their heirs; that is to say, **Jane Long, Elizabeth Howell** and the heirs of **William Y. Larkin,** dec'd, in three equal shares of $50.00 to each. Lastly, I do here-by appoint my sons **John** and **Anderson Larkin** my Executors to this my will.

Given under my hand & seal this 9th day of Sept.1842.

Signed sealed & delivered in presence of the subscribing witnesses.

                                    Henry x Larkin (seal)
James Amis, Benjamin Looney, John Armstrong   (his mark)

The foregoing will in regard to the tract of land is altered so far as to give **Mary Larkin** the right of possession of the dwelling house with five acres of land thereunto attached during her life, then the same is to be the property of said **Anderson Larkin** as provided in the will. Said alteration made before signed on day and date of will.

                                    Henry x Larkin (seal)
James Amis, Benjamin Looney, John Armstrong.   (his mark)

WILL OF ISAAC LAUDEBACK

Page 324   Dated: July 6, 1846
                                Proven: July 5, 1847

In the Name of God, Amen.

Now being called to mind the uncertainty of life and the certainty of death, and being weak of body but of sound mind and good memory to dispose of such of my worldly substance as it has pleased Almighty God to bless me with &c, I **Isaac Laudeback** on the 6th day of June in the year of our Lord one thousand eight hundred and forty six, I make this my last Will and Testament in manner and form as follows, to wit, Viz:

First. My will is that as soon after my decease as is convenient and necessary, I wish my Executors or either of them to sell or dispose of enough of my perishable property at private or public sale and the money arising from sale or sales to be faithfully applied to the payment of my just debts and funeral expenses.

Secondly. I give to my wife **Hannah** all my land that I die seized and possessed of and all of my household and kitchen furniture during her life, and after her death the household furniture to be equally divided between my three daughters, Viz: **Elizabeth Laudeback, Mahaly Logan** and **Louisa Landers.**

Thirdly. I give and bequeath unto my daughter **Elizabeth** my gray mare and a large, white cow and a white and red heifer calf, to be disposed of by my said daughter in her own way and manner &c.

Fourthly. As soon after the decease of my beloved wife **Hannah,** I desire that all my land be equally divided between my four children: **David Laudeback, Elizabeth Laudeback, Mahaly Logan** and **Louisa Landers.**

Fifthly. I do hereby nominate and appoint my friends **David Laudeback** and **David Reynolds** my Executors of this my last Will and Testament. In witness whereof I do to this my will set my hand and seal. The day and date above written.

                                    Isaac Laudeback (seal)
Signed, sealed and published in our presence and we have subscribed our names hereto in the presence of the Testator. This 6th day of June, 1846.
Attest: **Wm. Smith, Daniel Stewart**

A Codicil to my last Will and Testament. I here make in manner and form hereinafter mentioned in addition to what I have given to my wife **Hannah,** I give and bequeath to her all my standing crop that is growing, or will be raised on my farm this present year, also my sorrel horse and a pided cow, etc. Should my Executors fail to have enough perishable property to satisfy all my just debts, Executors to sell enough of the perishable property I leave to my wife to satisfy my just debts and no more &c.

                                    Isaac Laudeback (seal)

Signed and sealed and published and acknowledged in our presence, and we have subscribed our names hereto in the presence of the Testator. This 13th day of June, 1846.
Attest: **Wm. Smith, Daniel Stewart**

WILL OF HENRY LAUDEBACK

Page 326   Dated: August 26, 1846
                                Proven: June Term, 1854

I **Henry Laudeback** of the County of Hawkins and State of Tennessee, do make and publish this my last Will and Testament and thereby dispose of my property both real and personal in the following manner.

First. I give and bequeath unto my wife **Mary** one negro woman named **Eliza** and her increase and one horse worth $50.00, one side saddle and bridle and all the household furniture, during her life or widowhood, and then to be equally divided among my three childrens' heirs, to wit: **John, Sally,** and **Elizabeth.**

Second. I give and bequeath unto my son **John** one negro boy named **Samuel.** To my daughter **Sally,** $300.00 which she has already received. To the heirs of my daughter **Elizabeth,** one negro boy named **James.**

Third. The remainder of my personal property to be sold and the proceeds equally divided between heirs of my three children, the three children above named, to wit: **John, Sally** and **Elizabeth.**

Fourth. I give and bequeath unto my son **John** one half of all the land I may own at my death and the other half to be equally divided between heirs of my two daughters, **Sally & Elizabeth.**

Fifth. To **Nathaniel Grigsby** and his wife **Elizabeth,** $5.00.

Sixth. Should there be any money on hand, or notes after defraying the expenses of my burial and after paying my just debts, it should be equally divided between my son **John,** my daughter **Sally** and heirs of my daughter **Elizabeth.**

I hereby appoint my son **John** and _____ my Executors to this my last Will and Testament, hereby revoking all other wills heretofore by me made. in witness whereof I have hereunto set my hand and affixed my seal, This 26th day of August, 1846.

                                    Henry x Laudeback (seal)
                                          (his mark)
Signed, sealed and acknowledged in presence of witnesses: **James M. Hord, Sally Hord, William G. Hord**

WILL OF ELIZABETH LEEPER

Page 327   Dated: July 14, 1851

I **Elizabeth Leeper** do hereby make and publish this my last Will & Testament hereby revoking and making void all others heretofore made by me.

First. My will and desire is that so soon after my death as practicable my body be decently buried and my Executor pay my funeral expenses out of the first money coming into his hands.

Secondly. My will and desire is that my Executor pay all my debts if I should owe any at the time of my death out of any money that may come into his hands.

Third. I will and bequeath to my grand son **Francis L. Phipps** $50.00 to be paid by my Executor...

Fourthly. I will and bequeath to my grand daughter **Abenaida Phipps** $50.00.

Fifthly. I will and bequeath to my son Guion Leeper the balance of my property consisting of household and kitchen furniture, farming utensils, stock of all kind, and debts due and owing me at the time of my death, whether the same may be due by note, account or otherwise. All money that I may die seized and possessed of, my three negroes Mary, James and Fred and all the property, money whether bank notes or silver cho--- in action, and in short my will and desire is ... to my said son Guion. In fact everything that I may own at the time of my death, excepting the above mentioned bequest to my grandson Francis L. Phipps and my grand daughter Abenaida Phipps. And I do hereby appoint Guion Leeper to be my Executor of this my last Will and Testament.

Given under my hand and seal this the 14th day of July, 1851.

Elizabeth x Leeper (seal)
(her mark)

Signed sealed and published in our presence and we have subscribed our names in the presence of the Testator. This 14th day of July, 1851.

Sam Powel, Wm. Armstrong

WILL OF WILLIAM LONG

Page 328
Dated: August 5, 1853

I do make and publish this my last Will and Testament hereby revoking...all other wills by me made.

1st. I direct that my personal property of every description be sold.

2nd. I give and bequeath unto Phillip and Joseph Long all my lands to be equally divided between them after all my debts are paid.

3rd. I give and bequeath to my sister Cassander Duggan and her heirs $200.00. My Executor is to lay out said $200.00 in land for the benefit of Cassander and her heirs four years after my decease.

4th. My will is that my two nephews Nicholas and William Gasper Long when they become of age have $50.00 each.

Lastly. I do hereby nominate and appoint Phillip Long my Executor.

In witness whereof I do to this my will set my hand and seal. This 5th day of August, 1853.

Signed, sealed and acknowledged in our presence: R. Chesnutt, Wm Phillips

Wm Long (seal)

WILL OF JOHN LADY

Page 329
Dated: August 3, 1854
Proven May & June Term, 1857

I John Lady being of sound mind and memory do publish this my last Will and Testament hereby revoking and making void all other wills by me at any time made.

First. I direct that my funeral expenses and all my debts be paid as soon after my death as possible out of any money that I may die possessed of, or may first come into the hands of my Executor.

Secondly. I give and bequeath to my beloved wife Sarah all my real and personal property, my books and papers of every kind with all the money that I may die possessed of and every thing in any way that belongs to me at the time of my death, to my wife Sarah during her natural life.

Thirdly. I give and bequeath to my wife Sarah's two grandsons,

Orseneaus W. Peters and Samuel Peters at the death of my beloved wife, my lands, to be equally divided between them.

Fourthly. I give and bequeath to my wife's grandson Calvin B. Peters one horse to be worth $100.00, one new plow, single tree and clevis and one hoe, to be furnished to him when he becomes 21 years of age - to be furnished by my wife Sarah should she live until the s'd Calvin B. Peters arrives at 21 years...should my wife die before Calvin becomes 21, then to be furnished by my Executor.

Fifthly. I give and bequeath to Kissiah Cartell on condition she lives with me or with my wife, if I should die, until she arrives at the age of 18 years, the sum of $15.00 to be paid to her by my Executor out of any money that should come into his hands out of my Estate.

Sixthly. I give and bequeath all my moveable property at the death of myself and my wife to the above named Orseneaus W., Samuel and Calvin B. Peters either to be sold and the money divided equally or divided equally without selling, at their discretion, after my fourth and fifth bequest is complied with.

Seventh. I will and desire that my friend Benjamin Thurman shall be the Executor of this my last Will and Testament, and I hereby nominate and appoint him. In testimony whereof I have set my hand and seal, This twenty third day of August, 1854. Signed sealed and acknowledged in the presence of the sub-scribing witnesses.

(The araur made before signed)
John Lady (seal)
Test. Wm Hutchisson, Jeremiah Seavers

WILL OF THOMAS MARTIN

Page 330
Dated: Jan. 12, 1803

In the Name of God, Amen.

I Thomas Martin of the County of Hawkins and State of Tenn., being very sick and weak in body, but of perfect mind and memory, Thanks be to God, calling into mind the mortality of my body and knowing that it is appointed for all men once to die, do make and ordain this my last Will and Testament, that is to say: Principally and first of all, I give and recommend my soul into the hands of Almighty God that gave it and my body to the earth to be buried at the discretion of my Executors in decent Christian burial, nothing doubting but at the general resurrection I shall receive the same again by the mighty power of God. And as touching such worldly Estate as it hath pleased God to bless me with in this life, I give, devise and dispose of in the following manner, Viz:

First. I give and bequeath unto my dearly beloved wife Anney one bed and its furniture and the use of my plantation until my son John Martin arrives at the age of 21, or as long as she remains my widow for the express purpose or reason... the family on. And when my son John arrives at 21, my will is that the land be sold and the value equally divided amongst all my sons. Also, I give unto my dearly beloved son Daniel Martin my sorrel horse. Also, I give unto my dearly beloved daughter Phebe all her apparel known by the name of hers. Also, I give unto my dearly beloved daughter Johana all her apparel known by the name of hers. Also, I give unto my dearly beloved daughter Mary all of her apparel known by the name of hers. Also, my will is that my bay horse and all my cattle, all my household furniture be left with my wife for the express purpose of my family. My farming utensils and sheep, also my shop tools and shop afacs (effects?)

to be disposed of as my Executors think fit...to pay my just debts.

Also, it is my express will that my Executors ___convey all that part of the land to **Joseph McCollough** that he bought from me, agreeable to the bargain laid down between s'd **Joseph McCollough** and myself whenever they obtain the title from **Phelps Read**, or any other person for him.

And I do likewise constitute, make and ordain my dearly beloved wife **Annie** my Executrix and **Joseph McCollough** and **William Berry** Executors, and do hereby utterly disallow, revoke and disannul all and every other former Testaments, wills, legacies, bequests and Executors by me in any wise before named, willed and bequeathed: ratifying and confirming this and no other to be my last will and testament.

In witness whereof I have hereunto set my hand and seal. This twelfth day of Jan., 1803.

                                            Thomas Martin (seal)

Signed, sealed published, pronounced and declared by the said **Thomas Martin** as his last Will and Testament in the presence of us who in his presence and in the presence of each other have subscribed our names.

John x Walker, Daniel x Martin, Phebe x Martin
  (his mark)   (his mark)   (her mark)

WILL OF EDY LEONARD

Page 331   Dated: June 16, 1856
                                          Proven: Aug Term, 1856
State of Tennessee)
Hawkins County   ) In the Name of God, Amen.

        I, **Edy Leonard** of the County aforesaid, being weak and frail in body but of a sound and disposing mind and memory, do make and constitute this to be my last Will and Testament, that is to say (Viz). At my death, it is my desire to be decently buried and that my Executor pay the expense of the same. Secondly. My will is that **John** and **David Leonard**, my two brothers, and **Elizabeth Kyles**, my sister, each of them be paid within twelve months after my death one dollar. And also my brother **William Leonard's** children have one dollar between them. Thirdly. It is my will and desire that all of the balance of my Estate both real and personal be equally divided between my brother **Jacob Leonard** and my sister **Agnes Leonard**. In witness whereof I have hereunto set my hand and seal. This 16th day of June, 1856.

                                            Edy x Leonard (seal)
                                                    (her mark)

Witness: **John Reynolds, Rachael x Leonard**
                        (her mark)

WILL OF ABSALOM D. LOONEY

Page 332   Dated: April 9, 1862
                                          Proven: Jan'y Term, 1863

I, **A. D. Looney** of Hawkins County, State of Tennessee, do hereby make and constitute the following to be my last Will & Testament, that is to say: At my death, I wish to be buried in a plain, decent manner. I want the expense of same to be paid out of any money or valuable property I may have on hand. I further want all my just debts paid by my Executor and Executrix. I further desire that my beloved wife **Sally** have full control and possession of my house and 100 acres of land joining the same, and timber to keep the

same in good repair during her natural life, together with all my out buildings. She shall own and possess my negro boys **Jack, Calvin** and **Gran**, sometimes called **Kziah** during her natural life, and at her death to be sold on a credit of 12 months to the highest bidder, good security to be required, and the proceeds to be divided between my five daughters: **Louisa Hutchisson, Mary Ann Campbell, Margaret C. Looney, Sally Jane Looney & Susan Looney.** my son **Orville B. Looney** who is now in the army shall have and enjoy all the land I now own except what I have allotted to my wife, and at her death he is to have the portion that I have allotted to her. Also, provided always that a home for my single daughters should any there be at my wife's death have a home at my old homestead. And in course of Providence, my son **O. B. Looney** should not return from the army, then I desire that the land I have gave my son **O. B.** shall be equally divided between my three daughters, **Margaret C., Sally Jane** and **Susan Looney.** I desire that my wife shall have and own all my stock, and request her to dispose of a sufficient amount to set my three single daughters upon an equal footing with those that have married. I have about $3,000.00 in notes that I desire my two daughters **Margaret C.** and **Sally Jane Looney** to have and design to assigning the same to them – they are to share and share alike. I desire that my daughter **Susan** have two negroes, one girl called **Rosanah** aged about 12 years, one boy called **Nathan** about 10 years. The two slaves is given to my daughter **Susan** to be used by her and to enjoy the same, but them and their increase are to descend to her lawful heirs according to the laws of the State of Tennessee. I desire that my wife shall have full control of all household furniture, grain, bacon, farming utensils--in short, all on the plantation at my death, having full confidence in her. I desire that my sons, **William C., James G, Rufus G., John B., Absalom L.** and **Israel Looney** be paid as a present by my Executor, $10.00 each, I having heretofore provided for them.

        I do hereby nominate and appoint my wife **Sally Looney** and my son **O. B. Looney** Executrix and Executor of this my last will and testament. Witness my hand and seal this 9th day of April, 1862.

                                            Absalom D. Looney (seal)

Signed, sealed and delivered in presence of us:
Jacob Miller, John R. Charles

WILL OF HENRY LARKIN

Page 333   Dated: January 13, 1864

I **Henry Larkin** being weak in body but of sound mind and memory, do make and ordain this my last Will and Testament, hereby revoking all former wills by me made (to wit):

        First. I give and Bequeath unto my wife **Mary H. Larkin** one third part of my land during her natural life, including the dwelling and out houses, provided she lives on the same and also the bedding and other things she brought with her after we were married.

        Secondly. I give and bequeath unto my four daughters **Sally Ann Darter, Elizabeth E. Larkin, Mary J. Ford** and **Nancy P. Larkin** each an equal part of my estate after my just debts and funeral expenses are first paid, but my will and desire is that my daughter **Mary J. Ford** shall have the use of her part of my estate during her natural life, then I wish it to descend to the heirs of her body. My wish and desire is that my daughters that are unmarried remain with my wife and have the use of the house as long as they remain single.

Thirdly. I give and bequeath unto my son David B. Larkin such part of my estate as will be sufficient with the two negroes his grandfather left him to make him equal to the other heirs.

Fourthly. I give and bequeath unto my grandson Henry T. Ford my anvil and vice. My will and desire is that my negroes all be hired out with the exception of Eliza and her child until a sufficient amount is raised besides what the personal property will bring to pay my debts. I hereby nominate & appoint P. G. Hale, Sr. my sole Executor. Given under my hand and seal this 13th of January, 1864.

Henry x Larkin (seal)
(his mark)

Test. Andrew Tarter, William B. Porter

WILL OF JOSEPH MORRISETT

Page 334

Dated: Sept. 27, 1790

In the Name of God, Amen.

The 27th of September, 1790, I, Joseph Morrisett, of the State of North Carolina, in the County of Camden, being sick and very weak in body but of perfect mind and memory, thanks be given to God for the same, do make and ordain this my last Will and Testament, that is to say:

First of all, I recommend my soul unto the hands of God that gave it and my body to the earth to be buried at the hands of my Executors, and as touch-ing my worldly estate which it hath pleased God to bless me with in this life, I give and dispose of the same in the manner and form following:

Item. I give and bequeath unto my beloved son Jonathan Morrissett one cow and calf, one hand mill and the shop tools with sundry other things in possession for his full part of my estate and no more.

Item. I give and bequeath unto my beloved daughter Rhoda Gregory one side saddle now in (her) possession.

Item. I give and bequeath unto my beloved daughter Mary Gregory one feather bed and furniture, one chest with sundry other things in possession for her full part and no more.

Item. I give and bequeath unto my well beloved son Enoch Morrisett one bay horse named Stretchor, my wagon and cart and the use of my whole team to move the now intended voige and all my axes, hoes, nails and one plow.

Item. The remainder of my estate, goods or chattels, rights and credits to be equally divided between my two sons, Enoch & John. I recommend the use of as much of my estate for my well beloved wife Abiah as shall be a reasonable maintenance during her widowhood or natural life. I also appoint my well beloved sons John and Enoch my hole and sole Executors, denying, revoking, disannulling and disallowing all and every other will & testament, confirming this and no other to be my last Will & Testament. In witness whereof I ... have set my hand and seal this day & year above written. Sign-ed, sealed and declared by the said Morrisett to be his last...in the presence of us the subscribers.

Joseph Morrisset (seal)

John Ford, William Hughes, Thomas Burges

This is to certify that John & Enoch-Morrisset have this 4th day of Jan., 1791 div'd our father Joseph Morrisset, dec'd estate, have set apart for our mother, the wife of our late father one negro woman named Hannah with all other property set apart to her by Thomas Amis, Elijah Chisum & Benjamin Murrell, by us chosen to divide the said estate to be for her support during her life or widowhood.

John Morrisset, Enoch Morrisset

Test. James Maybury

WILL OF THOMAS MIDKIFF

Page 335

Dated: May 26, 1794

Territory South of the River Ohio, Hawkins County.

This last Will and Testament of Thomas Midkiff is as follows, to wit:

I give each of my children begotten by my wife Ruth on shilling sterling, and all the rest of my Estate I give to my wife Ruth during her life, and after her decease to be equally divided among my children whose names are here sot to it: Rachael, Jinny, John, Isaac, Jeremiah, Sarah. Given under my hand and seal This twenty six day of May and in the year of our Lord, one thousand, seven hundred and ninety four. As witness my hand.

Thomas "M" Midkiff (seal)
(his "M")

In presence of Isiah Midkiff, John Greene

WILL OF MICHAEL MORRISON

Page 335

Dated: July 6, 1795

In the Name of God, Amen.

I Michael Morrison of Hawkins County in the Territory South of Ohio River, being of sound and perfect mind and memory, blessed be God, do this 6th day of July, 1795, make and publish this my last Will and Testament in manner following:

First: Wheras I have mentioned a certain tract of land, which tract of land I hereby fully empower my Executors or either of them as here-after mentioned to make him the said John Morrison a lawful deed to s'd land agreeable to said article as lodg in the hands of Jacob Miller of Hawkins Co. To Robert Young's two youngest daughters Elizabeth and Mary, each five pounds and to his oldest daughter Ann I hereby give and bequeath ten pounds and to James King's two daughters five pounds each. To Thomas Henderson's two daughters five pounds each. To my brother Thomas Morrison's oldest daughter Ann, I bequeath to her twenty five pounds, and to Nancy King, wife of Thomas King five pounds. The above amounts to the different persons above mentioned to be discharged by my Executors in good trade out of my Estate, either money or good trade. The balance of my Estate real and personal I hereby bequeath unto my brother Thomas Morrison to him and his heirs' use forever, and I do by these presents constitute, make and ordain my trusty friends Thomas Morrison & Thomas Henderson Executors of this my last Will and Testament. In witness whereof I Michael Morrison have to this my last Will & Testament set my hand and seal the day and year above written.

Micheal Morrison (seal)

Signed, sealed, published and declared by the said Micheal Morrison the testator as his last will & Testament in presence of us who were present at the time of signing and sealing...

Elijah McAnally, Thos x Brandon, Thos King
(his mark)

WILL OF WILLIAM MORRISS/MANESS

Page 336

Dated: Aug. 22, 1808

In the Name of God, Amen.

I William Maness/Morriss of the County of Hawkins, State of Tennessee, being sick and weak in body but of sound mind and memory, thanks be to God for the same calling to mind the mortality of this life and knowing that it is appointed for all men once to die do make and ordain this my last Will and Testament, and the property of which I am possessed, I give and dispose of in the following manner, to wit:

Item. I give and bequeath to my beloved wife Sarah the use of all my land and property during her life.

Item. I give and bequeath to my daughter Mary Blackburne one shilling to be laid out of my present estate.

Item. I give and bequeath to my following children each one shilling to be laid out of my personal estate: Rebecca McCarmack, Edward Maness/Morris, Henderson Maness/Morris, John Maness/Morriss.

Item. I give and bequeath to my daughters Sarah Fisher and Elizabeth Maness/Morris after the death of my wife Sarah all my personal estate to be equally divided between them share and share alike, to them and their heirs forever in fee simple.

I do hereby appoint my son-in-law William Fisher to be the Executor of this my last Will & Testament. In witness whereof I have hereunto set my hand & affixed my seal the 22nd day of August, in the year of our Lord, 1808.

William Maness/Morris(seal)

Signed sealed published pronounced & declared as his last will & testament by the said William Maness/Morris the day and date above written, in the presence of

Hezekiah Hamblen McC--(illigible)

WILL OF PETER MILLER

Page 337   Dated: Jan. 31, 1809

In the name of God, Amen.

I Peter Miller of the State of Tennessee, County of Hawkins, being for some time past in a declining state of health, though of sound mind and memory, do make and ordain this to be my last Will and Testament in writing, in manner and form as follows (that is): After recommending my soul to God and my body to the dust from whence it came, to be buried in a plain, decent and Christian like manner (after my decease), and concerning such worldly goods as it has been pleasing to Almighty to bestow on me, I dispose of them as follows: First. I desire my funeral charges to be paid out of my goods and chattels at the discretion of my Executors whom I shall hereafter name, and my debts which are very few to be paid as above.

Item. I give to my beloved wife Polly all the property that she was seized of at our marriage and likewise all the clothing of any kind that she has made since, and likewise two hundred dollars in cash--one hundred to be paid to her at the expiration of six months after my decease. The other hundred to be paid to her at the expiration of twelve months after my decease.

Item. I do lend to my beloved wife the dwelling house and garden for the term of one year after my decease, together with out houses and other buildings.

Item. I give to my daughter Sally Lockmiller two hundred dollars--fifty dollars at the expiration of twelve months after my decease and fifty dollars yearly until the above sum be paid to her.

Item. I give to my son John my daughter Polly Buram, my daughter Darky Charles, my daughter Nancy Ingram, and my daughter Ebby Kepler (Klepper?) the sum of one dollar each.

Item. I give to my grandsons Pitzer Buram and Miller Ingram the sum of thirty dollars each, provided they live to the age of 21 years, and if they die before that time--either of them--this item to be void as to the one so deceased, but not as to the surviving one.

Item. I give to my beloved son Jacob Miller the tract of land I now live on, and likewise my island in Holston River, and all the remainder of my goods and chattels if any there be after the foregoing items is satisfied.

Item. I do appoint and request my beloved son Jacob Miller and my trusty friend (and brother in law) John Howel to be my Executors of this my last Will and Testament in writing, and do by these presents revoke, disannul and make void every other will or wills by me made.

In testimony whereof I have hereunto set my hand and affixed my seal This thirty first day of January, 1809.

Peter Miller (seal)

Signed sealed published and declared by Peter Miller Testator to be his last Will and Testament in writing, in presence of us who was subscribing witnesses thereto: J. Bagood (Jurat), John Francisco (Jurat), George Johnston (Jurat) Charles Hooks, James Francisco

COPY OF MARY MATHEWS' WILL

Page 338   Dated: July 6, 1809

In the Name of God, Amen.

I Mary Mathews of Grantsfield in the County of King George, State of Virginia, being in perfect sence and memory, but calling to mind the uncertainty of this life and that it is ordained that all the human family shall once die, do hereby make my last will and Testament, that is to say. In the first place, I will and desire that I may be decently buried in the family grave yard by the side of dear & ever beloved Father and Mother.

Secondly. I desire that my Executors herein named shall pay and satisfy as soon as possible all my just debts after the payment of my debts such real and personal estate as the Great Giver of all things has pleased in His goodness to entrust me with. I give, devise and dispose of as follows: First, I give and devise the tract of land called Grantsfield adjoining Boydshole in said county whereon I now reside unto John Mathews, son of Thomas Mathews of Charles County in the State of Maryland and his heirs forever, if the said Thos should have a son by the name of John, and if said Thos should not have a son by the name of John then and in that event, I give the s'd tract of land to Thomas Mathews also a son of the aforesaid Thomas Mathews and his heirs forever. Secondly, I give the tract of land containing by estimation 200 acres be the same more or less, lying and being in the said Charles Co., Maryland, being the tract of land that was granted to a certain Thomas Mathews by a patent bearing date, the eighth day of July, Seventeen hundred and forty three, and that descended to me by the death of my dear father John Mathews unto Thomas Mathews, son of said Thomas Mathews of Charles County and his heirs forever. Thirdly, I give the tract of land lying likewise in s'd County of Charles, granted to a certain Charles Meeks, my grandfather, by a patent bearing date the third of September, Seventeen hundred and thirty three and by said Charles devised unto me--unto Mary Mathews Posey of the said Charles County and her heirs and assigns forever. Fourthly. And whereas by the eternal and immutable laws of nature, man was born free and indepdent, evidenced by the unconquerable desire for liberty implanted in the human breast and as I have always considered the state of slavery in which the blacks are held by the laws of Virginia and Maryland as incompatible with justice and humanity, I will and desire that all my slaves--both in Virginia and Maryland--in whose hands soever they may be, be emancipated by my Executors so soon after my death as possible and that they be retained in slavery under no pretence whatever, but may be permitted to enjoy their liberty in as high a degree as if they had by the laws of the land been born free, and I further will and devise that my Executors shall laid out such of my infant slaves that may be incapable of maintaining and supporting themselves until they become to 21 years and the females until they come to 18 years if their mothers should be unable and unwilling to maintain and support them and that my Executors out of my Estate shall support and maintain such of my slaves as at the time of my death, from age or infirmity are incapable of maintaining and supporting themselves, and if those slaves which I own in Virginia and Maryland by the laws of s'd states cannot remain in said states respectively and enjoy their freedom, then it is my will and desire and I do hereby direct that such of my slaves as cannot remain in said states respectively & enjoy their liberty be removed to any other of the United States by my Executors which they may think best, at the expense of my Estate.

Fifthly. I give & bequeath unto my negro man named Bendley, my negro woman named Sarah and my negro maid named Clarissa the sum of fifty dollars each, and that my Executors pay the said sums of money to them respectively.

Sixthly. I give and bequeath unto Mrs. Fanny Armstead of Laudon County, Va. my gold watch and clasp and suit of nett curtains. Seventhly, I will and desire that my Executors shall sell and dispose of all my crops on hand, my tobacco and bank stock which may be on hand at the time of my death, and pay over the money arising therefrom, together with all my money on hand or due to me by bond or otherwise unto my first and second cousins and unto my friends Mrs. Hellen G. Foote & Mrs. Ann Seawick, their Executors, administrators or assigns, after paying therefrom my just debts, the legacies herein bequeathed & the expenses of executing this my will relative to my slaves. Eightly. It is my will & desire that my Executors shall have the family grave yard at Grantsfield inclosed with a good and substantial brick wall, if I should not do it during my life. Ninthly, I give and bequeath unto my Executors all my books and any article of household furniture they may choose, and it is my will that my Executors may be amply reimbursed for the trouble and expense in executing and carrying into effect this my will. And lastly, I constitute my friends Richard Stuart and Townshend L. Dade Executors of this my last will and testament.

In testimony whereof I have hereunto set my hand and seal this sixth day of July, 1809.

Mary Mathews (seal)

Signed sealed and published as the last will of the above named Mary Mathews

Laughorne Dade, Mary Ann Dade, Jane R. Yates

At a Monthly Court held for King George County, the 1st day of Dec., 1814, this last will & Testament of Mary Mathews, dec'd was proven by the oath of Laughorne Dade one of the subscribing witnesses thereto. In relation to the Codicil to the said will, no evidence was offered and on motion of Townshend L. Dade one of the executors named in said will who entered into bond according to law, certificate was granted him for obtaining probat. hereof in due form

of law, and at another Court held for said County the 6th day of July, 1815, the said will was further proved by the oath of Mary Ann Dade, another subscribing witness, and ordered to be recorded.

Test - Law. Betty, Clerk

State of Virginia, King George County, to wit:

I Lawrence Betty, Clerk of the Court of the County aforesaid do hereby certify that the foregoing is a true copy from the records of my office. In testimony whereof I have set my hand and affixed the Public Seal of my Office this 25th day of August, 1815, in the 40th year of our Common-wealth.

Law. Betty

I John Taliaferro presiding magistrate of King George County in the State of Virginia, do hereby certify that the above attestation is due the form of law. Given under my hand and seal This 26th day of August, 1815.

John Taliaferro (LS)

WILL OF JOSEPH MORRISET/MORRISSETT

Page 341   Dated: Nov. 26, 1812

In the Name of God, Amen.

I Joseph Morrisset of the County of Hawkins within the State of Tennessee, being of sound mind and memory do make this my last will and testament in the manner following: I give and bequeath to Margaret Kenner, daughter of Winder Kenner the sum of one hundred dollars. I give to my two brothers Richard Morrissett and Alexander Nelson Morrissett all the personal estate that I may die possessed of after the aforesaid sum of one hundred dollars, the sum to be equally divided between them.

I give and devise to my said brother Richard all my share, right, title & interest in and to the plantation whereon my mother Mary Morrissett now lives. I give and devise to my brother Alexander the tract of land that I purchased of Needham Lee adjoining the tract whereon my mother now lives. And I do appoint Samuel Powel Executor of this my last Will & Testament. In witness whereof I have hereunto set my hand & seal This 26th day of Nov., 1812.

Joseph Morrisset (seal)

Signed sealed acknowledged and published in the presence of us:

J. Amis, Rogers Michael, C. A. Hall.

WILL OF ABSALOM MORLAN

Page 342   Dated: Dec. 3, 1814

In the Name of God, Amen. The 3 day of December.

The last Will and testament of Absalom Morlan who is in perfect health and memory. First. I recommend my soul to God who gave it and my body to be decently buried, not doubting but at the Resurrection I shall receive the same by the Almighty power of God that gave it, and as to my worldly estate I order it to be in the following manner: First. Its my will that all my just debts and funeral charges to be paid. Then I order the rest of my property to be left on the land for the support of my wife Asanath, and the rents of my lands to support her as long as she remains my widow, and then I order my property remaining to be taken care of and divided amongst her daughter Abgail's children. I order my wife Asanath to have the house to live in and the renting of the land to who she pleases, only the land that James Boatman cleared, let James Boatman have that, and let him have liberty of clearing on any part of my land that he sees proper and have it to himself, and at my wife's decease I order my land to her daughter **Abigail** as long as she lives. And then one dollar apiece to be paid to all my brothers and sisters and the land to be divided amongst my wife's daughter **Abigail's** children if she has any living children, and if not, I do make and ordain my wife and **James Boatman** to be my whole and sole Executors of this my last Will and Testament. I hereby disannul every other will, former testament, wills, bequests, ratifying confirming this and no other to be my last Will and Testament. In witness I have hereunto set my hand and seal, December the 3rd, 1814.

Absalom Morlan (seal)

Test. **Nathan White, William White**

WILL OF JESSE McWILLIAMS

Page 342   Dated: Aug. 1818

In the Name of God, Amen.

State of Tennessee)   I, **Jesse McWilliams** of the State and County
Hawkins County   )   aforesaid, being in a low state of health,
                              but of sound mind and perfect memory and
calling to mind that it is appointed once for all men to die do make, constitute and ordain the following to be my last Will and Testament, revoking hereby all other heretofore by me made. And first of all I give and recommend my soul into the hands of God who gave it and my body to a decent Christian burial in certain expectation of the resurrection of the same and as to the goods and chattels with which it hath pleased God to bless me, moved by sundry good reasons it is my will to dispose of same after the following ways and manners, to wit:

Item 1st. I give to my beloved wife **Martha** all and singular my live stock of cattle, one bay horse colt which will be two years old in September next also all the household and kitchen furniture that **Martha** was possessed of at the time of our marriage. Likewise one trunk and one bed and furniture from among those beds that I was possessed of before our marriage.

Item 2nd. It is my will and desire that my land, horses, hogs, farming utensils, household and kitchen furniture (the above excepted) be sold at public sale to the highest bidder, and after paying my just debts out of same, the remainder of the profits to be disposed of as follows: Three hundred and seventy dollars I leave and bequeath to my youngest daughter **Eleanor**, together with the above-excepted bed and furniture. Moreover, it is my will that **Eleanor** at my decease shall live with my son **John** and the above money applied in the best manner that can be devised, that the said _____ may be maintained from the profits arising therefrom, and should **Eleanor** out live **John**, it is my will she live with my daughter **Margaret Shaver** and the above three hundred still to be applied to her use as before, and at the death of **Eleanor**, the said three hundred and seventy dollars shall be equally divided among her surviving brothers and sisters and their heirs.

Item 3rd. The remainder of the profits of the above mentioned sale shall be disposed of as follows: Three hundred dollars to my well-beloved wife to her own use, the remainder divided among my five children, to wit: **Robert, John, Nelson, Nancy** and **Margaret.**

Item 4th. My wife **Martha** shall have my present crop of wheat, and that part of the crop now growing shall be applied to winter the stock, the ensuing winter.

Item 5th. It is my will for the love and confidence I have in and for **John McAnnally, John Smith** (of Smith's Bent) and **John McWilliams** (son of **Hugh**),

I appoint the same my true and lawful Executors to this my last Will and Testament. In witness whereof I have set my hand and seal This first day of August in the year of our Lord one thousand eight hundred and eighteen, and of the American Independence, the Forty-third.

Jesse McWilliams (seal)

Signed, sealed and delivered in presence of:
Jeremiah McAnally, David McAnally, Mary x Medkeff
(her mark)

WILL OF THOMAS MOONEY

Page 344   Dated: October 12, 1815

In the Name of God, Amen.

The 12th day of October, 1815. I, **Thomas Mooney**, of the County of Hawkins, State of Tennessee, being sick and weak of body but of sound mind and memory, and calling to mind that it is appointed for all men once to die do make and ordain this to be my last Will and Testament in manner and form following, to wit:

First and principally of all, I give my soul unto care of Almighty God who created and gave it.

Second. My body to the earth to be buried in a decent and Christian-like manner at the discretion of my Executors, and

Third and lastly. My earthly Estate wherewith I may be seized or possessed of I give and bequeath as follows: To my beloved wife **Rebecca** all my household and kitchen furniture and farming utensils, together with as much of my stock as may be deemed sufficient for present family use which is to be judged of and set apart for that purpose by my Executors.

Item. It is my will that the remainder of my personal Estate be sold and the money arising therefrom to go in discharge of my debts.

Item. I will that my wife have the whole benefit of my plantation on which I now live, during her natural life, and the whole benefits of my plantation I purchased of **Hugh Chesnutt**, for the term of 10 years, to enable her to raise and educate her children. Then at the expiration of 10 years, the last named plantation to be equally divided among each of my children.

Item. It is also my will that at the time of the decease of my wife **Rebecca**, the other plantation on which I now live and all the stock that may then be, and household furniture be divided amongst my children, share and share alike.

Item. I will that all outstanding debts that may be indue me at the time of my decease be appropriated to assist in payment of my debts.

Item. I hereby constitute and appoint my beloved wife **Rebecca** Executrix and my brothers **George** and **Edmond Mooney** Executors of this my last Will and Testament.

Item. The foregoing I declare to be my last Will & Testament in all its parts, publishing and declaring it as such, disannulling and revoking all others. In testimony whereof I have hereunto set my hand and affixed my seal this day and year first before written.

Thomas x Mooney (seal)

Signed, sealed published & declared in   (his mark)
presence of: **Andrew Galbraith, Edward Williams, James Williams.**

WILL OF MARTHA McWILLIAMS

Dated: January 25, 1819
Proven: Aug. Term. 1819

In the Name of God, Amen. State of Tennessee, Hawkins County.

I Martha McWilliams being in a low state of health but of sound mind and perfect memory, and calling to mind that it is appointed once for all men to die, do make constitute and ordain the following to be my last Will and Testament. And first and principally, I bequeath and recommend my soul into the hands of my gracious God who gave it me and my body to a decent Christian burial in a full and certain hope of the Resurrection of the same.

Item 2nd. For sundry good causes moving me thereunto, it is declared to be my last will; and I appoint my well beloved brother John McAnally my sole heir in law to all and singular my live stock, household and kitchen furniture with all goods and chattels I may die possessed of. After my brother John shall have paid the expenses of my funeral out of the same the remainder shall be to and for his own use except one bed and furniture and one trunk which for special reasons I leave to my beloved niece Elizabeth McAnally (daughter of above said brother).

Item 3rd. Whereas by the will of my late husband Jesse McWilliams, I have a sum of money willed to me which may be seen by a reference to said will, I now hereby declare it my last will that as soon as the aforesaid money is collected that my brother John shall pay or cause to be paid out of the same all my just debts, likewise shall pay or give to my beloved sister Sally Burns the sum of twenty dollars, and the remainder of said money left me by my late husband's will—with all other monies or property that I may leave at my decease not otherwise disposed of, I leave and bequeath to my aforesaid brother John to his own use and behoof and for no other purpose whatsoever.

In testimony whereof I have hereunto set my hand and affixed my seal This Twenty fifth day of January in the year of our Lord, one thousand eight hundred and nineteen.

Martha McWilliams (seal.)

Witnesses present:
Test: Richard Moore, Thomas x Stubblefield, Jeremiah McAnally
(his mark)

WILL OF WILLIAM MARTIN

Dated: August 4, 1820

In the Name of God, Amen.

This the last Will and Testament of William Martin of the County of Hawkins and State of Tennessee is as follows, viz:

He, the said William Martin finding himself weak of body but in perfect mind and memory, Blessed be God therefore, and calling to mind the frailty of this life and the certainty of death, I do ordain and make this my last Will and Testament in form and manner as followeth:

Imprimis. I do recommend my soul unto the hand of God that gave it and my body to the Earth to be interred therein with decent and Christian burial at the discretion of my Executors hereafter to be made. And as for what worldly goods it hath pleased God to bless me with, all I do will and bequeath in manner and form as followeth, viz:

Item. I give and bequeath to my beloved wife Levey/Levey Martin all the rest of the whole of my worldly Estate during her natural life.

After her death, then my will is that my land shall be divided between my son in law Ephraim Winstead and my son in law Alexander Trent.

Item. After the decease of my beloved wife, I do give and bequeath to my son in law Ephraim Winstead the upper part of my land and the plantation where I do now live dividing my land and running from the line toward Clinch Mountain along the line between the two springs to the line towards Copper Ridge to him and his heirs forever.

Item. After the decease of my beloved wife I do give and bequeath to my son in law Ephraim Winstead whatever remains of my worldly Estate to him and his heirs forever.

Item. After the decease of my beloved wife, I do give and bequeath to my son in law Alexander Trent the lower part of my land and plantation from the said dividing line where Ephraim Winstead now lives to him and his heirs forever.

Item. At my decease I do give and bequeath to my son in law Alexander Trent one horse creature to him and his heirs forever. Also it is my desire that my son in law Ephraim Winstead and my beloved wife shall act for me after my decease in all my worldly concerns. Witness my hand and seal this August 4, 1820.

William x Martin (seal)
(his mark)

Test: Francis Winstead, Thomas x Martin, James Martin.
(his mark)

WILL OF GEORGE MAXWELL

Dated: November 14, 1821

In the Name of the Father, Son and Holy Ghost, Three persons but one God.

I, George Maxwell of the County of Hawkins and State of Tennessee, calling to mind the certainty of death and the uncertainty of the time when do make and ordain this my last Will and Testament in the words following, to wit: After commending my soul to God and my body to the dust to be buried in a decent and Christian manner hoping they will again be united at the Resurrection and enjoy a glorious immortality. I dispose of my worldly goods as follows: I allow my stock of all kinds to be sold—farming utensils and household furniture also. And all my debts paid out of the money arising from the sale – In the first place. The residue to be applied as hereafter directed. Next, I allow two tracts of land lying on Rice's or Howard's Creek to be sold containing two hundred acres each. I borrowed from my son Jesse in his lifetime $600.00. At his death he allowed it to be equally divided between his two sisters Matilda and Anne. I allow $600.00 of the price of that land to be paid to my two daughters Matilda & Anne agreeable to his direction. The residue of the price of that land, be it much or little, I allow to be equally divided between William Solomon, Matilda & Anne. My negro family I divide as follows: I give and bequeath to my son William and his children Ned and Nancy and her increase that she [Matilda] has had possession of for some time. Also, Anthony and Sampson I give, bequeath to my daughter Anne and her children. Winney and her children, and her increase. Also, Bob and Punch, Rose and her two youngest children & her increase. Rene and Casey either to be sold and their value to be equally divided among my four children—one of the Legatees may take them and pay three fourths of their value to the other three Legatees. The place I live on I allow to be sold and the price to be equally divided between my four children William,

Soloman, Matilda & Ann, except two hundred dollars of the first of it to be paid to William as the negroes left him was not so valuable as the others. After my debts is paid out of the net proceeds of stock and household furniture, I allow $50.00 to each of my grand children that was named for me. I leave $20.00 to the East Tennessee Bible Society. I leave my Bible and books to Anne. Should there still be a residue remaining from my stock, I leave $100.00 to Matilda, more than the rest as she has kept me in clothing some time, and probably will have more trouble yet. And should there be no residue left from the stock, I allow that $100.00 to be paid out of the price of the land. I leave a land warrant in the hands of John Snap, if recovered to be equally divided. I paid my money forty years ago for it and he never paid a cent for it—I never sold it to him.

I nominate & appoint my son Soloman and my son in law William Lyons to execute this my last Will & Testament. Witness my hand This 14th of Nov. 1821.

George Maxwell

Witness present: Abraham Rafter, John Loughmiller

WILL OF JACOB MANAS
Page 348   Dated: Aug. 14, 1824

In the Name of God, Amen.

I Jacob Manas of Hawkins County in the State of Tennesseee, being very weak in body but of perfect mind and memory, do make this my last Will and Testament in the manner following (to wit):

First. I give and devise unto my dear wife Margaret Manas one cow with all my household and kitchen furniture to her and her heirs forever, and likewise, a reasonable support out of my lands and tenements, goods and chattels to be named hereafter.

Item 2nd. I give unto my deceased daughter Elizabeth Manas' heirs one dollar to them and their heirs forever.

Item 3rd. I give unto my son Daniel Manas, one dollar to him and his heirs forever.

Item 4th. I give unto my son Ephraim Manas one dollar to him and his heirs forever.

Item 5th. I give unto my son Elijah Manas one dollar to him and his heirs forever.

Item 6th. I give unto my daughter Sarah Paine one dollar to her and her heirs forever.

Item 7th. I give unto my daughter Nancy Varnum one dollar, to her and her heirs forever.

Item Eighth. I give unto my daughter Annas Jones one dollar, to her and her heirs forever.

Item Ninth. I give unto my son Elisha Manas the 34 acre tract of land whereon I now live and likewise an 8 acre tract entry and two 1/2 acre entries including all my right, title and claims to all my land or lands whatsoever, and likewise give unto my son Elisha my horses, cattle, hogs, sheep, farming utensils, goods, chattels and effects that has not yet been mentioned, to him and his heirs forever, provided nevertheless that my son Elisha is to give my beloved wife a reasonable support during her life, and that he does likewise give to my grand daughter Eliza Jones a colt from the increase of a young sorrel mare that I have given him provided she should breed. I likewise constitute and ordain my son Elisha my sole Executor of this my last Will & Testament.

In witness whereof I have set my hand and affixed my seal this 14th day of August, 1824.

Jacob x Manas (seal)

Witnesses present: Edwin Hamblen, H. M. Bussell, John Jones

WILL OF JOSEPH McMINN
Page 349   Dated: Nov. 6, 1824

I, Joseph McMinn of the County of Hawkins in the State of Tennessee, now residing at the Cherokee Agency, being in the ordinary enjoyment of health of sound mind and disposing memory, but considering the uncertainty of life and the transitory nature of all human concerns, and being anxious from sufficient motives that my Estate should be disposed of agreeably to my views of justice and propriety do make, ordain and publish this my last Will and Testament hereby revoking and making void all former wills of a date preceeding this.

And whereas by an agreement made on the 9th day of October in the year of our Lord Eighteen hundred and twenty between myself and my wife Nancy McMinn for and on account of certain conditions therein expressed, and executed in the presence of the Hon. John Williams of the County of Knox, she the said Nancy became possessed of six certain negroes, a carriage and pair of horses, parcel of my personal estate. Now that the said agreement so as aforesaid entered into may be fully and completely carried into effect according to the true intent and meaning thereof after my death, and that the said Nancy may enjoy, have and hold the said property. First, I give and bequeath to my wife Nancy McMinn the six negroes, carriage and horses aforesaid to her own proper use and will, to dispose of forever, which is to lieu and satisfaction of dower, and all claims whatsoever of that kind upon my Estate, and I do hereby expressly require and direct the Trustees named in the deed on conveyance bearing date October 9, 1821 and by which I conveyed in trust the said negroes, carriage and horses to the use of the said Nancy to make an absolute Deed of Conveyance or Bill of Sale to her for the said property or so much thereof as may be expressed in the said deed of date 9th October, 1821.

Item. It is my will and desire that my Executors hereinafter named, as soon after my death as convenient, discharge all my debts and funeral expenses and in the next place proceed to sell all my Estate, real and personal. The real on a credit on one, two and three years, and the personal on a credit of one year, except all such parts or pieces of property as I may hereinafter otherwise dispose of.

Item. I give and bequeath to my sister Jane Kinkead, daughter of David and Mary Kindead, a mulatto woman named Milly, she being the same that I obtained by my marriage with Rebecca Kinkead, sister to the said Jane Kinkead, which mulatto woman with all her present and future increase of children, Josiah excepted, I bequeath as aforesaid to the said Jane and the issue of her body lawfully begotten, but in the event of her death without such issue living, any one or more of her brothers and sisters then the said Milly and her childred as above bequeathed to the said Jane Kinkead shall descend to and become the property of such surviving brothers and sisters, share and share alike, as tenants in common and not as joint tenants.

Item. I give and bequeath unto Rebecca McMinn Long, daughter of John and Nancy Long of Kentucky the said Josiah above excepted.

WILL OF JOHN McBROOM

Page 252   Dated: January 22, 1828

In the Name of God, Amen.

I John McBroom of the County of Hawkins, State of Tennessee, being sick and weak in body but of sound and disposing mind, considering the certainty of death and the uncertainty of the time thereof, and being desirous to settle my worldly affairs & thereby be the better prepared to leave this world when it shall please God to call me hence, do therefore make and publish this my last Will & Testament in the manner and form following, that is to say: First and principally, I commit my soul into the hands of Almighty God, and my body to the earth to be decently buried at the discretion of my Executors hereinafter named, after my debts and funeral charges are paid &c.

Item. I give and devise unto my eldest son James McBroom $5.00, together with what he has received more than a proportional share alike.

Item. I give and devise unto my eldest daughter Polly $5.00 together with what she has received a full proportional share alike.

Item. I give and devise unto my son Alexander McBroom's children--all that are lawfully begotten--all the tract of land that I now live on that lieth on the north side of the Carter Valley Road, to have and to hold each and severally to share alike in fee simple.

Item. I give and devise unto my daughter Jane McBroom all the tract that I live on & claims that lieth on the East side of the Carter Valley Road to have and hold in fee simple.

Item. I devise & bequeath all the rest & remainder of my Estate, that is, the money proceeds of the sale of my property after my death to be equally divided between my son Alexander and daughter Jane McBroom in shares and shres alike, with the exception of one negro woman called and known by the name of Pegg, which I wish to free as follows: To all whom it may concern, be it known that I John McBroom of the County and State aforesaid for divers good causes & considerations release from slavery, liberate, manumit from slavery my negro woman named Pegg and I do henceforth declare to be free and discharged from all manner of servitude forever after my death. And lastly, I do hereby constitute Absalom Looney & Jacob B. Groves to be sole Executors of this my last Will and Testament, revoking and annulling all former wills by me heretofore made, ratifying and confirming this and no other to be my last Will & Testament. In testimony whereof I have set my hand and affixed my seal this 22nd day of January, 1828.

John x M. McBroom (seal)
(his mark)

Signed sealed published & declared by John McBroom the above named Testator as and for his last Will & Testament, in the presence of us who at his request, in his presence & in the presence of each other have subscribed our names as witnesses thereto:

Absalom Looney
Aaron Williams   Attest:
John Charles   Jacob B. Groves
Andrew Gouldy   Executors

WILL OF CHRISTIAN MESSER

Page 353   Dated: May 28, 1831

I, Christian Messer of Hawkins County and State of Tennessee, being in sound mind and having a desire to dispose of my worldly affairs while I possess a full strength of mind, I constitute this my last Will and Testament. After committing my body to the dust and my soul to God, I do dispose of my

---

Item. It is my will and direction that the residue of my Estate be divided between the sons and daughters of my brothers and sisters respectively, share and share alike, except to my niece Betty Morrison to whom I have given such a portion of my New Canton tract as I consider will be fully equal to her and her husband Robert Morrison's interest in my whole Estate.

Item. I will and direct that my Executors pay to the trustees of McMinn Academy in the County of Hawkins for the use of said academy the sum of $300.00.

Item. I will and direct that my Executors where I do not make the donations myself, present to my friends hereafter named the following articles of property, to wit: To Sarah Gaines daughter of James Gaines, Esq. one set of silver teaspoons with the initials of her name thereon. To Hannah Cooper a like donation. To Hannah Larkins a like donation. To Mary Williams daughter of James G. Williams a like donation. To Willoughby Williams, son of s'd James G. Williams, one supertine fur hat. To Mrs. Mary Rogers, wife of ____ Rogersville ____, one black silk shawl. To Richard Mitchell blank ____. To Joseph McMinn Looney a riding horse worth $100.00.

Lastly. I do hereby nominate and appoint my trusty friends, Col. John Williams of Knox County and Orville C. Bradley, Esq. of Hawkins County executors to this my last Will and Testament, and direct that they need not give security as required by Act of Assembly. In witness whereof I have hereunto set my hand & seal this Sixth day of November 1824.

NB. The following words were written on the second page between the 28th and 29th lines and said pages before signing, sealing and delivering thereof to wit: Except to my niece Betty Morrison to whom I have given such a portion of my New Canton tract as I consider will be fully equal to her and her husband Robert Morrison's interest in my whole Estate.

Signed, sealed, published and declared in presence of us by the said Joseph McMinn to be his last Will & Testament.

James Cowan, James S Bridges, John L. McCarty, Jas. G. Williams, Wm. W. Cowan, Jas. Mitchell   Joseph McMinn

WILL OF ELIZABETH MOORE

Page 351   Dated: Feb. 28, 1825

In the Name of God, Amen.

I Elizabeth Moore of the County of Hawkins, State of Tenn., being in sound sense and memory do make this my last Will and Testament.

Item. I give and devise unto my daughter Elizabeth Yoe a negro girl named Sharlotte.

Item. I give and devise unto my daughter Sally Williams the tract of land whereon I now live, also a negro girl named Mourning.

Item. I free my negro Sela. The balance of my Estate I give to be equally divided between Hugh Moore, Galaher Moore, Cleon Moore, Ewell Moore, John Moore's heirs Elizabeth Yoe and Sally Williams.

And Lastly. I appoint my sons Hugh G. Moore and Cleon Moore to execute this my last Will and Testament. Signed sealed and delivered this 28th day of February in the presence of:

Daniel Taylor, James Taylor, William Taylor,   Elizabeth x Moore
(her mark)

worldly property as follows, to wit: In the first place, I allow my just debts to be paid. I will and bequeath to my wife **Sally Messer** her mainte- nance off the tract of land I now live on during her lifetime. I will and bequeath to my three sons **Jacob, John** and **Isaac Messer** the tract of land I now live on, to be equal divided among them, and I moreover allow my three sons, **Jacob, John** and **Isaac** within twelve months after my decease to pay to each of my other children the sum of five dollars. I also allow my movable property and stock to be sold and equally divided amongst the hole of my children. And I do empower **William Young, Stanwic Hord,** and **Samuel McFeeters, Jr.** my Executors of this my last Will & Testament.

Given under my hand and seal this 28th day of May in the year of our Lord, one thousand eight hundred and twenty-one.

Christian x Messer (seal)
(his mark)

Signed and sealed in the presence of:
James Young, Jacob Derick, John Derick   AB

WILL OF SAMUEL MOONEY

Page 354   Dated: August 31, 1832
    In the Name of God, Amen.

The 31st day of August in the year of our Lord, 1832, I **Samuel Mooney** of the County of Hawkins and State of Tennessee, being sick and weak in body but sound in mind and memory, and calling to mind that it is appointed for all men once to die, do make and declare this my last will and testament in manner and form following, Viz: My body to be buried in a decent and Christian-like manner at the discretion of my Executor herein- after named, and my soul I give to God who created and gave it, and my Earthly Estate I give and bequeath as followeth:

First. I allow all my just debts to be paid.

Second. I give my personal Estate that may remain after paying my just debts as follows: To my Sister **Faney** my bay horse and what may afterwards remain to be equally divided between my other three sisters, **Sally, Martha & Nancy.** And my land I give to my mother during her natural life, and at her death to be equally divided between all my brothers and sisters.

Lastly. I do hereby constitute and appoint my friend **Charles Mooney** my Executor to this my last Will & Testament.

In testimony whereof I have hereunto set my hand and seal The day and year first above written.

Samuel x Mooney (seal)
(his mark)

Signed sealed and published and declared in presence of
Merda [Meredith] Welliford, Andrew Galbraith, Sr., Wilson Brooks

WILL OF HENRY McCOLLOUGH

Page 354   Dated: Mar 20, 1834
                                               May Term, 1834

I **Henry McCollough, Sr.** of the County of Hawkins and State of Tenn., being of sound mind and memory doth make this my last Will & Testament in the following manner.

First. I give and bequeath to my son **Alexander McCollough** the planta- tion where I now live together with all my horses and hogs and farming utensils of every description whatsoever and my still and vessels belonging thereto,

one bed and furniture called his and one called mine with its furniture.

2nd. I give to my daughter **Nancy McCollough** all my household furni- ture of every description, together with all my cattel only my pot metal, and that to be divided equally between **Alexander** and **Nancy.** **Alexander** is to (buy) my son **Henry McCollough** a horse beast to be worth $60.00 when s'd **Henry** is 21 years of age—the horse to (be) valed equal to good trade. **Alexander** and **Nancy** to pay all my just debts equally between them out of their respective shares. I have lately given to my son **William** a mare and I was to have the colt that I allow to **Nancy.**

Lastly. I do constitute and appoint my brother **Joseph McCollough** my Executor and to enter on the administration without giving security. In testimony whereof I have set my hand and seal This 20th day of March 1834.

Henry x McCullough (seal)
(his mark)

Signed, sealed in the presence of:
Jonathan Huffmaster, Peter x Beale, Jonathan Morlan

WILL OF SOLOMON MITCHELL

Page 355   Dated: Jan'y 31, 1837
I **Solomon Mitchell** of the State of Tennessee and Hawkins County, being of sound and disposing memory, do make and ordain this my last Will & Testament, revoking all other wills heretofore by me made.

In the first place, I give and bequeath unto my wife **Nancy Mitchell** all my Estate if she should survive me, that is, all my personal and real prop- erty or estate of every kind whatever, of every debt due or owing that I may die seized and possessed of, to have and to enjoy her lifetime.

Secondly. I desire that at both our deaths that my two slaves **Betty** and **James** may receive their freedom, and I do hereby at [my] death and my wife **Nancy Mitchell's** death give them their freedom. That is, I desire that my Executors may get a special Act of Assembly passed if it can be done for them to receive their freedom according to the tenor of this my last Will and Testament. If they do not receive their freedom as above stated, I give and bequeath the above named slaves to **John Mitchell** my son forever, that is, in the following manner. I give the service of said two slaves to him one day in each week forever, and the other five days of each week during their life- time I give to said two slaves. During their services to him, I desire he shall not depart with said two slaves or trade his right of them away.

Thirdly. At my death and my wife's death I give and bequeath unto my eleven children, that is to say: **Rebeckah, Lewis, Jesse, Greenberry, Nancy Robert, Morris, Elizabeth, Polly, Susannah, Richard,** Fifty Cents each.

Fourthly, I give and bequeath to my son **John Mitchell** all my property which I have not before disposed of of every kind whatever that I may die seized and possessed (of) forever. I constitute and appoint **John Mitchell** my Executor.

In testimony whereof I have hereunto set my hand and seal This 31st day of January, 1837.

Solomon x Mitchell (seal)
(his mark)

Signed sealed and delivered in the presence of us:
William Gideons, Marshall M. Webb, W. W. Walker

Page 356

NUNCUPATIVE WILL OF SARAH MOONEY
Dated Aug. 27, 1837

We, John Walker and Ruth D. Mooney do state that the Nuncupative Will of Sarah Mooney was made by her on the 12th day of August, 1837, in our presence to which we were specially requested to bear witness by the Testator herself in the presence of each other, that it was in her last sickness at the house of Ruth Mooney where she had resided for several weeks previous to her death and the same is as follows, (Viz):

It was her will and desire that her effects should be disposed of after her decease in the following manner:

First. She wished and desired that Martha Mooney her niece should have her bed.

Secondly. That her clothes should be equally divided between Martha Mooney and Elizabeth Mooney, two nieces.

Thirdly. She stated that she had put into the hands of Hezekiah Davis for collection about the sum of forty dollars and it was her wish that James Mooney should be paid out of that money what she owed him, and that her Aunt Ruth Mooney should have the balance. Made out by us and signed This 22nd day of August, 1837.

John Walker
Ruth x D. Mooney
(her mark)

Page 357

WILL OF RHEUBIN MAYO
Dated: Jan'y 10, 1839

I Rheubin Mayo being of sound mind and perfect memory do make and publish this my last Will & Testament hereby revoking and making void all other wills by me made.

First. I direct and it is my wish that I should be buried decently.

Second. That all my funeral Expenses be paid.

Thirdly. That all my just debts be paid after my decease by my Executors out of any money I may have on my hands or may come into their hands after my decease.

Fourthly. I give and bequeath unto my beloved wife Jane Mayo her life-time estate out of my land where I now live, all the household and kitchen furniture to use it as she pleases, 100 acres lying on the branch.

Fifthly. After her decease, my wish is and I bequeath it to my youngest son Andrew Mayo.

Sixthly. After my decease my wish is for daughters that is single to remain on the land for their support until thay decease of my wife Jane Mayo.

Seventh. I do give and bequeath unto my grandson Rheubin Mayo for the love and affection I have for him sixty acres of land where his father now lives, thay son of Nelson Mayo.

Eighth. Provided that Nelson Mayo thay of Rheubin Mayo doth give Jane Mayo a home on the sixty acres of land by building her a good cabbin if it is her request.

Ninth. I do give and bequeath unto my eldest son John Mayo one dollar to be paid by Executors out of the Estate after my decease. I do give and be-queath unto my second son Richard P. Mayo one dollar to be paid by my Execu-tors after my decease. I do give and bequeath unto my third son Nelson Mayo one dollar to be paid by my Executors after my decease. I do give and be-queath unto my daughter Elizabeth Harlis one dollar to be paid by my Executors.

I do give and bequeath unto my daughter Polly Hagood one dollar to be paid by my Executors. I do give and bequeath unto my daughter Sally Hagood one dollar to be paid by my Executors. I do give and bequeath unto my daughter Ann Shoults one dollar to be paid by my Executors out of my Estate. It is my wish and I bequeath unto my four daughters, Jane Mayo, Susan Mayo, Rachael Mayo, and Matilda Mayo all the household and kitchen furniture after thay decease of my wife. It is also my request that so much of my property as will pay all my just debts and legatees be sold by my Executors and funeral expenses. I do hereby wish—and it is my desire—that if there is any more property than that will pay thay expense after my decease for my fore daugh-ters to have it for their use, then I want it to be divided equal among my fore daugh-ters Jane, Susannah, Rachael and Matilda Mayo to be valled (valued) by the Executors and equally dived.

Lastly, I do hereby nominate and appoint and it is my wish and desire that my youngest son Andrew Mayo and John Looney my friend be my Executors.

In witness whereof I do sine this my last Will & Testament with my seal.
January 10 day, 1839.

Rheubin Mayo (seal)

In the presence of us witess:
Lacy Armstrong, John Armstrong, James Armstrong

Page 358

WILL OF TABITHA C. MILLER
Dated: March 24, 1839
Proven: April 1839

I Tabitha C. Miller being weak of body and sound of mind and knowing death is certain and life uncertain, I do lawfully constitute the follow-ing to be my last Will & Testament. In the first place I want my body put away with as little superfluity as possible so it is decently done. In the next place I want the Doctor bill in case of my sickness and all other ex-penses and if there should be any small debts all to be paid. And I will and bequeath to my dear sister Darcas C. Miller all the personal property I have. And I also will that Jacob Miller my brother shall have all the land Estate I have which I heired from my father and he Jacob Miller is to pay $150.00 for the above named expenses and to get some tomb stones for my own & my father's graves and to put a stone wall round my own & my father's & mother's graves and he Jacob Miller is to do it within twelve months after my decease, and to be paid a reasonable price for so doing. And if there should be any thing yet left, I will that my dear sister Darcas C. Miller shall have it all and all the cash notes I have is to be applied in the above manner. I request my brother Jacob Miller to be my sole Executor of this my last Will & Testament and hereby nominate and appoint him for that purpose.

Given under my hand and seal This 24th day of March, Eighteen hundred and thirty nine.

Tabitha x C. Miller (seal)
(her mark)

Attest: William x Maness, James F. Miller
(his mark)

Page 359

WILL OF WILLIAM MOLSBEE
Dated: October 17, 1839

State of Tennessee, Hawkins County. In the name of God, Amen.

I **William Molsbee** of said county and state, being of sound mind and memory but weak in body, knowing the uncertainty of life and the certainty of death, do make and ordain this to be my last Will & Testament in manner and form following, that is to say.

First. I recommend my soul to Almighty God, and I request that all my just debts be paid.

2ndly. After my decease I will that all my personal property shall be sold by my Executor at public auction, and out of the proceeds, my Executor shall pay **John Stoely** my step son $30.00. And to **William Molsby** $30.00. And to my daughter **Polly** wife of **Jacob Bowman** $30.00. And the balance if any to be paid over unto the hands of my beloved wife **Nancy**, and my request is that at her death, if anything remains in her hands that it be paid over to **David Molsbey's** daughters. Having heretofore conveyed to my son **David** all my land in consideration of his maintaining & supporting myself & wife, I now state that that was the consideration alone that induced me to convey said land to him, and the $1,000.00 was only inserted as a mere matter of form by the person who drew the Deed of Conveyance, which I now again ratify by this my last Will & Testament. And should any defect or informality be discovered in said deed, my desire is and I now devise and bequeath to him all my title, right and interest in said land to said **David**, the balance to have enjoy & possess forever.

And I hereby appoint my son **David** my Executor, and also that he be excused from giving bond for the performance of his duties as Executor. My desire is that I may be buried on the farm where I now live, in a decent and plain manner and near where **Samuel Simmons** is buried. In testimony whereof I have hereto set my hand and seal. This 7th day of October AD 1839.

William x Molsbey (seal)
(his mark)

Test: **R. G. Fain, D. Alexander**

WILL OF WILLIAM MANIS

Page 359   Dated: June 12, 1842

This 12th Day of June, 1842 (In the Name of God, Amen).

I, **William Manis** being imperfect and unsound in body, but perfect and sound in understanding and mind, do make this my last Will and Testament.

1st. I will and request that all my just debts and contract be duly paid as soon after my death as possible out of money that I may die possessed of or may first come into the hands of my wife **Lydia Manis**.

2nd. I give and bequeath her—my beloved wife—155 acres of land whereon she now lives and seven head of horses and all other personal property and household furniture during her lifetime. And after my decease, I direct that she shall inherit and have the above during her life, and after her death, I request that my two youngest sons (to wit) **Carter Manis** and **Joseph Manis** have the aforesaid 155 acre tract of land and the premises thereunto belonging.

3rd. I will and bequeath that after the decease of my wife that all my heirs shall inherit their proportional part of the property porportioned to my wife and willed as aforesaid. All such property divided equally among my heirs Except my son **Campbell Manis** and him I will and bequeath the sum of $5.00 out of my Estate.

4th. I will that my wife shall hold all my notes now executed or heretofore executed to me for her own use and benefit, excepting one note on **Peter Bart** and **Mark Kenner**. And I also bequest that my wife have a receipt

that **John Starnes** has in possession, said receipt for the collection of $45.00 or thereabouts on **James Willis** and **James Sampson**, the receipt given to my wife. The receipt is on **John McCallia** for collection.

And lastly, I nominate my wife **Lydia Manis** and I appoint her my Executrix. In witness I do hereby to this my will set my hand and seal This 12th day of June as aforesaid 1842.

William x Manis (seal)
(his mark)

Signed, sealed and published in presence of us.
Witns: **Pleasant Begley, A. Anderson, Clinton Manis**

In addition to my last Will & Testament, I **William Manis** having made and willed the same do make and declare this as a Codicil thereto, to wit: I do hereby will and bequeath until **Zilphia Frazier** 50 acres of land with the present crops thereon, including the premises where she now lives, and also one gray mare and colt. And I also will and bequeath unto the said **Zilphia Frazier** six head of cattle, twenty three head of hogs and also all the household stuff with the before mentioned property that she is now in possession of, and also one side saddle and also six bee hives and I also give and bequeath to her the said **Zilphia** one note of hand on **Mark Kenner** and **Peter Bart** for $25.00 and interest thereon. And I being sound in mind ordain the before mentioned will my last desire. And lastly, it is my desire that this Codicil be attached to and constitute a part of my will to all intents and purposes. This 12th day of June as aforesaid 1842.

William x Manis (seal)
(his mark)

Test: **Pleasant Begley, Clinton Manis**

WILL OF JACOB MILLER

Page 361   Dated: September 27, 1842
                                  Proven: Feb'y 6, 1843

I **Jacob Miller** of Hawkins County, State of tennessee being of sound mind & memory do make and publish this my last Will & Testament in manner and form following:

To my faithful and loving wife I will and bequeath $300.00 per annum to be paid her by my Executor hereinafter named during her life. To my son **Peter Miller** I will $3,500.00, the same being already paid him. To my son **Willie B. Miller**, I will $3,500.00, the same being already paid him. To my son **John S Miller** I will the plantation on which he resides with its appurtenances & the negro man **Clinton** also now in his possession. To my daughter **Sarah Young** I will the negro girl **Alcy** now in her possession valued at two hundred dollars and the balance of three thousand dollars to be paid her as hereafter named. To my daughter **Elizabeth H. Miller** I will a negro girl at valuation and the balance of three thousand dollars as hereafter named. To my daughter **Rachael Forgey** I will the two negro girls **Jane** and **Lucinda** both now in her possession and valued at nine hundred and fifty dollars and three hundred dollars cash, making already an aggregate payment to her of twelve hundred and fifty dollars and the balance of three thousand dollars as hereafter named. To my daughter **Mary K. Weaver** I will two negroes at valuation, a horse at seventy-five dollars already delivered and the balance of three thousand dollars to be paid her as hereafter named, and further a Bureau with forty dollars provided she settles in this county. To my daughter **Susan Armstrong** I will the two negroes **Agnes** and **James** valued at one thousand dollars, a horse at seventy five dollars all now in her possession, and the balance of three thousand dollars to be paid her as hereafter named. I do hereby nominate and appoint Cornelius C. Miller my Executor to put this my last will in Execution, and do will and ordain that he pay to my daughters the respective ballances heretofore mentioned in the manner following: viz: Half of tive ballances in equal installments at twelve and eighteen months from the date of my demise in current funds. The other half in property at valua- tion—provided my Executor and each of my s'd heirs respectively can agree on and identify such property as it will suit both parties. They should have otherwise such balances or parts of the last named half to be paid them by said Executor at the end of two and three years from my demise in currency at legal installments; and further provided that they have the privilege of taking any part of the same property at the public sale of such property as Executor may not wish to keep.

To my son Cornelius C. Miller I will and bequeath all that may remain of my Estate after paying the foregoing legacies including all lands and property both real and personal.

In witness whereof I have hereunto set my hand & seal. This 27th day of September, the Year of our Lord one Thousand eight hundred and forty-two.

Jacob Miller

In presence of us who are subscribing witnesses to the same: R. W. Kinkead, D. Thurman

WILL OF MARY MORRISETTE

Page 362

Dated: May 19, 1843

Proven: 7 Sept., 1857 [R. p81]

I Mary Morrisette do make and publish this my last Will and Testament here- by revoking and making void all other wills by me at any time made. First, I direct that all my funeral Expenses and all my debts be paid as soon after my death as possible out of any moneys that I may die possessed of or may first come into the hands of my Executors:- Secondly, I give and bequeath to my sons Joseph, John and George Washington Morrisette twenty five cents each, more than I am able to give my other children. Thirdly, I give and bequeath to my son Richard Mitchell Morrisette my two negro boys named Henry and Frank. I give and bequeath to my daughter Nancy Everette my negro woman named Celia and my negro boy named Stephen during her natural life then said property to descend to her heirs. Fifthly, I give and bequeath to my son Richard Mitchell Morrisette and my daughter Nancy Everette all the other property or money I may die possessed of to be divided equally between them, the division to be made by themselves if they can agree or in case they cannot agree, the di- vision to be made by two dis-interested persons chosen by them as I do not wish any sale of property to be made. Lastly, I do hereby nominate and ap- point my son Richard Mitchell Morrisette and William Galbraith my Executors.

In witness whereof I do to this my will set my hand and seal. This 19th day of May, 1843.

Mary x Morrisette (seal)
(her mark)

Signed, sealed and published in our presence and we have subscribed our names hereto in the presence of the Testator. This 19th day of May, 1843.

Claiborne Walker, Edward Lee, Daniel H. Cockreham

WILL OF ZADOCK MOORE

Page 363

Dated: March 19, 1844

In the Name of God, Amen.

I Zadock Moore of the County of Hawkins and State of Tennessee, being in bad state of health but of sound mind and memory do make this my last Will and Testament in the words following, that is to say. I want all my funeral and burial expenses paid and all my just debts that is against me. I will and bequeath to my dear wife Barbary Moore all my household and kitchen furniture and peaceable & uninterrupted possession of the house & all the buildings as for as she may need and the profits and rents of the Land belonging to me, as much at least as she may need for a decent support with the exception of what may be needed hereafter. I want her to have a gentle horse to ride and two milk cows of her own choosing of the cows that belong to me and the clock now in the house and plow and pair of work gears and singletree and clevis. I want the wagon and gearing to remain on the farm for the use of the same and all the hodges belonging to me and suffi- cienty of the grain on the farm belonging to me for her support this year, and also one third of the wheat that is growing and the catting and flax wheels and the reel and one side saddle and riding bride and all the sheep and all my books. I want my son William Moore to take my sorrel horse named Challey and trade her in any way so as to get such a horse as named in the will for the use of his mother. I want Susannah McCullough to have uninterrupted possession of the house where she now lives and have the same privileges for support as she has heretofore had, during her lifetime. I want at the death of my before named wife, all the property sold & equally divided between the heirs of my daughter Susannah Moore, dec'd and my daugh- ter Rosannah Phillips & my daughter Ann Cane Bogart and the heirs of my daughter Winnea Keele, dec'd., and it is my will that John Rogers, William Shepherd and Isaac Phillips lay off to Thomas Moore my son, one third in value and in land of the place where I now live in satisfaction of his Deed made by Micajah Lee to him. And the above named valluenets is not to take the improvement that said Moore has made as any part of the value of said land, and the said valluetes is to lay off said land on the upper part of the tract so as to include his improvements and clear across the plantation the land to be valluered according to quality and quantity. And at the death of my wife as above named the balance of the land is to be equally divided between my three sons, William, Thomas and Samuel R. according to quality and quantity. The personal property not named in the will, after my death is to be sold, my debts as above named paid. The balance of any of said sale is to go to the use of my wife. I want William and Thomas Moore Executors of this my last will. This 19th day of March, 1844.

Zadock Moore

Test. Martin Phillips, James Moore

WILL OF GEORGE A. MATHES

Page 364

Dated: February 27, 1846

In the Name of God, Amen.

I George A. Mathes of the County of Hawkins and State of Tenn., being in feeble health but of sound disposing mind and memory, do hereby make and declare this to be my last Will & Testament. It is my will and desire in the first place that my just debts be paid and that all the debts owing to me be collected. It is also my will and desire that after the collection of the debts due to me and the payment of the debts which I owe, the balance of the money that may then _____ together with the money on hand remain, is to be equally divided between my beloved wife **Nancy L. Mathes** and my two dear children **Mary Jane** and **Margaret Elizabeth**, share and share alike. It is further my will and desire that all my other property and effects of every kind, both real and personal that may now or may hereafter in any way belong or descend or be bequeathed to me, shall in like manner be equally divided between my aforesaid wife and two children, share and share alike. It is further my will and desire that out of the respective shares of my Estate bequeathed as aforesaid to my two children, a sufficiency thereof shall at the discretion of their Guardian be set apart and devoted to their education. It is also my wish and desire that my aforesaid beloved wife **Nancy L** be the Guardian of my two (children) **Mary Jane** and **Margaret Elizabeth**. And I do hereby nominate and appoint my beloved brother **John P. Mathes** of the County of Jefferson in the state aforesaid to be the Executor of this my last Will and Testament, and it is my will and desire that my s'd brother **John P.** act jointly with my wife...in regard to the education of my two children...and I do hereby authorize and empower said Executor to sell and dispose of at any time, any of the property belonging to my Estate whenever in his opinion it may be to the advantage of my wife and children, and on such terms as he in his discretion may think best, upon consultation and with the assent and approbation of my wife. In testimony whereof I have hereunto subscribed my name and affixed my seal. This 27th day of February in the year of our Lord Eighteen Hundred and Forty Six.

G. A. Mathes (seal)

Signed, sealed and acknowledged the date
above written in the presence of:
S. D. Mitchell, J. R. Johnston, Nathaniel Hart

WILL OF JESSE MANIS

Page 365   Dated: May 25, 1846

A written Will and Testament, Hawkins, Co., Tennessee.
I **Jesse Manis**, do make and publish this as my last Will and Testament, hereby revoking and making void all other wills by me at any time made.

First. I direct that my funeral expense and all my debts be paid as soon after my death as possible out of any money that I may die possessed of or may first come into the hands of my Executors.

Second. I give and bequeath to **Clinton Manis**, my oldest son, the tract of land he now lives upon containing 150 acres more or less, lying adjacent to **Jefferson Kyle** and others.

Thirdly. I give and bequeath to **Donnelson Manis** my second son, $50.00 in personal property, to be paid out of the property now in my hands instead of his portion of land.

Fourthly. To **Jesse Manis** my third son, I give and bequeath the tract of land he now lives on lying adjacent to **John Sulivan** and **Pleasant Begley**, 50 acres more or less.

Fifthly. I give and bequeath to **Starlin (Sterling) Manis & Eldridge Manis** my two youngest sons the home tract of land containing 130 acres more or less, lying adjacent to the land of **John Kyle** and others to be divided as follows: Commencing on the top of a certain ridge below **James Goodman's** house, running with the said top to the cross fence, thence with the fence to the stables, then with the said fence to a ledge of rocks. Thence up the hill with the fence opposite a chestnut root and cross a chestnut log, a direct course to the top of the ridge that separates the tracts. **Starlin** to have the end where **Goodman** lives and **Eldridge** the home end. If either or both boys last mentioned should die before, I will that his or their part or parts should fall back and be equally divided between other heirs above mentioned and provided they should die before they become of age or have lawful heirs.

Sixthly. I give and bequeath to **Webby**, my youngest heir, a certain red cow. Likewise an equal part of all the household furniture.

Seventhly. I will and bequeath to my wife **Alsey Manis** a certain cow, red and white pided and that said wife has the liberty of disposing of the balance of the household furniture at her own pleasure. She also has the liberty of staying as long as she lives single or appears to act so as to promote the wellfare and interest of said children. Further, I appoint, give full power and control to **Clinton Manis** and as my Executor to bargain and sell or dispose of my part of two entries of land entered by **Abijah Anderson** and myself containing 200 acres lying adjacent **Swempfield Anderson** and others, one half of said land being my part—to be sold or disposed of and the proceeds therefrom to be equally divided between my 5 sons above mentioned. Said Executor to have control and management of **Starlin** and **Eldridge** and all the home affairs most suitable to the welfare, happiness & interest of said family, all made in and above a good supply for said family shall be sold and kept on interest for the benefit of **Starlin & Eldridge**, likewise all personal property except above mentioned and some excepted for other purposes shall be divided equally between the 5 sons above mentioned.

In witness whereof I do to this my will set my hand and seal This 25th day of may in the year of our Lord 1846.

Jesse x Manis (seal)
(his mark)

Signed sealed and published in our presence
and we have subscribed our names hereto in
the presence of the Testator This day above
mentioned. Witnesses: **Evan B. Spenser, Carter x Manis, William x Sulivan, John Sulivan.**   (his mark)   (his mark)
Proven the 1st day of June, 1846.

WILL OF THOMAS MARTIN

Page 367   Dated: May 17, 1847
                                    Proven: May 5, 1847

I, **Thomas Martin** of the County of Hawkins and State of Tennessee, being of sound, disposing mind and memory do make and ordain this my last Will and Testament in manner and form following:

First. I will and direct that all my just debts and funeral expenses be paid out of any money that I may die possessed of or may first come into the hands of my Executor from the sale of any of my personal Estate, or any debts that is due me.

Secondly. I will and desire that my wife **Elizabeth Martin** live on and be in the quiet possession and enjoyment of my houses and land and to be comfortably provided for out of my personal Estate, to be specially attended to by my Executors during her lifetime, and I desire that my smith tools be and remain unsold at any time but for the use of my several sons, and if there appears to be more of my personal property than will appear reasonable for my said wife's support, I will and desire that my Executors sell all the surplus property at a 12 months credit and the proceeds of said sale to be divided between my two daughters, namely **Mahaly Sullivan** and **Elizabeth Lawson** so as to make them equal in the property and **Elizabeth's** lot of land.

Thirdly. I give and bequeath to my daughter **Elizabeth Lawson** and her heirs a certain lot or parcel of my land. Beginning on a black____ed near a field called the Brag field and run a straight line to the SW corner of **William Martin's** field on the west side of the road going to town, then along the top of the ridge to my line westwardly with said line to my corner, then to the beginning.

Fourthly. I will and bequeath the balance of my land to be divided between my sons namely, **John Martin** and **William Martin** to have Lot No. 1. Beginning on a Spanish oak, the SW corner of my old tract, thence up bend to the SW corner of a field called the Brag field. Thence northwardly along the fence of said field to the top of a small ridge. Thence eastwardly along the top of said ridge to opposite a cross fence now between me and **John Martin.** Thence northwardly along said fence to another cross fence between me and **John Martin.** Thence with said fence to Mitchell's line and with that line to the mountain, to be divided as they may best agree next to the mountain. Lot No. 2. Beginning at the northwest corner of my home tract thence eastwardly to the branch, thence with my line to a lot of land I bought of **Ephraim Winstead.** Thence northwardly to a white oak, thence with said line to a stake on the south side of Copper Ridge. Then eastwardly to opposite a new cross fence. Then a straight line to said fence and with said fence to Ap's lot fence and with said lot fence to a small white oak in the edge of a field, then eastwardly along the top of a ridge to **Paschal Martin** to be divided between **Paschael & Aaron** as they may best agree. Lot No. 3, which includes my houses and improved land I will to my two sons **Absalom Martin** and **Abijah Martin** to be divided as they may agree. As to my two sons **James Martin** and **Thomas Martin** I (will) that my six sons above named pay the said James and Thomas Martin their portionable part of said land so as to make them all equal, but to deduct and have a credit from **James Martin's** part for $100.00 which I loaned him when he left this country. I also will and bequeath to my wife **Elizabeth Martin** my sorrel mare and colt. I also will to my son **Abijah Martin** my horsebeast, choice of my stock, and my rifle and shot pouch. And hereby revoke and disannul all former will by me made. And lastly, I hereby constitute and appoint my two sons **John** and **William Martin** my Executors to this my last Will and Testament. In witness whereof I have hereunto set my hand and seal, May 17, 1847.

Thomas x Martin (seal)
(his mark)

Signed sealed and acknowledged in the presence of us:
J. Mitchell, James Winstead, Wiley Cope

WILL OF JOSEPH MIDDLECOFF

Page 369
Dated: Sept. 20, 1847
Proven: Oct. 4, 1848
J. H. Vance, D. Clk

In the Name of God, Amen.

I **Joseph Middlecoff** being feeble in health but of disposing mind and memory do make & publish this my last Will and Testament. I give my body to be buried in a Christian-like manner at the discretion of my friends and my soul to return to God who gave it. Next, all my just debts to be

paid. I give and bequeath to my beloved wife **Patsy** all my property of every description, both real and personal for her comfortable support and the raising of my children so long as she shall remain my widow. It is my will that my son **George** have the tract of land which I purchased from **Pleasant N. Lee** and on which there is a saw mill. One-third of the saw mill is mine and the other **George's.** I wish the land and my interest in the mill to be valued and the final division of my property for my son **George** to pay to my other heirs the valuation of said land, together with my interest in said mill. I wish the line of the said tract of land to commence on a hornbeam corner to my old tract of land and corner to the said tract I purchased from Lee, running thence in a north direction straight with the fence to the corner and for this line to be the dividing line between the two tracts of land. If my said wife should ever marry, which I do not expect she will. It is my Estate to be divided between her and my children according to law. It is my will that my beloved wife **Patsy** should remain in the quiet and unmolested possession of all my property as before mentioned during her widowhood or her natural life and at her death I wish my property of every description both real and personal to be equally divided between my lawful heirs. It is my will that it be left to the choice of my son **George** whether he take the land and the mill as above mentioned. If he does not, I wish it to be disposed of as my other lands and for **George's** interest in the mill being two-thirds to be valued and for **George** to be paid the valuation by the other heirs when a final division shall take place. I wish my son **George** to have entire control of the saw mill and to pay his mother one-third of the proceeds thereof until the final division takes place and I do hereby nominate and appoint my sons **John Thomas** and **George** Executors to this my last Will and Testament. This 20th day of September in the year of our Lord, one Thousand eight hundred and forty-seven.

Joseph x Middlecoff (seal)
(his mark)

Witnesses: **Thomas J. Lee, A. W. Parris**

WILL OF JAMES MOORE

Page 370
Dated: June 5, 1849
Proven: Nov. & Dec. Term, 1852

State of Tennessee, Hawkins County. In the name of God.

I **James Moore, Sr.** of the County of Hawkins and State of Tennessee, being of sound mind and memory do hereby make my last Will & Testament.

First. My will is that I be decently buried and my funeral expenses paid out of my Estate.

Secondly. My will is that all my just debts be paid out of my Estate.

Third. That my wife **Elizabeth** to have all my personal Estate after my just debts and funeral expenses are paid, if she should out live me, for her support, and then at her death all the property to be sold and the proceeds equally divided between **Sally Beckners, Elizabeth McCollough** and **Polly Lane's** heirs which is my three daughters or their heirs as the case may be.

Fourthly. My will is that my son **James Moore** have a certain parcel or tract of land which is all my lands above the conditional line except herein mentioned.

Fifthly. My will is that my son **John Moore's** heirs have all my land below the conditional line, and his widow **Elizabeth Moore** have a support off the said land so long as she remains a widow and no longer.

Sixthly. My will is that my grandson **Barvey Moore** have 30 acres off the east end of my land across from line to line including where he now lives.

Seventhly. My will is that my son **James Moore** be — and I do appoint him—my Executor of my last Will & Testament. I do by these presents set my hand and seal this 5th day of June, 1849.

James Moore (seal)

In presence of us, **Nichilas Beckners, William Shepherd**

WILL OF CLEON MOORE

Page 370

Dated: August 18, 1852
Proven: Sept. Term, 1852
J. H. Vance, Clk

The State of Tennessee) I, **Cleon Moore** of the County and State aforesaid,
Hawkins County   ) being of sound and disposing mind and memory, make this my last Will & Testament.

First. It is my desire that all my just debts shall be paid.

Second. it is my desire that my beloved wife **Emily G. Moore** shall have all the negroes that I acquired by our marriage, to wit: **Eliza, Esther, Ellen, Robert, Carroll & Nancy** and their increase if any, and all the household and kitchen furniture that may be on hand at my decease which I acquired by our marriage. It is also my desire that my beloved wife **Emily** shall have the farm that I purchased of **William N. Cox** in Jefferson County, Tennessee, on condition that she—my wife **Emily G.**—pay to my heirs the sum of $1,000.00, it being money that I paid in part of the purchase money of said farm and other moneys advanced by me for debts contracted by my said wife before our marriage and that she shall have a bay mare (Fanny) now on the farm & a cow and calf on the farm in Jefferson, which cow I acquired by her by marriage. I desire further that should my wife **Emily** desire it she shall have laid off to her by my Executor hereinafter mentioned a sufficient quantity of grains &c from my farm in Jefferson County for one year's support.

Third. It is my desire that the remainder of the property it has pleased Almighty God to bless me with shall be sold by my Executors on a credit of twelve months and the proceeds therefor to be equally divided among the following persons, to wit: **Virginia McCarta** (now dead), **Sarah Moore, William Moore, John Moore, Margaret Moore, George Kendrick Moore, Moriah Bradford, Mary Moore, Eliza Ruth Moore, Josaphine G. Moore, Cleon R. Moore.** I have one other child, **Emiline Moore**, not named above but for whom I have heretofore provided. After deducting from **William Moore** $900.00 and from **Virginia McCarta's** heirs the sum of $1,300.00, from **George Kendrick Moore** the sum of $1,200.00 and from **John Moore** the sum of $900.00, all of said several sums having heretofore been advanced to my children in lands or money, which I have no doubt will be admitted by each of them.

Fourth. Should my Executors believe that it will be to the interest of my heirs to sell any or all of my land not disposed of my me on a credit of one, two or more years, they can do so.

Fifth. I desire that there shall be no misunderstanding about what is my will and intention in this my will. That is, that my wife shall have all the property herein before mentioned for her, on paying the sum of $1,000.00 above stated to the rest of my heirs not heretofore provided for, and that the remainder of the proceeds of the sale of all my property both real and personal shall be divided equally among my heirs not heretofore provided for,

after deducting the amounts hereinbefore specified from the heir's share who has received it.

Sixth. I hereby revoke all other wills that I may have heretofore made, adopt and radify this my last Will & Testament, and I hereby appoint **Absalom P. McCarta** and **Thomas [Theo. I] Bradford**, two of my sons in law my Executors to this my last will. Signed and sealed in the presence of:
James L. Etter   Cleon Moore
John B. Logan

WILL OF JOHN MANIS

Page 372

Dated: Sept. 15, 1855
Proven: June Term, 1856

I **John Manis** of the County of Hawkins and State of Tennessee, being somewhat advanced in life and rather of feeble health, but of sound and disposing mind and memory, considering the uncertainty of life and the certainty of death, do make, publish and declare the following to be my last Will and Testament, hereby revoking and making void all the other wills made by me heretofore at any time whatsoever.

First. It is my will and desire that of the money that may be on hand at my death, or which may first come into the hands of my Executors hereafter named, all my just debts should be paid and all the expenses attending my funeral.

Second. It is my will and desire that my two sons, **Nelson** and **George Manis** shall have all my lands which lie in the valley where they now live, except that portion of said lands which lie northwest of a line to be run hereafter from a bunch of gums corner of a 50 acre grant to run with a line down to ____ **Dubard's** line and to cross the valley so as to strike **Andrew Frost's** line at **Dubard's** corner. It being my intention to give to my said two sons or their heirs all the lands which lies east and north of said line and to contain 125 acres to be equally divided between them, share and share alike.

Third. It is my will and desire that my four grandchildren, to wit: **Sarah Manis, Rhoda Manis, Amanda Manis** and **Gathan Manis** shall have my 50 acre tract of land as is contained in Grant No. 19338 and issued on the 20th day of October, 1835, to be equally divided between them, share and share alike. But if it should be thought advisable and for the interest of said grandchildren, by my Executors to sell said 50 acre tract, they may sell the same and if sale should be made whilst said grand children are minors, the money arising from said sale shall be put at interest until the oldest may become of age or shall marry, and then his or her portion of said proceeds shall be paid over to him or her, and so on with the others.

Fourth. It is my will and desire that my son **Pleasant Manis** shall have the tract of land whereon he now lives which lies west of the main road which passes my house from Sneedville to Rogersville. The east line to run with the road from the SE corner thereof to the lower corner of the tract whereon I now live, to wit: To the lower corner of my meadow. Thence leaving the road to the left and running a straight line to a stake, a corner of my 50 acre tract. Thence along the line of said 50 acre tract to a black oak and maple corner of said 50 acre tract. Thence around various courses to include all my land west of the last mentioned line.

Fifth. It is my will and desire that my wife **Celia Manis** shall have the entire use and control of my home plantation and the two places on which

Washington Smith and John Robison now live for and during her natural life or widowhood, and after her death or marriage that said plantations shall belong entirely in fee simple to my two sons John and Gilbert Manis who are now minors, or their heirs, to be equally divided between them share and share alike. And it is my will and desire that my wife Celia shall also have my negro boy Rowe and my mare mule for and during her natural life or widowhood, and after her death, or should she marry, then and in that case, it is my will and desire that my Executors shall sell the said negro boy and mule and divide the proceeds equally between Nancy Manis, Betsy Fields, Polly Robertson, Celia Manis and Lucinda Manis, my daughters, share and share alike. It is also my will and desire that my wife Celia shall have all my household and kitchen furniture, and one third of the stock (of) hogs that may be on hand at the time of my death, one third of the cattle and one third of the sheep, all the farming utensils.

Sixth. It is my will and desire that my son John Manis shall have a bay mare colt now one year old past and a saddle and bridle. And my son Gilbert to have a bay mare colt, saddle and bridle likewise. And that my daughter Celia shall have one cow and calf, one side saddle, and my daughter Lucinda shall have a cow and calf and side saddle.

Seventh. It is my will and desire that all the balance of my personal estate shall be sold by my Executors on 12 month's credit and the money when collected shall be equally divided between my daughters Nancy Manis, Polly Robertson, Celia Manis and Lucinda Manis, and if any money should be on hand at the time of my death more than sufficient to pay my debts and funeral expenses, it is my will and desire that said monies shall likewise be divided equally between my said four daughters last above named.

Lastly. I do hereby nominate and appoint my son Pleasant Manis and my son-in-law Carter Manis Executors to this my last will and Testament. This 15 September, 1855.

John x Manis (his mark)

Signed, sealed and acknowled in the presence of us this 15th day of Sept., 1855. George R. Powel, Abijah Anderson, Wm. Sullivan, Clinton A. Manis.

Page 374

WILL OF JOHN McWILLIAMS

Dated: May 13, 1855
Proven: Oct. Term, 1855

I John McWilliams of the County of Hawkins and State of Tennessee do make this my last Will & Testament, hereby revoking and making void all other wills by me made at any time.

First - I direct that my funeral expenses and all my debts be paid as soon after my death as possible out of any money that I may die possessed of, or may first come into the hands of my Executor.

Item 2. I do will all my landed Estate consisting of one-third part of the tract of land that I now live on. Also, a small tract purchased of John Kinkead, and a small entry to my grandson Joseph McWilliams, a son of a legitimate child who I do acknowledge as my son whose name was James McWilliams.

Item 3. I will to Margaret Smith daughter of C. Smith one Bureau.

Item 4. I do will that all my personal property be sold by (my) Executor after giving ten days' notice to the highest bidder on a credit of twelve months.

Item 5. I do will that my two negro slaves, to wit: Dol & Masadamia shall be divided equally between my brother Andrew, sister Nancy, and the proceeds of the sale of my personally (sic) after my debts is paid to be equally divided between my (brother) Andrew McWilliams and Nancy my sister.

Lastly. I appoint Robert Cooper as my lawful Executor. In testimony whereof I do set my hand and seal, in presence of the subscribing witnesses. The Executor is not to be (required) to give security. This 13th day of May, 1855.

John McWilliams (seal)

Attest: H. Hamilton
P. Critz

Page 375

WILL OF THOMPSON McGEE

Dated: November 8, 1855
Proven: Oct. Term, 1857 [R.p92]

I Thompson McGee being weak in bodily health but of sound mind and disposing memory, knowing that all mortal beings have to leave this sublunary world for the realms of immortality, and in consideration of the same, do hereby make and ordain this my last Will & Testament.

In the first place, I bequeath to Almighty God my soul who gave it.

Secondly. That all my just debts be settled out of my effects that I may leave.

Thirdly. I bequeath and give unto Alfred Rhoton McGee my son my plantation on which I reside, conveyed to said Alfred R. McGee by John Coldwell for 350 acres more or less, also my slave Elizabeth with one half of all my household and kitchen furniture, together with all my interest in the farming tools including wagon & gears.

Fourth. I give and bequeath unto my daughter Barbara Ann McGee my slave Mary, together with one half of my household & kitchen furniture. Also, one cow and a sorrel mare & colt. My old slave Edith is to remain as the property jointly between my son Alfred and my daughter Barbara, and they are jointly bound to support her whenever she becomes unable to support herself. I further hereby provide that my daughter Barbara is to be supported out of the proceeds of my farm as long as she remains unmarried and single.

Fifth. I give and bequeath to Nancy Jane Lloyd, my daughter $400.00 to be paid out the amount her husband Wm. Lloyd is indebted to me. The rest-due of said debt I bequeath unto my son Alfred and my daughter Barbara equally to each for such support and attention which I may require while I live.

My claims of debt on John Copenhaver for $800.00 with the interest thereon is to be divided equally between Louisa W. Fudge, my daughter, and my son Alfred and my daughter Barbara: the other half to my daughter Susan Williams.

I give and bequeath out of the debt of $1,500.00 coming to me from John $250.00 unto the children of my daughter Sarah Rice, the sum of $250.00 to be paid out of said $1,500.00 debt. The balance of said debt will be $1,000.00 which I bequeath equally amongst my other six children or their heirs, to wit: my son John A. McGee & Joseph C. McGee and my daughters Elizabeth Harris, dec'd heirs, Livinia W. Wolfe & Anderson McGee my son & Lucy Henneger and her child or children, the conditions of Lucy's share except five dollars which is to be paid over to her, is to remain in the hands of my Executor to (be) paid over to a Trustee appointed by the Honorable County Court of Hawkins, to be paid over to said Lucy her child or children as the case may be as they may need the same by said Trustee for which service he is to be reimbursed out of said share.

I hereby request, constitute and appoint my son-in-law **Conrad Fudge** and my son **Alfred R. McGee** my Executors to this my last Will & Testament. In testimony whereof I hereunto set my hand and affix my seal This 8th day of November in the year of our Lord, 1855.

Thompson McGee(seal)

Witness: **John H. Ellis, Robert Cooper, James Amis**

WILL OF WILLIAM MOLSBEE

Page 376   Dated: March 28, 1856

                                          Proven: Apr. & May Term, 1856

I **William Molsbee** being of sound mind and memory but weak in body do hereby make this my last Will and Testament, that is to say, I hereby will my soul to Him who gave it praying that through the merits of Christ, He will mercifully accept the same. As to my property, &c, I will and bequeath the entire land of which I am possessed unto my wife **Mary Magaline** during her natural life or widowhood. Said land is case of her death or marriage to belong to my heirs. I also will unto her, my wife, one sorrel horse and bay colt, one saddle, bridle and blanket, two milch cows, and one yearlin to be selected by her, also twelve head of shoats and two sows and my entire farming utensils, two big bedsteads and beds and clothing, two trundle bedsteads, beds and clothing, and the balance of my household and kitchen furniture. I also will unto her (my wife) twelve old sheep, my entire oats except forty sheaves, and all my corn, all my wheat except two bushels which I have sold to Dr. **J. G. Gillenwaters**, also all my flax. Eight hundred pounds of bacon and all my lard. As to my money, I will it to be loaned at interest until my children are 21 years of age when it with interest shall be paid or handed to them as theirs, and whatever of money my property not willed specially may bring, I also will (after debts paid) to my children subject to the above provisions.

I hereby appoint my brother **Joseph Molsbee** my sole Executor of this my last Will & Testament. In witness whereof I have hereunto set my hand and seal this March 28 in the year of our Lord one Thousand eight hundred and fifty six.

(his mark)

William x Molsbee (seal)

The above instrument was now and here subscribed by **William Molsbee** the Testator in the presence of each of us and was at the same time after all erasures and interlining declared by him to be his last Will and Testament, and we by his request sign our names thereto as attesting witnesses.

E. E. Gillenwaters

J. G. Gillenwaters

NUNCUPATIVE WILL OF JOEL MATHIS

Page 377   Dated: Aug. 27, 1856

                                          Proven: Oct. Term, 1856

We, **R. M. Bishop, Ward Mustin, George R. Stubblefield** and **S. Brooks** do state the nuncupative will of **Joel Mathis** was made by him on the 28th day of August, 1856, in our presence to which was specially required to bear witness by the Testator himself in the presence of each other, that it was made in his last sickness in his own dwelling house where he had been living for several years, and the same is as follows, to wit: It was his last will and desire that his effects should be disposed of after his decease in the following manner:

1st. That all his just debts be paid out of his effects and the remainder of his estate be divided among his children in the following manner: That his daughter **Nancy** have a separate sum of $200.00. The remainder to be divided among his heirs, to wit: **Nancy, Mary, Joseph, Leannah, Nila,** share and share alike.

2nd. That my land that I bought a short time ago from **John Brooks** and his wife, my will is that my wife and children move to said lands, that my wife and above children have and hold the said lands during my wife's natural life. Then my desire is that my Executors sell said land at public or private sale as they may think best, but if my wife and children do not move to said land my desire is that my Executors sell said land as soon as the same can be sold as the law directs, either public or private as they may think best.

3rd. My will and desire is that my wife and children have my bay mare and that they use her for the benefit of all the family and if the said mare brings a colt next spring that my daughter **Nancy** is to have it.

4th. My will and desire is that my Executors sell all my personal property at public sale except one year's support for my wife.

5th. My will and desire is that all my effects remain in the hands of my Executors until after the death of my wife or be loaned out at interest and at the death of my wife to be paid over to my children as described above.

6th and last. I hereby nominate and appoint **William C. Kyle, John Altom** and **S. Brooks** my Executors of my last Will & Testament.

Made out by us and signed the 27th of August, 1856.

R. M. Bishop

Ward x Mastin and **S Brooks**

(his mark

WILL OF WILLIAM McCARVER

Page 378   Dated: Sept. 5, 1856

State of Tennessee, Hawkins County. In the Name of God, Amen.

...I **William McCarver, Sen'r** being weak in body but sound in mind, do make and ordain this to be my last Will and Testament, revoking all others heretofore by me made, to wit:

Item 1st. I recommend my soul to God and body to a decent burial.

2nd. A certain piece of land sold to **Thomas Amis** and a conditional line made by said **Amis** and myself, **William McCarver, Sen'r.**, beginning at a spring near the creek that **John Watts** now uses water out of. Thence with a straight line with the fence towards the river to a large forked white oak tree. Thence with the fence to river. All east of the above named line belongs to said **Amis**.

3rd. I give and bequeath to my beloved wife **Margaret McCarver** the lot around the house and garden and privilege to both apple orchards for fruit. I further will that she shall have all my household and kitchen furniture except one bed, and that my son **William** is to get equal to the one that my son **Alexander** has had. I further will that all the property that my wife brought here when we were married, that she may dispose of it at her own will. The balance to be divided between my two sons at her death, or if she should get married. I will that she shall have a horse worth $75.00 and a saddle and bridle during her life, then to be divided between my two sons. I further will that she may have a support out of the smoke house and corn crib and wheat that is on hand at my death. I will my wife one choice cow and calf and four choice hogs and one sow and shoats.

4th. I further will that my farm shall be equally divided between my two sons if they can agree themselves on dividing. If not, to choose three disinterested men to divide it for them. I will also that each of them shall have access to all waters on the farm and also to both apple orchards for fruit. Each privilege to the barn. All my loose property to be divided between my two sons if they can agree. If not, to sell and divide the money, and also the moneys on interest. I will my land to my sons and their heirs...

5th. I further will that my wife shall have a neat sustenance off the farm during her natural life or widowhood. In testimony whereof I have hereunto set my hand This 5th of September in the year of our Lord, 1856.

William x McCarver (seal)

Witnesses: **J. W. Cain, James B. Amis** (his mark)

WILL OF WILLIAM McCOLLOUGH

Page 379   Dated: October 16, 1856
                Proven: Sept. Term, 1861

I **William McCollough** do make and publish this as my last Will & Testament hereby revoking and making void all other wills by me at any other time made.

First. I direct that my funeral expenses and all my debts be paid as soon after my death as possible out of any moneys that I may die possessed of or may first come into the hands of my Executor.

Secondly. I give and bequeath to my wife **Elizabeth** the farm on which we now live, to have the possession of the same or enough of the proceeds of said farm for her maintenance during her lifetime.

Thirdly. That **Sarah** and **Nancy McCollough** have their support off said farm while living single or stays with their mother, and at the death of my wife **Elizabeth**, the lands to fall to **William, Samuel,** and **John McCollough**, provided the three boys herein named pay to each one of the heirs $100.00 when said farm comes into their hands, to wit: **Alexander McCollough, Eliza Headrick, Henry P. McCollough, Sarah & Nancy Jane McCollough.** In witness whereof I do to this will set my hand & seal This the 16th day of Oct., 1856.

William x McCollough (seal)
(his mark)

Signed, sealed and published in our presence and we have subscribed our names hereto in the presence of the Testator This the 16th day of October, 1856.
Test: **William McPherson & James Moore**

WILL OF WILLIAM MILLER

Page 380   Dated: June 28, 1858
                Proven: Dec. Term., 1859

I **William Miller** of Hawkins County, State of Tennessee, being weak of body but sound of mind and memory do hereby make and constitute this writing my last Will & Testament which is in the words and figures following, to wit:

Item First. My will and desire is that my body shall be decently buried in a metalic coffin at such a place as my wife may direct, and after said expense then I want my just debts paid out of my effects such as notes of hand or other evidences of debts due me.

Item 2nd. My will and desire is that my beloved wife **Susan Miller** shall have, possess and enjoy all my real and personal estate during her natural life, subject, however, to the following conditions, that is: She must pay

my debts &c out of my effects (always excepting my negro called **Ben**) who I will hereafter provide for, provided there may be enough except **Ben** to pay and satisfy all claims against me, after leaving in their hands full as much personal property as is exempt from Execution in a widow's hands by the laws of Tennessee, and should the property aforesaid fail to pay...then I desire my Executrix hereinafter appointed to sell so much of my land over the knob near andjoining **James Yonas** as will satisfy all claims against my Estate, which said land is to be laid off and sold by my Executrix and for which she is to make title, deed &c.

Item 3rd. I desire at the death of my wife that my servant man called **Ben** shall choose among all my children who would he rather live with and after such choice is made two dis-interested neighbors are to assess his value and the child so chosen is to have him at this valuation, which valuation is to be thrown in the price of my land hereafter provided for.

Item 4th. My will is that all the property my wife may get under this will is to be hers in fee simple, except **Ben**, and my land as I now provide for. That is to say, at her death, that is, the death of my wife **Susan**, I desire all my land sold to the highest bidder on a credit of one half the purchase money in one and the other half in two years, retaining a lien until the whole is paid for and the proceeds to be equally divided among all my children (or their children should one of them be dead) with the understanding that my wife has full control, use of, and receive all the rents, profit &c and labor of **Ben** my servant during her natural life, and I do hereby appoint my wife **Susan** my sole Executrix with the request that my brother **Jacob Miller** assist her in carrying into effect this will. Witness my hand and seal This 28th day of June, 1858.

William Miller (seal)

Signed, sealed and delivered
before signed. **Jacob Miller, Christian Sensabaugh** .

WILL OF GABRIEL McCraw

Page 381   Dated: July 21, 1858
                Proven: April 2, 1860

I **Gabriel McCraw** of the County of Hawkins and State of Tennessee, being of sound and disposing mind do make and publish this my last Will & Testament, hereby revoking and making void all former wills by me at any time made. And as to such worldly Estate as it hath pleased God to intrust me with, I dispose of the same as follows:

First. I give and bequeath unto my beloved wife **Susanna McCraw** during her natural life all the property both real and personal including all notes and accounts in my favor against all persons whosoever.

Second. I give and bequeath unto my grand daughter **Evaline M. Godby**, formerly **Evaline M. Forgey** who intermarried with **Crockett Godby**, at the death of my wife my negro girl **Ellen** and all the children the negro girl may have living at the death of my wife.

Third. I direct that the residue of my property both real and personal shall be sold at the death of my wife at public auction on a credit of 12 months and the proceeds of such sale divided equally between my three daughters **Minerva Etter, Susan Mayes** and **Adaline E. Senter**, the rest of my children being already provided for.

And lastly, I do hereby make, ordain and appoint **Samuel McCraw** and **William K. Mayes** Executors of this my last Will and Testament, which office it is my desire they shall hold without security. In witness whereof I, Gabriel McGraw, the Testator, have to this my last Will & Testament written on one sheet of paper only, set my hand and seal this 21st July, 1858.

Gabriel x McCraw (seal)
(his mark)

Signed, sealed and published in the presence of us who have subscribed our names in the presence of the Testator and of each other: John S. Cocke
Wm. Gro—   and Samuel x S. W. Webb
(his mark)

WILL OF OLIVER C. MILLER

Page 382

Dated: August 3, 1861
Proven: March, 1862

I Oliver C. Miller being of sound and perfect mind and memory do make and publish this my last Will & Testament in manner and form following:

First. I give and devise unto my elder daughter, Martha J. Shanks, and unto my elder son, Thomas C. Miller jointly, their heirs and assigns all that my messuage or tenement including the farm on which I now live, situated, lying and being in Carters Valley in the Eighth District, Hawkins County, Tennessee, together with my freehold estate whatsoever therein, to them the said Martha J. Shanks and Thomas C. Miller jointly and to their heirs and assigns forever. Also, I give and devise unto my said elder daughter, Martha J. Shanks and unto my elder son Thomas C. Miller jointly all that my messuage or tenement situated or lying and being on Caney Creek in the 10th Civil District of said county and state, together with my freehold estate whatsoever therein to them...jointly and their heirs and assigns forever.

Secondly. I give and devise unto my younger daughter Mary Frances Miller & unto my youngest son Samuel Goodson Miller jointly their heirs and assigns all that my interest, messuage or tenement which exists in the undivided shares purchased by me of Susan Felkner farm situated, lying and being in the above Eighth Civil District, county and state aforesaid, together with my freehold estate in the same whatsoever, to hold, to them, the said Mary F. Miller and Samuel G. Miller jointly and unto their heirs...Also, I give and bequeath unto my said younger daughter Mary Frances Miller and my younger son Samuel G. Miller to be divided equally between them when they...arrive at the age of 21 years respectively, the following slaves, namely, Hannah a woman, John Wesley a boy, Rosanna a child, together with their increase, but the guardian to have the control, use and benefit of the labor of said slaves without charge until the said Mary Frances and Samuel G. arrive at their majority.

Thirdly. I give and bequeath unconditionally unto my beloved wife Matilda Miller the following slaves, namely, Nancy Ann, Lucinda and her child James Franklin, together with their increase.

Lastly. I give and bequeath unto my said wife all debts or money due me together with all my stock of horses, cattle, hogs, sheep, etc., with all my farming utensils, wagons, ploughs, harrows &C, household furniture of every variety on hands and kitchen furniture, loom house furniture, blacksmith tools with all kinds of grains on hands or growing, to enable her—said wife Matilda—to wind up my estate successfully and to support herself and my two minor children Mary F. & Samuel G. comfortably and give each of them the schooling that she may find practicable. To this end I hereby appoint my beloved

wife Matilda Executrix of this my last Will & Testament without requiring her to ruled to security by the County Court for her faithful discharge of duties therein. Further, a discretionary authority is hereby lodged by me with said Matilda Executrix to sell and dispose of either by private or public sale so much of the above recited personal property placed at her disposal as will make a sum necessary when added to the available debts now outstanding to liquidate all legal demands against the Estate. The residue and remainder of the above personal property, after all my just debts are paid out of it as indicated above are to be held and controlled solely by said Executrix Matilda Miller for her own use and benefit and for the joint use and benefit of my younger daughter Mary Frances also my younger son Samuel Goodson both minors, and to which or by whom the said Matilda is hereby designated and is hereby appointed by me Guardian to both of them... until they arrive at the age of 21, without her being ruled to bond by the County Court...when the above minors...arrive at the age of 21, then the unconsumed residue and remainder of personal property in the hands of said Guardian or its proceeds when sold, shall be divided unto three parts equally— between Matilda and my younger children, Mary Frances & Samuel Goodson, each receiving one third part thereof. My elder daughter, Martha J. Shanks & also my elder son Thomas C. Miller have been heretofore and otherwise fully provided for. In testimony whereof I have ...set my hand and affixed my seal this 3rd day of August, 1861.

O. C. Miller (seal)

Interlined before signed. Signed, sealed, published and declared by the above named Oliver C. Miller to be his last Will & Testament in presence of us who have hereunto subscribed our names as witnesses in the presence of Testator.
H. Watterson, John Young

WILL OF DAVID MOLSBEE

Page 384

Dated: April 13, 1864
Proven: June Term, 1864

State of Tennessee, Hawkins County

I, David Molsbee, being of a sound mind and perfect memory do make and publish this my last Will & Testament as follows:

First. I give and bequeath unto my beloved wife Margaret one horse or mule and her maintenance off my land and one year's provission, two cows, my household and kitchen furniture during her widowhood, and at her death or marriage what there remains is to be sold and equally divided between my five daughters.

Secondly. I give and bequeath unto the dunker church the meeting house and one acre of land around the house.

Thirdly. I give and bequeath unto my three sons, Joseph, Samuel and Abraham the remainder of my land as follows: First, I will and bequeath to Samuel one third of my land included where he now lives, mansion house, out house lot and barnd. Secondly, I give and bequeath unto Abraham one third of my land including my mansion house, out house, lot and barnd where I now live. Thirdly, I gave and bequeath unto Joseph the other third if he ever get back from the army, but if he never get back, I give and bequeath that third to be equally divided between Anna and Rachael Molsbee. I gave and bequeath to my five daughters, to wit: Catherine Consinger, Margaret Consinger, Mary Isenberg, Anna & Rachael Molsbee $300.00 each to be paid two years after my death in _____ currency. This amount is to be paid by my three

WILL OF WILLIAM NELSON

Page 386

Dated: 1832

In the Name of God, Amen.

I **William Nelson** of the County of Hawkins and State of Tennessee and citizen thereof, do make ordain and constitute this my last Will & Testament and desire it may be received by all and such as my friends and neighbors.

First. I give and recommend my soul to Almighty God that gave it me, nothing doubting in my mind but that I shall receive the same again by the Almighty power of God.

Next. I do recommend my body to be buried in a Decent burial at the discretion of my Executor, namely **Thomas Johnson.**

Thirdly. I give and most freely bequeath unto my beloved wife **Rebecah** one mare and colt, two cows and calves and a number of hogs, too tedious to mention, together with all my personal property of all kinds including my household and kitchen furniture of every description, and all other properties now in my possession to be freely enjoyed by her the said **Rebecca Nelson** enduring her natural lifetime, and at her decease, then and in that case, to be disposed of as my Executor thinks fit or proper. And I do most solemnly enjoin it on my Executor before mentioned to excute the hole sence and true meaning of the above instrument of righting to its full and true contents. In testimony whereof the said **William Nelson** hath hereunto set his hand and seal ratifying, allowing and confirming the same to be his last Will and Testament and no other. Signed, sealed and delivered in the presence of us who in the presence of each other hath hereunto set our hands this _____ day of _____ A.D., 1832.

William x Nelson (seal)
(his mark)

Witness: **James Willis & Larkin Willis** (his mark)

WILL OF SAMUEL NEILL, SR.

Page 387

Dated: Feb. 5, 1857
Proven: Oct. Term 1860

I **Samuel Neill, Sr.,** of the County of Hawkins and Town of Rogersville, Tenn., do make and publish this my last Will & Testament hereby revoking all other wills by me heretofore made.

First. I direct and declare it to be my Will and purpose that my Exec-hereafter named shall out of the funds of my Estate existing or to be raised as hereafter directed shall pay all my just debts, funeral expenses and legal liabilities.

Second. Whereas I have heretofore advanced to and paid for my son **James K. Neill** sums which taken together with my liabilities as his security, make a full moiety of my estate. I therefore declare it to be my will, purpose and desire for the purpose of doing equal and impartial justice between my sons, **James K. & Samuel Neill,** that my son **James K. Neill** shall in no case receive any further advances or portions of my estate either real or personal.

Third. I am the owner of an undivided interest in a tract of land lying in Sullivan County known as the Pryor Place, near the north fork of Holston and perhaps adjoining the lands of **Joshua Phipps,** also an undivided interest in a tract of land in said country known as the Barger or Cain place, lying on the island road adjoining the lands of **Hawk** and others, supposed to contain some 475 acres. Also a tract of land in said County of Sullivan known as the Scott tract, supposed to contain two or three hundred acres in which tract I have an undivided interest. Also an undivided interest in a tract of land

---

sons. Each one hundred dollars to each daughter. If **Joseph** never git back, **Rachael** and **Anney** is to pay his part to the other daughters. I will and bequeath unto my five grand children, **William Molsbee's** children, $50.00 each to be paid two years after my death in currency to be paid out of the money and proceeds of the sayle of my property. I mean my stock and farming utensils it over that amount the remaining to be equally divided between my five daughters. The remains also to be paid two years after my death in common (?) currency.

Lastly, I do hereby nominate and appoint **D. D. Anderson** and **Abraham Molsbee** my sole Executors in this my last Will and Testament. In witness I have hereunto set my hand and affixed my seal this the 13th day of April in the year of our Lord, One thousand, Eight hundred and Sixty-four.

David x Molsbee (seal)
(his mark)

Signed sealed and delivered in the presents of the forenamed **David Molsbee** to be his last Will & Testament in witness hereunto we have subscribed our names as witnesses: **Joel C. Gillenwaters, Asbury Gillenwaters, Benjamin Isenberg**

WILL OF EDWARD NORTH

Page 386

Dated: Sept. 19, 1813

In the Name of God, Amen.

I **Edward North** of Hawkins County, State of Tennessee, being weak in body but of perfect mind and memory, thanks be to God. Calling into mind the mortality of my body and knowing that it is appointed for all men once to die, do make and ordain this my last Will & Testament, that is to say, principally and first of all, I give and recommend my soul to God that gave it and my body I recommend to the earth, to be buried in decent Christian burial at the discretion of my Executors; and as touching such worldly estate wherewith it has pleased God to bless me in this life, I give and devise & dispose of the same in the following manner and form:

First. I give and bequeath unto my (daughter?) **Elizabeth** one dollar, my sons **Tom & William,** daughter **Leah,** wife **Eliza,** daughter **Polly** and daughter **Nancy** all my movable property to be equally divided among the above named (viz) my wife **Eliza,** daughters **Polly & Nancy** and my son **Thomas** $50.00, being the last payment of my land. I give and bequeath unto my wife **Eliza** $100.00, and I do utterly disallow, revoke and dis-annul all and every other legacy will, Testament, Legacies, bequests and Executors before named, willed, be-queathed and I do hereby make constitute ordain and appoint my wife, **Eliza** and **James Hagood, Esq.** Executors of this my last Will and Testament. In wit-ness whereof I have hereunto set my hand and seal This 19th day of September, 1813.

Interlined before assigned.

Edward x North (seal)
(his mark)

Signed, sealed and pronounced by the s'd **Edward North** as his last will and Testament in the presence of us who in the presence of each other have hereunto subscribed our names.

Fielding Seals, Patrick Bray

in Obion County, Tennessee. Also an undivided interest in some town lots
in the town of Kingston, Tennessee. Also an undivided interest in some town
lots in the Crab Orchard in the State of Kentucky, all of which real estate
belonged to the firm of **Neill & Simpson**, and is now owned by myself and the
heirs of law of my former partner, the late **William Simpson**, and I hereby
declare it to be my will and desire that all of the above lands that shall
remain undisposed of at my death shall by my Executor be sold on such terms
as he may deem best and the proceeds applied as hereinafter directed, and to
enable him the more readily to execute this part of my will, I hereby devise
to my son **Samuel Neill** (hereinafter appointed Executor of this my will) the
legal title to my undivided interest in all of said lands and all other land
of which I may die seized and possessed not otherwise disposed of in this will.

Fourth. It is my will, and I hereby direct my Executor that out of the
funds arising from the sale of my said property he shall pay all my debts
&c as directed in the first clause of this will in which liabilities I desire
shall be included whatever sums I may have to pay as security for my son
James K. Neill.

Fifth. I will, desire & bequeath unto my wife **Sidney** all my property
both real and personal of every kind and description whatever including the
funds arising from the sale of lands as directed in the third clause of this
will, for and during her natural life.

Sixth. I will and bequeath unto my grand daughter **Penelopy Neill** my
negro girl **Mary**, to have and to hold as an Estate in fee after the death of
my wife **Sidney**.

Seventh. It is my will and desire that my son **Samuel Neill** after the
death of his mother and the payment of my debts &c have all the rest and
residue of my estate, both real and personal (excepting the slave **Mary**, devised to my grand daughter and I therefore bequeath and devise unto my son
Samuel Neill his heirs & personal representatives all of my real and personal
estate of every kind and description whatsoever except the slave **Mary**, of
which I may die seized and possessed, to have and to hold as an estate in fee
after the termination of the life estate of my wife **Sidney Neill**.

Eighth. I hereby constitute and appoint my son **Samuel**
Neill my Executor of this my last will and testament. The word "owned" interlined before signed. In witness whereof I have hereunto set my hand and
seal this 5th day of Feb'y, 1857.

                                        Samuel Neill (seal)

Signed, sealed and acknowledged and published in our presence by the Testator
at whose instance and in whose presence we have hereunto subscribed our names
as witnesses.
J. H. Vance & H. Carmichael

WILL OF NANCY NUGENT
(From County of West Meath, Ireland)

Page 389   Dated: November 25, 1858
                                  Proven: Dec. Term, 1858

I **Nancy Nugent** of the County of Hawkins and State of Tennessee, do make and
publish my last Will and Testament, hereby revoking all other wills heretofore made by me.

First. I desire that my Executor shall pay all of my just debts and
funeral expenses out of the first money that may come into his hands as
Executor. And after the payment of my debts and funeral expenses, I will &
bequeath all the residue of my money & property of every kind and description

of which I may die seized and possessed to be disposed of in the following
manner, to wit: My entire estate is to be equally divided between my beloved
brothers **John Nugent** and **Francis Nugent** and my beloved sister **Mary Nugent**
sons and daughter of **Edward Nugent** and **Mary Nugent** all of whom I left in
Ireland many years since. My sister **Mary** living with our dear mother in the
County of West Meath about five or six miles from the town of Mullingar. My
will is that my brothers **John** and **Francis** and my sister **Mary** each have one
third or an equal share of my Estate. It is further my will that if either
of my said brothers or my sister shall have departed this life before or at
the time of my death leaving issue that the share of the said decedent or
decedents shall be equally divided among his, her or their respective children, male and female, share and share alike. And in case either of my
brothers or sisters in this will mentioned shall have departed this life at
the time of my decease leaving no issue living at that time, my will is that
the portion or share to which that brother or sister would have been if living at the time of my death entitled under the provisions of this will,
shall go to the survivor or survivors or to the issue of such brothers and
sister as shall have died leaving issue, to be equally divided between said
brothers and sister or their issue, the issue if any taking per stirpes as
the representative of their parent or ancestor.

It is further my will that if there should be none of the relatives provided for in the foregoing will in being at the time of my decease, then my
Executor hereinafter named is hereby constituted a Trustee to hold in trust
my Estate for the benefit of the Catholic Church of Multifarnum (Multyfarrham)
in the County of West Meath, Ireland and to transmit the proceeds of my said
estate to the Parish Priest of said church, to be by him used for the benefit
of the Church.

And I do hereby appoint **Jas. W. Rogan** as the sole Executor of this my
last Will & Testament.

For reasons satisfactory to myself but which it is unnecessary for me
here to state, it is my will and desire that none of the issue or descendants
of **James Nugent** my brother who died many years since in Hawkins County shall
have any share or portion of my Estate and I do hereby dis-inherit them.

And it is my will and desire that my Executor do proceed as soon after
my death as possible to collect all money or monies that are due me, or
coming to me, and I desire that he shall be charged no interest on such sums
as may come into his hands from the time he shall receive the same until he
shall have ascertained who are the proper legatees under this will and until
said legatees shall have established their claims to receive the share which
they are entitled to receive according to the plan of distribution herein
specified or directed.

In testimony whereof I have hereunto set my hand and seal This the 28th
of October, 1857.

                                        Nancy Nugent (seal)

Signed, sealed and acknowledged in our presence, we affixing our signatures
hereto in the presence of this Testator and as witnesses thereto at her
request the day and date above written.
Witnesses: **James Johnston, Joseph A. Johnston**

I **Nancy Nugent** do hereby make and publish this my codicil to the within
last will and testament. My will and desire is that should my brothers **John**
Nugent and **Francis Nugent** and my sister **Mary Nugent** have no children living
at the time of my death but should have grand children, or any of them should
have grand children then my will and desire is that said grand children shall
take said property in the same way provided in my will - that the children

of the said brothers and sister should take my property, and if there should be no grand children of brothers and sister, then my will is that my property shall go to the Catholic Church as provided in my will, and it is further my will and desire that from the fact that Jas. W. Rogan, the person appointed in said will as my Executor is indebted to me and related to most of those who owe me money, I hereby revoke said appointment of James W. Rogan as my Executor, and I do hereby constitute and appoint Sam Powel my Executor of this my last will and testament and codicil to said will I revoke and annul the appointment of James W. Rogan as my Executor, the balance of said will to remain as it is except as altered by this codicil.

Witness my hand and seal this 25th day of November, 1858.

Nancy x Nugent (seal)
(her mark)

Signed, sealed and acknowledged and we have subscribed our names in the presence of the Testator.

Peter Joyce, Eliza McKnight

WILL OF MARY NOTHERN

Page 391

Dated: May 11, 1859

Proven: June Term, 1860

I Mary Nothern of the County of Hawkins and State of Tennessee, make and publish this my last Will & Testament revoking all others hereto-fore by me made.

First. My Executors are to pay my burial expenses and all my just debts out of my Estate.

Second. I give and bequeath to my son John Nelson Ballard the sorrel mare called Nelly, one white cow and calf, one sow and three pigs, one bed and furniture, bedstead &c, one wash kettle and three sheep.

Third. I give my daughter Edna Elizabeth Hambrick the black cow, one sow and six pigs, five shoats, one bed and furniture, stead &c, all the household furniture consisting of one loom, one wheel, on pair cards, one was _ pot (wash), cooking utensils, cupboard, ward, clothing &c, and one sheep.

I request what money I have on hand and also the proceeds of the sale of one sorrel mare to be applied to the payment of the balance due on the land I purchased of Adam T. Hileman as soon as a good and sufficient title is made by said Hileman. I request that the land remain unsold until my daughter becomes 21 years of age, then to be divided equally between my son Jno. Nelson Ballard and my daughter Edna Elizabeth Hambrick.

I further appoint Daniel J. Read my Executor to this my last will and testament. Signed the 11th day of May, 1859.

Mary x Nothern (seal)
(her mark)

Witnesses: J. L. RITTER, A. B. RITTER

WILL OF WILLIAM OWEN

Page 392

Dated: July 11, 1815

In the name of God, Amen.

I William Owen of Hawkins County in the State of Tennessee, being sick and weak of body but of perfect and sound mind and memory, do make and ordain this my last Will & Testament as follows: I give and bequeath unto my son Parr Owen all that tract of land whereon he now lives in the same

manner it has been run and laid off, only the line running towards the nobbs to be so extended as to include the spring on his part, supposed to contain 190 acres. I give to my son in law George Conway all that tract of land whereon he lives, as it has been run and laid off, supposed to contain 160 or 170 acres. I give to my son David Owen the tract of land whereon he now lives to begin on Joseph Bryan's line at a point where a straight line cross-ing the branch where the water works begins will strike the middle of the hollow that runs towards Mrs. Moore's and with that hollow to Moore's line. I give to my son William Owen all that part of my land between David Owen's line and William Patterson's old line, as run by David Stuart. I give to my daughter Sally Owen all that part of my land from Patterson's old line to the main road, and to my daughter Betsy Owen all my land on the south side of the road not interfering with the parts allotted to Farr Owen and George Conway. I leave to my son James Owens $10.00 to be paid out of my personal Estate, reserving the possession and property of the plantation whereon I now live, and what part I now rent to the use of myself and my wife during out natural lives, and after our decease to be held and enjoyed by the legatees according to the foregoing distribution. And it is further my will that all my legatees shall at all times thereafter enjoy and equal privilege in making use of any timber on any of the land allotted to any or either of them.

Signed, sealed and delivered this 11th day of July A.D. 1815

W. Owen (seal)

In presence of Thomas Henderson, Stephen x Stubblefield, Farr Owen, George Conway, Thomas Jones
(his mark)

WILL OF ELI OVERTON

Page 393

No Date Furnished

In the Name of God, Amen. This the last Will and Testament of Eli Overton of County of Hawkins and State of Tennessee is as followeth: Viz: He the said Eli Overton finding himself sick and weak of body, but in perfect mind and memory Blessed be God therefore and calling to mind the frailty of this life and the certainty of death, I do ordain and make this my last Will and Testament in form and manner as followeth:

Imprimis. I do recommend my soul unto the hand of God that gave it, and my body to the Earth to be interred therein with decent and Christian burial at the discretion of my Executors hereafter to be named. And as for what worldly goods it hath pleased God to bless me with, I do will and bequeath in manner and form as followeth, Viz:

Item. I give and bequeath all my land and plantation where I now live with all the rest of my whole Estate of every description of stock and house-hold and kitchen furniture to by beloved wife Miley Overton during her life-time and after her decease then my desire is that everything of my whole Estate that remains shall be equally divided between Sally Grantum and Sealy Grantum. I do give and bequeath it to them and their heirs forever. This I do make and ordain it my last Will & Testament. I do also leave my beloved wife Miley Overton and James Murrel my Executors to act for me.

Eli Overton

Francis Winstead, Mathew Winstead

WILL OF MILLA OVERTON

Page 393

Dated: August 19, 1855
Proven Oct. Term, 1858

I **Milla Overton** being of sound and disposing memory do hereby make and publish this my last Will and Testament hereby revoking all other wills by me made, and in regard to my little personal property, having nothing but what was bestowed upon me by the Government of the United States as a pension from the services of my husband in the Revolutionary War, and a claim that **Sam Powel** my agent is prosecuting before the Pension Officer of the United States for arrearages of pension.

I will and bequeath of the pension due me and arrearages of pension due, prosecuted by said **Powel** so much as will be sufficient to amply pay **Susan Wells** for taking care of me, nursing me in my sickness, so that she may be amply and fully indemnified for all her trouble. And believing that said moneys if obtained will not more than pay said **Susan Wells** for her trouble and pay my burial expenses, my will is that said **Susan Wells**, after paying said expenses have whatever may be coming to me as above stated. Witness my hand and seal This 19th day of August, 1858.

Milla x Overton (seal)
(her mark)

Executed and acknowledged in our presence:
F. Brewer, M. E. Wells, John Lawson

.

WILL OF GABRIEL PHILLIPS

Page 394

Dated: August 14, 1812

In the Name of God, Amen.

I **Gabriel Phillips** of the County of Hawkins and State of Tennessee, being of perfect mind and membery, thanks be to Almighty God for the same, doth ordain and establish this my last Will and Testament. That is to say,

First. I recommend my soul to God that gave it, my body to the dust of the Earth, to be decently buried in some Christian burying place at the discretion of my Executors.

Second. I give and bequeath to my beloved wife **Milly Phillips** all my household and kitchen furniture during her remaining my widow, and at her death or marriage it is to go to the use and support of my family to be disposed of as the rest of my property.

Whereas, I have a bond on **Abram Chapman** to make a title to a certain parcel of land lying in the County of Hawkins, my will is that my son **John Phillips** shall have the same by he, **John Phillips** paying one-half of the purchase money at the time it becomes due and my Executors paying the other half. And be it well understood that **John Phillips** is to pay into their hands at the expiration of four years, and then and in that case my Executors to make a Deed of Conveyance to said **John Phillips** and his heirs or assigns. I do give and bequeath unto my son **Thomas Phillips** a horse and saddle to be worth $65.00 when he arrives to the age of 21 years of age, and so in like manner, all my sons to receive a horse and saddle to be worth as much as that **Thomas** is to have, to be paid out of my estate when each of them shall arrive at the age of 21.

I due also give and bequeath to my daughter **Polly Phillips** a feather bed to weigh 25 pounds of feathers, and a cow to be worth eight dollars, to be paid within three months after my decease. And so, in like manner, I give and bequeath to each of my daughters as much and in the same property as

Polly is to have when they each of them shall arrive to the age of 18 years of age, to be paid out of my Estate.

Whereas I have give a bond to **William Keele** with certain conditions and I due enjoyne it on my Executors as a particular injunction to see that the bond is faithfully complied with and require my Executors to make a Deed of Conveyance to said **William Keele** according to the conditions laid down in said bond as soon as is convenient to have done.

And lastly, as to all the rest of my Estate, I allow my wife for the use and support of my family as long as she remains my widow, or until my younges son comes of age and then if my childing cannot agree on a division all my property is to be sold and equally divided between all my sons and daughters. I due also appoint my beloved wife **Milly Phillips, Isaac Barton, Jacob Coffman** and **David Byler, Esq.** Executors of this my last Will and Testament, revoking all others. August 14, 1812. (his mark)

Gabriel x Phillips (seal)

Signed, sealed, published and declared in the presence of us who was present at the signing of the same. **James McCollough, Zadoc Moore, Robert Phillips**

WILL OF CHRISTIAN PEARSON

Page 395

Dated: May 14, 1819

In the Name of God, Amen.

I **Christian Pearson** of Hawkins County, State of Tennessee, being of sound and perfect mind and memory (blessed be God) do this 14th of May in the year of our Lord 1819 make and publish this my last Will and Testament in the manner following that is to say. It is my will and desire to give all my Estate to all my sons and daughters to be divided equally between them provided nevertheless and upon condition that none of them attempt to raise an account against my Estate for work that they did for me after they arrived of age and in case any of them do attempt to raise an account as above stated, then, it is my will and intention that each one of them so raising an account shall have one dollar each to be levied out of my Estate and in that case, it is my will and intention that the balance of my Estate be equally divided among the rest of my sons and daughters...

First. Provided none of my sons and daughters attempt to raise accounts against my Estate...I give and bequeath all my Estate both real and personal to all my sons and daughters, namely **Michael Pearson, Betsy Jones, Polly Shanks, George Pearson, Christian Pearson, Caty Begley, Lawrance Pearson, John Pearson, Henry Pearson, Sally Pearson, Peggy Nash** and **Sassy Pearson** to be equally divided among them, share and share like to them and their heirs forever.

Secondly. Provided any of them raise an account as aforesaid, then I bequeath to each of my sons and daughters so raising accounts against my Estate as aforesaid the sum of one dollar...to be levied out of my estate to them and their heirs forever.

Thirdly. If any of my sons and daughters shall raise an account against my Estate for work done after they came of age as aforesaid, then and in that case I give and bequeath all the balance of my Estate after the one dollar apiece for such as raised accounts is taken out to all my sons and daughters that do not raise accounts...to be equally divided among them, share and share alike.

And I do hereby appoint my sons **Lawrance Pearson & Henry Pearson** Exec's of this my last will and testament. In witness whereof I, the said **Christian Pearson, Sr.** have to this...set my hand and seal the day and year above written.

Christian Pearson (seal)

Page 397

WILL OF JOHN PILANT

[Proven 1822]

In the Name of God.

Be it remembered that I John Pilant of the County of Hawkins and State of Tennessee, being weak in body but sound in mind and memory, considering the uncertainty of this mortal life, this my last Will and Testament in manner and as follows, that is to say. My wife Crsiah Pilant is to have all my property of every description, in her power to make sale of any of s'd property so far as to pay all my debts, and the balance she is to have her lifetime or widowhood, and let it be understood that the balance of my property is to support my wife and wrais the children that is not of age, and let it be remembered that my son Robert and my son George is to have all my land at the time that my wife marries or they become of age, and if one of them should die before they are of age, my son John is to have that one part, and if the both should die, my son Thomas is to have the other part.

And I give my son Joseph six shillings, my son James six shillings, my son William six shillings, my son Isaves six shillings, my son Kinching six shillings and I give my daughter Charlet foer six shillings, Nanna Gourley six shillings, and I give my daughter Polly six shillings, my daughter Milly six shillings, daughter Rachael six shillings, my daughter Betsy six shillings, my son Thomas six shillings, my son John six shillings.

In witness whereof I have hereunto set my hand and seal.

John x Pilant (seal)

(his mark)

Signed, sealed and delivered in the presence of Ozburn x Hale, John Jones, J. M. Charles

(his mark)

Page 397

WILL OF HENRY PEARSON

Dated: October 13, 1841

I Henry Pearson of the County of Hawkins and State of Tennessee, planter, do make and publish this my last will and testament, hereby revoking and making void all former wills by me at any time...made. And first, I direct that my body be decently interred in a manner suitable to my condition in life, and as to such worldly Estate as it hath pleased God to intrust with me, I dispose of the same as follows:

First: I direct that my debts and funeral expenses be paid as soon after my decease as possible out of any money that I may die possessed of, or may first come into the hands of my Executors from any portion of my Estate real or personal.

Secondly: I give and bequeath to my beloved wife all my Estate real and personal. I do also wish her to make sale of all the personal property immediately after my death if need requires it, to settle my debts, but if not I wish her to have the use of all the property real and personal so long as she lives or remains a widow. I wish her to give each of my children $150.00 out of my Estate so soon as they arrive to the age of 21 years of age, or sooner if they marry younger. The amount if not paid in money may be (paid)

in property at a cost valuation. I consider that Louisa Davis has already had her $150.00. But if my wife should marry at any time after my death I wish my Estate to be amediately disposed of as the Law directs in such cases. And after each getting $150.00, the balance equally divided.

I do hereby make ordain and appoint my esteemed wife and my beloved son Christopher Columbus Executors of this my last Will and Testament. In witness whereof I, Henry Pearson, have to this my will written on one sheet of paper, set my hand and seal this 13th day of October, 1841.

Henry x Pearson (seal)

(his mark)

Signed, sealed and published in the presence of us: Wm. Wilder, W. C. Wilder

Page 398

WILL OF JANE PATTERSON

Dated: February 28, 1842

In the Name of God, Amen.

I Jane Patterson of the County of Hawkins and State of Tennessee, being sick and weak in body but of sound and disposing mind and memory, thanks be to God for the same, and calling to mind the certainty of death and the uncertainty of this transitory life, do this day make, publish and declare this as and for to be my last Will and Testament in manner and form following:

Imprimis. I desire that all my just debts and funeral expenses be fully paid and satisfied.

Item. I give and bequeath unto my daughter Betty my old sorrel mare, one fallen leaf table, one walnut cupboard, and her equal part of the kitchen furniture, half a dozen of cheers, also an equal part of my hogs.

Item. I give and bequeath unto my son William my young sorrel mare, my smith tools, one bed and clothing, also one equal part of my hogs, an equal part of the kitchen furniture, an equal part of the cupboard furniture. I desire that my son William send my grandson Isaiah James Patterson to school to learn to read and write, and that he give said Isaiah J. Patterson one horse and saddle at the age of 20 years, provided he stays with him until that period.

Item. I give and bequeath unto my daughter Martha my Bureau, also my young bay hose two years old, half a dozen of cheers, an equal part of the cupboard and kitchen furniture, an equal part of my hogs.

Item. I give and bequeath unto my daughter Susannah Hunter Patterson my young bay horse one year old past, one walnut chest, one black cow and her calf, half a dozen of chairs, an equal part of the cupboard and kitchen furniture, one coffee kettle, an equal part of the hogs.

Item. I give my grand daughter Martha Patterson one bed and clothing, one flax wheel and a small trunk.

Item. I give and bequeath unto my grandson James Patterson one muley cow.

Item. I do further bequeath unto my daughter Martha one bed and clothing.

Item. I do further give and bequeath unto my daughters Betsy, Martha & Susannah Slaughter and my son William each one equal share of my table linning. I do further give and bequeath unto my son William Patterson my entry of 50 acres of land on the waters of Big Creek adjoining the lands of her son William's.

Item. I do further give and bequeath unto Betsy a pair of drawing chairs, and my wearing apparal to be equally divided between my three daughters heretofore mentioned.

Item. I further give and bequeath unto my four sons, to wit: **James, George, Adam** and **John Patterson** one dollar each.

Item. I do further give and bequeath unto my son **William** my large family Bible.

Lastly. I do hereby nominate and appoint **Charles Coffin Alexander** my Executor of this my last will and testament, revoking and declaring this to be my last will and testament. In witness whereof I have hereunto set my hand and seal. This 28th day of February, 1847.

Jane x Patterson (seal)

Signed, sealed and delivered in presence   (her mark)

of: **Wm. Alexander, Wm. x Smith,**

    John Patterson. (his mark)

(The word "part" in 19th line and the word "saddle" in 25th line were interlined before signing).

WILL OF WILLIAM PHIPPS

Page 400   Dated: August 12, 1845

                              Proven: Dec. Term. 1856

I **William Phipps** of the County of Hawkins and State of Tennessee, being of sound mind but feeling the uncertainty of this mortal life, also the necessity of preparing for death by making a necessary arrangement of my temporal affairs, do make and declare the following last Will and Testament, hereby revoking and annulling all others, to wit:

Item First. I will and bequeath unto my four grandsons, sons of my son **Edward E. Phipps**, dec'd, namely **Wm. Tivis Phipps, Joshua Lafayette Phipps, James Pulasky Phipps,** and **Edward E. Phipps** all the land lying on the south side of Holston River owned by me and now in the possession of my daughter **Jane Phipps**, widow of **Edward E. Phipps**, dec'd...to be equally divided between my four grandsons above named, share and share alike, to them and their heirs forever, but to be under the control of the widow during her natural life, but should any of the said heirs die before they arrive to lawful age without lawful issue then his or their share or shares in said land to descend to the surviving brothers.

Item 2nd. I give and bequeath to my daughter **Elizabeth G. Coldwell**, wife of **John Coldwell** one negro woman named **Rachael** and her increase, also stock, household and kitchen furniture and all of which she has heretofore received.

Item 3rd. To my daughter **Mary Whittenberg**, I will and bequeath my negro boy **Jim**, in addition to what she has heretofore received.

Item 4th. To my daughter **Margaret Gillenwaters**, wife of **Joel Gillenwaters**, I will and bequeath two negro children named **Clinton** and **Alice**, also stock and household furniture all of which she has before received of me.

Item 5th. I will and bequeath unto my daughter **Sarah**, wife of **John Miller** one negro woman called **Cinda** and also one negro girl, yellow complected, named **Roda**, stock, household and kitchen furniture, all of which she has heretofore received of me.

Item 6th. And my daughter **Willie Ann**, deceased wife to **Gaven Leeper** in her lifetime received of me one negro woman named **Alice**, also stock, household and kitchen furniture considered by me a full share with my other daughters above mentioned.

Item 7th. I will and bequeath to my daughter **Betty A.** wife of **John Shields** my negro woman **Emaline** and two of her children **Citty** and **George**

and all her increase from this date if there should be any, and the two young negroes that she now has in her possession, **Ambrose & Adaline**, to her and the heirs of her body forever.

Item 8. I will and bequeath to my grandson **Edward Erwin Shields**, son of **John** and **Betta A. Shields** my negro boy **Cain** (child of **Emaline**) to be held in trust by his father and his uncle **Wesley A. Phipps** until he, my grandson, shall have become 21 years of age. It is my will that the negro boy **Cain** be hired out to the highest bidder when he shall (reach) 14 years of age, year-after-year until my grandson becomes of age, and the proceeds of the hire of said boy to be applied to the use of schooling my grandson, and if said grandson should die before he comes of age, or without lawful issue, then said negro boy to (go) to my daughter **Betty A. Shields**, to her and the heirs of her body forever. Also, I will to my grandson **Edward E. Shields** a good feather bed and furniture for the same.

Item 9. To my son **Joshua Phipps** I will and bequeath in addition to what he has already received of me a negro boy named **Sam**.

Item 10. To my son **William P. Phipps**, I will and bequeath in addition to what he has already received of me a tract or parcel of land containing 50 acres be the same more or less, of the lower end of my home place. Beginning at a post oak and black oak conditional corner of my tract and the **Berrald** tract now owned by **Wm Lyons** or son, running south sixty, west with a new marked line to the back line of the old **Erwin** grant, thus south twenty five, east along the old line to the corner ash and beech near a small spring at the foot of a large hill, being the corner between the **Marsletter/Morrisette** tract and the tract on which I now live. Then north sixty six east along the old marked line to a black oak and sweet gum, then due north along the old line to the beginning, to him and his heirs forever.

Item 11. To my son **Thomas M. Phipps**, I will nothing more, he having already received his full share in cash, negro &c.

Item 12. To my son **James L. Phipps** I will and bequeath a tract or parcel of land purchased of **Margaret Surgoine** containing 140 acres more or less, bounded as follows: Beginning on the bank of Holston River in a small island on an ash tree for corner a mulberry **Lyons** & box elder pointers then along a marked line between **William Armstrong** and myself south sixty nine and a half, west to white oak on the old **Patton** line, sourwood, gum and hickory pointers, then with the old **Patten** line south twenty five, east fifty poles to a white oak corner black oak pointer, then along a marked line formerly the line between **Margaret Surgoine** and myself to the bank of Holston River to the corner elm, then up the meanders of the river to the beginning, to him and his heirs forever. Also three negroes, to wit: **Mima, Charles & Bob**, also one bed & furniture with a full share of stock and farming utensils &c, all of which he has received.

Item 13. I will and bequeath to my son **Wesley A. Phipps** the plantation that I now live on bounded as follows, to wit: Beginning at the corner elm on the river bank, then with the marked tree formerly between **Margaret Surgoine** and myself to a white oak corner and black oak pointer on the old **Patten Line**, then along the said **Patten** line south forty five degrees east to where **Wm. P. Phipps'** line intersects with the old **Patton** line, then along the said **Wm. P. Phipps'** line to the post oak and black oak corner, then along the said conditional line between **Lyons** and myself to the river on a black oak and hickory corner, then up the meanders of the river to the beginning, containing 400 acres more or less, to him and his heirs forever; also three negroes named **Caty, Powel** (and underlined deceased girl), **Julia**; also one bed and

furniture, stock of all kinds, farming utensils, &c, and at my death, I will
that he have all my personal property not otherwise disposed of. It is also
my will that my son Wesley A. Phipps' legacy be charged with all my lawful
debts which may be due from me at my decease & that he pay the same. Also
give me a decent and respectable support as long as I live with the use of
my old dwelling house or otherwise as I may choose.

Item 14. I will and bequeath to my grand daughter Sarah Jane, daughter
of Wesley A. & Eliza Jane Phipps my negro child Mary, child of Emaline, to
her and her heirs forever, it being full compensation to her father Wesley
A. Phipps for taking care of and raising Emaline's family of children. Also
one Bureau, feather bed & furniture for the same. It is also my will that
William Armstrong, my son Joshua Phipps and my son James L. Phipps be my
Executors to this my last Will and Testament.

In testimony whereof I have hereunto set my hand and seal This 12th day
of August, 1845.

Wm. Phipps (seal).

Witness: Wm. Armstrong, Alfred Armstrong, Mary Armstrong

Codicil to this my last Will and Testament

I William Phipps having heretofore made my last Will & Testament, do make and
declare this codicil thereto to wit: It is my will that my negro woman
Emaline that was willed to my daughter Betty Shields, I will and bequeath her
to my Wesley A. Phipps, and also my negro man named Sam that I had willed
to my son Joshua Phipps, I will and bequeath to my son Wesley A. Phipps, he
to pay to my son Joshua Phipps whatever sum the said boy Sam may be worth
at my death. If they should fail to agree on the price of said negro Sam,
to be valued by my Executors.

Lastly, it is my desire that this codicil be attached to and constitute
part of my will to all intents and purposes. This 8th day of September, 1851.

Signed, sealed in presence   Wm. Phipps (seal).
of: Wm. Armstrong, H. C. Armstrong

Page 403
WILL OF THOMAS POINDEXTER
Dated: Dec. 3, 1849
Proven: Sept. Term 1853

State of Tennessee, Hawkins County, December 2, 1849:
Know ye that I Thomas Poindexter being in very usual state of health
and of sound mind and memory but calling to mind the mortality of my body,
and it is appointed for all to die, do make, ordain and constitute the following to be my last Will & Testament.
First and principally, I give and recommend my soul of that gracious
God who gave it me, and my body to a decent burial.
2. I give unto my beloved son James Poindexter all my part of the land
which my father lived on which the said James Poindexter now lives on, to
have and to hold, him and his heirs forever, to make him equal to my daughter
Martha.
3. To make my son George and daughter Emaline equal with them, I give
and bequeath unto them my dry field tract of land to have and to hold forever
in law for equity.
4. I give to my son William L. Poindexter $500.00 to be raised out of
the balance of my property. Also my wife is to have all the rest of my lands,
the red house and the home house and all the balance of my lands during

her natural life or widowhood. Also is to kep with her all the blacks
which I shall have in possession, and after making those children that has
not had beds and furniture and one horse beast to make them equal with the
others, after this is done she is to have all the rest of the household and
kitchen furniture and all the horses and cattle and hogs, but I recommend
that she makes sales and sells all her surplus property and live on the
money. She is to keep my youngest son with her until he (Robert) becomes
of age and then to make him equal with the rest, and at her death everything
is to be equally divided between William Poindexter, George W. and James
Poindexter and Emaline Poindexter and Robert F. Poindexter, and if I hereafter make anything it is to be equal to them all, and if the money I have
on hand is not disposed of, it is to be equally divided between the above
written names.
This I subscribe to be my last Will & Testament. Given under my hand
and seal This 3rd day of December, 1849.

Thomas Poindexter (seal)

Witness: John L. Connose & Edmond Lovin

Page 404
WILL OF JOSHUA PHIPPS
Dated: July 3, 1861
Proven: Aug. Term, 1861

I Joshua Phipps of the County of Hawkins in the State of Tennessee, being in
feeble health but of sound and perfect mind and memory do make, publish and
declare this to be my last Will & Testament hereby revoking all former wills
by me at any time made, and as regards my Estate real and personal, I desire
to dispose of the same as follows:
First. I will and desire that all my indebtedness and my funeral expense
be paid as soon as practicable after my decease.
Secondly. I will and devise to my son Frank L. Phipps the farm called
and known by the title of the Hugh Leeper farm which property speaking would
belong to the said Frank L. Phipps and his sister Abenaida Netherland at my
death, but for the said Abenaida's share I promise hereinafter to fully compensate her with other property so as to give the entire farm to my son
Frank L. Phipps. I also will and devise to my son Frank L. Phipps the farm
known by the title of the James Leeper farm, also the William Lyons farm,
also the Samuel Henderson farm that I purchased of said Henderson. I also
will and devise to my son Frank L. Phipps the following named slaves which
he now has in his possession, including the increase if any born since (to
wit) one negro man named Jim, one negro boy named Henry, one negro woman
named Lucy and her infant child named Saul or Sal, one negro girl named
Laura, one negro man named Frank, one negro girl named Mary, daughter of
Lucy, one negro boy named Dick, one negro girl named Maria, also a negro boy
named Tom which the said Frank L. Phipps has never had in his possession.
I also will and devise to my son Frank L. all the stock of every description,
household furniture, monies advanced or loaned, and other charges entered
against him on my Memorandum Book marked "A", and release him from the charges
of the same. I also will and devise to my said son Frank L. Phipps the one
fourth part of all my cash on hand, notes, bonds and judgements remaining
after discharging any indebtedness, the said Frank L's proportion of the cash
on hand to be paid out of the proceeds of the notes &c when collected by my
Executors. I also will and devise to my son Frank L. the one half of a certain lot of horses to be hereinafter mentioned. Also one large ox wagon

which is to be repaired and paid for off my farm. Also, a full set of black smith tools now in **Fawbush's** shop that belongs to that shop, also my buggy and harness belonging to it.

Thirdly. I will and devise to my daughter **Abenaida Netherland** commonly called **Ida Netherland** and her husband **Robert G. Netherland** a certain tract or parcel of land lying on the north side of Holston River in Hawkins County adjoining the **Reed** farm and others. Beginning at the upper corner of **Reed** farm on the river, thence up the river with its meanders to the mouth of the in-branch or ditch at the lower end of the **Payne** field. Thence a straight line in a northwest direction to a corner that is to be marked twenty rods due east of what is known as the five pines corner as I believe a corner of the **Ripley** place on the **Ross** line. Thence a parallel line with the **Ross** line to the top of the ridge opposite a large field on the **Ripley** place in the lower end of which the **Widow Grady** lives. Thence a straight line to the back corner of the field now worked by **Banks**. Thence with the dividing fence between **Robert G. Netherland** and myself to the stage road, changing the course of the fence so as to run it out at the corner tree at the mouth of the lane. Thence running with the middle of the county road known as the Kincaid Road to the top of the ridge near the corner of **R. G. Netherland**'s woodland fence, at the point where the road to the campground leaves the Kincaid Road, thence a straight line, a west course to the **Bradley Bellamy** corner on the top of Pine Mountain. Thence with the meanders of the mountain to **Snow's** and **Bellamy** corner. Thence southward with the **Snow** and **Bellamy** lines so as to include the **Bellamy** place around with my lines to the **Hamilton** corner, on the dividing line between the **Hamilton** lands and **McMinn's** lands. Thence with said dividing line, south course to the end of said dividing line south of the stage road to the corner known as the corner between **Bradley & Hamilton**, so as to include pretty much all the **Hamilton** lands. Thence across the **Ripley** place a south course, a straight line to a corner to be made, two rods west of the spring where the **Widow Grady** lives. Thence a straight line to the **Reed** corners and **Ripley** corners at the corner of the woodland fence on the **Reed** place. Thence with the line of the **Reed** place to the beginning corner on the river.

I also will and devise to my daughter **Ida Netherland** and her husband R. G. **Netherland** my back tract of land known as the mill tract, including the mill, including 100 or 110 acres. Also my interest in the Island Factory property, but not in the proceeds of that business heretofore, only the site, building and machinery is included in this bequest to them. Also, I will and devise to the said **Ida** and her husband my houses and lots situated in Kingsport, Sullivan County, Tennessee, all of which property I devise to them to dispose of as they may think proper.

I also will and devise to the said **Ida Netherland** and her husband the following named negroes which they have now in their possession, and their increase if any (to wit) One negro woman named **Julia Ann**; one negro boy **Jack**, one negro girl named **Lucy**; one negro girl named **Amanda**; one negro girl named **Minta**; one negro man named **Anthony** (sold by R. G. **Netherland** to **Buchanan**), one negro man named **Ransom**; one negro girl named **Ann**, said negroes are all in their possession except **Anthony** heretofore sold to **Buchanan**. Also, one negro boy named **Amos** and one negro boy named **Walter** which they have not yet had possession of.

Also all the stock of every description--household and kitchen furniture, monies advanced or loaned including all the charges entered against them on my Memorandum Books marked "A", before referred to, and release them from the charges of the same.

I also will and devise to the said **Ida Netherland** and her husband... a two horse wagon to be finished in **Wyrick's** Shop and to be paid for off my cash on hand, notes, bonds and judgements remaining after the payment of my indebtedness. Their proportion of the cash on hand to be paid out of the proceeds of the notes when collected by my Executors.

After making the foregoing bequests of the island factory property and one fourth of my cash on hand, notes, bonds and judgements to the said **Ida** and **Robert G. Netherland** I design the same as full compensation for her interest in the **Hugh Leeper** place before mentioned, and it is my will and desire that the said **Ida** and her husband..., as soon after my decease as practicable, execute a deed in fee simple to the said **Frank L. Phipps** for their interest in the **Hugh Leeper** farm, but in the event that they are unwilling and refuse to execute such deed...then it is my will and desire that... **Frank L. Phipps** shall have my interest in the island factory property, and also the one-fourth part of the amount of my cash on hand--notes, bonds and judgements hereinbefore devised to the **Ida** and **Robert G. Netherland**, the one half of a certain lot of horses hereinafter mentioned, also my shotgun and the fixtures belonging thereto.

There is an unsettled transaction between The Honorable **Seth J. W. Lucky** and myself in which he proposes to convey to me the one half of his interest in the copper mines in Carroll County, Virginia to discharge an obligation I hold on him, and should such conveyances hereafter be made, I will and devise said copper interests--the one half to **Frank L. Phipps** and the other half to **Ida Netherland** and R. G. **Netherland**.

Fourthly. I will and devise to my daughter **Nancy B. Bynum**, wife of John G. **Bynum**, the following property now in her possession, to wit: one fine piano, $2,500.00 in money heretofore advanced for her benefit in relation to changing the administration of the Estate of **Orville Bradley**, dec'd. Also about 350 acres or what may remain of the **Ripley** place after taking off a small portion thereon hereinbefore devised to **Ida Netherland** and **Robert G. Netherland**. Also, I will and devise to her a small portion of the **Ross** place lying west of the lands devised to **Ida** and R. G. **Netherland**. I also will and devise to the said **Nancy B. Bynum** the following named negroes which are now in her possession, and their increase if any, to wit: One negro girl named **Queen**; one negro boy named **Ike**; one negro boy named **Dave**; one negro girl named **Rosetta**; one yellow man named **Madison**; one black woman named **Peachy** which property I devise to the said **Nancy B. Bynum** for her own separate use and control.

I also will to **Nancy B. Bynum** all the horses and stock of every description including all the charges made against her on my Memorandum Book marked "A" before referred to and release her from the charges of the same. Also,I will and devise to her a fine gold watch, known as her mother's watch.

I also will and devise to my said daughter **Nancy B. Bynum** and her husband John G. **Bynum**, all the copper interest I now own in Carroll County, Virginia with full liberty to dispose of same.

Fifthly. I will and devise to my son **William Joshua McKinney Phipps**, commonly called **"Mack Phipps"** the remainder of the tract of land on which I now live--lying in Hawkins County, south of the stage road, running from the present ferry landing, after taking off that portion of the same heretofore devised to **Ida** and **Robert G. Netherland**. Also, that portion of my lands known as the Camp Ground lands, and also that portion of my **Hamilton** lands remaining after taking off such portions of said lands as have hereinbefore been devised to **Ida** and **Robert G. Netherland**.

I also will and devise to the said Mack Phipps the one-half of my pre-sent crop on my lands, including all that may be received from my tenants. Also, all the old grain and bacon that may be on the place at my decease. Also, all my farming utensils not herein otherwise dis-posed of, including the thrashing machine, wheat fans &c. Also, a large four horse wagon and one two horse wagon and one horse wagon including every-thing now in use in the cultivation of the farm. Also, the one-half of all the iron that may be left after finishing the wagons herein before devised to Frank L. Phipps and Robert G. Netherland; also the one half of my entire stock of cattle, sheep and hogs. Also, five farm mules...my large gray mare and colt...two gray fillies known as the Miller fillies...one young, brown horse that has been worked, and my four oxen; also my iron safe, my rifle gun and fixtures...also my Colts pistol; also the one half of the hay and rough-ness on my farms. Also, the one half of the furniture—household and kitchen—not hereinafter otherwise disposed of.

I also devise to my son Mack Phipps the following named negroes, to wit: One negro man named Andy; one negro man named Lewis; one negro man named Jack; one negro man named Rufus and his wife Viney and child. Also one negro woman named Maria and her three children, to wit: Sal, Rufus and Mary. I also will and devise to my said son Mack Phipps the one fourth of cash on hand—notes, bonds and judgements that may remain after discharging my indebt-edness as herein before provided for, but the fourth to be paid so far as pos-sible out of the cash that may be on hand.

Sixthly. I will and devise to my wife Ann P. Phipps during her natural life all the lands purchased by me of the bank formerly owned by Rev'd T. A. Ross, lying north of the stage road running from the present ferry landing, including the Ratherwood Mansion, but excepting the factory property now owned by William Powel. And at the death of my wife, the same to descend to our son Mack Phipps, if he should survive her, but if...Mack Phipps should die before his mother, then...said tract of land shall descend to the lawful heirs of Frank L. Phipps and those of Robert G. and Ida Netherland, equally, i.e. each heir to take an equal share of the same.

It is also my will and desire that my wife Ann P. Phipps shall have the following slaves or negroes to be by her disposed of as she may see proper, to wit: one negro woman named Nancy and her child; one negro woman named Matilda and one negro boy named Harry, and Maria. Also one fourth of the amount of any cash on hand—notes, bonds and judgements remaining after dis-charging my indebtedness as herein before provided for. Also my carriage & harness, a two-horse wagon and harness, also my sorrel mare and mule colt, my gray filly known as the Netherland filly and my gray horse known as the "pacing gray", also the one-half of my entire stock of cattle not otherwise disposed of, also the one-half of all my sheep...entire stock of hogs, also one-half of the old grain and bacon on hand, also her sewing machine, also the one half of my household and kitchen furniture—all to be hers and to be disposed of as she may see proper.

It is also my will and desire that my wife shall have the use of the one half of the house we now live in, and the one half of all the furniture therein while she lives or remains single, provided the occupation of the one half of the house by her should be agreeable to our son Mack.

It is further my will and desire that my wife and our son Mack shall carry on their respective farms jointly, and the net proceeds thereof to be divided equally between them, after the payment of school accounts, store

accounts, taxes, physicians' bills &c and settlements thereof to be made an-nually with my Executors at her own house or place of residence.

In case of the death of our son Mack Phipps before his mother without lawful issue, then it is my will and desire that my wife should make her home in the Ratherwood house herein before devised to her, and that the farm lying south of the stage road and hereinbefore devised to Mack Phipps, together with the negroes and monies devised to him that may remain undisposed of shall descend to the lawful children and issue of Frank L. Phipps, and of Robert G. and Ida Netherland—to be equally divided between them share and share alike.

And no matter at what time Mack Phipps should die, if without lawful is-sue, then it is my desire that the farm lying south of the stage road and other lands, property and monies devised to Mack, or so much thereof as re-mains undisposed of, shall descend to the lawful children and issue of Frank L. Phipps and Robert G. and Ida Netherland. But it is not designed by this will to confer the power upon Mack to dispose of either the lands or negroes devised to him provided he should die without leaving issue.

It is further my will and desire that the remainder of my stock of horses, after satisfying the legacies of such stock hereinbefore given to my wife and son Mack shall be equally divided between Robert G. and Ida Netherland and Frank L. Phipps who shall make the division among themselves, excepting my mare called Lalla Rookh and the black horse known as Poney's colt which are not to be embraced in said division. The black horse, Poney's colt I will and devise to my nephew Nate Phipps and the mare Lalla Rookh I at pre-sent make no disposition of.

It is further my will and desire that my wife Ann P. Phipps shall have the control and management of our son Mack's estate until he shall become of age, or until she shall marry, and that she be not required to give bond un-less it should hereafter become manifest that his estate was likely to be lost or diminished for want of proper management, and upon the happening of such contingency, it is my will that she enter into bond and security as the law requires, or that she surrender the custody of the same to a properly ap-pointed Guardian. But before my wife shall receive from my Executors the Estate of our son Mack, a perfect inventory of everything she may so receive should be made out and filed with the papers of my Estate by my Executors, and she shall be required to make settlement annually with my Executors of the Estate of our son Mack Phipps at her own house.

It is further my will and direction that my Executors in making col-lections of the judgements now due me that they at least collect in gold or silver so much of said judgements as may be necessary to pay off and discharge the legacies herein before devised in money to my son Mack and my wife.

And lastly, I do hereby nominate and appoint Joseph B. Heiskell, Esq., Frank L. Phipps, my son, and Robert G. Netherland, Executors of this my last Will and Testament and direct that the said Heiskell shall be liberally com-pensated for the services he may render connected with the execution of my will.

In testimony whereof I have hereunto subscribed my name and affixed my seal on this 3rd day of July, 1861.

Joshua Phipps (seal)

Signed, sealed and acknowledged in our presence, and in the presence of the Testator the 3rd day of July, 1861.

James A. Neil, Wm. Powell, J. Netherland.

Codicil to Will of Joshua Phipps

For the purpose of avoiding any difficulty in the construction of my foregoing will and of making some further provision in relation to my property, I do further make and publish this codicil to my foregoing will.

1st. In specifying the property given to **Robert G. Netherland** and **Ida Netherland** his wife, in lieu of the **Leeper** place, I desire to include the Mill place in addition to the other property mentioned...and in case they fail and refuse to make the conveyance therein before provided, the said mill with the other property devised over in that event shall go to **Frank L. Phipps.**

2nd. In the several devises to the children of **Frank L. Phipps** and **Robert G. & Ida Netherland**, in the event that my son **Mack** dies without issue, it is intended that each child of **Frank L. Phipps** shall take equally with each child of **Robert G. & Ida Netherland** per capita, and that all the children by **Ida**--whether by **Robert G. Netherland** or any future husband, shall be included and take equally with the children of **Frank L. Phipps**, and in the event any of the said children now living or to be hereafter born, shall die before the said **Mack** leaving issue, then such issue shall take the share such deceased child would have taken on the death of said **Mack** without issue in the life time of such child.

3rd. As it may become necessary for **Mack Phipps** to dispose of his negroes from time to time for mis-conduct, power is hereby conferred on him to sell or exchange such negroes as may become refractory, and in the event other causes exist for a sale of any of said negroes, such sale may be made by said **Mack** with the concurrance...of my Executors, or a majority of them, or of the survivor of them, and in that event they shall require the fund arising therefrom to be invested to be held according to the provisions of my will.

4th. In the devise of my lands to the said **Robert G. Netherland** and wife **Ida**,it is not my intention to make the Estate of **Robert G. Netherland** in the event he survives **Ida**, a fee simple Estate, but he shall hold the same for his natural life only, and upon his decease the same shall descend to the children of **Ida**, or her heirs at law.

5th. It is not my intention that the Guardian of my son **Mack** shall dispose of the stock bequeathed to him so much as may be necessary as his proportion to stock the farm, and the increase or such stock as it may from time to time be advisable to sell shall be by the Guardian disposed of in her discretion, at private or public sale. The stock of **Mack** and my wife **Ann P. Phipps** may be kept in common or divided as shall be considered best by my Executors.

6th. In drawing the bequest to my wife of cattle, a different mode of expression is adopted from that and as to other stock said bequest is intended to give to her one half of my whole stock of cattle, the other half being given **Mack.**

7th. I enjoin it upon the Guardian of my son **Mack** to take good care of my old servant **Andy**, that he be not overworked or exposed, but be employed in the oversight and feeding of stock, attending to the fields &c, lighter duties suited to his age and faithful character.

8th. It is my desire that my Executors named in my will shall not be required to give security for the performance of their duties, unless some event subsequent to my decease shall in the opinion of the Court make the same necessary and proper.

10th (there was no 9th). It is my desire that my son **Mack** be liberally educated and so much of his property as may be necessary to carry out this object to the fullest extent practicable shall be appropriated by his Guardian to that purpose.

11th. **Robert G. Netherland** and wife **Ida** shall have power during their joint lives to dispose of the lands devised to them by deed executed by them jointly and proved and acknowledged according to the law for disposing of the Estates of married women.

12th. I give and bequeath to **Robert G. Netherland** and **F. L. Phipps** my interest in the apparatus purchased for the **Ratherwood** Seminary.

13th. I give to **Robert G. Netherland** my gold-headed cane.

In testimony whereof I have set my hand and seal This 4th of July, 1861.

Joshua Phipps(seal)

Signed and sealed in presence of us, we attesting the same in presence of the Testator and of each other by his request.

Eldridge Hord, J. Netherland

COPY OF JONATHAN ROBERTS' WILL

Page 413   Dated: September 28, 1789

In the Name of God, Amen.

I **Jonathan Roberts** of Hawkins County on Holston River and State of North Carolina, am very sick and weak in body, but of perfect mind and memory, thanks be given unto God. Calling to mind the mortality of my body and knowing that it is appointed for all men once to die, do make and ordain this my last Will & Testament, that is to say: principally and first of all, I give and recommend my soul unto the hands of Almighty God that gave it and my body I commend to the Earth to be buried at the discretion of my Executors, nothing doubting but at the General Resurrection I shall receive the same again by the mighty power of God, and as to touching such worldly estate wherewith it has pleased God to bless me in this life, I give and devise and dispose in the following manner and form.

I give and bequeath to **Phebey** my dearly beloved wife 100 acres of land whereon I now dwell, together with my movable estate by her freely to be possessed and enjoyed, and I do hereby utterly disallow, revoke and disannul all and every other Testament, will, legacies, bequeaths & Executors by me before in anywise made.

In witness whereof I have set my hand and seal This 28th day of Sept. in the year of our Lord one thousand seven hundred and eighty nine.

Jonathan x Roberts (seal)
(his mark)

Signed sealed and delivered.

John x Roberts, Wm. x Mooney, Moses x Dodson
  (his mark)   (his mark)   (his mark)

(No Certificate Attached)

WILL OF THOMAS ROGERS

Page 414   Dated: Sept. 9, 1811

In the Name of God, Amen.

I, **Thomas Rogers** of the County of Hawkins and State of Tennessee, being very sick in body and in perfect mind and memory, being given up to God, calling unto mind the memory of my body and knowing that it is appointed for all men once to die, do make and ordain this to be my last Will & Testament, that is to say; principally and first of all, I give and recommend my soul unto the hand of God that gave it & body I recommend to the earth, to be buried in a decent Christian burial <u>to</u> the discretion of my friends, nothing doubting but at the General Resurrection I shall receive the same again by the mighty power of God, and as touching such worldly estate wherewith it hath pleased God to bless me in this life, I give, devise & dispose of the same in the following manner & form:

First. I give and bequeath to my dearly beloved wife a sartain brown mare and one red cow and one feather bed and furniture, together with all my household goods and furniture by her to be possessed.

Second. I give and bequeath unto my two sons **Daswel** and **Thomas Rogers** all my lands and buildings and possessions to be equally divided between them, the said **Daswel** and **Thomas** forever firmly to be possessed by them.

Also my still and (?) fixing &c.

Thirdly. I give and bequeath unto my four daughters, to wit: **Martha, Betty & Susanna & Maley** all the remainder of goods and livestock and all just debts that are owing to me after paying all just debts that I owe, unto the four above mentioned girls, by them forever to be possessed. And I do hereby truly disallow, revoke & disannul all other forever Testaments, wills, legacies, bequaths & Executors by me in any wise before named, willed, bequeathed, ratifying and confirming this and no other to be my last Will and Testament. In witness whereof I have hereunto set my hand this 9 day of September in the year of our Lord 1000 eight hundred and eleven. Signed, published and delivered in presence of:

Thomas Rogers (seal)

Wm. Nichols
John Monk

WILL OF JOHN RICE, SEN'R.

Page 415

Dated: Sept. 18, 1811.

In the Name of God, Amen.

I **John Rice, Sen'r**, being for some time past in a declining state of health but of sound mind and memory, and calling to mind the mortality of all men—that it is appointed unto all men once to die—do by these presents declare, ratify and announce my last Will & Testament in the manner following, to wit: After commending my soul to God and my body to the dust from whence it came, to be buried in a decent and Christian manner, hoping they will be again united at the General Resurrection and received into the favor of God. I do bequeath and dispose of all my worldly goods and chattels in the following manner.

First. I allow all my just debts to be paid. I give and bequeath to my daughter **Sally** three dollars, thirty-three cents. To my son **Edward**, three dollars, thirty-three cents. To my son **William** three dollars, thirty-three cents. To my daughter **Elizabeth** three dollars, thirty-three cents. To my son **John** three dollars, thirty-three cents. To my daughter **Anney**, one hundred dollars. To my son **Shelton**, three dollars and thirty-three cents. To my daughter **Polly**, one hundred dollars. To my son **Dangerfield**, three dollars, three cents. To my son **Reuben**, three dollars, thirty-three cents. To my son **Drury**, three dollars, thirty-three cents. The balance of my Estate I give to my daughter **Agness**.

I do nominate and appoint my trusty friends **Michael Looney** and **David Coldwell** to execute this my last Will & Testament, revoking all former wills by me made heretofore to be null and void and declaring this to be my last Will & Testament. Given under my hand and seal this 18th day of September in the year of our Lord, 1811.

John x Rice (seal)
(his mark)

Witness: Michael Looney, David Coldwell, B. Coldwell.

Page 416

WILL OF BARTHOLIMEW REASON

Dated: December 3, 1814

Bartholimew Reason desires that December the 3rd, 1814: know all men by these presents that I make **Ezekiel Sullivan** lawful power of atturnie in all that he posses, lands and bons, notes on due bills and all that he now possesses and after all his contracts settled, all cousts and charges settled the remainder of my astate I leave in the hands of said **Sullivan** to dispose of as his own property until **Benjamin Reason**, son of **Bartholimew Reason** - 20 one years of age the 24th day of October last, comes to take it of my hands when of set lay.

Bartholimew x Reason (seal)
(his mark)

Test: James Anderson, Peter Anderson

And if said Reason recovers health this will be his one [agent] [see original].

Page 416

WILL OF CORNELIUS REGAN

Dated: May 19, 1816

In the name of the Blessed Almighty Father, son and Holy Ghost, Amen. I, **Cornelius Regan** of Hawkins County and State of Tennessee, considering the uncertainty of this mortal life and being of sound and perfect mind and memory, blessed be Almighty God for the same, do make and publish this my last Will & Testament in the manner and form following, viz: I will and bequeath unto my dearly beloved wife **Annie Regan** all my Estate both real and personal of what nature and kind soever, that is to say, household and kitchen furniture, the service of my negro girl **Lucy**, my debts due, my stock of cattle and hogs &c, and the benefit of all, to be enjoyed by her during her natural life, all to be taken care of by my Executor for her use. Also the money due upon bonds when received to be put out to use and the interest thereof to be applied to her support and maintenance by my Executor. And after her—my said wife's decease—all that exists or remains of my said estate or any increase thereof to pass to my son in law, **Henry Sampson Larkin** whom I constitute my sole heir and my Executor of this my last Will and Testament. It is also my will that my just debts be paid and it is likewise my request and most earnest desire that my said heir, **Henry S. Larkin** at his decease will not leave—now mine—then his poor servant **Lucy** in bondage nor send her away empty, but according as God may bless him in this world to contribute to her support in the evening of her life, and if she should have any increase to issue to let all them go free at the age of 30 years or sooner. And I hereby revoke all former wills by me made. In witness whereof I have hereunto set my hand and seal this 10th day of May, 1816. Interlined by the Testator.

Cornelius Regan (seal)

Signed, sealed published & declared by the above said **Cornelius Regan** to be his last Will & Testament in our presence who at his request and in his presence have hereunto subscribed our names as witnesses to the same.
John Galbraith, William King, Philip King

Page 417

WILL OF JOSEPH RUSSELL

Dated: November 20, 1811

In the Name of God, Amen.

I **Joseph Russell** of the County of Hawkins and State of Tennessee, being of sound mind and perfect memory, but of infirm health have thought it expedient to make this my last Will & Testament, and have bequeathed unto my widow during her natural life her choice of the building she now occupies or to have such made for her on any part of the land I have left to my son **Joseph Russell** as shall be comfortable, and at his expense. Also two negro slaves by the names of **Jinny** and **Tennessee**, to be disposed of as she may think proper at her death. Also one riding creature and two cows, to be delivered her out of my Estate, and my son **Joseph** is to find her a good sufficient maintenance. I also appoint her Executrix to this my last Will and Testament.

I give and bequeath unto my son **William Russell** $100.00; also unto my son **Alexander Russell**, I give and bequeath $200.00. Also unto my son **Benjamin Russell**, I give and bequeath $300.00. Also unto my son **James Russell**, I give and bequeath $300.00. Also unto my daughter **Betsy Myers**, wife of **Jacob Myers**, I give and bequeath $300.00, to be paid in two years. But should the said **Jacob Myers** remove himself and family sooner, the foregoing sum to be paid on leaving the country. I also give to her husband an anville, vice and bellows which are now in his possession. Also, unto my son **Moses Russell**, I give and bequeath $300.00. All the foregoing sums are exclusive of (what) has already been paid. Also, I give and bequeath unto my daughter **Polly Russell** a negro girl named or called **Lucy**, a mare called hers, two cows, a bed with sufficient furniture or a horse to (be) valued at $100.00, and $100.00 to be paid in four years. Also I give and bequeath to my son **Joseph Russell** all my real and personal Estate except that which has heretofore been named, and desire him to be my Executor to act with his mother who has been appointed Executrix in a foregoing clause, and desire them to pay all debts justly due from my Estate and collect all debts due and faithfully pay off and perform all things required by this my last Will & Testament. To all which I have hereby set my hand and seal this 20th day of November, 1816

Joseph x Russell (seal)
(his mark)

Test: **Jno A. Rogers, James Bagan,**
     William Bradley

WILL OF ROBERT ROBINSON

Page 418   Dated: June 16, 1828

Be it remembered that I, **Robert Robinson** of Hawkins County, State of Tenn., considering the uncertainty of this mortal life and the certainty of death, and being much afflicted and diseased in body yet sound in mind and memory, do make the following my last Will & Testament and being duly impressed with the belief of a state of Immortality beyond the grave, I would first command my Immortal Spirit to God who gave it, and after death that my mortal remains be decently interred.

All my property I wish disposed of in the following manner, to wit:

1st. I give and bequeath unto my wife **Polly Lewis Robinson** all my household furniture consisting of three beds and furniture, 1 Bureau, the kitchen furniture with all the other articles not here mentioned. I give and bequeath unto her the Loom and all the necessary implements for weaving – of my farming utensils I give unto her, 1 shovel plough, 1 set of gears & necessary implements for ploughing. I give unto her 2 hoes, 1 mallock, 1 log chain, 1 handsaw, 1 chopping axe, 1 drawing knife & 2 chisels, and of my stock I give unto her one horse creature--her choice-- 2 cows & calves, 5 head of sheep, 15 head of hogs, the flock of geese & all the poultry. I also give unto her the present crop now growing consisting of wheat, rye, oats, corn & flax &

all other things not herein mentioned now growing on the farm. The rest of my personal property I will that it be sold according to law & after all my just debts are paid the residue to be divided equally between my wife **Polly Lewis** & my three children, namely: **Emaline, John Ellis & Nancy**. I also bequeath unto my wife **Polly Lewis (Robinson)** two tracts of land containing 50 acres each, adjoining the place where I live, her to dispose of them at her own discretion &c. In testimony whereof I have hereunto set my hand and seal This 16th day of June, 1828. In presence of:

William Armstrong, Jacob Felkner,   **Robert Robinson** (seal)
James Amis

WILL OF HORACE RICE

Page 419   Dated: October 8, 1830

I **Horace Rice** of the County of Hawkins and State of Tennessee, being of sound mind and memory but somewhat afflected in body and being desirous of settling my Estate by devise while in perfect memory, do make, ordain and publish this my last Will & Testament in manner and form following, to wit:

First. It is my will and desire and I hereby will and bequeath unto my mother **Keziah Rice** a decent maintenance during her natural life--in sickness and in health--to be paid by my Executor hereinafter named out of my effects that may come to his hands or mine.

Second. I will and bequeath to my brother **Orville Rice** in consideration of the natural love and affection I have for him, my tract of land commonly known as the **McAlister** tract, situated--lying and being in the County of Monroe and State of Tennessee, between the Little Tennessee and Hiwassee Rivers, adjoining Lickrot on the east, containing about 320 acres, more or less, to him and his heirs forever.

Third. I will and bequeath and it is my desire that my Executor hereinafter named pay to **Robert Carden** the sum of $500.00 in consideration of services rendered by the said **Carden** to me, while debilitated in body. Yet, I wish it distinctly understood that if a settlement takes place between said **Carden** and myself and I should make what I consider satisfaction to him for said services, then and in that case, nothing is to pass by this devise.

Fourth. I will and bequeath unto my brother **Orville Rice** all the rest and residue of my estate both real and personal and mixed of whatever kind, after all my just and lawful debts are paid. To him and his heirs forever. I hereby nominate and appoint my brother **Orville Rice** Executor to this my last Will and Testament, but wish it understood that no security is to be required of him for the true performance of the trust.

Witness my hand & seal this Seventh November, 1829.

Horace Rice (seal)

James M. Hawery, P. Parsons

I, **Horace Rice**, having (according to the conditions of the foregoing will mentioned in the third bequest giving unto **Robert Carden** the sum of $500.00 in consideration of services rendered me while in a state of debility) made a settlement with the said **Robert Carden** and having paid...(him) in full for all services rendered to me up to this date, do hereby revoke the said third bequest in the foregoing will and do declare the same null and void to all intents and purposes.

In testimony whereof I have hereunto set my hand & seal This 8th day of October in the year of our Lord, one thousand eight hundred and thirty.

Horace Rice (seal)

Signed, sealed and published and declared in presence of:
Test: **P. Parsons, James M. Hawery**

WILL OF JAMES ROSE

Page 420

Dated: June 1, 1831

In the Name of God, Amen

I James Rose of the County of Hawkins and State of Tennessee, now being well stricken in years, considering the uncertainty of life and the certainty of death, do at this time feel myself possessed of sound mind and memory and being possessed with a small portion of worldly affairs, I am desirous to dispose of the same as hereunder written, and I do avow and own this my last Will & Testament, revoking all former Testaments by me heretofore made or acknowledged as I wish to dispose of my property as her described. First, I bequeath my soul to God and secondly, after my death, if I should be indebted, all my just debts to be paid. After my funeral expenses is paid if anything is required, then the balance I will and bequeath to Benjamin Bunch my trusty friend consisting of a tract of land lying and being in the County of Grayson and State of Virginia on the waters of New River, estimated at 140 acres of land being the same I purchased from John Welch, Senr., and also a variety of notes and accounts due me in said County of Grayson and in the County of Hawkins, State of Tennessee, and all and singular my worldly affairs that I now am possessed of with the exception of a pension allowed me for my services as a soldier in the Revolution War which I will and bequeath to my trusty friend Benjamin Bunch, and acknowledge this my last Will and decree. Witness my hand and seal. Sealed signed dated and delivered in presence of this the first day of June in the year of our Lord one thousand eight hundred and thirty one.

NB The pension above described I reserve for my own use free from this will. Witness my hand and seal.

James x Rose (seal)
(his mark)

Test: William x Goodman, Neill x Goodman
(his mark)   (his mark)

WILL OF RICHARD ROBERTSON

Page 421

Dated: June 21, 1831

In the Name of God, Amen.

I, Richard Robertson of Hawkins County, State of Tennessee, one of the United States of America, being of sound mind and memory, do make, ordain and declare this instrument which is subscribed with my own name to be my last Will & Testament, revoking all others.

Imprimis. All of my debts of which there are but few and none of magnitude are to be punctually and speedily paid, and the legacies hereinafter bequeathed are to be paid as soon as circumstances will permit, and in the manner directed.

Item. To my dearly beloved wife Mary Robertson, I give and bequeath my whole estate both real and personal during her natural life or widowhood. My wife Mary is required to raise and school my son Caleb out of the aforesaid personal property until he is 21 years of age, then he is to have a good horse, saddle and bridle out of the personal property which I have left in the hands of my wife. Also, my son Caleb is to have a good feather bed and furniture, also a good cow and calf when he arrives at the age of 21. Also my said wife with my Executors hereinafter named is hereby empowered to collect and receive all money due me on bonds, notes or otherwise. Also, my s'd wife and Executors are empowered to sell any of the personal property they may think proper &c after my son Caleb has received what is above named to him.

I will that my wife Mary have, hold possess &c the balance of my estate both real and personal during her natural lifetime or widowhood, and if my s'd wife Mary should marry, my will is that my Executors shall take charge of s'd Estate until my son Caleb become 21 years of age, at which time my will is that my real Estate be equally divided between my sons, to wit: John, Richard T., James, William, Hezekiah, Jesse and Caleb Robertson. And further, I will that my personal estate be equally divided between my daughters, to wit: Nancy Boatman, Dorcas Perkpile, Sary Austin, Jane Crosby, Mary Talley, Elizabeth Talley, Laming Harriet and Matilda Harrier. And further, I appoint my loving wife Mary Robertson my lawful Executrix, and John Robertson and Charles Talley Executors of this my last Will & Testament, hereby disannulling all former wills by me made, and ratify and confirm this my last Will & Testament. Signed, sealed, published and declared by the said Richard Robertson to be his last Will & Testament in the presence of us this twenty first day of June in the year of our Lord, eighteen hundred and thirty-one.

Richard x Robertson
(his mark)

Witness:
John Donaldson, Benoni Talley, Richard T. x Robertson
(his mark)

WILL OF MICHAEL ROARK/ROCK

Page 422

Dated: August 25, 1834
Proven: Feb. 4, 1839

In the Name of God, Amen. I Michael Roark of the County of Hawkins and State of Tennessee, being somewhat weak of body but of sound mind and memory, and knowing the uncertainty of life, do make and ordain this my last Will & Testament in manner following, to wit:

Item 1st. I bequeath to my son James Rock one dollar and no more.

Item 2nd. To my daughter Sally Combs who intermarried with Elijah Combs I bequeath one dollar and no more.

Item 3rd. To my son Michael Rock I bequeath one dollar and no more.

Item 4th. To my daughter Rebecca Tunnel who intermarried with William Tunnel, I bequeath one dollar and no more.

Item 5th. To my daughter Betsy who intermarried with Thomas Self, I bequeath one dollar and no more.

Item 6th. To my daughter Sally Reynolds who intermarried with George Reynolds, I bequeath one dollar and no more.

Item 7th. To my daughter Julia Kirkpatrick who intermarried with John Kirkpatrick, I bequeath one dollar and no more.

Item 8th. To my daughter Polly Morrisett who intermarried with George Morrisett, I bequeath one dollar and no more. And it is my wish and desire that she remain on the plantation on which I now reside as long as I or my wife survive should she choose so to do.

Item 9th. It is my wish and I so will it that my wife—should she survive me—is to remain on my plantation, use and enjoy it as long as she lives.

Item 10th. To my well beloved grandson James Rock (son of John Rock), I will and bequeath the tract or parcel of land on which I now reside, to him and his heirs forever, but he is not to have possession until the death of myself and wife—reserving the use of it for our maintenance. Also, I bequeath to him all my personal effects of every description, subject to the payment of my just debts.

Item 11th. To my well beloved son John Rock, I bequeath four shares of the tract of land I bought of the heirs of Charles Campbell joining the tract

I live on and containing about 150 acres.

Item 12th. I do hereby appoint my well-beloved son John and my beloved grandson James Rork my Executors to this my last Will & Testament, and I wish them to qualify and enter upon their duties without giving bond and security, in believing that they will faithfully perform the trust hereby imposed on them. I hereby commit my soul unto the hands of a merciful God before whom I must shortly appear.

In testimony whereof I have hereunto set my hand & seal This 25th day of August, 1834.

Signed, sealed delivered &   Michael Rork
published as the last Will
& Testament of Michael Rork
in our presence date above.
D Alexander, Joseph Mooney

WILL OF ELLEN ROGERS

Page 424   Dated: August 17, 1837
In the Name of God, Amen.

I Ellen Rogers of the County of Hawkins and town of Rogersville, being in feeble health but of sound mind & memory do make and publish this my last Will & Testament.

First. I give and bequeath to Eliza Cocke, wife of Frederick Cocke the tract of land willed to me by my father James Forgey, lying on the south side of Holston River above Surgoinesville to her, her heirs and assigns forever.

Second. I give and bequeath to my daughter Matilda Rogers my negro girl Elsey which was willed to me by my father James Forgey, to her, her heirs and assigns forever.

Lastly. I constitute and appoint Frederick Cocke Executor to this, my last Will & Testament. In testimony whereof I have hereunto set my hand and seal The 17th day of August, 1837.

                                    Ellen Rogers (seal)
Signed, sealed published and declared in
the presence of: John Cocke, G. McCraw

WILL OF THOMAS ROBERTS

Page 424   Dated: June 6, 1841
                                    Proven: Aug. Term, 1842

In the Name of God, Amen.

I, Thomas Roberts of Hawkins County, the State of Tennessee, being of bad health but of sound mind, I make this my last Will & Testament in words following, to wit: I will and bequeath to my beloved wife Matilda Roberts during her lifetime or widowhood, the plantation where I now live, to have all profits arising from the same. Also, all my personal property of all kinds out doors and in the house, not to be sold nor squandered by any person with the exception of some things hereafter mentioned. I will and bequeath to my son James Roberts one sorrel filly the one that he claims, also one rifle gun. And at my death to a saddle and bridle and martins gills and my great coat. I will and bequeath to my daughter Elizabeth one bed and furniture and one cow. And I also upon the condition that William Pety lives here till he is 21, he is to have a colt worth $20.00

or $25.00. And I will that at the death of my wife that Mary Mooney have $10.00 worth of property. The heirs of Theoffolous Roberts to have $10.00 worth of property, William Roberts $10.00 worth of property. Tomson Roberts to have $10.00 worth of property. Nathaniel Roberts to have $10.00 worth of property, and Wiley Roberts to have $10.00 worth of property, and I also will if my daughter Elizabeth and my son James lives with and takes care of me and my wife during our lifetime, then at our death James is to have all my farming tools and all the balance of my   and all the personal property to be divided equally between the said Elizabeth & James Roberts. Whereof I have hereunto set my hand and affix my seal. This 6th day of June, 1841.

                                    Thomas x Roberts (seal)
Witness: Martin Phillips, Abram Baun   (his mark)

WILL OF NANCY ROUSE

Page 425   Dated: June 13, 1842

I Nancy Rouse do make and publish this my last Will and Testament hereby revoking and making void all other wills by me at any time made. First of all, I direct that my funeral expenses and all my debts be paid as soon after my death as possible out of any money that I may die possessed of, or may first come into the hands of my Executors. Secondly, I give and bequeath to my beloved son, John Rouse, my tract of land, lying on the south side of Clinch Mountain in Little Poor Valley, also on the left prong of Cove Creek, beginning and running as follows:

Beginning on a poplar and hickory on or near Michael's corner, then south forty one, east fifty poles to an oak and beech. Then north fifty five, east two hundred and eight poles to a stake. Then north thirty, east one hundred poles to a stake. Then north sixty five, east twenty poles to a stake on Shanks' line. Then north thirty, west forty poles to a stake. Then south fifty, west three hundred and thirty five poles to the beginning. And, thirdly, I will and bequeath to Mary Smith & Elizabeth Purcell & Nancy Hart my beloved daughters, equally, all my household and kitchen furniture, and fourthly, I will and bequeath that all my horses and cattle and hogs and all other plantation property that I may die possessed of may be equally divided between all my children.

In witness whereof I do set my hand and seal This June 13th, 1842.

                                    Nancy x Rouse (seal)
Signed and sealed and published   (her mark)
in our presence & we have subscribed
our names here in the presence of the Testator: James Y. Campbell(seal) and
Silas Campbell (seal)

WILL OF JOHN RIGGS

Page 426   Dated: January 31, 1849
In the Name of God, Amen.

I, John Riggs of the County of Hawkins and State of Tennessee, being in a bad state of health, but of sound mind and memory, blessed be God, do make and publish this my last Will & Testament in manner and form following, to wit:

First. After all my funeral expenses and all my debts are paid, I do then give and bequeath unto my beloved wife Mary W. Riggs all the land that I am now seized and possessed of. I also do give and bequeath unto my said wife Mary W. Riggs my black girl named Emily during her natural life or widowhood.

It is also my will that after my funeral expenses and debts are paid that the residue of my personal property go to my s'd wife Mary W. Riggs during her natural life or widowhood for the purpose of enabling her to raise and school my children with the exception of such negroes as I may now set a-part: It is my will that my black boy named Major and my black girl named Tabitha be sold at public sale to the highest bidder on a twelve months' credit: the proceeds of sale applied to the use of paying my debts. After my debts are paid to be put at interest for the benefit of my heirs, namely: William E. D. Johns, a son that my wife had by her former husband: Samuel T. Riggs, James V. Riggs, Pleasant Marion Riggs, and my daughter Louisa J. Riggs, my heirs at law. After the death or marriage of my said wife Mary W. Riggs, it is my will that all my personal property shall be sold by my Executor and the proceeds equally divided amongst my s'd sons and daughters, share and share alike.

Lastly. I do nominate and appoint Franklin G. Taylor my Executor.

In witness whereof I do to this my last Will set my hand and seal this 31st day of January, 1849. Interlined before signing.

John Riggs (seal)

Signed, sealed and published in our presence and we have subscribed our names hereto in the presence of the Testator this 31st day of January, 1849.

John H. Cockerham, William x Roberson
(his mark)

WILL OF WILLIAM ROBERTS

Page 427   Dated: None given

Know all men by these presents that I William Roberts do by these presents, now being in my proper mind, as my last Will & Testament. I do give to my three children, Claiborn, Susanna and Elizabeth Roberts an equal portion of estate when they grow to the years of maturity that the rest of my children has had which sum I now estimate at $120.00 each and the balance of my estate real and personal I bequeath to my wife Jane Roberts and my three children during her widowhood, at which time my wife Jane doth marry again after my three above described children shall have received their part of my Estate as above directed then my wife is to have an equal part with my children.

Witness my hand and seal.   (his mark)
William x Roberts (seal)

Test: Joseph Baker, Daniel Bloomer, Ezekiel Robinson
NB I do by these presents constitute and appoint Daniel Bloomer, William Willing, Joseph Roberts Trustees of my Estate.

Joseph Baker   William x Roberts
(his mark)

WILL OF GEORGE ROGERS, SR.

Page 427
Dated: Mar. 23, 1853
Proven: July Term, 1853

In the Name of God, Amen. I George Rogers, Sen. being called to mind the uncertainty of life and the certainty of death and now of being of sound mind and disposing mem—ory, I now make this my last Will and Testament, to wit:

First. I direct that all my just debts and funeral expenses be paid out of any moneys that I may die seized and possessed of. Should I not have on hand money enough to pay and satisfy the above mentioned expenses, then I direct my Executor to first collect my debts and if there is not enough to pay my just debts, I desire that my Executor sell enough of the personal property that will come into his hands hereafter to ____ the remainder if there should be any.

Secondly. I will it and it is my will that my negro man Peter be free at my death.

Thirdly. I will it and it is my will that my son Robert Rogers have all my personal property at my death, to wit: Three head of horses and their increase and about eleven head of cattle and their increase and some sheep and thirty five or forty head of stock hogs and their increase, and all the other personal property that I may die seized or possessed of or may come in-to my hands hereafter.

Fourthly. I will and it is my will that my daughter Manila, wife of Pleasant Bigley, have one good feather bed and furniture.

Fifth and Lastly. I do hereby appoint my son Robert Rogers Executor of my last Will and Testament.

In witness whereof I do to this my last will set my hand and seal. This the twenty third of March in the year of our Lord one thousand eight hundred and fifty-three. Signed and sealed in our presence and we have subscribed our names hereunto in the presence of the Testator this 23rd March, 1853.

George x Rogers (seal)
(his mark)

Witnesses: Samuel Amyx, F. W. Burton, Elizabeth x Everhart, J. A. Wilder
(her mark)

WILL OF EMELINE ROGERS

PAGE 428
Dated: Nov. 5, 1856
Proven in Part Aug. & Sept, 1857
[Rec'd p. 67 and p. 81]

I, Emeline Rogers of the County of Hawkins and State of Tennessee, do make and publish this my last Will and Testament hereby revoking and making void all former wills by me at any time made.

First. I direct that my body be decently interred at Robert Rogers' in said county in a manner suitable to my condition in life and that my funeral expenses be paid as soon after my decease as possible out of any money that I may die possessed of or may first come into the hands of my Executor from any portion of my Estate, real or personal.

Secondly. I give and bequeath to my only son Anderson C. Rogers the re-mainder of all my Estate real or personal consisting of notes and receipts and one rone mare, a quantity of sheep with household and kitchen furniture. My wish and desire is that all my Estate shall be sold, every part thereof on a credit of twelve months, and the money loaned at interest and that my Executors renew the notes every twelve months for the benefit of my only son Anderson C. Rogers who was born the 25th day of May, 1851.

Thirdly. It is my will and desire that my son Anderson C. Rogers remain and live with my mother until he is 21 years old provided she lives until that time, and if she should die before my son arrives at the age of 21, I want my son to live with Prutlee Pearson provided he Prutlee has a home and is settled, and if he has not a home, I want my son to live with my sister and

Catherine Burton, if she has a home. If not with **Matison Cope** and his wife Jane.

Fourthly. It is my wish and desire for **John H. Pearson** to be Guardian of my son until **Prurlee Pearson** arrives at the age of 21 years, then my wish is that **Prurlee Pearson** be appointed Guardian in place of **John H. Pearson**.

Fifthly. It is my wish and desire in case my son **Anderson C. Rogers** should die before he arrives at the age of 21 years, that my beloved mother **Elizabeth Pearson**, if living, shall have my entire Estate, and if she is not living, then to be equally divided between my brothers and sisters that may be living.

And, lastly, I appoint my friend **John H. Pearson** my Executor of this my last Will and Testament.

In testimony whereof I, **Emeline Rogers** have set my hand and seal This 8th day of November, 1856.

Emeline Rogers

Attest: **John Starnes, Wm. Hutchisson**

WILL OF ROBERT ROGERS

Page 430

Dated: March 14, 1858
Proven: Apr. Term. 1858

Hawkins County, Tennessee

I, **Robert Rogers, Sen'r.** do make and publish this as my last Will and Testament hereby revoking and making void all other wills by me made at any time.

First. I direct that all my funeral expenses and all my debts be paid as soon after my death as possible out of any money that I may die possessed of or may first come into the hands of my Executor.

Second. I give and bequeath to **A. L. Rogers**, my son, a tract of land No. 1 in District No. 2, containing 80 acres more or less. There is a note to be credited out of the value of the said land for $150.00, or over perhaps, I think that is now in the hands of **George Powel**. This I give and bequeath to **Pleasant L. Rogers**, my son. The same number of acres in district No. 2 in being a portion of the same lot. Credits out of the same for the sum of between fifty and sixty dollars I think. The amount of the said credits to be paid to **Mariah Rogers** and her two children, to wit: _____? **Rogers** and **Arthur Rogers**.

Fourth. I give and bequeath to my son **Robert Rogers** 120 acres more or less out of the old home. Same tract of land in District No. 2. The land to be divided by a surveyor and marked.

Fifth. I give and bequeath to **Mariah Rogers** my daughter being part of the same tract of land, fifty acres be the same more or less. It is my wish that the County Court of this county will appoint a County Surveyor and three impartial free holders to lay off and divide the same lands in proportion to the amount herein given to each one. It is my will that my son **John Rogers** be allowed $1,200.00 out of the property sold at my sale, or that may come into the hands of my Executors hereafter. It is my will and desire that **Anderson C. Rogers** my grandson be allowed $500.00 whenever he becomes the age of 21 years or more. Now if the said **Anderson C. Rogers** should die before he arrives at the age of 21 years, then the amount that is given him to be divided between my heirs equally. It is my will and desire that my black girls **Mandy** and **Margaret** be sold at my death on a credit of twelve months to the highest and best bidder. It is my will and desire that my upper tract of land from the marked line on the top of the ridge running

with the spur to the top of Clinch Mountain be sold on a twelve months' credit to the highest bidder—supposed to be 200 acres more or less. It is my will and desire that my wife **Catherine Rogers** shall have the following named slaves, to wit: **Silvey, Albert, William** and **Tom** and their increase, during her natural lifetime or widowhood, and if she should marry, then the property is to be taken and sold on a credit of twelve months to the highest bidder to pay the debts then on hand, and the residue to be equally divided between my lawful heirs. Now, if there is not property enough sold to pay my debts in the amount that I have willed to be sold, and to pay the amount that is given in money, it is my will and desire that there should be a sufficient number of slaves sold to pay the amount that is due. I will to my wife **Catherine Rogers** one gray mare and colt. I furthermore will to my son **Robert Rogers** one sorrel colt. The balance of my stock to be sold and all other property except that my wife is entitled to by law to be sold on a twelve months' credit to the highest bidder. My daughter **maria** has a filly that she is entitled to by law. **Peter Rogers**, a man of color owes me $100.00, his part for prosecuting a suit where he was a party concerned, and it is my will that my Executors should collect the same and apply it to paying my debts and...

Secondly. I appoint my son **A. L. Rogers** and **John A. Wilder** my Exec's. In witness whereof I do to this my will set my hand and seal This 24th day of March, 1858.

Robert Rogers (seal)

Signed, sealed and published in our presence and we have subscribed our names hereto in the presence of the Testator This 14th day of March, 1858.

Test: **John Vaughan, William Faris**

WILL OF SAMUEL SMITH

Page 432

Dated: Sept. 6, 1798

In the Name of God, Amen.

I, **Samuel Smith** of State of Tennessee, County of Hawkins, being in a low state of health, but of sound, disposing mind and memory, do make this my last will in manner and form as follows, to wit:

First, I will my body to the dust from whence it came and my soul to God who gave it. Next, I will all debts and funeral charges be paid by my Executors hereinafter named. Next, I will to my son **Samuel Smith** one negro man named **Jack** and all my household furniture. Next, I will a child's part to my wife **Ann Smith**, as the law directs, if she has not forfeited it by her conduct. Next, I will an equal division between **Henry Law, Joseph Hite**, and the children of **Thos. Smith** of all the balance of my estate. Next, I will and appoint my son **Samuel Smith** and **James Lea** of Jefferson County my Executors, and also renders reasons why I do not make an equal divide among the whole heirs, my son **Samuel** has tended more on me in my infirmities than any of the rest, and **Henry Law, Joseph Hite** and **Thomas Smith** has had less of my property than the rest and is poorer.

Given under my hand and seal this 6th day of September, 1798.

Samuel Smith L.S. (seal)

Test. **Jas. Lea, Benjamin Cloud, Wm. Henderson**

WILL OF JOHN SAUNDERS

Page 432

Dated: June 30, 1807

In the Name of God, Amen.

I, **John Saunders** of the County of Hawkins and State of Tennessee, being in a low state of health, but perfect mind and memory Thanks be to God, and calling to mind the mortality of my body and knowing that it is appointed for all men once to die, I do make & ordain this my last Will and Testament, that is to say, principally and first of all, I give and recommend my soul unto the hands of Almighty God who gave it and my body to the earth to be buried in decent Christian burial at the discretion of my Executors, not doubting but at the general resurrection I shall receive the same by the mighty power of God, and as touching my worldly Estate wherewith I am possessed, I give and devise and dispose of in the manner following, to wit:

Item 1st. I give to my son **George Saunders** all that tract of land of 400 acres on Honeycut's Creek that **William Jeffers & Stephen Parten** is now living on to him and his heirs forever.

Item 2nd. I give to my son **James Saunders** the tract of land whereon I now live, with the appurtenances to the same belonging to him and his heirs forever, only the benefits arising from the same, I wish to be disposed of in the following manner. I wish the said farm to be for the use and maintenance of my said son **James** and my two daughters **Betsy & Polly**, equally amongst them until they are grown up, after which time the whole of the premises belongs to **James**. I also wish my two daughters **Betsy** and **Polly** to be with their sister **Tabitha Chesnutt** and being under her jurisdiction until they are capable of acting for themselves and I wish **Henry** and **Bitha** to live on my farm and keep all the things together and as to my other Estate, I give and dispose of in the following manner (to wit): All my negroes and stock of every kind I divide equally, share and share alike between **George Saunders, Tabitha Chesnutt, James Saunders, Betsy Saunders & Polly Saunders** with all the rest of my household furniture & utensils of every kind only. I give two daughters **Betsy & Polly** a bed and furniture apiece which is to be considered in the division as a part of their share and what past property of any kind that any of my children has already received is to be counted to them a part of their share. To **Willie Saunders** I give five shillings, knowing that he is no child of mine, and as to my wife **Tisha Saunders**, I give nothing as she has left my bed and eloped with another man. I appoint Richard Mitchell & **Joseph McMinn** Referees and request of them to divide my said Estate among my legatees agreeable to the tenor of my last Will and Testament. I do also appoint my son **George Saunders** and **Henry Chesnutt** Executors. In witness whereof I have hereunto set my hand and seal this 30th day of June in the year of our Lord one Thousand eight hundred and seven, 1807.

John x Saunders (seal)
(his mark)

Signed, sealed & acknowledged in presence of:
Wm. Paine, Sam'l Smith, Michael Rock

Page 433: October 8, 1808

WILL OF PETER SMITH

In the name of God, Amen.

I, **Peter Smith** of the County of Hawkins and State of Tennessee, being indisposed in body, but perfect in mind and memory and knowing that it is appointed for all men once to die, I do make and ordain this my last Will & Testament, running and being in the following form, to wit:

First: I commit my soul to Almighty God who gave it me and my body I recommend and desire _____ decently buried in the Earth at the expense of my Estate.

Second. That all my just debts should be paid.

Third. I give unto **Joshua & Samuel Smith** the tract of land I now live on, each an equal share. Should **Able Smith** outlive me, my desire is that **Joshua Smith** should take care of him: I give unto my son **Able Smith** that bed and furniture which is called his own to go to use of **Joshua Smith**, my desire be the fourth part of my Estate. And should I be the longest liver, my desire (is that) my movable property be equally divided amongst my children. I further desire that my son **John Smith** be the Executor of my Estate. Signed, sealed and delivered in presence of   Peter Smith (seal)
October the eighth day, 1808.

Test:
_____

Page 434: March 4, 1817

WILL OF ROBERT L. STUBBLEFIELD

In the Name of God, Amen.

I, **Robert Loxley Stubblefield**, of the County of Hawkins and State of Tennessee, being of sound and perfect mind and memory, blessed be God for the same. I do this fourth day of March in the year of our Lord one thousand, eight hundred and seventeen, make and publish this my last Will & Testament in manner and form following.

Item First. I do give and bequeath unto my son **Thomas Stubblefield** the tract of land whereon I now live containing 300 acres, to hold, possess and enjoy, to him and his heirs forever—under the following conditions and reserve (Viz): That my well beloved wife **Sarah** shall have a sufficient supply from the profits arising from said land to maintain her comfortably and decently and free from want, during her natural life or widowhood and that my daughter **Winnefred** shall have a comfortable maintenance and support out of the profits arising from said land so long as the said **Winnefred** shall remain single. But when she marries her maintenance and support shall cease, and after the death of my wife, and the marriage of my daughter, the said **Thomas Stubblefield** shall have full possession of the aforesaid tract of land without reserve to him and his heirs forever.

Item Second. I do give unto my well beloved wife **Sarah** one good horse, saddle and bridle, feather bed and furniture, she making her own choice of beds.

Item. I do give and bequeath unto my daughter **Winnefred** above named, out of my goods and chattels a portion equal to the others of my daughters that is married and settled off.

Item. I have already given my son **Stephen** a tract of land containing 400 acres as his full share of my Estate.

Item. I have also given my son **George** 300 acres of land as his full share of my Estate.

Item. I have also given my son **William** a valuable stud horse which he chose instead of land.

Item. And it is my will and desire that all my property not yet disposed of—the same consisting of live stock, household furniture and farming utensils—shall be sold at public sale and the profits thereof be equally divided between my wife **Sarah**, my son **William** and my daughters **Nancy, Mary, Keziah, Anna, Sarah, Susannah, Betsy** and **Winnefred.**

And I do hereby make and appoint my sons **William, Thomas** and **George** my Executors to this my last Will and Testament. In witness whereof I the said Robert Loxley Stubblefield to be his last Will & Testament in presence of us who were present at the time of signing and sealing the same.

Robert Loxley x Stubblefield (seal)
(his mark)

Felps Read, Martin Stubblefield,
Joseph Lebow, Thomas Read

WILL OF DANIEL SYESTER

Page 435

Dated: July 18, 1821
Proven: Aug. 1, 1821

In the Name of God, Amen.

I, **Daniel Syester** of Hawkins County, Tennessee, being a low state of health but of sound mind and memory and knowing that all men must die, do make this my last Will & Testament in manner and form following. I will my soul to God who gave it, and my body to the earth from whence it came, to be buried in a decent Christianlike manner and as to what world goods it hath pleased the Almighty to bless me with, I give and bequeath in the following manner, to wit: It is my will that all my just debts be paid out of my Estate, and as I did remove from Virginia, Barkley County about twenty one or two years ago, leaving there a wife and eight children in possession of a good tract of land with a considerable stock of horses, cattle, hogs and sheep, farming utensils, wagons &c, with all my household and kitchen furniture--in fact--everything that I did own, I left on said plantation for the use and benefit of my said wife and children, and owing to some unhappy differences between myself and said wife, I never returned there since, and having heard that my said wife has been dead for several years, but not knowing that it is the truth and supposing it is probable for her yet to be alive, it is therefore my will and desire that if my said wife **Hannah Syester** is yet alive that she shall have the sole use of my said plantation, with all the stock of every kind and all the other property that I left behind me during her natural life and at her death (if she is still living) it is my will that my Executors hereafter named shall sell the tract of land whereon my wife **Hannah** did live when I left her with all my other estate both real and personal that I have in the State of Virginia or Maryland. After the death of my wife **Hannah** if not already dead, and whereas a certain woman formerly **Caty Shook** but now my wife **Caty Syester**, and the said **Caty Syester** has been my best friend and one that has aided and assisted me in making of what property I now possess in the State of Tennessee, and being desirous to provide for her future maintenance, it is therefore my will and desire that she the said **Caty Syester** shall have the use and benefit of the plantation whereon I now live with all my stock of every description, and my household and kitchen furniture, all my farming tools of every kind, waggon and still &c, with every other article belonging to the premises for use and benefit for the maintenance of herself and children, and at her death the lands and other property left her to be sold by my Executors. It is my will that my Exec's sell the property on twelve months' credit and the land and property sold in Virginia to be equally divided between **John, Daniel, David, Jacob, Betsy, Susannah, Polly, Peggy Syester** (being the children of my wife **Hannah**). **Caty Syster** (my present wife) **Nancy, Sally, Elias and Sophia Syster**, share and share alike, making thirteen shares or legatees, and it is my wish that the amount of the sales of the land property in Tennessee be equally divided between my twelve children, **John, David, Daniel, Jacob, Betsy, Susannah, Polly, Peggy, Nancy, Sally, Elias** and **Sophia**, share and share alike, and if my present wife **Caty** should die before the sale and division of the money arising from my property in Virginia and Maryland that my twelve children

before named shall each have an equal share of said money, and it is further my will that if any of my children die before a division take place and have lawful heirs that their share or part of my Estate shall go to the heirs of such deceased person or persons, and if no heirs, to be equally divided between the surviving children before named. It is my will that my Executors shall have a reasonable allowance made them for all their trouble and expense, and I do hereby appoint my friends **Richard Mitchell** and **Stokley D. Mitchell** of Hawkins County, Tennessee and **Peter Light, Sen'r** of Virginia, Berkley Co., my Executors to this will, revoking all others by me made, and I the said **David Syester** do hereby acknowledge this and no other to be my last Will and Testament. In witness whereof I hereunto set my hand and seal this 18th day of July 1821. The words "In the State of Tennessee" on the second page of this will was interlined before signing.

Daniel Syester (seal)

Signed, sealed and acknowledged before:
Nicholas Long, James Long

WILL OF LOUTHER SMITH

Page 437

Dated: August 13, 1821

in the Name of God, Amen.

I, **Louther Smith** of County of Hawkins and State of Tennessee, being in a low state of health at present, but of perfect mind and memory, and calling to mind that I have once to die, I now do make and ordain this to be my last Will and Testament, that is to say, principally and first of all, I recommend my soul unto the hands of them that first gave it and my body I recommend to the Earth to be buried at the discretion of my Executors, and as touching such worldly Estate which it has pleased God to bless me with, I give, devise and dispose of the same in the following manner and form:

First. I want so much of my Estate sold as will be of value sufficient to satisfy all my just debts.

Second. I give and bequeath unto my son **David Smith** my young horse and a cow to be by him disposed of as he pleases. And all the rest of my estate, together with the household furniture and everything that I possess, both real and personal, I leave in the hands of my beloved wife **Barbary**, to have and to hold the same and to dispose of it as she sees proper amongst my children as long as she lives single or departs this life, and then to be equally divided amongst my children, and I do hereby utterly disallow, revoke and dis-annul all and every other former Testament but willed and bequeathed, ratified and confirming this and no other to be my last Will and Testament. In witness wherefore I have hereunto set my hand and seal this 13th day of August in the year of our Lord one thousand, Eight Hundred and Twenty-one.

Louther x Smith (seal)
(his mark)

Signed, sealed, published pronounced and delivered in the presence of us and in the presence of each other.
Isaac Laudeback, Henry Laudeback

WILL OF WYETH STUBBLEFIELD

Page 438

Dated: July 1, 1821

In the Name of God, Amen, or be it remembered that I, **Wyeth Stubblefield** of Hawkins County, East Tennessee, being weak in body but of sound and perfect mind and memory, or you may say this considering the uncertainty of this mortal life, and being of sound memory &c blessed be the Almighty God for the same, I do make and publish this my last Will and Testament in manner and form following, that is to say.

First. I give unto my beloved wife Sarah Stubblefield her maintenance of the land where I know live during her lifetime or widowhood. Also one bed and furniture and all the dressure furniture except the pature, and also the kitchen furniture and one black colt, one cow and calf and five good killen hogs such as the said Sarah Stubblefield wants, and also two sows sheep &c. I also do give unto my eldest son Joseph Stubblefield the tract of land where he now lives on. I do also give unto my son Robert Stubblefield the tract of land where Lewis Jarrell know lives, running along the ridge down and taking half of the valley of woodling land to that tract. I do also give unto my younger son Richard Stubblefield the tract of land where I know live, and also one cow and calf and half of the waggon and also an equal share of hogs as the others had when they left me, one bed and furniture, and also half of the puter, after the widow death, and farming tools equal to those of the other children, and two sheep. I do also give unto my youngest daughter Polly Stubblefield one large sorrel mare call. Pilot and one bed and furniture, one cow and calf, and also an equal part of the hogs as the others had when left me. And one half of the puter after the widow death and also two sheep and to be maintained of. the three plantations as long as she remains single. And all the rest of the property is to be sold and divided amongst the three girls after my debts is paid, and all the property that is left to the widow is to be divided amongst all my children after her death, of whom I hereby appoint Thomas Stubblefield and William Mays my Exec's of this my last will and testament, hereby revoking all former wills by me made. In witness whereof I have hereunto set my hand and seal this day of being the first day of July, in the year of our Lord, one thousand eight hundred and twenty one.

Signed, sealed published and declared by the above named Wyeth Stubblefield to be his last will & Testament in the presence of us who at his request and at his presence have hereunto subscribed our names as witnesses to the same.

Wyeth x Stubblefield (seal)
(his mark)

Lewis Jarrel, Gideon Harris, John McAnnally

WILL OF MARTIN SHANER

Page 439
Dated: May 24, 1827

I Martin Shaner of the County of Hawkins, State of Tennessee, being aged and infirm, but of sound mind and memory, do make publish and declare this to be my last Will & Testament. After recommending my soul to God from whence it came, by body to the dust, I bestow such worldly goods as it has been the Lord's will to bestow on me in the following manner, that is:

First. I wish all my honest debts to be paid. First, I give unto my beloved wife two beds and furniture, together with her clothing and kitchen furniture, one cow and calf, and one yearling calf cald Polly Kelley's. Also, I lend to my wife the plantation whereon I now live, together with all the land that I am seized and possessed of during her natural life and at her decease. I give and bequeath to my soning law James Harmak/Harmack all that part of my plantation lying S. E. of a line to be run from a corner beech—

Ben Hutchenson's corner to a scaly back hickory about 20 poles from my spring for the benefit of my daughter Lidia and her children. And in the same manner I give--that is--at the death of my wife, I give unto my grandson Lewis Davis the plantation that his father John Davis now lives on, by his paying his mother and brothers $200.00 in trade, in three annual installments at my decease. And the balance of my land that is the balance of the 400 acre tract that I have not given to James Harmak/Harmack and wife and children, I give and bequeath unto my three sons, Jacob, Henry & John Shaner in equal portions. Further, I wish my Executors whom I will hereafter name to bring to sale all the property not herein named - and when the Estate is fully settled, the balance which may remain in their hands to pay over to my wife Caty for her own disposal.

For the purpose of putting this my last Will & Testament in Execution, I nominate and appoint my worthy friends, Samuel Wilson, Sen'r and Jacob Miller my Executors. In witness whereof I, the said Martin Shaner, have hereunto set my hand and affixed my seal This 24th day of May, 1827.

Martin Shaner (seal)

Signed, sealed published and declared in presence of us who are subscribing witnesses thereunto.

Edward x Eidson, Wm. Mill(er)
(his mark)

WILL OF BARTLET SIMS

Page 440
Dated: Jan'y 11, 1793 -
January 11, 1793

This is my will that after paying of my just debts, the balance of my estate I do leave to my wife Elizabeth, (at) her decease then for every thing to be sold and equally divided amongst my children.

Bartlet x Sims
(his mark)

Test: Thos. Murrell (Jurat), Houston Johnson, Elisabet Morras/Morris (Jurat)

WILL OF THOMAS STUBBLEFIELD

Page 441
Dated: June 15, 1833

In the Name of God, Amen. I, Thomas Stubblefield, being in a low state of bodily health, but of sound memory and calling to mind it is appointed once for men to die, do constitute, ordain and appoint the following to be my last Will & Testament, to wit: I give my body to a decent Christian burial with a certain hope of the resurrection of the same, and my soul I commend unto the hands of God who gave it me. As to lands, good, and chattels with which it pleased God to Bless me it is my will and desire they shall be disposed of in the following manner, that is to say:

First. Out of the proceeds thereof my just debts to be paid be hereafter directed.

Secondly. I give and bequeath to my wife Patsey Stubblefield all my household and kitchen furniture (except one bed and furniture), all my farming utensils, two cows and calves, ten head of my best pork hogs, one sow and seven shoats, one sorrel mare called Sal and her colt, one wagon and gear, two work oxen, three ewes and three lambs and what quantity of geese and ducks there are belonging to the farm.

Thirdly. I give and bequeath to my daughter **Sally** one sorrel horse colt three years old this spring past, one cow and calf, one sow and pigs, one ewe and lamb, one feather bed and furniture.

Fourthly. It is my will and desire that the Court of Hawkins in session shall appoint one, two or three disinterested persons to lay off and designate to my wife **Patsey Stubblefield** so much of my land where she may choose the same provided the same be in one plot and of as convenient form as may be, as shall be sufficiently adequate for her support in raising my family of children 'till they be grown to men and women estate, and after the children are raised as aforesaid that wife **Patsey** shall possess and hold said land as laid off for her use during her natural life or widowhood, provided nevertheless my will is out of the proceeds of the land so laid off there shall be an ample provision made for the maintenance of my daughter **Willemoth** (who is in a helpless condition) during her natural life as well as to maintain my wife **Patsey**, and should my wife hereafter marry a second time and good reason thereafter appear that the land and property hereby devised to her is likely to become embezzled, or destroyed, it is my will that my Executors hereafter named shall so interpose as effectually to take care of the same, that it may be applied to raising my children and the maintenance of my aforesaid daughter **Willemoth** during her life.

Fifthly. It is my will that the balance of my stock of horses, cattle, hogs, sheep &c not specially hereby devised otherwise shall be sold at public sale and my debts to be paid out of the proceeds thereof; if not sufficient, my Executors are hereby empowered to sell to the highest bidder and convey to him or her so much of the extreme lower end of my old tract of land as may be sufficient to satisfy the balance of debt and no more.

Sixthly. It is my will that the balance of land not hereby otherwise appropriated shall be equally divided amongst all my children as soon as may be convenient.

Seventhly and lastly. It is my last will and desire that **Martin Moore** and **William Thompson** of Granger County and **William Mayes**, Hawkins County to be and they are hereby constituted my true and lawful Executors and are hereby authorized to carry into effect this my last Will & Testament according to the true intent and meaning of the same. In testimony whereof I have hereunto set my hand and seal the fifteenth day of June in the year of our Lord one thousand eight hundred and thirty-three.

Thomas x Stubblefield(seal)
(his mark)

Witnesses present: **John McAnally, Arthur x Bond, Flemming x Mayes**
(his mark)   (his mark)

WILL OF MICHAEL SHANKS

Page 442   Dated: May 15, 1833
In the Name of God, Amen.

I **Michael Shanks** of the County of Hawkins and State of Tennessee, being in a low state of health, but of perfect sound mind and memory (Blessed be God) do this the 15th day of May, 1833, make and publish this my last Will and Testament in manner following, that is to say. I give to my beloved wife **Elizabeth** the use of the lease of the tract or parcel of land that I got from **Absalom Kyle** and **James McCarty**, including the buildings thereon, the use of my household and kitchen furniture, the use of my farming utensils, the use of three beds and furniture, the use of all my cattle and hogs, and whereas I have notes of hand on **James P. McCarty** and **Absalom Kyle**, I believe seven notes of hand, fifty dollars each with a credit on one of them for twelve dollars which notes fall due yearly. I will that my beloved wife **Elizabeth** have as much of the money arising from said notes of hand as she may think proper to make use of. I will that my beloved son **Christian Shanks** keep the possession of the above named notes of hand and pay the money as it falls due arising from them to my beloved wife **Elizabeth**—or as much thereof as she may think proper. I will that my son **Christian Shanks** pay no interest on the notes of hand above stated and that he be allowed a reasonable sum for his attention to my wife **Elizabeth** during her natural life. All the before-mentioned property my wife is to have the use of during her natural life. I will that at my wife's death the property to be sold and equally divided amongst my sons and daughters, and should there be any money arising from s'd notes of hand before stated that it to be equally divided amongst my sons and daughters after paying all my just debts. I hereby make and ordain my son **Christian Shanks** Executor to this my last Will & Testament.

In witness whereof I have hereunto set my hand and affixed my seal.

Michael Shanks (seal)

Signed, sealed and delivered in the presence of **A. Kyle, James Nugent, Wm. C. Kyles**

WILL OF STUFFLE SHOULTZ

Page 443   Dated: April 15, 1834

I **Stuffle Shoultz** of the County of Hawkins and State of Tennessee, being old and infirm in body but sound mind and memory, knowing the uncertainty of human life, ordain this to be my last Will and Testament.

First. I wish to be buried in a plain and Christian manner.

Secondly. It is my desire that the tract of land on which I live to be equally divided between my son **Phillip Shoultz** and **Caty Shoultz** my daughter. **Phillip** to have that part adjoining the place where **Mrs. McKergon** lives, including the field on the creek. **Caty** to have the part where I now reside or live. **Phillip** is to keep my son **Isaac** or provide for him, and **Caty** is to keep **Christian**. **Phillip** is to live with **Caty** and assist in managing the farm until he marries or until **Caty** marries, and in that case **Phillip** is to go to his own place and give up the house place to **Caty**. I give to each of my other children one dollar to be paid out of my Estate. The balance of my Estate to be divided between **Phillip & Caty**. And I do hereby revoke all other wills and testaments heretofore made. In testimony whereof I have hereunto set my hand and seal This 15th of April, 1834.

Stuffle x Shoultz (seal)
(his mark)

Test: **A. L. Burem, Jno. A. Rogers, Thos. Thomas, Lewis C. Barmer John H. Dammer**

WILL OF ELIZABETH SWAIN

Page 444   Dated: Jan. 31, 1836
State of Tennessee)   January 31st, 1836, Be it remembered that I,
Hawkins County   )   **Elizabeth Swain** of the county and state aforesaid doth this day give and will unto to boys, her grandsons by the names of **John Swain** and **Joshua Barnet**, both of the County and State aforesaid the following property, Viz: Two beds and furniture and one

oven and tea kettle and four puter basins, six puter plates, two puter dishes, one jug and two bottles, and one flax wheel and one cotton wheel; one fall leaf table, one hachet, one smoothing iron and saddle and one looking glass and two bibles and one hymn book and two axes and one weeding hoe and also if Dix Alexander should get my pension money for me the same boy is to have hit as well as the property. This I do in my right elemets and in my best senses. I do this as my last will and testament. Signed and sealed in the day and year above mentioned, and in the presence of

Witnesses: Riley Jones, James Jones

Elizabeth x Swain (seal)
(her mark)

WILL OF OWEN SIZEMORE
(See Original)

Page 444
Dated: March 12, 1836

I, Owen Sizemore, being of sound and perfect mind and memory do make and publish this my last Will and Testament in manner and form as follows:

First. I give and bequeath unto my loving wife all my real and personal estate her lifetime except (   ).

Secondly. I give and bequeath unto my daughter Alcey a sorrel mare, a saddle and bridle, and a young cow, also two feather beds and furniture. I further give and devise unto my two youngest children Solomon and Alcey my plantation where I now live—one hundred to my son Solomon, one hundred to my daughter Alcey. Solomon's hundred of the lower end next to my manshen. I want at my wife's death all my personal property to be equally divided between my two sons Solomon and Owen, and my eight daughters, to wit: Elizabeth Willis, Pheraby Hausher, Saley Brown, Nancy Stapleton, Abillrey Anderson and Alcey. Also my daughters Lidda Sizemore and Aggy Stapleton. This is my last Will & Testament by me made. In witness whereof I have hereunto set my hand and fixed my seal This 12th day of March, 1836.

Owen x Sizemore (seal)
(his mark)

Signed, sealed published and delivered by the above named Owen Sizemore to be his last Will and Testament in the presence of us who have hereunto subscribed our names as witnesses in the presence of the Testator.

Lewis Click, Samuel x Brown
(his mark)

WILL OF WILLIAM STASY/STASEY

Page 445
Dated: March 16, 1838

I William Stasy of Hawkins County and State of Tennessee, being weak in body but of sound mind and memory do put in writing this piece of paper as my last Will & Testament, that is to say: My Will and desire is that my well beloved wife Dolley Stasy, if she shall live longer than me, have the privilege of house and as much of the use of the plantation negroes and stock that I may die possessed of as she may want so as that she may live comfortable as long as she lives after me. Also that she may have the command at any time or all times of any one or as many of the negroes as she may choose to have to wait on her for her convenience during her natural life and not to let or be hindered therefrom at any time by any person or persons whatsoever.

Item. Whereas I have heretofore given to my daughter Elizabeth Morelock two negroes and other property that was as much as I thought she ought to have or as much as would be her proportion of my Estate, all of which I hereby

bequeath unto her and I now give and bequeath unto her the sum of five dollars to be paid out of my estate.

Item. Whereas I have heretofore given to my daughter Sarah Mullins (?) and her heirs two negroes and other property that was as much as I thought she ought to have or as much as would be her proportion of my Estate, all of which I hereby bequeath unto her the sum of five dollars to be paid out of my estate.

Item. Whereas I have heretofore given to my son Thomas Stasey two negroes and other property that was as much as I thought would be his proportion of my Estate, all of which I now give and bequeath unto him, and I now give and bequeath unto him the sum of five dollars to be paid out of my Estate.

Item. Whereas I have heretofore given to my daughter Judith Morelock two negroes and other property as much as I thought would be her proportion of my Estate, all of which I now give and bequeath unto him and bequeath unto her the sum of five dollars to be paid out of my Estate.

Item. Whereas I have heretofore given to my son Zachariah a piece of land and other property as much as I thought would be his proportion of my Estate, and I now give and bequeath unto him the sum of five dollars more to be paid out of my Estate. Also, I give and bequeath unto my two grand children, the children of my son Zachariah, to wit: Elizabeth and John Stasey the sum of five dollars apiece to be paid out of my Estate.

Item. As to my son Richard Henry Stasey, whereas he having lived with me from youth up and taken charge of me and his mother, and if his mother should outlive me, my will and desire is that he superintend the plantation negroes and stock as long as his mother shall live if he should out live her and take charge of her in her old age as a dutiful son, not to suffer her to want when in his power to prevent, and at the time of her death, my will and desire is that whatever of my property may be on hand at the time of the death of my said wife then and in that case, he my said son Richard Henry to have and to hold all my land, negroes, and all the property belonging to me that may be on hand at the time of my death or at the death of my...wife to be his forever.

And I hereby nominate and appoint by these presents my said son Richard Henry Stasey to be my Executor of this my last Will & Testament, and to see that it be faithfully done.

In witness whereof I have hereunto set my hand and affixed my seal This 16th day of March, 1838.

William x Stasey (seal)
(his mark)

Signed, sealed in the presence of us: Joseph Britton, John x Cavern,
(his mark)

William x Stasey,
(his mark)

WILL OF GEORGE STIPE

Page 447
Dated: May 6, 1841

In the Name of God, Amen.

I, George Stipe, Snr. of County of Hawkins & State of Tennessee, being in sound and perfect mind and memory, do make this my last Will & Testament in manner and form following that is to say:

First. I give to my beloved wife Catharine the use of all my tract of land whereon I now live, during her natural life. I also give to my said wife Catharine the use of all my personal Estate during her natural life.

Secondly. I give to my son **George Stipe, Jr.** one dollar to be levied out of my Estate.

Thirdly. I give one horse to my son **Henry Stipe** to be equal in value to the horse that I gave to my son **John Stipe**, to be delivered to him by my Executrix when he shall arrive at the age of 21 years.

Fourthly. I give to my son **James Stipe**, one horse to be equal in value to the...horse that I gave to my son, **John Stipe**, to be delivered to him by my Executrix when he shall arrive at the age of 21 years.

Fifthly. I give and bequeath all my land and personal property after the death of my said wife to my sons and daughters, namely, **John, Henry, James, Jacob Stipes** and **Elizabeth Shell, Polly Davis, Kitty Davis, Nancy Ford, Julia Anne Stipe** and **Sally Leath**, to them and their heirs forever, to be e- qually divided among them share and share alike. I give to my son **Jacob** one horse to be equal to the horse I gave **John Stipe**.

Lastly. I do hereby appoint my...wife **Catharine Stipe** Executrix of this my last Will and Testament and I do hereby direct that she be not required to give security for her execution. In witness whereof I have hereunto set my hand and seal this 6th day of May A.D. 1841.

George x Stipe, Sen'r (seal)
(his mark)

Signed, sealed and pronounced by the said **George Stipe, Sen'r** in the presence of us as his last Will and Testament who were in the presence of each other at the signing and sealing thereof.
Hezekiah Hamblin, James Nugent

WILL OF JACOB SENSABAUGH

Page 447   Dated: october 19, 1841
State of Tennessee)   I, **Jacob Sensabaugh** do make and publish this
Hawkins County   )   my last Will & Testament hereby revoking and
making void all other wills by me at any time
made.

First. I direct that my funeral expenses and all my debts be paid as soon after my death as possible out of any moneys that I may die possessed of or may first come into the hands of my Executor.

Secondly. I give and bequeath to my beloved wife **Susannah** my plantation on which I now live to have and to hold during her natural life, subject, however, to these restrictions: First, I do not authorize her to sell, bargain or trade it off on any condition whatever. Secondly, if she marries she forfeits all claim to the land. At her death the land is to be sold, provided the youngest child has attained the age of 21 years, and the proceeds of the sale of the land, together with all the other property that may be in her hands at the time of her death is to be equally divided amongst all of my children: 1st, **Betsy**; 2nd, **Sally**; 3rd, **Rosana**; 4th, **Anne**; 5th **Jacob**; 6th, **Absalom**; 7th, **Jefferson**; 8th, **John**; 9th, **Prescilla**; 10th, **William**; and 11th, **Nicholas**. It is likewise my will that any surplus property that I may die possessed of may be sold provided my wife sees fit to spare it, and the pro- ceeds of such sale to be equally divided between my wife and the above named children.

And lastly, I do hereby nominate & appoint my wife **Susannah** my Executrix. In witness whereof I do to this my will set my hand and seal This 19th day of October, 1841.   **Jacob Sensabaugh** (seal)
Signed, sealed and published in our presence, and we have subscribed our

names hereto in the presence of the Testator. This 19th October, 1841.
Joshua Phipps, John Sprowl, D. K. Smith

WILL OF ALEXANDER SMITH

Page 448   Dated: August 10, 1842
                                       Proven: Sept. 1842

State of Tennessee)
Hawkins County   )   I, **Alexander Smith**, do make and publish this as my last will and testament hereby revoking and making void all other wills by me at any time made.

First. I direct that my funeral expenses and all my debts be paid as soon as possible after my death out of any money that I may die possessed of or may first come into the hands of my Executor, and that all my personal property be sold and the money arising from such sale be applied to the pay- ment of said expenses and debts or so much thereof as will defray them all.

Secondly. I give and bequeath to my son **John Smith** the land whereon he now lives, it being and lying in District No. 17, joining the lands of **Hamilton's** heirs and **Samuel McPheeters'** heirs, containing by estimation 50 acres more or less.

Thirdly. I give and bequeath to my son **Alexander Smith** the land whereon he now lives adjoining the above described land, and the land of **John Patterson's** heirs.

Fourthly. I give and bequeath to my son **Joseph Smith** the land whereon I now live lying in the above named district and joining the lands of **Lewis C. Patterson, William Pickens** and others containing by estimation 50 acres...

Fifthly. I give and bequeath to my daughter **Elizabeth Hicks** and her children the land whereon **Riley Hicks** now lives joining the above described land and lands of **Samuel McPheeters'** heirs and others containing by estima- tion 50 acres...

Sixthly. I bequeath to my sons **William Smith** and **George Smith** the sum of one dollar each. And I further direct that if there should not be money enough arising from the sale of my personal property to discharge the above named expenses, debts, bequeaths &c, that **John, Alexander** and **Joseph Smith** and **Elizabeth Hicks** shall each of them pay an equal part of such unsatisfied balances and that the above described lands be bound for the same equally, and if there should remain any money arising from the sale of my personal property after paying the above named expenses, debts &c, that it be equal- ly divided among the above named heirs (Viz) **John, Alexander** and **Joseph Smith** and **Elizabeth Hicks, William** & **George Smith**.

Lastly, I nominate and appoint **Alexander Smith, Jr.** my Executor. In witness whereof I do to this my last Will & Testament set my hand and seal This 10th day of August, 1842.

Alexander x Smith Sr. (seal)
(his mark)

Signed, sealed and published in our presence, and we have subscribed our names hereto in the presence of the subscribers the day and date above written.
Samuel Smith
Archibald Patterson

WILL OF WILLIAM SKELTON
Dated: November 9, 1843

I, **William Skelton,** do make and publish this as my last Will & Testament hereby revoking and making void all other wills by me at any time made.

First. I direct that my funeral expenses and all my debts be paid as soon as possible out of any moneys that I may die possessed of or may first come into the hands of my Executor.

Secondly. I give and bequeath to my daughter **Nancy Christian** my bed and furniture.

Thirdly. I give to my brother **James Skelton** my saddle.

Fourthly. I give unto my grandson **William L. Christian,** his heirs and assigns forever all my landed estate containing 232 acres, more or less, ly-ing in Hawkins County, State of Tennessee, on the south side of Holston River, on Grassy Creek, District No. 17, whereon I now live to have and to hold the same forever, with the exception of the land whereon my brother **John Skelton** now lives and occupies, which land I give and bequeath the use of unto the said **John Skelton** for the term of his natural life, and his wife, **Elizabeth Skelton,** should she be the the longest liver, the possession of which after their deaths shall belong to the said **William L. Christian,** his heirs &c; and I further give and bequeath to the said **William L. Christian** all my personal property consisting of one sorrel mare, one cow, my stock of hogs, farming utensils &c, &c.

Lastly. I do hereby nominate and appoint **William L. Christian** my Executor.

In witness whereof I do to this my last Will & Testament set my hand and seal this 9th day of November, 1843. Interlined before signed.

William x Skelton (seal).
(his mark)

Signed, sealed and published in our presence and we have subscribed our names hereto in the presence of the Testator, day and date above written.

Witness: Samuel Smith: Proven 4th March, 1844.
Emanuel Rutledge: 1st July, 1844.

Page 450

WILL OF EZEKIEL SULLIVAN
Dated: March 31, 1847
Proven: May 3, 1847

I, **Ezekiel Sullivan,** of the County of Hawkins and State of Tennessee, being of sound, disposing mind and memory do make and ordain this my last Will & Testament in manner and form following.

First. I will that all my burial expenses be paid and all my just debts out of any money that may come into the hands of my Executors out of my Estate.

Secondly. I want all my personal estate except my saddle to be sold and the proceeds to be equally divided between my four daughters, namely, **Peggy Bloomer, Elizabeth Bray, Polly Herd** and **Nancy Barrett.** And I will that my son **William Sullivan** have my saddle and to have $100.00 out of the proceeds of the sale of the tract of land that I sold to **Solomon Sizemore.** And the balance to be equally divided between my son **John Sullivan's** two children.

Thirdly. I will that my old tract of land to be divided between my two sons **Thomas** and **William Sullivan:** I will that **Thomas Sullivan** have the upper end, and **William** to have the lower end, beginning on a white oak on the south side of the pine ridge, running across the plantation with a cross fence to a black oak and dogwood in the gap of a ridge, thence south-

wardly to his line, and I hereby revoke and disannul all former wills here-tofore by me made.

And lastly, I hereby appoint and constitute my son **Thomas Sullivan** and **John Mitchell** my Executors of this my last Will and Testament. In witness whereof I have hereunto set my hand and seal, March 31, 1847.

Ezekiel x Sullivan (seal)
(his mark)

Sealed and acknowledged in presence of:
Wm. L. Hartley, James Kenner, Ezekiel Anderson

Sworn to in open Court by Wm. L. Hartley, James Kenner & Ezekiel Anderson on 3rd day of March, 1847.

J. K. Vance, Dep'ty Clk.

Page 451

WILL OF WILLIAM SMITH
Dated: May 7, 1805
Proven: May Term, 1805

In the Name of God, Amen.

I, **William Smith,** of the County of Hawkins & State of Tennessee, being of sound and perfect mind and memory, blessed be God, do this seventh day of May, in the year of our Lord, one thousand eight hundred and five, make and publish this my Will and Testament in the manner following, that is to say:

First. I give and bequeath unto my loving wife **Elizabeth Smith** the 220 acres during her life or widowhood, then to have the thirds. I also bequeath unto her three negroes named **Prince, Jack & Jim,** during her life or widowhood. Then the said negroes and increase to be equally divided between her and the children which are at this time seven in number, namely, **Sally, George, William, Joel, Betsy, Peter & John**--now about three months, eleven days old, the household furniture of every description, together with the farming uten-sils & tools of all kinds, to be at her disposal. I have a bond on Col. **Thomas King** and tested by **John Robbisson** for 300 acres of land which if ob-tained, to be equally divided. My stock of all kinds to be sold and equally divided.

Signed, sealed published and declared by the said **William Smith** the Testator as his last Will & Testament in the presence of us who were present at the time of signing and sealing thereof. I do also make and ordain my loving brother **Samuel Smith** Executor of this my last Will and Testament.

William Smith (seal)

Test: John Burts (Jurat)
Robert McMinn (Jurat)

Page 452

WILL OF JAMES SIMMONS
Dated: July 17, 1847
Proven: May Term, 1851

In the Name of God, Amen.

I, **James Simmons** of the County of Hawkins and State of Tennessee, being weak in body but of sound and perfect mind and memory, for which I thank God, considering the uncertainty of this mortal life do make this my will & Testament as follows, which shall make void all wills which I may have made heretofore. First. I give my soul to him who made it, hoping to enjoy eternal happiness at the resurrection of the dead and my body to be deposited in the grave in a plain and Christian style, and as to my worldly concerns and affairs, I wish them to be disposed of in the following manner (Viz). I do give and bequeath unto my son **James G. Simmons** all my land. Again it is my sincere desire and will that my black boy **Ben** at my decease receive his freedom, and inasmuch as I hold the only right and title to said black boy **Ben**, be it known to all men that I make no transfer of my title to any person or persons. I pronounce him free at my death, and I request my Executors to see that said black boy according to my will be freed at my death. Again, I wish my stock, farming utensils and household and kitchen furniture to be sold to the highest bidder and the amount received for said property be equally divided among my children (Viz) **Polly Acuff's** heirs, my son **John Simmons'** heirs, my daughter **Nancy Williams**, my daughter **Frances Patterson**, my daughter **Betsy Lewis**, my son **Thomas Simmons'** heirs, Lucinda, Matilda & **Thomas**; my son **James G. Simmons**, my daughter **Rachael Spears**. Now it is my will and wish that my son **James G. Simmons** and **Andrew Spears** be the Executors.

In testimony whereof I have hereunto set my hand and seal This 17th day of July, 1847.

                    James x Simmons (seal)
                         (his mark)
Signed and sealed in the presence of us: **William Gillenwaters, George A. Gillenwaters**.
N.B. The following articles now in my house belong to **Alcey Wheeler** upon which I have no claim: One bed and bed clothes, one bedstead and card, one cotton wheel and flax wheel, one loom, one oven & hooks, all the geese and ducks.

                    James x Simmons (seal)
                         (his mark)

WILL OF JAMES SKELTON

Page 453   Dated: Dec. 8, 1847
                           Proven: Aug. Term. 1848
State of Tennessee, Hawkins County, December 8th, 1847.
In the Name of God, Amen.

I, James Skelton of the County of Hawkins, State of Tennessee, considering the uncertainty of this mortal life and being of sound mind and memory do make and publish this my last Will & Testament in manner and form following. That is to say. First, after my just debts be paid, I give and bequeath to my beloved wife **Mary Skelton** the tract of land whereon I now live, lying and being in the County of Hawkins and State of Tennessee during her widowhood. Then to be equally divided between my four youngest sons Viz: **William, Robert, James & Reuben Skelton**. And I hereby appoint my beloved wife **Mary Skelton** Guardian of my youngest children during her widowhood, also I desire that after paying all just debts the remainder of my perishable property be equally divided between my youngest three daughters, Vic: **Anna, Katherine & Matilda**. I also desire that my beloved wife **Mary Skelton** give to each of my oldest children the sum of one dollar and in witness whereof I have hereunto set my hand and seal the eighth day of December in the year of our Lord, one thousand eight hundred and forty-seven.

                    James x Skelton (seal)
                         (his mark)
Witness: **James Feagins, Stephen Christian, John Skelton**

WILL OF ALCY STURM

Page 454   Dated: July 17, 1849
                           Proven: July Term, 1850
In the Name of God, Amen.

I **Alcy Sturm** being of sound and disposing mind and memory but feeble in body, do make and publish this as my last Will & Testament, hereby revoking and making void all other wills by me at any time made.

First. I give and bequeath to my beloved daughter **Catharine** $150.00 to be paid out of any monies that I may die seized and possessed of or may first come into the hands of my Executors. And it is also my will and desire that my said daughter **Catharine** have all my interest in the stock on hand in a tan yard in which **James L. L. McCall** and myself are jointly interested, and that this shall be her portion of my property. It is my will and desire that my slave **Harry** who has been an obedient and faithful servant and who I have always intended should be liberated at my death, shall be privileged and allowed to live with any of my children whom he chooses and that he shall not be sold by my Executors, nor be confined to any particular place of residence by them but that he may remain with my children in common.

Thirdly. It is my will and desire that all my personal property except the above mentioned be sold by my Executors, and that the proceeds of said sale be equally divided between my six other children Viz: **Mariah**, who intermarried with one **Montgomery S. Wells**; **Nancy** who intermarried with one **Samuel Snapp**; **Eliza** who intermarried with one **James L. L. McCall**, **Sarah** who intermarried with one **M. T. Cox**, **William** and **Jacob**, and that my Executors pay **George W. Alexander** one dollar therefrom.

Lastly. I hereby nominate and appoint **Montgomery S. Wells** and my son **Jacob Sturm** my Executors. In witness whereof I do to this my will set my hand and seal This seventeenth day of July, 1849.

                    Alcy Sturm (seal)
Signed, sealed and published in our presence and we have subscribed our names hereto in the presence of the Testator This seventeenth day of July, 1849.
Edw. J. Aston, Francis Goodman

NUNCUPATIVE WILL OF NANCY SHOUGH

Page 455   Dated: April 29, 1850
We, **Michael Reynolds** and **Hannah Reynolds** do state that the nuncupative will of **Nancy Shough** was made by her in the month of February, the day of the month not recollected, in the year 1850, in our presence to which we were specially required to bear witness by the Testator herself in the presence of each other, that it was made in her last sickness in her own habitation or dwelling house, and the same is as follows, to wit:

It was her will and desire that her effects should be disposed of after her decease in the following manner. First, it was her wish and desire that her daughter **Margaret** shall have her saddle. Second. It was her wish and desire that the balance of her effects, after paying all her just debts should be equally divided between her daughter **Margaret**, her son **Pleasant** and her son **William's** wife and children. Her daughters **Nancy** and **Elizabeth** having heretofore been provided for. Made out by us and signed This 29th day of April, 1850.

     Michael x Reynolds, Hannah x Reynolds. Signed in my presence,
        (his mark)   (her mark)   **Jos. B. Galbraith**

WILL OF WILLIAM SKELTON/SHELTON

[See Original]

Page 455

Dated: Nov. 15, 1850
Proven: July 6, 1851

State of Tennessee)
Hawkins County)   In the Name of God, Amen. I William Skelton/
Shelton being of sound mind and memory, knowing at the same time the uncertainty of life and the certainty of death, I wish now to dispose of my property such as has been pleased (sic) God to bless me with. I, William Skelton/
Shelton do make this and publish this as my last Will and Testament, hereby
revoking and making void all other wills by me made at any other time.
   1st. I direct that my funeral expenses and all my just debts be paid
as soon after my death as possible out of any moneys that I may die possessed of or may first come into the hands of my Executors.
   2nd. I will one hundred dollars to my sister Polly Chesnutt.
   3rd. I will to my sister Nancy Williams $50.00.
   4th. I will to my sister Winney White one dollar to her or to her heirs.
   5th. I will my interest in the land to William Chesnutt; the land
where William now lives and also $250.00, and also three head of cattle.
   6th. I will one third of my interests in land to Thomas Chesnutt, the
land where Thomas now lives.
   7th. I will that the Executors to my will sell to the highest bidder
the balance of my interest in the tract of land where Thomas Chesnutt lives
and the proceeds be equally divided among the heirs of Polly Chesnutt, my
sister.
   8th. And last, I will that Thomas Chesnutt & David Reynolds be my
Executors to manage my affairs and in witness whereof I do to this my will
set my hand and seal. This 15th day of November, 1850.

William x Skelton/Shelton
(his mark)

Witness: Thos. Smith, David Reynolds
(his mark)

Page 456

WILL OF DAVID SENSABAUGH

Dated: April 27, 1856
Proven: May Term, 1862

I, David Sensabaugh of the County of Hawkins, State of Tennessee, hereby revoking and making void all other wills by me heretofore made.
   First. I direct that my funeral expenses and all my debts be paid out
of any monies I may die possessed of or that may first come into the hands
of my Executors.
   Secondly. I will and bequeath to my sons Christian Sensabaugh and
Richard Sensabaugh equally all of my property of every kind and description,
both real and personal that I may die possessed of viz. land, my negro man
Edward, household and kitchen furniture, stock, grain, farming utensils and
all effects belonging to me of every kind. But I require that the said
Christian and Richard to do the following things. They must maintain, support, provide for and take care of my wife Nancy during her life. I also require them to pay out to my son Michael Sensabaugh $300.00: to my son David
Sensabaugh $300.00: to my daughter Susan Amis $300.00: to my daughter Nancy Sensabaugh
$150.00: to the children of my son Joseph Sensabaugh $200.00 which shall be
the share of each in my Estate. And to my daughter Elizabeth Bowman, as her
share, $200.00 to be held as a trust fund in the hands of my Executors here-
inafter named, during her life to be loaned out by them and the interest to

be paid to her annually, and at her death it is my will and desire that it
shall go to her daughter Susan Jane Bowman. I have already paid to each of
my sons, John Sensabaugh, Henry and Jacob all that I wish them to receive
out of my Estate.
   Lastly. I hereby constitute and appoint my son Christian and my son-
in-law James Amis Executors of this my Will and Testament. In testimony
whereof I have hereunto subscribed my name and affixed my seal. This 27th
day of April, 1856.

David x Sensabaugh (seal)
(his mark)

Signed by David Sensabaugh the Testator in the presence of us who in his
presence have subscribed our names as witnesses.
Hiram Fain, Thomas P. Harlen

Page 457

WILL OF JOHN SHANKS

Dated: May 16, 1853
Proven: April Term 1855

I John Shanks do make and publish this my last Will and Testament hereby revoking and making void all other wills by me at any time made.
   First. I direct that my funeral expense and all my debts be paid as
soon as after my death as possible, out of any moneys that I may die possessed of or may first come into the hands of my Executors.
   Secondly. I give and bequeath to my son Anderson Shanks, my son Jacob
and my son Daniel Shanks all the home plantation together with the several
parcels of land adjoining it which belong to me, equally between them.
   Thirdly. I give and bequeath to my daughters Elizabeth Starnes and
Polly Shanks $150.00 each, which sum of money is charged on the lands in the
second bequest. Nancy Davis, my daughter, also having been heretofore provided for fully and $50.00 over which is to be deducted from her share of
my personal property.
   Fourthly. I give and bequeath to my son Michael Shanks $200.00 charged
also on the lands named in the second bequest. My son John Shanks and my
son David Shanks having been heretofore fully provided for in their interest
in my home lands named in the second bequest.
   Fifthly. I desire that all my personal property be sold and the proceeds of it, together with any money that may remain at my decease and I
direct that the same be divided equally among all my children named above,
due respect being observed to the deduction to be made in Nancy Davis' share.
   Lastly. I do hereby nominate and appoint Andrew Shanks and Joseph B.
Galbraith my Executors. In witness whereby I do to this my will set my
hand and seal this 16th day of May A.D. 1853.

John Shanks (seal)

Signed, sealed and published in our presence and we have subscribed out
names hereto in the presence of the Testator this 16th day of May, 1853.
H. Watterson, O. C. Miller, Edward Watterson, Wm. Hutchisson.

Page 458

WILL OF CHRISTIAN SHANKS

Dated: Nov. 13, 1858
Proven: Jan'y Term, 1859

In the Name of God, Amen.
I Christian Shanks of the County of Hawkins and State of Tennessee,
being of sound mind and memory and considering the uncertainty of this trail."

transitory life do therefore make, ordain, publish and declare this to be my last will and testament. That is to say.

First. After all my lawful debts are paid and discharged the residue my my Estate real and personal I give, bequeath and dispose of as follows, to wit: To my beloved daughter **Catharine** and her husband **William Williams** the land and appurtenances situated thereon where I now live known and described as the **Cole** Tract containing about 136 acres, but in doing this it is expressly understood and I hereby make it incumbent upon them to provide for my beloved wife **Polly** a house and support her decently and comfortably for and during the term of her natural life and at the death of said **Polly** to bury her decently and furthermore, after the death of the said **Polly**, the said **William & Catharine** likewise must pay to the other heirs the sum of $700.00 to be equally divided amongst them, and to be paid in annual installments of $200.00 a year without interest...I furthermore give to my beloved wife **Polly** all my household & kitchen furniture of every kind and description for and during her natural life, and at her death to be sold by my Executors, hereinafter to be appointed and the proceeds thereof to be equally divided amongst my lawful heirs. It is further my will that the blacksmith shop that was erected by the joint labor of my sons and son-in-law shall be free to be used by them as they have heretofore used it until the death of my beloved wife **Polly** and then, I will that the tools of every kind and description in said shop be sold and the proceeds thereof equally divided among my heirs. To my son **Henry** I give & bequeath the **Peggy Pearson** tract of land containing about 14 or 15 acres.

To my son **George** I give and bequeath the lower end of the **Mack Kenner** tract of land on which is the house and orchard. The upper end of said tract of land I give and bequeath to the sole and separate use of my daughter **Betsy Kenner** and her heirs forever. The line between said upper and lower end of said farm shall commence on the south bank of Poor Valley Creek at the mouth of a ditch and run with the orchard fence to near the corner of the barn and then with the fence running from the barn to the foot of the Stone Mountain, and thence continuing the direction of the last named fence to **George Rider's** line at or near the top of Stone Mountain.

It is further my will that all of my lands not herein before disposed of, together with my half of a town lot in Rogersville of every kind and description shall be sold at my death and divided equally among all my children. I have heretofore given all my children about $200.00 each and I have by this my will provided for my son **Henry**, my son **George**, and my two daughters **Betsy Kenner & Katy** and her husband **William Williams** by giving them lands as herein before set forth. Now it is my wish to provide for my sons, **Michael, John, William** and **Christian**, not herein given any land and therefore give to each of my last named sons the sum of $200.00 each to be paid by the first day of January, 1859. It is my will that the four last named sons shall have, in addition to the sum of $200.00...an equal share with my other children of the proceeds of property to be sold after the death of my wife **Polly.**

It is my will further that all my property not herein before disposed of shall be sold at my death by my Executor & the proceeds equally divided among all my children. I hereby constitute and appoint my son-in-law **William Williams** my Executor.

In witness whereof the said **Christian Shanks** have hereunto subscribed my name and affixed my seal This 13th day of November, 1853.

Christian Shanks (seal)

(his mark)

The above and foregoing instrument was subscribed by the s'd **Christian**

Shanks in our presence and acknowledged by him to each of us, and he at the same time declared the said instrument so subscribed, to be his last Will & Testament, and we at the Testator's request and in his presence have signed our names as witnesses hereto.

A. A. Kyle, S. R. Russell

WILL OF WILLIAM SMITH

Page 460   Dated: September 3, 1859
                             Proven: October, 1859

In the Name of God, Amen.

I **William Smith, Senr.** of the County of Hawkins and State of Tenn., being of sound mind and memory, and considering the uncertainty of this frail and transitory life do therefore make, ordain, publish and declare this to be my last Will & Testament, that is to say:

First. After all my lawful debts are paid and discharged, the residue of my Estate, real and personal, I give, bequeath and dispose of as follows (to wit):

1st. I give and bequeath to my daughter **Elizabeth Kennon**, her heirs & assigns forever about 50 acres of land off the east end of my tract of land including where **Thomas Kennon** now lives, also my little black boy named **Caswell.**

2nd. All the balance of my land whereon I now live adjoining the lands of **David Reynolds, John Reynolds** and others, I give and bequeath to my son **Sevier Smith** on the following conditions, that the said **Sevier Smith** is hereby bound to support me and his mother **Winney Smith** decently and clear of want during our natural lives, or during my wife's widowhood.

3rd. I give and bequeath to my daughter **Cassander Couch** one negro girl Hannah together with some money that I have heretofore given her.

4th. In addition to what I have heretofore given **Mahlon** and **Nancy White**, $400.00--$200.00 apiece--to be paid to their Guardian, and to be paid by my Executor so soon as my property is disposed of and my Estate settled up.

5th. I also give to my son **John Rufus Smith** my town lot in the town of Rogersville about five eights of an acre adjoining **McKnight's** lot and others, on the main road to the Court House. Also $400.00 in money.

6th. I also give to **Minerva Kirkpatrick** my negro girl **Jane**, to have and to hold the right to her and her heirs forever.

7th. It is my desire also that my three negro boys, **Bob, Sandy** and **John** be kept in the family and it is my request that **David Kirkpatrick, Sevier Smith, Calvin Smith** and **Lazarus Couch** take the three boys and keep them among them at the price I have here set on them; that is, **Bob** at $500.00; **Sandy** at $400.00; and **John** at $200.00, and the money to be applied to the uses hereinbefore mentioned, and the balance of the money to go into the hands of my Executors and be applied to other uses.

8th. It is also my will and desire that my black girl **Eliza** be free at my death, and that she is not to be subject to be sold by none of my heirs, and that none of my children nor wife is to have any claim on her as being a slave, and she is to have the privilege of living on the land that I have given to my son **Sevier**, or to live with any of the connection, as the case may be.

9th. It is my wish also that my son **Calvin M. Smith** have in addition to what I have heretofore given him, some claims and receipts that I hold on him and have paid for him to the amount of some one hundred and twenty odd dollars, and the claims to be given up to him.

10th. In addition to what I have given **Sevier**, I also give him my sorrel mare and two beds, bedsteads and furniture. I have a small piece of land joining **John Saunders John Fitzpatrick** which I wish to be sold and the money to go towards paying my debts.

11th. It is also my wish that after my just debts is paid, the balance of property both household and kitchen furniture and stock of every kind be left with my wife for her use and support during her widowhood.

Lastly. I make, constitute and appoint **David Reynolds** and **Lazarus Couch** to be Executors of this my last Will & Testament, hereby revoking all former wills by me made. In witness whereof I have herewith subscribed my name and affixed my seal. This 18th day of July in the year of our Lord, one thousand eight hundred and fifty nine.

William x Smith (seal)
(his mark)

Witness:
John Reynolds, J. R. Saunders

A Codicil to the above named will whereas I **William Smith** of the County of Hawkins and State of Tennessee, have made my last Will & Testament bearing date of 18th July, 1859, in which I have disposed of the greater part of my effects. Now, therefore, I do by this my writing which I hereby declare to be a codicil to my last Will and Testament and to be taken as a part thereof, order and declare and it is my will and desire that **Aslee** and **Waltman White** my two grand children have as addition to what I have heretofore given them $100.00 more each of them, making $300.00 apiece. Also, in addition to what I have given my son **Sevier**, I also give him my wagon and gearing. It is also my wish and desire that all the balance of my effects after my just debts are paid, which I left to my wife in my first will, still be left in her possession and to be used for her support during her widowhood, and not to be wasted or disposed of in any other way whatsoever. And whatever is left during her widowhood or at her death to be equally divided amongst my lawful heirs. It is also my will that my black girl **Eliza** be not free until the death of my wife. In witness whereof I have hereunto set my hand and seal. This 3rd day of September in the year of our Lord one thousand eight hundred and fifty nine.

William Smith(seal)
(his mark)

Witness: John Reynolds, J. R. Saunders

Page 462

WILL OF DAVID SHANKS

Dated: October 27, 1859
Proven: November 1859

I, **David Shanks** do make and publish this as my last Will and Testament hereby revoking and making void all other wills by me at any time made.

First. I direct that my funeral expenses and all my debts be paid as soon after my death as possible out of any moneys that I may die possessed of or may first come into the hands of my Executor.

Second. I give my land to my wife **Nancy Shanks** during her life and if she should die before my youngest child comes of age, I want the land to remain together until it comes of age, and then I want the land sold and the proceeds equally divided between all my children.

Thirdly. I give to my wife **Nancy Shanks** one horse and two cows and all my sheep and all my stock (of) hogs, all my household and kitchen furniture. After leaving my wife one year's provision, I want the balance of the grain

and the remainder of stock of horses and cattle sold and the money after paying my debts &c to go to the use of my family.

Lastly. I nominate and appoint **William Sullivan** my Executor.

In witness whereof I do to this will set my hand and seal. This the 27th day of October, 1859.

David x Shanks
(his mark)

Signed, sealed and published in our presence, and we have subscribed our names hereto in the presence of the Testator. This the 27th day of October, 1859.

John Vaughn, William Wyatt

Page 463

WILL OF WILLIAM SHANKS

Dated: November 18, 1861
Proven: Feb'y Term, 1862

In the Name of God, Amen.

I **William Shanks** of the County of Hawkins and State of Tennessee, being of sound mind and memory & considering the uncertainty of this frail and transitory life do therefore make, ordain, publish and declare this to be my last Will and Testament, that is to say:

First. After all my lawful debts are paid and discharged, the residue of my Estate real and personal, I give, bequeath and dispose of as follows, to wit:

To my dear beloved wife **Catharine Shanks**, all my property and effects, both real and personal during her widowhood, and at her death, the entire property and effects (except one dollar which I give to my daughter Louisiana **Hawkins**). The entire balance to be equally divided between my several other children, to wit: **Martin V. Shanks, Eliza Ruth P. Shanks, Cyrena G. Shanks, Amanda Shanks, Hannah H. Shanks, Mary Shanks & Roxannah Shanks**. I further will that after my death my wife **Catharine Shanks** be at liberty to sell any of the property she does not wish to retain.

I appoint my wife **Catharine Shanks** my Executrix. This, the eighteenth day of November, 1861.

William Shanks (seal)

Witness: Henry Stipe, W. P. Armstrong

Page 463

WILL OF JAMES SANDERS

Dated: February 26, 1863

I, **James Sanders**, do make and publish this my last will and Testament, hereby revoking and making void all other wills by me at any time made.

First. I direct that my funeral expenses and all my debts be paid as soon after my death as possible, out of any moneys I may die possessed of, or may first come into the hands of my Administrators.

I give to my son **James Allen Sanders** 150 acres of land, and to my son **Nelson Sanders** 150 acres of land, under the following provisions: **James** is to take **Nelson** at my death and keep him well fed and comfortably clothed, and is to take care that he is well treated, for which he shall give bond and security to my administrators if he shall well and truly carry out these provisions as here stated he is to have the use of **Nelson's** land during his life and at his death, it shall belong to **James**. If **James** should die before **Nelson** then **Nelson's** land to be sold and the proceeds is to provide him a comfortable home during life.

I give to my daughter **Tabitha** $1,600.00 which amount is to be put on interest to be appropriated to her support, and at her death, the principal is to be divided equally among the heirs.

I have given to each of my sons **William** and **John** the sum of $600.00, which amount with interest is to be charged to them from the time they received it it up to the time of my decease, and after deducting that amount, they are to share equally with my four daughters, Viz: **Rebecca's** heirs, **Eleanor, Elizabeth, Salitz** and the child of **George M. Sanders.**

Lastly, after the foregoing bequests have been arranged, the land is to be divided, giving **James** his choice of the upper or lower end of the **Lee** farm from which to take his own and **Nelson's** part allowing them also a fair portion of woodland. Then the balance of the land and property to be sold and divided equally according to the instructions in this will, between the heirs of **John Sanders**, the heirs of **Rebecca Morrisett**, **William Sanders**, **Eleanor Cockerham**, **Elizabeth Smith**, **Salitz Drake**, and the child of **George M. Sanders**. and in the event of the death of **George's** child, its share is to be divided equally among the heirs. Also, during my wife's lifetime, I sold her part in some lands for $530.00, which she directed me to pay to her three daughters, **Eleanor, Elizabeth & Salitz**. I have paid $300.00 of this amount and intend to pay the balance if I can before my death, but if I should not, I want My Administrator to pay it.

In witness whereof I do to this my will set my hand and seal. This the 26th day of February, 1863.

                     James Sanders (seal)

Signed, sealed and delivered in our presence. This the 26th day of February, 1863. Witness: **D. M. Sheffey, J. J. Carroll**

WILL OF THOMAS TAYLOR

Page 465   Dated: Feb'7 26, 1813
In the Name of God, Amen.

I, **Thomas Taylor** of the State of Tennessee, now residing in Hawkins County, being much afflicted in body but yet in perfect mind and memory, thanks be to God for it. Calling to mind the mortality of my body and knowing that it is appointed for all men once to die, do make and ordain this my last Will & Testament. That is to say, principally and first of all. I do give and recommend my soul to God who gave it, and my body I recommend to the Earth, to be buried in a decent manner, agreeable to the Christian rule, but at the general resurrection, I shall receive the same again by the power of God. And as touching such worldly Estates wherewith it has pleased (God) to bestow on me in this life, I do give, devise and dispose of in the following manner.

First. I recommend all my just debts be paid.

Secondly. I recommend all my perishable property to be sold and equally divided in my family of boys and girls, one black cow excepted, and allowed for **Catrena Brown.**

Thirdly. I recommend my land to be for the use of my son **James Taylor** for five years, and he is to scool **Beckey** and **Ann** to read and write their name, and to keep the plantation in repair, and at the expiration of five years to be sold and equally divided between **John, Thomas, James** and **Wilson Taylor**, and the said sons to pay to **Becky** and **Ann** $150.00 each that is to come out of the price of the land, either in money or in property. I allow **Joseph Long's** note 100 dollars, **William Logan's** note 50 dollars and **Andrew Forgey's** note to be collected by my Executors and give to suits of clothes

to **Beckey** and two to **Ann**, at the age of 15 years.

And I do constitute my sons **Thomas** and **James** to be my Executors. And I do hereby disallow, revoke and utterly disannul all quiths, and every other Testament that mite been heretofore been mead, and I do hereby ratify and confirm this to be my last Will & Testament.

In witness whereof I have set my hand and seal This 26th day of February, 1813.

Signed, sealed, published and delivered by the said **Thomas Taylor** to be his last Will & Testament in the presence of us who in his presence and in the presence of each other have subscribed our names.

                     Thomas Taylor (seal)

Test. **John Long** , **James Y. Long**

N.B. That part of my will saying that **James Taylor** is to live on my plantation five years is done away and the land is to be sold. (blank space) will allow and that part of **James Taylor** scooling my daughters **Ann** and **Rebeckey** is done away, and there is a note on **James Surgian (Surgion)** of 110 dollars and sixty-five dollars out of said note which is mine.

And I do certify that the above signed will to be my last Will and Testament with these under amendments.

                     Thomas Taylor (seal)

Test: **Aaron Wells, John Long**

WILL OF NOTTLEY THOMAS

Page 466   Dated: Apr. 4, 1836

I **Nottley Thomas** of the County of Hawkins and State of Tennessee, planter, do make and publish this my last Will and Testament hereby revoking and making void all former wills by me at any time heretofore made. And First, I direct that my body be decently buried at the grave yard where my first wife is buried, on my own plantation, in said County in a manner suitable to my condition in life, and as to my worldly Estate as it hath pleased God to intrust me with, I dispose of the same as follows:

First. I direct that all my debts and funeral expenses be paid as soon after my decease as possible, out of any money that I may die possessed of or may first come into the hands of my Executors from any portion of my Estate, real or personal.

Secondly. I give and bequeath unto my beloved wife **Temperance** and to my daughter **Mary Thomas** the plantation that I now live upon. Also, one sorrel mare, also my flock of sheep, also my stock of hogs. I do also will and bequeath unto my beloved wife **Temperance** and my daughter **Mary**, all my household and kitchen furniture with the exception of my bed and furniture that belongs to the said bed--and that I give to my wife alone. And also, I give all my farming utensils that belongs on and to my farm to my wife and daughter **Mary** as the above said property and also my bee stands. I do will and bequeath all the above named property to my wife **Temperance** and to my daughter **Mary** so long as the two above mentioned can agree and whenever disagrees the administrators below chosen is to proceed to sell the said property in such manner as they think proper and divide the moneys arising therefrom equally between the said two persons to wit: My lawful wife **Temperance** and daughter **Mary**. And as to my son **John Tomas** and my daughter **Elizabeth Toman** but now **Elizabeth Bassett** I do think in Justice that I have done all for them that I can, but yet for the love and affection that I have for them, I do will and bequeath unto them one dollar each out of the money arising from the sale of my property after my decease.

I do hereby make, ordain and apoint my assteemed neighbors and friends **Lewis Click & Beverly C. Ford** Executors of this my last Will & Testament. In witness whereof I set my hand and seal. This, the fourth day of April, one thousand, eight hundred and thirty-six.

Nottley x Thomas (seal)
(his mark)

Signed, sealed and published in the presence of us who have subscribed in the presence of the Testator and of each other.
Beverly C. Ford, Lewis Click

Proven by oath of **Beverly C. Ford** at August Term, 1852. The handwriting of **Lewis Click** proven at August Term, 1853.

J. H. Vance, Clk.

WILL OF JESSE TRENT

Page 467   Dated: July 25, 1837

I, **Jesse Trent, Sr.** of the County of Hawkins and State of Tennessee, being weak in body, but of sound, disposing mind, ordain and desire this to be my last Will & Testament. I give and bequeath to my wife **Elizabeth Trent** all of my Estate both real and personal to be at her disposal and control forever - out of which she is to pay all my just debts. It is my desire that my said wife be Executrix of this my last Will & Testament and that no security be required of her for the execution of the same. In testimony whereof I have hereunto set my hand and seal. This 25th day of July, 1837.

Jesse x Trent, Sr. (seal)
(his mark)

Signed, sealed and acknowledged in our presence the date above written.
Jas. A. Rogers, Larkin Willis, James Willis, Wm. D. Kenner

WILL OF WILLIAM TUCKER (SR.)

Page 468   Dated: February 6, 1843
                        Proven: Nove. 6, 1843

In the Name of God, Amen.

I, **William Tucker, Senr.** of the County of Hawkins and State of Tennessee, being of a sound and disposing mind and memory, bringing to mind the mortality of this life, knowing it is appointed to all men once to die, and having a desire to dispose of such worldly Estate as wherewith it hath pleased God to bless me, do make and publish this my last Will and Testament in manner following to wit:

Item First. I give and bequeath to my beloved wife **Nancy**, during her natural life, all and every part and parcel of the land and tenements whereon I now live, and at her death aforesaid lands to be equally divided between my two sons, **William J.** (junior?) **& Hyram Tucker.**

Item Second. After disposition or sale having been made of a sufficiency of my stock of horses and hogs and cattle as will satisfy all debts, dues or lawful demands against me, I give and bequeath to my wife **Nancy** all the remainder of my said stock and all farming utensils and all other such property as shall or may not otherwise be disposed of. Said property be converted to her use in raising her children.

Item 3rd. I give and bequeath to my daughters (eight in number) as follows: **Jane, Matilda, Oltha, Rebecca, Ruth, Myra, Elizabeth, Minerva,** unto each of the above named girls, my lawful daughters, I give and bequeath a good bed and all appurtenances pertaining thereto: bed clothes &c.

Item 4th. To my oldest son **George** I give and bequeath a two-year-old heifer, two sheep and a sow.

Item 5th. I give and bequeath to my second son **John** my oldest tract of land lying on or near the creek above this. I give and bequeath to my son **John** all said land held in or by title of two deeds when he becomes to be 21 years of age. Over said lands he is to have no power until he becomes 21 years of age, but the profits, products or produce of said lands shall be converted to the use and support of my wife **Nancy** and family.

Item 6th. To my sons **William** and **Hyram Tucker**, I give and bequeath a certain tract whereon I now live, held by title of one deed, termed the Middle Tract. The profits or products or produce of said land to be converted to the use and support of their mother **Nancy Tucker** and family until said **William** and **Hyram** shall become 21, at which time said land is to be equally divided between **William** and **Hyram Tucker.**

It is further my will and desire that my son **John Tucker** should remain with his mother, assisting her in having charge of raising her children.

Lastly, I do hereby constitute and appoint my trusty friends **Barnet Cantwell** and **John Cantwell** of the said County of Hawkins, my sole Executors of this my last Will & Testament.

In witness whereof I have hereunto set my hand and seal. This 6th day of February A.D. 1843.

(his mark)
William x Tucker (seal)

Signed in presence of **George Tucker, John S. Wells**

WILL OF D. THURMAN

Page 469   Dated: March 15, 1845
                        Proven: Apr. 7, 1845

In the Name of God, Amen.

I, **Dickinson Thurman**, of the County of Hawkins and State of Tennessee, being weak in body but of sound and perfect mind and memory, do make and publish this my last Will and Testament in manner and form following, that is to say:

First. That after the payment of all my just debts, (I) bequeath to my wife **Ann** all my real and personal property to remain in her hands and under her control until my son **William D.** obtains the age of 21 years, then the plantation I formerly lived on joining **C. C. Miller**, be sold and the proceeds of said sale of land to be equally divided between my two sons, **James F.** and **William D.** and daughter **Mary Gillenwaters.**

The black woman **Emeline** and children I give and bequeath to my wife **Ann**, together with the residue of my money, notes & dues of every kind, after paying all my just debts. My father and mother are to have their support on the products of the lands gotten from my father & where he now lives. And at the death of my wife **Ann**, or when she may choose to relinquish her claims to the plantation I now live on & also the plantation where **Silas Williams** now lives, I give and bequeath to my son **William D.** All my stock of every kind and farming utensils to remain on the farm and for the use of the same except a certain sorrel mare which I give to my wife **Ann** for her exclusive benefit. I will that my black man **Barry** remain in the family during my father and mother's lifetime & then so long as my wife **Ann** chooses to remain living with **William**, but then to be sold and the proceeds of the sale to be divided between **James F.** and daughter **Mary.** I will and bequeath to my wife **Ann** also, such of the household and kitchen furniture as she may want and the residue to be divided between **James F. & William D.** as my wife may think best.

I do hereby appoint **James R. Forgey** and my wife **Ann** Executor and Executrix of this my last Will & Testament, hereby revoking all former wills by me made. In testimony whereof I have hereunto set my hand and seal. This 15th March, 1845.

D. Thurman(seal)

Signed, sealed and published and declared by the above named **Dickinson Thurman** to be his last Will & Testament in the presence of:
H. Watterson, Robert Johnson

WILL OF SARAH TARTER

Page 470   Dated: Dec. 27, 1854
                                  Proven: July Term, 1860
In the Name of God, Amen.

I, **Sarah Tarter,** of the County of Hawkins and State of Tennessee, being of advanced age, but in good health and of sound and disposing mind and memory, and considering the uncertainty of life and the certainty of death, do make, publish and declare the following to be my last Will and Testament hereby making void all wills that may have been made by me at any time heretofore.

First. It is my will and desire that out of any monies that may be on hand at the time of my death, or out of the first monies that may come into the hands of my Executor hereinafter named, all the expenses attending my funeral shall be paid.

Secondly. It is my will and desire should I owe any debts at the time of my death, said debts shall be paid by my said Executor.

Thirdly. To my much esteemed and well beloved son in law, **Robert A. Hounshell** and his wife **Elizabeth** my well beloved daughter, I will and bequeath all the Estate that I may be possessed of at the time of my death, whether the same consists of monies, goods, lands, real, personal or mixed Estate, to them and their heirs or assigns forever.

Lastly. I do hereby nominate and appoint said **Robert A. Hounshell** my Executor of this my last Will & Testament. In witness whereof I have hereunto set my hand and affixed my seal. This 27th day of December, 1854.

Signed, sealed, published   **Sarah x Tarter** (seal)
and delivered in presence   (her mark)
of us the undersigned:
Geo. R. Powel, James G. Armstrong

WILL OF JOHN VAUGHAN

Page 471   Dated: Apr. 10, 1820
In the Name of God, Amen.

I **John Vaughan**, being very weak in body but of sound mind and memoroy, calling to mind that it is appointed for all men to die doth make this my last Will & Testament. In the first place, I give and bequeath unto my beloved wife **Judy Vaughan** all my housel furniture and with my horses, cattle and hogs as long as she lives, and then for her to divide all that property

equally between **Polly Wilson, Benjamin** and **Isham**, a son of my daughter **Clary's** to have his part equal to the other three, and there is **William** and **Agathe** and **Jonathan**—shall have five shillings each. Whereof I have hereunto subscribed my hand and caused my seal to be affixed. This 10th day of April, 1820.

John x Vaughan (seal)
(his mark)

Witness Present:
Thomas Hammon (Jurat)
Howel Brewer

WILL OF ABRAHAM VERNON

Page 472   Dated: January 8, 1825
In the Name of God, Amen.

I, **Abraham Vernon**, of the County of Hawkins, State of Tennessee, being of sound mind and memory, blessed be God, do this eighth day of January in the year of our Lord, One Thousand eight hundred and twenty-five, make and publish this my Will & Testament in manner following, that is to say:

First. I give and bequeath unto my loving wife **Rebecca Vernon**, after paying my debts, all my free hold and personal Estate, except my elder brother **Nathan Vernon**, I give and bequeath $20.00. Also my younger brother **Harland Vernon**, I give and bequeath the same sum of $20.00, each out of my Estate, and the residue to be at the disposal of my wife as she wishes, and my negroes named **Jacob, Junie** and her two children **Jack** and **Malinda**, I wish her to keep them if they are obedient to her, and at my wife's death I wish them to be set free, and if they should be disobedient to my wife, she may dispose of them as she pleases.

And also, I appoint my said wife **Rebecca Vernon** sole Executrix of this my last Will & Testament in the presence of us who are present at the time of my signing and sealing thereof, the year and date first above written.   **Abraham Vernon** (seal)
Witness: **Nicholas Long, Jesse Dowell**

WILL OF JOHN M. VAUGHAN

Page 472   Dated: November 22, 1834
                                  Proven: Feb'y 23, 1835

Know all men by these presents, I **John M. Vaughan** of Hawkins County, Tennessee, taking into consideration the uncertainty of human life and being desirous of settling and regulating my own affairs in the event of my death, do make and publish this my last Will & Testament, revoking and annulling all others.

Imprimis. It is my will and desire that my body be decently committed to the Earth from whence it came.

Item. It is my will and desire that the tract of land on which I now live consisting of the tract that was allotted to my wife out of her father's Estate composed of lot of five or six acres south of the stage road on which my houses stand and of a lot of about 68 acres north of the stage road and also consisting of a lot bought of **Jacob Wills** for which I hold his title bond, of about 40 acres lying north of the road and adjoining **J. Francisco** on the east and also consisting of another tract bought of **Critz** on both sides of the stage road joining the lands of **O. Bradley & J. Wills** & others containing about 81 acres, and said tract on which I live is supposed to contain in all about 195 acres. Now, it is my will that said tract of land, together with all my household and kitchen furniture, farming utensils and stock go to my wife Elizabeth Vaughan during her life, to raise, educate and support her children, and support and maintain herself during her natural life, and at her death the same to be equally divided among my children by her; and at her death the same purposes as above, and at her death to also (be) equally divided among my said three children, John H. Vaughan, Elizabeth & William P. Vaughan.

Vaughan, Jr., and William P. Vaughan.   It is my will that my slaves go to my said wife during her natural life, for the same purposes as above, and at her death to also (be) equally divided among my said three children, John H. Vaughan, Elizabeth & William P. Vaughan.

Item.   It is my will that all my debts be collected by my Executors and the proceeds applied to the settlement of all just claims against my Estate.

Item.   It is my will that my plantation called the McMinn Place, consisting of the lands I bot of Robert Morrison & F. A. Ross containing by supposition about 500 acres, more or less, be sold by my Executors on a credit of one and two years, at public sale to the highest bidder on bond and security good and sufficient, and that the proceeds thereof after paying any debts that may not be discharged by the claims I hold on others shall be equally divided, share and share alike among my four children by my first wife, viz: Henry H. Vaughan, James M. Vaughan, Thomas J. Vaughan, George W. Vaughan & Florintha Vaughan.

Item.   It is my will and desire that any portion of the Estate of their grandfather, Jeremiah Cloud coming to me in right of their mother shall be confirmed to my said children and be vested in them.

Item.   It is my will that James Francisco and my wife Elizabeth Vaughan be Executor and Executrix of this my last Will and Testament and that no security be required unless my wife Elizabeth should marry again.   In testimony whereof I have hereunto set my hand and seal.   This 22nd day of November, 1834.

John M. Vaughan (seal)

Witnesses present who witnessed the same at the request and in the presence of the -

Testator: Orville Bradley, Randolph Burris, George Cloud, George Morrison

WILL OF JAMES VAUGHAN

Page 474
Dated: Sept. 8, 1840

In the Name of God, Amen.

I, James Vaughan of Hawkins County, being in moderate health, knowing that it is appointed that all men has to die, therefore, I commit my soul to God who gave it, and I do constitute this my will & Testament in manner and form as follows, viz: My will and desire is that my son John Vaughan shud pay all my just debts and shud hold all the perishable property, the one half to be kept for the well support of my beloved wife, Sally Vaughan. Then my will and desire is that my son John shud have the land and plantation whereon I now live containing 100 acres, also 30 acres known by the (name of) Wooten Place, also an entry of 30 acres lying on the north side of the copper ridge which has not been surveyed, then my will and desire is that the part of my land lying on Clinch River shud be rented till the death of my beloved wife Sally Vaughan for her support; and at her death my son John may sell the same or keep it, tho my will and desire is it my just debts are paid at the death of my wife Sally, and my son John sees

cause to keep said river tract of land, my will and desire is that he shud pay William Vaughan, Allen Vaughan, Nancy Donnelson, Patsy Rogers, Elizabeth Hartel $50.00 each in money or good trade, if they see cause to take such.

And lastly, I appoint my son James Vaughan, Joseph Vaughan, and Benjamin Vaughan Executors of this my last Will & Testament.   Signed, sealed.   In witness whereof I have hereunto set my hand and seal this 8th day of September, 1840.

James Vaughan (seal)

Witness: James Payne, George Payne

WILL OF JOHN VAUGHAN

Page 474
Dated: Dec. 27, 1841
Proven: Aug. Term, 1842

I, John Vaughan of the County of Hawkins and State of Tennessee, do make this my last Will & Testament hereby revoking and making void all former wills by me heretofore made.

First.   My will and desire is that all my just debts be paid out of any money that I may die possessed of, or that may first come into the hands of my Executors.

Second.   My will and desire is that my son George Washington, for and in consideration of the bequests hereinafter made to him do keep and support my wife Nancy Vaughan during her natural life.

Third.   I do give and bequeath unto my sons Samuel N. Vaughan and Benjamin Vaughan during their natural lives and then to their lawful heirs forever all my lands on the north side of Clinch Mountain, it being about 110 acres and 10 acres on the south side of the copper ridge whereon the said Samuel N. Vaughan now lives, to be equally divided between them according to quality.

Fourth.   I do will and direct that the above named Samuel N. and Benjamin Vaughan for and in consideration of the above bequest shall within 12 months after my death jointly pay unto my son John Vaughan $100.00.

Fifth.   I give and bequeath unto my son George Washington Vaughan all my land whereon I now live and joining it being about 170 acres, together with all my personal estate that I may die possessed of or entitled to, and all money and debts due me except so much as may be necessary to supply the bequests made in this will in money.

Sixth.   Whereas my sons Beverly Vaughan and James L. Vaughan has gone to parts unknown, if they should return within two years after my death, I do give and bequeath to them one dollar each.

Seventh.   I do give and bequeath unto the heirs of my daughter Mahala Dickerd one dollar.

Eighth.   I do give and bequeath unto my daughter Mary Gilliam one dollar.

Ninth.   I do give and bequeath unto my daughter Rebecca Roller $1.00.

Tenth.   I do give and bequeath unto my daughter Nancy Hickman $1.00.

Eleventh.   I do give and bequeath unto my daughter Martha Davis $1.00.   And for the performance and execution of this my will, I do appoint Robert W. Kinkead my Executor.   In testimony whereof I have hereunto set my hand and seal.   This 27th day of December, 1841.

John x Vaughan (seal)
   (his mark)

In presence of: William Carmack, James T. Brice, William E. Carmack

WILL OF HARLEN VERNON

Page 476

Dated: Aug. 16, 1849
Proven: Feb'y 1850

I, **Harlen Vernon** of the County of Hawkins and State of Tennessee, being of sound disposing mind and memory do make and ordain this my last Will and Testament in manner and form following.

First. I will that all my just debts be paid by my Executors out of moneys that I may die possessed of or that may first come into their hands from any property.

Secondly. I will that my three negro slaves, namely, **Mary, Marinda & James**, be free at my death and remain citizens of this state as other free slaves do.

Thirdly. I do not know that I have any lawful heirs or legal representatives living, but should there be any unknown to me and should apply to my Executors and make known that fact, I will that my Executors pay to each the sum of one dollar out of my Estate.

Fourthly. As to my personal property, I have but little, but such as I may be possessed of I will that my three slaves above named have the same.

And lastly, I nominate and appoint my friend **Robert Rogers** Executor of this my last Will & Testament.

In witness whereof I have hereunto set my hand and seal August 16, 1849.

Harlen Vernon (seal)

Robert Rogers, J. Mitchell, George Rogers

WILL OF NATHAN VERNON

Page 476

Dated: Jan. 12, 1851
Proven: Feb. 1854

Now, I, **Nathan Vernon**, in the Name of God, Amen, and being called to mind the uncertainty of life and the true certainty of death, and having been blessed with a small portion of property for which I am very thankful to my Creator for, and being of sound mind at this time which will enable me to dispose of such of my property as I am at this time desirous of doing which is as follows, Viz:

First. I will and desire and my will is that as soon after my decease as is practicable, I desire that my Executor or Administrator should my Executor refuse to serve, pay all my just debts and funeral expenses out of any money that may first come into the hands of my Executor or Administrator.

Second. My will and desire is that should I decease before my wife, then and in that case, I desire that my wife **Elizabeth Vernon** be well supported out of any means that is thought best by my Executor or Adm'r during her natural life. Should there be that much of my Estate in the hands of my Executor or Administrator, and should my wife **Elizabeth Vernon** choose to leave my house or houses where I now live after my decease, then and in that case I desire that my wife have ten dollars out of any money that may remain or be in the hands of my Executor or Adm'r., and all further support and supplies stopped from my said wife **Elizabeth.**

Third. My will is: Should there be any lawful heir or heirs that have a lawful claim or claims to any portion of my Estate after my decease, for some of them are unknown to me at this time, my desire is for them to have one dollar each and no more of my Estate.

Fourth. My will and desire is that after the death of myself and my wife **Elizabeth**, should there be any of my Estate left or unexpended, then

and, in that case I give and bequeath the balance of my Estate to **Thomas Coward** an ediot boy, son of **Patsy Coward**, both relatives and are living with me at this time and have been for many years, taking care of me and my wife... My will and desire is that **Patsy Coward**, mother of **Thomas Coward** whom I willed the remainder of my Estate to be, and I hereby appoint her the said **Patsy Coward** Guardian for her said ediot son **Thomas Coward**, and to receive from my Executor or Administrator all such Estate as may be coming to the said **Thomas Coward**, after all other expenses are paid and settled of. And to have full power and authority in dealing it out to her son, as thou it belonged to her, the said **Patsy Coward**, in every way, manner and form in taking care of her son, **Thomas.**

Fifth. Know ye that this is my last Will & Testament, revoking all other or former wills heretofore made by me, or all other deeds of gift or deeds of trust of any kind previous to the making of this will.

Lastly, I do hereby nominate and appoint my friend ___blank space___ my Executor of my last Will & Testament. In witness whereof I do hereunto set my hand and affix my seal. This 12th day of January, 1851.

Nathan Vernon(seal)

Signed, sealed and published in the presence of the Testator This__ blank space__ 1851.
Attest: **Hugh Kirkpatrick, Joseph Coward**

WILL OF ALLEN VAUGHAN

Page 478

Dated: Feb'y 7, 1858
Proven: March 1st, 1858

I, **Allen Vaughan**, do make and publish this as my last Will and Testament, hereby revoking and making void all other wills by me at any time made.

First. I direct that my funeral expenses and all my just debts be paid as soon as possible out of any money that I may die possessed or, or may first come into the hands of my Executor.

Secondly. I give and bequeath to my beloved wife **Nelly** all my land, being the tract on which I now live, for and during her natural life and no longer.

Thirdly. The land mentioned in the above bequest at the death of my wife, I give and bequeath to my three children (to wit), my son **Allen**, my daughters **Rebecca** and **Susan**, to be equally divided between them on account of their having helped me to pay for said land.

Fourthly. I give and bequeath to my daughter **Rebecca** one large pot.

Fifthly. I give and bequeath to my son **Allen**, my daughters **Rebecca** and **Susan** all my personal property that may be on hand, if any, after paying all my just debts, to be equally divided between them.

Last. I do hereby nominate and appoint my son **Allen** my Executor. In witness whereof I do to this my will set my hand and seal. This 7th day of February, 1858.

Allen x Vaughan (seal)
(his mark)

Signed, sealed and published in our presence, and we have subscribed our names hereto in the presence of the Testator. This 7th day of February, 1858.

Jas. B. Galbraith, P. L. Henderson, Michael Looney

WILL OF ROBERT WILLIAMS

Page 479   Dated: September 30, 1786

In the Name of God, Amen.

I, Robert Williams of Sullivan County, being weak in body, yet of perfect mind and memory, thanks to God for his mercies, do make and constitute this my last Will and Testament as follows, viz:

First. I commit my soul into the hands of God who gave it, and my body to the dust to be buried in Christian decency at the discretion of my Executor, in hopes to receive it again at the general resurrection by the mighty power of God, and as for that portion of things which God has been pleased to bestow upon me, I dispose of in the manner following:

I give and bequeath unto my beloved wife Ann the use of my plantation and the service of my slaves during her widowhood; also, I leave her all my farming utensils, two work horses named George and Jack, two mules such as she shall choose, and all my household furniture, cattle, sheep and hogs. To my daughter Ann I give one young horse known by the name of the Orphan Colt. To my daughter Mary I give one horse creature or fifteen pounds. To my daughter Rebekah, I leave one horse creature or fifteen pounds Virginia money. To my sons Robert and Samuel, I leave my plantation to be equally divided between them, quantity and quality and improvements considered; likewise, my negroes to be valued and equally divided between them, and if the negro wench should ever have issue, the first two children, or if but one, to be equally divided between my two daughters, Mary and Rebekah. Moreover, I will that the remainder of my horse creatures be sold and the money raised thereby be equally divided between my two sons Robert and Samuel. Likewise, all bonds, notes and book debts except so much as pays all my lawful debts. And further, I appoint and nominate my wife Ann, her son David Kinkead, and David Kinkead her sister's son (sic) to be my sole Executors of this my last Will & Testament, making void all other wills and Testaments heretofore made. In witness whereof I do hereunto set my hand and seal. This 13th day of September in the year of our Lord, one thousand seven hundred and eighty-six.

Robert x Williams (seal).
(his mark)

Signed sealed and acknowledged in presence of us: (1st name illegible), James Berry, David Kinkead

WILL OF REUBEN WEBSTER

Page 480   Dated: December 19, 1790

The Nuncupative Will of
Reuben Webster
Who Departed this Life December 19, 1790

1st. That his land and plantation should remain in the possession of his widow during her natural life, for the purpose of raising and maintaining his children, and at her death to be equally divided among all his children.

2nd. That all his movable property remain likewise in the hands of his widow towards the support of the orphans until they come to full age and then to be equally divided among them all.

3rd. That the tract of land which he sold John Hammond should have a right and title to the same.

Territory of the United States of America, South of the River Ohio, Hawkins County.

We do hereby certify that the above was proved to be the will of Reuben Webster, deceased—delivered from his own mouth in his last sickness before Isaac Lane, Bartlett Marshall, John Hammond & Joseph Webster.

Thos Henderson
James Blaiy/Blaiy/Blair
21st Dec., 1790

WILL OF REUBEN WINDHAM

Page 480   Dated: Oct. 15, 1795

In the Name of God, Amen.

I, Reuben Windham of Hawkins County, in the Territory of the United States South of the Ohio River, being weak in body but in perfect sound mind & memory, do make and ordain this my last Will & Testament as follows, to wit:

I leave to my son William Windham my negro man named Witshaw as soon as he is settled in a way of living for himself. I leave to my daughter Charlotte Windham Rose & Leanor until Leanor is grown and then Rose is to return to the rest of my Estate; the said negroes to be in Charlotte's possession as soon as she is in a settled way of living for herself.

And all the rest of my property I leave for the support of my wife and family until my children are grown to be able to maintain themselves, unless my Executors should think it necessary that a division should take place sooner, and then all my Estate is to be equally divided between my wife and all my children, share and share alike, and the shares of such of my children as shall not be of age when such division shall take place, to be put in the hands of guardians appointed according to law to prevent waste or fraud of their parts of such Estate.

I leave and appoint my wife Rachael Windham, my son Wm. Windham and Thos. Henderson Executors of this my last Will & Testament. In testimony whereof I have hereunto set my hand and seal. This 15th day of October, A.D., 1795.

Reuben Windham (seal)

Signed, sealed, published and declared in presence of:
James Blair, Jesse x Strand
(his mark)

Be it further remembered that the portion allotted to my son William Windham shall be considered as his part without any more when a division of my Estate shall take place, agreeable to the foregoing will, and Charlotte is to keep Rose as her property without her ever returning this schedule to be considered as a part of my Estate, and I do ratify and confirm this schedule to be a part of my last Will & Testament. In witness whereof I have hereunto set my hand and seal. This 16th day of October, 1795.

Reuben Windham(seal.)

Signed in presence of:
James Blair
Jesse Strand

WILL OF ANDREW WINDGAR

Page 481   Dated: Aug. 21, 1810   [See Original Will]

In the Name of God, Amen.

I, Andara Winegar, Sen't of the County of Hawkins and State of Tenn., being in a languishing state of health, wish to commit my soul to God who gave it and my body to the dust for to be buried in Christian decency at the discretion of my Executors, and for my portion of worldly things that God in his Providence has bestowed on me, I wish for to dispose of in the following manner, after paying my just debts. I leave to my well beloved wife **Catrin** my dwelling house and all my household goods, one gray mare and colt, two milch cows, the third of my land and all of the orchard, my stock of hogs, during her life or widowhood. My land above to my sons **Andara** and **Fredric** equally, quantity and quality considered. I leave my land on condition that **Andara** pay unto **Phillip** and **William Winegar** $160.00 in trade equal to corn at two shillings a bushel, when convenient to **Andara**. And on the same conditions, **Frederic** pay unto **Peter**, **Phillip** and **William Winegar** $200.00 to divide $10.00 when convenient to **Frederic**.

N.B. There is $20.00 of the above money in **Phillip Winegar's** hand, and a certain black horse I leave to my wife **Catrin**. I appoint my sons **Andara** and **Frederic Winegar** for to be my Executors to this my last Will and Testament. Signed with my hand and dated This 21 day of August, in the year of our Lord, 1810.

Andrew x Winegar (seal)

(his mark)

Test: **David Kinkead**
(name of witness here illegible)
Johannes Winninger(in German Script)

WILL OF CHARLES WOLFE

Page 482

Dated: March 17, 1813
Proven: May Term, 1819

In the Name of God, Amen.

I, **Charles Wolfe** of Hawkins County, State of Tennessee, being very sick and weak in body, but of perfect mind and memory, thanks be given to God, calling unto mind the mortality of my body and knowing that it is appointed for all men once to die, do make and ordain this my last Will and Testament, that is to say. Principally and first of all, I give and recommend my soul unto the hand of Almighty God that gave it and my body, I recommend to the Earth to be buried in a decent Christian burial at the discretion of my Executors nothing doubting but at the general resurrection, I shall receive the same again by the mighty power of God. And as touching such worldly Estate wherewith it has pleased God to bless me in this life, I give, devise and dispose of the same in the following manner and form.

First. I give and bequeath to **Susan**, my dearly beloved wife all my lands and tenaments, stock and household furniture of every description. Also, I give and bequeath to my son **Jacob Wolfe** one good horse. To my son **Phillip Wolfe** one shilling sterling. To my daughter **Catharine Davis**, I give one shilling sterling. To my son **Peter Wolfe**, I give one shilling sterling. To my daughter **Elizabeth**, I give one shilling sterling. To my daughter **Hannah McGinnis**, I give one shilling sterling. To my daughter **Barbara** I give one horse and cow and her bed. To my son **Charles Wolfe**, I give one grown horse a colt, one plow and one axe. I give to my son **George** one grown horse and a colt, one plow and one axe. I give to my well beloved wife **Susana Wolfe** whom I constitute my sole Executrix of this my last Will

and Testament, all and singular my lands, messuages and tenaments, by her freely to be possessed and enjoyed. And I do hereby utterly disallow and disannul all and every other former testaments, wills, legacies, bequests and Executors by me in anywise before named, willed and bequeathed, ratifying and confirming this and no other to be my last Will & Testament. In witness whereof I have hereunto set my hand and seal. The 17th day of Mar. in the year of our Lord one thousand eight hundred and thirteen.

Charles Wolfe (seal)

Signed, sealed, published, pronounced and declared by the said **Charles Wolfe** as his last Will & Testament in the presence of us who in his presence and in the presence (of each other) have heretofore subscribed our names. **Archibald McCoy, Adam Wolfe, Jesse Epperson.**

WILL OF CHRISTOPHER WILLFLE/WILFLE

Page 483

Dated: May 17, 1817
Proven: May Term, 1817

In the Name of God, Amen.

I, **Christopher Wilfle** of the County of Hawkins in the State of Tenn., being of sound mind but infirm of body, do make this instrument my last Will and Testament.

Item 1st. I give and bequeath unto my son **John Wilfle** that part of my tract of land on which he now resides, to begin in the great road where **John Critz** lives, crosses the same, thence down the road to the first fence of the lot now occupied as a calf pasture, thence a south course with s'd fence to the outside of the plantation, thence a westerly course with the fence back of the barn to the line of **John Burris'** tract, to include all that lays south of the before described lines, also one negro woman slave named **Easter**, provided she may choose to go to him, and in the case she does not, she is to be sold and the amount of sale paid to my son as aforesaid. Also, one bay mare called Tam.

Item 2nd. I give unto my three daughters, **Mary, Elizabeth** and **Pheby**, all the remaining part of my land lying principally on the north side of the great road, to be equally divided between them, and in case they cannot agree among themselves, it is my will that **James T. Gaines, Robert McMinn & John Critz** divide the same into three lots of as near equal value as they can, and that my said daughters draw lots...I also give and bequeath unto my daughter **Mary** two negro slaves, to wit: a boy named **Ceaser**, and a girl named **Emeline**. I also give and bequeath unto my daughter **Elizabeth** two negro slaves, one a woman named **Milley**, the other a girl named **Mariah**. I also give and bequeath to my daughter **Pheby** two negro slaves, to wit: **Carson** and **Winney**. I give and bequeath unto said daughters aforesaid, all my stock (except the mare before mentioned), together with all my farming tools of every description. And in case there should be more of either than they may wish to keep on the farm, they are to be sold at public sale by my Executors and the proceeds divided equally amongst them. I also give my said daughters all my household and kitchen furniture, and if more than they wish to keep, to be divided as the last above-mentioned articles are to be, or in case of a separation taking place between them by marriage—in that case, the stock on hand, household and kitchen furniture to be equally divided so that the one going off may have her share with her. I wish my two stills and vessels sold and the money arising therefrom after paying my debts to be equally divided amongst my four children.

In testimony whereof I have hereunto set my hand and affixed my seal. This 17th day of May in the year of our Lord, 1817. I constitute and appoint the before point the before James T. Gaines, Robert McMinn & John Critz Exec's of this my last Will & Testament.

Christopher Willlie(seal)

(note: someone has written "supposed to be" below his signature, suggesting that Willlie is the correct spelling)

Signed and acknowledged in the presence of:
John M. Vaughan, John Akaid

Page 484

WILL OF JOHN WALKER

Dated: Aug. 19, 1818

In the Name of God. Amen.

I, John Walker of the County of Hawkins and State of Tennessee, being weak in body but of sound and perfect mind and memory, considering the uncertainty of this mortal life, blessed be Almighty God for the same, do make and publish this my last Will & Testament in manner and form following(viz):

First. After paying all just debts, I give and bequeath unto my eldest children (viz) Joshua Walker, John Walker, Walter Walker, Edward Walker, Elizabeth Walker, Jane Epperson and James Walker each one dollar, which several legacies I will and order to be paid to the said respective legatees after my decease. And the rest of the Estate to be equally divided between my beloved wife Elizabeth Walker and my four youngest children (viz) Cinthia Walker, Sarah Walker, Frances Walker and Andrew Walker. And, also, I hereby appoint Elizabeth Walker my wife sole Executrix of this my last Will and Testament, hereby revoking all former wills by me made. In witness whereof I have hereunto set my hand and seal. This 19th day of Aug.. One Thousand eight hundred and eighteen.

John Walker(seal)
(his mark)

Signed, sealed and declared by the above named John Walker to be his last Will & Testament in the presence of us who have hereunto subscribed our names as witnesses in the presence of the Testator.

James x Walker, Nicholas Long
(his mark)

Page 485

WILL OF BUTSON/BATSON WHITEHURST

Dated: March 26, 1823

In the Name of God. Amen.

I, Batson Whitehurst, of the County of Hawkins and State of Tennessee, being in perfect health of body and of perfect mind and memory, thanks be to God for his mercies, and calling into mind the mortality of my body and knowing that all men sooner or later must die, do make and ordain this my last Will and Testament, that is to say. Principally and first of all, I give and recommend my soul into the hand of Almighty God that gave it, and my body I recommend to the Earth, to be buried in a decent Christian order at the discretion of my Executors here named which are Hillery Whitehurst of North Carolina and John Burkhart of Hawkins, Tennessee.

And as touching such worldly Estate wherewith it has pleased God to bless me with in this life, I give, devise and dispose of the same in the following manner and form.

First. I give and bequeath my negro boy George and negro woman Siller to my brother Hillery Whitehurst and Henry Whitehurst, heirs to Sarah Camper and Nancy Cox, to be equally divided.

Secondly. I give to my four grandchildren, namely Patsy, Batson, John and Thomas Whitehurst the following two negroes, Charles and Nancy, to be equally divided, as they come to the age of maturity. My Executors to hire out the same for their benefit; and the balance of my personal property divided equally with these four children, leaving sufficient to defray all debts and expenses, and:

Thirdly. For divers good reasons good will and full compensation which I bear for my friend John Burkhart, I do will, give and devise to him my negro girl Hannah which is now in his possession, to keep her as long as he sees cause, to dispose of as he may (think) proper, and as his property forever. And I do hereby utterly disallow, revoke and disannul all and every other (testament), will, legacies bequeathed by me in any way before named, willed or bequeathed, ratifying and confirming this and no other to be my last Will and Testament. In witness whereof I hereunto set my hand and seal. This 26th day of March in the year of our Lord one thousand eight hundred and twenty three.

Batson Whitehurst (seal)

Signed, sealed, published and declared by the said Batson Whitehurst as his last Will and Testament in the presence of us who in his presence and in the presence of each other have hereunto subscribed our names:
Attest: Carter Mason, Edward William

Page 486

WILL OF ELIZABETH WELCH

Dated: June 30, 1825

In the Name of God. Amen.

I, Elizabeth Welch of Hawkins County and State of Tennessee, being sick and weak in body but of sound and perfect mind and memory (blessed be God), calling to mind the mortality of this life and knowing that it is appointed for all people once to die, do make and ordain this my last Will & Testament in manner and form following, (viz):

First. In consideration that my son Robert Welch and daughter Elizabeth Reynolds have received advances from me, I therefore give them twenty-five cents each.

Second. I give and bequeath to my two sons William Welch & John Welch my mare and colt, stock of hogs and the crop of corn now growing to be equally divided between them, share and share alike to them and their heirs forever.

Third. I give and bequeath to my two daughters Peggy Welch and Polly Welch my cow heifer and calf and all my household furniture to be equally divided between them, to them and their heirs forever. In witness whereof I the said Elizabeth Welch have hereunto set my hand and fixed my seal. This 30th day of June, 1825.

Elizabeth x Welch (seal)
(her mark)

Signed, sealed, published and declared by the said **Elizabeth Welch** as her last Will and Testament in the presence of us who were present at the signing and sealing thereof.
R. D. Young, James Long

WILL OF SOLOMAN WALTERS

Page 487   Dated: June 12, 1823
I, **Soloman Walters**, considering the uncertainty of this mortal life and being of sound and perfect mind and memory, blessed be the Almighty God for the same. I do make and publish this my last Will and Testament in manner and form following, that is to say:
   First. I give and bequeath unto my beloved wife **Fanney Walters** all my household and kitchen furniture or as much of it as she wants. I also give her one horse beast—she is to have choice of horses and two cows and six hed of sheep and six head of hogs, and she is to have privilege of the house and garden and orchard, and she is to have a piece of ground or land laid off or set apart containing two or three acres wherever she wants to have it for a truck patch and she is to keep the negro garrel or woman named **Luzesey**. All these things she is to hold or keep during her natural life time, and after her death, it is to be sold and equally divided amongst my five daughters, **Margaret, Elizabeth, Nancy & Christeney** or **Frankey & Mary**, except **Nancy** and **Margaret**. I give **Nancy** $73.00 and **Margaret** $70.00 that is to be taken out of their share and the balance is to be equally divided. My stock and household and kitchen furniture, negroes and everything I own except the land, is to be sold and the money is to be equally divided amongst them. The land I give it unto my two sons, that is to say: I give and bequeath unto my son **Elijah**, the land or plantation I bought of **John Forgey**, and the land or plantation I live on I give or bequeath unto my son **George**. And the lines are to remain the same as when I bought it of **John Forgey**. There is a consideration of **Elijah's** part. He bought a negro boy at **McMinn's** sale called or named **Harrey** and the bill of sale was given in his name and I paid the money for him. Now, if he takes the negro he is not to get the land and if he takes the land he is not to get the negro and the negro is to be sold and the money equally divided amongst my daughters. And if he takes the negro the land is to be sold and the money equally divided amongst them and if he keeps the land he is not to have it any longer than his lifetime, then it is to fall back to his children, and it is to be equally divided amongst them and if he keeps the land he must pay unto his mother yearly 33 bushels of corn and seven bushels of wheat and sixteen bushels of oats and he must furnish her with hay and fodder accordingly, during her lifetime. And **George** must pay unto his mother yearly 66 bushels of corn and 14 bushels of wheat and 32 bushels of oats and to furnish her with hay and fodder accordingly. And **George** is to be made equal with the balance of my children in household furniture and such as hogs and sheep and cows, other utensils as I gave them when they left me before anything can be sold. And the balance is to be equally divided amongst my daughters and **George** is to have the wum mill that is in the barn and **George** is to keep his mother as long as she wishes to live with him, or during her lifetime and as to my daughter **Margaret**, what I give her she is to keep it during her lifetime, then it is to return back to her children and to be equally divided amongst them, and I hereby appoint my son son **George** and **Andrew Winegar, Jr.** my sole Executors of my last Will and Testament, hereby revoking all former wills by me made.

   In witness whereof I have hereunto set my hand and seal this 12th day of June, 1833.

Test:
John Spangler, Robert Johnson
John Winegar

                                    Soloman x Walters (seal)
                                              (his mark)

WILL OF JAMES WEST

Page 488   Dated: February 5, 1834
In the Name of God, Amen.
   I, **James West** of the County of Hawkins and State of Tennessee, being weak in body but in perfect mind and memory, thanks be given to God. Calling into mind the mortality of my body and knowing that it is appointed for all men once to die, do make and ordain this my last Will and Testament. That is to say: Principally and first of all, I give and recommend my soul into the hand of Almighty God that gave it and my body I recommend to the Earth to be buried in decent Christian burial at the discretion of my Executors, nothing doubting but at the general resurrection I shall receive the same again by the mighty power of God. And as touching such worldly Estate wherewith it hath pleased God to bless me in this life, I give, devise and dispose of the same in the following manner and form:
   First. I give and bequeath to **Nancy** my dearly beloved wife all my household and kitchen furniture and farming utensils and movable effects and all my stock, horses, cattle, sheep and hogs and ten negroes, to wit: **Joe, Cate, Sind, Sall, Anderson, Looney, Jeff, Bets, Lisa** and **Sook** and their increase, which she is to have her lifetime and at her death all to be equally divided amongst my heirs to wit: **John, William, Bayless, Samuel, Winney, Elizabeth, James, Polly, Calvin, Gideon, Lucy & Nancy**. Also, my lands which is to be equally divided among the said heirs at my wife's death by her freely to be possessed and enjoyed, and I do hereby utterly disallow, revoke and disannul all and every other former testaments, wills, legacies, bequests and Executors by me in any ways before named, willed and bequeathed, ratifying and confirming this and no other to be my last Will and Testament. in witness whereof I have hereunto set my hand and seal this fifth day of February in the year of our Lord one thousand, eight hundred and thirty four.

                                    James West (seal)
Signed sealed published pronounced and declared
by the said **James West** as his last Will and Testament in the presence of us who, in the presence of each other, have hereunto subscribed our names.
Beverly Smith

WILL OF ANDREW WINEGAR

PAGE 489   Dated: April 5, 1835
Knowing the destinies of Providence on the bed of my affliction; knowing that death is the common lot of mankind, therefore, I **Andrew Winegar**, being of rational mind but of feeble body do ordain and make this my last Will and Testament, to wit: In the first place, I desire that my just debts be paid. Therefore, it may be necessary that my Executor or Executrix sell a sufficiency of my personal property to discharge the same. The residue of my property I give and bequeath unto my beloved wife **Frances**, my son **Soloman** share and equal alike, consisting of land and stock, together with my servant boy **Burton**. It is my desire that my wife **Frances** be my Executrix and Guardian to our son **Soloman**, waiving the necessity of her giving security

WILL OF JOSEPH WHITE

Dated: May 11, 1835

State of Tennessee, Hawkins County, May the 11th day, 1835 -

I, Joseph White, in the name of God, Amen. Being frail in body but sound in memory do make and A doing this my last Will & Testament.

To all whom these presents may come greetings.

First of all. After my death, I desire my body to be buried decently and the expenses paid out of my Estate. Then secondly, I give and bequeath to my youngest daughter, Elizabeth, a certain tract and parcel of land that I bought of my son George White, and he from William Moore, being in said county war (where) I now live for her only proper use and to her heirs. And I give and bequeath to my son William Gilmore White 100 acres of land, Burd's old Survey adjoining my daughter Elizabeth, be the same more or less, and I give and bequeath to my son in law Abram Shuttles 100 acres of land in said county, it being the tract whereon he now lives, it being sarvied by warrant. I give and bequeath unto my son George White $400.00, and I give and bequeath to my daughter Jemina White the sum of $20.00, to be paid to her or her acres out of a certain tract of land lying jointn old Alexander Ballard when sold. And the money maid out of said land, and I give and bequeath to my daughter Sally $20.00 to be paid out of said land when sold and the balance of money arising from the s'd land. And the balance of money arising from the s'd land. And the expenses arisen on said Estate and the land to be sold by my Executors. And also, it is my will that my youngest daughter Elizabeth shall have her bed and furniture. And this I make and doain (ordain) my last will and testament wherunto I set my hand this day and date above written. And it is my will that my son George White shall be my Executor.

Joseph White (seal)

Signed, sealed, published, pronounced by the Testator in the presence of:

James Lee, James Pangle

WILL OF GEORGE WOLFE, SEN'R.

Dated: April 15, 1837
Proven: Sept. 2, 1839

In the Name of God, Amen.

I George Wolfe, Sen'r of the State of Tennessee and County of Hawkins, being very sick and weak in body, but of perfect mind and memory thanks be given unto God, calling to mind the mortality of my body and knowing that it is appointed for all men once to die, do make and ordain this my last Will and Testament, that is to say.

Principally and first of all. I give and recommend my soul unto the hands of Almighty God that gave it and my body I recommend to the Earth to be buried in decent Christian burial at the discretion of my Executors,

---

nothing doubting but at the general resurrection I shall receive the same again by the mighty power of God. And as touching such worldly Estate wherewith it has pleased God to bless me in this live, I give, devise and dispose of the same in the following manner.

First. As I have already given to my two sons Volentine and John Wolfe as much of my real and personal Estate as I intend for them, I dispose of the remainder as follows. I give and bequeath to my two other sons George and Nicholas Wolfe 100 acres of land each, joining John Mill, Hiram Mills, Hiram Tucker, John Wolfe's and Volentine Wolfe's lines, and it is my request if my two sons George and Nicholas Wolfe cannot agree on the division of their land between themselves, they are to get a jury of disinterested men to divide it equal for them, and I do further will that myself and my wife Polly are to keep possession of the land for our maintenance during our natural lifetimes. I further give and bequeath unto my four daughters that are at home with me, Viz: Barbara, Polly, Margaret, and Ally Wolfe, to each of them one horse beast to be worth $50.00 each, and to each of the said daughters $10.00 in moncy when they leave home or marry.

I further will that my wife Polly Wolfe, if I should die before her, is to keep possession of my negro boy named Bob to work for her maintenance during her natural life, and at her decease the said negro boy Bob is to be sold and the money for his purchase is to be divided equally among all my daughters, Hannah, Katherine, Elizabeth, Barbara, Sarah, Polly, Susanah, Margaret and Ally, and the girls that are at home, Viz: Barbara, Polly, Margaret and Ally to have equal with the others and I also give to my daughters, Viz: Hannah, Katherine, Elizabeth, Barbara, Polly, Sarah, Susannah, Margaret and Alta all of my land from the top of the copper ridge, running with the top of said ridge an east and west direction north of said ridge bounded by Volentine Wolfe, Ausbrun/Osborne Coffee, David Wilders' line, to be equally divided among all of the above named girls, and all the land belonging to me south of the copper ridge, I give to my two sons George and Nicholas Wolfe to be equally divided between them, and all my household and kitchen furniture to be at the disposal of my wife Polly, and at her decease be at her disposal. I also constitute, ordain and appoint my wife Polly Wolfe my sole Executrix of this my last Will and Testament, and I do hereby utterly disallow, revoke and disannul all and every other Will and Testament by me heretofore, confirming this only to be my last Will and Testament. In witness whereof I have hereunto set my hand and seal. This fifteenth day of April in the year of our Lord, one thousand eight hundred and thirty seven.

George x Wolfe
(his mark)

Signed sealed published and declared by the s'd George Wolfe as his last Will & Testament, in the presence of us who in his presence and in the presence of each other have hereto subscribed our names.

Moses McGinnis, Jacob Wolfe, Samuel Timonds (may be)

WILL OF FRANCIS WINSTEAD

Dated: Sept. 20, 1842
Proven: Nov. 7, 1842

In the Name of God, Amen.

I, Francis Winstead, of the County of Hawkins in the State of Tenn., being weak of body but of sound mind and memory, knowing the uncertainty of life and the certainty of death, do make and ordain this my last Will and Testament, that is to say: I do recommend my soul to Almighty God who gave it and desire that my mortal body shall be decently committed to the earth with the usual Christian rites according to the discretion of my Executors hereinafter to be named, and as to the worldly Estate or property it hath pleased Almighty God to bless me with, I dispose of it in the following manner, to wit:

I give and bequeath unto my dearly beloved daughter-in-law, **Margaret Winstead**, widow of my son **Ephraim Winstead**, dec'd late of said County and State, all my estate or property of every description now owned by me or which may be hereafter owned by me, to be at her absolute disposal and control forever, in consideration of my love and affection for her and also in consideration of the love and affection she has always bestowed upon me, and am only sorry that I have not more to give unto her to remunerate her for her kindness and attention shown to me by her in my old age.

And it is my desire and I do request and ordain that my said daughter-in-law **Margaret Winstead**, together with my grand son **James Winstead** shall be my Executor and Executrix to this my last Will and Testament. And I do hereby request that the County Court shall qualify them as such without requiring from them bond and security, having full confidence that they will discharge their duties and discharge any debts which may be contracted on account of my funeral &c. Wherefore in witness whereof I have hereto set my hand and seal this 20th day of September, 1842.

Francis Winstead (seal)

Signed, sealed and published in the presence of us as the last Will and Testament by him.
Jesse Cope, Paschal Martin

WILL OF LARKIN WILLIS

Page 493   Dated: October 14, 1846
                                    Proven: Feb. 7, 1859
                                    [Recorded P. 238]

I, **Larkin Willis** of Hawkins and State of Tennessee being of sound disposing mind and memory, do make and ordain this my last Will and Testament in manner and form following, to wit:

First. After my just debts are paid, I want my wife **Elizabeth Willis** to have control of the tract of land where we now live on for her support during her lifetime, said land containing 200 acres more or less. I also want her to have my gray horse and a mare and two of the choice cows out of my stock of cattle. Also my yoke of oxen, also all my stock (of) hogs and my stock of sheep and all my farming tools, together with all my household and kitchen furniture to have during her lifetime. I want my black boy **Lige** to remain with my wife to serve her during her lifetime; also my black girl **Juda** to live with and serve my said wife as long as she may live. And I want **William Berry** to have the whole use and benefit of the tract of land whereon he now lives rent free that is to the line of my old tract of land.

2nd. After my said wife's death, I want my Executors to attend to selling what of my estate remains at my wife's death and equally divide the proceeds of the same between my heirs and legatees; namely, **James Willis, Samuel Willis, Patsy Kyle** and **Soloman Willis**. And lastly, I do hereby constitute and appoint my friends **John Mitchell** and **Swempfield Anderson** Exec's of this my last Will and Testament, revoking all other former wills and

bequests by me made. In witness whereof I have hereunto set my hand and seal this 14th day of October in the year of our Lord, 1846.

Larkin Willis (seal)

Signed, sealed and delivered in presence of us:
James Payne, George Payne, James M. Moneyhew

WILL OF FRANCIS H. WALKER

Page 494   Dated: January 30, 1847

Know all men by these presents that I **Francis H. Walker** of the County of Hawkins and State of Tennessee, being of sound mind and memory and understanding to make and ordain and establish this as my last Will and Testament in words following, that is to say:

First. After my decease, I desire my body to be buried decently and the expenses thereof paid out of my Estate, and all just debts be paid.

Second. I give and bequeath to my beloved wife **Lucinda Walker** the <u>hole</u> of my Estate both real and personal during her life, provided she remains my widow, and if she should marry, it is my wish that she have one fifth part of my estate, that is to say—one child's part.

3rd. It is my wish and desire that my daughter **Polly Ann Walker** shall have a horse, saddle and bridle, a cow, a bed and furniture.

4th. It is my wish that my son **William Walker** shall have a horse, saddle and bridle, a cow, a bed and furniture, when he comes to be 21 years of age.

5th. It is my wish that my daughter **Martha Caroline Walker** shall have a horse, saddle and bridle, a cow and bed and furniture when she comes to be 21 years of age, and it is also my wish that all my property both real and personal be sold in such ways and in such manner as my Executors hereafter named may think most advantageous, and the moneys arising therefrom to be equally divided between my children, namely: **Elizabeth Jane Horner, Polly Ann Walker, William Walker** and **Martha Caroline Walker**. My wife **Lucinda Walker** included. I also nominate and appoint my wife **Lucinda** and my son-in-law **Thomas N. Horner** my Executors.

I acknowledge this to be my last Will & Testament. This 30th day of January, 1847.

Francis H. x Walker (seal)
(his mark)

Signed, sealed and acknowledged in the presence
of us: **William Cobble, John C. White, George White**

WILL OF FANNY WALTERS

Page 495   Dated: Sept. 14, 1848
                                    Proven: January Term: 1852

Mediating on the uncertainty of human events being of advanced age, but of sound mind and disposing memory do make this my last Will & Testament, hereby revoking all others heretofore made by me.

In the first place, I give unto Almighty God the care of my soul.

I bequeath and give unto my daughter **Nancy** and her husband **Daniel Harrell** all my property and effects of every kind and description, consisting of debts, money and every other description of property I may die siezed and possessed of. I hereby constitute and appoint my son-in-law **Daniel Harrell** my Executor to this my last Will & Testament, authorizing my said Executor to act without the requirement of security.

In testimony of which I have hereunto set my hand and seal. This 14th day of September in the year of our Lord one thousand eight hundred and forty eight.

Fanny x Walters (seal)
(her mark)

Attest: James Amis, Thomas Purcell, Clemens x Winegar
(his mark)

Page 496

WILL OF THEODERIC WEBB

Dated: December 28, 1850 (THEORDRICK)
Proven: May Term, 1857

State of Tennessee, Hawkins County.

I, Theoderic Webb do make and publish this my last Will & Testament hereby revoking and making void all other wills by me at any time made.

First. I direct that my funeral expenses and all my debts be paid as soon after my death as possible out of any moneys that I may die possessed of or may first come into the hands of my Executors.

Secondly. I give and bequeath to my three children that is under age (to wit): Theodore, Henry and Catharine, as much property as will make them equal with those that is of age.

Thirdly. I give and bequeath to my wife Catharine all the rest of my property, real and personal, during her lifetime or widowhood (to wit) my plantation and plantation utensils and all my stock of every kind, household and kitchen furniture, &c.

Fourthly. I give and bequeath at the death or marriage of my wife Catharine all the property that remains both real and personal to my children (to wit) John Webb, Elijah Webb, Patsy Price, Susannah Price, Lucinda Shanks, Samuel Webb, Gabriel Webb, David Webb, and the above named minors (to wit), Theodore, Henry and Catharine, their heirs or assigns forever to be divided equally among them.

Fifthly. I give and bequeath to my daughter Polly one dollar and no more.

Lastly. I do hereby nominate and appoint John Webb and Elijah Webb my Executors. In witness whereof I do to this my last will set my hand and seal. This 28th day of December, 1850.

Theodore Webb (seal)

Signed, sealed and delivered in presence of
R. D. Young, Willie B. Kenner

Page 496

WILL OF JAMES WEBSTER

Dated: January 12, 1853
Proven: May Term, 1853

I, James Webster do make and publish this my last Will & Testament, hereby revoking and making void all other wills by me at any time made.

First. I direct that my funeral expenses and all my debts be paid as soon after my death as possible out of any money that I may die possessed of or may first come into the hands of my Executor or Administrator.

Secondly. I give and bequeath to my wife Elizabeth all my lands, it being in two tracts--one on which I now live the other adjoining there-unto, together with all my personal property consisting of horses, cattle,

hogs, sheep & poultry, together with all my household and kitchen furniture, farming utensils and to have and to hold during her natural life, an dispose of as she may think proper.

Thirdly through Ninthly. I give and bequeath one dollar (only) to each of my children as follows: Daughter Delila Jane; son Eldridge C; son James C; son Catnaro G; son Alexander H; son Absalom L. B.

In witness whereof I do to this my will set my hand and seal. This 11th day of January, 1853.

James Webster (seal)

Signed sealed published in our presence and we have subscribed our names hereto in the presence of the Testator this 11th day of January, 1853.

Codicil to the last Will & Testament of James Webster. First, my will and desire is that my beloved wife Elizabeth be—and I do hereby constitute her my sole Executrix, and that she be not required to give security for her performance of said Trust. In testimony whereof I have hereunto set my hand and seal. This 12th day of January, 1853.

James Webster
J. M. Charles, John Parish, W. B. Charles

John Parish, W. B. Charles

Page 497

WILL OF GEORGE WILLIAMS

Dated: Sept. 27, 1855

I, George Williams, of the County of Hawkins and State of Tennessee, being in perfect health and of sound mind and disposing mind and memory (sic), but considering the uncertainty of life and the certainty of death do make, publish and declare the following to (be) my last Will and Testament, hereby revoking and making void all wills heretofore made by me at any time.

First. It is my will and desire that my Executors hereafter to be appointed, as soon after my death as practicable, shall discharge all my just debts and the expenses attending my funeral.

Secondly. It is my will and desire should my dearly beloved wife Sophia T. Williams survive me, that she shall have the use of $1,500.00 in cash, over and above what is contained in our marriage contract heretofore executed by us. The said $1,500.00 to be and remain in the hands of my Exec's and paid over to her for her own separate use and support for and during her natural life, and after her death, the same $1,500.00 shall be equally divided between my children, nine in number, to wit: Margaret E. Xoe, Cleon H. Williams, Stokley D. Williams, Christopher C. Williams, Ethelbert C. Williams, Franklin E. Williams, Sally E. Williams, James M. Williams and Cornelia F. Montcastle or to their heirs, share & share alike, after paying to my said Executors the necessary expenses attending the same.

Thirdly. It is my will and desire that my two grandchildren Hugh G. Williams and George Williams, sons and heirs of my son John Williams, dec'd, shall be paid by my Executors the sum of $1,000.00 each, the same to be and remain in the hands of my Executors and placed by them at interest and the interest of the same to be collected annually and principal and interest thereof to be kept at interest until the eldest of said children shall become of lawful age, then the said $1,000.00 with all the proceeds thereof shall be paid over to him after paying all necessary expenses attending the same, and the other $1,000.00 hereby devised to the youngest of said children together with the proceeds thereof shall be kept at interest until the youngest of said children shall have arrived at lawful age, at which time the remaining $1,000.00 with proceeds thereof after paying all necessary expenses attending the same shall be paid over to him. But if either of said children of **John Williams**, dec'd. hereinbefore mentioned shall die without children, then it is my will and desire that the other being the survivor shall have the money hereby devised to both under the same limitations and restrictions as hereinbefore set forth. But should both of said grand children...die before they shall have attained the lawful age and without children—heirs of their bodies—then and in that case it is my will and desire that the said sums of money hereby devised to them, together with the proceeds thereof shall be equally divided between my said children or their heirs hereinbefore named.

Fourthly. It is my desire that my Executors hereinafter named—after giving the usual notice and as soon after my death as practicable shall sell all my real estate at public auction on one, two and three years' credit, purchasers giving bond with approved security, bearing interest from the day of said sale and a lien retained upon the land until the purchase money is fully paid, and the same to be sold in the following manner, to wit: My home tract containing about 800 acres in one lot. My **Kyle** tract of land containing about 200 acres in the second lot, and my **Libo** tract of land containing aobut 130 acres in the third lot. And my mill tract containing about three acres more or less with the appurtenances all to be sold separately and separate bonds to be taken for the same. In the sale of said real estate, the graveyard on the home tract is to be reserved and to be kept in repair by the purchaser.

Fifthly. It is my will and desire that my said Executors shall as shortly after my death as practicable sell and dispose of all my personal property, my negro slaves excepted, at public auction on 12 months' credit, taking bond with approved security for the purchase money.

Sixthly. It is my will and desire that all my slaves shall be equally divided between my said nine children, hereinbefore named, share and share alike. The said slaves to be divided by three disinterested persons to be chosen by my Executors unconnected with any of the parties either by affinity or consanguinity and the slaves thereof to be determined by lot, and if in the division of said slaves the shares should be considered unequal by said commissioners then and in that case, it is my will and desire that my said Executors shall make said slaves equal by paying cash to the owners of such share or shares as are deficient.

Seventhly. After retaining out of my Estate the said sum of $1,500.00 for the separate use of my said wife and the said sums of money hereinbefore devised to my two grand children **Hugh G.** and **George Williams**, it is my will and desire that all the proceeds or money arising from the sale of my lands and other property hereinbefore mentioned, and all the notes, monies, goods and chattels, all the chose in action or possession, all monies on hand after paying all my just debts in <u>fieri</u> (<u>fieri</u> <u>facias</u> ?). All my estate not herein before disposed of shall be equally divided between my s'd nine children hereinbefore named, or their heirs, share and share alike after taking into account the advances heretofore made by me to my children which will be found exhibited and set forth in my day book, fully and entirely—my intention being to make my said nine children as near equal as may be in the division of my estate. Inasmuch as I have heretofore given to my said son **John Williams**, dec'd a considerable amount of money and property and have devised in this my last Will and Testament $1,000.00 each with the proceeds thereof to my said two grand children, **Hugh G.** and **George Williams**

and heirs of the said **John Williams**, dec'd,making in my estimation about an equal share with my other children hereinbefore named. Therefore, in the division of my property, it is expressly understood and I do so ordain and direct, that they are to have no part or parcel of my Estate except the $1,000.00 and the proceeds thereof-to each of them as hereinbefore devised.

Lastly. I do hereby nominate and appoint my two friends **Absalom P. McCarty** and **James M. Moore** Executors of this my last Will and Testament. In witness whereof I have hereunto set my hand and affixed my seal this 26th day of September, in the year of our Lord one thousand eight hundred and fifty-four.

George Williams (seal)

Signed sealed published acknowledged and declared in presence of us the undersigned. This 26th day of September, 1854. The word "**Montcastle**" on first page interlined before signed.
George R. Powel, Sam Powel & R. G. Fain

Codicil

Inasmuch as **Absalom P. McCarty** one of the Executors named and appointed in this my last Will & Testament has since the execution thereof departed this life, and as I am desirous to have another Executor appointed to act with **Col. James M. Moore**, my other Executor, I do hereby nominate, constitute and appoint **William Etter** of Hawkins County said Executor of this my last Will & Testament to act in connection with my other Executor, **Col. James M. Moore**, and I do hereby declare this to be a codicil to my last will and testament. In witness whereof I have hereunto set my hand and seal This 27th September, 1855.

George Williams

Witness: R. G. Fain, George R. Powel

I desire that my wife, **S. T. Williams** shall have and use my negro girl **Charlotte** during her natural life, and at her (my wife's) death, I desire that she revert to my nine children as specified in my will. I moreover, in my will have given her the interest on $1,500.00, but I now desire that she have the use of the same or as much as she may desire for the building of her house upon condition that she give bond and security for the forthcoming of the same at her death as specified in my will. I moreover will that my son **Jas. M. Williams** shall have a young bay horse that I now have and be charged for the same, $100.00. I will also that my son-in-law **A. J. Montcastle** shall take my negro man **Tom** to his house and sell the same to go out of the country and account to my Executors for the proceeds of the same Sept. 4, 1856: These requests are parts of our father's will; were made to us two days previous to our father's (**George Williams**) death when his mind was clear and sane. Witness our hands, date above given.

S. D. Williams

Jas. M. Williams

WILL OF JONADAB WADE

Page 501   Dated: Jan'y 18, 1857
                                          Proven: Feb. 1857 & R'd p 25
I, **Jonadab Wade** do make and publish this my last Will & Testament, hereby revoking and making void all other wills by me at any time made.

First. I direct that my funeral expenses and all my debts be paid as soon after my death as possible out of any money that I may die possessed of or may first come into the hands of my Executor.

Secondly. I want a respectable set of tombstones erected at my grave, also I wish to have my grave enclosed by a post and plank fence.

Thirdly. I wish and desire to have all my personal property disposed of by public sale as soon as possible.

Fourthly. I wish and desire that my Executor pay to my brother John the sum of $40.00 due him by account.

Fifthly. My wish and desire is that my brothers and sisters have the remainder of my Estate after my Executor has paid all my debts.

Lastly. I do hereby nominate and appoint William E. Carmack my Exec. In witness whereof I do to this my will set my hand and seal. This 18th day of January, 1857.

Jonadab **Wade** (seal)

Signed sealed and published in our presence and we have subscribed our names hereto in the presence of the Testator. This 18th day of January, 1857.
Attest: J. B. C Edmondson, C. C. Brice, J. C. Miller

A codicil to the last will —

I, Jonadab **Wade**, having heretofore made and published my last Will and Testament do make and declare this a codicil thereto, to wit: **First.** My will and desire is that my Executor be required to act only on the property that I have in this county. **Lastly,** it is my desire that this codicil be attached to and constitute a part of my will to all intents and purposes.
This 18th day of January, 1857.

Jonadab **Wade** (seal)

Signed and sealed and published in our presence and we have subscribed our names hereto in presence of the Testator this 18th day of January, 1857.
Attest: J. B. C. Edmondson, C. C. Brice, J.C. MILLER

WILL OF JOHN WILLIAMS

Page 502
Dated: August 18, 1860
Proven: Jan. Term, 1864

The last Will & Testament of John Williams of the County of Hawkins and State of Tennessee.

I, John Williams, considering the uncertainty of human life and being of sound mind and memory do make and publish this my last Will & Testament, that is to say:

First. I give unto my beloved wife **Ruth** one third part of the farm on which I now live, or on which she may be living at the time of my decease, including the dwelling and out-buildings, one horse, one cow and such other stocks & household and kitchen furniture as may be necessary for her comfort. Also one black girl named **Nep** to keep and enjoy during the period of her natural life. At her death whatever property she may have is to be disposed of according to the directions given hereinafter.

Second. I give to my daughter **Anna** $150.00. Note: I have heretofore paid to my daughter **Nancy** $900.00; to my son **James** $500.00; to my **Ruthy** $200.00; to my son **Elisha** $150.00; to my son **John N.** $150.00; to my daughters **Harriet N. Helen W. & Eliza** each $150.00. Other former bequests to my daughter **Anna** is to make her up equal to those who have received $150.00. I then give to **Anna McCauley, John N., Elisha, Mollie K. Carroll** my grand daughter **Helen W.** each $50.00 to equal the amount paid to **Ruthy.** I then give to my daughters **Anna McCauley, Eliza Ballard,** the heirs of **Ruthy Ballard,** the heirs of **Harriet N. & to Helen W. Seaver & to my sons Elisha, John N.** each $300.00 to equal the amount paid to **James Williams.**

I then give to **Anna McCauley, Eliza Ballard,** the heirs of **Ruthy Ballard,** and the heirs of **Harriet N. & to Helen W. Seaver;** also to my sons **James, Elisha & John N.** each $400.00 to equal the amount paid to **Nancy Robinson.** If there shall be enough of my Estate. If not, then same proportion must be observed and if more after these bequests, then the remainder is to be divided equally among the heirs. I give to my son **Joseph** a full heir's part of my Estate which is to be governed and controlled by **Elisha & John N. Williams** whom I do hereby appoint his Guardians and he is to have the sole benefit of said share during his natural life. At his death, it is to be paid over to the heirs as directed with my other Estate. And my directions are for my Executors to value whatever slaves there may be, as near as they can to those already sold, and the heirs who have not already slaves from the estate shall have the refusal of them.

And (I) do hereby appoint and constitute **Elisha & John N. Williams** Executors of this my last Will & Testament. In witness whereof I have hereunto set my hand and affixed my seal. This 18th day of August, 1860.

John **Williams** (seal)

This instrument consisting of one sheet was now here subscribed by the Testator John Williams in presence of each of us, and was at the same time declared by him to be his last Will & Testament, and we at his request signed our names hereto as attesting witnesses.

J. J. Carroll, H. C. Seaver.

WILL OF R. D. WELLS

Page 504
Dated: April 9, 1860
Proven: May Term, 1860

I Randolph Dulaney **Wells** of the County of Hawkins and State of Tennessee, being of sound and disposing mind and memory, but weak and feeble of body, considering the uncertainty of life and the certainty of death and for the purpose of settling my worldly affairs as far as may be, do make, publish and declare the following to be my last Will & Testament, hereby revoking and making void all wills which I may have made any time heretofore.

First. It is my will and desire that my Executor hereinafter named shall out of the first money that may come into his hands defray my funeral expenses and pay all my just debts.

Secondly. It is my will and desire and I do direct that my dearly beloved wife **Matilda Wells** shall have all the property that belonged to her at the time of our marriage—consisting of the following negroes, to wit: **Eveline** and her two children **Sally & Margaret; Caroline & her child Mary, Nancy or Nan** and that she have all other property whether it consisted of goods, chattels, money or any other valuable thing whatsoever that belonged to her at the time of the marriage aforesaid.

Thirdly. It is my will and desire that all the balance of my property, with the exception hereafter named, shall be divided between my wife **Matilda** and my little son **John R. Wells** as follows: One third thereof to my said wife...and two thirds thereof to my said son **John R. Wells,** reserving, however, to the said John R. Wells the household furniture that belonged to his mother and reserving to my wife **Matilda** $25.00 in cash.

Lastly. I do hereby nominate, constitute and appoint my friend **Richard S. Horner** my Executor of this my last Will & Testament.

In witness whereof I have hereunto subscribed my name and affixed my seal. This 9th day of April, 1860.

R. D. **Wells** (seal)

Witness: George R. Powel, A. Carmichael.

WILL OF NATHAN WELLS

Page 505

Dated: Nov. 15, 1861
Proven in part at July Term, 1863

In the event that it should please God to remove me from time to Eternity during the present ware with the Government of lincon, The following is a disposition I wish to be made of my property, Viz: One hundred dollars to be put in the hands of some safe person and the interest arising therefrom to be paid over——The Southern Missionary Cause of the Methodist and one hundred dollars to be put at interest and the interest annually to be pade to seport of the gospel at home, fifty dollars to be paid to Nathan Ratcliff as a present on account of his misfortunes, & if John Minderwood (or Winderwood?) shall return home after he has served out the time for which he volunteered in defense of the rites of his Country and if he sits in & servs out the balance of his time that deducting the time he was in the ware, he shall have in the stead of horse & saddle worth seventy five dollars. That they shall be worth one hundred and twenty five dollars, and affer Nancy Wells & Rosanah Wells shall have the land I have and all the cash nots I have on hand and all the property of all kinds, except paying Fanney Bradshaw one hundred twenty five dollars when she is 21 years old and if she saye (stay) with N. Nancy or Rosanah Wells until she is or if they should not live until she is 21 years she is in that event to have the amount. Please give Emaline Wells fifty dollars for the care she tuck of her father. This given under my hand and seal November 15, 1861.

Nathan Wells

Attest: Reason Wells, Joseph B. Bradshaw

WILL OF WILLIAM WHITE

Page 505

Dated: July 1, 1813
Proven: Oct. 1863

I, William White, of the County of Hawkins & State of Tennessee, do make and publish this my last Will & Testament, hereby revoking and making void all other wills by me at any time made.

First. I direct that my funeral expenses and all my debts be paid as soon after my death as possible out of moneys that I may die possessed of or may first come into the hands of my Executor.

Secondly. And I bequeath to my dear wife Rebeka my house and household and kitchen furniture with the privilege or access to any timber for fewel or comfort of any kind, and the milk cow that is on hand so long as she remains my widow or remains here on the premises.

Thirdly. The remains of my property both real and personal to be equally divided between my lawful heirs. Furthermore, my will is that my wife be entitled to one half of the rents of the farm as means of support. Also, that she in case that she becomes dissatisfied and leaves this residence that she takes nothing with her or is entitled to nothing only the personal property that she brought with her and no more.

Likewise, I _____ constitute and appoint my son Isaac White to be my lawful Executor of this my last Will & Testament, hereby revoking all others or former wills by me made, and that he be appointed and is authorized to manage and conduct the farm and keep the same in repair, and to defray the expenses of the same out of the other half of the rents of the farm. In witness whereof I now subscribe my name and affix my seal. This February 1, 1863.

William White (seal)

Attest: Thos. N. Price, John Walker, Jnr.

WILL OF ROBERT YOUNG

Page 506

Dated: _____ 1804
Proven: August, 1804

I, Robert Young, Senr. of Hawkins County and State of Tennessee, do constitute and ordain this my last Will & Testament, wrote with my own hand.

First. Committing my body to the earth and my life to God who gave it, &c. It is my will that all my just debts be first paid and then my worldly Estate to be divided thusly. I will and devise to my oldest son John Young my survey of land less or more lying, joining his place he live on, on the upper end of John Thompson's place on the lower end in Carter's Valley, known by the name of the Big Spring Place. I will & devise unto my two sons, Robert and William Young the plantation I now live on lying on the north bank of Holston River joining Henry Price on the upper end and ___? Carter on the lower end, to be equally divided in quantity between them, by a line drawn from the middle of the line on the river crossing the middle of the land to the side line. The lower end to belong to Robert and the upper end...to William. I likewise will and devise unto my said two sons Robert and William my negro man named Wilson at my wife's decease. They are to have an equal right to him and then they are to have my farming tools, my carpenter tools and my smith tools equally between them. I will and devise unto my son-in-law Henry Larkins the place he lives on containing 200 acres of land more or less, lying between John Young's land and John Armstrong's land in Carter's Valley. I will and bequeath unto my wife Jenny Young my house and furniture, the household furniture she is to have that part at her own disposal. She is to have what is called Old Meadow corn field, the brier field and the field by the barn, and my two negroes Wilson and Hannah as long as she lives. William Young is to have the big fields on the river, the meadow excepted. She is to have all my stock as long as she lives, but if she thinks there is too much stock for her to support she is to put a part into the Executors' hands which they are to make sale of for the purpose of raising $120.00 which my Executors is to divide as follows: Twenty dollars to be paid to each of Nathaniel Henderson's four children when they are come to the years of maturity: Sally, Jenny, John and Nath. And my Executors is to put $40.00 into John Cooper's hands to assist in raising his son Young Cooper.

If there is any more money raised out of my stock than will pay this $120.00, the overplush is to be equally divided between my two daughters, Ann Larkins and Mary Cooper. I will and devise unto my said two daughters Ann Larkins and Mary Cooper my negro woman Hannah, and they are to have an equal right to her and her offspring. And whereas I have a bond of Stokley Donaldson for a preemption of 640 acres of land in Cumberland, and I have a Patent for 100 acres of land lying on the mouth of Buffalo Creek, Grainger County, and a Military Warrant of 640 acres of land in Cumberland which I lett Burnet Suong (?) have who lives in Cumberland, and I have got no account of it wherefore I give my two sons Robert and William full power and authority to sue at law or any other method they think best and they are to hold whatever they get, only if that preemption from Stokley Donaldson be all obtained, they are to make my brother William Young a right to 200 acres of it. I do constitute and appoint my two sons Robert Young and William Young to be my Executors of this my last Will and Testament to which I sett my hand and seal. This_____in the year of Our Lord, One Thousand eight hundred and four.

Robert Young (seal)

WILL OF JOHN YOUNG

Dated: June 17, 1834

Page 508

I, John Young, of Hawkins County in the State of Tennessee, being of sound mind and memory and taking into consideration the uncertainty of life and the necessity for the prevention of trouble and difficulty to those who are to come after me of settling and providing for the settlement of my own affairs, do make, ordain and publish this my last Will & Testament, revoking and annulling all others.

It is my Will that my decease, after my body decently committed to that earth from whence it was taken.

Item. I give and bequeath to my beloved wife Peggy Young a negro woman named Judy and her two children, Leonard & Maria and her offspring herein to be born, to hold in absolute property during her life and to dispose of as she may please among her children.

Item. I give and bequeath to my said wife all my household and kitchen furniture and all my stock of sheep to dispose of according to her own pleasure among her children.

Item. It is my Will that my said wife have her maintenance and support together with the necessary lots and rooms out of my plantation and houses, according to the reservations contained in a deed made by me to my son John Young, Jr., all of which are more particularly set forth in said deed and are hereby confirmed to her.

Item. To my daughter Harriet, I give and bequeath a negro woman named Hester and her two children Geoff & Matilda and her offspring, hereafter to be born, also one good horse and saddle and three cows and calves.

Item. To my daughter Caroline, married to Nathaniel I. Carter, I confirm the negro girl Elvy of whom she now has possession and I give and bequeath to her a negro girl Prudy yet in my possession, together with the offspring of said girls hereafter to be born, and in addition to those she has already received, I give and bequeath to my s'd daughter another cow and calf.

Item. I give and bequeath to my daughter Juliet two negro girls named Mary Ann & Rill Anne and their offspring hereafter to be born, and one good horse & saddle and three cows and calves. (This item should have proceeded the last one above but was overlooked by Copier).

Item. I give and bequeath to my son John Young, Jr., all my stock not otherwise disposed of, all my farming tools and utensils, the shop tools and the grain or crop on hand, also a negro girl Emaline and two negro boys Wesley & Richard, but in consideration of my son John receiving by this will and by a deed for my plantation, heretofore executed by me to him (which deed with its reservations and conditions is hereby confirmed) a better share of my Estate than my other children, he is required out of his legacy as a condition thereof, and as a condition and reservation in the above named deed to pay all the just debts that may be due and arising from my Estate or from me at the time of my decease.

Item. I give and bequeath to my son John my negro man Cain to do with as he may choose, but subject to these conditions, that he pay to my son Clairbourne $200.00 and to my son George $100.00 and it is my will that my said sons Clairbourne & George receive said legacies out of the proceeds of said negro man Cain.

Item. I give and bequeath to my son John five old negroes, viz: Dan,

Wilson, Will, Jude & Sarah, to be kept by him on the plantation, and supported during their lives, and to be worked according to their reasonable ability and not to be disposed of or parted from out of the family of my own children.

Item. To my son Robert Young, to my son William Young, to my son Arthur G. Young, to my son Hord Young, to my daughter Polly Armstrong, and to my daughter Betsy Young, in addition to the gifts and advancements heretofore bestowed, I hereby give and bequeath one dollar each——they being already sufficiently provided for according to my ability.

Item. It is my Will that my son John Young & Orville Bradley be Executors of this my last Will & Testament. It is my Will that my son John take upon himself the burden of the general execution of this Will, but that in all cases of difficulty if any should arise, that he have the assistance of my other Executor, Orville Bradley.

Item. My son John being charged by this Will with the payment of all my debts, it is my will that all my Estate or rights if any such there may be not otherwise disposed of, be vested in him as general residuary legatee.

In testimony whereof I the said John Young (sr.) have hereunto set my hand and affixed my seal. This 17th day of June, 1834.

John Young (seal)

Signed, sealed in our presence and witnessed at the request of the Testator.
H. Watterson, Benjamin Looney, John Looney (March 18, 1840), Charles C. Watterson, William McKitryan

Codicil.
I, John Young, Sen., do this 18th day of March, 1840, make and publish this Codicil to my last Will and Testament in manner following: Whereas in my last Will & Testament I have given and bequeathed to my wife Margaret Young and also to my daughters, Harriet, Juliet & Caroline to each and severally the negroes therein named and described to them and whereas they being of mature age and knowing the negroes whom I had given and bequeathed to them, each and severally in my said last Will and Testament, have made some exchanges of those said negroes among themselves with my full approbation and it is my desire that those exchanges of negroes among themselves may not affect at all hereafter the equality of distribution therein made to each of the above named legatees. And lastly, it is my desire that this my present Codicil be annexed to and made a part of my last Will and Testament to all intents and purposes.

In witness whereof I have hereunto set my hand and affixed my seal. This 18th day of March, A.D. 1840.

John Young (seal)

Signed sealed published and declared by the above John Young, Sen., to be his last Will & Testament in the presence of us who have hereinto subscribed our names as witnesses in the presence of the Testator.
H. Watterson, Charles C. Watterson, William McKitryan

Sealed and acknowledged in presence of:

_____ (Name of witness here illigible)

Thomas Armstrong (Jurat), William Maxwell,

WILL OF MARGARET YOUNG

Page 510

Dated: August 28, 1852
Proven: August, 1853

I, **Margaret Young,** of sound and perfect mind and memory do make and publish this my last Will & Testament in manner and form following:

First. I give and bequeath unto my daughter **Caroline Carter's** daughters one negro girl named **Daphne** and her increase, but the said **Caroline** to have the use of her labor during her natural life, and also the said **Caroline** to have the disposal of said negroes to her daughters respectively. Also, I give and bequeath to the said **Caroline Carter** one negro boy named **Jacob,** with the provision the said boy **Jacob** is to be valued at $200.00 ($100.00 of which $200.00 is paid and the said **Caroline Carter** is to pay unto my son **George B. Young** $70.00 of said valuation. And the said **Caroline** is to pay unto my son **Arthur G. Young's** daughter **Caroline Francis** $30.00 of said valuation.

Item. I give and bequeath to my daughter **Harriet DeWolfe** during her natural life, one negro girl **Josephine** and her increase, with the provision that at the said **Harriet DeWolfe's** death, the negro girl **Josephine** and her increase shall descend to my son **Claibourne Young's** children.

Item. I give and bequeath to my son **Hord Young** one negro boy named **Charles.**

Item. I give and bequeath to my son **John Young** and **Cornelias C. Miller** my son-in-law, or to which of them who will give the highest price for the two boys, two negro boys named **Wesley** and **Jackson,** and the proceeds of said two boys to be paid over unto my son **Claiborne Young.** Then I give and bequeath to my son **John Young's** daughter, **Susan Catherine** one negro girl named **Sarah Ann.**

Item. I give and bequeath to my son **John Young** one negro woman named **Elva** with this proviso--that he pay all my just debts.

My other sons and daughters, namely, **Robert Young's** heirs, **William Young, Polly Armstrong, Arthur G. Young, Betsy Young** and **Juliet Miller** have all been heretofore amply provided for.

I appoint my son **John Young** Executor of this my last will and testament, hereby revoking all former wills by me made. In witness whereof I have hereunto set my hand and seal. This 28th day of August, 1852.

Margaret Young (seal)

Signed, sealed, published and declared by the above **Margaret Young** to be her last Will and Testament in the presence of us who have hereunto subscribed our names as witnesses in the presence of the Testator.

H. Watterson
James L. McKirgan
James. B. Gailbraith

End of Volume One

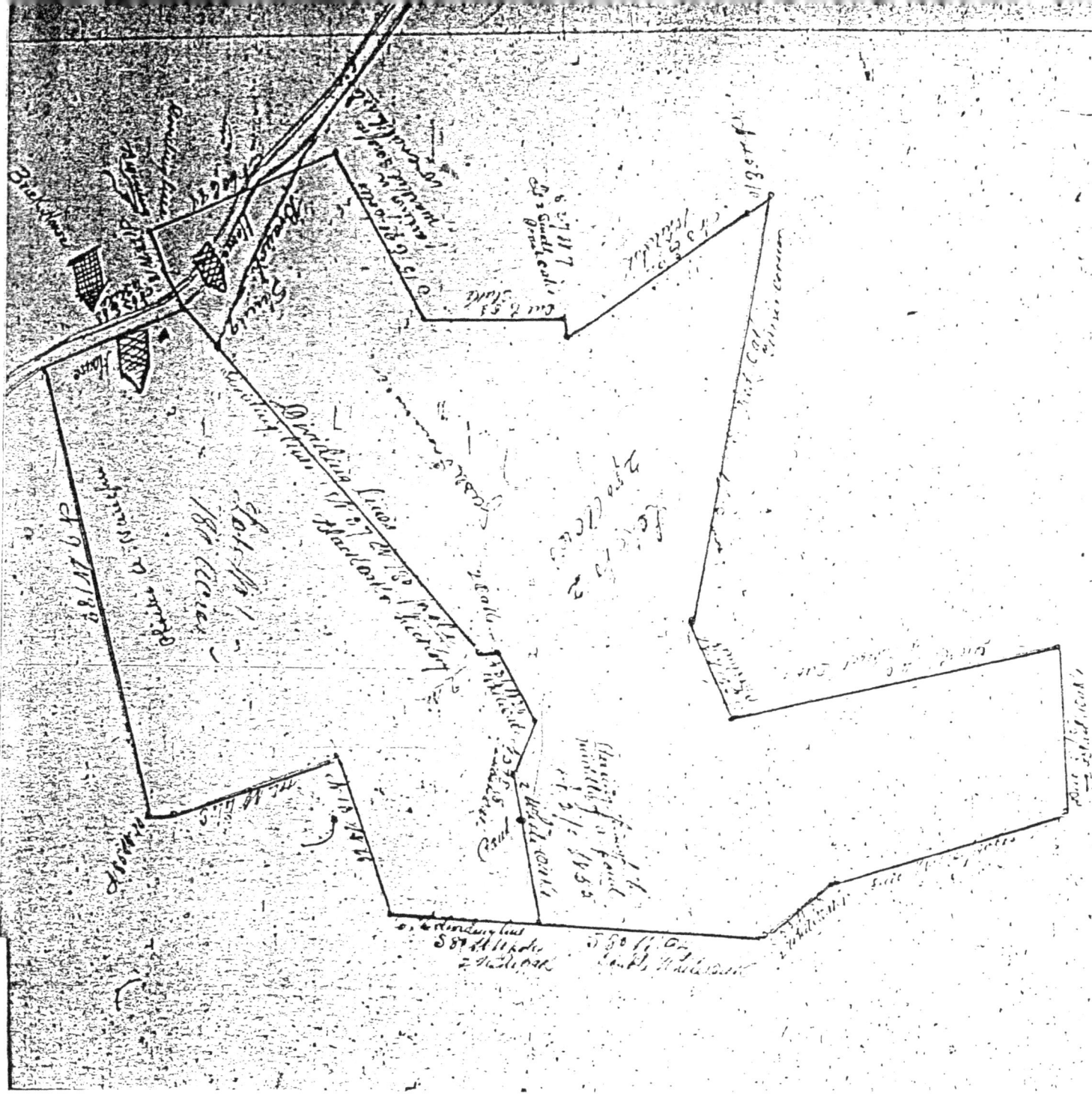

TWO SEPARATE LISTINGS OF NAMES GIVEN - Implied and Actual

(NAME) = indicates the surname was implied from reading

AGGY, 3
AMBROSE, 3
CATT, 3
DAPH, 2
FRANK, 2
JESSE, 4
JOE, 2
LYD, 5
MILLY, 2, 3
MINOR, 3
NANCY, 3
SAL, 4
SALL, 3
SPENCER, 4
TOM, 2

-(-

(BAKER),
  CATHERINE, 128
  CHARLOTTE, 128
  TWEDAY, 128
(BRYANT),
  LUCINDA
    CORNELIA, 57
(BURNS),
  JOHN, 58
  WILLIAM, 58
(CALDWELL),
  ANN, 65
  JANE, 65, 66
  JOHN, 65, 66
  SILAS, 65(2)
  ST. CLAIR,
    65(4), 66(2)
(CARDEN),
  JUDITH, 74
  L. JOSEPHPHENE,
    74(3)
(CAREY),
  MARY AN(-), 72
  SUSANNAH, 72
(CARMACK),
  CATHARINE, 70
  CATHERINE, 70
  CORNELIUS,
    70(3), 101
  CORNELIUS,
    (JR.), 70
  ELIZABETH, 70
  ISAAC, 70
  JOHN, 70
  NANCY, 70(2)
  NELLY, 70
  POLLY, 70
  RACHEL, 70
  SALLY, 70

SUSANNAH, 70
WILLIAM, 70(2)
(CARMACK-LONG),
  POLLY ANN, 101
(CARMICHAEL),
  ANN, 100
  MATTIE ELLEN,
    100
  WHITFIELD, 100
  WILLIAM ANDREW,
    100
(CARPENTER),
  JACKSON, 89(2)
  JAMES, 90
  JOHN, 90
  WILLIAM, 90
  WILSON, 89
(CARTER),
  TEMPYRANCE
    (TEMPEY), 105
(CHAMBERS),
  SARAH, 93
(CHARLES),
  DARCUS JANE, 84
  JASPER, 84
  LUCINDA, 84
  MALINDA, 84
  MANECY, 84
(CHESTER),
  ARCHIBALD, 79
  CATHARINE, 79
  MARY, 79(3)
(CHESTNUT),
  INDIANA, 92(2)
  JAMES, 92
(CHESTNUTT),
  CAROLINE, 103,
    104(3)
  RODHAM, 104
  SAMUEL, 103,
    104(5)
  THOMAS, 104(2)
(CHRISTIAN),
  (S)INDY, 73
  ALLEN, 72
  BETSY, 72
  CINDY, 73
  DAVID, 103(2)
  ELDRIDGE, 103
  ISAAC, 103
  JAMES, 72
  JESSE, 103
  JOHN, 72
  JR., 72
  LEWIS, 72, 73
  LUCINDA, 72
  NANCY, 72(2), 85
  PEGGY, 72, 73(4)

POLLY, 72
SALLY, 73
STEPHEN, 103
THOMAS, 72,
  73(4)
WILLIAM, 73(4)
WILLIAM L., 103
(COLLINS),
  FRANKEY, 82(2)
  SIMEON, 82
(COX),
  BETSY, 64
  EMMALINE, 64
  JOHN, 64(2)
  LUCY, 64(2)
  MARY, 64
  NANCY, 64
  PHAROAH, 64(2)
  POLLY, 64
  SAMUEL, 64
  THOMAS, 61
  WITNER, 64(2)
(CROZIER),
  ELIZABETH, 86
(CURREY),
  GEORGE, 77
  JAMES C., 77
  JOHN, 77
  WILLIAM G., 77
(CURRY),
  ANN, 71
  GEORGE, 71
  MARGARET, 71
  REBECCA, 71
  SAMUEL, 71
(DALZELL),
  WILLIAM, 109
(DAVIS),
  JAMES MADISON,
    112
  LARKIN, 112
  LEANIER JANE,
    112
  LOUISA, 112(3)
  MARY, 112
  POLLY, 119
  WILLIAM HENRY,
    112
(DICKSON),
  ELIZA D., 114
  JANE S., 114
  WILLIAM S., 114
(DOBSON),
  JANE, 111(2)
  JOHN A., 111
  MARY ANN, 111
  NANCY JANE, 111
(DODSON),
  JAMES, 108

JAMES, 92(4),
  93(3)
JOHN, 81(2)
NATHANIEL, 81(2)
(COLE),
  MARGARET, 75
(COLLINS),
(CHRISTIAN)?,
  CINDY, 73
(CHURCH),
  ENOCH, 85
  FEORGE, 66
  GEORGE, 66, 85
  HENRY, 66(2), 85
  MATILDA, 85
  SARAH, 85
  THOMAS, 66(2)
(CLICK),
  ARTHUR, 95
  ELIZA, 95
  ELIZABETH, 68
  GEORGE, 68,
    95(2)
  JACOB, 68
  JAMES, 95
  JOHN, 68, 95(2)
  KATHARINE, 68
  MARGARET, 68
  MARY, 95
  MATTHIAS, 68
  MICHAEL, 68
  PETER, 95(2)
  ROBERT, 95(2)
  ROSANNAH, 95(2)
  WILLIAM, 94, 95
(COBB),
  BARSHABA, 106(2)
  CATHARINE, 97
  DYER, 97(2)
  ELIZA, 106(2)
  ELIZABETH, 97(3)
  JACKSON, 97(2)
  JESSE, 106,
    107(3)
  JOSEPH, 97(4)
  MARY, 97(2), 98
  SALLY, 106(2)
  THOMAS, 97(2)
  WILLIAM, 106(2),
    107(2)
(COCKE),
  LUCINDA, 90
(COCKREHAM),
  SALLY, 83(2)
(COLDWELL),
  ABRIAM, 93
  BENONI, 92(5)
  INDIANA, 93(2)

(DODSON)
  (continued)
  JOHN, 111(2)
  LAZARUS, 108
  ROLLY, 110
  WILLIAM, 113
(DODSON-SAUNDERS),
  NELLY, 107
(ELLIS),
  BETSEY, 123, 125
  FISHER, 125
  JOANNA, 123,
    124, 125(2)
  JOHN, 123,
    124(2), 125
  WILLIAM, 123,
    124, 125
(ELLIS-FISHER),
  NANCY, 124
(EPPERSON),
  NANCEY, 122
(EPPERSON-BEARD),
  PHANNY, 122
(EPPERSON-BRADSHAW),
  SINA, 122
(EPPERSON-DICKARD),
  SUSANNAH, 122
(EPPERSON-McCLEANE),
  KASSIA, 122
(EVERHART),
  JOHN, 122
  SAMUEL, 122
  WILLIAM, 122
(FORGEY),
  ANDREW, 127(4),
    128(2)
  JAMES, 127
  JOHN, 128
(GAINES),
  BEHETHELAND, 148
  CHILDRESS,
    148(4)
  EDMOND, 148
  ELIZABETH,
    148(2)
  FRANCES, 149
  HENRY, 148
  JAMES, 148
  MARY, 148
  PHEBE, 148
(GALBRAITH),
  AENEAS, 147
  ANDERSON, 161,
    162
  ANDREW, 161,
    162(4)
  JOHN, 147
  JOSEPH, 161,
    162(3)
  JULIANN, 153
  MOTTLENIA, 146
  WILLIAM, 162
(GIBSON),

MATILDA, 156
(GIDDIONS),
  EDWARD, 149
  ISHAM, 149
  JAMES, 149
  WILLIAM, 149
(GIDEONS),
  ISHUM, 149, 150
(GILLENWATERS),
  CALVIN M., 156
  GEORGE, 160(2)
  POLLY, 156
  THOMAS, 156
(GODDARD),
  CATY, 152
  ELENOR, 152
  NANCY, 152
  POLLY, 152
  REBECCA, 152
  SALLY, 152
  SARAH, 152
  SUTEARY, 152
(GRIGSBY),
  BETSY JANE,
    163(3)
  ELIZABETH,
    163(3)
  FRANK, 155
  GIPSON, 155
  HENRY, 163
  JAMES, 163(6)
  JESSE, 163(3)
  JOHN, 163
  SAMUEL, 163
  SARAH, 155
  SARENA, 163(3)
(GROSS),
  CORNELIUS, 152
  JAMES, 152
  NANCY, 152
  WILLIAM, 152
(GROVES),
  JACOB B., 154(5)
(GULLY),
  NANCY, 154
  NATHAN, 154
(HAGAN),
  ALEXANDER, 169
  ALICE, 169
  ELIZABETH, 169
  FRANCES, 169
  JOHN, 169
  MARGARET, 169
  MARY, 169
  THOMAS, 169
(HAGOOD),
  BENJAMIN F.,
    172, 173(4)
  JAMES M., 172,
    173(5)
  NANCY, 173(2)
  STEPHEN D., 172,
    173(3)

WILLIAM, 173
(HALE),
  ALIS, 176
  MARTHY, 176
(HAMBLEN),
  ABNER, 179(2)
  HENRY, 179(2)
  JOHN, 179(3)
  MARY, 179
  NANCY, 179(3)
  WILLIAM, 179(2)
(HAMILTON),
  CATHARINE, 164
  ELENOR, 164
  ELIZABETH, 164,
    165
  JAMES, 164
  JOHN, 164
  MARGARET, 164
  ROBERT, 164(2)
(HAMLEN),
  EDWIN, 165(2)
  FRANK, 165(3)
  HENRY, 165(3)
  PASCAL, 165(2)
  POLLY, 165
  ROSAMOND, 165
  SALLY, 165
  SUSANNAH, 165
(HARLAN),
  CORNELIUS,
    181(12)
  ELIZABETH,
    181(2)
  MARY ELIZA,
    181(4)
  MATILDA, 181(3)
  RACHAEL, 180(3),
    181(3)
  TABITHA, 181(4)
  THOMAS, 180
(HARLIN),
  JOHN, 166
(HARRIS),
  ELIZABETH, 171
  ISAM, 171
  JANNY, 171
  LUTEY, 171
  POLLY, 171
  RACHAEL, 171(2)
  SALLY, 171
  WILLIAM, 171
(HAYNES),
  CHRISTOPHER,
    172(2)
  FRANCIS, 172(2)
  JESSE, 172(2)
  JOHN, 172(2)
  SARAH CHARLES,
    172
(HENDERSON),
  AMANDA, 176(2)
  BALLDY, 176

BETSY, 176
GEORGE, 176
JOHN, 176
LUCINDA, 176
MILLY, 176
SAMUEL, 176
SAMUEL L., 176
THOMAS, 176
WILLIAM, 176
(HERREL),
  POLLY, 166
(HORD),
  ELDRIDGE, 174
  STANWIX, 174
  THOMAS, 174
  WILLIAM, 174(2)
(HOWEL),
  BETSY, 168(3)
  CLARK, 168(2)
  ELIZABETH, 168
  JAMES, 168(2)
  MATTISON, 168(3)
  NANCY, 168(2)
  SALLY, 168(3)
  SARA, 168
  WILLIAM, 168
  WILLY, 168(3)
(HUFFMASTER),
  ANNY, 171
  BARBARY, 171
  BETSY, 171
  DANIEL, 171
  JOHN, 171(2)
  JONATHAN, 171
  JOSEPH, 171
  MARY, 171
  SALLY, 171
(HUTCHISSON),
  MARGARET, 178(3)
  REBECCA, 178(3)
  RUDOLPH, 178(2)
(JACKSON),
  BETHUNIA, 183
  JAMES, 183(2)
  JOE, 184(2)
  ROBERT, 183(2)
(JOHNSON),
  ABNER, 187
  ANDERSON, 187
  ANNA, 187
  BENONI P.C., 188
  BETSY, 184(2)
  CHARITY, 184(2)
  DELPHA C., 188
  ELIZABETH, 187
  HANER, 187
  JAMES, 184
  JEREMIAH, 184
  LUCY, 184(3)
  MARY, 184
  PATSY, 187
  POLLY, 184
  ROBERT EMET, 188

SALLY, 184, 187
THOMAS, 184, 187
(JONES),
 ENECH, 183
 MARTIN, 183
(KARNES),
 ANDREW, 190
 GEORGE, 190
 JACOB, 190
(KENNER),
 JAMES, 199(5), 200(3)
 LUCY, 194
 RODHAM, 199(5), 200(2)
 WILLIAM, 195
(KINCHELOE),
 ELIZABETH, 198(2)
 JAMES, 198(3)
 JAMES B., 198
 JOHN, 198(2), 199
 LOUISA, 198(2), 199(2)
 MARGARET, 198, 199(3)
 NANCY, 198
 NANCY LOUISA, 198
 POLLY, 198, 199
 RACHAEL, 198(3), 199(2)
 SARAH, 198(2), 199
(KINCHOELOE),
 JAMES B., 197
 POLLY, 197
(KING),
 ADAM, 196
 ELIZABETH, 196
 SARY, 197
(KIRKPATRICK),
 DAVID, 202
(KLEPPER),
 BETSY, 156
(KLINE),
 JACOB, 189
(KYLE),
 ABSALOM, 193
 BARSHEBA, 205
 LEAH, 193
 LEONIDAS, 205(6)
(LAUGHMILLER),
 ABRAM, 211
 DAVID, 211(2)
 FREDERICK, 211
 GEORGE, 211
 HENRY, 211
 JACOB, 211(2)
 JOHN, 211
 JONAS, 211(2)
 PHILLIP, 211

(LEMAR),
 BENJAMIN, 211
 HENNEY, 211
 MARINE, 211
 RACHAEL, 211
 RICHARD, 211
 SALLEY, 211
 SUSANNAH, 211
(LOYD),
 BENJAMIN, 208
 JOHN, 208
 POLLY, 208
 THOS., 208
 TOM, 208
(McCARTY),
 AMANDA, 161
(PHILLIPS),
 MARGARET, 104
(SENSABAUGH),
 SUSAN, 128
(SHOTTS),
 ELIZABETH, 128
(SMITH),
 CAROLINE, 179
 MOSES, 179
(STAPLES),
 MARY ANNE, 66
 NANCY, 66
(WINSTON),
 LUCY, 195

ABRAHAM, 193
ABRAM, 165
ABSOLOM, 78
ADALINE, 140, 274
AGNES, 246
AGNUS, 78
ALBERT, 147, 294
ALCY, 151, 246
ALEXANDER (ELLICK), 137
ALFRED, 13, 220
ALICE, 273(2)
ALMIRA, 169
ALSY, 133
AMANDA, 103, 104(2), 277
AMBROSE, 274
AMOS, 277
ANDERSON, 334
ANDREW, 210
ANDY, 281
ANN, 104, 277
ANNA, 69
ANTHONY, 236, 277
APP, 65
ARAMINTHA, 153
ARAMINTO, 147

ARCHABEL, 201
ARRON, 36, 147
ARTHUR, 19(2)
ATNE, 21
BACCHUS, 128
BAPTIT, 193
BARNEY, 169
BASS, 192, 193
BECKEY, 179
BEN, 7, 15, 78, 148(2), 181, 260, 309
BERRY, 183, 184
BETS, 334
BETSY, 172, 184
BETTIE, 193
BETTY, 13, 19(3), 192, 193(2), 242
BILL, 8, 176
BOB, 65(2), 92, 104, 157, 179, 184, 236, 274, 314, 336
BURTON, 62, 63, 334
BUSH, 205(3)
CAIN, 274, 347
CAIRY, 105
CALVIN, 226
CAROLINE, 186, 195(3), 344
CARROLL, 253
CARSON, 140, 330
CASEY, 236
CASWELL, 314
CATE, 169, 334
CATHARINE, 90
CATHERINE, 186
CATY, 179, 274
CEALY, 75
CEASER, 330
CELIA, 247
CHARITY, 106(3), 165, 186, 220
CHARLES, 5, 93(2), 94, 104, 274, 332, 349
CHARLOTT, 26(4)
CHARLOTTE, 218
CHERRY, 170(2)
CINDA, 273
CITTY, 273
CIZ, 65(2)
GLARISA, 7
CLARISSA, 7, 231
CLINT, 205
CLINTON, 246, 273
COMFORT, 192, 193(2)
COOK ELIZA, 204
COOK ELIZA'S

LUCY, 204
CYNTH, 92
DAN, 120, 347
DAPHNE, 349
DAVE, 278
DAVID, 18
DICK, 36(3), 79, 88(2), 118, 148, 170, 179, 276

DINER, 148
DOL, 256
EASTER, 26(2), 330
EDE, 151
EDITH, 256
EDWARD, 81, 220, 311
EDY, 172
ELBERT, 104(2), 216
ELIZA, 8, 105, 129, 170(2), 179, 192, 194, 195, 222, 227, 253, 314
ELIZABETH, 256
ELLEN, 92, 179, 253, 260
ELSEY, 289
ELVA, 349
ELVY, 347
EMALINE, 273, 274, 275, 347
EMELINE, 320, 330
EMILY, 290
ESTER, 103
ESTHER, 106(2), 253
EVE, 184
EVELINE, 344
FAN, 93(2)
FANNY, 7
FELL, 193(2)
FILL, 217
FLORIDA, 179
FRANCIS, 10, 123
FRANK, 92, 150, 179, 184, 247, 276
FRANKEY, 62, 106
FRANKY, 106, 172
FRED, 170, 223
GEOFF, 347
GEORGE, 8, 123, 124, 144, 205(2), 212, 273, 332
GIBB, 176
GIBSON, 150
GIDEON, 198, 199
GILBERT, 148

(continued)
GRAN, 226
HAMILTON, 106(2)
HANNAH, 66(2), 174, 227, 261, 314, 332, 346
HARDY, 216
HARREY, 333
HARRIET, 8, 10, 19, 123, 161(3), 179
HARRISON, 62
HARRY, 179, 193, 279, 310, 320
HENDERSON, 216
HENDLEY, 231
HENRY, 80, 181, 184, 247, 275
HENSTON, 186
HESTER, 347
HILYON, 88
HOUSTON, 114, 115, 117, 205(2), 220
IBB, 146(3)
ICEHAM, 198(2)
IKE, 278
ISAAC, 7(3), 94
ISABEL, 81
ISHAM, 199
JACK, 10, 118, 140, 148, 172, 193(2), 197(2), 199, 210, 226, 277, 279, 294, 308, 322
JACKSON, 349
JACOB, 165, 184(2), 322, 349

JAKE, 180
JAMES, 25, 62, 63, 216, 222, 223, 242, 246, 325
JAMES FRANKLIN, 261
JANE, 19, 212, 246, 314
JEAN, 21
JEFF, 207, 334
JEFFERSON, 19(2)
JENNY, 193
JESSE, 172, 179
JESSY, 204
JIM, 163, 273, 275, 308
JIN, 129(2)
JINNY, 285
JO, 104
JOE, 5, 10, 77, 88, 172, 184, 334

JOHN, 78, 148, 172, 181, 195(3), 206(2), 314
JOHN WESLEY, 261
JOSEPH, 132
JOSEPHINE, 349
JOSIAH, 238
JUDA, 337
JUDE, 348
JUDY, 347
JULIA, 94, 172, 181, 274
JULIA ANN, 157, 277
JUNIE, 322
KADER, 162
KATE, 193(2)
KATHARINE, 184
KZIAH, 226
LAUNAR, 144
LAURA, 161, 199(2), 200, 276
LEANOR, 328
LEIS, 15
LEONARD, 347
LEROY, 81
LEWIS, 62, 63, 94, 184, 206(2), 279
LIGE, 337
LILBOURN, 104
LILBOURNE, 104
LILLA, 168
LIND, 210
LINDA, 8, 219
LISA, 334
LIZA, 198
LOONEY, 334
LOUSANNA, 19
LUCE, 168
LUCINDA, 246, 261
LUCY, 62, 63(3), 81, 105, 140, 205(3), 276, 277, 284, 285
LUZESEY, 333
LYDIA, 104, 172
MADISON, 278
MAJOR, 291
MALINDA, 148, 199, 220, 322
MALL, 144
MALVINA, 181
MANDY, 184, 293
MANSON, 172
MARCH, 219
MARCIA, 179
MARGARET, 172, 293, 344
MARIA, 74, 276,

279(2), 347
MARIAH, 78, 120, 330
MARIE, 179
MARINDA, 325
MARK, 209
MARTHA, 62, 170(2), 186
MARTIN, 194
MARY, 10, 62, 78, 92(2), 93, 104, 124, 140, 157, 179, 192(2), 193, 219, 220, 223, 256, 265, 275, 276, 279, 325, 344
MARY ANN, 157, 347
MASADAMIA, 256
MATILDA, 279, 347
MELINDA, 199
MELVINA, 216
MICHAEL B., 216
MILES, 172
MILL, 217
MILLA, 219
MILLE, 61(2)
MILLEY, 330
MILLY, 5, 80, 238
MIMA, 274
MINERVA, 148
MINGO, 192(3), 193(3)
MINNA, 147
MINNE, 176
MINTA, 183, 277
MITCHELL, 147
MOLLEY, 179
MORIAH, 157
MOSES, 17
MOURNING, 239
NAN, 344
NANCE, 216
NANCY, 8, 10, 26, 90, 147, 169, 193, 236, 253, 279, 332, 344
NANCY ANN, 261
NANN, 195(3)
NATHAN, 226
NED, 179, 236
NELLY, 206(3)
NELSON, 80, 114, 115, 117
NEP, 343
NICE, 118(2)
NICEY, 113, 114(2)

NOAH, 219
OLD GEORGE, 184
OLD LUCY, 205
OLD PHILLIS, 198
ORANGE, 161
PACK, 176
PAGE, 161
PAGEY, 15
PARK, 65
PEACHY, 278
PEGGY, 132, 172
PETER, 105, 179, 219, 292
POCAHONTAS, 7
POLLY, 5, 113, 137
POMPEY, 92
POWEL, 274
PRESTON, 157
PRI(S)E, 66
PRICE, 66
PRINCE, 308
PRUDY, 347
PUNCH, 236
QUEEN, 278
RACHAEL, 184(3), 200(2), 212, 220, 273
RANSOM, 277
RENE, 236
REUBEN, 157
RHODA, 17
RICETON, 17
RICHARD, 347
RIL--ANNE, 347
RINDA, 7
ROBERT, 78, 133(2), 253
ROBING, 144
RODA, 273
ROSANAH, 226
ROSANNA, 261
ROSE, 151, 197(2), 199(2), 236, 328
ROSETTA, 278
ROWE, 255
RUFUS, 8, 148, 279(2)
RUTH, 168
SAL, 276, 279
SALL, 334
SALLIE, 193
SALLY, 176, 344
SAM, 21, 34, 179, 183, 275
SAMPSON, 236
SAMUEL, 222
SAMUEL J., 216
SANDY, 179, 183, 314
SARAH, 79(2), 94, 121, 125(2),

161, 192(2), 231, 348

SARAH ANN, 349
SAUL, 276
SEALAH, 157
SELA, 239
SHARLOT, 20(2)
SHARLOTTE, 239
SID, 129
SIDEA, 36(2)
SIDNEY, 19(2), 199(2), 200
SILLA, 164
SILLER, 332
SILVE, 144
SILVEY, 294
SIMON, 26(3)
SIND, 334
SIS, 118, 184
SOOK, 334
SPENCER, 78, 153
STEPHEN, 7, 19(3), 105, 247
STOKLEY, 179
SUDY, 181
SUSAN, 92, 94, 150
SYDNEY, 104
TABITHA, 291
TENNESSEE, 285
TILDA, 216
TOM, 131, 135, 193, 210, 276, 294, 342
TONA, 210
VICEY, 65
VINCENT, 204
VINEY, 279
VIOLET, 193
WALKER, 144
WALTER, 277
WESLEY, 161, 347, 349
WILEY, 8, 78
WILL, 150(2), 348
WILLIAM, 78, 157, 184, 294
WILLIAM HENRY, 20
WILLIS, 179
WILSON, 346, 348
WINNEY, 36, 236, 330
WITSHAW, 328
WYLY, 106(2)
YOUNG GEORGE, 184
-(?),
GEORGE, 69
---DAY,
ANN, 23

-MINNE,
VALENTINE, 35

-A-

ACUFF,
POLLY, 309
AKAID,
JOHN, 331
ALEXANDER,
CHARLES COFFIN, 273
D., 47, 154, 159, 180, 220, 245, 289
DEBORAH, 6(3)
DICKS, 6(3), 109
DIX, 303
GEORGE W., 310
MR., 185
WILLIAM, 6(2)
WILLIAM DICK, 17
WM., 273
WM. M., 124(2), 125
ALEXANDER'S,
(land), 148
ALTOM,
JOHN, 14(3), 49, 258
WILLIAM, 13, 14(2), 89
ALVIS,
CHARLES D., 19, 20
ELIAS H., 20
GEORGE W., 20
JOHN M., 20
JOSEPH H., 20
SUSANNAH, 20(2)
THADDEAS J., 20
THOMAS J., 20
WILLIAM A., 20
ALVIS, JR.,
CHARLES D., 20(4)
ALVIS, SR.,
CHARLES D., 20
AMIS,
FANNY, 1
HAYMES, 168
HAYNES, 1, 2(3), 5, 9(3), 10, 172
J., 232
JAMES, 2, 5, 9, 10, 216, 221, 257, 286, 335, 339
JAMES B., 259
JAMES H., 10
JOHN, 1(2), 5
LINCOLN, 1,

5(3), 165, 185
LUCY, 1, 2, 5(2)
LUCY H., 10
LUCY N., 5
MARTHA, 10
MARY, 1, 10
NANCY, 2
POLLY, 7
SARAH, 10
SUSAN, 311
TABITHA, 1
THOMAS, 1, 2, 5, 10(2), 227, 258
THOMAS G., 5
THOMAS GALE, 1
THOMAS J., 10(2), 172
THOS. J., 48
WILLIAM, 2, 8
WILLIS, 1, 5
WM., 2
WM. A., 9
AMIS, JURAT,
JAMES, 147
AMYX,
-, 12
ELIZABETH, 11, 12
ISAAC, 11, 12
MARY, 12(3)
POLLY, 11
PRISSILLA, 12(2)
SAMUEL, 11(2), 12(5), 292
AMYZ,
SAMUEL, 11
ANDERSON,
-, 12, 13(3), 38
A., 246
AARON, 12(2), 13
ABIJAH, 250, 255
ABILLREY, 303
AUDLEY, 100
BITHA, 13
CARTER, 11
CATHERINE, 11
D., 183
D.D., 263
DAVID, 5(2), 6(2), 39
DAVID M., 6
ELEN, 11
ELIZABETH, 6(2)
EZEKIEL, 308
JAMES, 284
JONATHAN, 10(2), 11
MARY, 11
PETER, 284
RHODY, 11
SWEMPFIELD, 250, 337
WILLIAM, 118

ANTRIKIN,
NICHOLAS, 150
APERSON,
JOHN, 189
ARGENBRIGHT,
GEORGE, 129
SALLY, 129
ARMSSTRONG,
WILLIAM, 132
ARMSTEAD,
FANNY (MRS.), 231
ARMSTRONG,
ABINAH, 2, 3
ALFRED, 18(2), 19(3), 275
ALFRED L., 19
ALICE LOUISIANA, 7
ANN, 5(2), 15
ANNA, 5
ARTHUR, 7, 8
ARTHUR GALBRAITH, 129
B., 4
BAKER, 3, 4, 18(3), 23
CARRY, 7
CARRY A., 7(2)
CARY, 9(2)
CLINTON, 7(5), 149
ELIZABETH, 4, 7(2), 15, 147(2)

H.C., 19(2), 275
HARRY C., 18
HENRY, 18, 19
HENRY C., 17
HUGH, 36
J.R., 59
JAMES, 1, 4, 5, 244
JAMES G., 321
JAMES M., 10
JANE, 3(2), 5(3)
JAS., 4
JAS. M., 134
JEAN, 4
JOHN, 3(2), 4(8), 5(3), 221, 244, 346
JOSEPH ROGERS, 7
JULIA, 8(3), 9(3)
LACY, 244
LOUISIANA, 10
LUCY ANN, 10
MARGARET, 9(2)
MARY, 3, 7, 18, 19(5), 275
POLLY, 348
RACHAEL, 6, 7

ARMSTRONG
(continued)
RACHEL, 5, 7
SAM'L, 4
SARRY CATHERINE, 15
SARRY CHRISTIAN, 15
SARY CATHERINE, 15
SETH, 14(2), 15
SUSAN, 246
THOMAS, 3, 4(3), 5, 347
W., 9(2), 129
W.P., 316
W.T., 5
WILLIAM, 1, 2, 4, 5, 7(3), 8(2), 17(2), 43, 66, 215, 274, 275, 286
WILLIAM L., 18(2), 19(5)
WILLIAM PITT, 7
WM., 3, 4, 19, 131, 223
WM. R., 136
ARMSTRONG (JURAT),
A.G., 129
ARMSTRONG,,
WILLIAM, 7
ARMSTRONG, JR.,
WILLIAM, 7, 9
ARMSTRONG, SR.,
WILLIAM, 6(2), 9
ARNALD,
MARGARET, 85
ARNOLD,
ALFRED, 16
ANDREW J., 16
ELIZA, 16
GEORGE, 15, 16
GEROGE P., 16
HARVEY, 16
JACKSON, 16(2)
JOHN H., 126
JOHN K., 15, 16(2)
JULIANN, 16
MARTHA, 16(2)
SARAH, 16
WILLIAM, 16(2)
ARNOLT,
SALLY, 17
WILLIAM, 16, 17
WILLIAM M., 16(2), 17
ARNOTT,
FANNY, 200
JAC, 126
JIM, 123
THOS. M., 88

WM. M., 120(3)
ASTON,
EDW. J., 310
ATHEY,
JOHN, 190
AUBRAKEN,
FRANCIS, 121
AUSTIN,
SARY, 288
AYERS,
JAMES, 88(2)

-B-

BABB,
ELIZABETH, 144
BACHUS, 130
BACON,
CATHERINE, 24(3), 25
ISABELLA, 24(2)
MARY, 24
MICHAEL, 24(2), 25
SARAH, 24
BAILEY,
CARR, 32
D., 56
DAVID, 57
HENERETTA, 201
JAMES, 31, 32(3), 74
JOHN, 32
POLLY, 103
SAMUEL, 32, 73
THOMAS, 32
WILLIAM, 31, 32
WINNFRED, 213
ZILPHA, 213
BAILEY, JR.,
WILLIAM, 31
BAILEY, SR.,
WILLIAM, 31
BAINES,
J.M., 163
BAKER,
ANTHONY, 128
GEORGE, 128
JACOB, 189, 190
JOSEPH, 291
PHILLIP P., 128
BALDWIN,
AILCY, 40, 41
CASSANDER, 50
ELIZABETH JANE, 46
ESTHER, 46
JOHN, 45
MARY, 45
MARY ANN, 46
NICHOLAS, 40(2), 41, 45(2)
BARB,
JACOB, 199
BARGER,

50(2), 51
WILLIAM, 45(2), 46
BALDWIN (JR.),
WILLIAM, 45
WILLIAM K., 46
BALL,
BENNETT, 33(2)
JANE, 56
JESSE, 34
JOHN, 34, 55, 56(3), 57(2), 103
JONATHAN, 33(3), 34
MOLLY, 33(2)
MOSES, 33(2), 34
NANCY, 56
PATSY (MORELOCK), 56
POLLY, 34
ROBB, 33
S.H., 56
SPENCER, 2, 33, 56, 57
SPENCER H., 56, 57(2)
THOMAS, 33(2), 34
WESLEY, 34, 56(2), 57(2)
WILLIAM, 33(2)
BALL, SR.,
JOHN, 56
BALLARD,
ALEXANDER, 335
DAVID, 40
ELIZA, 344
ELLIZA, 343
GEORGE, 40
JAMES M., 40
JAMES MAULEY, 40(2)
JANE, 40
JESSE, 40
JOHN, 40
JOHN NELSON, 267
JOSHUA, 40
RUTHY, 344
SARA ANN, 40
SARAH ANN, 39
WILLIAM, 40
BALLARD, JR.,
ALEXANDER, 39, 40(2)
BALLARD, SR.,
ALEXANDER, 39(2), 40(3)
BARB,
JACOB, 199
BARGER,

ISAAC, 190
BARMER,
LEWIS C., 302
BARNARD,
JOHN, 214
JONATHAN, 56
LEWIS, 214
REUBEN, 69, 212, 214
ZADPC, 214
BARNES, 140
BARNET,
JOSHUA, 302
BARNETT,
ADALINE, 50(2)
JOHN, 49(2), 50, 200
LUCY, 50
TEMPY, 50(2)
BARNETT, JR.,
JOHN, 50(2)
BARR,
BARBARY, 31(2)
DEBOROUGH, 31(2)
EDY, 30, 31(2)
ELIZABETH, 51
GEORGE, 31
HENRY, 31
JACOB, 30, 31(4)
JAMES, 30, 31(3)
MATHEWS, 31
MICHAEL, 31
NANCY, 31(2)
PETER, 30, 31(2)
SUSAN, 31(2)
BARR, SR.,
EDY, 30
PETER, 30
BARRETT,
A.P.K., 52, 53
ALFRED, 38(3)
CLINTON, 39(2)
ELIZABETH, 52(2)
ELIZABETH LAURIE, 52
EZEKIEL HAYNES, 53
HUGH, 38(2), 52(3)
JAMES ARTHUR, 53
JIM, 39
JOHN, 38(3), 39(2), 52(4)
JOHN NELSON, 52(3)
LOUISA, 52
MALINDA, 38(2), 39
MARIA, 52(2)
MARTHA CORNELIA, 53
MARY, 52
MARY ELIZABETH,

53
MATILDA, 52
NANCY, 38(2),
39, 53(2), 307
NELSON, 38(3),
39(2)
ORLENA, 52(2)
PEGGY JANE, 53
PLEASANT, 38(2)
POLLY, 38(2), 39
SALLY, 52(2)
SARAH ADALINE,
53
T.T., 52, 96
THOMAS, 38(5),
39, 52
THOMAS ORVILLE,
53
THOMAS T., 52,
53, 178
tract, 8
WILLIAM, 52
WILLIAM N.,
53(3)
WINEFRED, 38
WM. C., 53
BARTON,
ISAAC, 25, 270
BARTON, ESQ.,
ROBERT M.,
116(5)
BASSETT,
ADALINE, 35, 42
ALEXANDER, 35,
42
BURRELL, 35(4)
BURWELL, 34, 35,
36(2), 42(2)
BURWELL W., 43
ELIZABETH TOMAN
(THOMAS), 318
ELVIRA, 35, 42,
43
GEORGE, 35
HELEN, 42
HUGH, 35(2), 36
ISAAC, 35
JAMES N., 42
JOHN, 35
JOSEPH, 35
KETTURAH, 35,
36, 42
LOUISA, 35
MARTHA, 42(5),
43
NATHANIEL,
34(2), 35, 36
RICHARD, 35
RICHARD
NATHANIEL, 42
SPENCER, 35(5),
43
SUSANNAH, 49

WILLIAM, 35
BAUGH,
VALENTINE, 190
BEAL,
ELIAS, 96
JACOB, 134
BEALE,
PETER, 242
BEAN,
JOHN, 61
KATHERINE, 48(2)
MORDECAI, 48(3),
49
BEARD,
PHANNY, 122
BECKNER,
A., 54
ABRAHAM, 53
ABRAHAM B.,
54(2)
JACOB, 111
JOHN F., 54
JOSEPH D., 53(2)
NANCY, 54
NICHOLAS, 87,
112
RHODA, 54
SARAH, 54
BECKNERS,
NICHILAS, 253
SALLY, 252
BEEIL,
CATHERINE, 42
DAVID, 42(2)
EVE, 42(2)
JOHN, 41(2),
42(2)
MARTIN, 42
BEEL,
SARAH, 200
BEGLEY,
CATY, 270
JOHN, 12(2), 13
PLEASANT, 118,
136, 246(2), 249

BELCHER,
RUSSEL F., 136
BELL,
REBECCA, 144
THOMAS W., 75
BELLOMY,
JAMES M., 98,
128
BERNARD,
JOHN, 56
POLLY, 56
REUBEN, 34, 110
BERRY,
FRANCIS, 29
HANNAH, 29
JAMES, 327
JOHN, 29, 112

LAW., 232
LAWRENCE, 232
MARY, 29
SUANNE, 29
THOMAS, 29, 111,
212
WILLIAM, 29(4),
225, 337
BERSHIRE,
JOHN, 164
WILLIAM, 164
BIGLEY,
PLEASANT, 292
BISHOP,
R.M., 14, 257,
258
BLACK,
ROB'T, 21
BLACKBURN,
A., 162
B., 58
BLACKBURNE,
MARY, 229
BLACKWELL,
ANNY, 39
DAVID, 39(3)
BLAIR,
JAMES, 328
BLARY/BLAIRY/BLAIR,
JAMES, 328
BLEVINS,
JOHN, 88, 159
BLINCOE,
GEO. W., 167(2)
BLOOMER,
DANIEL, 37(3),
291
ELIZABETH, 37
ISAAC, 126
JAMES, 37(2)
JESSE, 37
JESSE D., 185
JOSEPH, 37
LUCY, 37(4)
MARTHY, 37
MARY, 37
MILLY, 37
NEHEMIAH, 37
PEGGY, 307
PHEBE, 37
WILLIAM, 37
BOATMAN,
JAMES, 232
NANCY, 288
BOGART,
ANN CANE, 248
BOLIN,
JAMES, 41(4)
JOHN, 41(2)
BOLTZELL,
JENNY, 170(2)
BOND,
ARTHUR, 301

BOWMAN,
ANNA, 48
DAVID, 47(2)
ELIZABETH, 311
JACOB, 47(3),
48(2), 245
JOHN, 48
MARY, 47, 48
POLLY MOLSBEE,
245
REBECCA, 48
SAMUEL, 48
SUSAN JANE, 312
WILLIAM, 47, 48
BOYD,
BENJAMIN, 80
HULDY, 122
JOHN, 82
BOYLES,
JOEL, 34
BRADFORD,
ELIZABETH, 7,
8(2)
MORIAH, 253
THOMAS (THEO.
I), 254
BRADLEY,
JAMES, 17, 77,
172(2)
JAMES P., 203
JAS., 200
O., 125, 322
ORVILLE, 44(4),
45(4), 46(2),
47, 124(3),
125(2), 133,
173(2), 176,
278, 323, 348
ORVILLE C., 239
REUBEN, 190
WILLIAM, 18(2),
43(2), 45(2),
285
WM., 80
BRADSHAW,
FANNEY, 345
JOSEPH B., 345
SINA, 122
BRAMHALL,
JACOB, 30
JUDITH, 30
THOMAS, 30(4)
BRANDON,
THOS., 228
WILLIAM, 165
BRAY,
ELIZABETH, 307
HENRY, 25(3)
MARGARET, 25
PATRICK, 263
POLLY, 97
THOMAS, 132
BRAY, JR.,

BRAY, JR.
(continued)
BENJAMIN, 25
BRAY, SR.,
BENJAMIN, 25
BREDENS' (line),
JAMES, 150
BREEDEN,
JAMES, 25(2),
27, 184
BREWER,
F., 269
FREDERICK, 207
HOWEL, 322
BRICE,
C.C., 343
JAMES T., 20,
324
JOHN T., 45
BRIDGES,
JAMES S., 239
BRITTON,
ABRAHAM, 179
JOSEPH, 304
BROOKS,
ALBERT, 49(2)
EBENEZER, 22, 23
GEORGE, 49, 208
JAMES, 20, 49(2)
JOHN, 49(2),
194, 258
JOSEPH, 41(2)
LAFAYETTE, 49
LEAH, 49, 192
NANCY, 49
POLLY, 1, 162
S., 49, 257, 258
S.D., 14
SUSANNAH, 49
THOMAS, 49
WILLIAM D.,
49(2)
WILSON, 241
WM. D., 49
BROOM,
ALEXANDER M.,
132
BROWN,
-, 21
HENRY, 147
HUGH, 21(3)
JESSE, 3
JOHN, 21
JOHN J., 34
MARGARET, 21
POLLY, 189
REBECCA, 21
REBECKA, 21
SALEY, 303
SAMUEL, 303
SARAH, 21
WILLIAM, 21
BROWN, SEN'R JURAT,

HENRY, 147
BRUSHIRE,
ROBERT, 164
BRUTHINTON,
BETSY, 32(2), 33
CATHARINE, 32
HENRY, 32(2),
33(2)
JACOB, 32(3)
JINNY, 32
POLLY, 32
BRYAN,
BETSY, 81
JOSEPH, 268
BRYANT,
JAMES, 189
LUCINDA
CORNELIA, 57
MARTHA A., 57
MARTHA ANN, 57
MARY E., 57
MARY ELIZABETH,
57(2)
SAMUEL, 57(2),
58
SARAH, 57(2)
BUCHANAN,
---, 277
JOHN, 190
BUCKHART,
JOHN, 170
BUCKNER,
PRESLEY, 65
BUNCH,
BENJAMIN, 287
BUNCH (Jurat),
JOHN, 39
BURAM,
HENRY, 165
MARY, 165
PITZER, 230
POLLY, 229
BURCHELL,
CATHERINE, 51
JOHN, 51(4)
REBECCA, 51
BURD,
---, 335
BUREM,
A.L., 302
ABSALOM, 27(2),
28
ABSALOM L.,
29(2)
C. PITSER, 28,
29
CHARLES P., 29
HENRY, 27(4),
28(2), 29(5),
165
JOHN, 27(2), 28,
29(2)
PASKIL, 28

PASKIL H., 27
PASKILL H.,
29(3)
PETER, 27, 29
PITSER, 27, 28
BURGES,
THOMAS, 227
BURHEM,
ABSALOM, 28
CHARLES PITSER,
28
HENRY, 28(3)
JOHN, 28
PASKILL H., 28
PETER, 28
BURKE,
JOSHUA, 189
BURKHART,
JOHN, 331, 332
BURNS,
JOHN, 58(2)
MARY, 58, 59
MARY M., 58
ROBERT, 58
SALLY, 235
WILLIAM, 58
BURRIS,
JACOB, 176
JOHN, 308, 330
RANDOLPH, 323
BURTON,
CATHERINE, 293
ELIZABETH, 55(2)
F.W., 292
REBECCA, 55(3)
SAMUEL, 67
BURUM,
PETER, 2
BUSSELL,
ABSALOM T., 54,
55(2)
B.L., 55
BENJAMIN L.,
54(2)
BENJAMIN
SANFORD, 54, 55
BURWELL W., 54,
55
CALVIN P., 54,
55(2)
GEORGE W., 54,
55
H.M., 238
JAMES M., 54, 55
JOHN R., 54, 55
POLLY, 54(2), 55
VIRENDA CHARLES,
55(2)
BYLER,
DAVID, 270
BYNUM,
JOHN G., 278
NANCY B., 278

BYRD,
ANN, 24
CHARLES, 23, 24
DAVID, 23(2), 24
ELIZABETH,
23(2), 24(2)
HENRY, 41
JAMES, 23, 24(2)
JANE, 24
JOHN, 23, 24,
41(2), 46
MARY, 23, 24
MICHAEL, 23, 24,
25
RICHARD, 23(3),
24(3)
WILLIAM, 23,
24(2)

-C-

CAIN,
J. W., 259
CAIN, JR.,
HIGH, 91
CALDWELL,
DAVID, 22, 23
JAMES, 22, 65(2)
JANE, 65
CAMP,
A.J., 101
CAMPBELL,
ANDERSON, 46, 77
ANNA, 77(2)
CHARLES, 288
DAVID, 23(2)
JAMES (V.), 77
JAMES V., 152
JAMES Y., 290
JOHN, 23(2),
190(3)
MARY ANN, 226
N., 207
NELSON, 96
ROBERT, 77,
190(2)
SILAS, 290
CAMPBELL'S,
JOHN, 22(2)
CAMPER,
SARAH, 332
CANNON,
DENNIS, 208
CANTWELL,
BARICE, 112
BARNET, 320
JOHN, 320
CARDEN,
BEVERLY J., 195
C. COLUMBUS, 74
C.C., 74(3)
CHARLOTTE, 74
CHRISTOPHER

COLUMBUS, 74
COLUMBUS, 194,
195
FRANK, 74
J.W., 75, 271
JAMES, 271
JAS, 77
JOSEPH, 74,
194(2)
JOSEPH W., 74
JUDITH, 194, 195
ROBERT, 271, 286
CARDEN & RUBEL,
-, 74
CARDIN,
JUDITH, 192
CAREY,
DANIEL, 71(2),
72(4)
MARY AN(-), 71
REBECCA, 71
SALLY, 71
SOLOMAN, 71
CARMACK,
C.E., 101
CORNELIUS,
70(4), 101, 166
EPPS, 101(2)
JAMES, 101(2),
158
JOHN, 166(2)
WILEY, 101(2)
WILLIAM, 70,
101(3), 324
WILLIAM E.,
101(3), 324, 343

CARMACK, JR.,
CORNELIUS, 70
CARMICHAEL,
A., 99, 100,
137, 161, 181,
207, 344
ARCHIBALD, 99
DANIEL, 88(3)
DR. ARCHIBALD,
99
H., 265
HAMILTON, 88(2)
JAMES, 88, 145
PLEASANT, 88
CARPENTER,
ALLEN, 89
ANDERSON, 89,
90(2)
HANNAH, 89(2)
JESSE, 89, 90
JOHN, 90
NANCY ORLENA,
89(2)
WILSON, 89
YELBERTON,
89(2), 90

CARRELL,
KISSIAH, 224
CARRINGTON,
JOSEPH, 146(3)
LUCINDA, 147
CARROLL,
J.J., 182, 317,
344
MOLLIE K., 343
CARTER,
---, 346
ALLEN, 95,
105(4)
BETSY, 27, 28,
29
CAROLINE, 347,
349
CHARLES, 95
HAMILTON J.,
95(2)
HIGHLEY, 95
HILA, 96
LUCINDA, 96
MRS., 9
NATHANIEL, 347
SIBBRINEY, 201
CASE'S (grave),
THOMAS, 202
CASNER,
DAVID, 168
CATER,
HAMELTN (sp), 96
CAVERN,
JOHN, 304
CAVIN,
ELIZABETH, 178
JOHN, 178
LUCY, 178
CELEY,
WILLIAM, 168
CHAMBERLAIM,
JEREMIAH, 145
CHAMBERLAIN,
JEREMIAH, 145
CHAMBERS,
DANIEL, 93, 94
DAVID, 168
SARAH, 93(2)
WILLIAM S.,
93(2), 94(2)
CHANBERS,
DANIEL, 173
CHAPMAN,
ABRAM, 269
CHARLES,
BARSHABA J., 92
C.A., 119
CARSHA J., 91
CLINTON A., 174
DARKY, 229
E.W., 92
ELDRIDGE, 84
ETHELDRIDGE,

91(2)
HEZEKIAH, 119
HUGHY J., 91
J.M., 55, 271,
340
JACOB M., 175
JAMES, 84(2),
177
JOHN, 240
JOHN R., 96, 226
MARY, 84
MRS., 154
SALLY, 27, 28,
29, 175
SARAH, 84(3)
SUSANNAH, 91
SUSANNAH E., 91
W.B., 340
WILLIAM A., 16,
91
CHARLTON,
JACOB, 80(3)
CHESNUT,
A., 271
CHESNUTT,
ELIZA, 202
HENRY, 295
HENRY D., 51
HUGH, 234
POLLY, 311
R., 223
RODHAM, 220
SALLY, 216
SAMUEL, 216(2)
TABITHA, 295
THOMAS, 134, 311
WILLIAM, 311
CHESTER,
JOHN, 79(2), 80
JOHN K., 80
SAM'L G., 80
CHESTNUTT,
ELIZA, 202
INDIANA, 92
RICHARD, 202
RODHAM, 200, 205
SAM'L, 104
SAMUEL, 103(2),
177
SUSAN, 103, 104
CHILDRESS,
G.S., 102
GEORGE S.,
101(2)
JAMES, 148
JAMES M., 101(2)
SARAH T., 101
CHISOLM,
BETSY, 143
CHISUM,
ELIJAH, 227
CHRISTIAN,
ALLEN, 86(2)

BETSY, 32
CINDY, 73(2)
DAVID, 102
ELDRIDGE, 103
ELIZABETH, 6,
102, 103
GEORGE, 86
JAMES, 74,
102(3), 103(2)
JAS, 86
JESSE, 103(2)
JOHN, 85(3),
86(3)
JOSEPH F., 103
LEWIS, 72, 74,
85
MARGARET, 74(2)
MARY E., 103
NANCY, 86(2),
307
RACHAEL M., 103
SALLY, 73
SETH, 86
STEPHEN, 103(2),
309
THOMAS, 74(2),
85
THOMAS J., 86
WILLIAM, 74(2)
WILLIAM L., 85,
86, 102(3),
103(2), 307
CHRISTIAN, JR.,
LEWIS, 73
CHRISTIAN, SR.,
LEWIS, 72,
73(5), 74(2)
CHURCH,
ALLICE, 85(2)
ELEANOR, 66
HENRY, 84(2), 85
JOHN C., 66(3)
JOHN CHRISTIAN,
66
WILLIAM, 85
CLADWELL,
JAMES, 66
CLAIBORNE,
County, 89
CLAP,
EARL B., 190
CLARK,
BENJAMIN, 190
JOSEPH W., 141
PETER, 190
POLLY, 204
CLARKE,
JAMES W., 95
CLAYTON,
PETTUS C., 190
CLECK,
MATTHEW, 65
CLICK,

CLICK (continued)
JACOB, 68
LEWIS, 94(2),
95, 303, 319
MARGARET, 68
MICHAEL, 67(2),
68(2)
ROSANNAH, 94(3)
CLILPPER,
JOSEPH, 143
CLOUD,
BENJAMIN, 294
GEORGE, 323
JEREMIAH, 141,
142, 323
JESSY, 140
COBB,
ARTHUR, 105,
106(3)
BARSHA, 105(2)
BARSHABA, 106(3)
CATHARINE, 104
EDWARD, 100
JESSE, 106(4)
JOEL, 97, 100(3)
P.A., 104
PHAROAH, 105,
107(2)
RICHARD C., 106
RICHARD
CASEWELL, 106
RICHARD CASWELL,
105
WILEY, 97(2),
98, 100(2)
WILLIAM, 105
WINSTED D.,
100(2)
WINSTON D., 100
COBBLE,
WILLIAM, 338
COCKE,
ELIZA, 289
ELIZA M., 135,
136
FREDERICK, 289
JOHN, 289
JOHN S., 261
SALLY, 68
THOMAS, 90(2),
91(2)
WILLIAM E, 5
COCKERHAM,
ELEANOR, 317
COCKREHAM,
ABNER W., 83(2)
AMANDA, 83
DANIEL H.,
83(2), 247
EMILY H., 83
JOHN, 83(2),
84(2)
JOHN H., 83(2),

84, 291
THOMAS, 83
THOMAS G., 83,
84
WILLIAM H.,
83(2)
COFFEE,
AUSBRUN/OSBORNE,
336
COFFIN,
CHARLES, 200
COFFMAN,
ANDREW, 40(2)
ELIZABETH, 201
JACOB, 270
COLDWELL,
ABRIAM, 92
ANDERSON F.,
92(2), 93
B., 82, 130, 283
BENONI, 80(2),
127, 128(2),
189(2)
BENONI F., 81
DAVID, 283
DELPHI ANN, 81
ELIZA, 81
ELIZABETH, 80,
81
ELIZABETH G.,
273
JAMES, 136
JOHN, 132, 133,
256, 273
JULIA ANN, 81
N.H., 50
PERCY C., 81
RACHAEL, 81(2)
SALLY, 92
T., 94
THOMAS, 81,
92(2), 93, 130,
132, 133(2), 173

THOMAS K., 81
THOS., 131
VOLNEY, 81
COLDWELL, JR.,
T., 173
COLE,
---, 313
JAMES, 75
JOHN, 75(3), 189
JOSEPH, 75
JOSIAH, 189
MARGARET, 75
COLEY,
BETSY, 63
FRANK, 63
JAMES, 62(2), 63
JOHN, 62, 63
MOLLY, 62, 63
NANCY, 62, 63
PEGGY, 62, 63

SALLY, 62(2),
63(2)
WM, 62
WM., 63
COLLINS,
ALLEN, 83
CHARLOTTY, 83
JANE, 51
MILLENTON, 83
MORGAN, 83
SARDY, 83
SHEPARD, 157
SIMEON, 82(2)
VARDY, 157(2)
COMBS,
ELIJAH, 288
SALLY, 288
COMES,
LIDY, 166
CONDRAY,
DENNIS, 65
CONN,
GERRARD T., 189
CONNER,
-, 105
JAMES, 90
JULIAS, 105, 106
MALVINA M., 135,
136
CONNILLY,
THOMAS, 71
CONSINGER,
CARTHERINE, 262
MARGARET, 262
CONWAY,
GEORGE, 268(2)
COOK,
MARGARET, 8
MARGARET E.,
8(2)
COOKE,
-, 35
STERLING, 35
COOPER,
ABSOLOM, 78
ELIZABETH,
76(3), 78(2), 79
HANNAH, 239
HENRY, 78(2)
JAMES, 76(3),
78(4), 79, 217
JANE, 78(2), 79
JOHN, 78(5),
79(2), 346
MARY, 78(2), 346
PEGGY, 217
PRISSILLA, 109
ROB'T, 126
ROBB, 16
ROBERT, 78(3),
79, 140, 141(2),
158, 256, 257

WILEY, 78, 79
WILLIAM, 78(2),
79
YOUNG, 346
COOPER, ESQ.,
ROB'T, 158
COPE,
JANE, 293
JESSE, 337
MATISON, 293
WILEY, 251
COPENHAVER,
JOHN, 256
COUCH,
CASSANDER, 314
LAZARUS, 314,
315
MARTHA, 163
MARY ANN, 163
COUCH'S,
Line, 113
COURTNEY,
JAMES, 175
WILLIAM, 175
COWAN,
JAMES, 239
WM. W., 239
COWARD,
ANNA, 111, 113
JOSEPH, 326
PATSY, 326
THOMAS, 326
COX,
ABSALOM, 68
BENJ., 59
BENJAMIN, 59(3)
E., 99
EDWARD, 61(2),
77
ELIACUIM, 99
ELIAKENN, 98(2)
ELIZABETH, 77,
99(2), 145
ELIZABETH V., 77
ELLICE, 61(2)
FRANCES, 68
FRANCIS, 77
GEORGE, 68(2),
96, 97
GEORGE VAN, 96
HUGH, 99
ISCAA D., 152
JACOB, 64(4)
JAMES, 77, 96,
97
JAMES M., 96, 97
JAS, 2
JESSE, 59
JOHN, 61(3), 64,
68(3), 69, 77
JOHN JAMES, 96
JOHN T., 96(5),

97(2)
JOSIAH, 68
M.T., 310
MARJERY, 59
MARTIN, 99
MARY, 64(4)
MATHER, 99
NANCY, 332
RUSSEL, 68
SARAH, 310
SARAH S., 96, 97
SOLOMON, 59
TABITHA, 5,
  77(2)
TATBITHA, 77
THOMAS, 61, 194
THOMAS G.A., 77
THOMAS H., 77
THOMAS T., 97
TIBITHA, 61
WILLIAM, 59(2),
  99
WILLIAM N., 253
WM., 165
ZACHARIAH, 9
COX (HALE),
  ALICE, 77
COZIER,
  AGNES, 86
  CASANDER, 86
  JOHN, 87
  NANCY ISABELLA,
    86
  SUSANNAH, 86
CRAFT,
  REBECCA, 69(4)
CRAIG,
  ROBERT, 190
CRAIG, JR.,
  ROBERT, 189
CRAUDER,
  JOSEPHINE A.,
    125
CRAWFORD,
  MARGARET, 130
  WILLIAM, 62(4)
CRAWLEY,
  HENRY, 121
CRAYCRAFT,
  RUBEN, 59(2), 60
  WILLIAM, 60
CREECH,
  B.A., 52
  JESSE, 151
CREED,
  MARY A., 91
  MARYANER, 91
  WILLIAM S.,
    91(3)
CRILLY,
  COLLIN, 60(3)
  JANE THOMPSON,
    60

WILLIAM, 60
CRITZ,
  ---, 322
  JOHN, 82, 330,
    331
  P., 256
  PHILLIP, 140,
    141
  SUSANNAH, 98(3)
CROBARGER,
  GEORGE, 82(3)
  HETTY, 82
  MARY, 82(2)
CROCKETS,
  COL. JOSEPH, 22
CROSBY,
  JANE, 288
CROSIER,
  CASANDER, 87(3)
  ELIZABETH, 87
  NANCY ISABELLA,
    87
CROSON,
  DR(E)WSILLER, 67
  DURSILLER, 67
  JOHN, 67(5)
CROSS,
  DEANER, 61
  EDWARD, 60(2),
    61
  ELIZABETH, 61
  GIBBINS, 61
  JAMES, 61
  MARY, 61
  NANCY, 61
  PATTY, 61
  REBECKER, 61
  ROBBER(D), 61
  ROBERT, 61
  WILLIAM, 61
CROZIER,
  JOHN, 86(2)
CUMMING,
  DAVID B., 213
CUNNINGHAM,
  BETSY, 22
  DAVID, 22
  JAS., 21
  JOHN, 22
  POLLY, 22
CURR(Y),
  JANE, 76
CURREY,
  SAMUEL, 76(4)
CURRY,
  GEOR., 73
  GEORGE, 165
  JAMES, 71
  JOHN, 71
  MARY, 71(2)
  SAMUEL, 71(3),
    77
CURRY/CURREY,

SAM'L, 77

-D-

DADE,
  LAUGHORNE, 231
  MARY ANN, 231,
    232
  TOWNSHEND L.,
    231
DALTON,
  LEWIS, 214
DALZELL,
  FRAN'S, 109
  FRANCIS, 108(2)
  NANCY, 108(2)
DAMMER,
  JOHN H., 302
DANIEL,
  POLLY O., 135
DARTER,
  SALLY ANN, 226
  STEPHEN, 105
DAUGHERTY,
  -, 189
  JOHN, 189
DAVIS,
  ASA, 119(4)
  CATHARINE, 329
  ELIZABETH, 149
  GEORGE, 163
  HEZEKIAH, 243
  JANE E., 58(2)
  JEAN, 22(2)
  JOHN, 46, 300
  JOSEPH, 121
  JULIA, 146, 147
  KITTY, 305
  LARKIN, 112(2)
  LEWIS, 300
  LILBORN, 119
  LOUISA, 272
  MADISON, 112(2)
  MARTHA, 324
  MARY, 218
  NANCY, 51, 312
  POLLY, 305
  PRISSILLA, 12(2)
  SARAH, 12
  WILLIAM, 51(2),
    218
DAVIS, JR.,
  JAMES, 112(2)
DAVISON,
  JAMES W., 95
DAZEAL'S,
  (entry), 196
DEANE,
  JAMES, 170
  MARY, 170
DECHERT,
  MICHAEL, 190
DECK,

DANIEL, 211
DELP,
  ANDREW J.,
    117(2)
  DANIEL, 117(3)
  MARGARET, 117(2)
  ROBERT, 189
  STEPHEN, 117
DERIAUX,
  RACHAEL, 201
DERICK,
  JACOB, 241
  JOHN, 241
DeWOLFE,
  HARRIET, 349
  LOUISIANA, 8(3)
DICKARD,
  SUSANNAH, 122
DICKERD,
  MAHALA, 324
DICKSON,
  JANE S., 113(2)
  JOHN, 116
  WILLIAM S.,
    113(2)
  WM. S., 117(2)
DOBSON,
  ROBERT, 111(2)
DODSON,
  ANN, 113
  ARTHUR, 113,
    120(2)
  ELISHA, 91, 110,
    185
  ELIZA, 118
  ELIZABETH, 113
  GEORGE, 111(2),
    118
  JAMES, 110(2)
  JAMES H., 118
  JAMIMA, 110(5)
  JOHN, 111,
    112(3), 113, 120

  LANY (DELANEY),
    113
  LAZARUS, 107
  MARTHA, 118(3)
  MARY, 113
  MOSES, 282
  PATSEY, 118
  RAWLEIGH, 107,
    108
  REBECCA, 112,
    120(3)
  ROLLY, 110
  SANFORD, 118
  SARAH, 110
  THOMAS, 110(4)
  THOMAS L., 118
  TOLLIVER, 107
  WILLIAM, 113,
    120(3)

DODSON (continued)
  WILLIAM E., 118
  WINNIE, 120
  WINNY, 113, 120
DODSON, (SR.),
  RALEIGH, 107
DODSON, SENR.,
  JOHN, 111
DODSON, SR.,
  RAWLEIGH, 107
DONALDSON,
  JOHN, 288
  STOKLEY, 346
DONALSON,
  tract, 38
DONELSON,
  JAMES, 38
DONNELSON,
  NANCY, 324
DOUGHERTY,
  JAMES, 61
DOWDALL,
  EDWARD, 108(2)
DOWELL,
  JESSE, 322
DRAKE,
  R.H., 51
  SALITZ, 317
DRINNEN,
  WILLIAM, 12
DRINNON,
  ELENOR, 12
DUBARD,
  ---, 254
DUFF,
  WILLIAM, 189
DUGGAN,
  CASSANDER, 223
DUGUARD,
  MARGARET, 190
DUKES,
  ROBERT, 190
DUNLAP,
  JOHN, 206
DYKES,
  HENRY, 119
  ISHAM, 119(2)
  ISUM, 109
  JAMES, 109, 119
  JOHN, 109(2),
    118(2), 119(2)
  JOSEPH, 110, 119
  SUSANNAH, 109(2)
  THOMAS, 119
  WILLIAM, 109(2),
    110, 119(2)
DYKES (MULLENIX),
  MARY, 119
DYKES (SIMPSON),
  SUSANNAH, 119
DYKES, SENR.,
  WILLIAM, 109

-E-

EAVIN,
  MARY, 201
EDISON,
  C., 118
EDMONDSON,
  J.B.C., 343
EDWARDS,
  -, 95
EIDSON,
  CRETON, 126, 127
  EDWARD, 300
  JOHN, 127
  LARKIN W., 126,
    127(3)
  MARTHA, 127(2)
  SAMUEL, 126
  SWINEFIELD, 126,
    127
  THOMAS, 154(3)
  WILLIAM, 127
  WILLSON, 126
  WM., 126
EIDSON, SR.,
  WILLIAM, 126(2)
ELLIS,
  BETSEY, 124(2)
  BURRIS, 124
  GUY, 124(2), 125
  JANE, 124(2)
  JOANNA, 123,
    125(4)
  JOHN, 123,
    124(4), 125(5)
  JOHN H., 257
  WILLIAM, 124(3),
    125
  WM., 124, 125
ELLIS, SR.,
  JOHN, 123
ELLIS,CLK.,
  JOHN H., 112
ELLISON,
  EDMOND, 126
  ELIZABETH,
    125(2), 126(2)
  FRANCES, 126
  THOMAS, 125(2),
    126(2)
ELMORE,
  SARAH, 161(2),
    162
  WILLIAM PROTER,
    161
ELY,
  SUSANNAH, 179(2)
ELZEY,
  W., 61
ELZY,
  WILLIAM, 132
ENART,
  ISABELLA, 116(2)

EPPERSON,
  ALLEN, 121
  BETSY, 121
  HARRISON, 122(2)
  HESTER, 121
  HOPSON, 122
  JANE, 121(2),
    331
  JESSE, 121, 330
  JOHN, 121(2)
  JOSEPH, 121(4)
  NANCY, 121, 122
  PATSEY, 121
  PEGGY, 121
  POLLY, 121
  STEPHEN, 122(2)
  THOMAS, 121
  THOS., 121
  WILLIAM, 122(3)
EPPERSON (BOYD),
  HULDY, 122
ERWIN,
  ---, 274
  ANDREW, 120
  BENJAMIN, 120
  EDWARD, 120(3),
    121(2)
  ELIZABETH, 120
  FRANCES, 120
  JOHN, 120
  MARGARET, 121
  MARY, 120
  ROBERT, 120
  SAMUEL, 120
  SARAH, 120
  WILLIAM, 120
ESTILL,
  BENJAMIN, 189
ETTER,
  A. H., 267
  C.C., 162
  FRANKEY, 135
  GEORGE H., 190
  J. L., 267
  JAMES, 162
  JAMES L., 36,
    43, 90, 254
  MINERVA, 260
  WILLIAM, 342
ETTER, JR.,
  WILLIAM W., 162
EVERETT,
  JOSEPH, 148(2)
EVERETTE,
  NANCY, 247
EVERHART,
  CHRISLEY, 122,
    123
  ELIZABETH, 292
  JACOB, 122
  JAMES, 122, 205
  JOHN, 122
  LIZZY, 122(2)

POLLY, 122,
  126(3)
SAMUEL, 122
WILLIAM, 122(2),
  126, 205

-F-

FAIN,
  ELIZA R., 139
  ELIZABETH, 137,
    138
  ELIZABETH R.,
    137
  GEORGE C., 139
  GEORGE G., 137,
    138(2), 139
  HIRAM, 137(2),
    138, 139, 312
  JOHN H., 137,
    138, 139
  N., 139, 174
  NANCY, 139
  NICHOLAS, 137
  R. G., 137, 245
  R.G., 342
  RICHARD G., 137,
    138, 139
FAIN, JR.,
  HIRAM, 139
FALKERSON,
  JAMES L., 220
FARIS,
  E.D., 96
  WILLIAM, 294
  WM., 204
FARMER,
  ELIZABETH, 129
  WILLIAM, 130
  WM., 129
FARQUHAR,
  AMOS, 6
FARR,
  ABIAL H., 204
FARRIS,
  A.W., 252
FAWBUSH,
  ---, 277
FEAGINS,
  JAMES, 74, 103,
    309
  WILLIAM, 30,
    73(2), 74, 152
FEGINS,
  WILLIAM, 152
FELCKNOR,
  GEORGE, 128, 129
  HENRY, 128(2),
    129
  JACOB, 128(2),
    129(3)
  LOUIS, 128
  MARTIN, 129(2)

PHILLIP, 128,
129
POLLY LEWIS,
128(2)
ROSANNA, 128
FELKEN/FELKNER,
RUTHY, 85
FELKNER,
GEORGE, 130, 131
JACOB, 43, 131,
286
JOHN, 131
PHILIP, 131
SUSAN, 130, 131,
261
FELKNER'S,
Island, 85
FIELDS,
BETSY, 255
POLLY, 32
FINDLEY,
CONNALLY, 190
MARGARET, 195
FINLEY,
JAMES, 129(3)
PRUDENCE, 129(5)
SAMUEL, 129(3)
WILLIAM, 129
FINLEY'S DOCTOR,
(line), 188
FISHER,
-, 124, 125
JAMES, 124(2)
NANCY, 123, 124,
125
SARAH, 229
WILLIAM, 229
FITZGERALD,
GARRETT, 144
MOLLY, 144
FITZPATRICK,
EDMOND, 155
JOHN SAUNDERS,
315
FLETCHER,
CHRISTINE, 136
HENRY, 136
JAMES, 135
JOHN, 136
JOHN G., 165
JOHN P., 135
PEGGY, 135
RICHARD, 165
THOMAS, 135
THOMAS A., 134
WILLIAM, 135
FLIPPERE,
THOS, 145
FLORA,
ABRAHAM, 134(2)
CHARLOTTE,
134(2)
DANIEL, 134(2)

EVLINE, 134
JACOB, 134
JOSEPH, 134(2)
LUCINDA, 134
NANCY, 134(2)
POLLY, 134
FOOTE,
HELLEN G.
(MRS.), 231
FORD,
B.C., 85
BEVERLEY O., 135
BEVERLY C., 11,
85, 319
ELIZABETH, 152
HENRY T., 227
HOLLY, 38
JAMES C, 11
JAREL, 11
JOHN, 227
MARY J., 226(2)
MILTON, 2
NANCY, 305
FORGEY,
ANDREW, 127(2),
128(2), 130, 317

BETSY, 132, 133
ELLEN, 131, 133
EVALINE M., 260
GABRIEL, 139,
142
HUGH, 128(2)
ISABELLA, 130
JAMES, 127(2),
128(2), 131,
132, 136, 289
JAMES (R) 133
JAMES (R.), 132
JAMES R., 133,
135, 136, 139,
142, 321
JAMES REYNOLDS,
131, 132(2)
JAS, 189
JOHN, 127, 128,
130(2), 333
MANERVA, 142
MARGARET, 128,
131, 132, 133,
135
MATILDA, 132,
133, 142
NANCY, 5
POLLY, 131, 132
RACHAEL, 131,
132, 133(2),
142, 246
SUSAN, 142
FORGEY, JR.,
ANDREW, 127
FOSTER,
MARIAH, 99

RACHAEL, 99
FOX,
RICHARD, 71
SAMUEL, 71
FRANCIS,
CAROLINE, 349
FRANCISCO,
AMANDA, 93,
94(3)
DANIEL, 94
G., 173(2)
GEORGE, 173, 174
J., 322
JACKSON, 141(2)
JACKSON W., 140,
142
JAMES, 140, 230,
323
JAS., 76
JOHN, 230
P.A., 140, 141
SARAH, 94
THOMAS, 94
WILLIAM B., 140
FRAZIER,
POLLY, 100
ZILPHIA, 246
FROST,
ANDREW, 254
ELIZABETH, 126
ROBERT, 129,
130, 136
SARAH, 130
SIMEON, 129
THOMAS, 129
WILLIAM, 129
FUDGE,
CONRAD, 19, 257
LOUISA W., 256
FULKERSON,
-, 136
ABRAM, 136
ALICE G., 136,
137
CATHARINE, 137
FRANCIS M., 137
HARRIET, 137
JAMES L., 136,
137
MARGARET, 137
SAM'L V., 137

-G-

G. LYON,
grist mill, 44
GAILBRAITH,
JAMES B., 349
GAINES,
FRANCES G., 149
JAMES, 239
JAMES T., 148,
149, 330, 331

JAMES TAYLOR,
148
JOHN G., 149
SARAH, 148, 239
GALBRAITH,
A., 162
AENEAS S., 146,
147(2), 153
ALEXANDER M.,
161, 170
ANDERSON, 162
ANDREW, 107,
146(3), 147,
153, 161(3),
162, 170, 216,
219, 234
ANDREW L., 153
ANDREW, SR., 241
ANNA MARIA, 161
ARTHUR, 147(3)
ARTHUR W., 153
ARTHUR WRIGHT,
153
AUDLEY, 161(2),
162
ELIZABETH, 147
ENEAS S., 146
FREDERICK A.,
162
HARVEY, 162
J.B., 7
JAS. B., 326
JOHN, 147(2),
153(3), 284
JOHN M., 161
JOHN SHARP, 153
JOS. B., 19, 310
JOSEPH, 145(2),
147, 161, 162
JOSEPH B., 312
JULIANN, 153
MARY, 81
MARY T., 162
MOTTLENIA, 146
WILLIAM, 161,
162, 247
WM., 162
GALBRAITH(SR.),
ANDREW, 161(2)
GALBRAITH, SR.,
A., 162
GALBRAITH'S,
line, 106, 107
GARLAND,
JOSEPH, 46
GARRISON,
ELIZABETH, 200
GETSER,
NELSON, 161(2)
GIBBINS, SR.,
W. THOMAS, 61
GIBBONS,
-, 217

GIBBONS (continued)
EDMOND, 143,
144(2)
EPPS, 143
JAMES, 144,
157(3), 158
JOHN, 82, 122,
144, 157(2), 158

ROBERT, 157(2),
158(2)
THOMAS, 143(3)
THOS., 144(2)
WILLIAM, 143,
157(2), 158
GIBLEY,
MANILA, 292
GIBSON,
SHEPARD, 156(2)
GIDEONS,
ISHAM, 149(2)
JAMES, 149(2),
150(2)
JAMES H., 150
JOHN, 149(2)
MARTHA, 150
WILLIAM, 149(2),
242
GIFORD,
JACOB, 185(3)
JUDITH, 185
MRS., 185
GILL,
THOS. J., 204
GILLENWATER,
WILLIAM, 156
GILLENWATERS,
ASBURY, 263
C., 153
CALVIN, 156(3)
E.E., 257
EILJAH C., 161
ELIJAH C., 160
ELIJAH D., 39
ELIZABETH, 157,
207
GEO., 156
GEORGE, 160
GEORGE A., 309
J.G., 257
J.G., DR., 257
JOEL, 156, 273
JOEL C., 263
MARGARET, 273
MARY, 155,
160(3), 320
MARY ANN, 157,
158, 207
POLLY, 156, 160
RACHAEL, 156
ROBERT, 156
SALLY, 143,
160(2)

SUSAN ADALINE,
207
SUSANNAH A.,
157, 158
THOMAS, 156(2),
160(4), 166
WILLIAM, 156(2),
160, 309
WM., 161
GILLENWATERS
(JURAT),
JOEL, 144
GILLENWATERS (SR.),
THOMAS, 155(2)
GILLIAM,
JOHN, 80(2)
MARY, 324
POLLY, 80
SALLY, 152
GLADSON,
ELIZABETH, 162
JOSHUA, 162
LEVIN, 162(2),
163(2)
MARK S., 162
NATHAN, 162(3)
WILTON, 162
GLEN,
SAMUEL, 189, 190
GODARD,
FRANCIS, 73
GODBY,
CROCKETT, 260
EVALINE M., 260
GODDARD,
FRANCIS, 152(3)
SARAH, 152
SOLOMAN, 152
GODSEY,
MARY, 157(2),
158
GOING,
ANDREW, 151
SHEARD, 151
WILLIAM, 151(3)
GOLDEN,
B., 58
GOLDING,
WILLIAM, 31
GONNOSE,
JOHN L., 275
GOODMAN,
-, 11
E. S., 219
FRANCIS, 310
JAMES, 249, 250
NEILL, 287
WILLIAM, 287
GOODSON,
JOHN, 190
GORDON,
ALLA, 5
JAMES, 165

GOULDY,
ANDREW, 240
GOURLEY,
NANNA, 271
GRADY,
--- (WIDOW), 277
GRAFT,
JACOB, 60
GRANT,
ALEX'R, 143
ALEXANDER,
143(3)
ELLINOR, 143
MARY, 143(2)
THOMAS, 143(2)
GRANTHAM,
FRANCIS, 5
JAMES, 77
RICHARD, 10
GRANTUM,
SALLAY, 268
SEALLY, 268
GRANVILLE,
JOHN, 16
GRAY,
NATHAN, 199
ROBERT, 173
ROBERT D., 199
WILLIAM, 190
GREEN,
DAN, 96
PRISCILLA,
179(2)
THOMAS, 16
GREENE,
JOHN, 228
PRISCILLA, 179
SUSANNAH, 179
WILLIAM, 179
GREENWAY,
SALLY, 81
GREGORY,
ABIAH, 227
ENOCH, 227
JOHN, 227
MARY, 227
RHODA, 227
GRER(CHESTER?),
SAM'L, 80
GRIFFIN,
JAMES, 210
JONES, 213, 214
MARY, 213
GRIGSBY,
AARON, 9
ASHBY, 150(2)
ELIZABETH, 222
JAMES, 150, 151
JOHN, 150(4),
151
MR., 8
NATHANIEL,

150(3), 163(3),
222
SAMUEL, 150
WILEY A., 16
WILLIAM, 87,
150, 155
WINNEY, 150(2)
GRIGSBY SEN.,
WILLIAM, 87
GRIGSBY, COL'D,
WILLIAM, 155
GRILLS,
ELBERT, 145(3)
ELBERT (ELLET),
145
JOHN, 144,
145(4)
PHILADELPHIA,
144(2), 145(6)
RICHARD, 145(2)
GRISGBY,
WILLIAM, 155
GRO --,
WM., 261
GROSE,
CHRISLEY, 144
CHRISLEY
(CHRISTLEY), 144

CHRISTLEY, 144
LOUISA, 38
POLLY, 151
GROSS,
CORNELIUS,
152(3)
JAMES, 152(3)
JOHN, 152(2)
LEWIS, 152
MARY, 152
NANCY, 151(2),
152
WILLIAM, 151(2),
152(3)
GROVE,
ELIZABETH,
143(2)
JACOB, 70
JOHN, 167
GROVES,
(farms), 180
-, 180
FANNY, 154
JACOB B.,
154(5), 240
JOHN, 180
MR., 154
GULLY,
ISAAC, 155
LAZARUS, 154,
155
NANCY, 154, 155
NELSON, 155
PRAINT, 155

187(2), 188
ELIZABETH, 187
HARDY, 185
HOUSTON, 300
J. S., 218
J.L., 335
JAMES, 6, 12,
110, 184, 185,
186(4), 218
JAMES T., 184,
185
JAMES THOMAS,
184
JOHN F., 6
JOHN WESLEY, 187
LUCINDA, 99
MARGARET, 99
MATILDA, 135
MILDRED, 145(3)
NANCY, 185(3)
NATHANIEL WILEY
McBRIDE, 187,
188
NATHANIEL WILLEY
McBRIDE, 187
ROB'T, 82
ROBERT, 176,
187(2), 188(2),
321, 334
ROBERT EMET,
187(2)
ROBERT ENET, 187
SANFORD, 36
STEPHEN, 135,
187
SUSANNAH, 184(2)
THOMAS, 118,
186(2), 187, 264

THOS., 118
VIRGINIA
REBECCA, 20
WALTER, 186(3)
WASHINGTON, 145
WILLIAM D., 135
WILLIAM W., 50,
187, 188
JOHNSTON,
GEORGE, 230
J.R., 249
JAMES, 266
JOSEPH A., 266
JONES,
-, 11
ANNAS, 237
AQUILA, 183
AQUILLA, 170,
183(2)
BETSY, 270
ELIZA, 237
ENEC, 183
JAMES, 303
JOHN, 54, 238,

271
MARTIN, 183
MARY, 183
RIAL, 207
RILEY, 177, 303
SUSANNAH, 12
THOMAS, 268
WILLIAM, 163,
189
JOYCE,
PETER, 267

-K-

KARNES,
-, 190
ANDREW, 190
ELIZABETH,
190(2)
GEORGE, 190(4)
JACOB, 190(5)
JOHN, 190
WILLIAM, 190
KARNE'S (line),
GEORGE, 190
KARNES, SR.,
GEORGE, 190(5)
KEELE,
A.B., 201(4),
208
ANTHONY B., 201,
207
JESSE, 201(2),
207
LIVY ANN, 201(2)
WILLIAM, 201(3),
208(3), 270
WINNEA, 248
KEELER,
WILLIAM, 42
KELLER,
WILLIAM, 42
KELLEY,
BARBABAS, 203(2)
BARNABAS, 203
JOSEPH D., 203
MARY, 203(2)
POLLY, 299
KELLY,
ANNE, 175
BARNABAS, 176
KENNER,
BETSY, 313
DARCUS, 27, 28,
29
ELIZABETH, 206
HOUSON, 207
JAMES, 199,
207(2), 308
JUDITH, 190(2),
192(2), 194(2),
195(2)
LAWRENCE STERNS,

192
MACK, 313
MALINDA, 199(2),
200(2)
MARGARET, 232
MARK, 207, 245,
246
MRS., 88
NEWTON, 207
ROAHAM BEVERLY,
192
RODHAM, 108(2),
194(4), 195
WILEY B.,
206(2), 207
WILLIAM, 207(2)
WILLIAM M., 194
WILLIAM W.,
194(5), 195(5)
WILLIAM WINSTON,
192
WILLIE B., 207,
339
WINDER, 232
WM. D., 319
KENNER, DR.,
JASPER, 207
KENNEY,
GEORGE, 96
KENNON,
ELIZABETH, 314
THOMAS, 314
KEPLER (KLEPPER),
EBBY, 229
KERSHNER,
JOHN, 10
JOHN H., 172
KESTREN,
DAVID, 81
KEY,
JAMES, 190
KEYS,
JOHN, 335
KILLENBARGER,
JOSEPH, 210
KINCADE,
BUROUGH, 183
KINCHELOE,
ELIJAH, 133,
197(2)
GEORGE W., 198
JAMES B., 197
JOHN, 198(2)
LIJAH, 131, 132,
199(4)
MARGARET, 197,
198(3)
POLLY, 197, 199
SARAH, 197,
198(2)
THOMAS O., 198
KING,
ADAM, 196(2),

200
ANDREW, 195(2),
197(2)
BARBARA, 195
BARBARY, 200(3),
201
C.H., 197
CHARLES, 196(2),
200
ELIZABETH, 205
JACOB, 196, 200
JAMES, 189(2),
196, 200,
205(3), 228
JNO, 143
JOHN, 151
LES, 140
MALVINIA, 160
MARY, 228
NANCY, 228
PHILIP, 284
THOMAS, 228
THOMAS, COL.,
308
THOS., 143, 228
WILLIAM, 189(6),
190, 228, 284
KING CAID'S,
line, 78
KING, COL.,
JAMES, 189
KING, SR.,
JAMES, 190
KING'S,
Old Line, 123(2)
KINKEA, ESQ.,
DAVID, 164
KINKEAD,
-, 207(3)
ANDERSON, 207
DAVID, 98, 148,
165, 183, 238,
327, 329
JANE, 238
JOHN, 255
MARY, 98(2), 238
MARY ANN, 207
NANCY, 157
R. W., 247
REBECCA, 238
ROBERT W., 174,
324
SAMUEL A., 98
WILLIAMS, 207
WMS, 207
KINKEAD, SR.,
WILLIAM, 207
KIRKEAD,
SAMUEL A., 186
KIRKPATRICK,
DAVID, 202(3),
314
HUGH, 202(4),

KIRKPATRICK
(continued)

HUGH L., 204(3)
JAMES, 202(4)
JOHN, 201(2),
202(3), 288
JUDITH, 202(2)
JULIA, 288
MARY, 204
MINERVA, 314
POLLY, 103
KITE,
JOHN, 203(2)
MARTIN, 203
KITE, SR.,
JOHN, 203(2)
KLEPPER,
BARNEY M., 20
BETSEY, 156
MARY ANN SUSAN,
20
NANCY, 156
WILLIAM, 127
KLINE,
JACOB, 189
MOTTENA, 188,
189
KLINE, JR.,
JACOB, 188
KNEELAND,
JOHN W., 204(3)
MARY B., 204(2)
KYLE,
---, 341
A., 205, 302
A.A., 314
ABSALOM, 106,
193, 301, 302
ABSOLOM, 194(3)
ABSOLOM A., 206
BARSHABA,
106(3), 204(2),
205
GALE, 193(3)
JEFFERSON, 249
JOHN, 249
LEAH, 192
LEONIDAS, 204,
206
MARY, 206
NANCY, 193
PATSY, 337
RACHAEL, 156
ROBERT, 156(4),
192(2), 193(2),
194(2)
ROBERT P.,
206(3)
THOMAS, 193(2)
WILLIAM, 193(6),
194
WILLIAM C., 258

WILLIE B., 35
WM. C., 206
KYLE, SEN'R,
ABSOLOM, 89
KYLES,
ELIZABETH, 225
WM. C., 302

-L-

LACKEY,
JAMES, 142
JOSEPH, 77
LADY,
JOHN, 223, 224
SARAH, 223
LAMBERT,
ISAAC, 2
LANDERS,
LOUISA, 221(2)
LANE,
ISAAC, 328
JOHN, 214(2)
POLLY, 252
SARAH, 214
LANGLEY,
BENJAMIN, 190
JAMES, 190
LARKIN,
ANDERSON, 220,
221
ANN, 217
DAVID, 217, 218
DAVID H., 227
ELIZABETH, 157
ELIZABETH E.,
226
HENRY, 60, 76,
217, 220, 221,
226, 227
HENRY SAMPSON,
284
JAMES C., 217
JOHN, 10, 68,
217, 220
MARGARET, 217
MARY, 217, 218,
220, 221
MARY H., 226
NANCY P., 226
ROBERT, 218
ROBERT R.,
217(2)
THOMAS, 68,
217(2)
WILLIAM, 217(2),
218
WILLIAM Y., 220
WM. Y, 188
LARKINS,
-, 18
ANN, 346
DOCK, 18

HANNAH, 239
HENRY, 346
WM. Y, 188
LARSON,
BANKS, 100
THOMAS, 100
LAUDERBACK,
DAVID, 221(2)
ELIZABETH, 221,
222
HANNAH, 221
HENRY, 222, 298
ISAAC, 33, 221,
298
JOHN, 222(2)
MARY, 222
SALLY, 222
LAUDERBACK,
HENRY, 203
ISSAC, 171
JANE, 179(2)
LAUGHMILLER,
DAVID, 34(2),
131, 136, 139,
142
ELIZABETH, 208
FREDERICK, 212
GEORGE, 208
JOHN, 28, 69,
208(2), 211(2),
212
JONAS, 211, 212
REBECCA, 208
SARAH, 212
SAVANA, 211(2)
LAVIN,
BENJAMIN, 220
FENAY, 220
LAW,
HENRY, 294
LAWSON,
A.O., 98
ADERSON, 187
ALFORD C., 187
ALFORD E., 187
CLEMENT, JR.,
219
DYER, 97
DYER D., 97, 98
EDWARD, 218, 219
ELIZABETH, 251
H.E., 98
JOHN, 269
NANCY, 12
PATSY, 219
LEA,
JAMES, 294
LEATH,
SALLY, 305
LEBOW,
JOSEPH, 297
LEE,
---, 317

BURRELL, 209,
219
CADOR, 209
CLINTON, 213,
219
EDWARD, 210,
213, 214, 216,
247
ELIZABETH, 161,
210, 216
GREGORY, 220
HOPKINS, 219
JAMES, 212, 213,
216, 219, 220,
335
JOHN, 209(2),
210(3), 219
JOHN, SR., 213
KADER, 209
MARTHA, 210(5)
MARY, 25, 209,
210(3), 212,
213, 214(2), 219

MICAJAH, 248
NEEDHAM, 212,
232
NICHOLAS, 216
PLEASANT N.,
216, 252
POLLY, 216
POLLY ANN,
216(2)
ROBERT, 210,
213, 219, 220
SAMUEL, 25
THOMAS, 25(2),
209, 212,
213(2), 216(3)
THOMAS J., 51,
252
THOS. J., 99,
104(2)
WILLIAM, 106,
210(3), 212, 213

WILLIAM D., 216
WM. F., 118
LEE, SR.,
JOHN, 209(2)
LEEPER,
---, 281
ELIZABETH, 222,
223
FRANCIS, 215
G., 44
GAVEN, 273
GUION, 215(2),
223
HUGH, 215, 275,
278
HUGH, SR., 216
JAMES, 214, 215,

216, 275
JANE, 215
JOHN, 215
MARGARET, 215
NANCY J., 215
RUTHE, 215
RUTHE A., 215
SALLY, 215
TAHPENA, 215
WILLIE ANN, 273
LEMAR,
  BENJAMIN, 210(2)
  BENJAMIN S., 210
  MARINE, 210
  MARINE T., 210
  RICHARD, 210(2)
  RICHARD S., 210
  THOMAS, 211
  THOS, 210
  WILLIAM, 210(2),
    211
  WILLIAM B., 210
  WILLIAM BISHOP,
    211
LEONARD,
  AGNES, 225
  DAVID, 225
  EDY, 225
  JACOB, 225
  JOHN, 225
  RACHAEL, 225
  WILLIAM, 225
LESLIE, ESQ.,
  ANDREW, 102
LEWIS,
  BETSY, 309
  HENRY, 39
  JOHN, 210(2)
LIBO,
  ---, 341
LIGHT,
  ELENOR, 212
  GEORGE, 212
  JACOB, 109, 212
  JOHN, 212
  JOSHUA, 212
  MICHAEL, 212
  PATIENCE, 212
  PETER, SR., 298
  SARAH, 69(2)
  VACHEL, 69(2),
    212
  WILLIAM, 212
  WRIGHT, 212
LIPES,
  DANIEL, 190
LIVINGSTON,
  JACOB, 129
LLOYD,
  NANCY JANE, 256
  WM., 256
LOCKMILLER,
  JOHN, 229

JONAS, 209
SALLY, 229
LOGAN,
  JOHN B., 117,
    254
  MAHALY, 221(2)
  WILLIAM, 317
LONG,
  ALEX R, 180
  ALN, 32
  DAVID, 220
  GEORGE M., 119
  JACOB, 190
  JAMES, 220, 298,
    333
  JAMES Y., 318
  JANE, 220
  JOHN, 111,
    220(2), 238, 318
  JOHN K., 34(2)
  JONATHAN, 220
  JOSEPH, 223, 317
  NANCY, 85, 220,
    238
  NICHOLAS, 151,
    223, 298, 322,
    331
  PHILLIP, 223
  POLLY, 220
  REBECCA McMINN,
    238
  SARAH, 34, 220
  SIBBY, 34(2)
  T.A., 103
  WILLIAM, 223
  WILLIAM GASPER,
    223
  WINNY, 163
LOONEY,
  A.D., 225
  ABSALOM, 186,
    218, 240
  ABSALOM D., 153,
    225, 226
  ABSALOM L., 226
  BENJAMIN, 218,
    221, 348
  ISAM, 128, 218
  ISRAEL, 226
  JAMES G., 226
  JOHN, 218, 348
  JOHN B., 226
  JOSEPH McMINN,
    239
  KATY, 68
  MARGARET C., 226
  MARY, 218
  METILDY, 218
  MICHAEL, 283,
    326
  O.B., 226
  ORVILLE B., 226

POLLY, 147
ROB'T J., 188
ROBERT, 218
ROBERT J., 187
RUFUS G., 226
SALLY, 225, 226
SALLY JANE, 226
SUSAN, 226
WILLIAM C., 226
LOONEY'S (line),
  ABSOLOM, 151
LOUGHMILLER,
  GEORGE, 209
  JOHN, 237
LOVIN,
  EDMOND, 275
  EDMUND, 90
  R. W., 130
LOYD,
  THOMAS, 208(2)
LUCAS,
  N., 56
  NANCY, 56
LUCINDA,
  DRINNON, 12
LUCKY,
  SETH J.W., 278
LUSTER,
  -, 32(3)
  FRANKEY, 32
  S.D., 32
LUTHOLTZ,
  ELIZABETH,
    211(2)
LYNCH,
  MATHEW MARCUS,
    141
LYNN,
  JAMES, 76(2)
McCARMACK,
  REBECCA, 229
LYON,
  - DAVID, 19
  JAMES, 190
  JOHN, 132
LYON'S,
  corner, 19
LYONS,
  G.M., 9
  GEORGE M., 174
  JAMES, 73(2)
  JESSE, 45
  JESSE M., 19,
    93, 96
  JIM, 96
  WILLIAM, 7, 9,
    132, 199, 212,
    237, 275
  WM., 18, 274
LYONS, JR.,
  DAVID, 86, 176

-M-

McADOW,

JOHN, 145
MARTHA, 145(2)
McALISTER,
  ---, 286
McANALLY,
  DAVID, 234
  ELIJAH, 228
  ELIZABETH, 235
  JEREMIAH, 234,
    235
  JOHN, 235, 301
McANNALLY,
  JOHN, 233, 299
  MARY E., 57
McBRIDE,
  LOUISA, 83(2)
McBROOM,
  ALEXANDER, 240
  JAMES, 240
  JANE, 240
  JOHN, 240
  JOHN M., 240
McC-----,
  HEZEKIAH
    HAMBLEN, 229
McCALL,
  ELIZA, 310
  JAMES L.L.,
    310(2)
McCALLIA,
  JOHN, 246
McCANN,
  M., 108
  MICHAEL, 108
  PATSY, 156
McCANNA,
  -, 196(2)
McCANSE,
  LOUISA, 161
McCARMACK,
  REBECCA, 229
McCARTA,
  ABSALOM P., 254
  VIRGINIA, 253(2)
McCARTY,
  (heirs), 193,
    194
  -, 193
  ABSALOM P., 342
  AMANDA, 161, 162
  J.P., 45
  JAMES, 301
  JAMES P., 206,
    302
  JAMES R., 138
  JOHN L., 239
  NANCY, 138(2),
    139
  WILLIAM, 193
McCARVER,
  ALEXANDER, 258
  MARGARET, 258
  WILLIAM, 258,

McCARVER
  (continued)
  WILLIAM, SR.,
    258
McCATLEY,
  DAVID, 109
McCAULEY,
  ANNA, 343, 344
McCLEANE,
  KASSIA, 122
McCLURE,
  BARSHA, 205
  BARSHABA, 205
  BARSHEBA, 205
  MITCHELL, 205
McCOLLOUGH,
  ALEXANDER, 241,
    242, 259
  ELIZABETH, 252,
    259
  HENRY, 242
  HENRY P., 259
  HENRY, SR., 241
  HEZEKIAH, 192
  JAMES, 270
  JOHN, 259
  JOSEPH, 225, 242
  MARIA, 83(2)
  NANCY, 129, 242,
    259
  NANCY JANE, 259
  SAMUEL, 259
  SARAH, 259(2)
  WILLIAM, 242,
    259(2)
McCORDE,
  ELIZA H., 204
McCORMICK,
  JOHN, 190
McCOY,
  ANANIAS, 21
  ARCHIBALD, 330
  WILLIAM, 168
McCRA,
  AR. G., 121
McCRAIN,
  G., 119
McCRAW,
  -, 45
  G., 31, 43, 289
  GABRIEL, 36,
    167(2), 260, 261
  SAMUEL, 260
  SUSANNA, 260
  WILLIAM, 43
McCULLAH,
  WILLIAM F., 176
McCULLOCK,
  JOHN, 190
  ROBERT, 190
McCULLOUGH,

SUSANNAH, 248
McDANIEL,
  -, 34(2)
  JEAN, 23
  WILLIAM, 34(2)
McFARLAND,
  JNO D., 180
  WILLIAM, 116
McFARLAND & DICKSON,
  -, 116
McFEETERS,
  SAMUEL, 241
McGEE,
  ALFRED R., 257
  ALFRED RHOTON,
    256
  ANDERSON, 256
  BARBARA ANN, 256
  JOHN A., 256
  JOSEPH C., 256
  THOMPSON, 256,
    257
McGINNIS,
  HANNAH, 329
  MOSES, 336
McGURNEY/McGUNERY,
  MICAL, 189
McHENRY,
  WILLIAM, 190
McKERGON,
  ---, MRS., 302
McKINNEY,
  A., 109
  CHAS. J., 47
  JOHN A., 108,
    109
McKINNEY'S,
  Line, 125
McKINNEY'S (land),
  JOHN A., 88
McKINNEY'S Line,
  C., 124
McKIRGAN,
  JAMES L., 349
McKNIGHT,
  ---, 314
  ELIZA, 267
McLAUGHLIN,
  THOMAS, 60
McMINN,
  ---, 323
  JAMES, 1
  JOSEPH, 121(2),
    148, 211, 238,
    239, 295
  NANCY, 238
  ROB'T, 122
  ROBERT, 62, 82,
    217, 308, 330,
    331
McPHEETERS,
  JOHN, 71
  SAMUEL, 71, 121,

164, 306
McPHERSON,
  WILLIAM, 259
McVAY,
  -, 144
  JAMES, 144(2)
  PATRICK, 144
McWILLIAMS,
  ANDREW, 256
  ELEANOR, 233(2)
  HUGH, 233
  JAMES, 164, 255
  JESSE, 164, 167,
    233, 234, 235
  JOHN, 176,
    233(3), 235,
    255, 256
  JOSEPH, 255
  MARGARET, 233
  MARTHA, 233, 235
  NANCY, 233, 256
  NELSON, 233
  ROBERT, 164(2),
    233
MALLORY,
  ELIZABETH, 182
MALORY,
  JACOB J., 182
  MARY M., 182
  MORIAH A., 182
MANAFEE,
  PEGGEY, 107
MANAS,
  DANIEL, 237
  ELIJAH, 237
  ELISHA, 237
  ELIZABETH, 237
  EPHRAIM, 237
  JACOB, 237, 238
  MARGARET, 237
MANESS,
  WILLIAM, 244
MANESS/MORRIS,
  EDWARD, 229
  ELIZABETH, 229
  HENDERSON, 229
  JOHN, 229
  WILLIAM, 229
MANESS/MORRISS,
  SARAH, 228
MANIS,
  ALSEY, 250
  AMANDA, 254
  C.A., 118, 127
  CAMPBELL, 245
  CARTER, 245,
    250, 255
  CELIA, 254,
    255(2)
  CLINTON, 246(2),
    249, 250
  CLINTON A., 255
  DONNELSON, 249

ELDRIDGE, 249,
  250
GATHAN, 254
GEORGE, 254
GILBERT, 255
JESSE, 249, 250
JESSE, JR., 249
JOHN, 117, 254,
  255(3)
JOSEPH, 245
LUCINDA, 255
LYDIA, 245, 246
MARY/MASY, 111
NANCY, 255
NELSON, 254
PLEASANT, 254,
  255
RHODA, 254
SARAH, 254
STARLIN, 250
STARLIN
  (STERLING), 249
WEBBY, 250
WILLIAM, 245,
  246(2)
MAPLES,
  -, 193
  JOHN, 193
  PATTY, 193(3),
    194(2)
  POLLY, 193(3),
    194(3)
MARRISETT,
  ENOCH, 209
MARSHALL,
  BARTLETT, 328
  HENRY, 3
  JOHN, 71
  THOMAS, 15
MARSLETTER/MORRISET
  TE,
  ---, 274
MARTIN,
  AARON, 251
  ABIJAH, 251
  ABSALOM, 251
  ANNEY, 224
  ANNIE, 225
  DANIEL, 224, 225
  ELIZABETH, 250,
    251
  JAMES, 236, 251
  JOHN, 224, 251
  JOHNANA, 224
  LEVEY/ LEWEY,
    235
  MARY, 224
  PASCHAL, 251,
    337
  PHEBE, 224, 225
  THOMAS, 224,
    225, 236, 250,
    251(2)

www.ingramcontent.com/pod-product-compliance
Lightning Source LLC
Chambersburg PA.
CBHW080238270326
41926CB00020B/4286

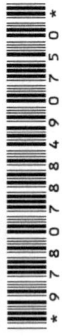